LOVE LETTERS TO
Jane's World

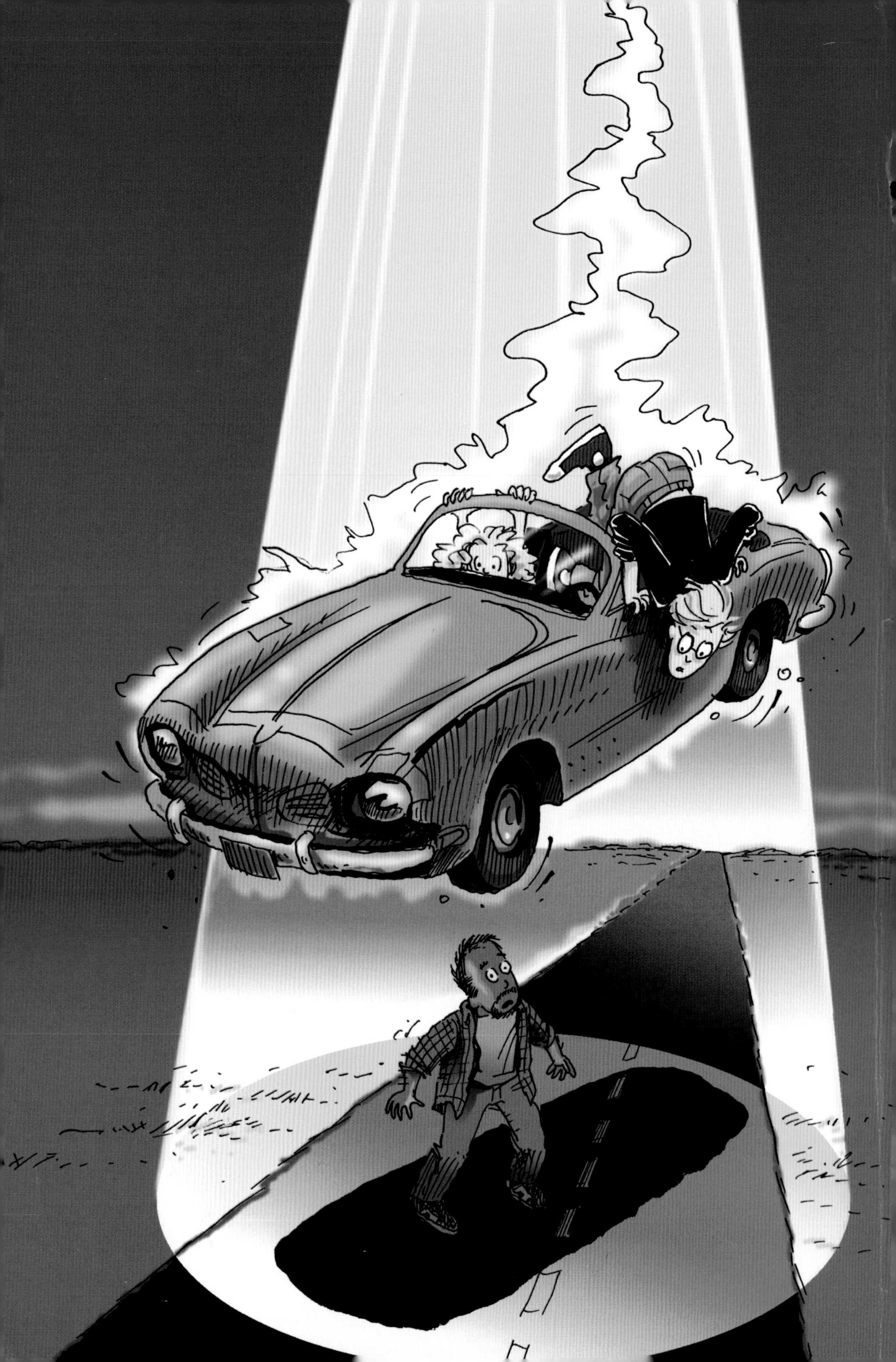

LOVE
LETTERS TO
Jane's
World

PAIGE BRADDOCK

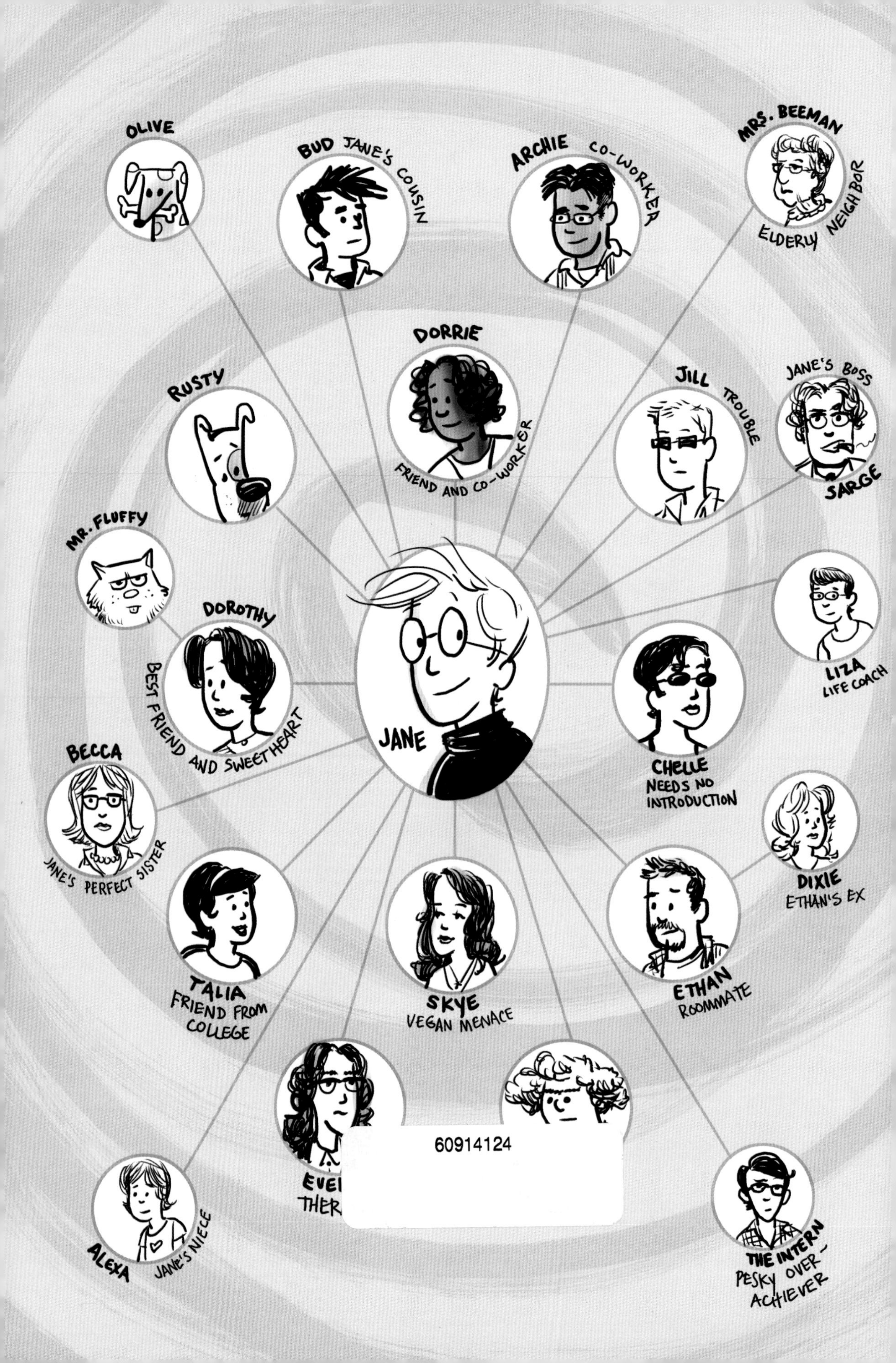
OLIVE
BUD JANE'S COUSIN
ARCHIE CO-WORKER
MRS. BEEMAN
ELDERLY NEIGHBOR
DORRIE
FRIEND AND CO-WORKER
RUSTY
JILL TROUBLE
JANE'S BOSS
SARGE
MR. FLUFFY
DOROTHY
BEST FRIEND AND SWEETHEART
JANE
LIZA
LIFE COACH
CHELLE
NEEDS NO INTRODUCTION
BECCA
JANE'S PERFECT SISTER
DIXIE
ETHAN'S EX
TALIA
FRIEND FROM COLLEGE
SKYE
VEGAN MENACE
ETHAN
ROOMMATE
ALEXA JANE'S NIECE
THE INTERN
PESKY OVER-ACHIEVER

Contents

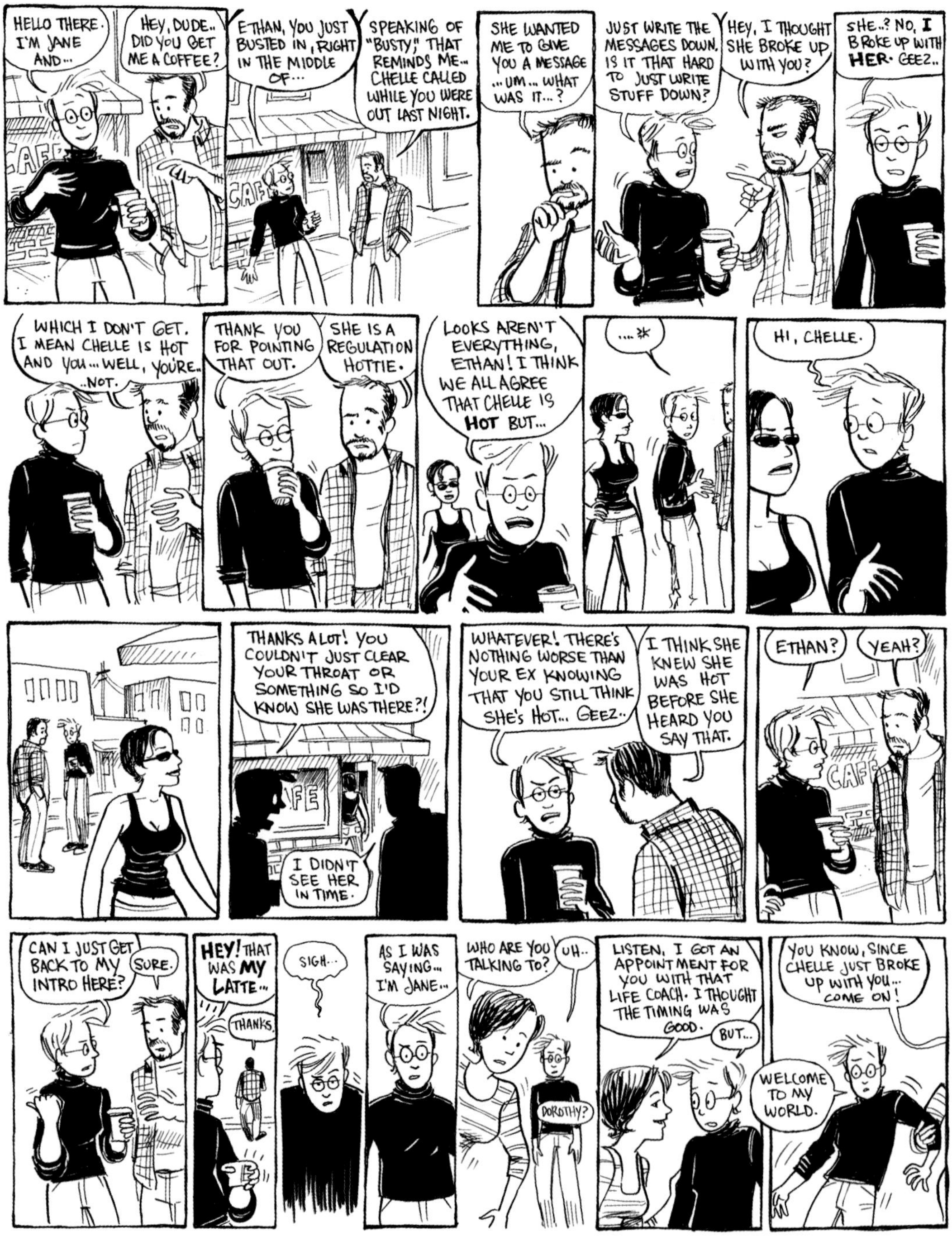

HELLO THERE. I'M JANE AND...
HEY, DUDE.. DID YOU GET ME A COFFEE?
ETHAN, YOU JUST BUSTED IN, RIGHT IN THE MIDDLE OF...
SPEAKING OF "BUSTY," THAT REMINDS ME.. CHELLE CALLED WHILE YOU WERE OUT LAST NIGHT.
SHE WANTED ME TO GIVE YOU A MESSAGE ...UM... WHAT WAS IT...?
JUST WRITE THE MESSAGES DOWN. IS IT THAT HARD TO JUST WRITE STUFF DOWN?
HEY, I THOUGHT SHE BROKE UP WITH YOU?
SHE..? NO, I BROKE UP WITH HER. GEEZ..
WHICH I DON'T GET. I MEAN CHELLE IS HOT AND YOU... WELL, YOU'RE.. ..NOT.
THANK YOU FOR POINTING THAT OUT.
SHE IS A REGULATION HOTTIE.
LOOKS AREN'T EVERYTHING, ETHAN! I THINK WE ALL AGREE THAT CHELLE IS HOT BUT...
....*
HI, CHELLE.
THANKS A LOT! YOU COULDN'T JUST CLEAR YOUR THROAT OR SOMETHING SO I'D KNOW SHE WAS THERE?!
I DIDN'T SEE HER IN TIME.
WHATEVER! THERE'S NOTHING WORSE THAN YOUR EX KNOWING THAT YOU STILL THINK SHE'S HOT... GEEZ..
I THINK SHE KNEW SHE WAS HOT BEFORE SHE HEARD YOU SAY THAT.
ETHAN?
YEAH?
CAN I JUST GET BACK TO MY INTRO HERE?
SURE.
HEY! THAT WAS MY LATTE...
THANKS.
SIGH...
AS I WAS SAYING... I'M JANE...
WHO ARE YOU TALKING TO?
UH..
DOROTHY?
LISTEN, I GOT AN APPOINTMENT FOR YOU WITH THAT LIFE COACH. I THOUGHT THE TIMING WAS GOOD.
BUT...
YOU KNOW, SINCE CHELLE JUST BROKE UP WITH YOU... COME ON!
WELCOME TO MY WORLD.

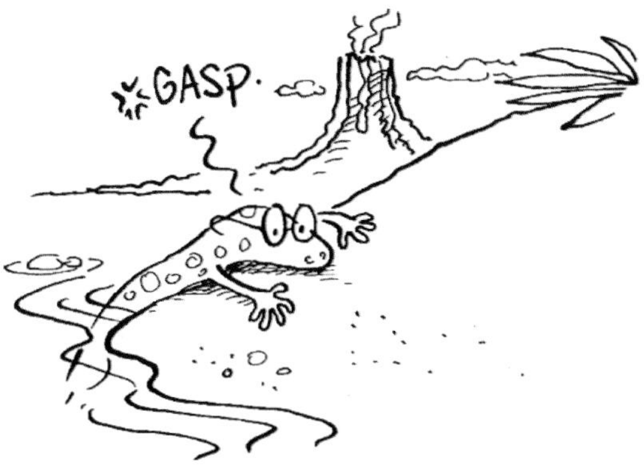
GASP.

Introduction

At one time I thought it would be cool to be the first openly gay cartoonist to land a nationally syndicated daily comic strip populated with gay characters. How the homophobes would squirm!

There would be a daunting downside, though. Once I had achieved the glory of being a true LGBT pioneer, I would then have to actually start thinking up and drawing a new strip every day, day after day, for years on end. The stress of facing constantly impending deadlines could drive a laid-back fellow like me crazy.

Fortunately, I was saved from enduring this glory-tinged nightmare by openly lesbian Paige Braddock, who got there ahead of me by launching her great LGBT-populated strip *Jane's World* in 1998. Since then, Paige has had to bear the consequences of unending creative labor that unnerved me. All things considered, she deserves every bit of the glory that comes with cracking a syndication barrier that once seemed insurmountable—and doing so with a level of skill, universal accessibility, and unforced humor that should make all of us in the queer community beam with pride.

When United Features (now United Media) first picked up *Jane's World* for syndication, its sales staff probably hoped that the feature would find a home somewhere between *Garfield* and *Doonesbury* on newspaper "funny pages." But such expectations were upended by the strip's explosive popularity online. The Internet, with its worldwide reach unencumbered by the cautious advertisers who have historically held most truly challenging comic strip innovations at bay, has allowed anyone anywhere—gay, straight, bi, cis, or gender-nonconforming—to hang out in Paige Braddock's queer-inclusive universe with no sense of not belonging.

Paige's enviable skills as a cartoonist are immediately obvious. Her lines seem effortlessly expressive; her characters talk the way people we all know talk. The appeal of Paige's title character is neither dependent on nor hampered by her lesbian identity. Jane is simply fun to spend time with, a fictional but easily relatable individual with whom most readers can identify. Her friends are fun to be around, too. As is her dog, Rusty.

Everyday humanity seen through a prism of humor is the enviable hallmark of *Jane's World*. As a fellow comics creator I'm especially impressed by the graceful flow, from strip to strip, of Paige's overarching narratives. Interesting comedic incidents make us chuckle from time to time, but Paige is no prisoner of punchlines. Her creation resembles real life, even if Jane's is a reality depicted with pen and ink.

It's a special treat to indulge in one *Jane's World* episode after another, presented in their proper sequence as opposed to on a catch-as-catch-can basis. It's hard to imagine a better way to experience Paige's creation than the one this book provides.

Prepare to binge-read.

Howard Cruse
Author of *Wendel* and *Stuck Rubber Baby*

SHE TOOK OFF WITH ALL MY STUFF!

Clown Princess

Jane thought she had the perfect plan to help Ethan avoid a potentially awkward situation. Of course, as is typical with most "Jane schemes," things went a bit off the rails. There was this unfortunate incident with a falling sign, then there was Jane's short trip to a universe inhabited only by female superheroes, but I am sure no one is interested in that. What this chapter is really about is how Jane met Chelle.

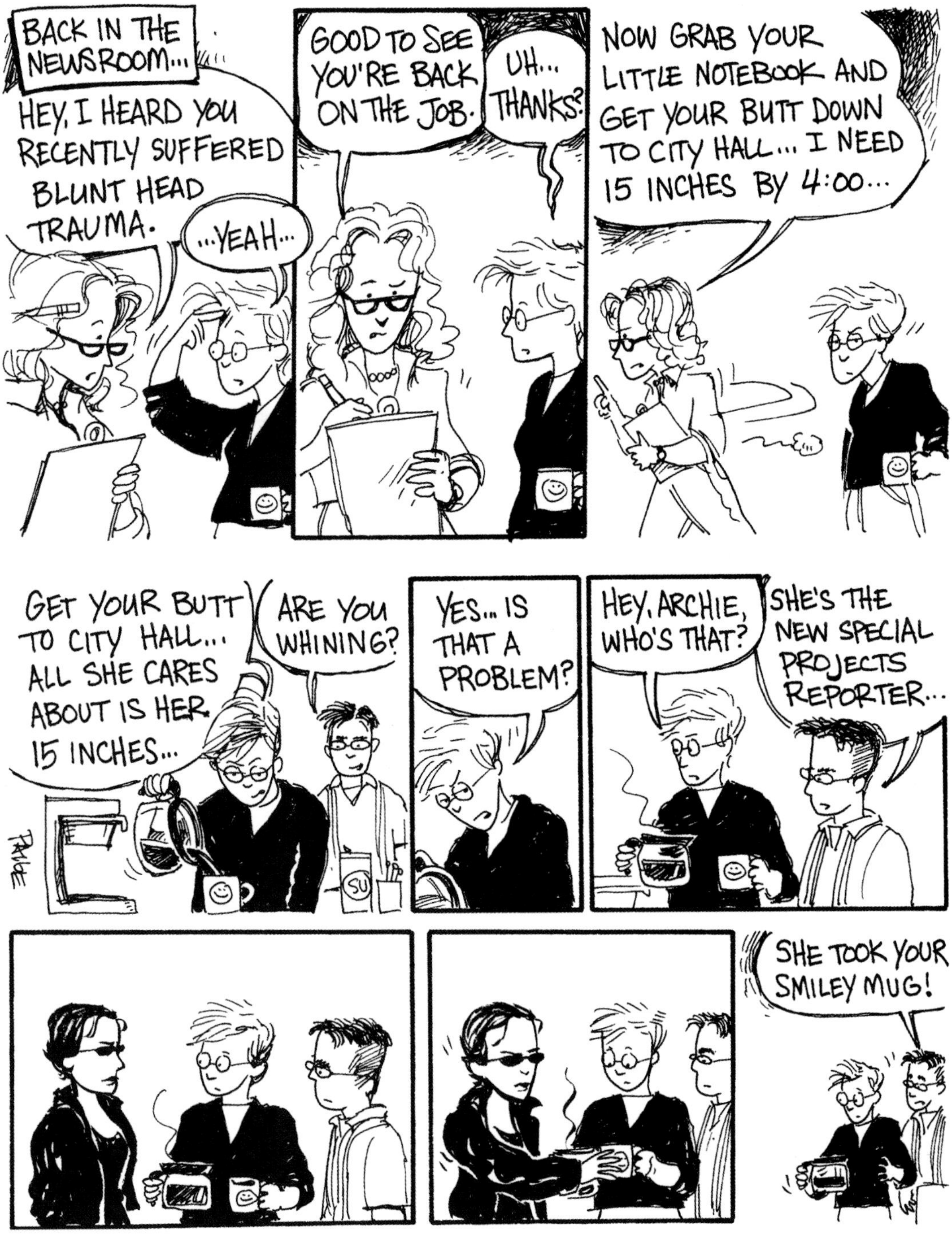
BACK IN THE NEWSROOM...
HEY, I HEARD YOU RECENTLY SUFFERED BLUNT HEAD TRAUMA.
...YEAH...
GOOD TO SEE YOU'RE BACK ON THE JOB.
UH... THANKS?
NOW GRAB YOUR LITTLE NOTEBOOK AND GET YOUR BUTT DOWN TO CITY HALL... I NEED 15 INCHES BY 4:00...
GET YOUR BUTT TO CITY HALL... ALL SHE CARES ABOUT IS HER 15 INCHES...
ARE YOU WHINING?
YES... IS THAT A PROBLEM?
HEY, ARCHIE, WHO'S THAT?
SHE'S THE NEW SPECIAL PROJECTS REPORTER...
SHE TOOK YOUR SMILEY MUG!

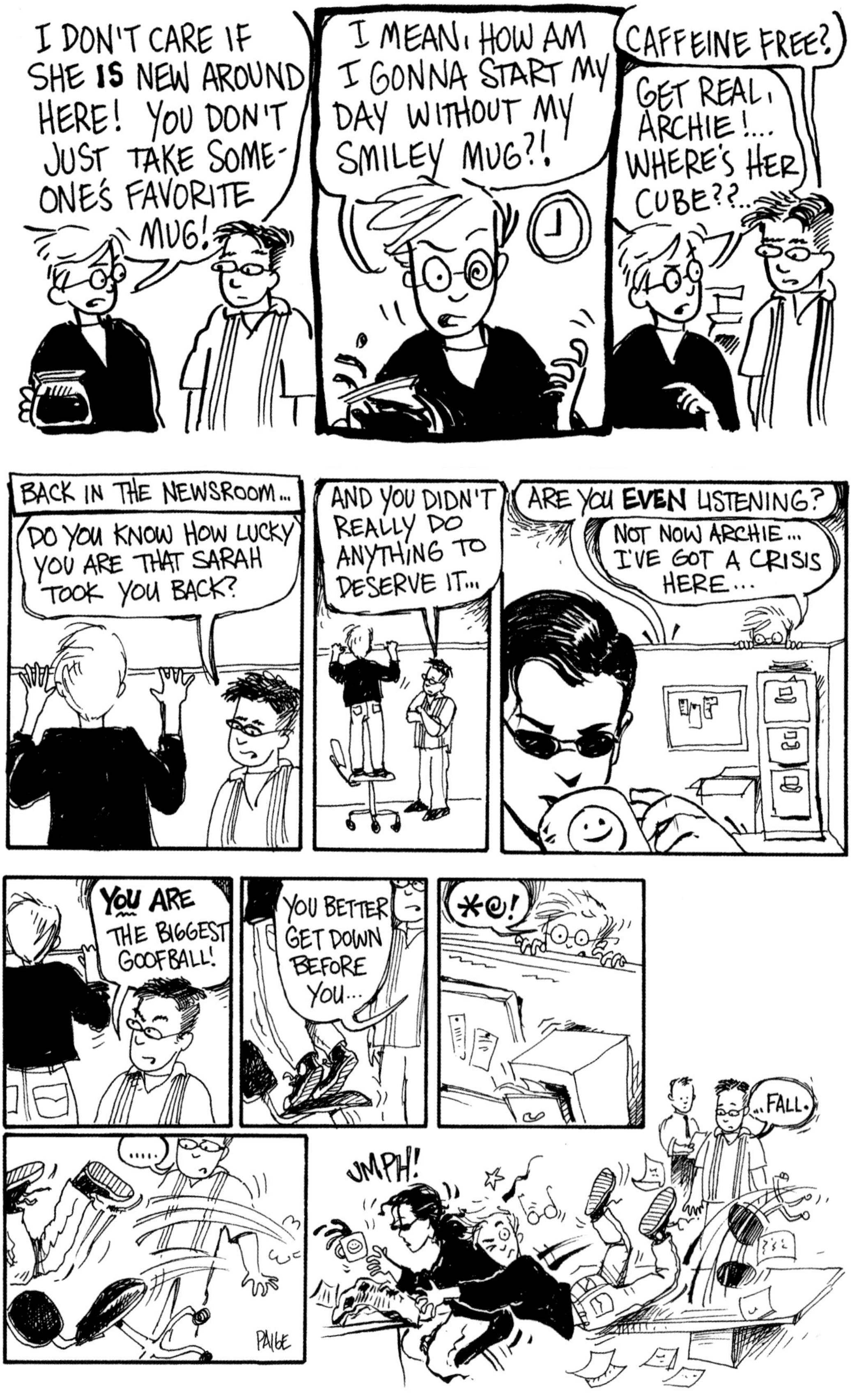

I DON'T CARE IF SHE IS NEW AROUND HERE! YOU DON'T JUST TAKE SOMEONE'S FAVORITE MUG!
I MEAN, HOW AM I GONNA START MY DAY WITHOUT MY SMILEY MUG?!
CAFFEINE FREE?
GET REAL, ARCHIE!... WHERE'S HER CUBE??...
BACK IN THE NEWSROOM...
DO YOU KNOW HOW LUCKY YOU ARE THAT SARAH TOOK YOU BACK?
AND YOU DIDN'T REALLY DO ANYTHING TO DESERVE IT...
ARE YOU EVEN LISTENING?
NOT NOW ARCHIE... I'VE GOT A CRISIS HERE...
YOU ARE THE BIGGEST GOOFBALL!
YOU BETTER GET DOWN BEFORE YOU...
*@!
.....
UMPH!
...FALL.
PAIGE

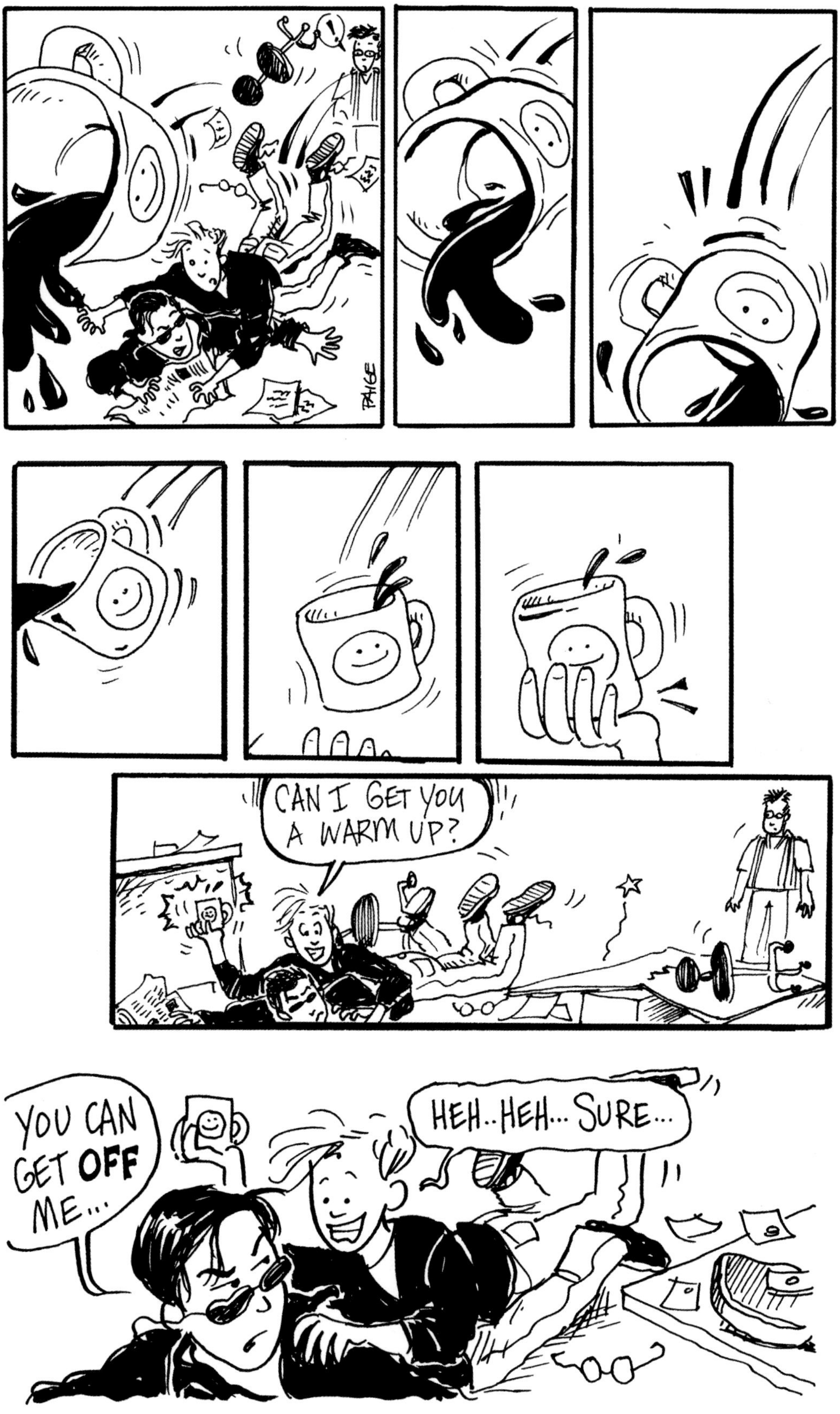
!
PAIGE
CAN I GET YOU A WARM UP?
YOU CAN GET **OFF** ME...
HEH..HEH...SURE...

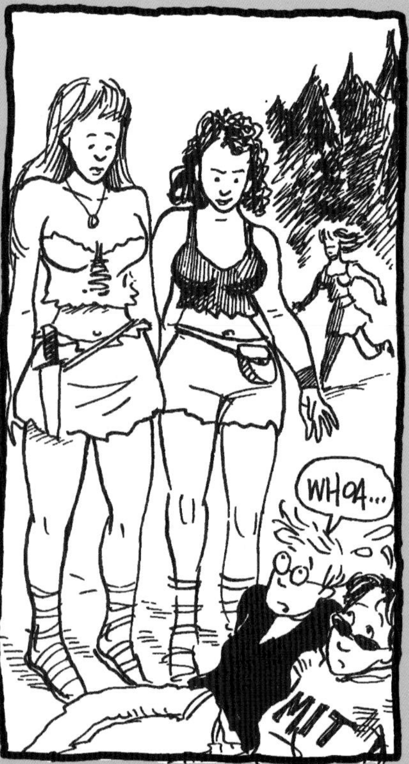
WHOA...
MIT

Amazon Island

Someone once said adversity can be character building. Adversity can also be annoying. At any rate, Jane has begun to think Chelle started to work at the paper just to make her life more difficult. In truth, sometimes Jane is a bit self-absorbed and thus assumes everyone's motives revolve around her. This next story, a seafaring tale gone wrong, throws cold water on some of Jane's theories about Chelle.

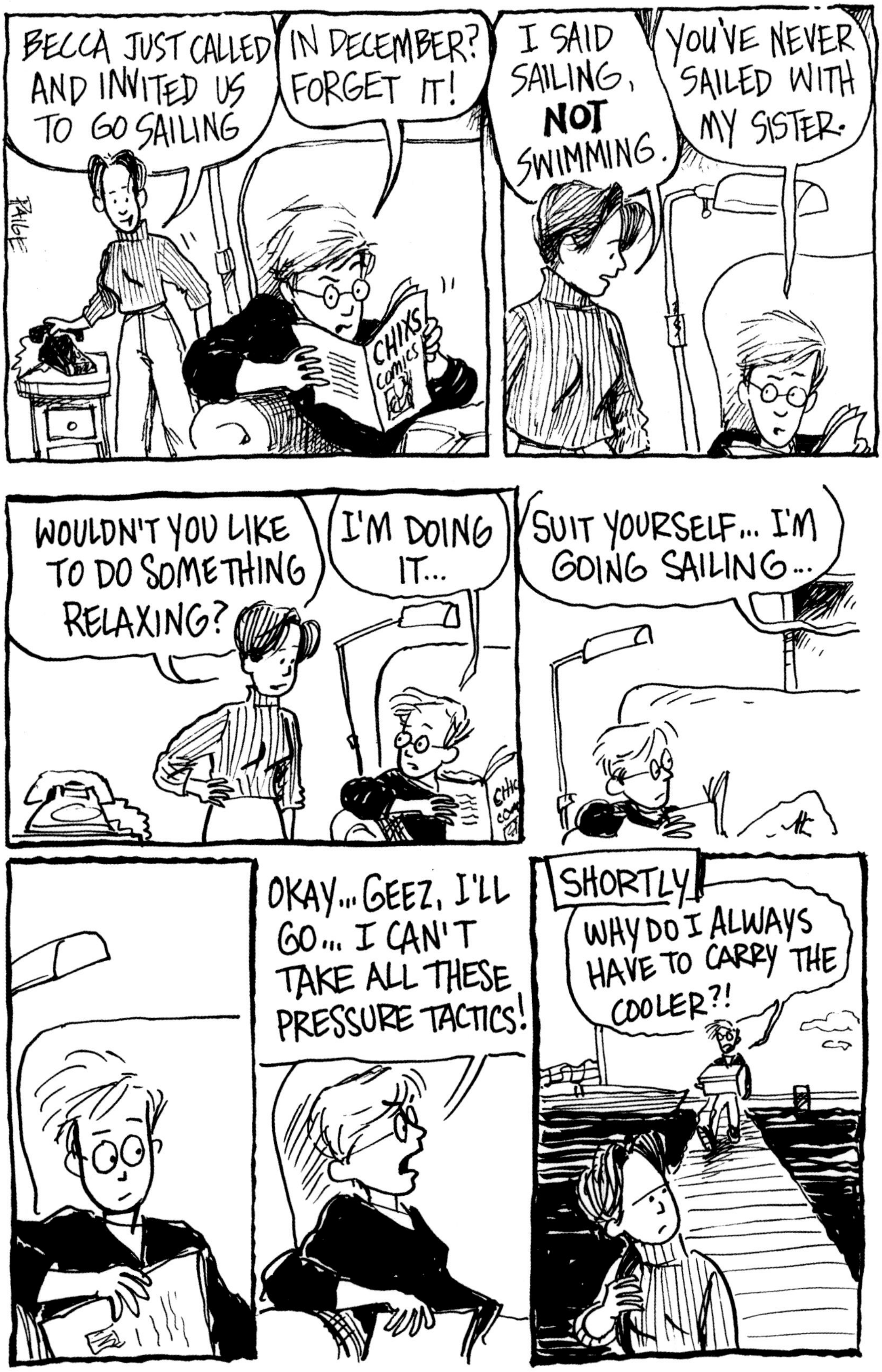
BECCA JUST CALLED AND INVITED US TO GO SAILING
IN DECEMBER? FORGET IT!
I SAID SAILING, **NOT** SWIMMING.
YOU'VE NEVER SAILED WITH MY SISTER.
CHIXS COMICS
WOULDN'T YOU LIKE TO DO SOMETHING RELAXING?
I'M DOING IT...
SUIT YOURSELF... I'M GOING SAILING...
OKAY... GEEZ, I'LL GO... I CAN'T TAKE ALL THESE PRESSURE TACTICS!
SHORTLY
WHY DO I ALWAYS HAVE TO CARRY THE COOLER?!

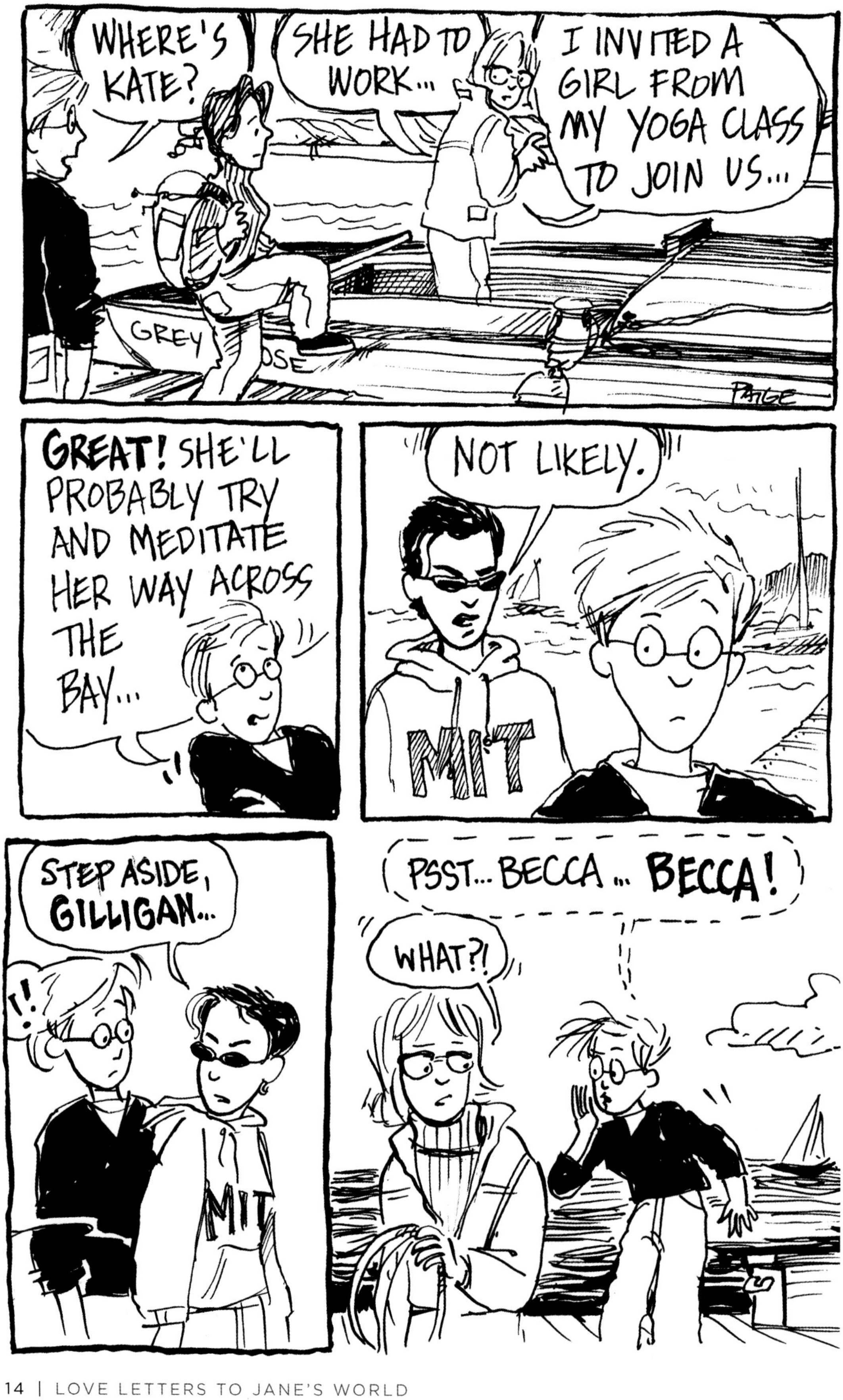
WHERE'S KATE?
SHE HAD TO WORK...
I INVITED A GIRL FROM MY YOGA CLASS TO JOIN US...
GREY
OSE
PAIGE
GREAT! SHE'LL PROBABLY TRY AND MEDITATE HER WAY ACROSS THE BAY...
NOT LIKELY.
MIT
STEP ASIDE, GILLIGAN...
MIT
PSST... BECCA ... BECCA!
WHAT?!

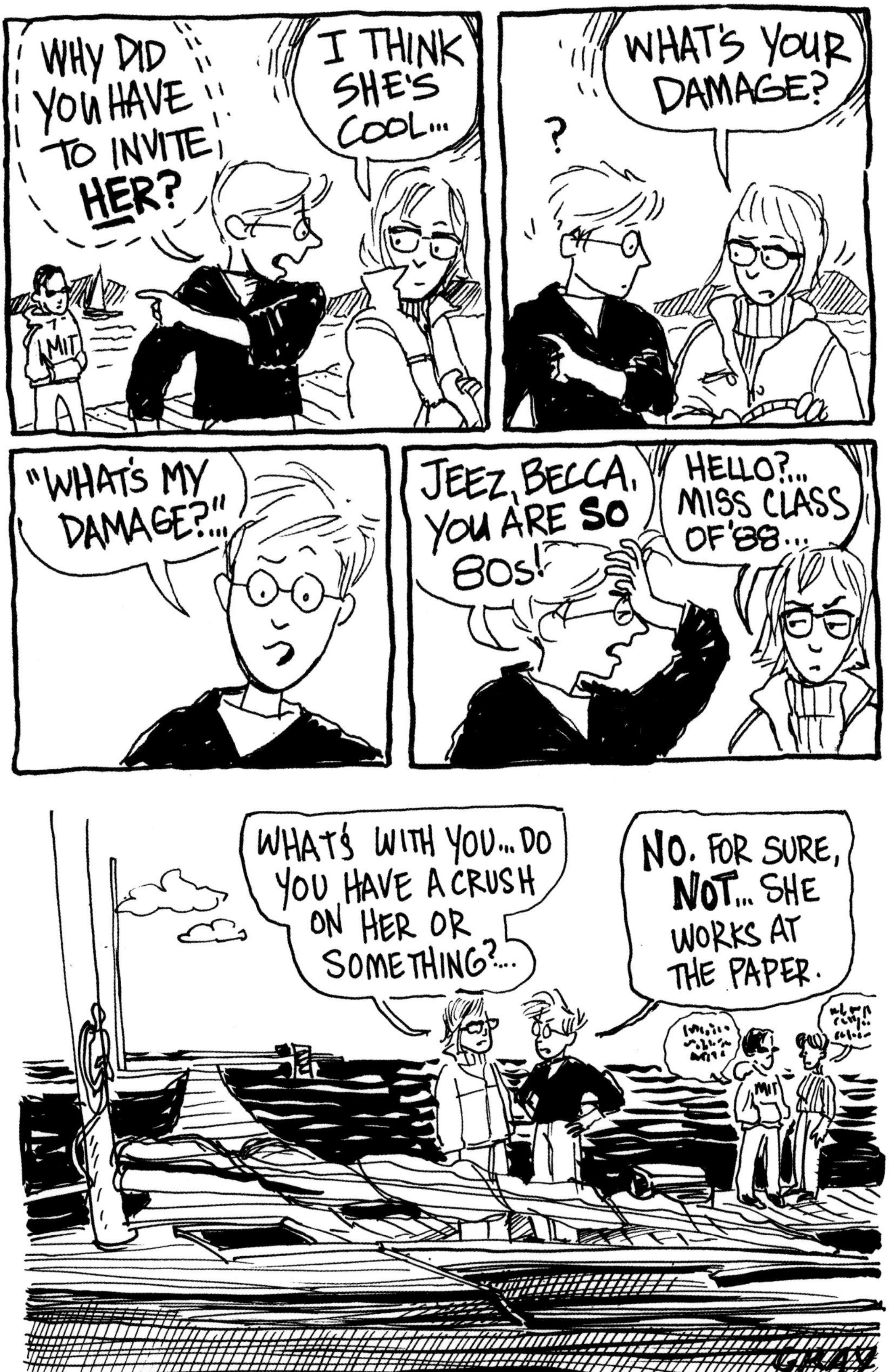
WHY DID YOU HAVE TO INVITE HER?
I THINK SHE'S COOL...
?
WHAT'S YOUR DAMAGE?
"WHAT'S MY DAMAGE?"...
JEEZ, BECCA, YOU ARE SO 80s!
HELLO?... MISS CLASS OF '88...
MIT
WHAT'S WITH YOU... DO YOU HAVE A CRUSH ON HER OR SOMETHING?...
NO. FOR SURE, NOT... SHE WORKS AT THE PAPER.
GRAY

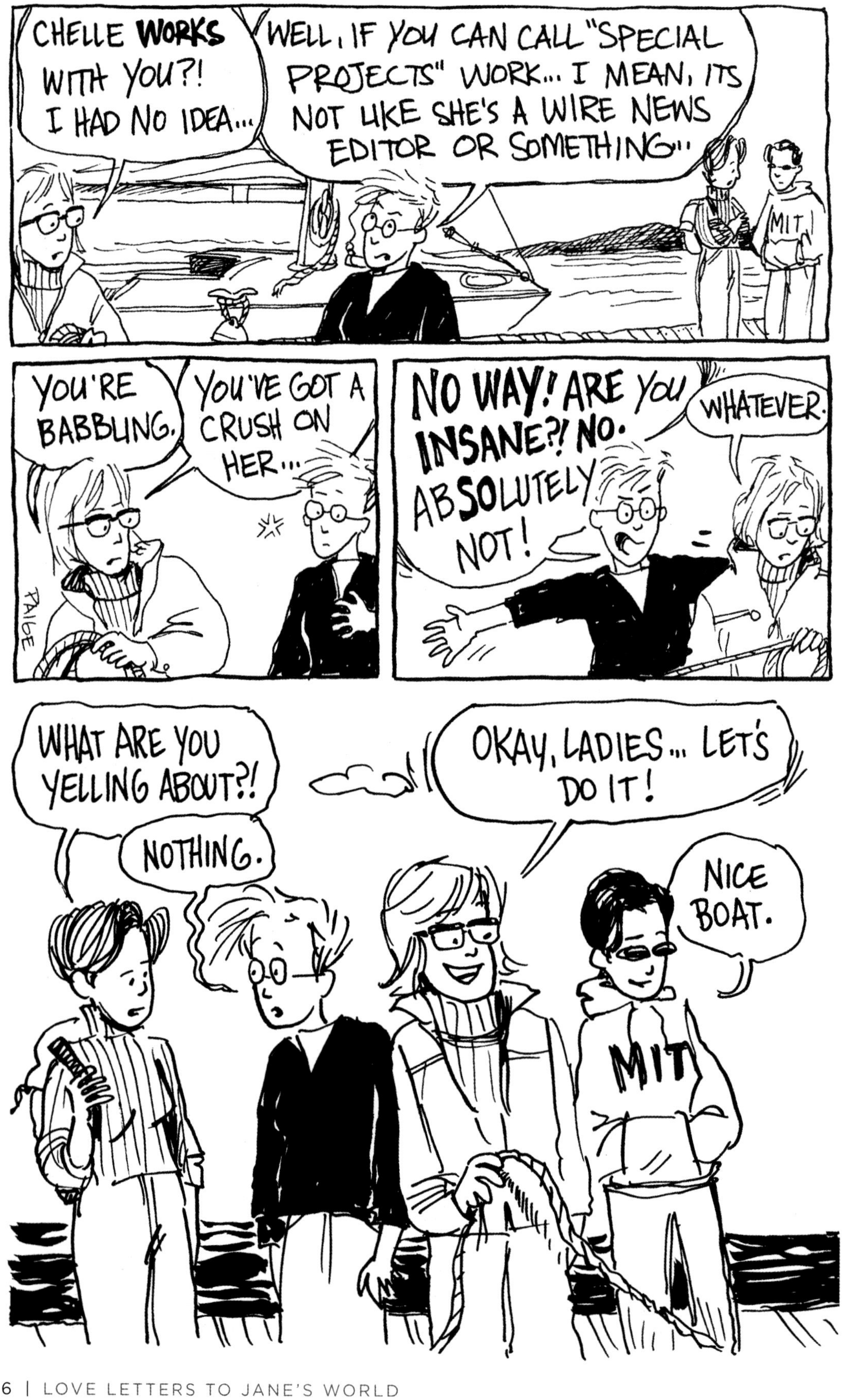
CHELLE WORKS WITH YOU?! I HAD NO IDEA...
WELL, IF YOU CAN CALL "SPECIAL PROJECTS" WORK... I MEAN, ITS NOT LIKE SHE'S A WIRE NEWS EDITOR OR SOMETHING...
MIT
YOU'RE BABBLING.
YOU'VE GOT A CRUSH ON HER...
PAIGE
NO WAY! ARE YOU INSANE?! NO. ABSOLUTELY NOT!
WHATEVER.
WHAT ARE YOU YELLING ABOUT?!
NOTHING.
OKAY, LADIES... LET'S DO IT!
NICE BOAT.
MIT

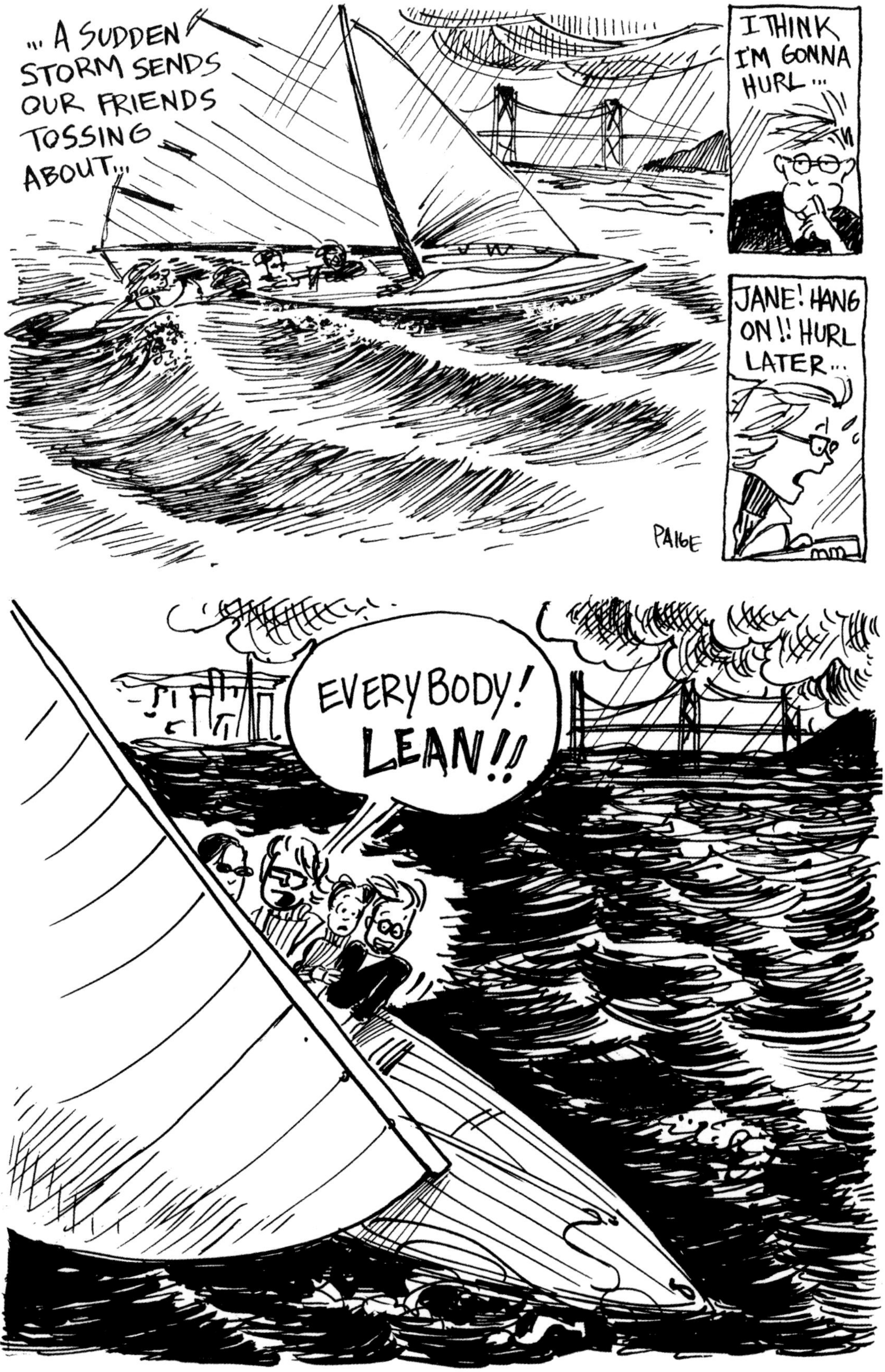
... A SUDDEN STORM SENDS OUR FRIENDS TOSSING ABOUT...
I THINK I'M GONNA HURL...
JANE! HANG ON!! HURL LATER...
PAIGE
EVERYBODY! LEAN!!

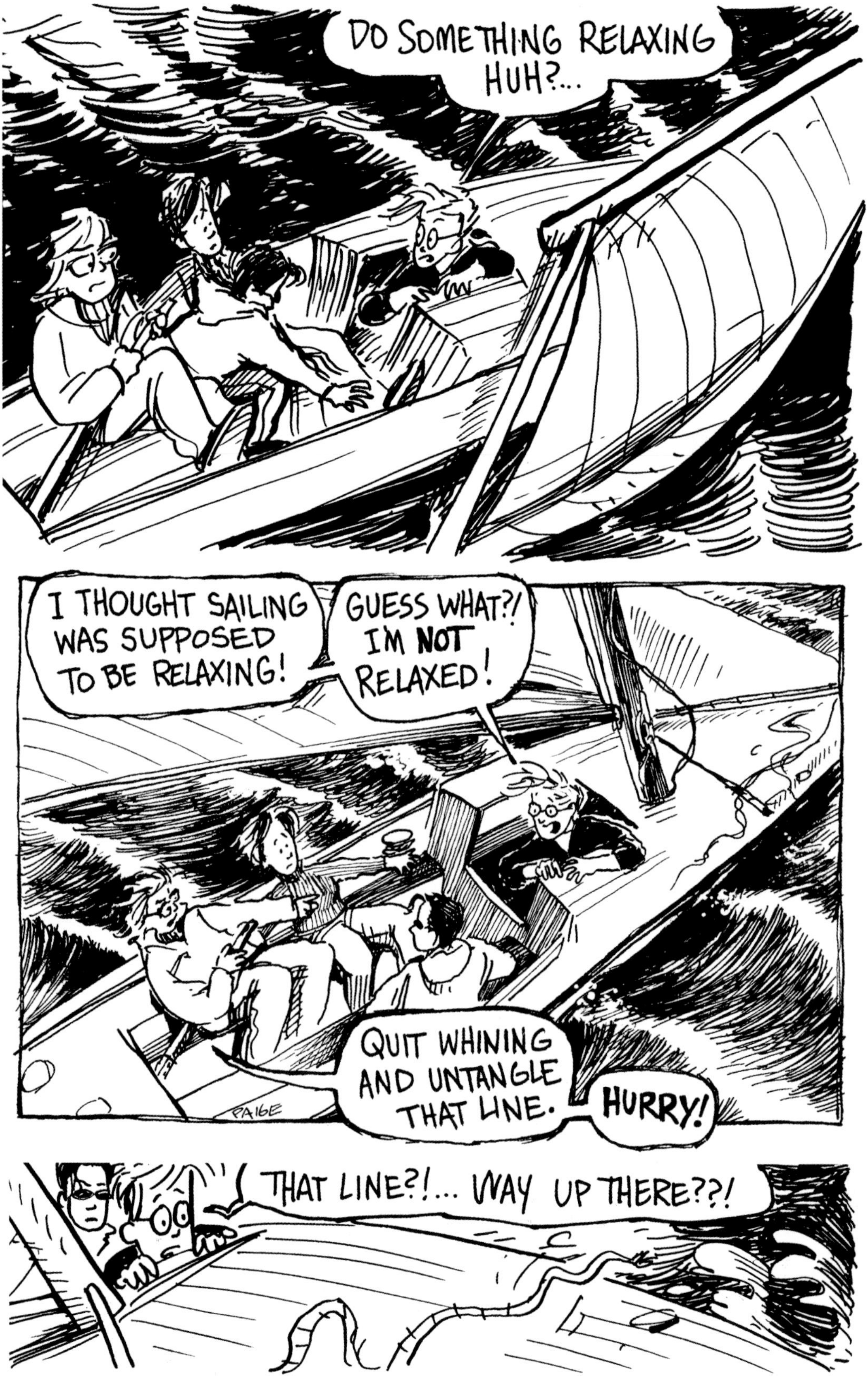
DO SOMETHING RELAXING HUH?...
I THOUGHT SAILING WAS SUPPOSED TO BE RELAXING!
GUESS WHAT?! I'M **NOT** RELAXED!
QUIT WHINING AND UNTANGLE THAT LINE.
HURRY!
PAIGE
THAT LINE?!... WAY UP THERE??!

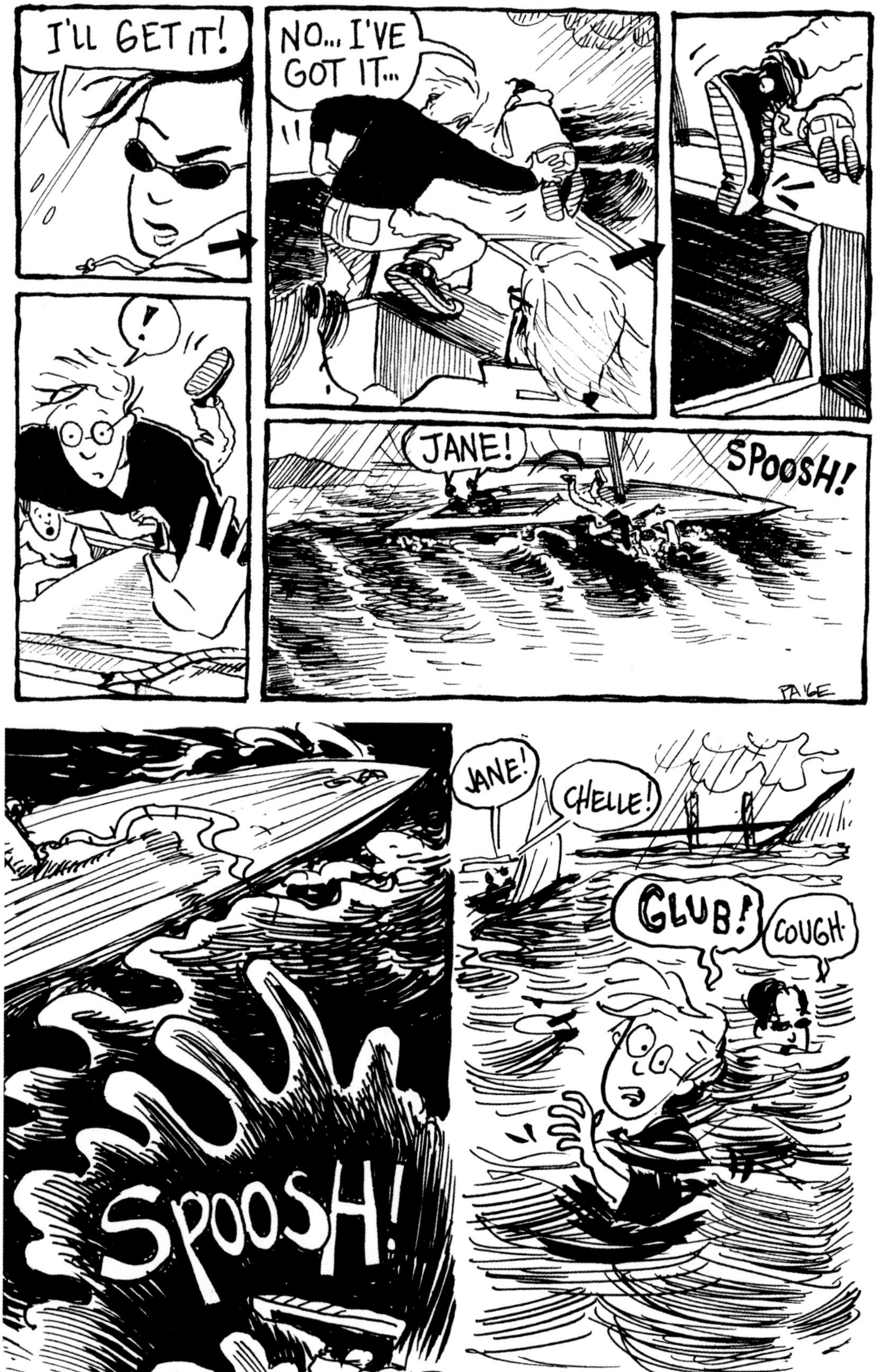

I'LL GET IT!
NO... I'VE GOT IT...
!
JANE!
SPOOSH!
PAIGE
SPOOSH!
JANE!
CHELLE!
GLUB!
COUGH

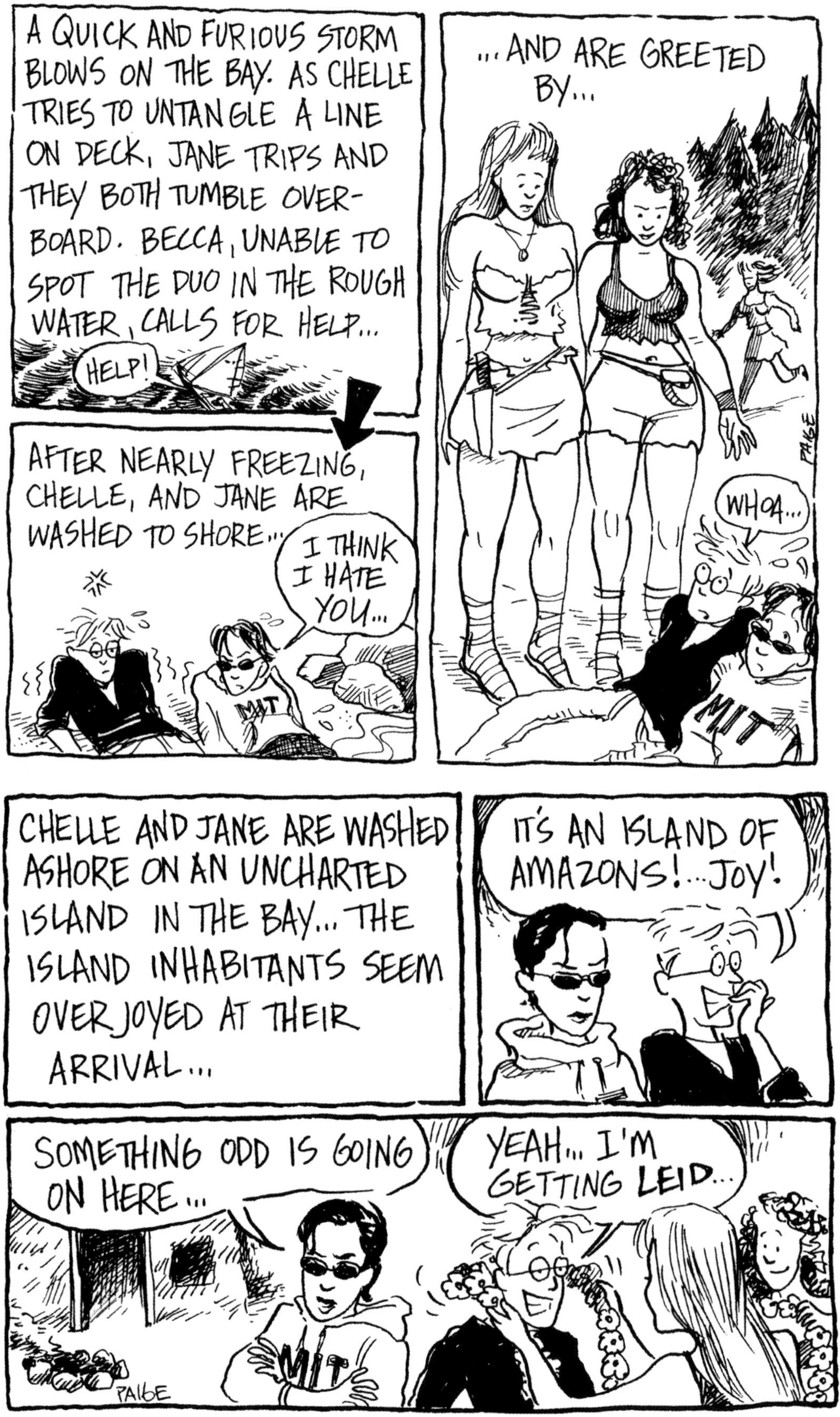
A QUICK AND FURIOUS STORM BLOWS ON THE BAY. AS CHELLE TRIES TO UNTANGLE A LINE ON DECK, JANE TRIPS AND THEY BOTH TUMBLE OVERBOARD. BECCA, UNABLE TO SPOT THE DUO IN THE ROUGH WATER, CALLS FOR HELP...
HELP!
AFTER NEARLY FREEZING, CHELLE, AND JANE ARE WASHED TO SHORE...
I THINK I HATE YOU...
...AND ARE GREETED BY...
WHOA...
PAIGE
CHELLE AND JANE ARE WASHED ASHORE ON AN UNCHARTED ISLAND IN THE BAY... THE ISLAND INHABITANTS SEEM OVERJOYED AT THEIR ARRIVAL...
IT'S AN ISLAND OF AMAZONS!...JOY!
SOMETHING ODD IS GOING ON HERE...
YEAH... I'M GETTING LEID...
PAIGE

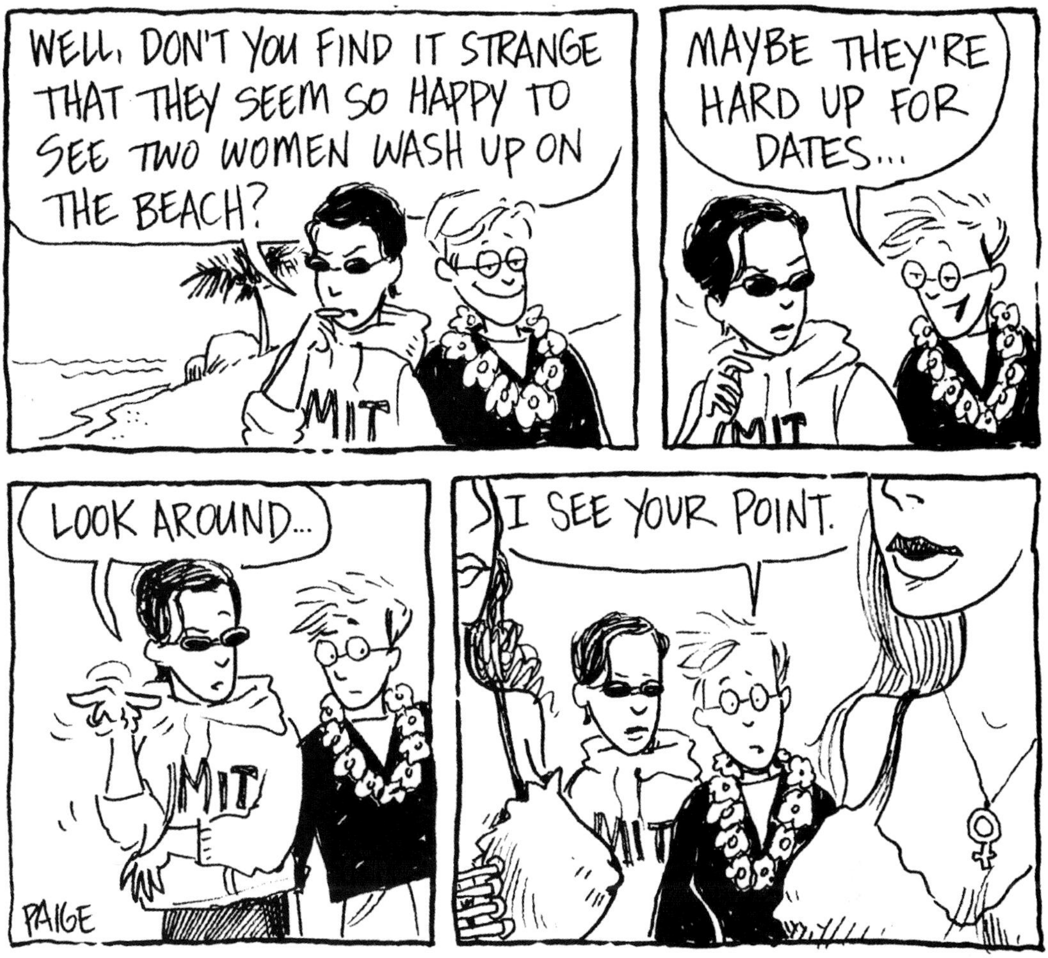
WELL, DON'T YOU FIND IT STRANGE THAT THEY SEEM SO HAPPY TO SEE TWO WOMEN WASH UP ON THE BEACH?
MIT
MAYBE THEY'RE HARD UP FOR DATES...
MIT
LOOK AROUND...
MIT
PAIGE
I SEE YOUR POINT.
MIT

“*Jane’s World* is a funny, fearless strip. The characters are funny, vulnerable, witty, and sexy (not necessarily in that order), and the relationships explored in the strip feel real, even when the circumstances get a little outrageous. I wholeheartedly recommend spending some time in *Jane’s World*.”

SHENA WOLF, Senior Editor, Digital and Creator Relations, Andrews McMeel

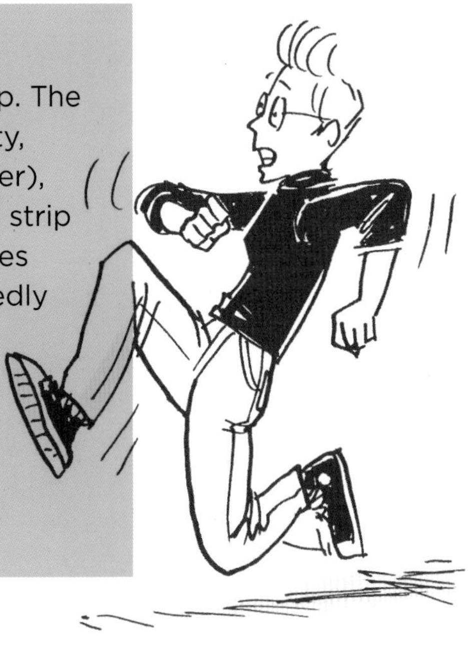

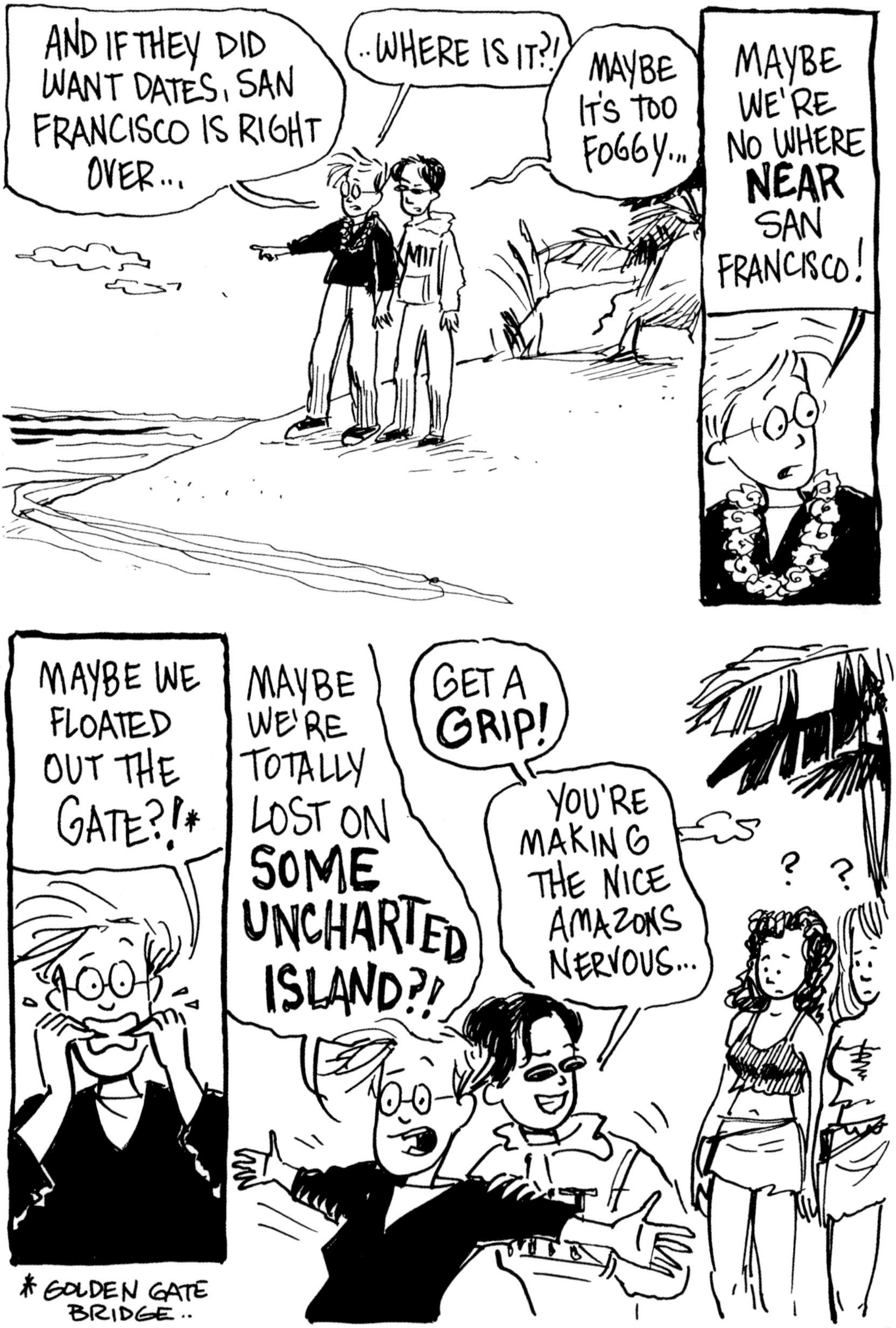
AND IF THEY DID WANT DATES, SAN FRANCISCO IS RIGHT OVER...
..WHERE IS IT?!
MAYBE IT'S TOO FOGGY...
MAYBE WE'RE NO WHERE **NEAR** SAN FRANCISCO!
MAYBE WE FLOATED OUT THE GATE?!*
MAYBE WE'RE TOTALLY LOST ON **SOME UNCHARTED ISLAND?!**
GET A **GRIP!**
YOU'RE MAKING THE NICE AMAZONS NERVOUS...
? ?
* GOLDEN GATE BRIDGE..

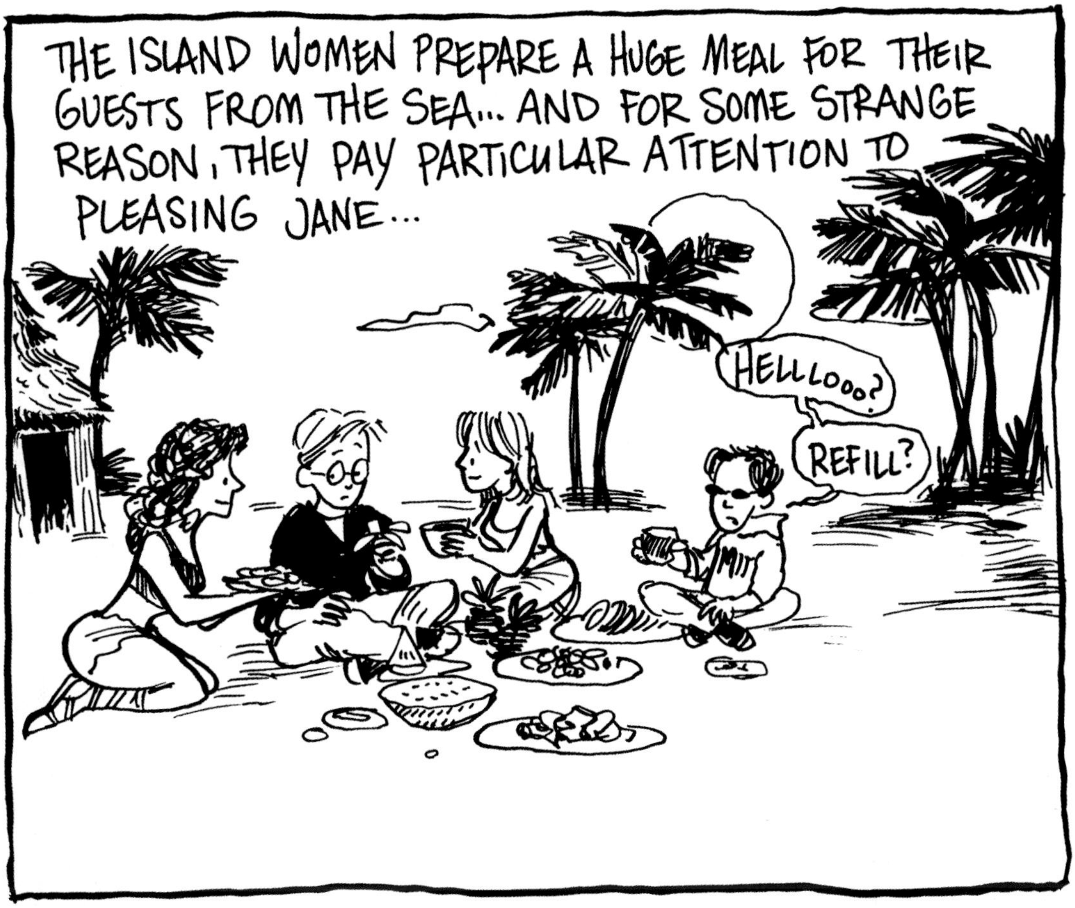
THE ISLAND WOMEN PREPARE A HUGE MEAL FOR THEIR GUESTS FROM THE SEA... AND FOR SOME STRANGE REASON, THEY PAY PARTICULAR ATTENTION TO PLEASING JANE...
HELLLOOO?
REFILL?
MIT

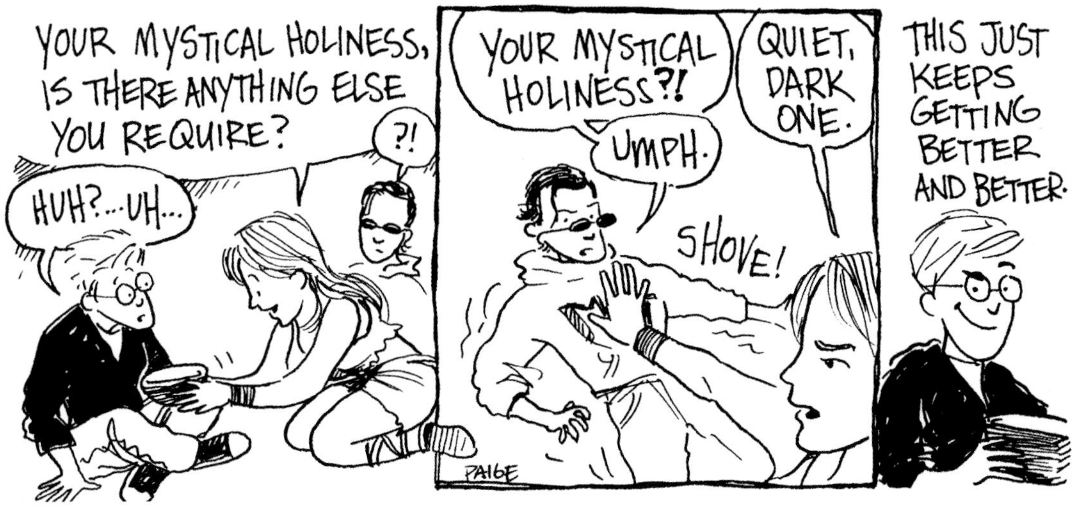
YOUR MYSTICAL HOLINESS, IS THERE ANYTHING ELSE YOU REQUIRE?
?!
HUH?...UH...
YOUR MYSTICAL HOLINESS?!
QUIET, DARK ONE.
UMPH.
SHOVE!
PAIGE
THIS JUST KEEPS GETTING BETTER AND BETTER.

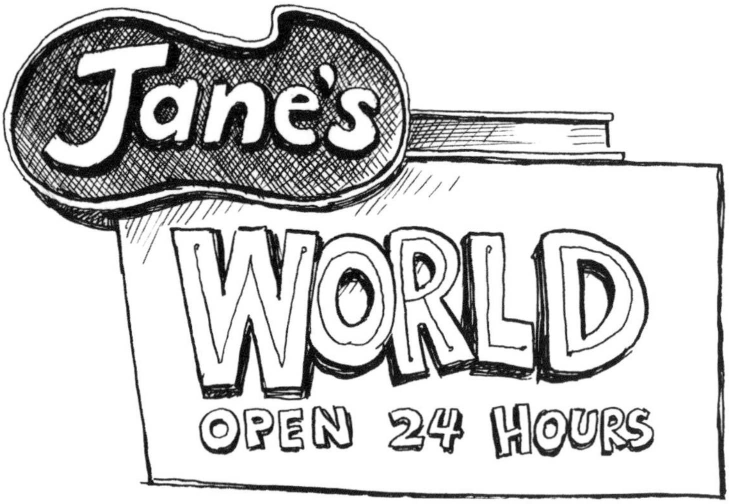
Jane's
WORLD
OPEN 24 HOURS

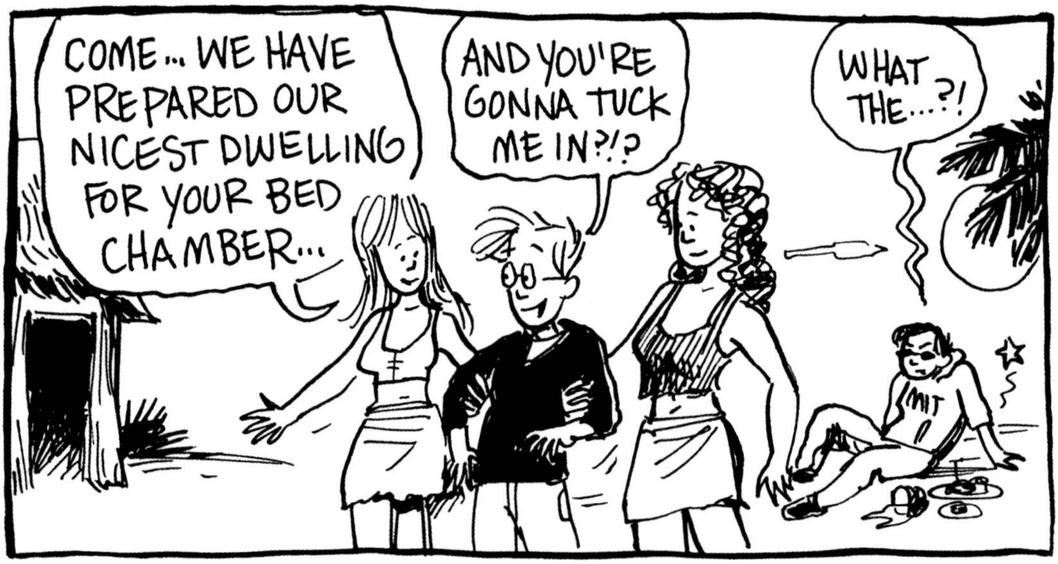
COME... WE HAVE PREPARED OUR NICEST DWELLING FOR YOUR BED CHAMBER...
AND YOU'RE GONNA TUCK ME IN?!?
WHAT THE...?!

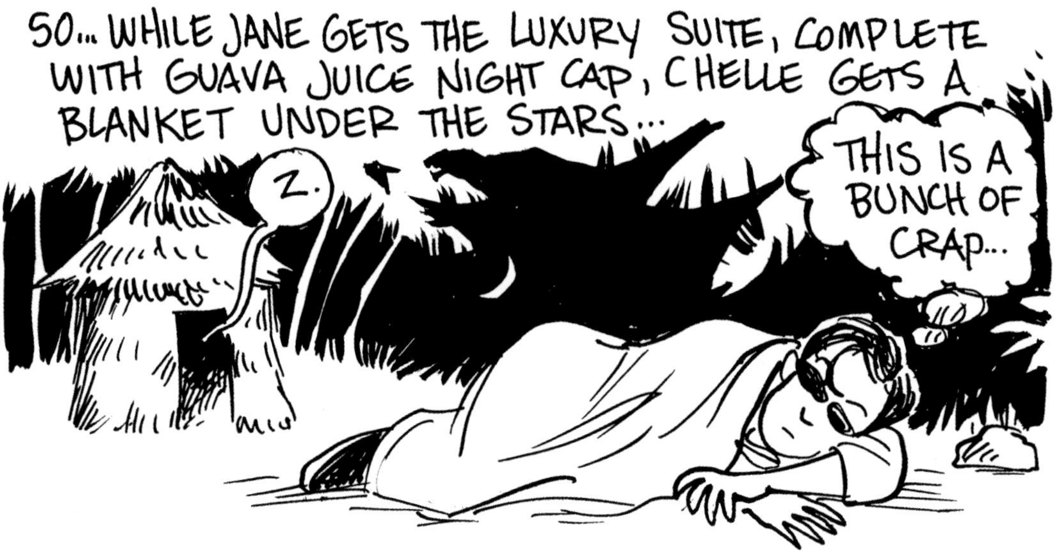
SO... WHILE JANE GETS THE LUXURY SUITE, COMPLETE WITH GUAVA JUICE NIGHT CAP, CHELLE GETS A BLANKET UNDER THE STARS...
Z.
THIS IS A BUNCH OF CRAP...

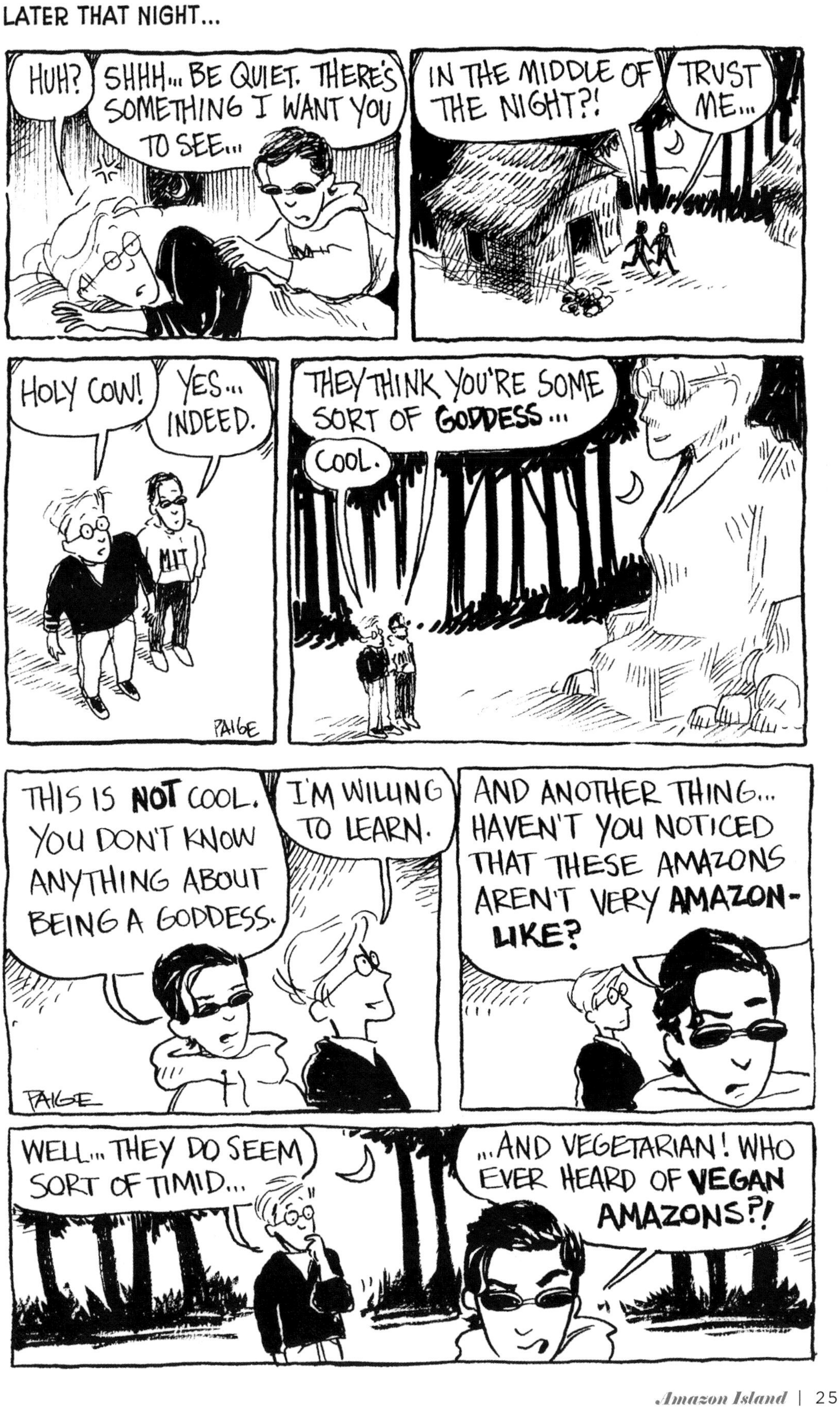
LATER THAT NIGHT...
HUH?
SHHH... BE QUIET. THERE'S SOMETHING I WANT YOU TO SEE...
IN THE MIDDLE OF THE NIGHT?!
TRUST ME...
HOLY COW!
YES... INDEED.
PAIGE
THEY THINK YOU'RE SOME SORT OF **GODDESS**...
COOL.
THIS IS **NOT** COOL. YOU DON'T KNOW ANYTHING ABOUT BEING A GODDESS.
I'M WILLING TO LEARN.
PAIGE
AND ANOTHER THING... HAVEN'T YOU NOTICED THAT THESE AMAZONS AREN'T VERY **AMAZON-LIKE?**
WELL... THEY DO SEEM SORT OF TIMID...
...AND VEGETARIAN! WHO EVER HEARD OF **VEGAN AMAZONS?!**

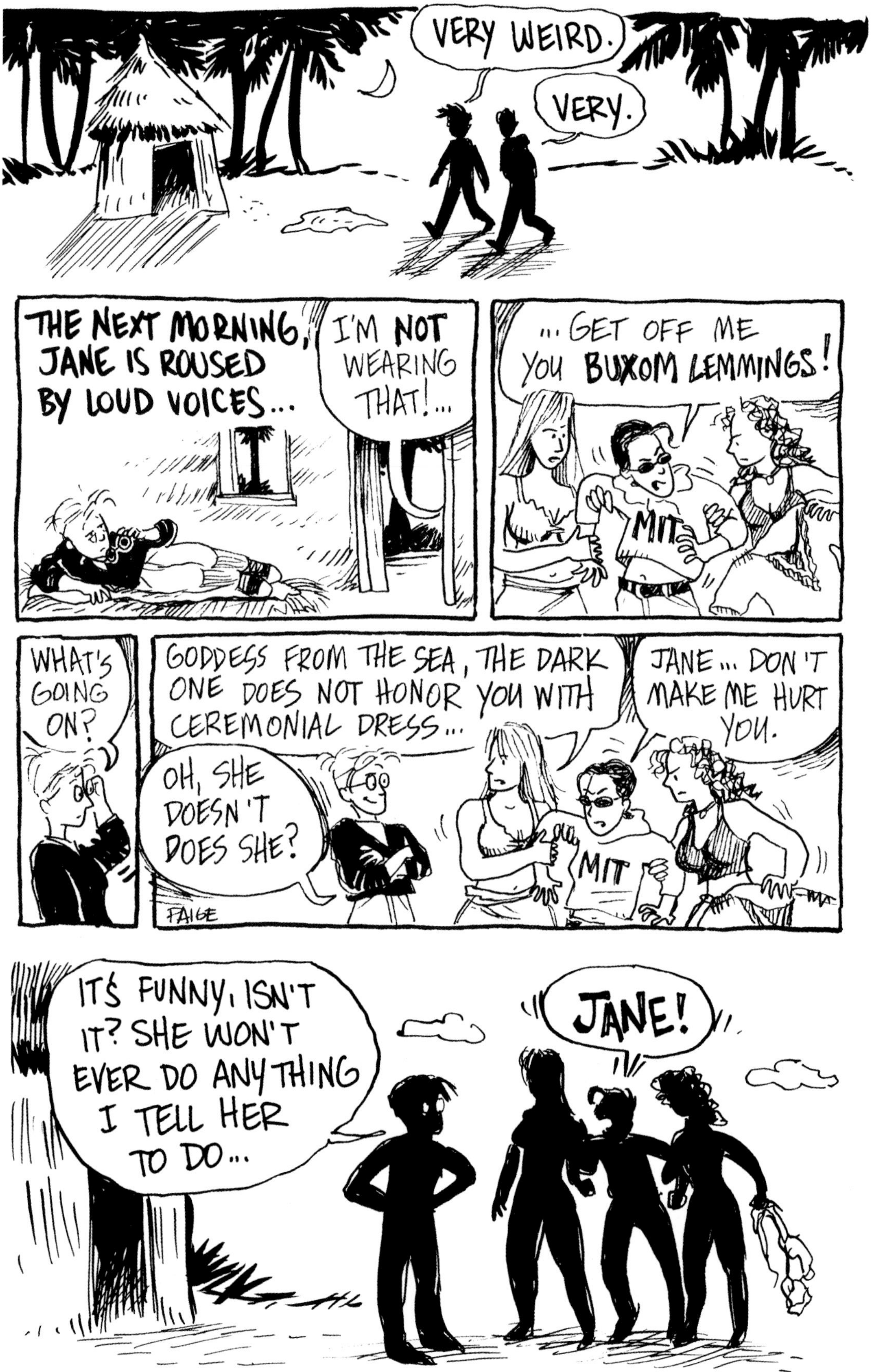
VERY WEIRD.
VERY.
THE NEXT MORNING, JANE IS ROUSED BY LOUD VOICES...
I'M NOT WEARING THAT!...
...GET OFF ME YOU BUXOM LEMMINGS!
MIT
WHAT'S GOING ON?
GODDESS FROM THE SEA, THE DARK ONE DOES NOT HONOR YOU WITH CEREMONIAL DRESS...
JANE... DON'T MAKE ME HURT YOU.
OH, SHE DOESN'T DOES SHE?
MIT
IT'S FUNNY, ISN'T IT? SHE WON'T EVER DO ANYTHING I TELL HER TO DO...
JANE!

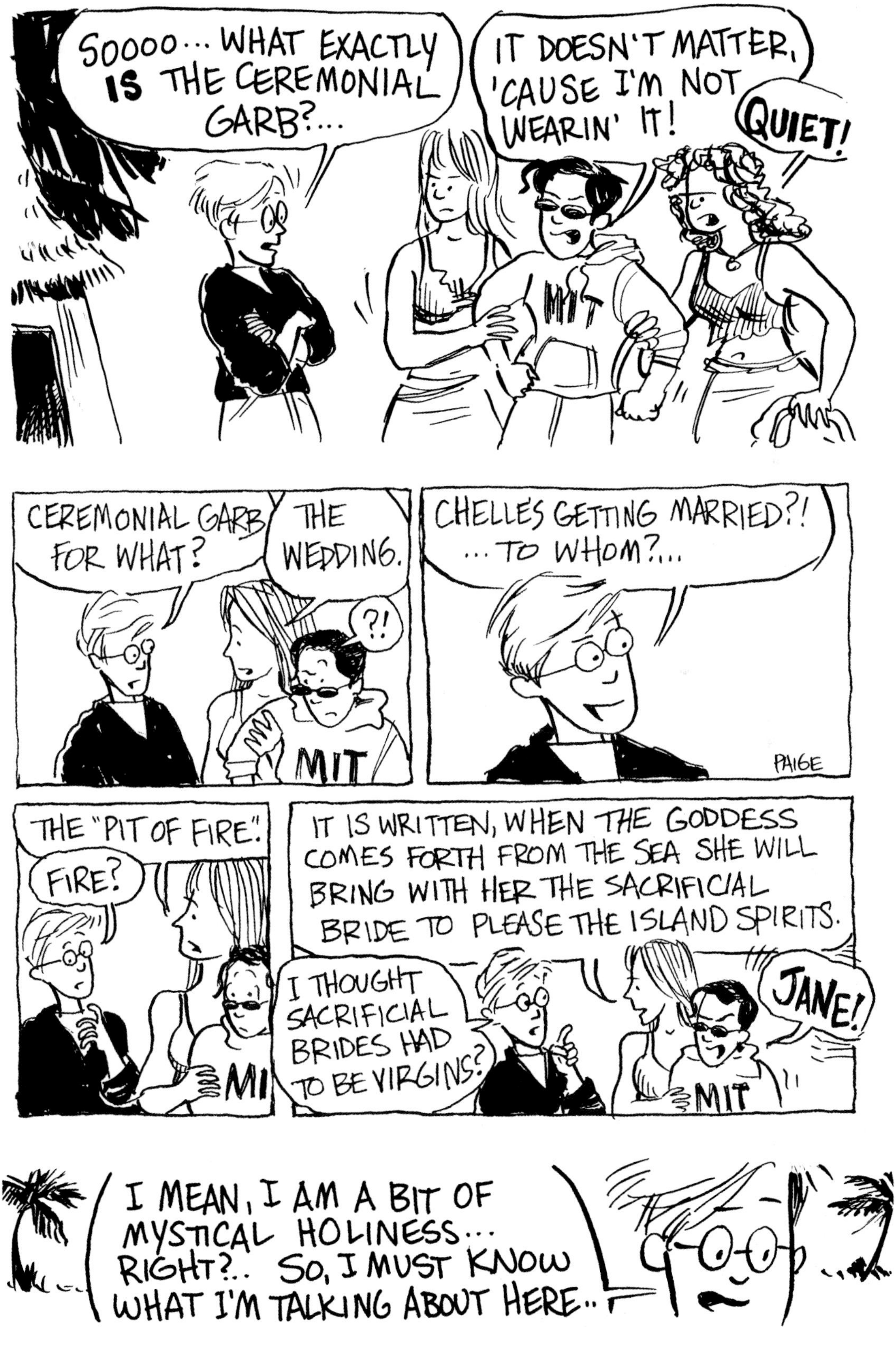
SOOOO... WHAT EXACTLY IS THE CEREMONIAL GARB?...
IT DOESN'T MATTER, 'CAUSE I'M NOT WEARIN' IT!
QUIET!
MIT
CEREMONIAL GARB FOR WHAT?
THE WEDDING.
?!
MIT
CHELLE'S GETTING MARRIED?! ...TO WHOM?...
PAIGE
THE "PIT OF FIRE".
FIRE?
MI
IT IS WRITTEN, WHEN THE GODDESS COMES FORTH FROM THE SEA SHE WILL BRING WITH HER THE SACRIFICIAL BRIDE TO PLEASE THE ISLAND SPIRITS.
I THOUGHT SACRIFICIAL BRIDES HAD TO BE VIRGINS?
JANE!
MIT
I MEAN, I AM A BIT OF MYSTICAL HOLINESS... RIGHT?.. SO, I MUST KNOW WHAT I'M TALKING ABOUT HERE..

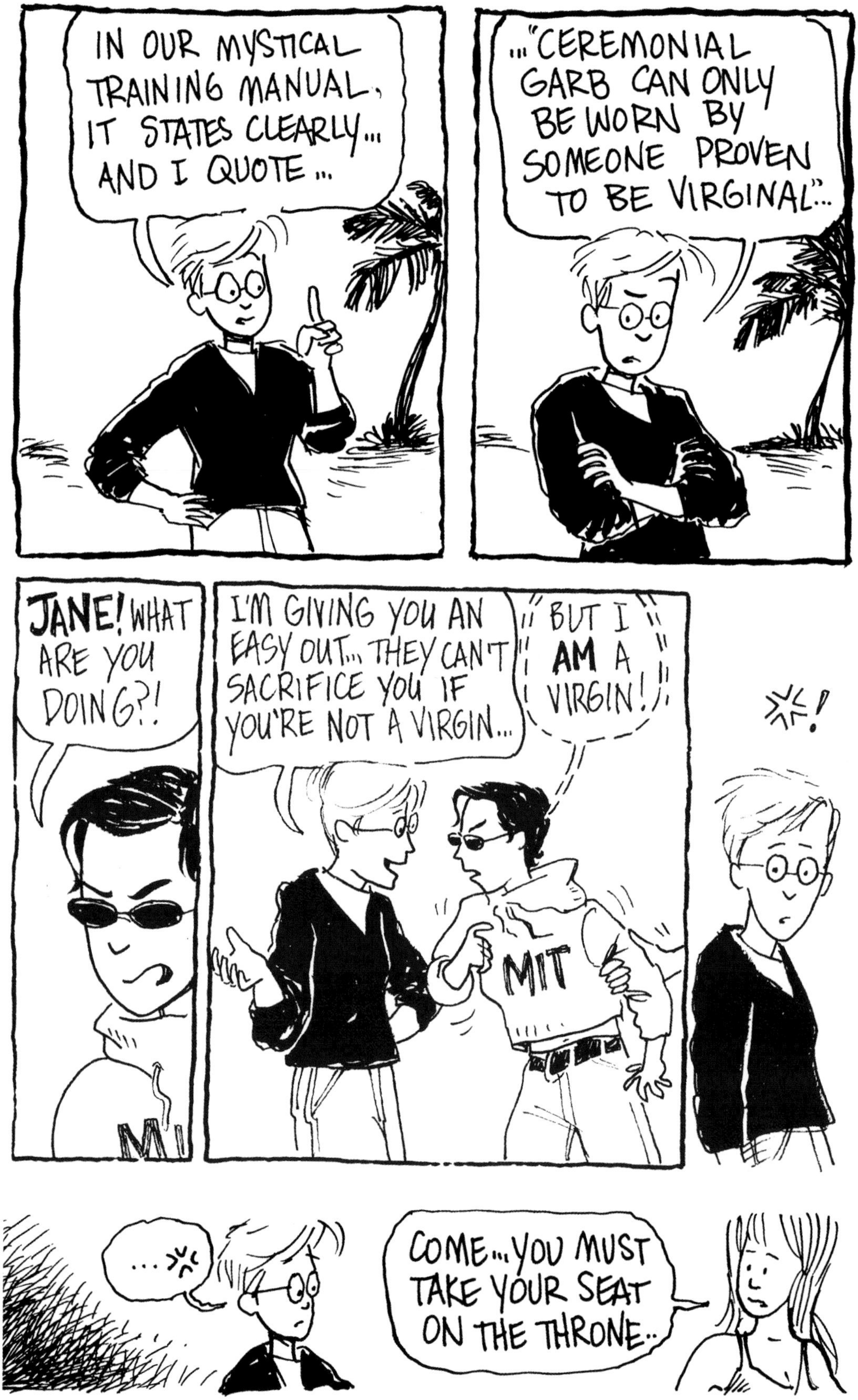
IN OUR MYSTICAL TRAINING MANUAL, IT STATES CLEARLY... AND I QUOTE...
..."CEREMONIAL GARB CAN ONLY BE WORN BY SOMEONE PROVEN TO BE VIRGINAL"...
JANE! WHAT ARE YOU DOING?!
I'M GIVING YOU AN EASY OUT... THEY CAN'T SACRIFICE YOU IF YOU'RE NOT A VIRGIN...
BUT I **AM** A VIRGIN!
MIT
...
COME... YOU MUST TAKE YOUR SEAT ON THE THRONE..

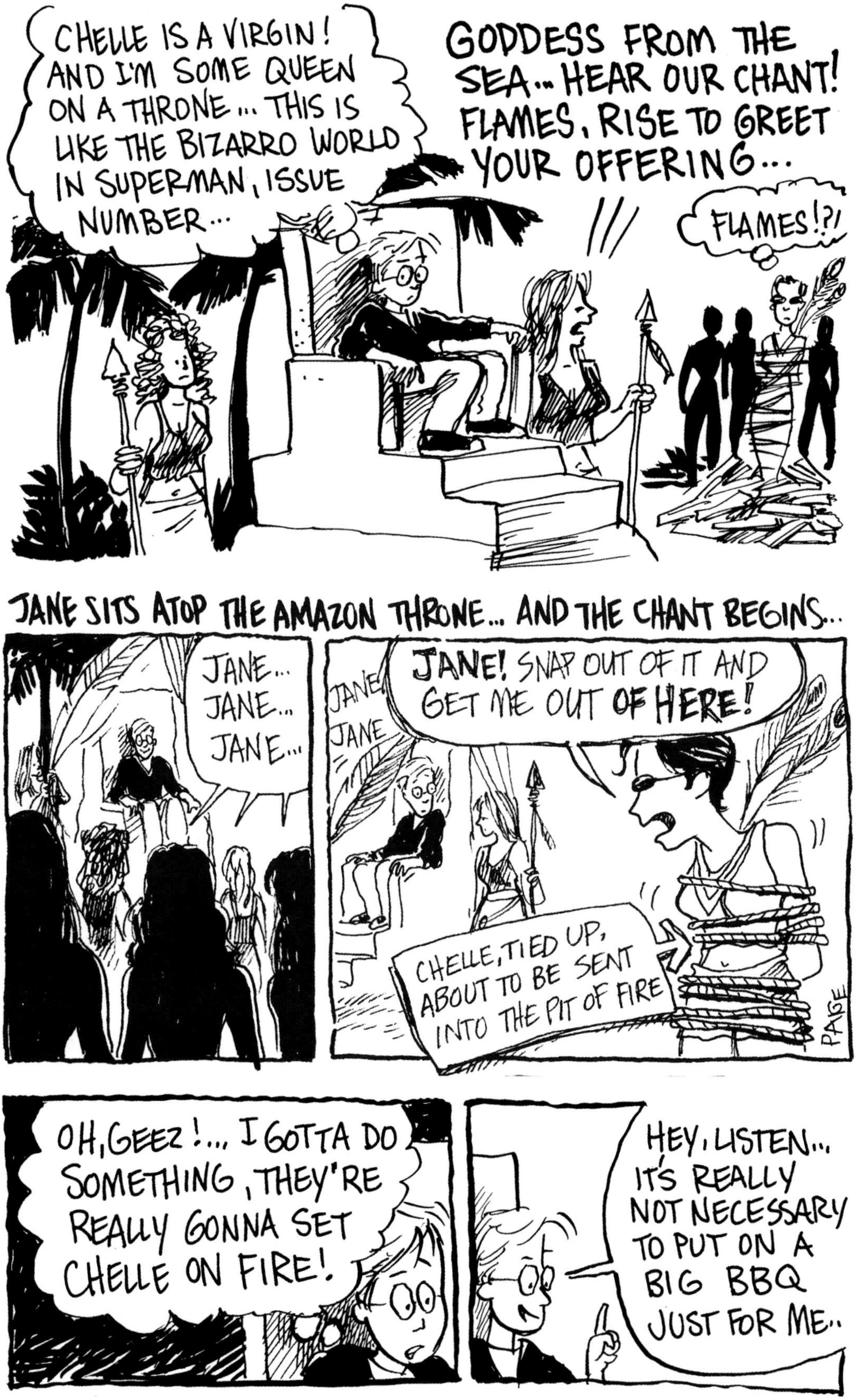
CHELLE IS A VIRGIN! AND I'M SOME QUEEN ON A THRONE... THIS IS LIKE THE BIZARRO WORLD IN SUPERMAN, ISSUE NUMBER...
GODDESS FROM THE SEA... HEAR OUR CHANT! FLAMES, RISE TO GREET YOUR OFFERING...
FLAMES!?!
JANE SITS ATOP THE AMAZON THRONE... AND THE CHANT BEGINS...
JANE... JANE... JANE...
JANE JANE
JANE! SNAP OUT OF IT AND GET ME OUT OF HERE!
CHELLE, TIED UP, ABOUT TO BE SENT INTO THE PIT OF FIRE
PAIGE
OH, GEEZ!... I GOTTA DO SOMETHING, THEY'RE REALLY GONNA SET CHELLE ON FIRE!
HEY, LISTEN... IT'S REALLY NOT NECESSARY TO PUT ON A BIG BBQ JUST FOR ME..

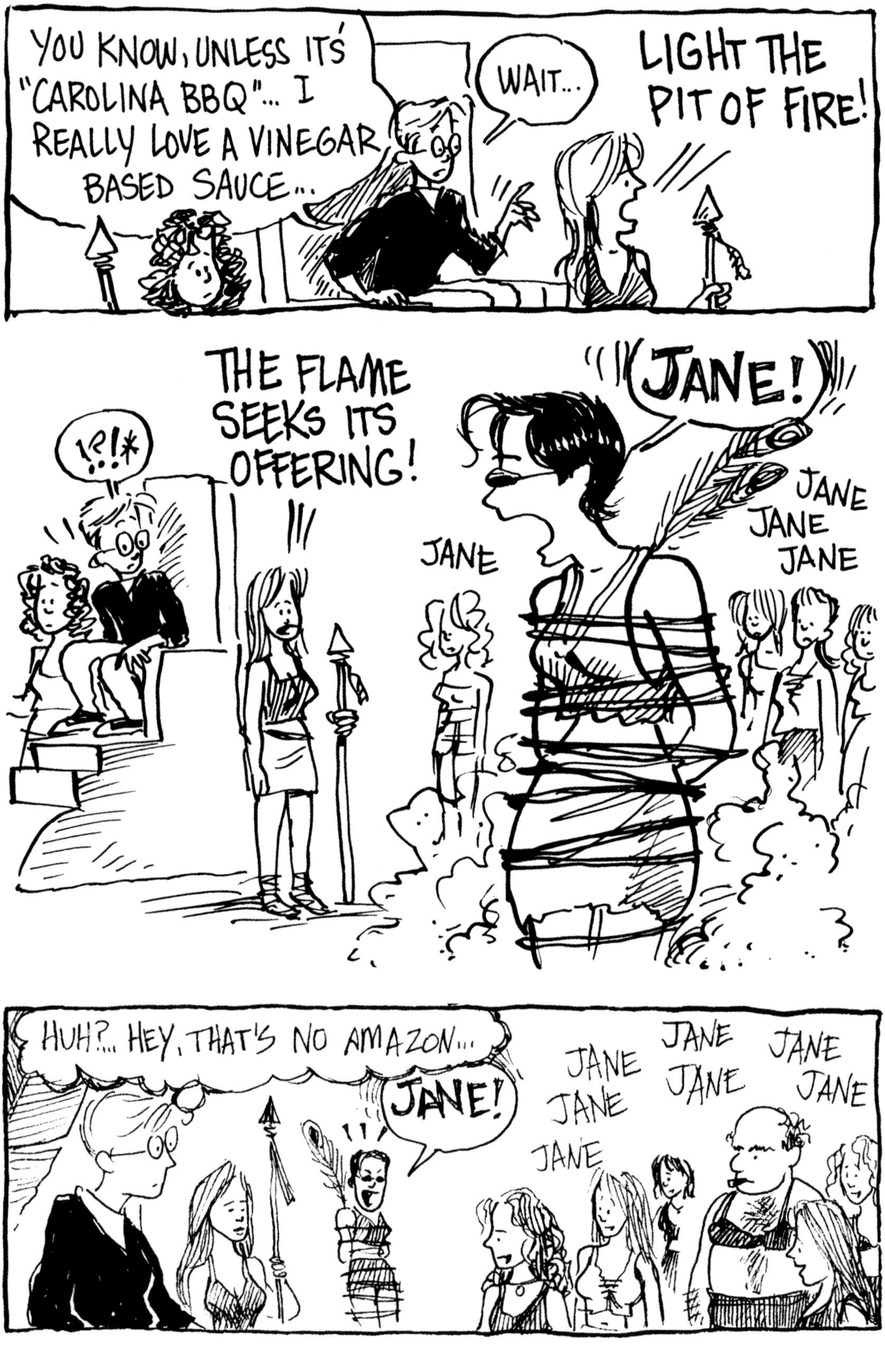
YOU KNOW, UNLESS ITS "CAROLINA BBQ"... I REALLY LOVE A VINEGAR BASED SAUCE...
WAIT...
LIGHT THE PIT OF FIRE!
!?!*
THE FLAME SEEKS ITS OFFERING!
JANE!
JANE
JANE
JANE
JANE
HUH?... HEY, THAT'S NO AMAZON...
JANE!
JANE
JANE
JANE
JANE
JANE
JANE
JANE

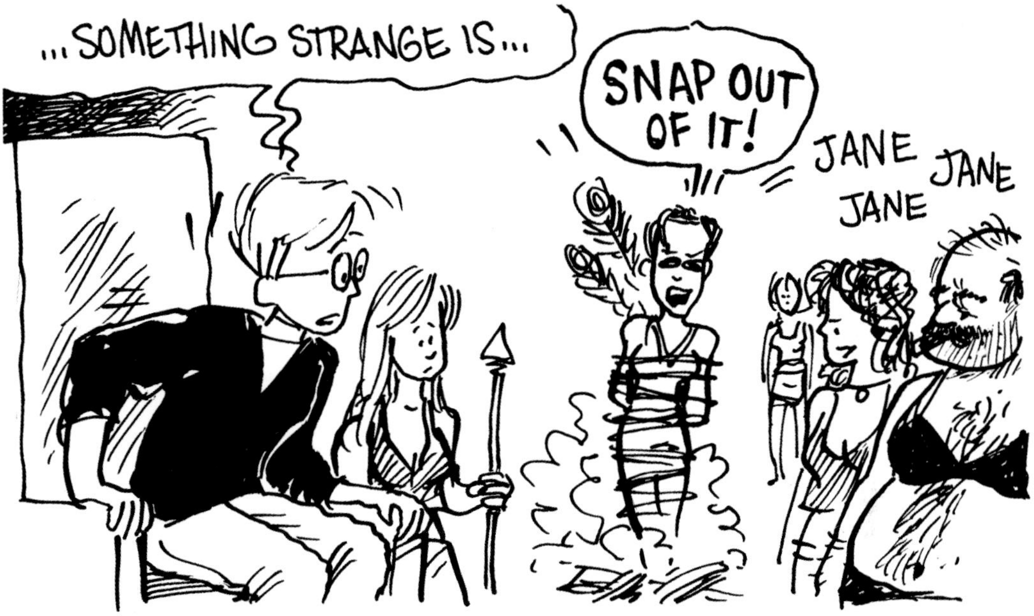
...SOMETHING STRANGE IS...
SNAP OUT OF IT!
JANE
JANE
JANE

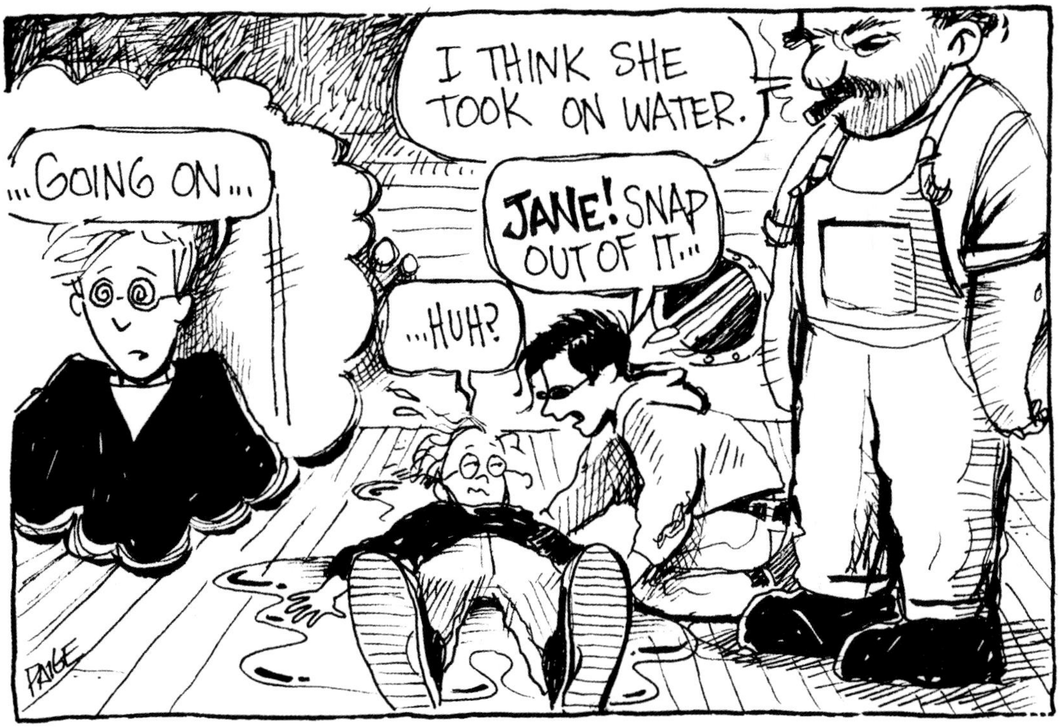
I THINK SHE TOOK ON WATER.
...GOING ON...
JANE! SNAP OUT OF IT.
...HUH?
PAIGE

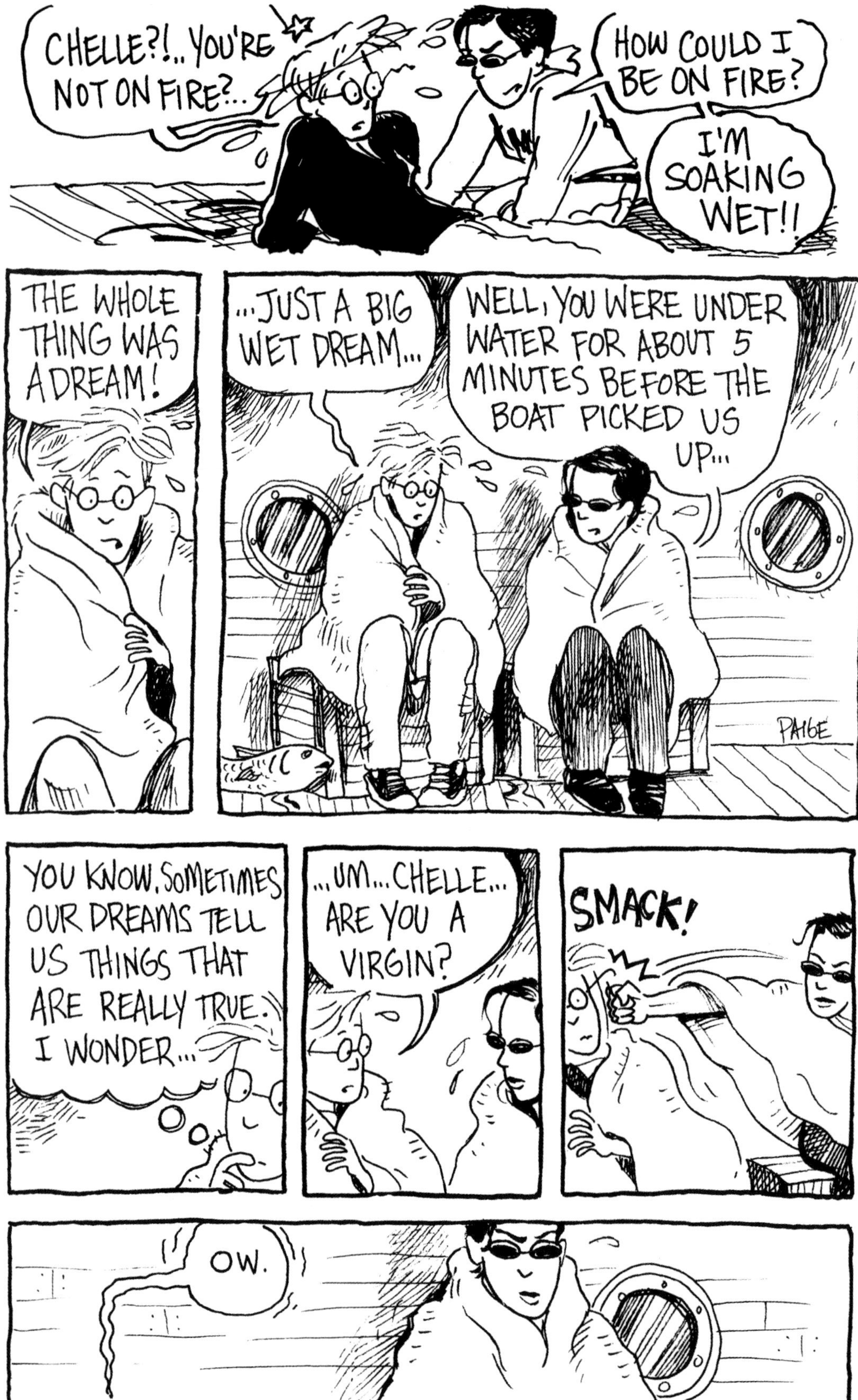
CHELLE?!.. YOU'RE NOT ON FIRE?...
HOW COULD I BE ON FIRE?
I'M SOAKING WET!!
THE WHOLE THING WAS A DREAM!
...JUST A BIG WET DREAM...
WELL, YOU WERE UNDER WATER FOR ABOUT 5 MINUTES BEFORE THE BOAT PICKED US UP...
PAIGE
YOU KNOW, SOMETIMES OUR DREAMS TELL US THINGS THAT ARE REALLY TRUE. I WONDER...
...UM...CHELLE... ARE YOU A VIRGIN?
SMACK!
OW.

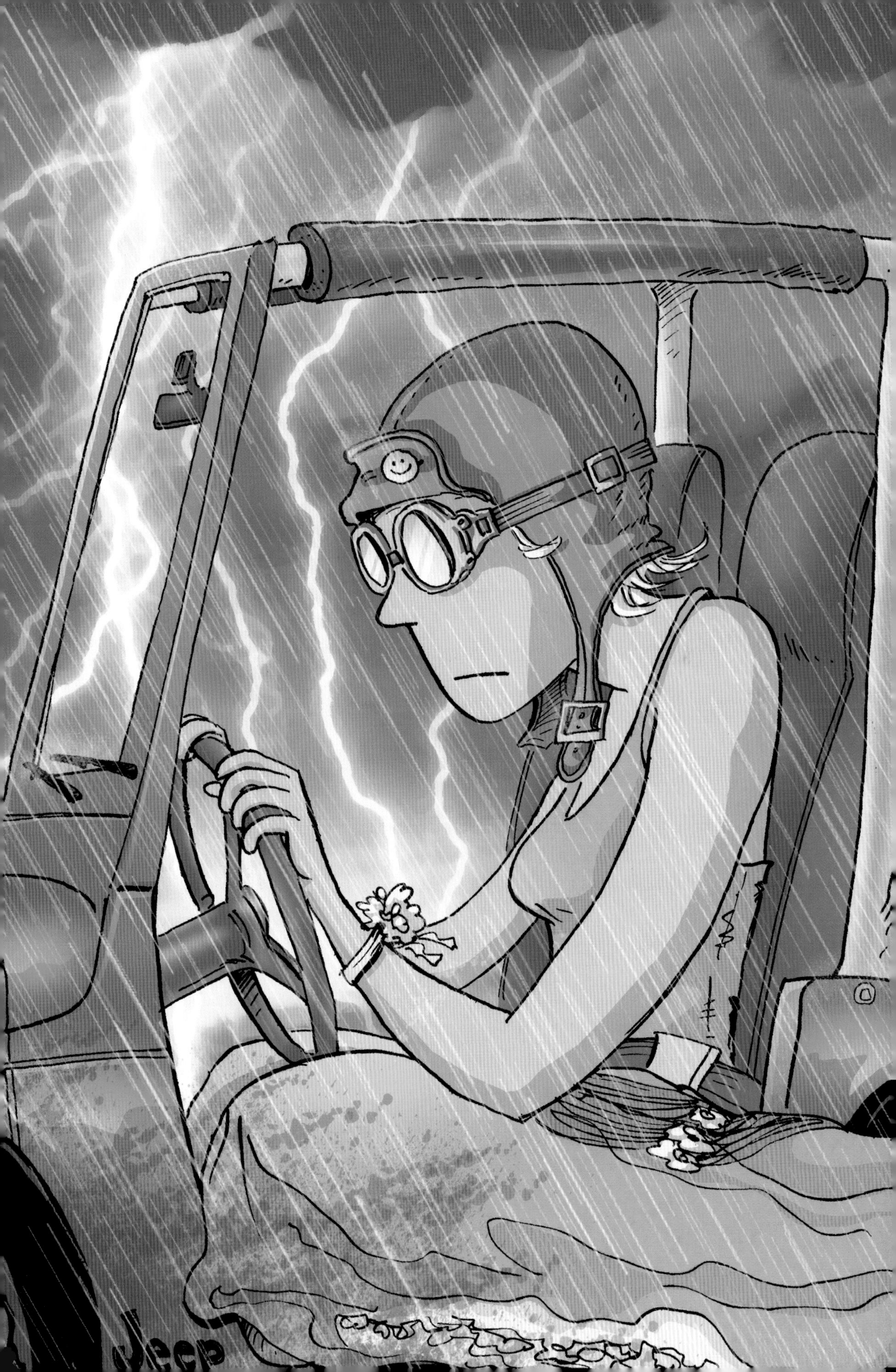

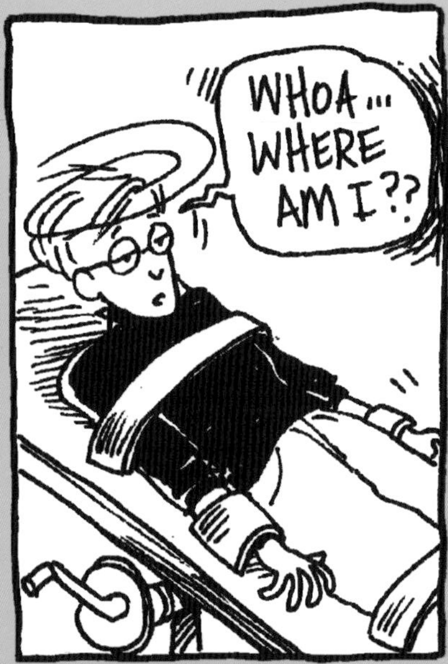
WHOA... WHERE AM I??

Close Encounters

Jane's managing editor at the newspaper decides it would be good for her to do a little community outreach at a small, rural paper. Jane has no choice but to follow orders and cover community news for *The Poultry Times*. The assignment is supposed to last two weeks but fourteen days without her morning espresso turns out to be more than Jane can stand. She bails on her duties at *The Poultry Times* and ends up in Memphis where she bumps into some old friends and has a close encounter of the weird kind. Actually, more than one.

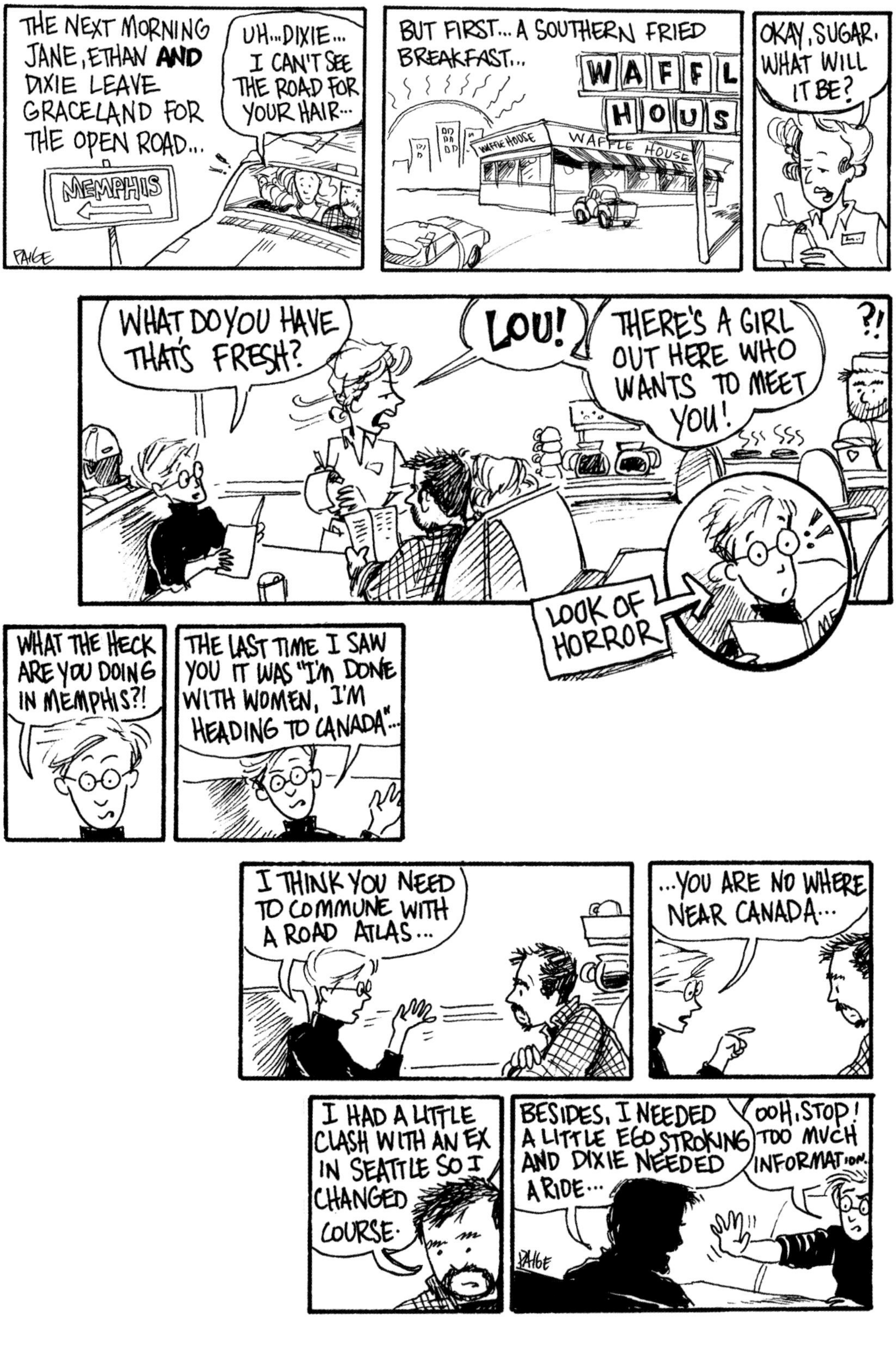
THE NEXT MORNING JANE, ETHAN **AND** DIXIE LEAVE GRACELAND FOR THE OPEN ROAD...
UH...DIXIE... I CAN'T SEE THE ROAD FOR YOUR HAIR...
MEMPHIS
PAIGE
BUT FIRST... A SOUTHERN FRIED BREAKFAST...
WAFFL
HOUS
WAFFLE HOUSE
WAFFLE HOUSE
OKAY, SUGAR. WHAT WILL IT BE?
WHAT DO YOU HAVE THAT'S FRESH?
LOU!
THERE'S A GIRL OUT HERE WHO WANTS TO MEET YOU!
?!
LOOK OF HORROR
WHAT THE HECK ARE YOU DOING IN MEMPHIS?!
THE LAST TIME I SAW YOU IT WAS "I'M DONE WITH WOMEN, I'M HEADING TO CANADA"...
I THINK YOU NEED TO COMMUNE WITH A ROAD ATLAS...
...YOU ARE NO WHERE NEAR CANADA...
I HAD A LITTLE CLASH WITH AN EX IN SEATTLE SO I CHANGED COURSE.
BESIDES, I NEEDED A LITTLE EGO STROKING AND DIXIE NEEDED A RIDE...
OOH, STOP! TOO MUCH INFORMATION.
PAIGE

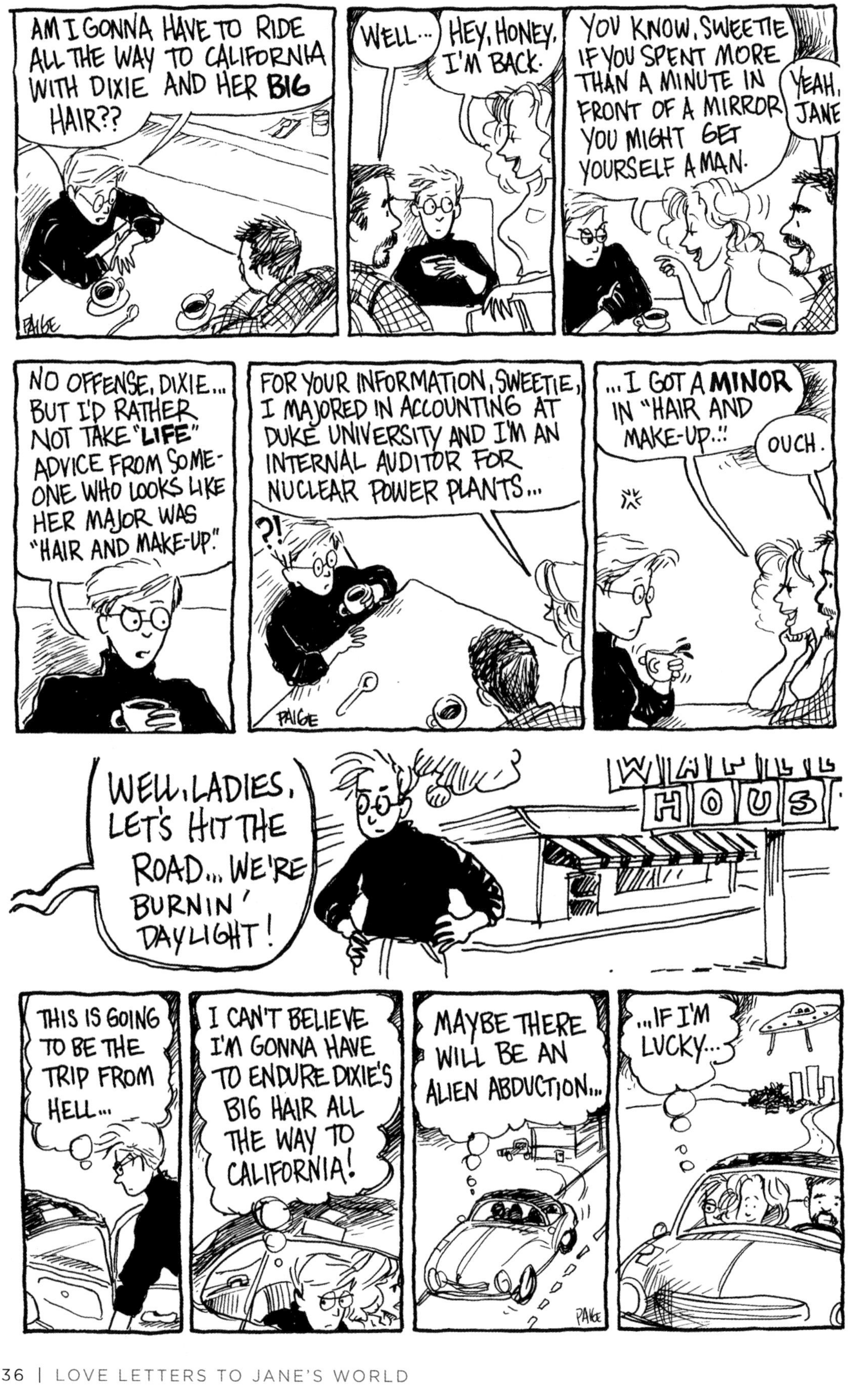
AM I GONNA HAVE TO RIDE ALL THE WAY TO CALIFORNIA WITH DIXIE AND HER **BIG** HAIR??
WELL...
HEY, HONEY, I'M BACK.
YOU KNOW, SWEETIE IF YOU SPENT MORE THAN A MINUTE IN FRONT OF A MIRROR YOU MIGHT GET YOURSELF A MAN.
YEAH, JANE
NO OFFENSE, DIXIE... BUT I'D RATHER NOT TAKE "**LIFE**" ADVICE FROM SOMEONE WHO LOOKS LIKE HER MAJOR WAS "HAIR AND MAKE-UP."
FOR YOUR INFORMATION, SWEETIE, I MAJORED IN ACCOUNTING AT DUKE UNIVERSITY AND I'M AN INTERNAL AUDITOR FOR NUCLEAR POWER PLANTS...
?!
...I GOT A **MINOR** IN "HAIR AND MAKE-UP..."
OUCH.
WELL, LADIES, LET'S HIT THE ROAD... WE'RE BURNIN' DAYLIGHT!
HOUS
THIS IS GOING TO BE THE TRIP FROM HELL...
I CAN'T BELIEVE I'M GONNA HAVE TO ENDURE DIXIE'S BIG HAIR ALL THE WAY TO CALIFORNIA!
MAYBE THERE WILL BE AN ALIEN ABDUCTION...
...IF I'M LUCKY...

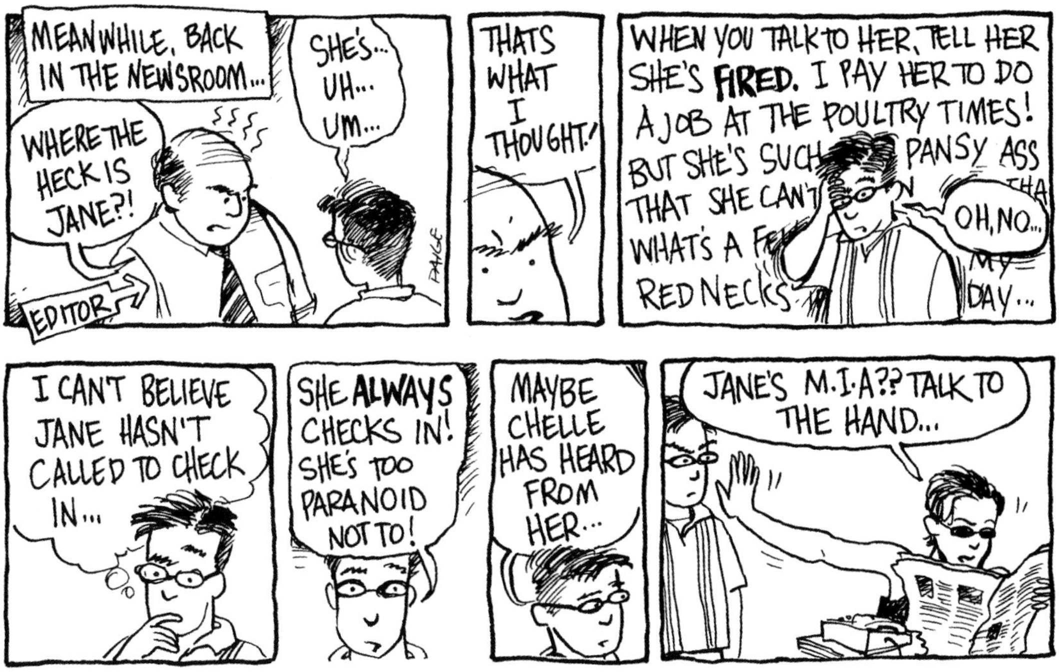
MEANWHILE, BACK IN THE NEWSROOM...
WHERE THE HECK IS JANE?!
EDITOR
SHE'S... UH... UM...
PAIGE
THATS WHAT I THOUGHT!
WHEN YOU TALK TO HER, TELL HER SHE'S **FIRED.** I PAY HER TO DO A JOB AT THE POULTRY TIMES! BUT SHE'S SUCH PANSY ASS THAT SHE CAN'T WHAT'S A RED NECKS DAY...
OH, NO...
I CAN'T BELIEVE JANE HASN'T CALLED TO CHECK IN...
SHE **ALWAYS** CHECKS IN! SHE'S TOO PARANOID NOT TO!
MAYBE CHELLE HAS HEARD FROM HER...
JANE'S M.I.A.?? TALK TO THE HAND...

MEANWHILE, ON THE OPEN ROAD, OUR TRIO DRIVES INTO THE DESCENDING OKLAHOMA DUSK...

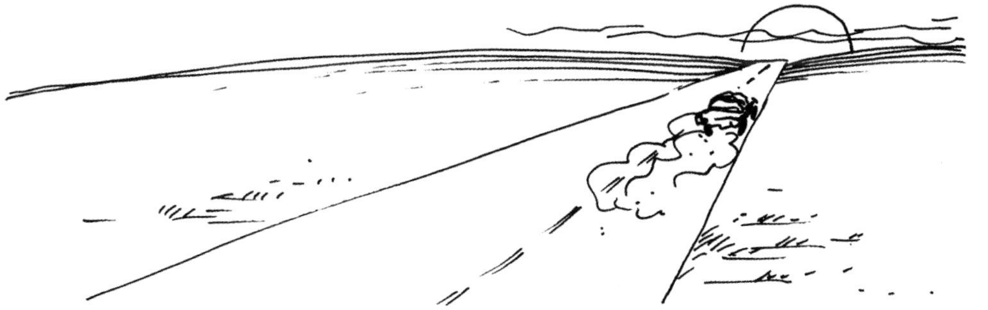

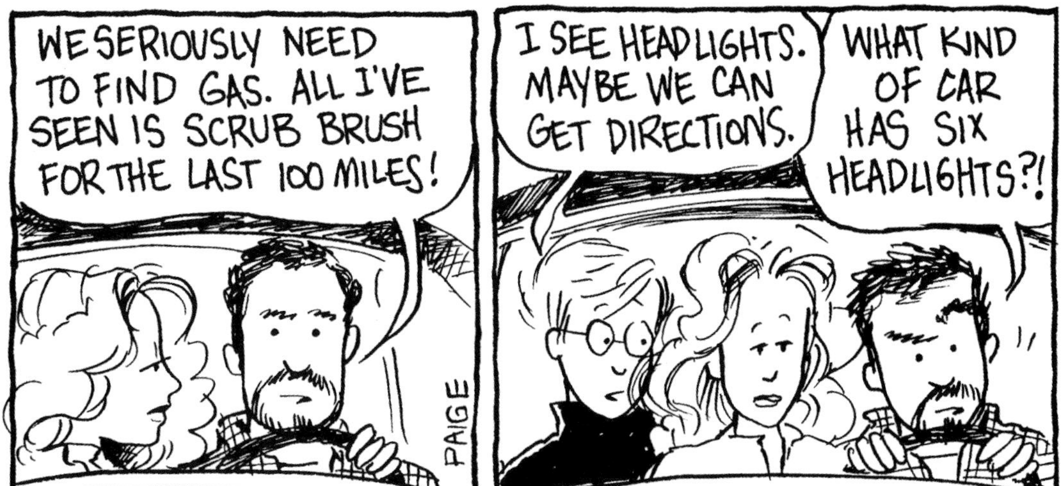
WE SERIOUSLY NEED TO FIND GAS. ALL I'VE SEEN IS SCRUB BRUSH FOR THE LAST 100 MILES!
PAIGE
I SEE HEADLIGHTS. MAYBE WE CAN GET DIRECTIONS.
WHAT KIND OF CAR HAS SIX HEADLIGHTS?!

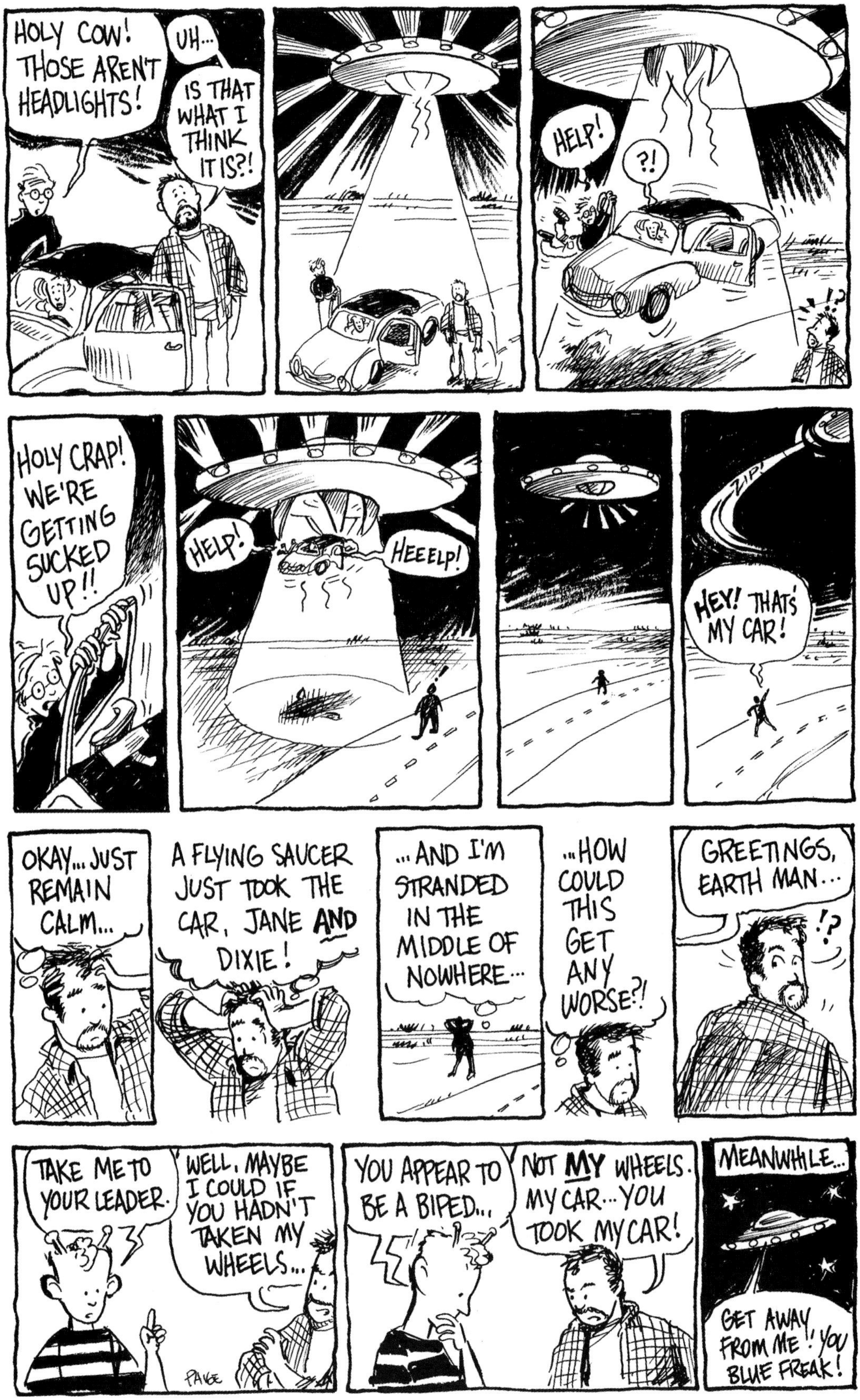
HOLY COW! THOSE AREN'T HEADLIGHTS!
UH...
IS THAT WHAT I THINK IT IS?!
HELP!
?!
!?
HOLY CRAP! WE'RE GETTING SUCKED UP!!
HELP!
HEEELP!
ZIP!
HEY! THAT'S MY CAR!
OKAY... JUST REMAIN CALM...
A FLYING SAUCER JUST TOOK THE CAR, JANE AND DIXIE!
...AND I'M STRANDED IN THE MIDDLE OF NOWHERE...
...HOW COULD THIS GET ANY WORSE?!
GREETINGS, EARTH MAN...
!?
TAKE ME TO YOUR LEADER.
WELL, MAYBE I COULD IF YOU HADN'T TAKEN MY WHEELS...
PAIGE
YOU APPEAR TO BE A BIPED...
NOT MY WHEELS. MY CAR... YOU TOOK MY CAR!
MEANWHILE...
GET AWAY FROM ME! YOU BLUE FREAK!

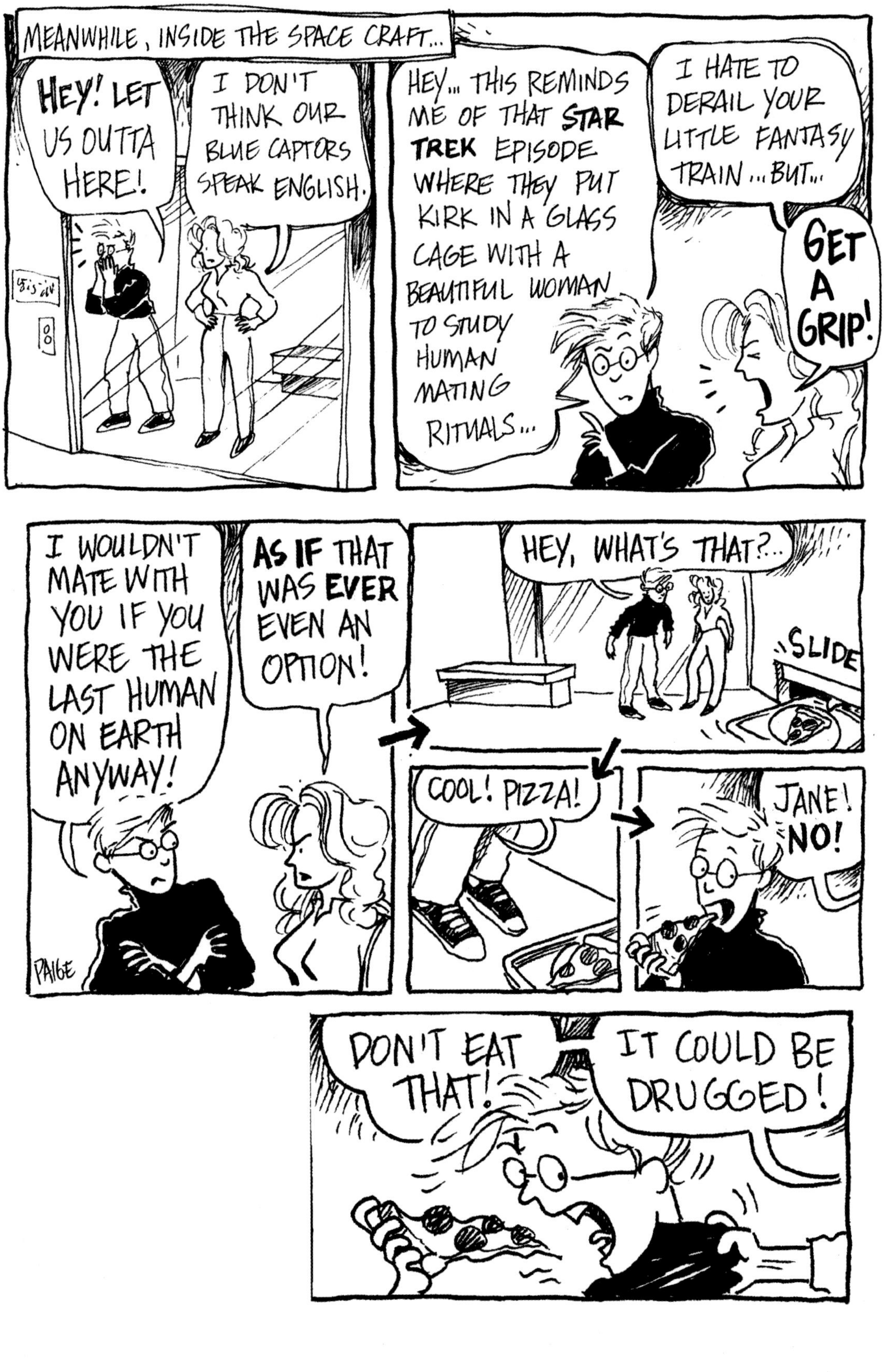
MEANWHILE, INSIDE THE SPACE CRAFT...
HEY! LET US OUTTA HERE!
I DON'T THINK OUR BLUE CAPTORS SPEAK ENGLISH.
HEY... THIS REMINDS ME OF THAT STAR TREK EPISODE WHERE THEY PUT KIRK IN A GLASS CAGE WITH A BEAUTIFUL WOMAN TO STUDY HUMAN MATING RITUALS...
I HATE TO DERAIL YOUR LITTLE FANTASY TRAIN... BUT...
GET A GRIP!
I WOULDN'T MATE WITH YOU IF YOU WERE THE LAST HUMAN ON EARTH ANYWAY!
AS IF THAT WAS EVER EVEN AN OPTION!
PAIGE
HEY, WHAT'S THAT?...
SLIDE
COOL! PIZZA!
JANE! NO!
DON'T EAT THAT!
IT COULD BE DRUGGED!

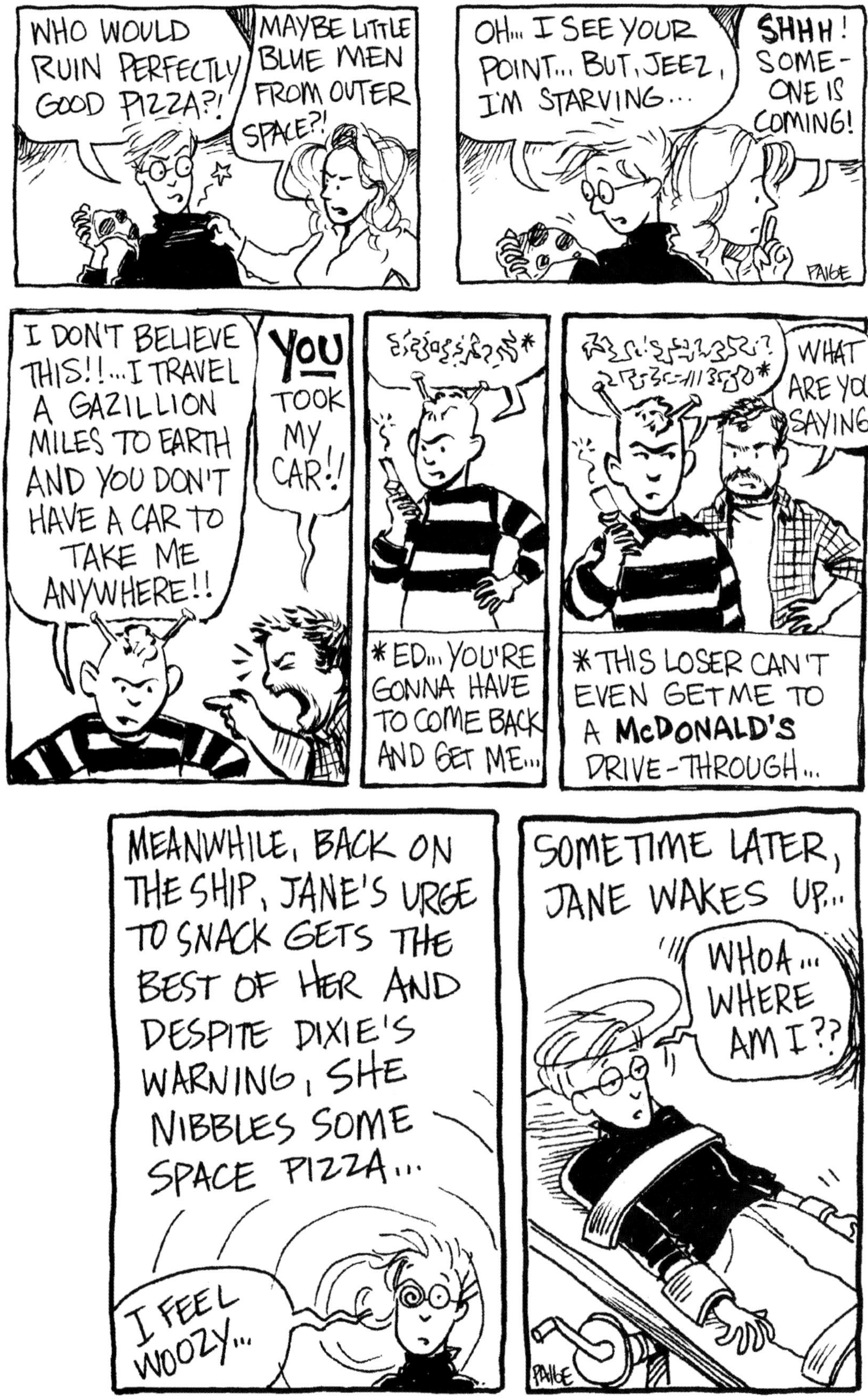
WHO WOULD RUIN PERFECTLY GOOD PIZZA?!
MAYBE LITTLE BLUE MEN FROM OUTER SPACE?!
OH... I SEE YOUR POINT... BUT, JEEZ, I'M STARVING...
SHHH! SOMEONE IS COMING!
PAIGE
I DON'T BELIEVE THIS!!...I TRAVEL A GAZILLION MILES TO EARTH AND YOU DON'T HAVE A CAR TO TAKE ME ANYWHERE!!
YOU TOOK MY CAR!!
*ED... YOU'RE GONNA HAVE TO COME BACK AND GET ME...
WHAT ARE YOU SAYING?
*THIS LOSER CAN'T EVEN GET ME TO A McDONALD'S DRIVE-THROUGH...
MEANWHILE, BACK ON THE SHIP, JANE'S URGE TO SNACK GETS THE BEST OF HER AND DESPITE DIXIE'S WARNING, SHE NIBBLES SOME SPACE PIZZA...
I FEEL WOOZY...
SOMETIME LATER, JANE WAKES UP...
WHOA... WHERE AM I??
PAIGE

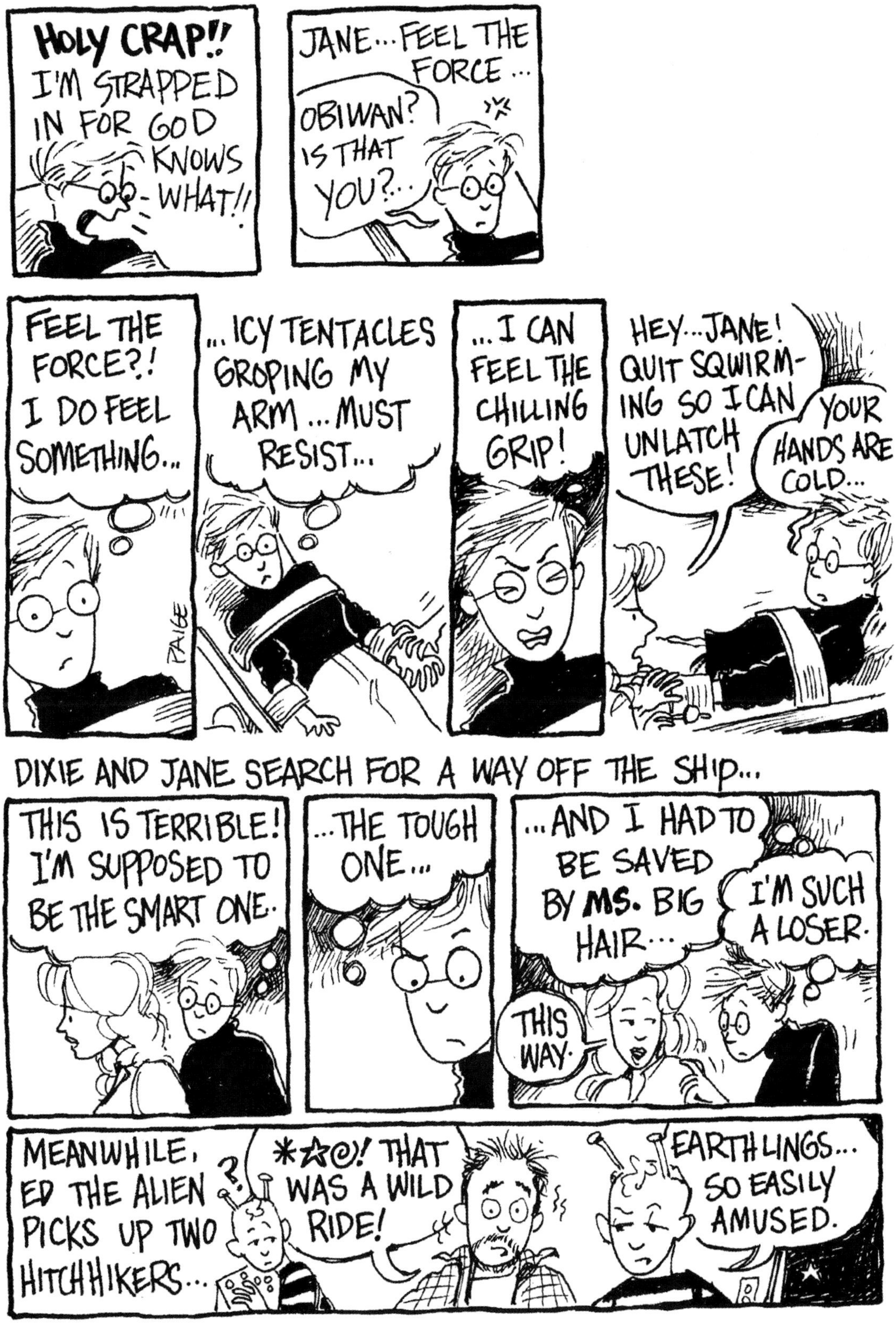
HOLY CRAP!! I'M STRAPPED IN FOR GOD KNOWS WHAT!!
JANE... FEEL THE FORCE...
OBIWAN? IS THAT YOU?...
FEEL THE FORCE?! I DO FEEL SOMETHING...
PAIGE
...ICY TENTACLES GROPING MY ARM ... MUST RESIST...
...I CAN FEEL THE CHILLING GRIP!
HEY...JANE! QUIT SQWIRMING SO I CAN UNLATCH THESE!
YOUR HANDS ARE COLD...
DIXIE AND JANE SEARCH FOR A WAY OFF THE SHIP...
THIS IS TERRIBLE! I'M SUPPOSED TO BE THE SMART ONE.
...THE TOUGH ONE...
...AND I HAD TO BE SAVED BY MS. BIG HAIR...
I'M SUCH A LOSER.
THIS WAY.
MEANWHILE, ED THE ALIEN PICKS UP TWO HITCHHIKERS...
?
*☆@! THAT WAS A WILD RIDE!
EARTHLINGS... SO EASILY AMUSED.

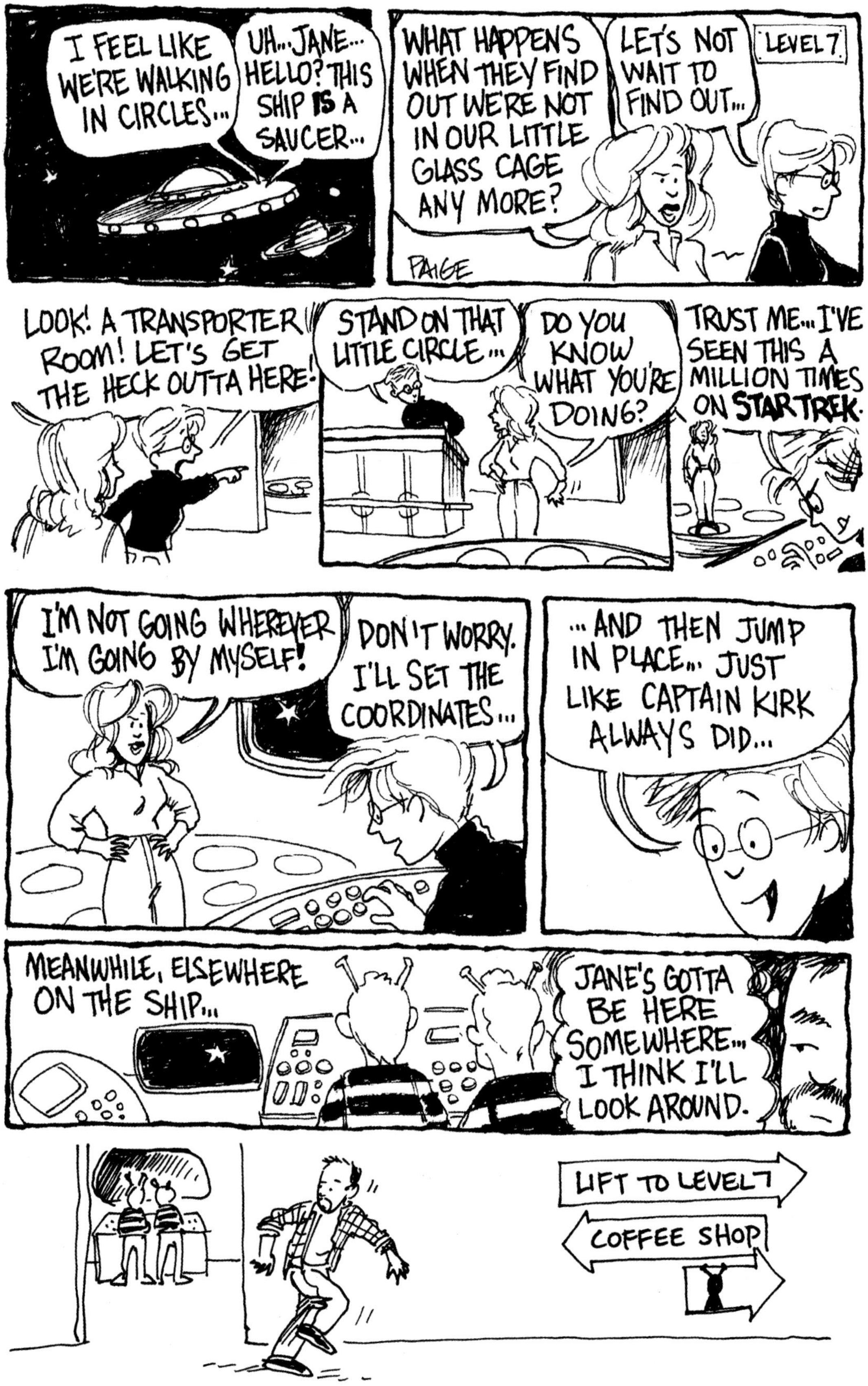
I FEEL LIKE WE'RE WALKING IN CIRCLES...
UH...JANE... HELLO? THIS SHIP IS A SAUCER...
WHAT HAPPENS WHEN THEY FIND OUT WE'RE NOT IN OUR LITTLE GLASS CAGE ANY MORE?
LET'S NOT WAIT TO FIND OUT...
LEVEL 7
PAIGE
LOOK! A TRANSPORTER ROOM! LET'S GET THE HECK OUTTA HERE!
STAND ON THAT LITTLE CIRCLE...
DO YOU KNOW WHAT YOU'RE DOING?
TRUST ME...I'VE SEEN THIS A MILLION TIMES ON STAR TREK.
I'M NOT GOING WHEREVER I'M GOING BY MYSELF!
DON'T WORRY. I'LL SET THE COORDINATES...
...AND THEN JUMP IN PLACE... JUST LIKE CAPTAIN KIRK ALWAYS DID...
MEANWHILE, ELSEWHERE ON THE SHIP...
JANE'S GOTTA BE HERE SOMEWHERE... I THINK I'LL LOOK AROUND.
LIFT TO LEVEL 7
COFFEE SHOP

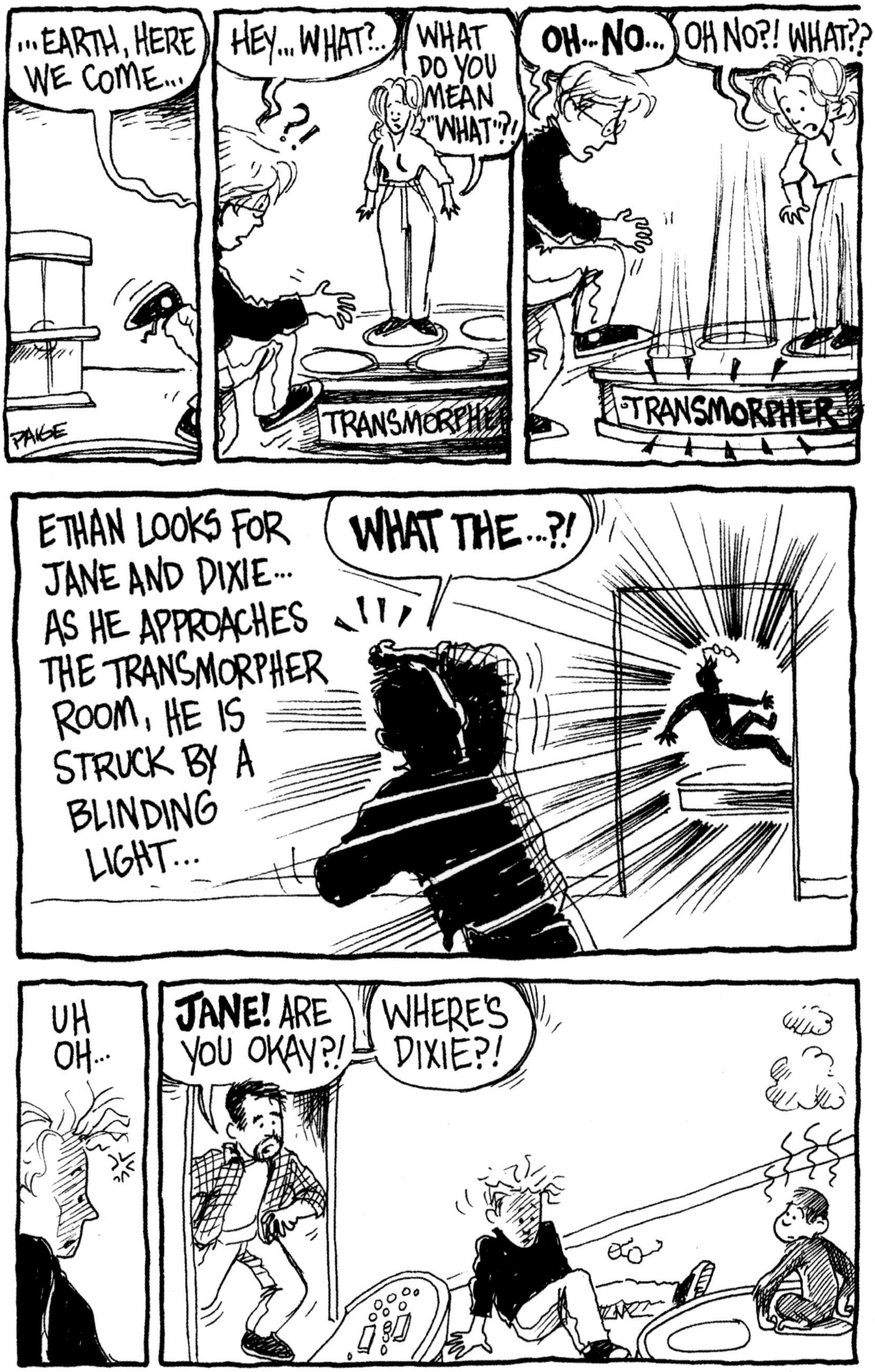
...EARTH, HERE WE COME...
PAIGE
HEY... WHAT?...
?!
WHAT DO YOU MEAN "WHAT"?!
TRANSMORPHER
OH...NO...
OH NO?! WHAT??
TRANSMORPHER
ETHAN LOOKS FOR JANE AND DIXIE... AS HE APPROACHES THE TRANSMORPHER ROOM, HE IS STRUCK BY A BLINDING LIGHT...
WHAT THE...?!
UH OH...
JANE! ARE YOU OKAY?!
WHERE'S DIXIE?!

YOU ARE UN**BE**LIEVABLE! YOU... YOU...

YOU TURNED DIXIE INTO A **CHIMP!!**

GROAN

WELL...TECHNICALLY, SHE'S A **MONKEY**...

?

PAIGE

IT WAS PASSIVE AGGRESSIVE TRANSMORPHING ...THAT'S WHAT IT WAS...

LOOK! A USERS MANUAL!

MAYBE THERE'S A WAY TO REVERSE THIS...

WHY DIDN'T YOU READ THAT FIRST?!

NOBODY READS THE USERS MANUAL UNTIL THERE'S A PROBLEM.

USERS MANUAL

WHAT'S IT SAY?

UH... IT'S NOT GOOD...

IT SEEMS THE TRANSMORPHER CHANGES ANY PERSON INTO THEIR NEAREST DNA RELATIVE.

...AND ONCE YOU LOSE A CHROMOSOME THERE'S NO GOING BACK...

USERS MANUAL

?

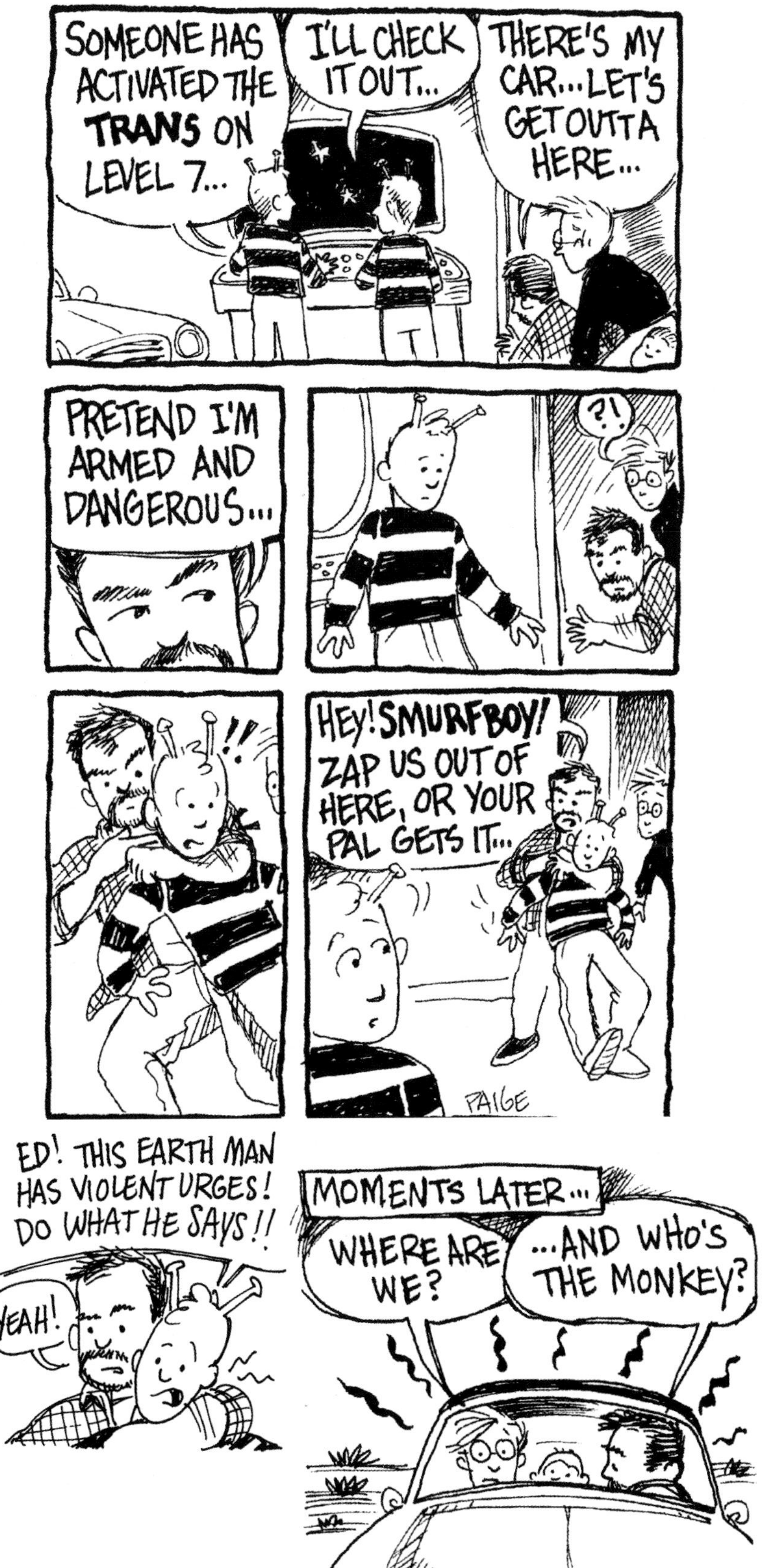
SOMEONE HAS ACTIVATED THE **TRANS** ON LEVEL 7...
I'LL CHECK IT OUT...
THERE'S MY CAR...LET'S GET OUTTA HERE...
PRETEND I'M ARMED AND DANGEROUS...
?!
!!
HEY! **SMURFBOY!** ZAP US OUT OF HERE, OR YOUR PAL GETS IT...
PAIGE
ED! THIS EARTH MAN HAS VIOLENT URGES! DO WHAT HE SAYS!!
YEAH!
MOMENTS LATER...
WHERE ARE WE?
...AND WHO'S THE MONKEY?

Camp Disaster

Jane, Ethan, and Dixie—who has been turned into a chimp—make it back from Oklahoma. Dixie is stuck being a chimp for now, which Ethan is super annoyed with Jane about. He agrees to go on a camping trip with Jane anyway, because she needs backup, and because she begged. Nothing says "lesbian" like a weekend in the great outdoors with your ex.

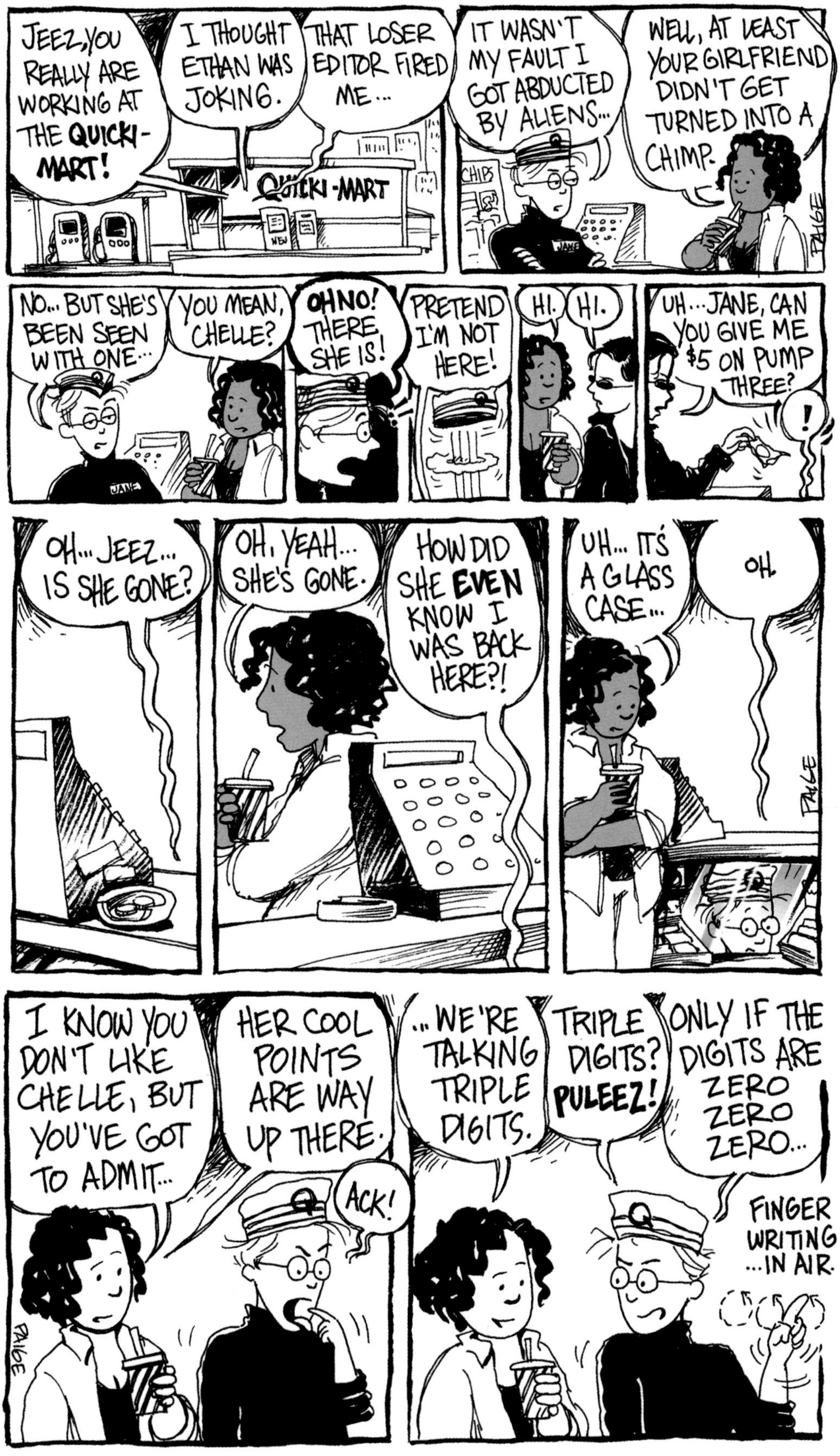
JEEZ, YOU REALLY ARE WORKING AT THE QUICKI-MART!
I THOUGHT ETHAN WAS JOKING.
THAT LOSER EDITOR FIRED ME...
QUICKI-MART
IT WASN'T MY FAULT I GOT ABDUCTED BY ALIENS...
WELL, AT LEAST YOUR GIRLFRIEND DIDN'T GET TURNED INTO A CHIMP.
NO... BUT SHE'S BEEN SEEN WITH ONE...
YOU MEAN, CHELLE?
OH NO! THERE SHE IS!
PRETEND I'M NOT HERE!
HI.
HI.
UH... JANE, CAN YOU GIVE ME $5 ON PUMP THREE?
!
OH... JEEZ... IS SHE GONE?
OH, YEAH... SHE'S GONE.
HOW DID SHE EVEN KNOW I WAS BACK HERE?!
UH... IT'S A GLASS CASE...
OH.
I KNOW YOU DON'T LIKE CHELLE, BUT YOU'VE GOT TO ADMIT...
HER COOL POINTS ARE WAY UP THERE.
ACK!
...WE'RE TALKING TRIPLE DIGITS.
TRIPLE DIGITS? PULEEZ!
ONLY IF THE DIGITS ARE ZERO ZERO ZERO...
FINGER WRITING ...IN AIR.

JANE PLANS A CANOE OUTING, HOPING TO GENERATE A LITTLE **LOVE-IN**... ...BUT...

SO, YOU INVITED DOROTHY AND SARAH...

...AND YOU, AND ME.

...A LITTLE WILDERNESS FOURSOME.

?!@

HI, JANE... THANKS FOR THE INVITE.

CHELLE!

THAT WAS REALLY BIG OF YOU TO INVITE ME.

MAYBE YOU AREN'T AS LAME AS I THOUGHT YOU WERE...

SARAH?

I ASSUME IT'S OKAY THAT I BROUGHT A DATE?

DATE?...

LATER...

CAMPGROUND

PHONE

ETHAN! YOU'VE GOTTA COME!

SARAH BROUGHT A DATE! I DON'T WANT TO CANOE ALONE!

PAIGE

IT'S YOUR DREAM COME TRUE... YOU, AND 5 WOMEN ON A CAMPING TRIP!

PHONE

NO, THAT'S **YOUR** DREAM...

...IN MY DREAM THE 5 WOMEN ARE NAKED AND IN A HOT TUB...

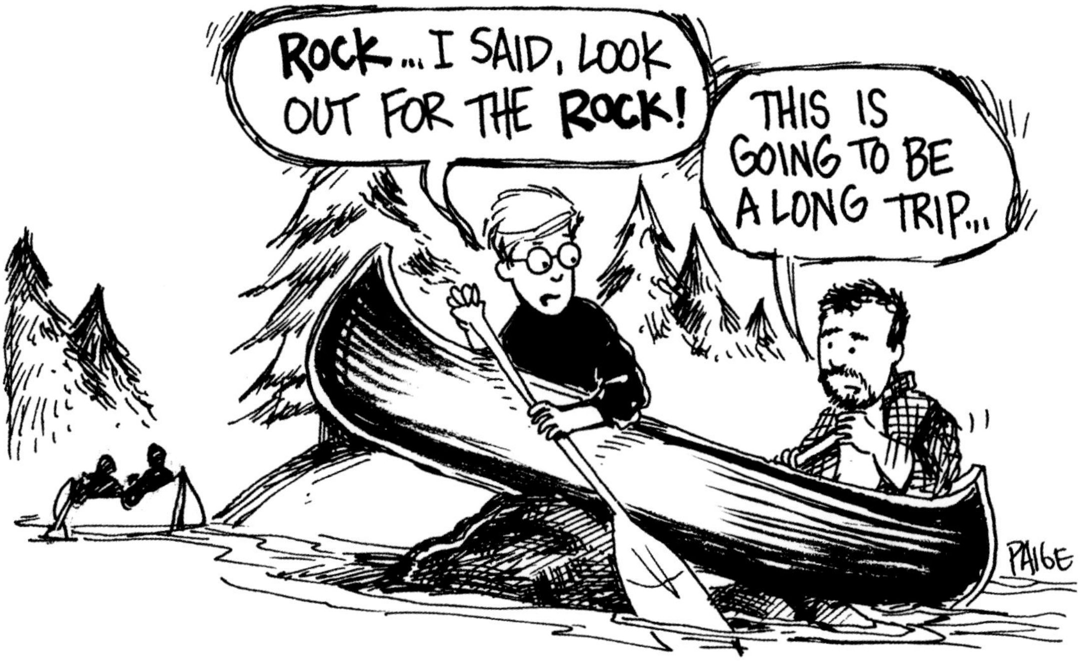
ROCK... I SAID, LOOK OUT FOR THE ROCK!
THIS IS GOING TO BE A LONG TRIP...
PAIGE

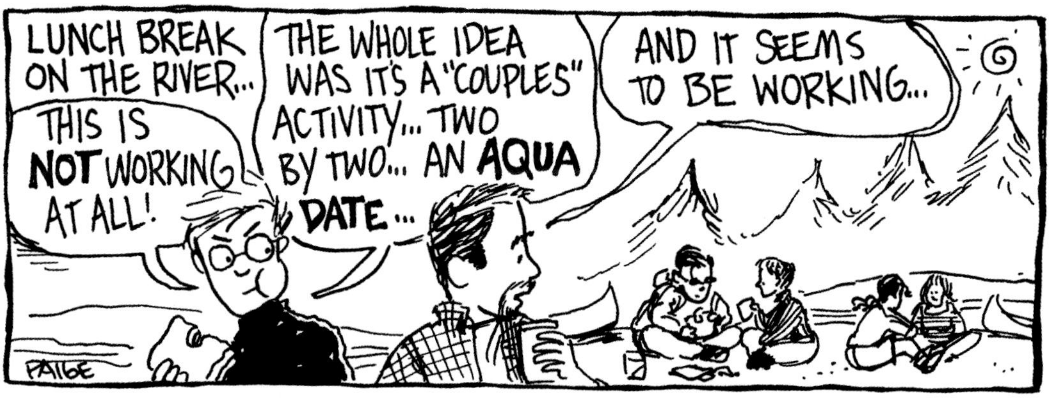
LUNCH BREAK ON THE RIVER...
THIS IS NOT WORKING AT ALL!
THE WHOLE IDEA WAS IT'S A "COUPLES" ACTIVITY... TWO BY TWO... AN AQUA DATE...
AND IT SEEMS TO BE WORKING...
PAIGE

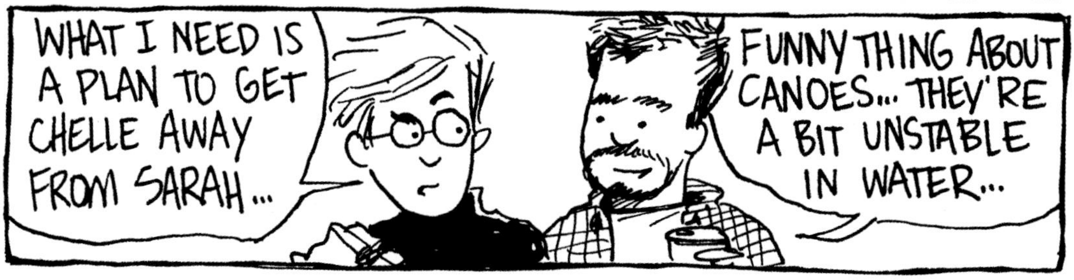
WHAT I NEED IS A PLAN TO GET CHELLE AWAY FROM SARAH...
FUNNY THING ABOUT CANOES... THEY'RE A BIT UNSTABLE IN WATER...

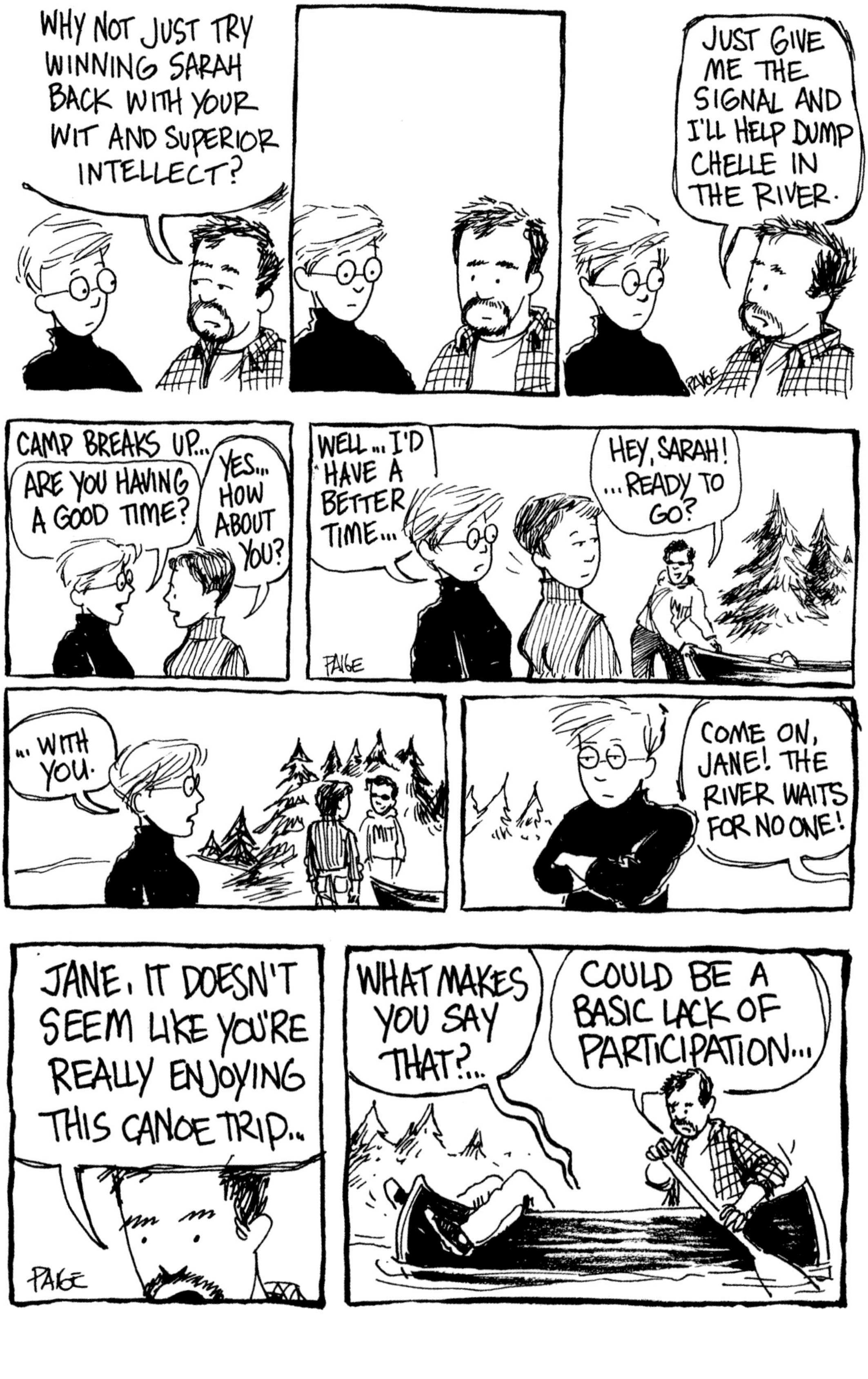
WHY NOT JUST TRY WINNING SARAH BACK WITH YOUR WIT AND SUPERIOR INTELLECT?
JUST GIVE ME THE SIGNAL AND I'LL HELP DUMP CHELLE IN THE RIVER.
PAIGE
CAMP BREAKS UP...
ARE YOU HAVING A GOOD TIME?
YES... HOW ABOUT YOU?
WELL... I'D HAVE A BETTER TIME...
HEY, SARAH! ...READY TO GO?
PAIGE
... WITH YOU.
COME ON, JANE! THE RIVER WAITS FOR NO ONE!
JANE, IT DOESN'T SEEM LIKE YOU'RE REALLY ENJOYING THIS CANOE TRIP...
PAIGE
WHAT MAKES YOU SAY THAT?...
COULD BE A BASIC LACK OF PARTICIPATION...

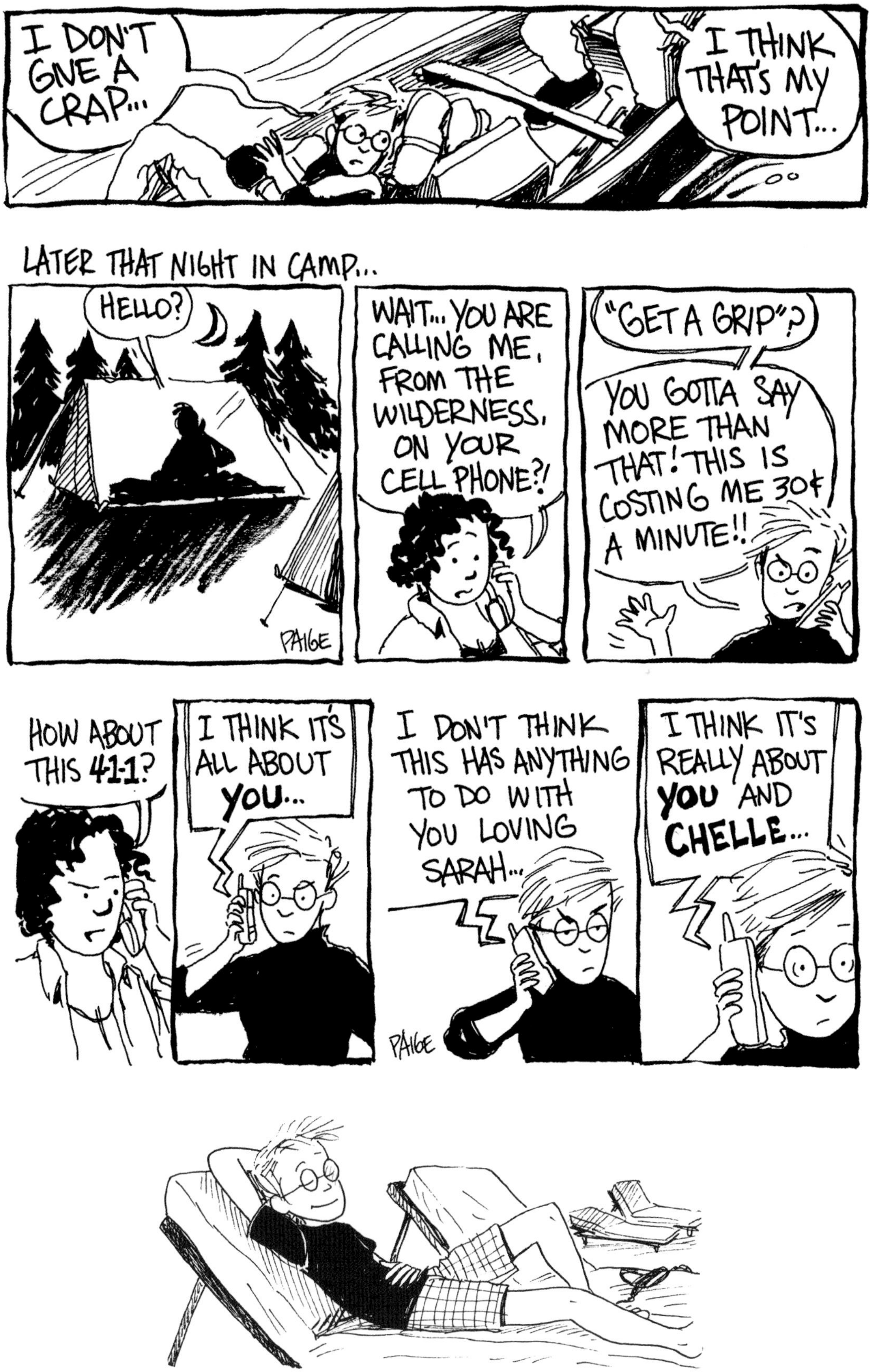
I DON'T GIVE A CRAP...
I THINK THAT'S MY POINT...
LATER THAT NIGHT IN CAMP...
HELLO?
PAIGE
WAIT... YOU ARE CALLING ME, FROM THE WILDERNESS, ON YOUR CELL PHONE?!
"GET A GRIP"?
YOU GOTTA SAY MORE THAN THAT! THIS IS COSTING ME 30¢ A MINUTE!!
HOW ABOUT THIS 411?
I THINK IT'S ALL ABOUT **YOU**...
I DON'T THINK THIS HAS ANYTHING TO DO WITH YOU LOVING SARAH...
PAIGE
I THINK IT'S REALLY ABOUT **YOU** AND **CHELLE**...

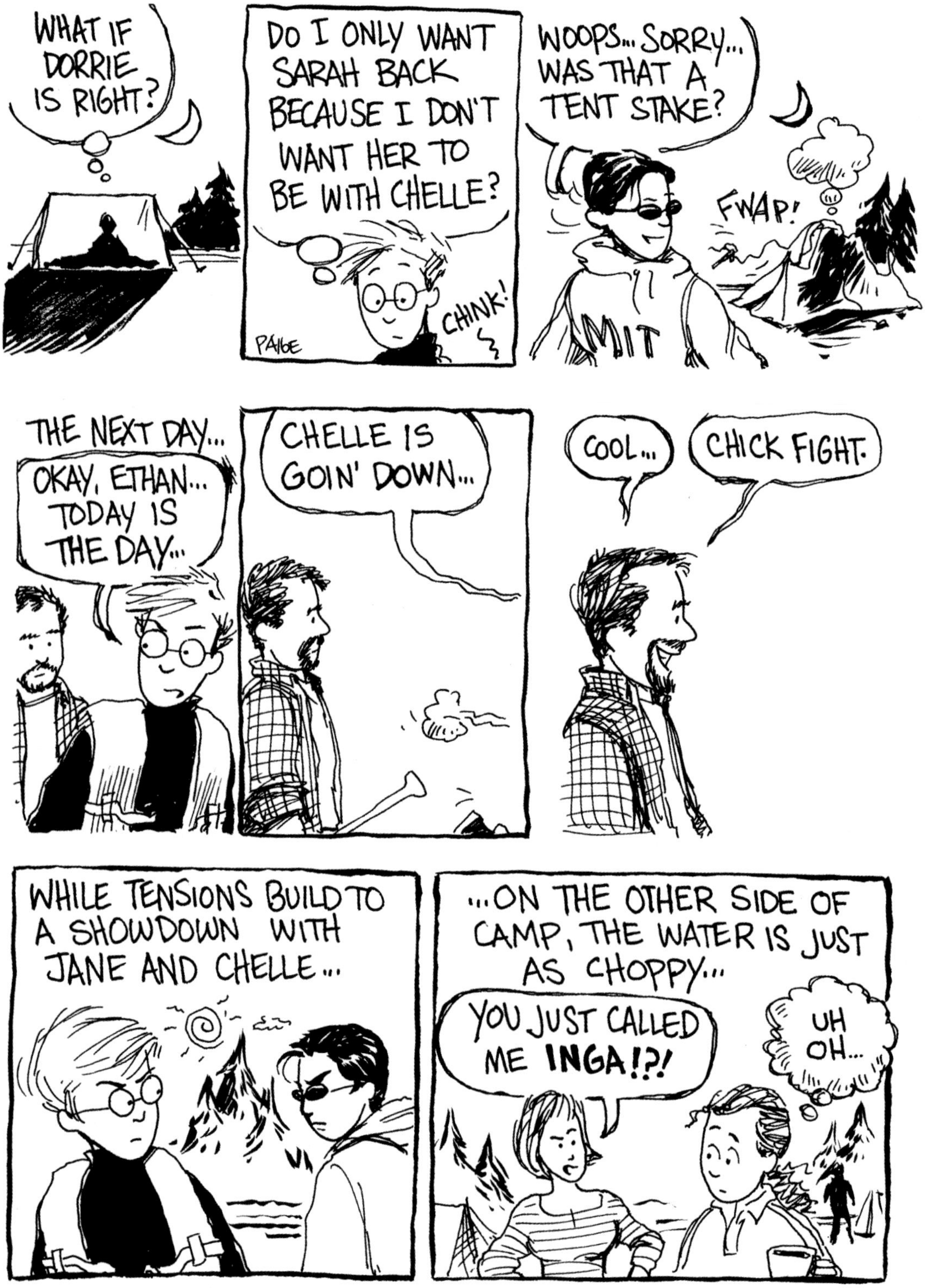
WHAT IF DORRIE IS RIGHT?
DO I ONLY WANT SARAH BACK BECAUSE I DON'T WANT HER TO BE WITH CHELLE?
CHINK!
PAIGE
WOOPS... SORRY... WAS THAT A TENT STAKE?
FWAP!
MIT
THE NEXT DAY...
OKAY, ETHAN... TODAY IS THE DAY...
CHELLE IS GOIN' DOWN...
COOL...
CHICK FIGHT.
WHILE TENSIONS BUILD TO A SHOWDOWN WITH JANE AND CHELLE...
...ON THE OTHER SIDE OF CAMP, THE WATER IS JUST AS CHOPPY...
YOU JUST CALLED ME **INGA!?!**
UH OH...

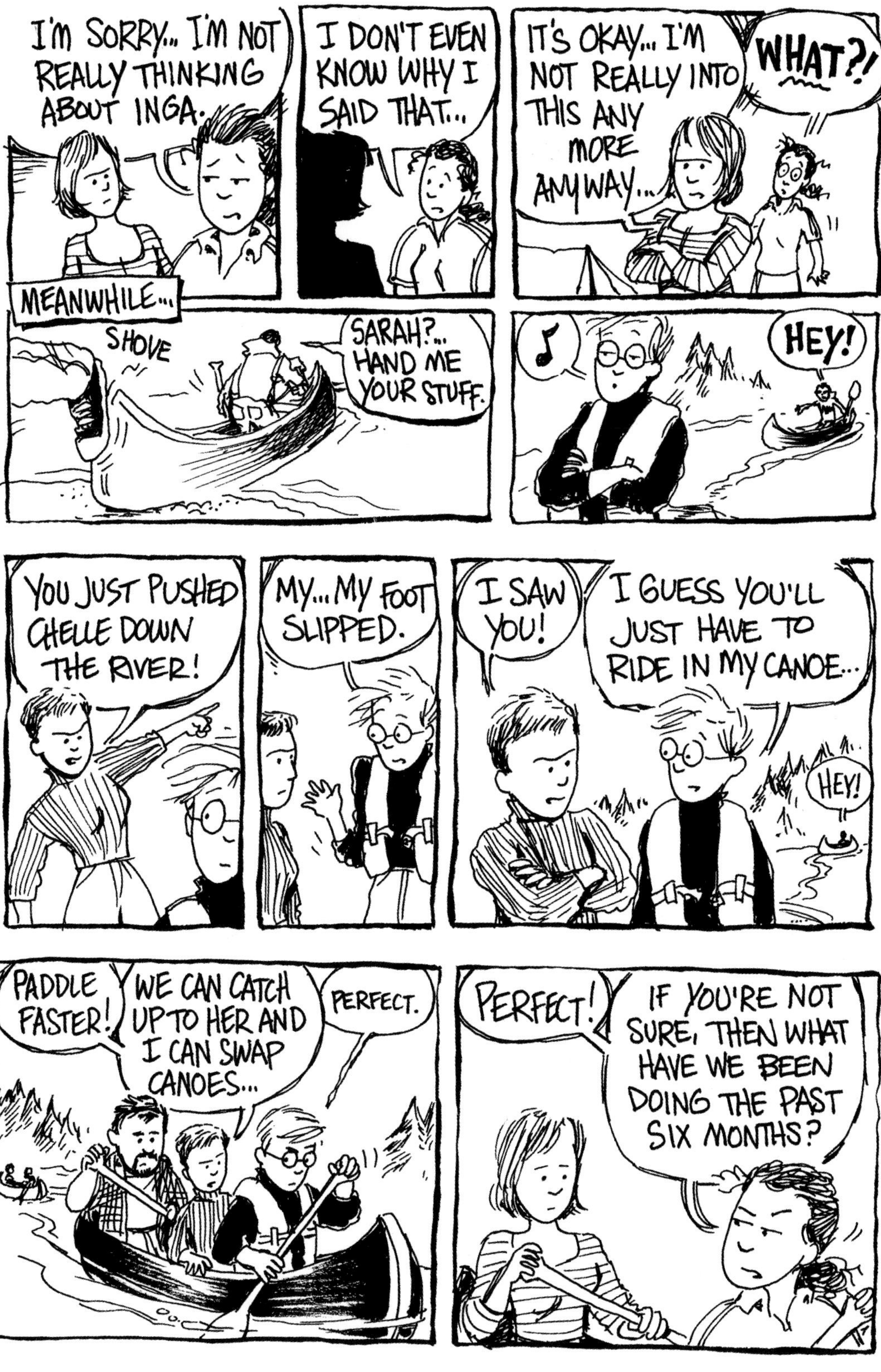
I'M SORRY... I'M NOT REALLY THINKING ABOUT INGA.
I DON'T EVEN KNOW WHY I SAID THAT...
IT'S OKAY... I'M NOT REALLY INTO THIS ANY MORE ANYWAY...
WHAT?!
MEANWHILE...
SHOVE
SARAH?... HAND ME YOUR STUFF.
HEY!
YOU JUST PUSHED CHELLE DOWN THE RIVER!
MY... MY FOOT SLIPPED.
I SAW YOU!
I GUESS YOU'LL JUST HAVE TO RIDE IN MY CANOE...
HEY!
PADDLE FASTER!
WE CAN CATCH UP TO HER AND I CAN SWAP CANOES...
PERFECT.
PERFECT!
IF YOU'RE NOT SURE, THEN WHAT HAVE WE BEEN DOING THE PAST SIX MONTHS?

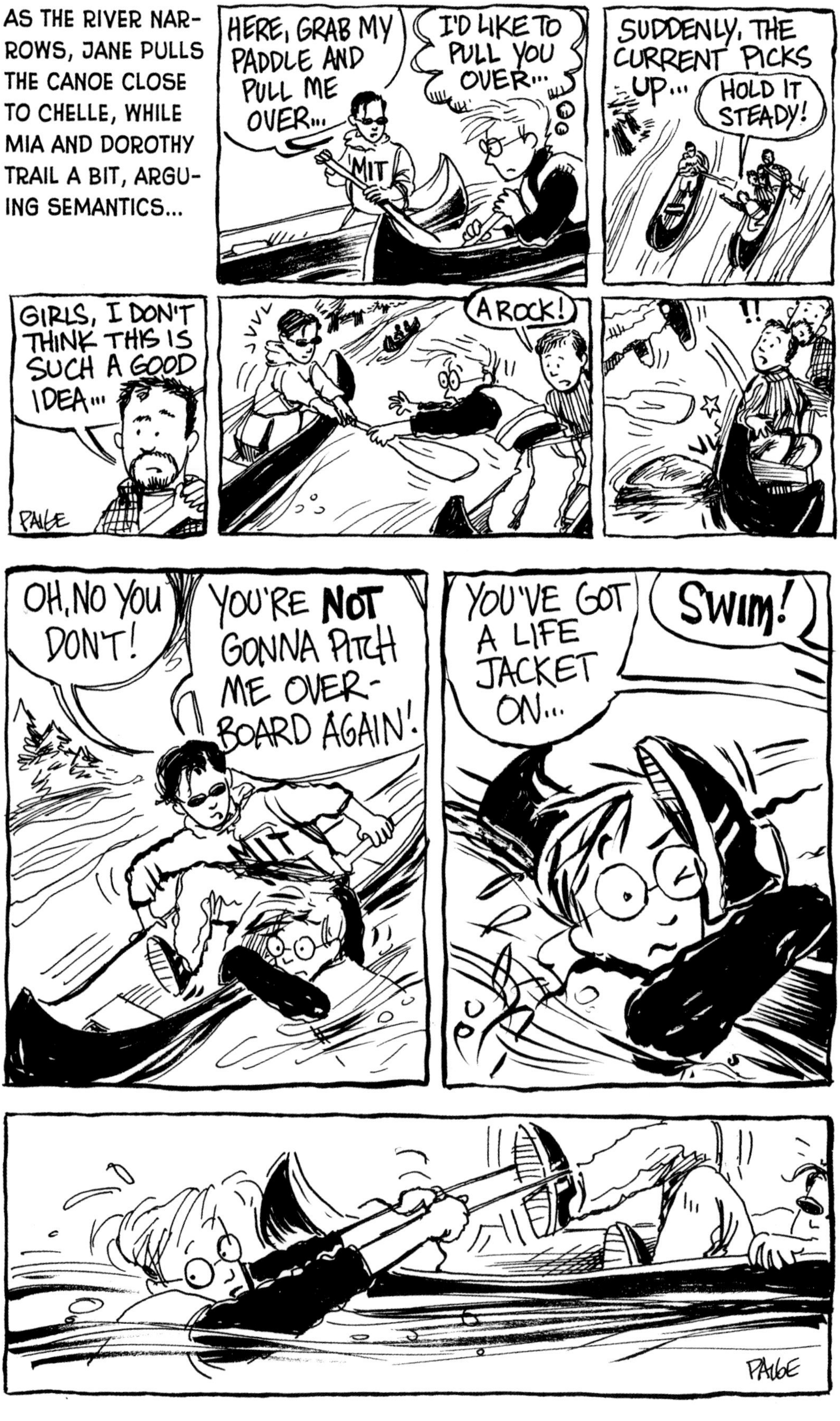
AS THE RIVER NARROWS, JANE PULLS THE CANOE CLOSE TO CHELLE, WHILE MIA AND DOROTHY TRAIL A BIT, ARGUING SEMANTICS...
HERE, GRAB MY PADDLE AND PULL ME OVER...
I'D LIKE TO PULL YOU OVER...
MIT
SUDDENLY, THE CURRENT PICKS UP...
HOLD IT STEADY!
GIRLS, I DON'T THINK THIS IS SUCH A GOOD IDEA...
PAIGE
A ROCK!
!!
OH, NO YOU DON'T!
YOU'RE **NOT** GONNA PITCH ME OVER-BOARD AGAIN!
MIT
YOU'VE GOT A LIFE JACKET ON...
SWIM!
PAIGE

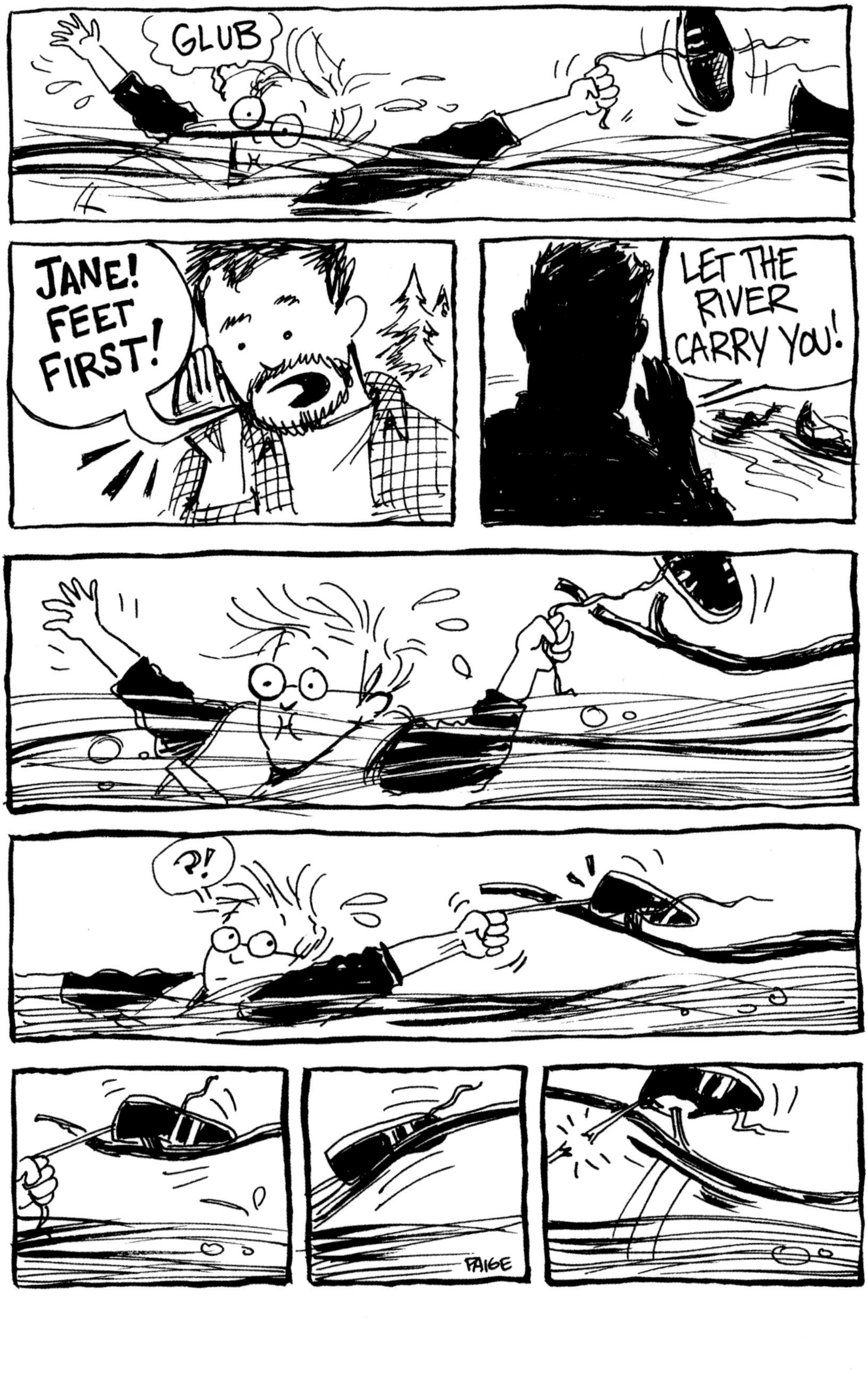
GLUB
JANE! FEET FIRST!
LET THE RIVER CARRY YOU!
?!
PAIGE

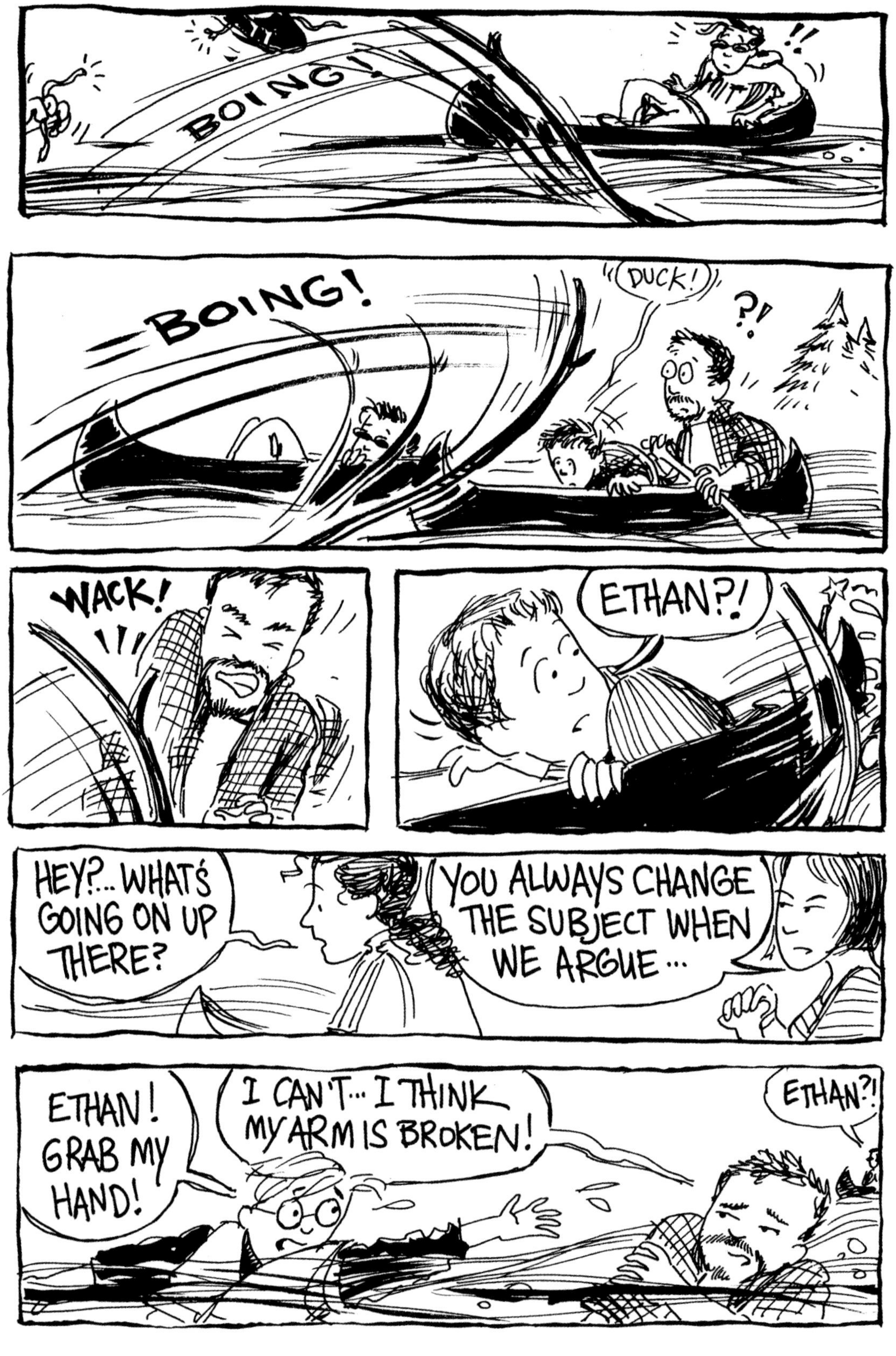
BOING!
!!
BOING!
DUCK!
?!
WACK!
ETHAN?!
HEY?... WHAT'S GOING ON UP THERE?
YOU ALWAYS CHANGE THE SUBJECT WHEN WE ARGUE...
ETHAN! GRAB MY HAND!
I CAN'T... I THINK MY ARM IS BROKEN!
ETHAN?!

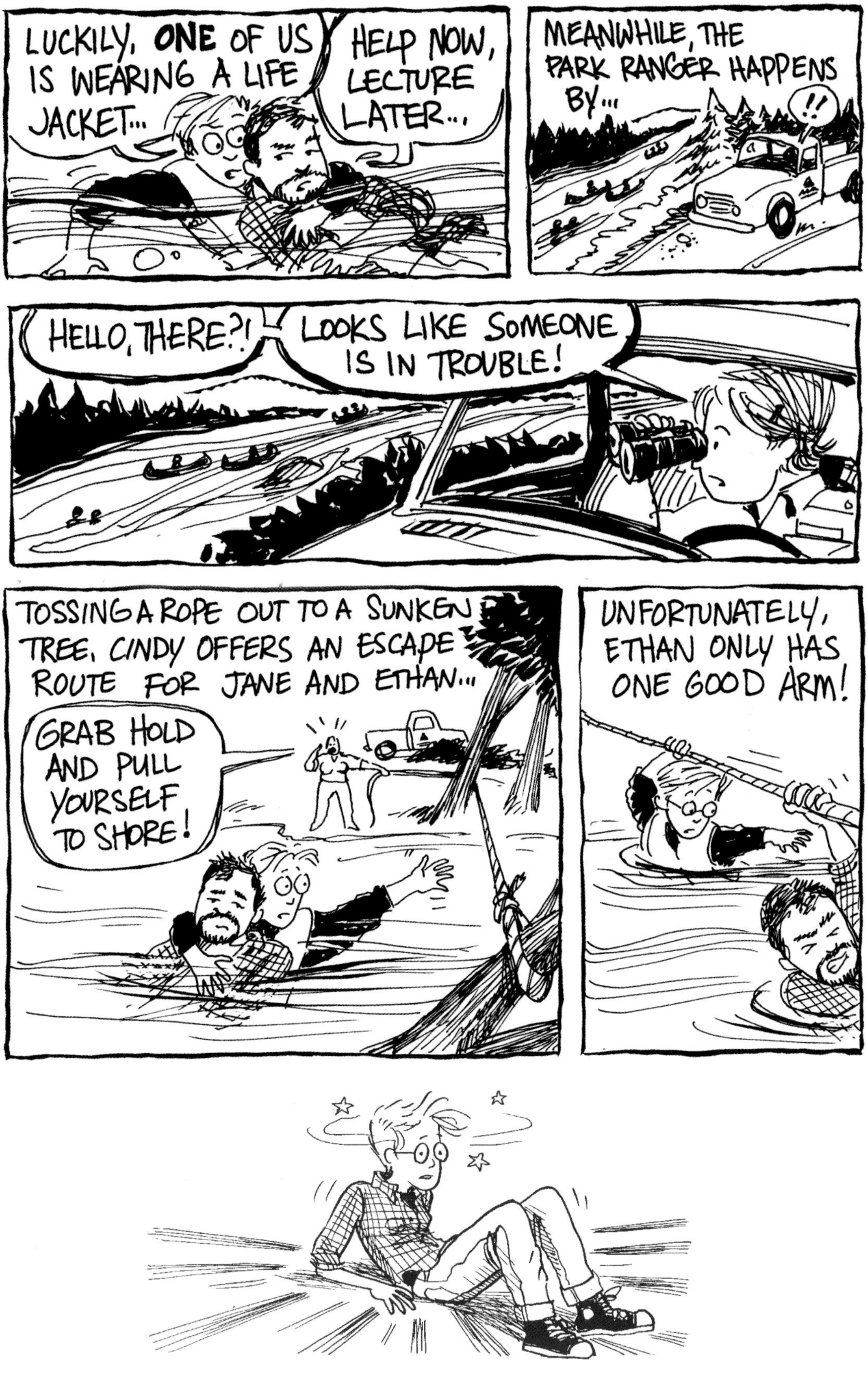
LUCKILY, ONE OF US IS WEARING A LIFE JACKET...
HELP NOW, LECTURE LATER...
MEANWHILE, THE PARK RANGER HAPPENS BY...
!!
HELLO, THERE?!
LOOKS LIKE SOMEONE IS IN TROUBLE!
TOSSING A ROPE OUT TO A SUNKEN TREE, CINDY OFFERS AN ESCAPE ROUTE FOR JANE AND ETHAN...
GRAB HOLD AND PULL YOURSELF TO SHORE!
UNFORTUNATELY, ETHAN ONLY HAS ONE GOOD ARM!

HANG ON I'LL COME GET YOU!
COUGH
DON'T WORRY... I'VE GOT YOU!
PAIGE

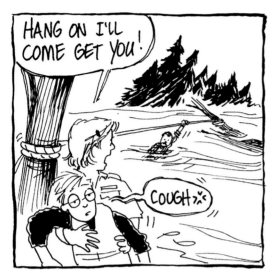

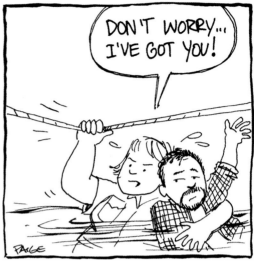

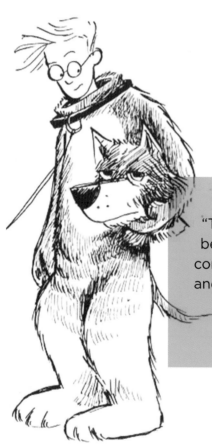

“True fact ...I had such total recall of being a younger me and seeing your comics in my local shop and feeling seen and valid for the first time. It meant so much. Still does.”

FOLEY, Portland (via Twitter)

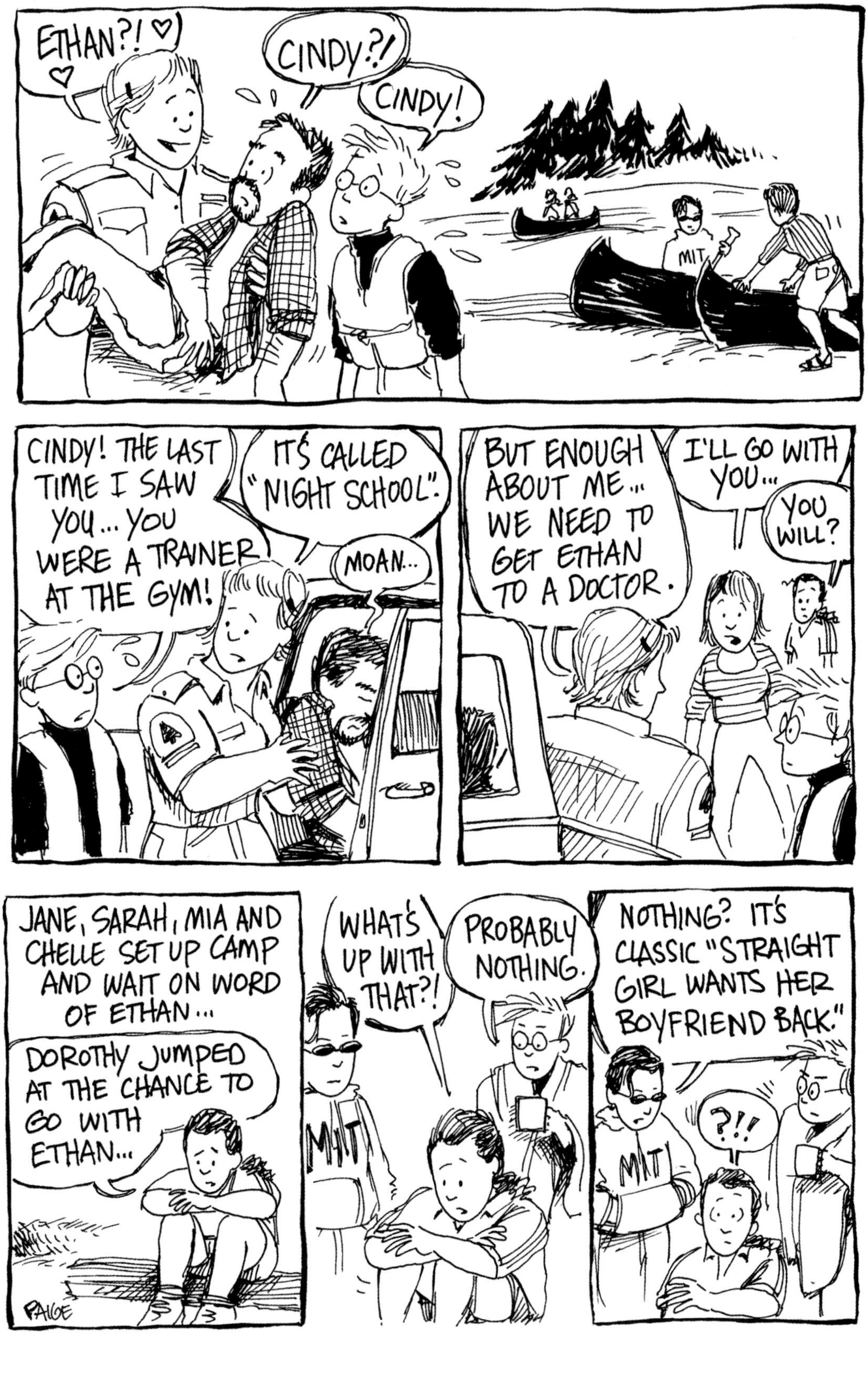
ETHAN?!
CINDY?!
CINDY!
MIT
CINDY! THE LAST TIME I SAW YOU... YOU WERE A TRAINER AT THE GYM!
IT'S CALLED "NIGHT SCHOOL".
MOAN...
BUT ENOUGH ABOUT ME... WE NEED TO GET ETHAN TO A DOCTOR.
I'LL GO WITH YOU...
YOU WILL?
JANE, SARAH, MIA AND CHELLE SET UP CAMP AND WAIT ON WORD OF ETHAN...
DOROTHY JUMPED AT THE CHANCE TO GO WITH ETHAN...
PAIGE
WHAT'S UP WITH THAT?!
PROBABLY NOTHING.
MIT
NOTHING? IT'S CLASSIC "STRAIGHT GIRL WANTS HER BOYFRIEND BACK."
MIT
?!!

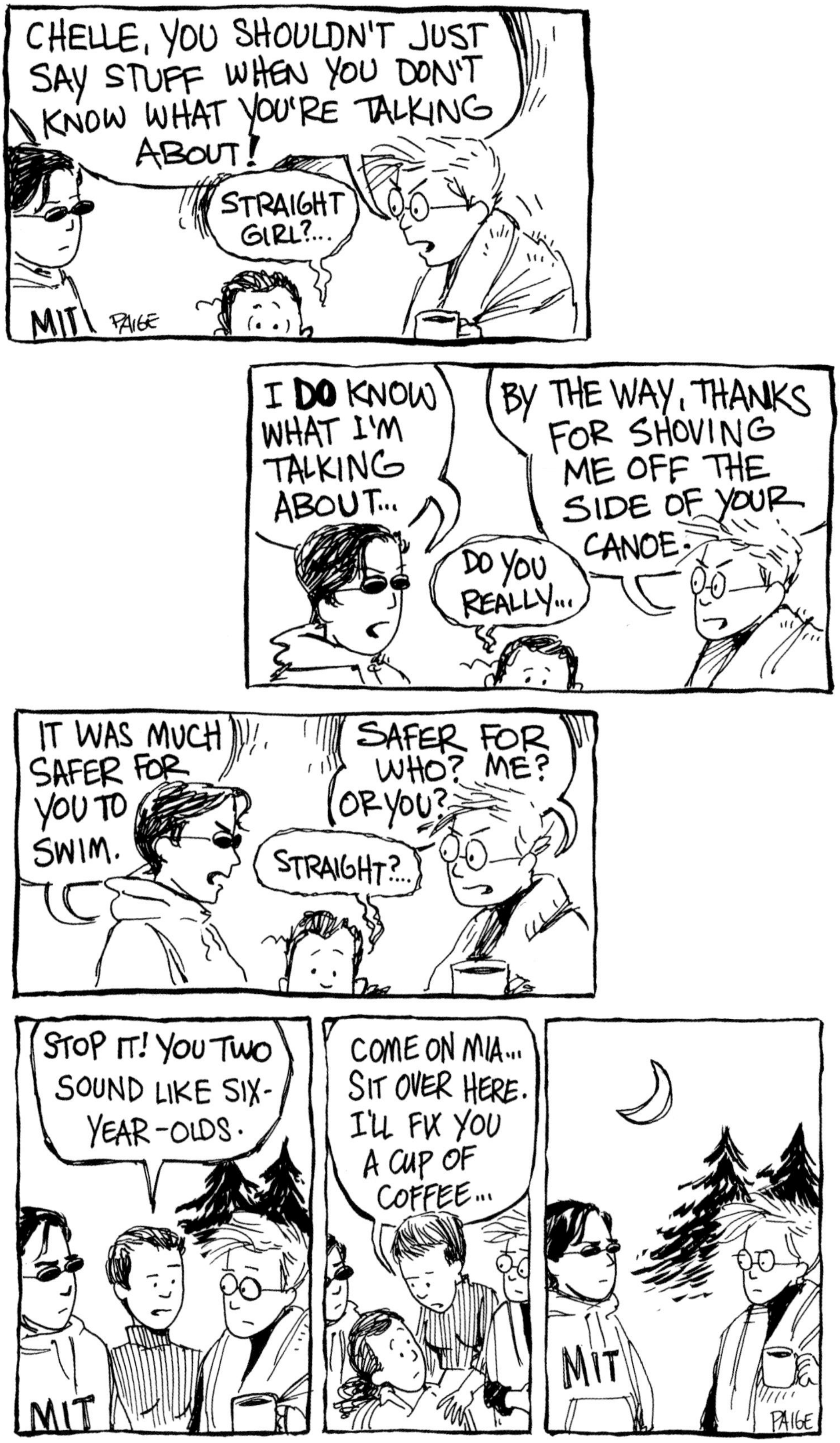
CHELLE, YOU SHOULDN'T JUST SAY STUFF WHEN YOU DON'T KNOW WHAT YOU'RE TALKING ABOUT!
STRAIGHT GIRL?...
MIT
PAIGE
I DO KNOW WHAT I'M TALKING ABOUT...
BY THE WAY, THANKS FOR SHOVING ME OFF THE SIDE OF YOUR CANOE.
DO YOU REALLY...
IT WAS MUCH SAFER FOR YOU TO SWIM.
SAFER FOR WHO? ME? OR YOU?
STRAIGHT?....
STOP IT! YOU TWO SOUND LIKE SIX-YEAR-OLDS.
MIT
COME ON MIA... SIT OVER HERE. I'LL FIX YOU A CUP OF COFFEE...
MIT
PAIGE

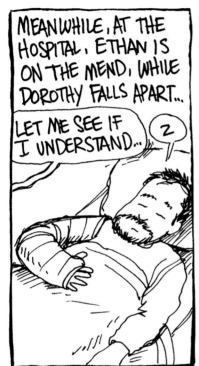

MEANWHILE, AT THE HOSPITAL, ETHAN IS ON THE MEND, WHILE DOROTHY FALLS APART...

LET ME SEE IF I UNDERSTAND...

Z

YOU **WERE** WITH ETHAN, BUT NOW YOU'RE **WITH** MIA...

SO... UM... WHY ARE YOU **HERE?**

I DON'T KNOW.

I THINK I'M HAVING A CRISIS OF PERSONALITY!

THE PSYCH WARD IS ON 4...

Z

YOU'VE CHANGED. MAYBE I'VE CHANGED.

YOU WENT FROM PERSONAL TRANER TO FOREST RANGER...

THE GYM WAS ALWAYS TEMPORARY... I KNEW I WANTED MORE.

MAYBE MIA AND I WERE JUST MEANT TO BE TEMPORARY TOO....

PAIGE

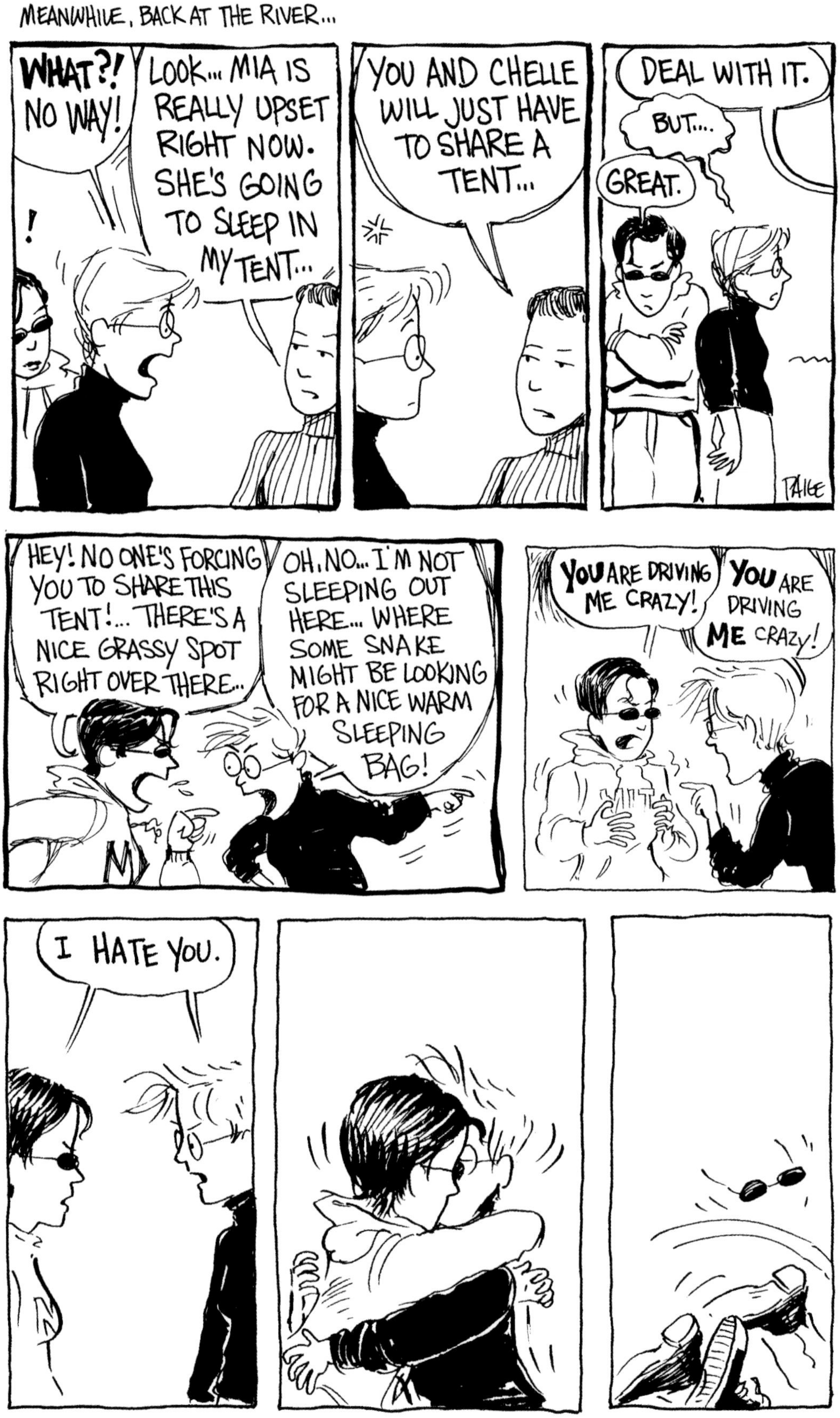
MEANWHILE, BACK AT THE RIVER...
WHAT?! NO WAY!
!
LOOK... MIA IS REALLY UPSET RIGHT NOW. SHE'S GOING TO SLEEP IN MY TENT...
YOU AND CHELLE WILL JUST HAVE TO SHARE A TENT...
DEAL WITH IT.
BUT....
GREAT.
PAIGE
HEY! NO ONE'S FORCING YOU TO SHARE THIS TENT!... THERE'S A NICE GRASSY SPOT RIGHT OVER THERE...
OH, NO... I'M NOT SLEEPING OUT HERE... WHERE SOME SNAKE MIGHT BE LOOKING FOR A NICE WARM SLEEPING BAG!
YOU ARE DRIVING ME CRAZY!
YOU ARE DRIVING ME CRAZY!
I HATE YOU.

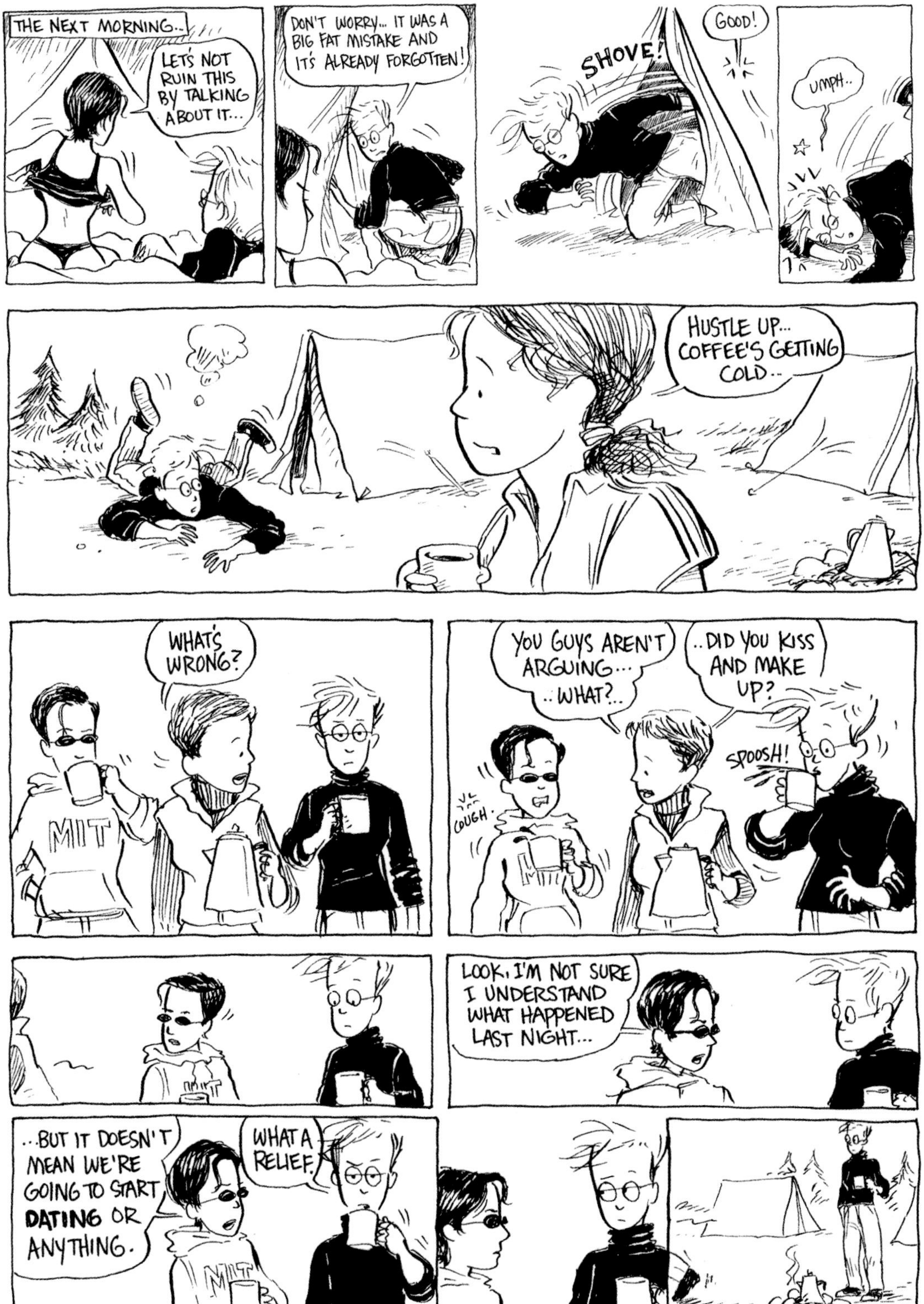

THE NEXT MORNING..
LET'S NOT RUIN THIS BY TALKING ABOUT IT...
DON'T WORRY... IT WAS A BIG FAT MISTAKE AND IT'S ALREADY FORGOTTEN!
SHOVE!
GOOD!
UMPH..
HUSTLE UP... COFFEE'S GETTING COLD..
WHAT'S WRONG?
YOU GUYS AREN'T ARGUING... ..WHAT?..
..DID YOU KISS AND MAKE UP?
COUGH.
SPOOSH!
MIT
LOOK, I'M NOT SURE I UNDERSTAND WHAT HAPPENED LAST NIGHT...
...BUT IT DOESN'T MEAN WE'RE GOING TO START **DATING** OR ANYTHING.
WHAT A RELIEF.

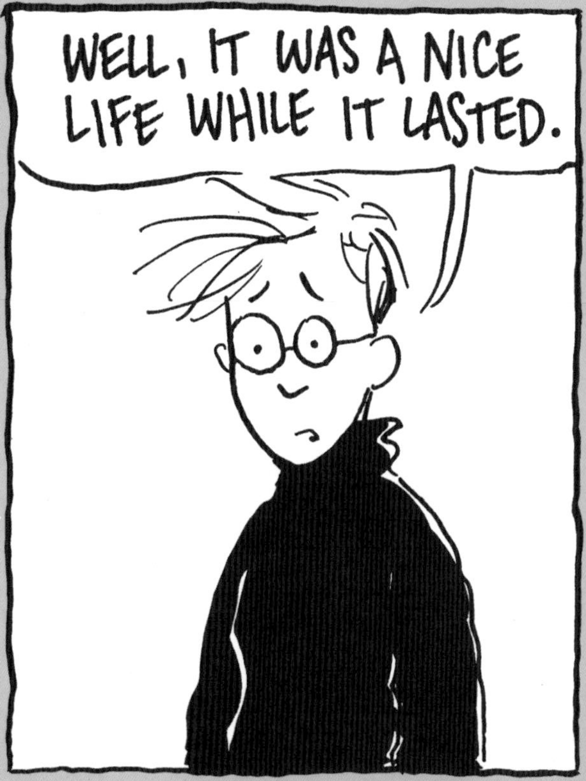
WELL, IT WAS A NICE LIFE WHILE IT LASTED.

Hard Fall

It turns out that being abducted by aliens has wreaked havoc on Jane's career. She's missed too much work and is fired from her job at the newspaper. In desperation she takes a downwardly mobile job at the local Quicki Mart. Oh, and Dixie is back. Turns out the transmorphing she suffered on the spaceship was only temporary. But that's not the only looming disaster. Jane is dumbfounded by Chelle's request to go to couples counseling. They aren't even a couple! But everyone has issues, and it's always nice when you can blame those issues on someone else.

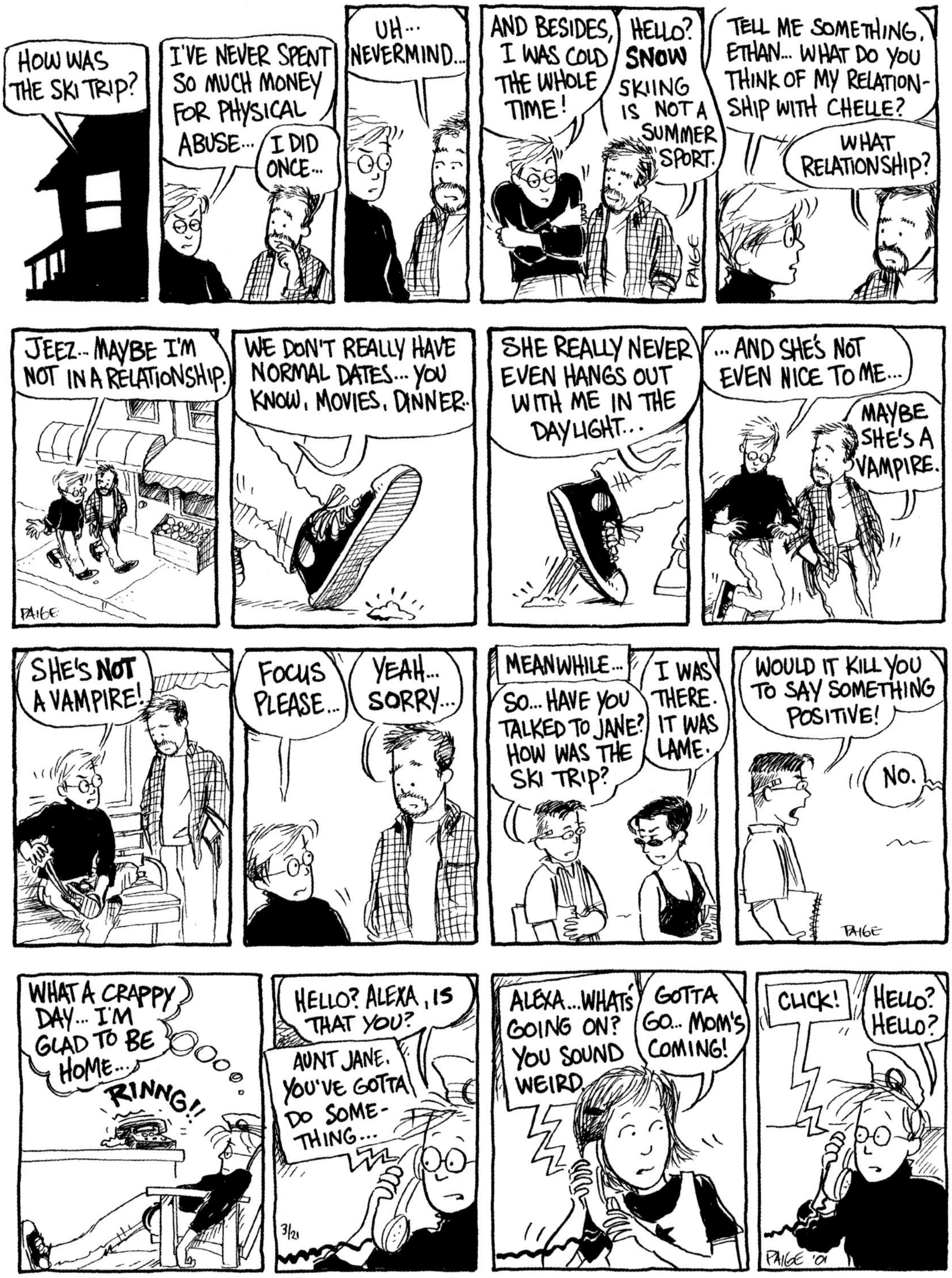
HOW WAS THE SKI TRIP?
I'VE NEVER SPENT SO MUCH MONEY FOR PHYSICAL ABUSE...
I DID ONCE...
UH... NEVERMIND...
AND BESIDES, I WAS COLD THE WHOLE TIME!
HELLO? SNOW SKIING IS NOT A SUMMER SPORT.
PAIGE
TELL ME SOMETHING, ETHAN... WHAT DO YOU THINK OF MY RELATIONSHIP WITH CHELLE?
WHAT RELATIONSHIP?
JEEZ... MAYBE I'M NOT IN A RELATIONSHIP.
PAIGE
WE DON'T REALLY HAVE NORMAL DATES... YOU KNOW, MOVIES, DINNER..
SHE REALLY NEVER EVEN HANGS OUT WITH ME IN THE DAYLIGHT...
...AND SHE'S NOT EVEN NICE TO ME...
MAYBE SHE'S A VAMPIRE.
SHE'S NOT A VAMPIRE!
FOCUS PLEASE...
YEAH... SORRY...
MEANWHILE...
SO... HAVE YOU TALKED TO JANE? HOW WAS THE SKI TRIP?
I WAS THERE. IT WAS LAME.
WOULD IT KILL YOU TO SAY SOMETHING POSITIVE!
NO.
PAIGE
WHAT A CRAPPY DAY... I'M GLAD TO BE HOME...
RINNG!!
HELLO? ALEXA, IS THAT YOU?
AUNT JANE, YOU'VE GOTTA DO SOMETHING...
3/21
ALEXA...WHAT'S GOING ON? YOU SOUND WEIRD
GOTTA GO... MOM'S COMING!
CLICK!
HELLO? HELLO?
PAIGE '01

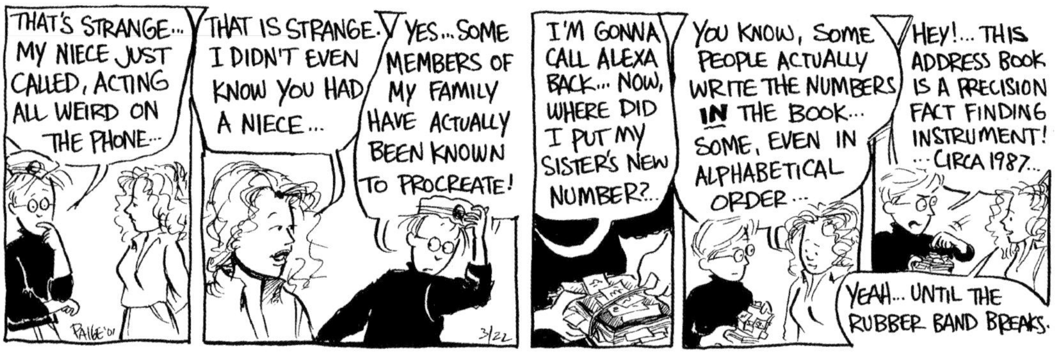
THAT'S STRANGE... MY NIECE JUST CALLED, ACTING ALL WEIRD ON THE PHONE...
THAT IS STRANGE. I DIDN'T EVEN KNOW YOU HAD A NIECE...
YES... SOME MEMBERS OF MY FAMILY HAVE ACTUALLY BEEN KNOWN TO PROCREATE!
I'M GONNA CALL ALEXA BACK... NOW, WHERE DID I PUT MY SISTER'S NEW NUMBER?...
YOU KNOW, SOME PEOPLE ACTUALLY WRITE THE NUMBERS **IN** THE BOOK... SOME, EVEN IN ALPHABETICAL ORDER...
HEY!... THIS ADDRESS BOOK IS A PRECISION FACT FINDING INSTRUMENT! ...CIRCA 1987...
YEAH... UNTIL THE RUBBER BAND BREAKS.
PAIGE '01
3/22

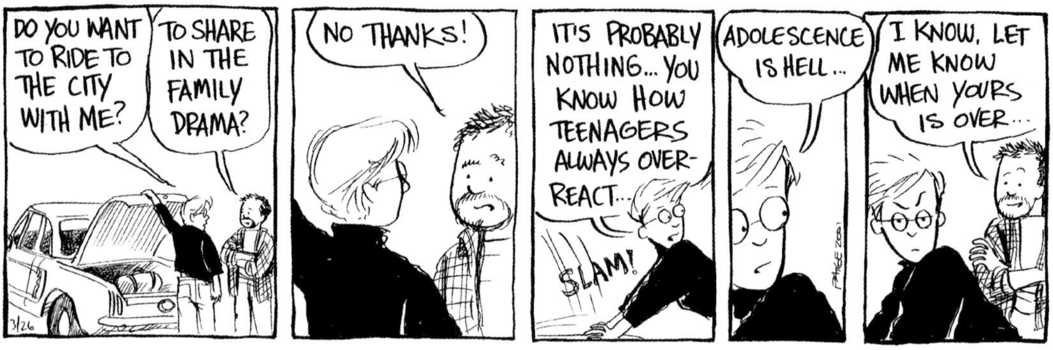
DO YOU WANT TO RIDE TO THE CITY WITH ME?
TO SHARE IN THE FAMILY DRAMA?
NO THANKS!
IT'S PROBABLY NOTHING... YOU KNOW HOW TEENAGERS ALWAYS OVER-REACT...
SLAM!
ADOLESCENCE IS HELL...
I KNOW. LET ME KNOW WHEN YOURS IS OVER...
3/26
PAIGE 2001

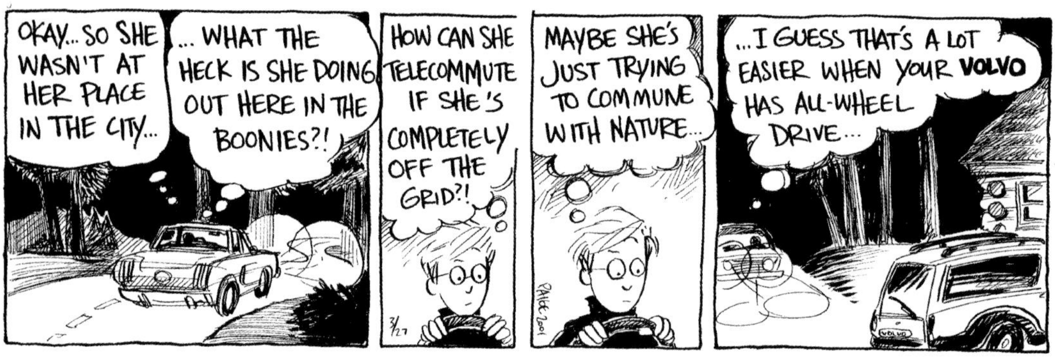
OKAY... SO SHE WASN'T AT HER PLACE IN THE CITY...
... WHAT THE HECK IS SHE DOING OUT HERE IN THE BOONIES?!
HOW CAN SHE TELECOMMUTE IF SHE'S COMPLETELY OFF THE GRID?!
MAYBE SHE'S JUST TRYING TO COMMUNE WITH NATURE...
...I GUESS THAT'S A LOT EASIER WHEN YOUR **VOLVO** HAS ALL-WHEEL DRIVE...
VOLVO
3/27
PAIGE 2001

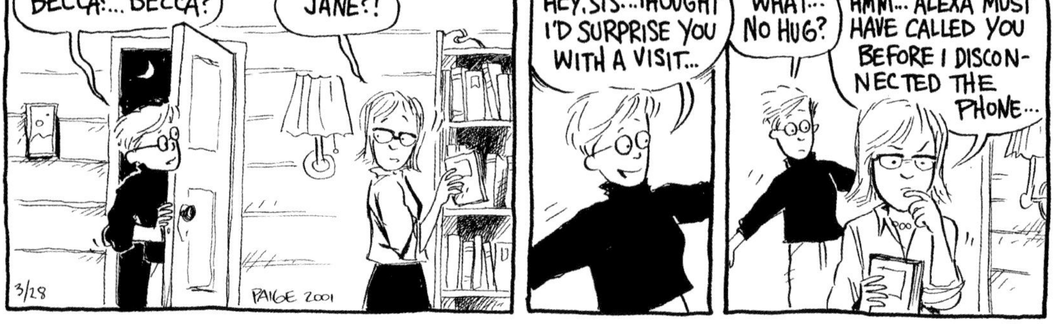
BECCA?... BECCA?
JANE?!
HEY, SIS... THOUGHT I'D SURPRISE YOU WITH A VISIT...
WHAT... NO HUG?
HMM... ALEXA MUST HAVE CALLED YOU BEFORE I DISCON-NECTED THE PHONE...
3/28
PAIGE 2001

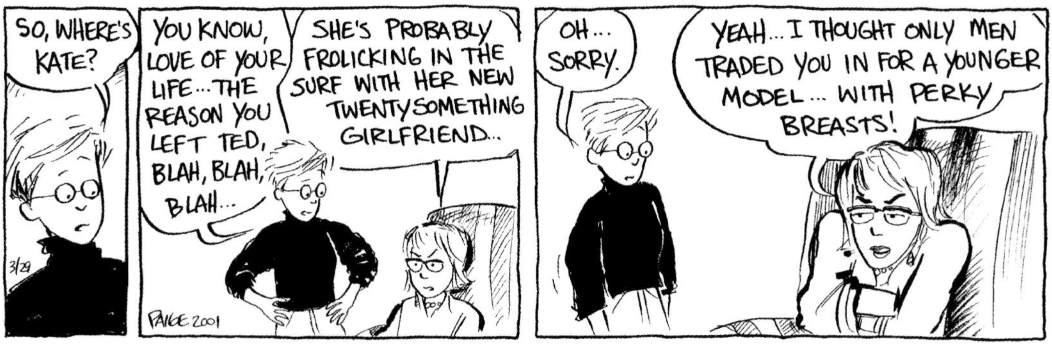
SO, WHERE'S KATE?
3/29
YOU KNOW, LOVE OF YOUR LIFE... THE REASON YOU LEFT TED, BLAH, BLAH, BLAH...
SHE'S PROBABLY FROLICKING IN THE SURF WITH HER NEW TWENTYSOMETHING GIRLFRIEND...
PAIGE 2001
OH... SORRY.
YEAH... I THOUGHT ONLY MEN TRADED YOU IN FOR A YOUNGER MODEL... WITH PERKY BREASTS!

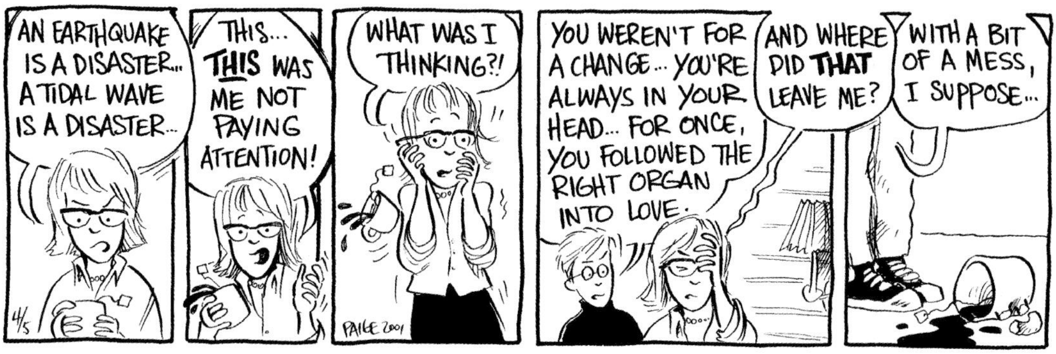
AN EARTHQUAKE IS A DISASTER... A TIDAL WAVE IS A DISASTER...
4/5
THIS... THIS WAS ME NOT PAYING ATTENTION!
WHAT WAS I THINKING?!
PAIGE 2001
YOU WEREN'T FOR A CHANGE... YOU'RE ALWAYS IN YOUR HEAD... FOR ONCE, YOU FOLLOWED THE RIGHT ORGAN INTO LOVE.
AND WHERE DID THAT LEAVE ME?
WITH A BIT OF A MESS, I SUPPOSE...

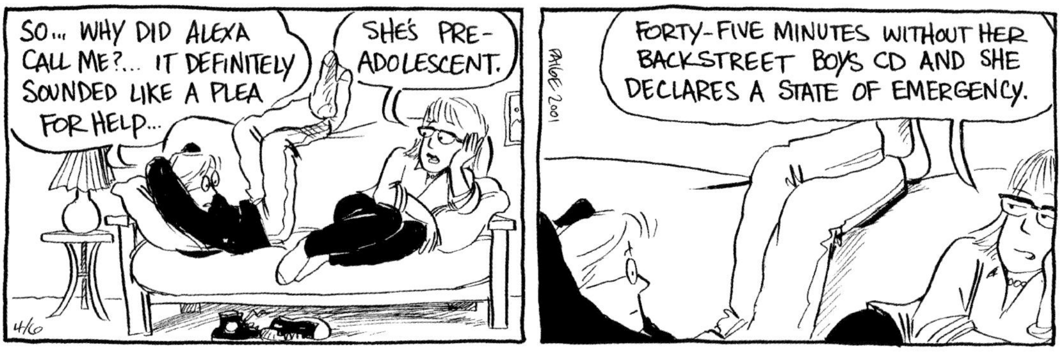
SO... WHY DID ALEXA CALL ME?... IT DEFINITELY SOUNDED LIKE A PLEA FOR HELP...
SHE'S PRE-ADOLESCENT.
4/6
PAIGE 2001
FORTY-FIVE MINUTES WITHOUT HER BACKSTREET BOYS CD AND SHE DECLARES A STATE OF EMERGENCY.

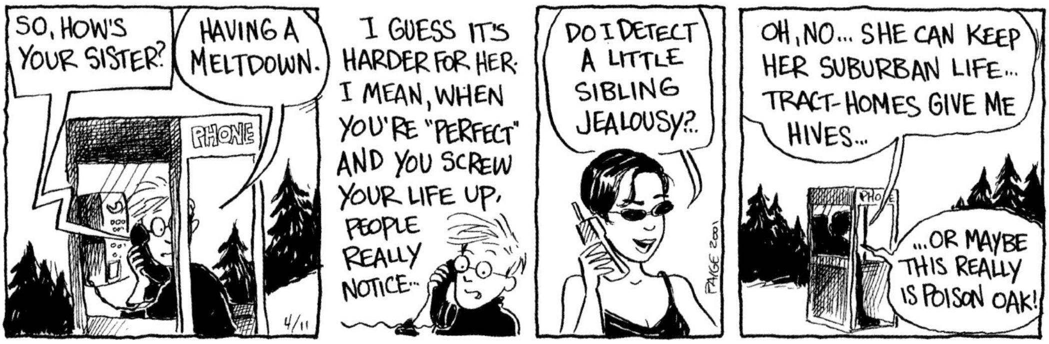
SO, HOW'S YOUR SISTER?
HAVING A MELTDOWN.
PHONE
4/11
I GUESS IT'S HARDER FOR HER. I MEAN, WHEN YOU'RE "PERFECT" AND YOU SCREW YOUR LIFE UP, PEOPLE REALLY NOTICE...
DO I DETECT A LITTLE SIBLING JEALOUSY?..
PAIGE 2001
OH, NO... SHE CAN KEEP HER SUBURBAN LIFE... TRACT-HOMES GIVE ME HIVES...
...OR MAYBE THIS REALLY IS POISON OAK!

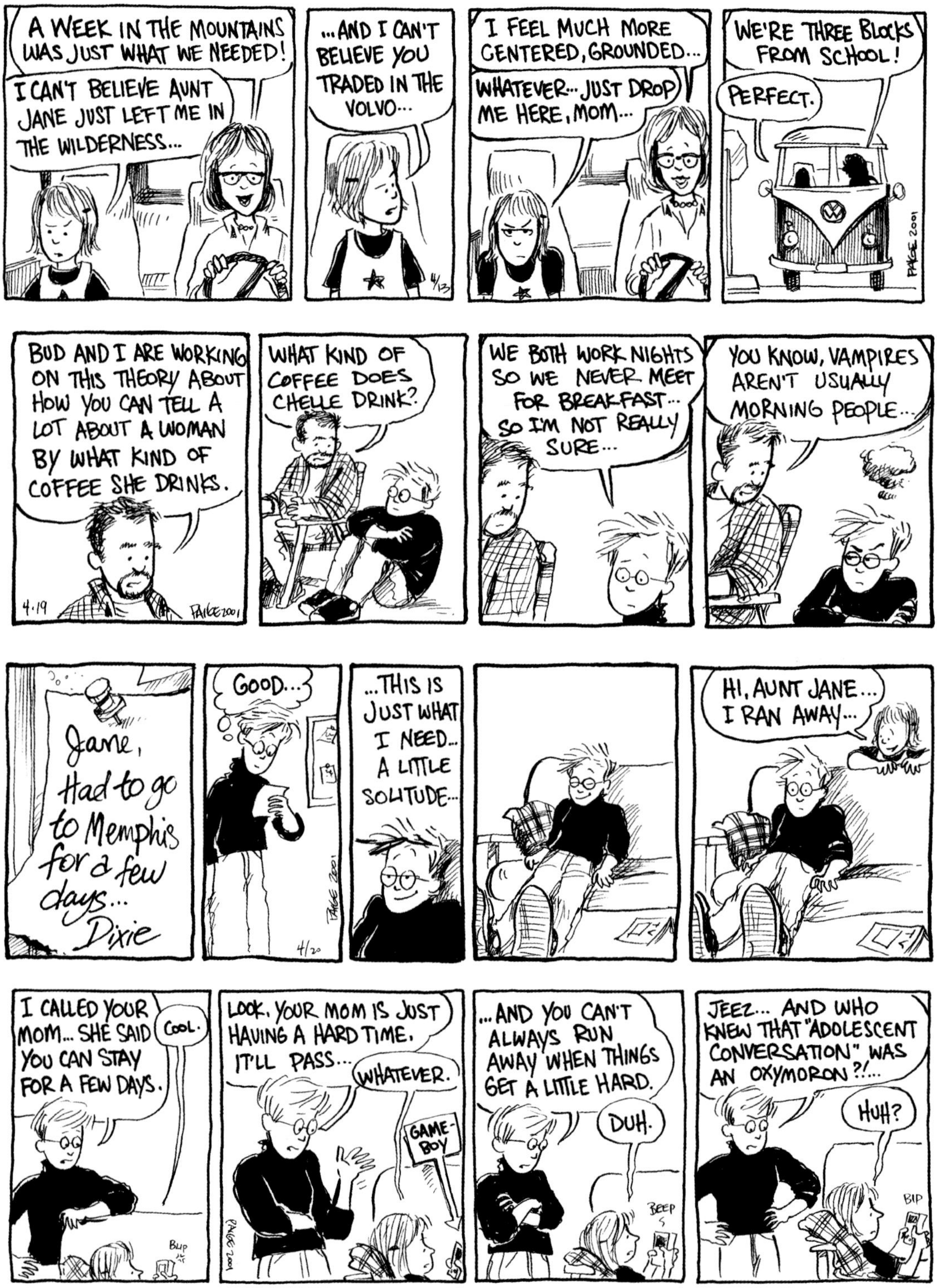
A WEEK IN THE MOUNTAINS WAS JUST WHAT WE NEEDED!
I CAN'T BELIEVE AUNT JANE JUST LEFT ME IN THE WILDERNESS...
...AND I CAN'T BELIEVE YOU TRADED IN THE VOLVO...
4/13
I FEEL MUCH MORE CENTERED, GROUNDED...
WHATEVER... JUST DROP ME HERE, MOM...
WE'RE THREE BLOCKS FROM SCHOOL!
PERFECT.
PAIGE 2001
BUD AND I ARE WORKING ON THIS THEORY ABOUT HOW YOU CAN TELL A LOT ABOUT A WOMAN BY WHAT KIND OF COFFEE SHE DRINKS.
4.19
PAIGE 2001
WHAT KIND OF COFFEE DOES CHELLE DRINK?
WE BOTH WORK NIGHTS SO WE NEVER MEET FOR BREAKFAST... SO I'M NOT REALLY SURE...
YOU KNOW, VAMPIRES AREN'T USUALLY MORNING PEOPLE...
Jane, Had to go to Memphis for a few days... Dixie
GOOD...
PAIGE 2001
4/20
...THIS IS JUST WHAT I NEED... A LITTLE SOLITUDE...
HI, AUNT JANE... I RAN AWAY...
I CALLED YOUR MOM... SHE SAID YOU CAN STAY FOR A FEW DAYS.
COOL.
BLIP
LOOK, YOUR MOM IS JUST HAVING A HARD TIME. IT'LL PASS...
WHATEVER.
GAME-BOY
PAIGE 2001
...AND YOU CAN'T ALWAYS RUN AWAY WHEN THINGS GET A LITTLE HARD.
DUH.
BEEP
JEEZ... AND WHO KNEW THAT "ADOLESCENT CONVERSATION" WAS AN OXYMORON?!...
HUH?
BIP

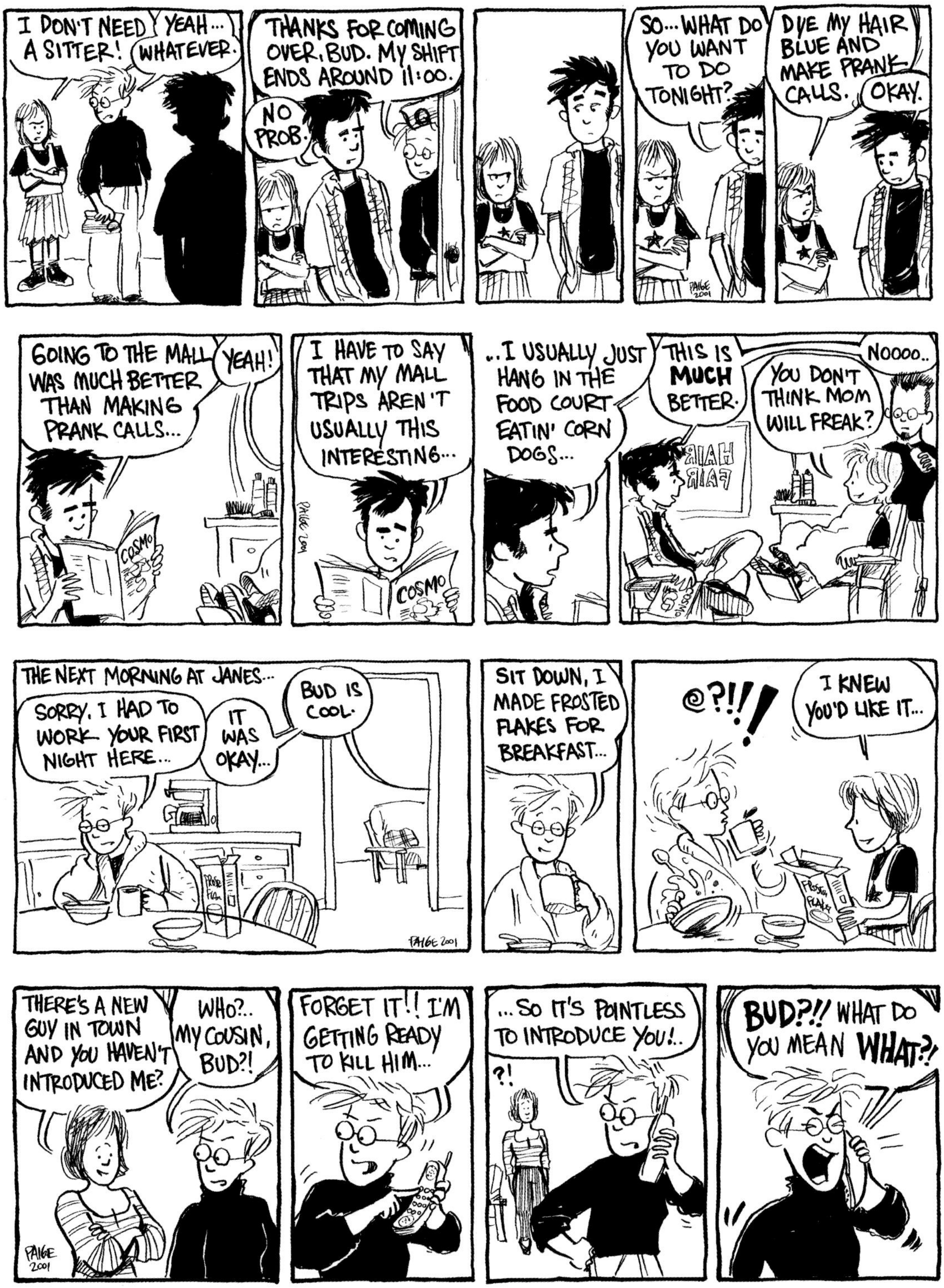
I DON'T NEED A SITTER!
YEAH... WHATEVER.
THANKS FOR COMING OVER, BUD. MY SHIFT ENDS AROUND 11:00.
NO PROB.
SO... WHAT DO YOU WANT TO DO TONIGHT?
DYE MY HAIR BLUE AND MAKE PRANK CALLS.
OKAY.
GOING TO THE MALL WAS MUCH BETTER THAN MAKING PRANK CALLS...
YEAH!
COSMO
I HAVE TO SAY THAT MY MALL TRIPS AREN'T USUALLY THIS INTERESTING...
COSMO
...I USUALLY JUST HANG IN THE FOOD COURT EATIN' CORN DOGS...
THIS IS **MUCH** BETTER.
NOOOO..
YOU DON'T THINK MOM WILL FREAK?
THE NEXT MORNING AT JANES...
SORRY. I HAD TO WORK YOUR FIRST NIGHT HERE...
IT WAS OKAY...
BUD IS COOL.
SIT DOWN, I MADE FROSTED FLAKES FOR BREAKFAST...
@?!!!
I KNEW YOU'D LIKE IT...
THERE'S A NEW GUY IN TOWN AND YOU HAVEN'T INTRODUCED ME?
WHO?.. MY COUSIN, BUD?!
FORGET IT!! I'M GETTING READY TO KILL HIM...
...SO IT'S POINTLESS TO INTRODUCE YOU!..
?!
BUD?!! WHAT DO YOU MEAN **WHAT?!**

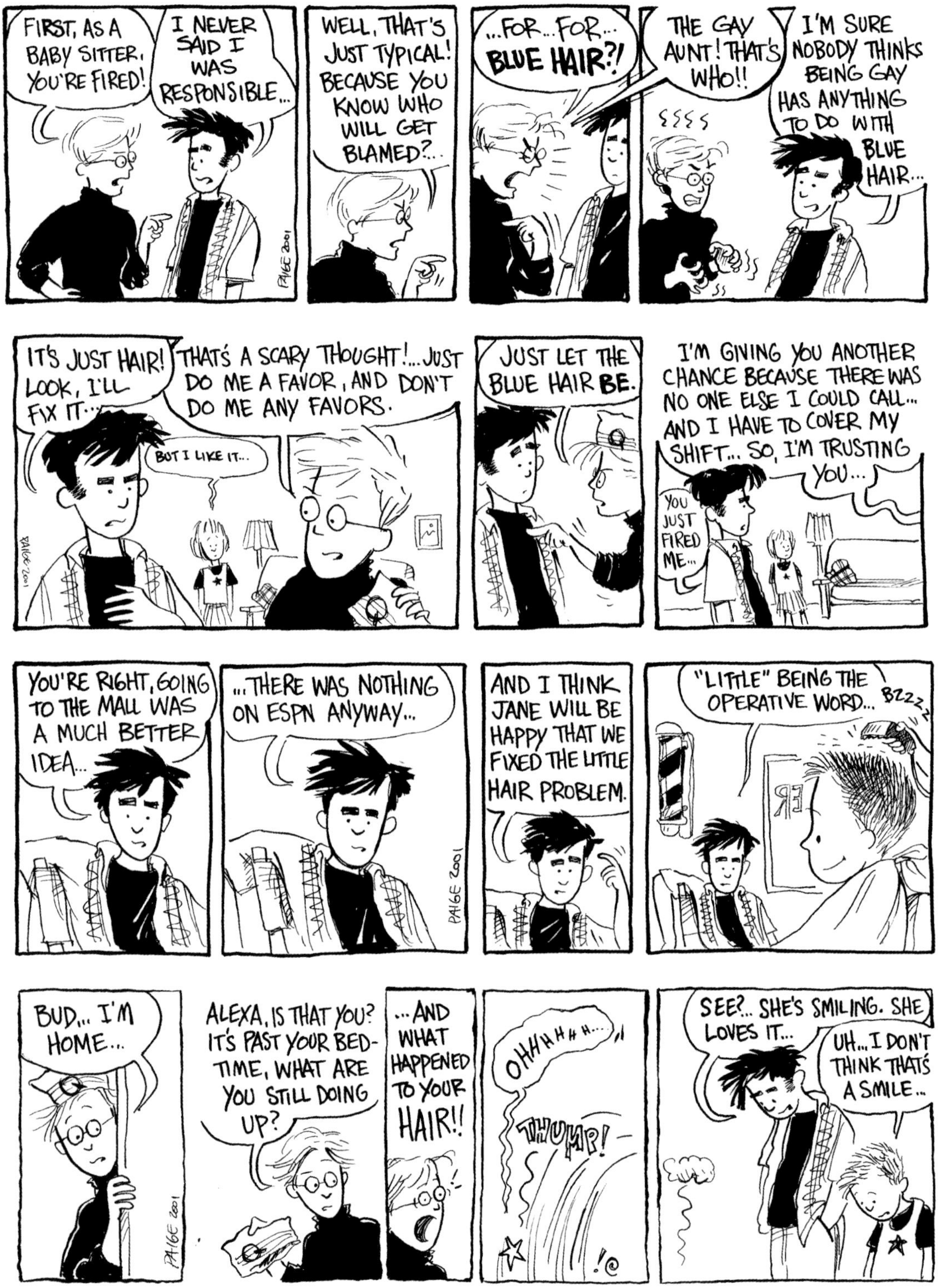
FIRST, AS A BABY SITTER, YOU'RE FIRED!
I NEVER SAID I WAS RESPONSIBLE...
WELL, THAT'S JUST TYPICAL! BECAUSE YOU KNOW WHO WILL GET BLAMED?...
PAIGE 2001
...FOR...FOR... BLUE HAIR?!
THE GAY AUNT! THAT'S WHO!!
I'M SURE NOBODY THINKS BEING GAY HAS ANYTHING TO DO WITH BLUE HAIR...
IT'S JUST HAIR! LOOK, I'LL FIX IT...
BUT I LIKE IT...
THAT'S A SCARY THOUGHT!... JUST DO ME A FAVOR, AND DON'T DO ME ANY FAVORS.
PAIGE 2001
JUST LET THE BLUE HAIR BE.
I'M GIVING YOU ANOTHER CHANCE BECAUSE THERE WAS NO ONE ELSE I COULD CALL... AND I HAVE TO COVER MY SHIFT... SO, I'M TRUSTING YOU...
YOU JUST FIRED ME...
YOU'RE RIGHT, GOING TO THE MALL WAS A MUCH BETTER IDEA...
...THERE WAS NOTHING ON ESPN ANYWAY...
PAIGE 2001
AND I THINK JANE WILL BE HAPPY THAT WE FIXED THE LITTLE HAIR PROBLEM.
"LITTLE" BEING THE OPERATIVE WORD...
BZZZZ
BUD... I'M HOME...
PAIGE 2001
ALEXA, IS THAT YOU? IT'S PAST YOUR BED-TIME, WHAT ARE YOU STILL DOING UP?
...AND WHAT HAPPENED TO YOUR HAIR!!
OHHHHHH...
THUMP!
SEE?... SHE'S SMILING. SHE LOVES IT...
UH... I DON'T THINK THAT'S A SMILE...

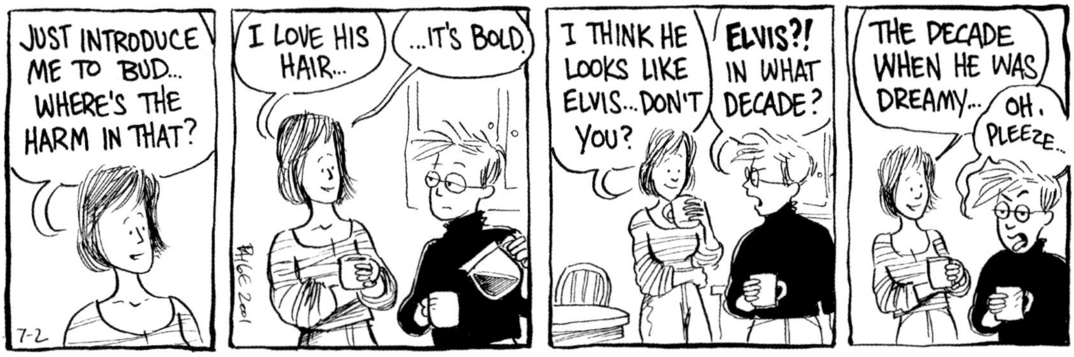
JUST INTRODUCE ME TO BUD... WHERE'S THE HARM IN THAT?
7-2
I LOVE HIS HAIR...
...IT'S BOLD.
PAIGE 2001
I THINK HE LOOKS LIKE ELVIS... DON'T YOU?
ELVIS?! IN WHAT DECADE?
THE DECADE WHEN HE WAS DREAMY...
OH, PLEEZE...

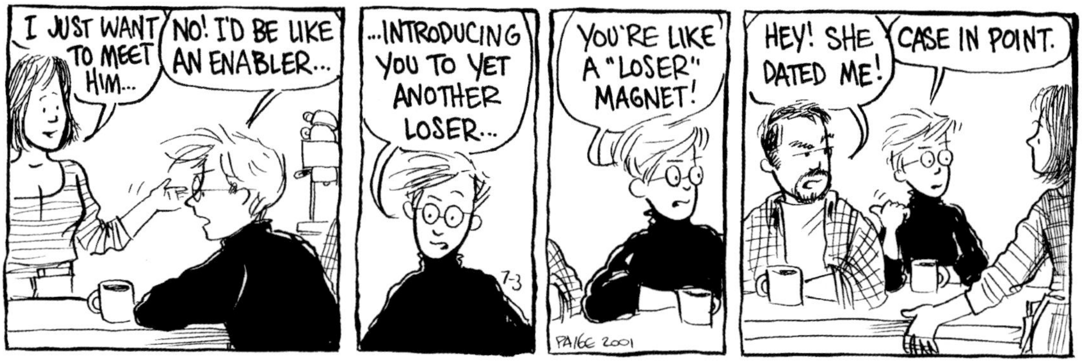
I JUST WANT TO MEET HIM...
NO! I'D BE LIKE AN ENABLER...
...INTRODUCING YOU TO YET ANOTHER LOSER...
7-3
YOU'RE LIKE A "LOSER" MAGNET!
PAIGE 2001
HEY! SHE DATED ME!
CASE IN POINT.

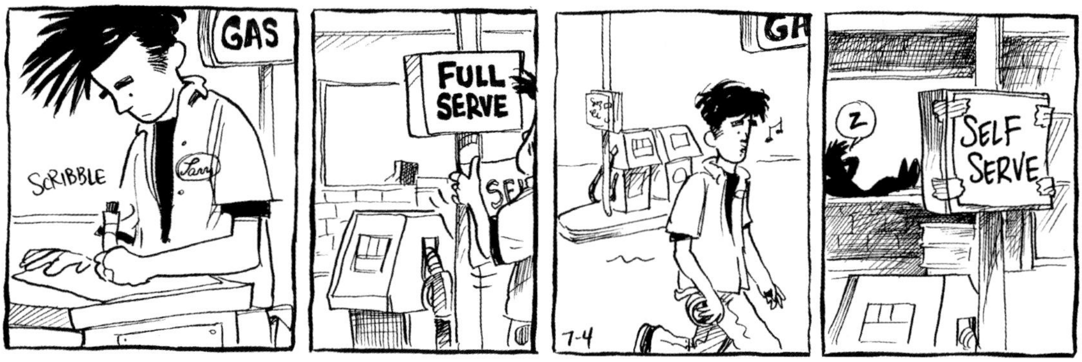
GAS
SCRIBBLE
FULL SERVE
7-4
Z
SELF SERVE

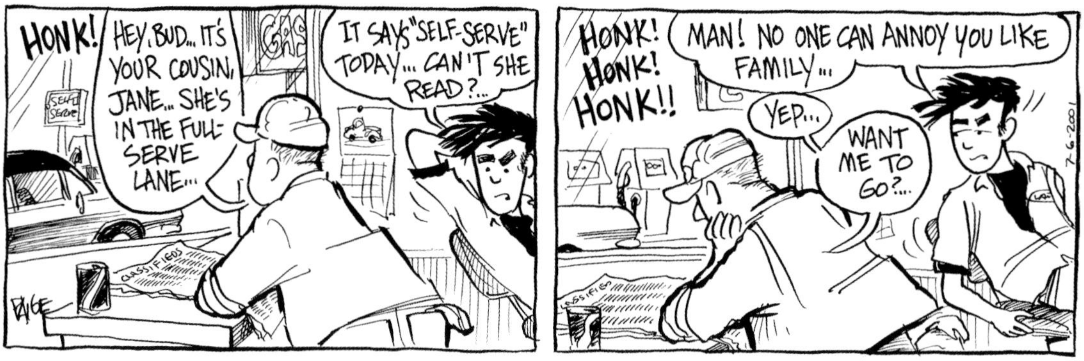
HONK!
HEY, BUD... IT'S YOUR COUSIN, JANE... SHE'S IN THE FULL-SERVE LANE...
IT SAYS "SELF-SERVE" TODAY... CAN'T SHE READ?...
PAIGE
HONK! HONK! HONK!!
MAN! NO ONE CAN ANNOY YOU LIKE FAMILY...
YEP...
WANT ME TO GO?...
7-6-2001

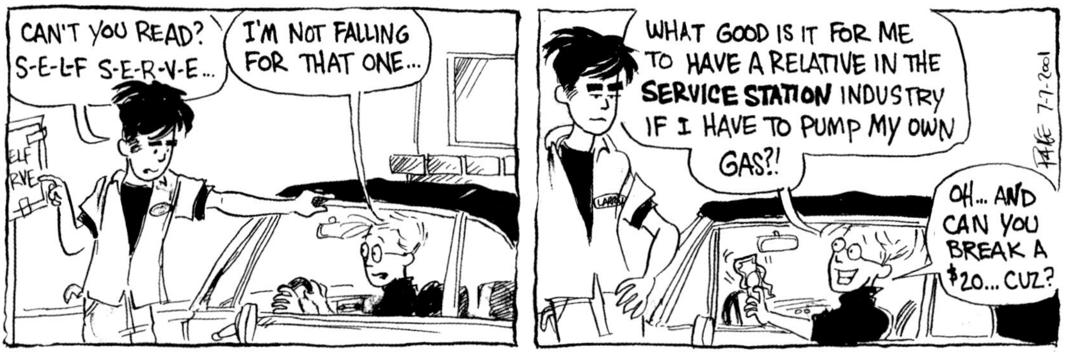
CAN'T YOU READ? S-E-L-F S-E-R-V-E...
I'M NOT FALLING FOR THAT ONE...
WHAT GOOD IS IT FOR ME TO HAVE A RELATIVE IN THE **SERVICE STATION** INDUSTRY IF I HAVE TO PUMP MY OWN GAS?!
OH... AND CAN YOU BREAK A $20... CUZ?
PAIGE 7-7-2001

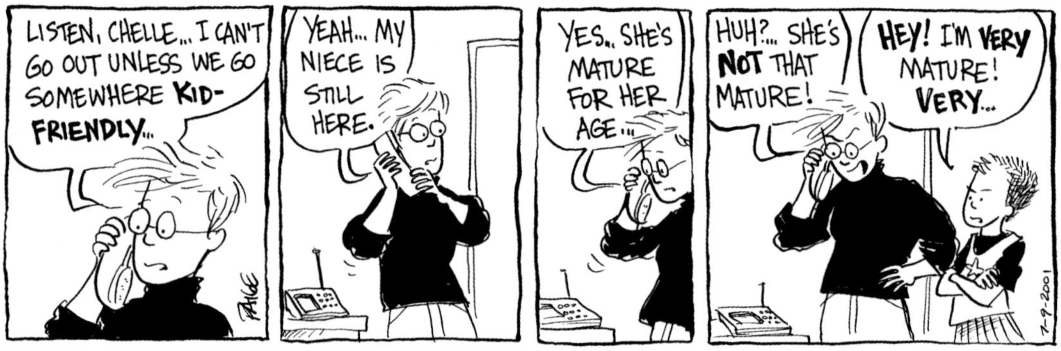
LISTEN, CHELLE... I CAN'T GO OUT UNLESS WE GO SOMEWHERE **KID-FRIENDLY**...
YEAH... MY NIECE IS STILL HERE.
YES.. SHE'S MATURE FOR HER AGE...
HUH?... SHE'S **NOT** THAT MATURE!
HEY! I'M **VERY** MATURE! **VERY**...
PAIGE
7-9-2001

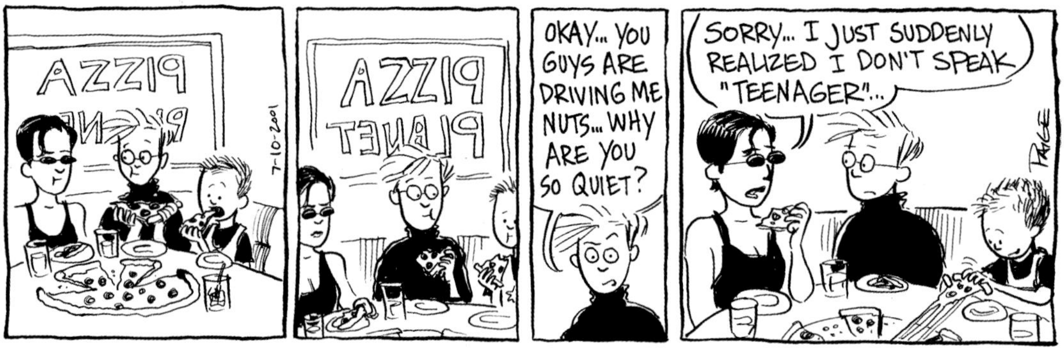
PIZZA
7-10-2001
PIZZA PLANET
OKAY... YOU GUYS ARE DRIVING ME NUTS... WHY ARE YOU SO QUIET?
SORRY... I JUST SUDDENLY REALIZED I DON'T SPEAK "TEENAGER"...
PAIGE

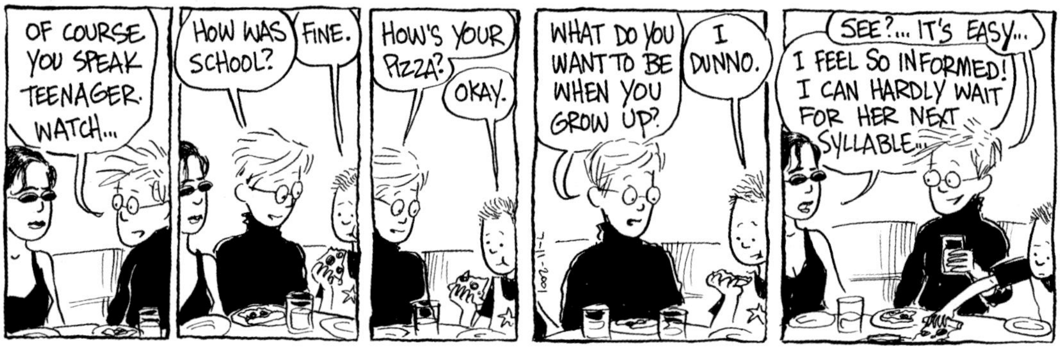
OF COURSE YOU SPEAK TEENAGER. WATCH...
HOW WAS SCHOOL?
FINE.
HOW'S YOUR PIZZA?
OKAY.
WHAT DO YOU WANT TO BE WHEN YOU GROW UP?
I DUNNO.
7-11-2001
SEE?... IT'S EASY...
I FEEL SO INFORMED! I CAN HARDLY WAIT FOR HER NEXT SYLLABLE...

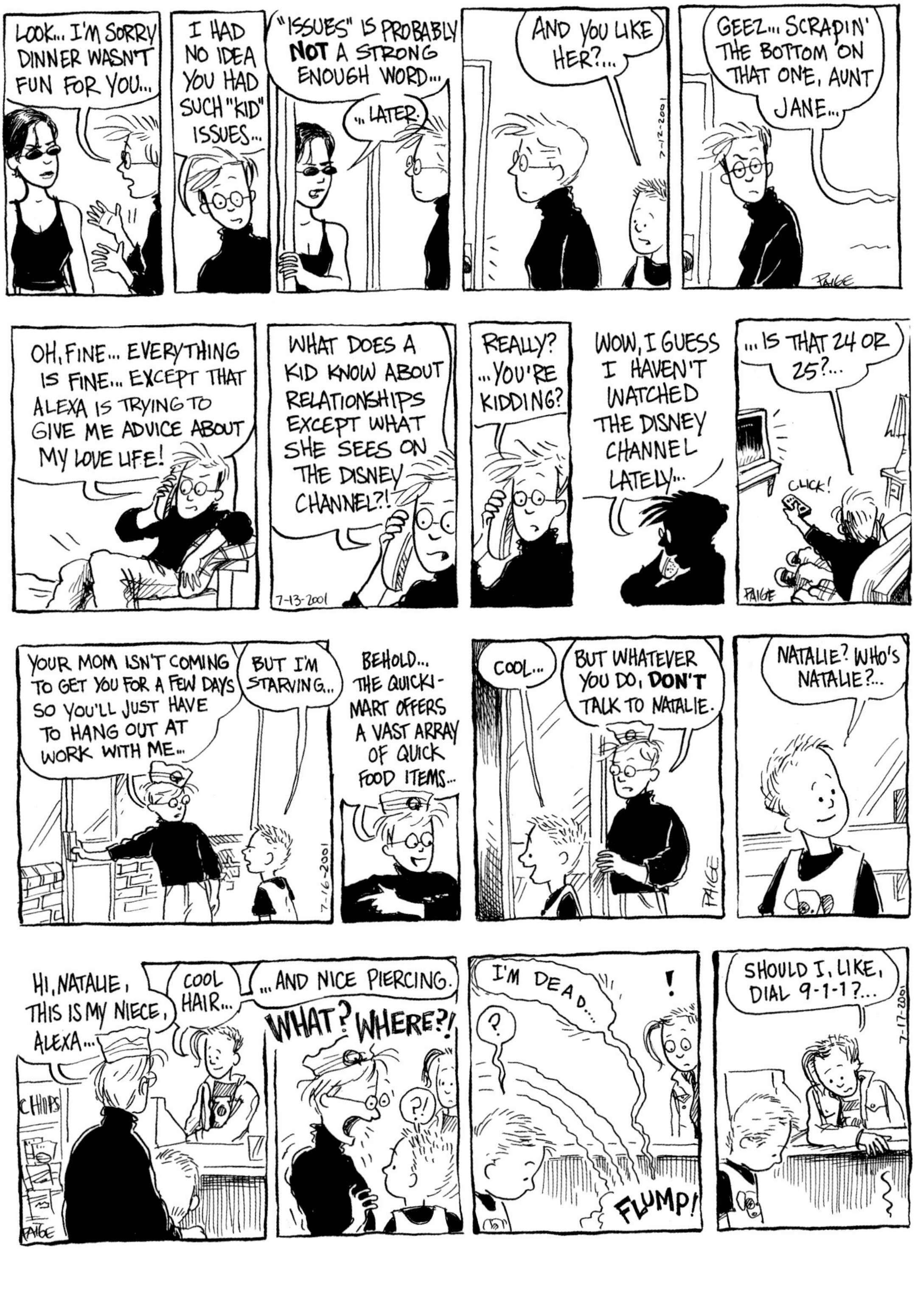
LOOK... I'M SORRY DINNER WASN'T FUN FOR YOU...
I HAD NO IDEA YOU HAD SUCH "KID" ISSUES...
"ISSUES" IS PROBABLY **NOT** A STRONG ENOUGH WORD...
... LATER.
AND YOU LIKE HER?...
7-12-2001
GEEZ... SCRAPIN' THE BOTTOM ON THAT ONE, AUNT JANE...
PAIGE
OH, FINE... EVERYTHING IS FINE... EXCEPT THAT ALEXA IS TRYING TO GIVE ME ADVICE ABOUT MY LOVE LIFE!
WHAT DOES A KID KNOW ABOUT RELATIONSHIPS EXCEPT WHAT SHE SEES ON THE DISNEY CHANNEL?!
7-13-2001
REALLY? ...YOU'RE KIDDING?
WOW, I GUESS I HAVEN'T WATCHED THE DISNEY CHANNEL LATELY...
... IS THAT 24 OR 25?...
CLICK!
PAIGE
YOUR MOM ISN'T COMING TO GET YOU FOR A FEW DAYS SO YOU'LL JUST HAVE TO HANG OUT AT WORK WITH ME...
BUT I'M STARVING...
7-16-2001
BEHOLD... THE QUICKI-MART OFFERS A VAST ARRAY OF QUICK FOOD ITEMS...
COOL...
BUT WHATEVER YOU DO, **DON'T** TALK TO NATALIE.
PAIGE
NATALIE? WHO'S NATALIE?...
HI, NATALIE, THIS IS MY NIECE, ALEXA...
COOL HAIR...
... AND NICE PIERCING.
CHIPS
PAIGE
WHAT? WHERE?!
?!
I'M DEAD...
?
!
FLUMP!
SHOULD I, LIKE, DIAL 9-1-1?...
7-17-2001

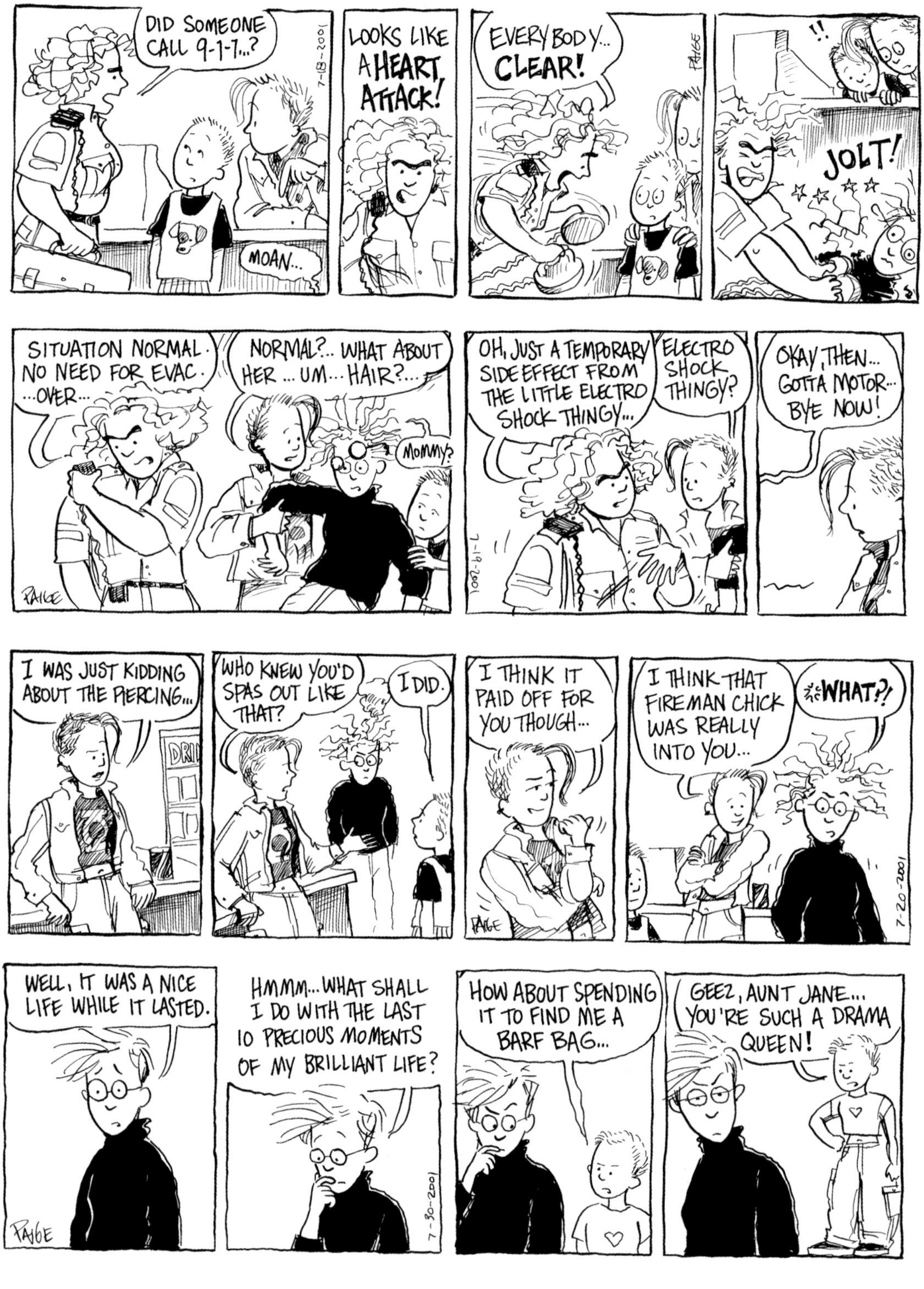
DID SOMEONE CALL 9-1-1...?
7-18-2001
MOAN...
LOOKS LIKE A HEART ATTACK!
EVERYBODY... CLEAR!
PAIGE
!!
JOLT!
SITUATION NORMAL. NO NEED FOR EVAC. ...OVER...
NORMAL?... WHAT ABOUT HER ... UM... HAIR?...
MOMMY?
PAIGE
OH, JUST A TEMPORARY SIDE EFFECT FROM THE LITTLE ELECTRO SHOCK THINGY...
ELECTRO SHOCK THINGY?
7-19-2001
OKAY, THEN... GOTTA MOTOR... BYE NOW!
I WAS JUST KIDDING ABOUT THE PIERCING...
WHO KNEW YOU'D SPAS OUT LIKE THAT?
I DID.
I THINK IT PAID OFF FOR YOU THOUGH...
PAIGE
I THINK THAT FIREMAN CHICK WAS REALLY INTO YOU...
WHAT?!
7-20-2001
WELL, IT WAS A NICE LIFE WHILE IT LASTED.
PAIGE
HMMM... WHAT SHALL I DO WITH THE LAST 10 PRECIOUS MOMENTS OF MY BRILLIANT LIFE?
7-30-2001
HOW ABOUT SPENDING IT TO FIND ME A BARF BAG...
GEEZ, AUNT JANE... YOU'RE SUCH A DRAMA QUEEN!

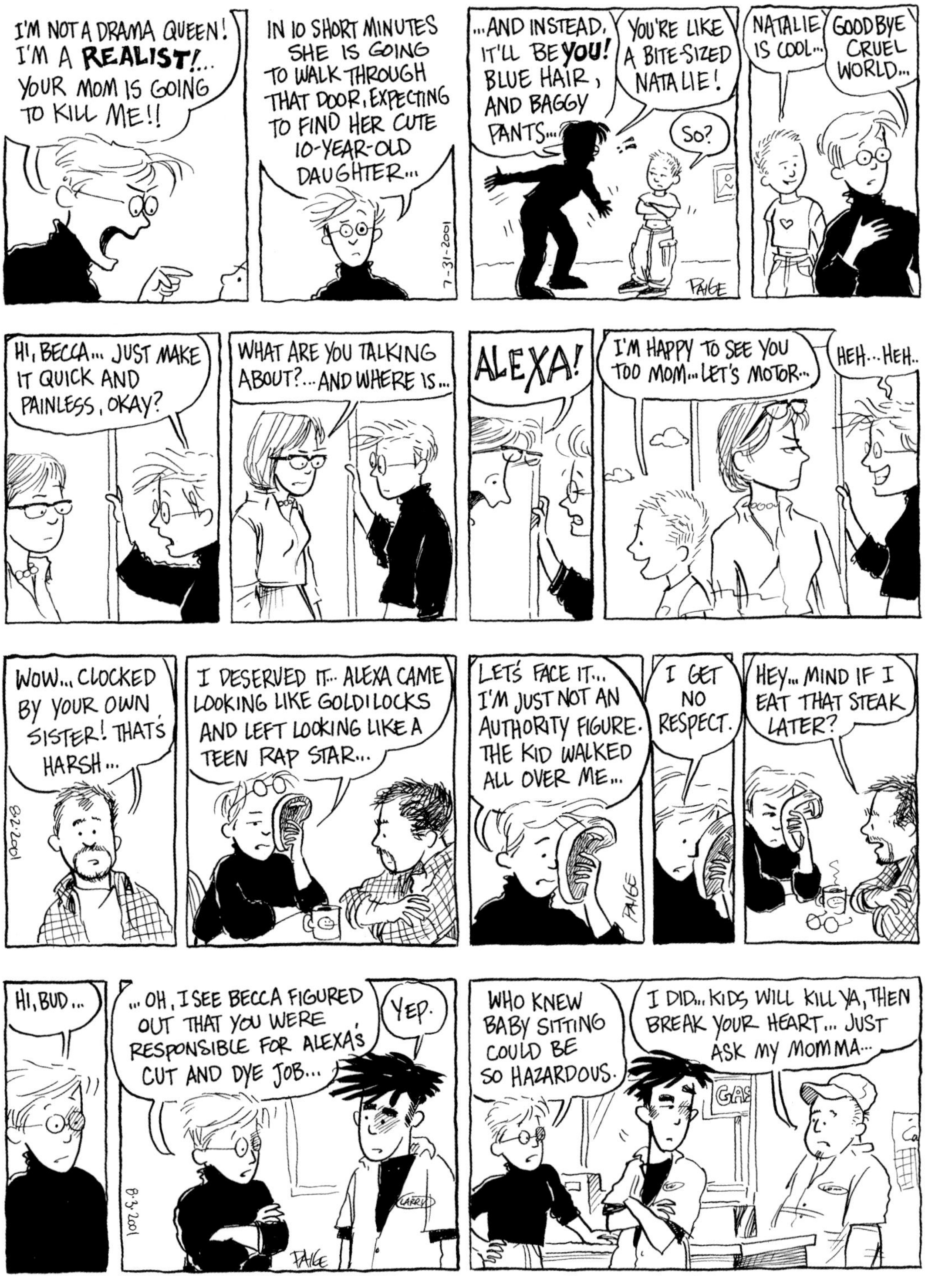
I'M NOT A DRAMA QUEEN! I'M A **REALIST!**... YOUR MOM IS GOING TO KILL ME!!
IN 10 SHORT MINUTES SHE IS GOING TO WALK THROUGH THAT DOOR, EXPECTING TO FIND HER CUTE 10-YEAR-OLD DAUGHTER...
7-31-2001
...AND INSTEAD, IT'LL BE **YOU!** BLUE HAIR, AND BAGGY PANTS...
YOU'RE LIKE A BITE-SIZED NATALIE!
SO?
PAIGE
NATALIE IS COOL...
GOODBYE CRUEL WORLD...
HI, BECCA... JUST MAKE IT QUICK AND PAINLESS, OKAY?
WHAT ARE YOU TALKING ABOUT?... AND WHERE IS...
ALEXA!
I'M HAPPY TO SEE YOU TOO MOM... LET'S MOTOR...
HEH... HEH...
WOW... CLOCKED BY YOUR OWN SISTER! THAT'S HARSH...
8-2-2001
I DESERVED IT... ALEXA CAME LOOKING LIKE GOLDILOCKS AND LEFT LOOKING LIKE A TEEN RAP STAR...
LET'S FACE IT... I'M JUST NOT AN AUTHORITY FIGURE. THE KID WALKED ALL OVER ME...
PAIGE
I GET NO RESPECT.
HEY... MIND IF I EAT THAT STEAK LATER?
HI, BUD...
...OH, I SEE BECCA FIGURED OUT THAT YOU WERE RESPONSIBLE FOR ALEXA'S CUT AND DYE JOB...
YEP.
8-3-2001
LARRY
PAIGE
WHO KNEW BABY SITTING COULD BE SO HAZARDOUS.
I DID... KIDS WILL KILL YA, THEN BREAK YOUR HEART... JUST ASK MY MOMMA...

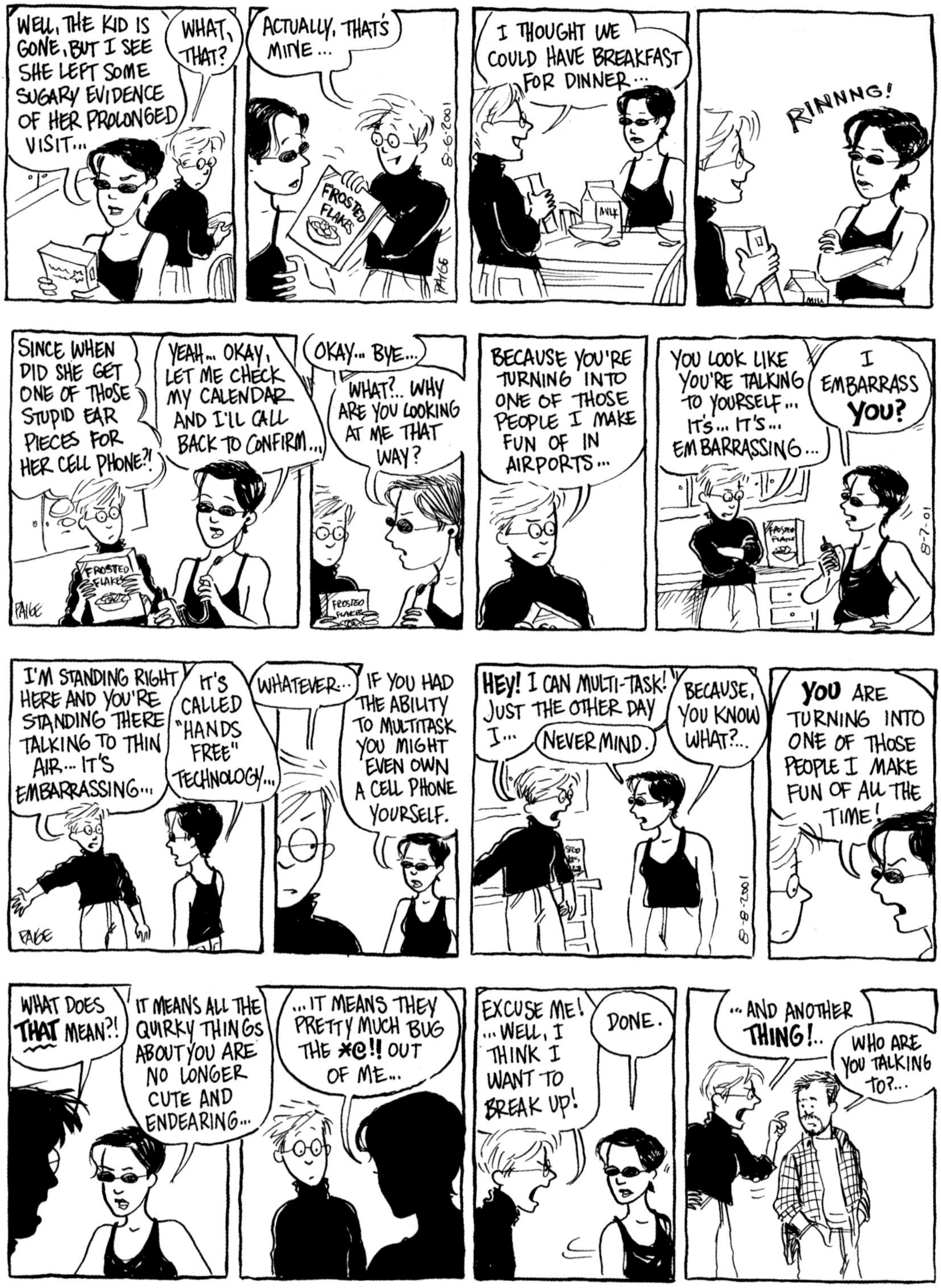
WELL, THE KID IS GONE, BUT I SEE SHE LEFT SOME SUGARY EVIDENCE OF HER PROLONGED VISIT...
WHAT, THAT?
ACTUALLY, THAT'S MINE...
FROSTED FLAKES
8-6-2001
PAIGE
I THOUGHT WE COULD HAVE BREAKFAST FOR DINNER...
MILK
RINNNG!
SINCE WHEN DID SHE GET ONE OF THOSE STUPID EAR PIECES FOR HER CELL PHONE?!
FROSTED FLAKES
PAIGE
YEAH... OKAY, LET ME CHECK MY CALENDAR AND I'LL CALL BACK TO CONFIRM...
OKAY... BYE...
WHAT?... WHY ARE YOU LOOKING AT ME THAT WAY?
BECAUSE YOU'RE TURNING INTO ONE OF THOSE PEOPLE I MAKE FUN OF IN AIRPORTS...
YOU LOOK LIKE YOU'RE TALKING TO YOURSELF... IT'S... IT'S... EMBARRASSING...
I EMBARRASS **YOU?**
8-7-01
I'M STANDING RIGHT HERE AND YOU'RE STANDING THERE TALKING TO THIN AIR... IT'S EMBARRASSING...
IT'S CALLED "HANDS FREE" TECHNOLOGY...
PAIGE
WHATEVER...
IF YOU HAD THE ABILITY TO MULTITASK YOU MIGHT EVEN OWN A CELL PHONE YOURSELF.
HEY! I CAN MULTI-TASK! JUST THE OTHER DAY I...
NEVER MIND.
BECAUSE, YOU KNOW WHAT?...
8-8-2001
YOU ARE TURNING INTO ONE OF THOSE PEOPLE I MAKE FUN OF ALL THE TIME!
WHAT DOES **THAT** MEAN?!
IT MEANS ALL THE QUIRKY THINGS ABOUT YOU ARE NO LONGER CUTE AND ENDEARING...
...IT MEANS THEY PRETTY MUCH BUG THE *@!! OUT OF ME...
EXCUSE ME! ...WELL, I THINK I WANT TO BREAK UP!
DONE.
...AND ANOTHER **THING!**...
WHO ARE YOU TALKING TO?...

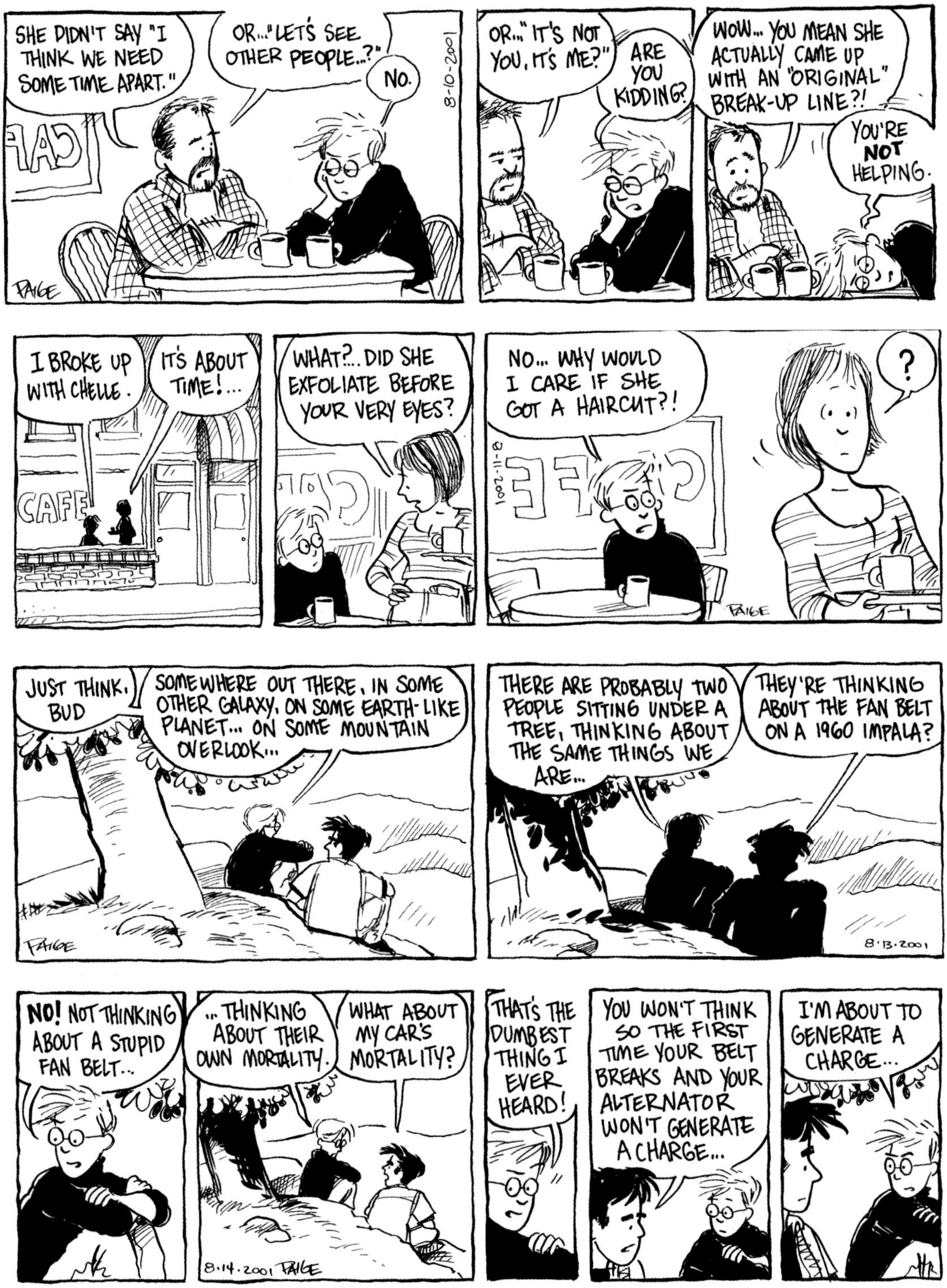
SHE DIDN'T SAY "I THINK WE NEED SOME TIME APART."
OR..."LET'S SEE OTHER PEOPLE..?"
NO.
8-10-2001
PAIGE
OR..."IT'S NOT YOU, IT'S ME?"
ARE YOU KIDDING?
WOW... YOU MEAN SHE ACTUALLY CAME UP WITH AN "ORIGINAL" BREAK-UP LINE?!
YOU'RE **NOT** HELPING.
I BROKE UP WITH CHELLE.
IT'S ABOUT TIME!...
CAFE
WHAT?... DID SHE EXFOLIATE BEFORE YOUR VERY EYES?
NO... WHY WOULD I CARE IF SHE GOT A HAIRCUT?!
8-11-2001
?
PAIGE
JUST THINK, BUD
SOMEWHERE OUT THERE, IN SOME OTHER GALAXY, ON SOME EARTH-LIKE PLANET... ON SOME MOUNTAIN OVERLOOK...
PAIGE
THERE ARE PROBABLY TWO PEOPLE SITTING UNDER A TREE, THINKING ABOUT THE SAME THINGS WE ARE...
THEY'RE THINKING ABOUT THE FAN BELT ON A 1960 IMPALA?
8·13·2001
NO! NOT THINKING ABOUT A STUPID FAN BELT...
...THINKING ABOUT THEIR OWN MORTALITY.
WHAT ABOUT MY CAR'S MORTALITY?
8·14·2001 PAIGE
THAT'S THE DUMBEST THING I EVER HEARD!
YOU WON'T THINK SO THE FIRST TIME YOUR BELT BREAKS AND YOUR ALTERNATOR WON'T GENERATE A CHARGE...
I'M ABOUT TO GENERATE A CHARGE...

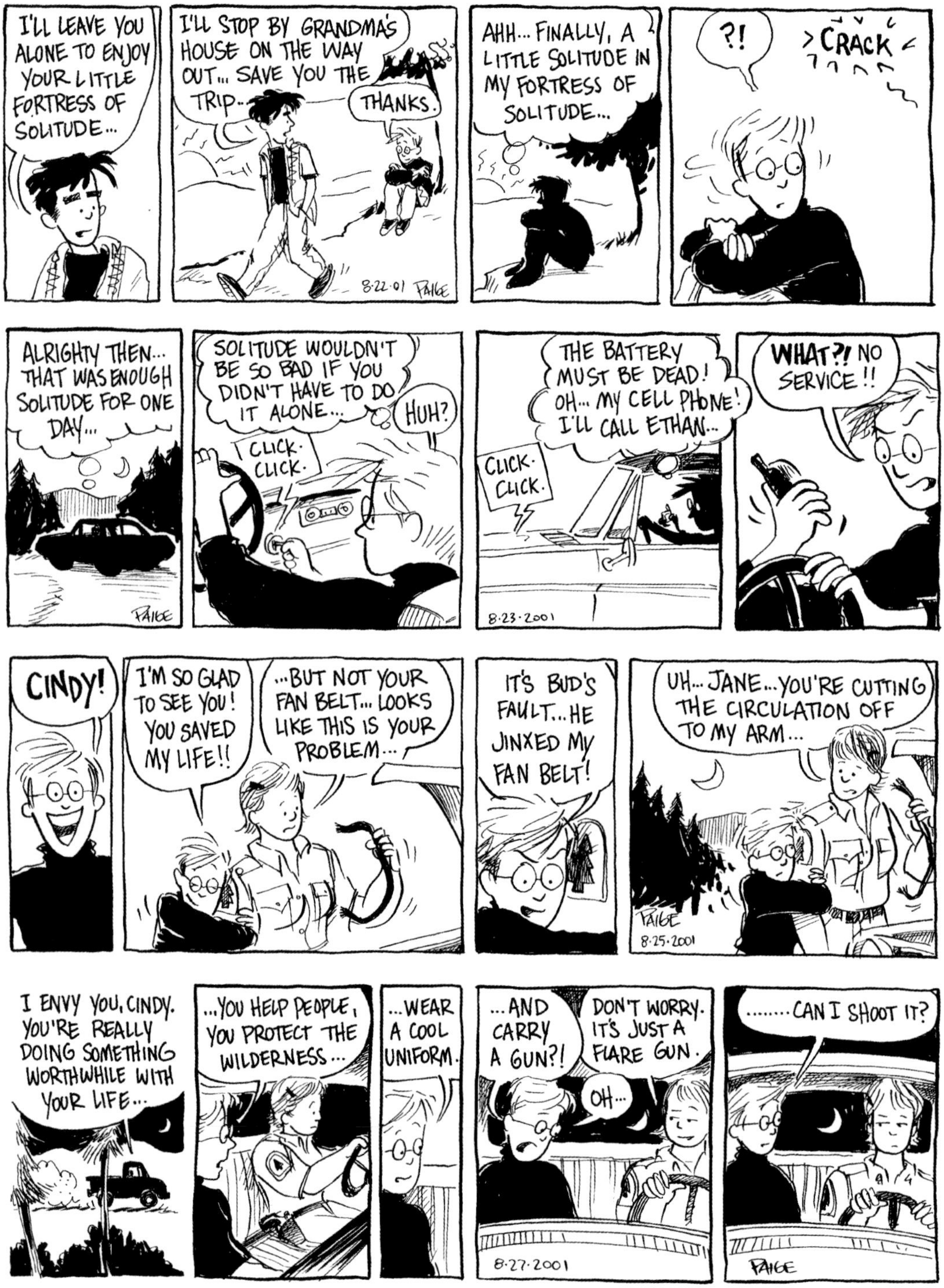
I'LL LEAVE YOU ALONE TO ENJOY YOUR LITTLE FORTRESS OF SOLITUDE...
I'LL STOP BY GRANDMA'S HOUSE ON THE WAY OUT... SAVE YOU THE TRIP...
THANKS.
8.22.01 PAIGE
AHH... FINALLY, A LITTLE SOLITUDE IN MY FORTRESS OF SOLITUDE...
?!
CRACK
ALRIGHTY THEN... THAT WAS ENOUGH SOLITUDE FOR ONE DAY...
PAIGE
SOLITUDE WOULDN'T BE SO BAD IF YOU DIDN'T HAVE TO DO IT ALONE...
HUH?
CLICK. CLICK.
THE BATTERY MUST BE DEAD! OH... MY CELL PHONE! I'LL CALL ETHAN...
CLICK. CLICK.
8.23.2001
WHAT?! NO SERVICE!!
CINDY!
I'M SO GLAD TO SEE YOU! YOU SAVED MY LIFE!!
...BUT NOT YOUR FAN BELT... LOOKS LIKE THIS IS YOUR PROBLEM...
IT'S BUD'S FAULT... HE JINXED MY FAN BELT!
UH... JANE... YOU'RE CUTTING THE CIRCULATION OFF TO MY ARM...
PAIGE
8.25.2001
I ENVY YOU, CINDY. YOU'RE REALLY DOING SOMETHING WORTHWHILE WITH YOUR LIFE...
...YOU HELP PEOPLE, YOU PROTECT THE WILDERNESS...
...WEAR A COOL UNIFORM...
...AND CARRY A GUN?!
DON'T WORRY. IT'S JUST A FLARE GUN.
OH...
8.27.2001
........CAN I SHOOT IT?
PAIGE

SO... SPEAKING OF NIGHT-LIFE, IS ETHAN STILL SINGLE? I ALWAYS HAD A CRUSH ON HIM...
NO JOKE!
REALLY?
8·29·01
WELL, HE WAS KINDA SEEING DIXIE...
THE BIG-HAIRED GIRL?!
WHAT'S SHE GOT THAT I DON'T HAVE?!
PAIGE
BESIDES ESTROGEN?
I SHOULD JUST GIVE HIM A CALL...

YOU AND ETHAN ARE STILL ROOMMATES RIGHT?
YEAH.
SHOULD I CALL HIM?
YOU'RE ASKING THE **WRONG** PERSON FOR ROMANTIC ADVICE...
8·30·01
HEY... THERE'S SOMETHING IN THE ROAD UP THERE...
PAIGE
WHAT DO YOU MEAN, "SOMETHING?"...

WHAT IS IT?! IS IT DEAD?! ...OR ALIVE??
WELL... IT'S STANDING, SO I ASSUME IT'S ALIVE...
8·31·2001
SEND UP A FLARE!
NO... DON'T PULL THE...
FFFZZZZZZZ
POP!
PAIGE

FFZZZ
9·3·2001
I CAN'T SEE!!
VARROOM!!
*@☆!!
?
PAIGE

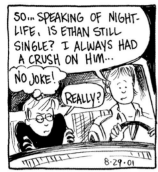

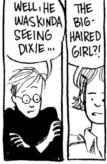

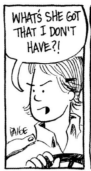

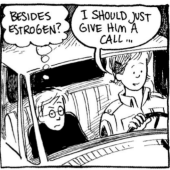

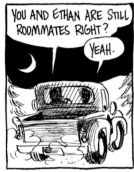

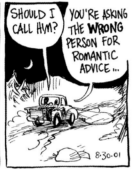

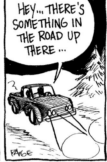

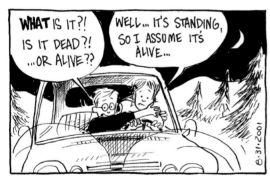

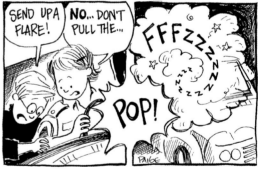

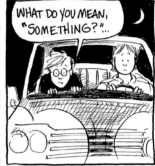

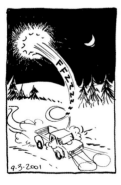

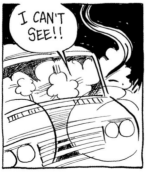

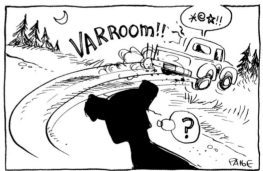

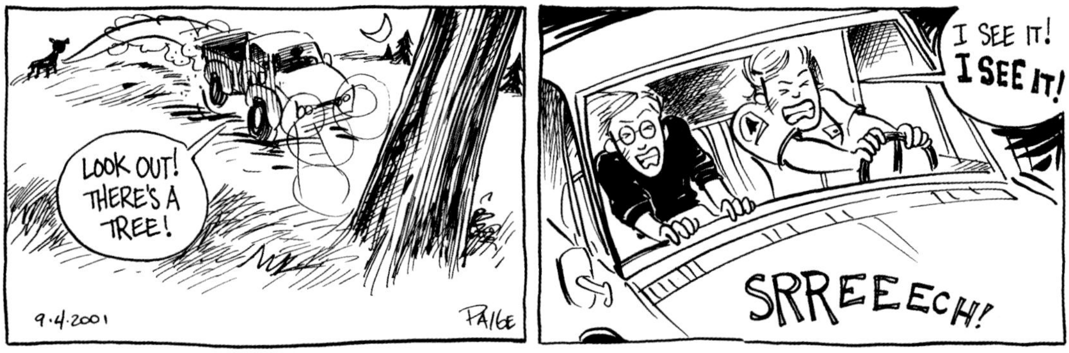
LOOK OUT! THERE'S A TREE!
9·4·2001
PAIGE
I SEE IT! **I SEE IT!**
SRREEECH!

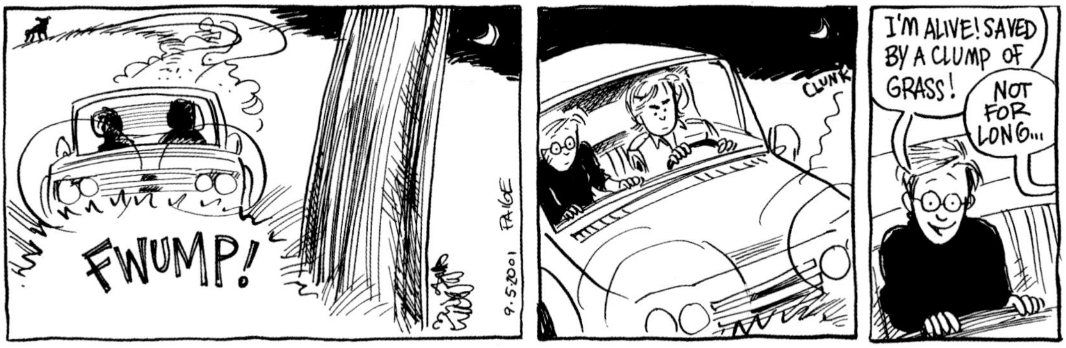
FWUMP!
PAIGE
9·5·2001
CLUNK
I'M ALIVE! SAVED BY A CLUMP OF GRASS!
NOT FOR LONG...

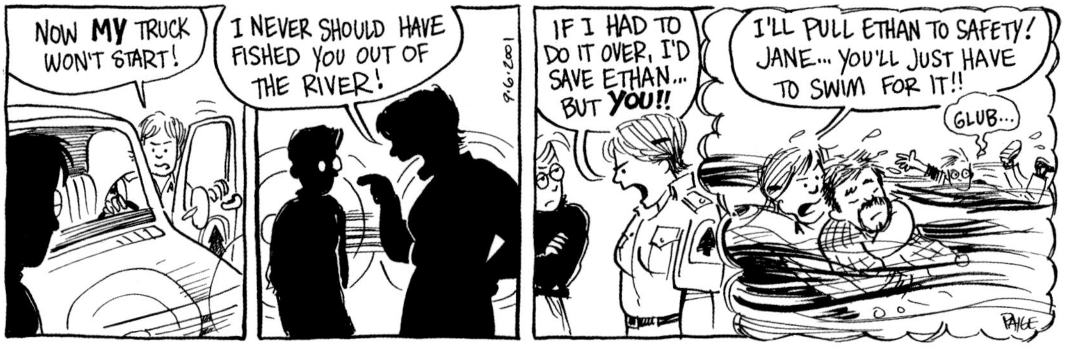
NOW **MY** TRUCK WON'T START!
I NEVER SHOULD HAVE FISHED YOU OUT OF THE RIVER!
9·6·2001
IF I HAD TO DO IT OVER, I'D SAVE ETHAN... BUT **YOU!!**
I'LL PULL ETHAN TO SAFETY! JANE... YOU'LL JUST HAVE TO SWIM FOR IT!!
GLUB...
PAIGE

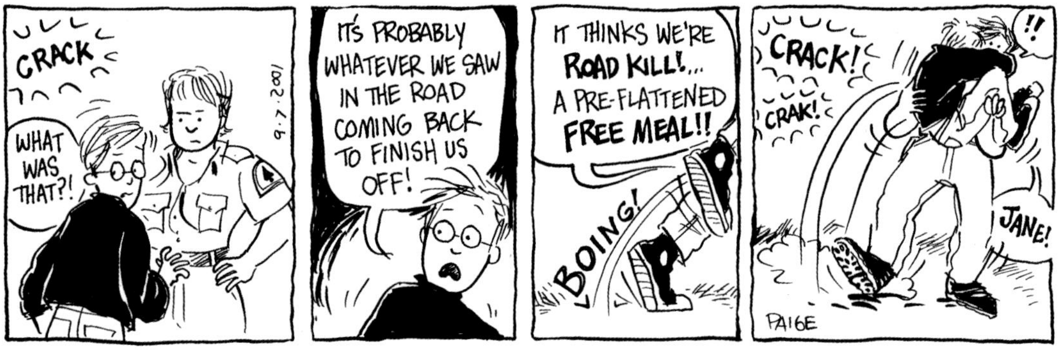
CRACK
WHAT WAS THAT?!
9·7·2001
IT'S PROBABLY WHATEVER WE SAW IN THE ROAD COMING BACK TO FINISH US OFF!
IT THINKS WE'RE **ROAD KILL!**... A PRE-FLATTENED **FREE MEAL!!**
BOING!
CRACK!
CRAK!
!!
JANE!
PAIGE

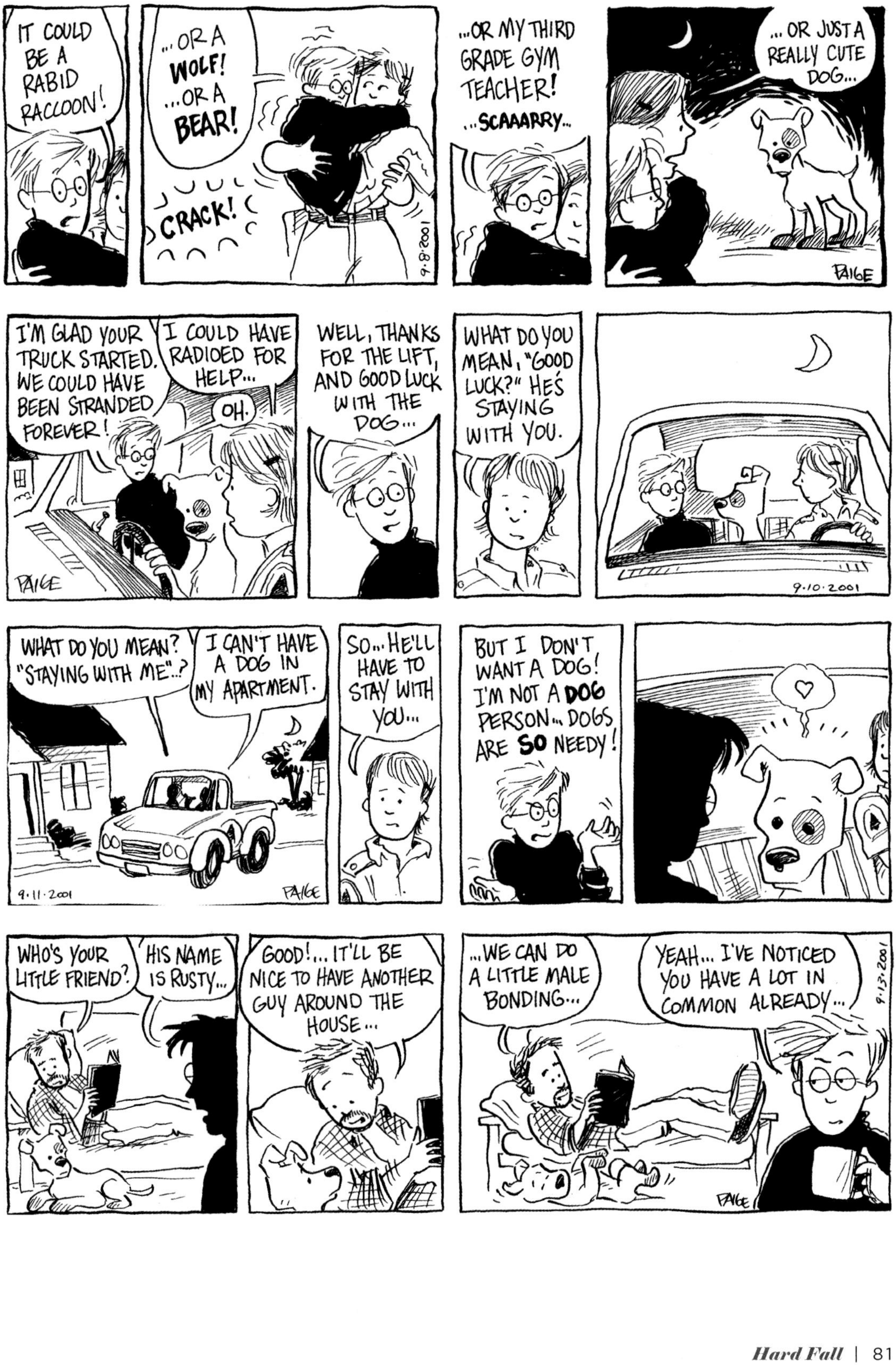
IT COULD BE A RABID RACCOON!
...OR A WOLF! ...OR A BEAR!
CRACK!
9·8·2001
...OR MY THIRD GRADE GYM TEACHER!
...SCAAARRY...
...OR JUST A REALLY CUTE DOG...
PAIGE
I'M GLAD YOUR TRUCK STARTED. WE COULD HAVE BEEN STRANDED FOREVER!
I COULD HAVE RADIOED FOR HELP...
OH.
PAIGE
WELL, THANKS FOR THE LIFT, AND GOOD LUCK WITH THE DOG...
WHAT DO YOU MEAN, "GOOD LUCK?" HE'S STAYING WITH YOU.
9·10·2001
WHAT DO YOU MEAN? "STAYING WITH ME"..?
I CAN'T HAVE A DOG IN MY APARTMENT.
9·11·2001
PAIGE
SO... HE'LL HAVE TO STAY WITH YOU...
BUT I DON'T WANT A DOG! I'M NOT A DOG PERSON... DOGS ARE SO NEEDY!
WHO'S YOUR LITTLE FRIEND?
HIS NAME IS RUSTY...
GOOD!... IT'LL BE NICE TO HAVE ANOTHER GUY AROUND THE HOUSE...
...WE CAN DO A LITTLE MALE BONDING...
YEAH... I'VE NOTICED YOU HAVE A LOT IN COMMON ALREADY...
9·13·2001
PAIGE

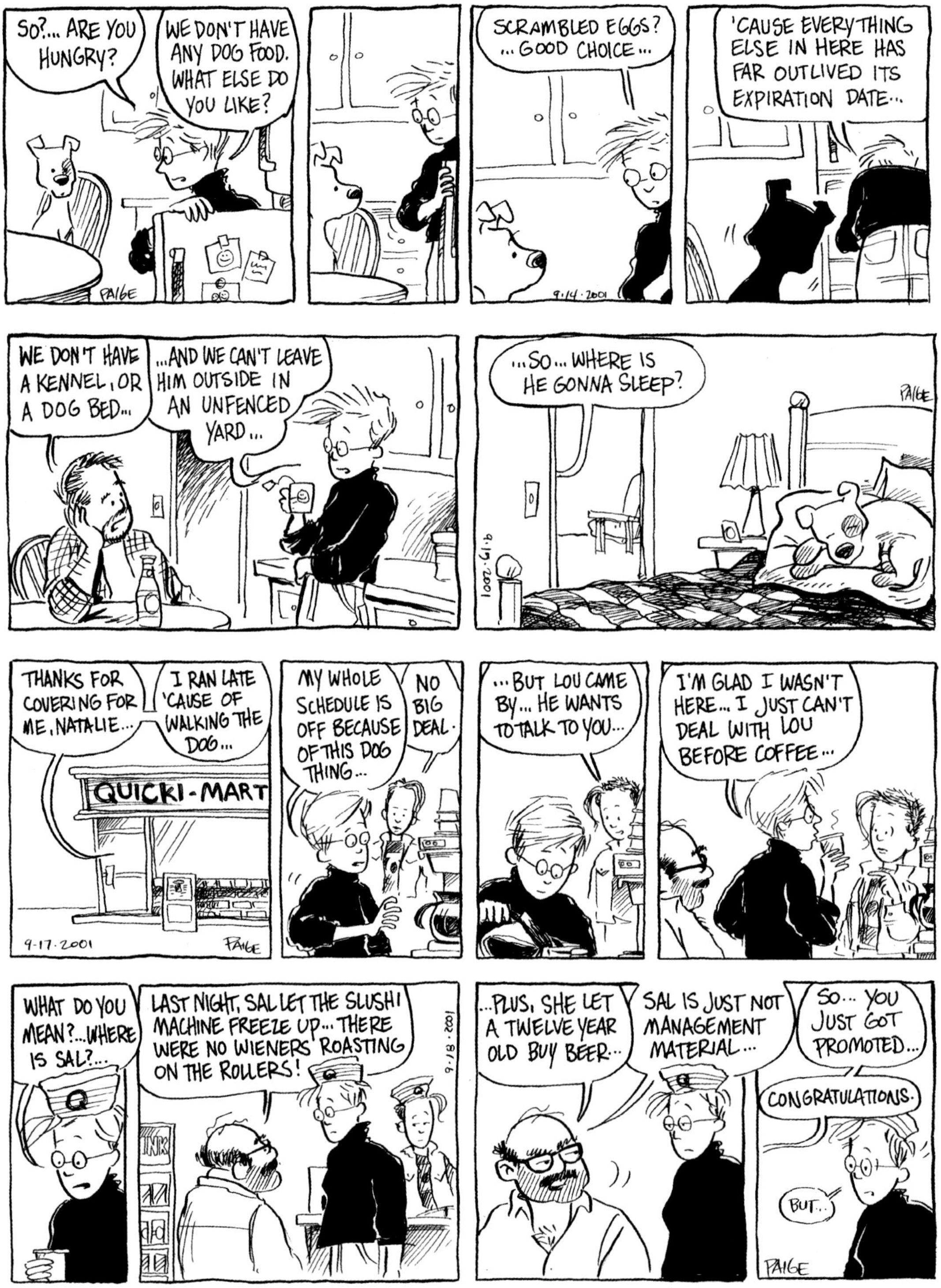
SO?... ARE YOU HUNGRY?
WE DON'T HAVE ANY DOG FOOD. WHAT ELSE DO YOU LIKE?
PAIGE
SCRAMBLED EGGS? ...GOOD CHOICE...
9·14·2001
'CAUSE EVERYTHING ELSE IN HERE HAS FAR OUTLIVED ITS EXPIRATION DATE...
WE DON'T HAVE A KENNEL, OR A DOG BED...
...AND WE CAN'T LEAVE HIM OUTSIDE IN AN UNFENCED YARD...
...SO... WHERE IS HE GONNA SLEEP?
PAIGE
9·15·2001
THANKS FOR COVERING FOR ME, NATALIE...
I RAN LATE 'CAUSE OF WALKING THE DOG...
QUICKI-MART
9-17-2001
PAIGE
MY WHOLE SCHEDULE IS OFF BECAUSE OF THIS DOG THING...
NO BIG DEAL.
...BUT LOU CAME BY... HE WANTS TO TALK TO YOU...
I'M GLAD I WASN'T HERE... I JUST CAN'T DEAL WITH LOU BEFORE COFFEE...
WHAT DO YOU MEAN?...WHERE IS SAL?...
LAST NIGHT, SAL LET THE SLUSHI MACHINE FREEZE UP... THERE WERE NO WIENERS ROASTING ON THE ROLLERS!
9·18·2001
...PLUS, SHE LET A TWELVE YEAR OLD BUY BEER...
SAL IS JUST NOT MANAGEMENT MATERIAL...
SO... YOU JUST GOT PROMOTED...
CONGRATULATIONS.
BUT...
PAIGE

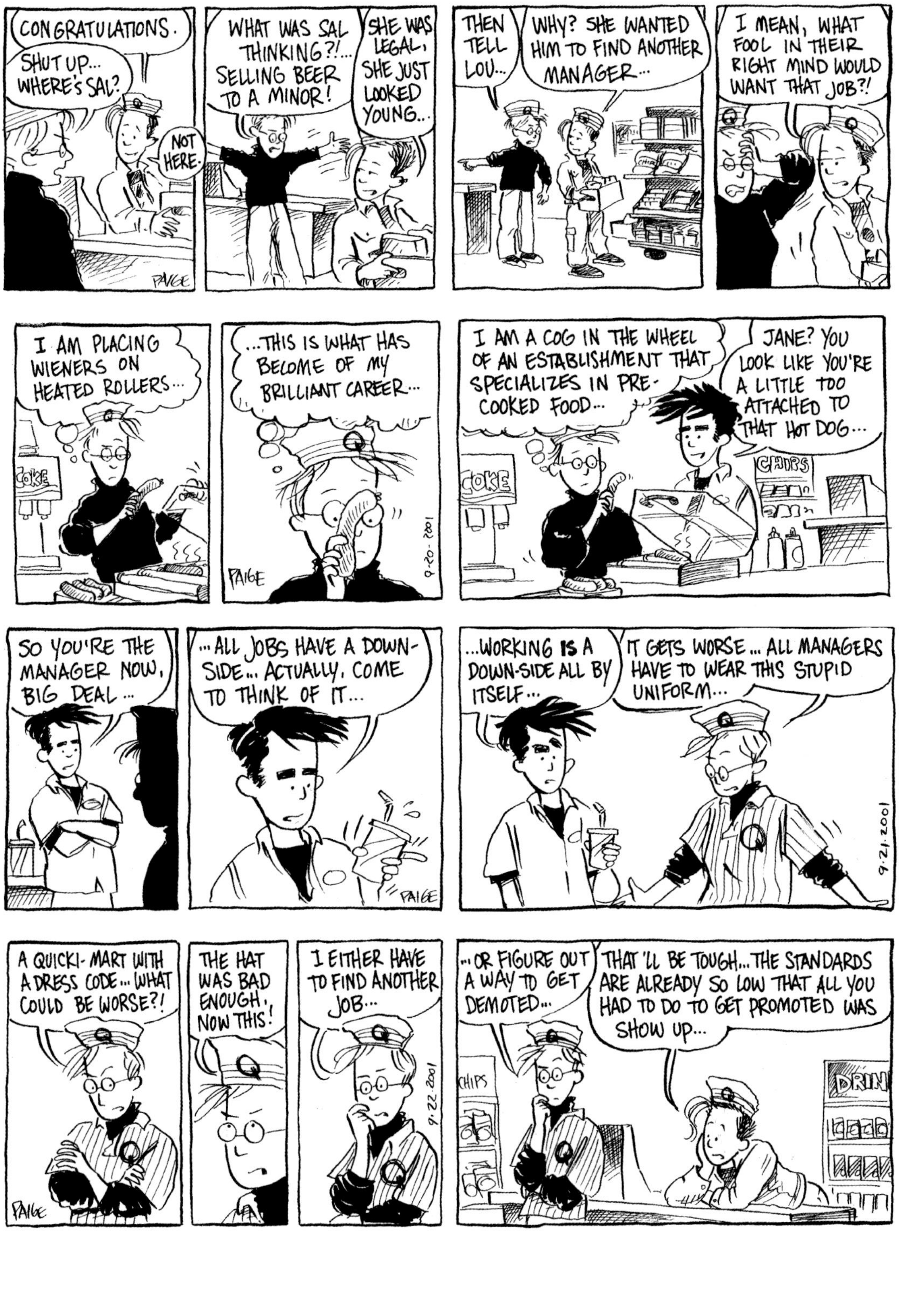
CONGRATULATIONS.
SHUT UP... WHERE'S SAL?
NOT HERE.
WHAT WAS SAL THINKING?!... SELLING BEER TO A MINOR!
SHE WAS LEGAL, SHE JUST LOOKED YOUNG...
THEN TELL LOU...
WHY? SHE WANTED HIM TO FIND ANOTHER MANAGER...
I MEAN, WHAT FOOL IN THEIR RIGHT MIND WOULD WANT THAT JOB?!
PAIGE
I AM PLACING WIENERS ON HEATED ROLLERS...
...THIS IS WHAT HAS BECOME OF MY BRILLIANT CAREER...
PAIGE
9-20-2001
I AM A COG IN THE WHEEL OF AN ESTABLISHMENT THAT SPECIALIZES IN PRE-COOKED FOOD...
JANE? YOU LOOK LIKE YOU'RE A LITTLE TOO ATTACHED TO THAT HOT DOG...
COKE
CHIPS
SO YOU'RE THE MANAGER NOW, BIG DEAL...
...ALL JOBS HAVE A DOWN-SIDE... ACTUALLY, COME TO THINK OF IT...
PAIGE
...WORKING IS A DOWN-SIDE ALL BY ITSELF...
IT GETS WORSE... ALL MANAGERS HAVE TO WEAR THIS STUPID UNIFORM...
9-21-2001
A QUICKI-MART WITH A DRESS CODE... WHAT COULD BE WORSE?!
PAIGE
THE HAT WAS BAD ENOUGH, NOW THIS!
I EITHER HAVE TO FIND ANOTHER JOB...
9-22-2001
...OR FIGURE OUT A WAY TO GET DEMOTED...
THAT'LL BE TOUGH... THE STANDARDS ARE ALREADY SO LOW THAT ALL YOU HAD TO DO TO GET PROMOTED WAS SHOW UP...
CHIPS
DRIN

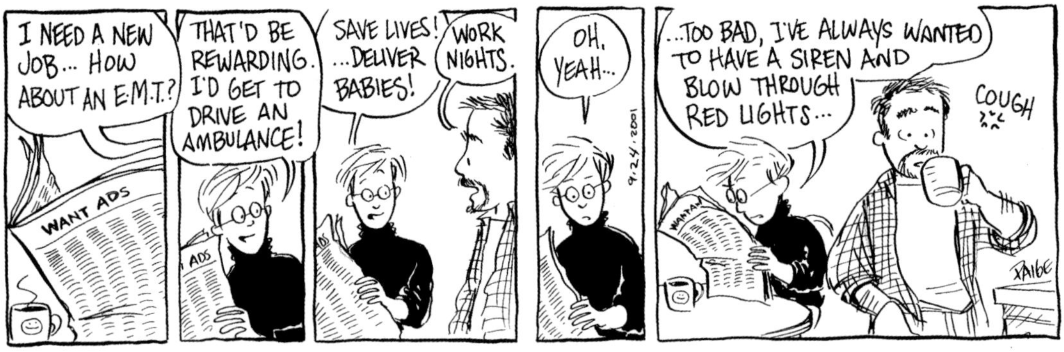
I NEED A NEW JOB... HOW ABOUT AN E.M.T.?
WANT ADS
THAT'D BE REWARDING. I'D GET TO DRIVE AN AMBULANCE!
ADS
SAVE LIVES! ...DELIVER BABIES!
WORK NIGHTS.
OH, YEAH...
9-24-2001
...TOO BAD, I'VE ALWAYS WANTED TO HAVE A SIREN AND BLOW THROUGH RED LIGHTS...
COUGH
PAIGE

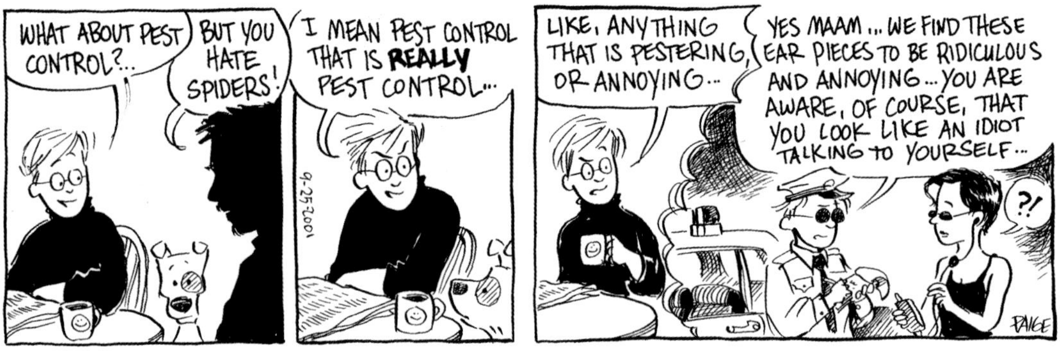
WHAT ABOUT PEST CONTROL?...
BUT YOU HATE SPIDERS!
I MEAN PEST CONTROL THAT IS **REALLY** PEST CONTROL...
9-25-2001
LIKE, ANYTHING THAT IS PESTERING, OR ANNOYING...
YES MAAM... WE FIND THESE EAR PIECES TO BE RIDICULOUS AND ANNOYING... YOU ARE AWARE, OF COURSE, THAT YOU LOOK LIKE AN IDIOT TALKING TO YOURSELF...
?!
PAIGE

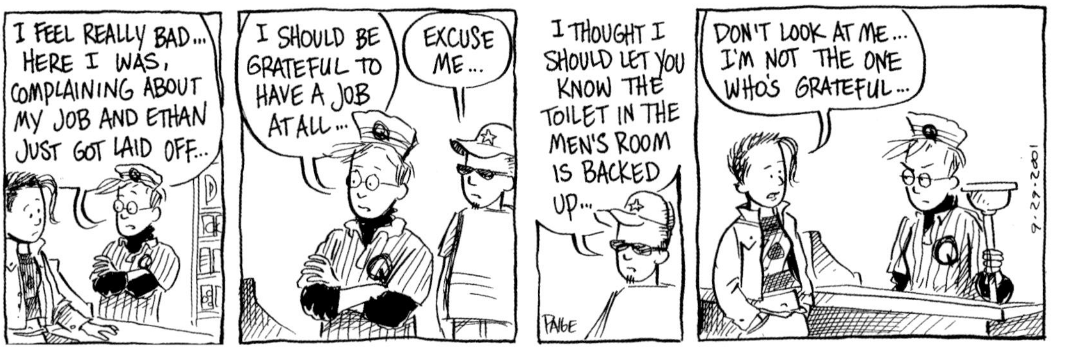
I FEEL REALLY BAD... HERE I WAS, COMPLAINING ABOUT MY JOB AND ETHAN JUST GOT LAID OFF...
I SHOULD BE GRATEFUL TO HAVE A JOB AT ALL...
EXCUSE ME...
I THOUGHT I SHOULD LET YOU KNOW THE TOILET IN THE MEN'S ROOM IS BACKED UP...
PAIGE
DON'T LOOK AT ME... I'M NOT THE ONE WHO'S GRATEFUL...
9-27-2001

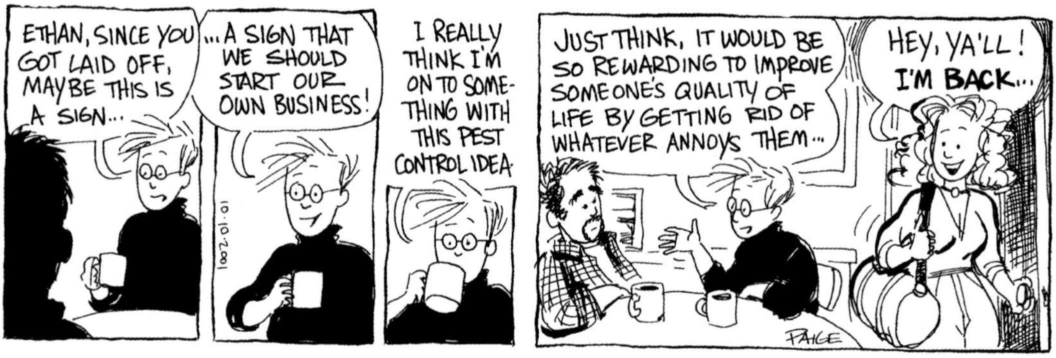
ETHAN, SINCE YOU GOT LAID OFF, MAYBE THIS IS A SIGN...
...A SIGN THAT WE SHOULD START OUR OWN BUSINESS!
10.01.2001
I REALLY THINK I'M ON TO SOMETHING WITH THIS PEST CONTROL IDEA.
JUST THINK, IT WOULD BE SO REWARDING TO IMPROVE SOMEONE'S QUALITY OF LIFE BY GETTING RID OF WHATEVER ANNOYS THEM...
HEY, YA'LL! **I'M BACK**...
PAIGE

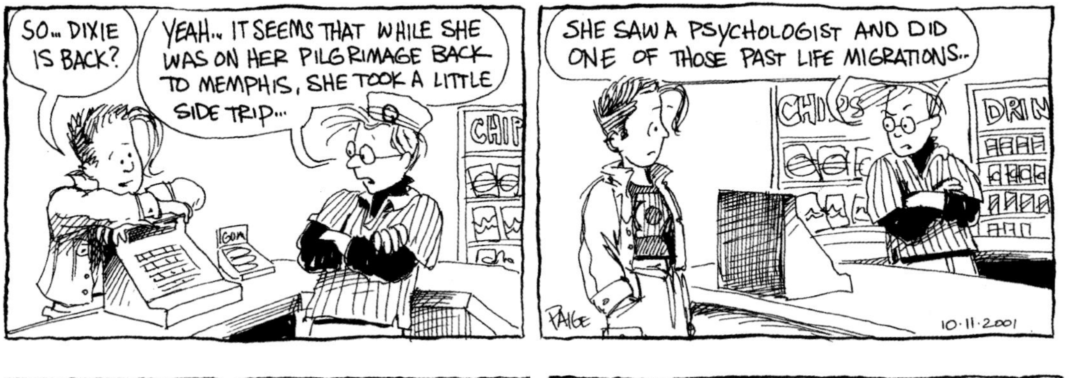
SO... DIXIE IS BACK?
YEAH.. IT SEEMS THAT WHILE SHE WAS ON HER PILGRIMAGE BACK TO MEMPHIS, SHE TOOK A LITTLE SIDE TRIP...
GUM
SHE SAW A PSYCHOLOGIST AND DID ONE OF THOSE PAST LIFE MIGRATIONS..
PAIGE
10·11·2001

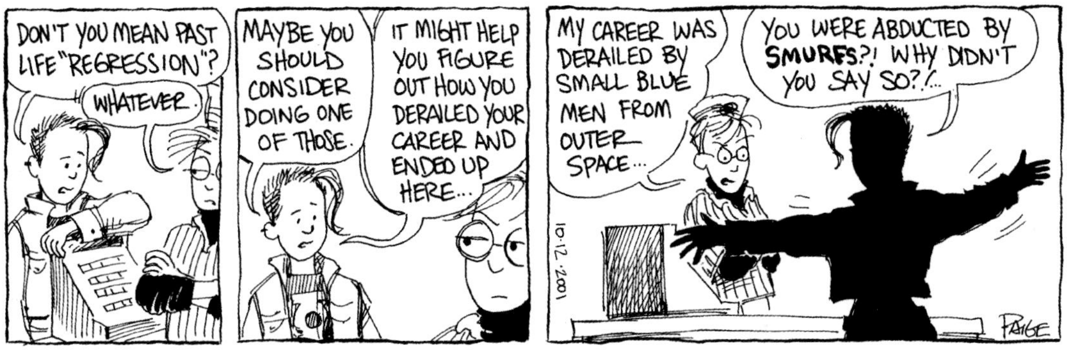
DON'T YOU MEAN PAST LIFE "REGRESSION"?
WHATEVER.
MAYBE YOU SHOULD CONSIDER DOING ONE OF THOSE.
IT MIGHT HELP YOU FIGURE OUT HOW YOU DERAILED YOUR CAREER AND ENDED UP HERE...
MY CAREER WAS DERAILED BY SMALL BLUE MEN FROM OUTER SPACE...
YOU WERE ABDUCTED BY **SMURFS**?! WHY DIDN'T YOU SAY SO?!...
10·12·2001
PAIGE

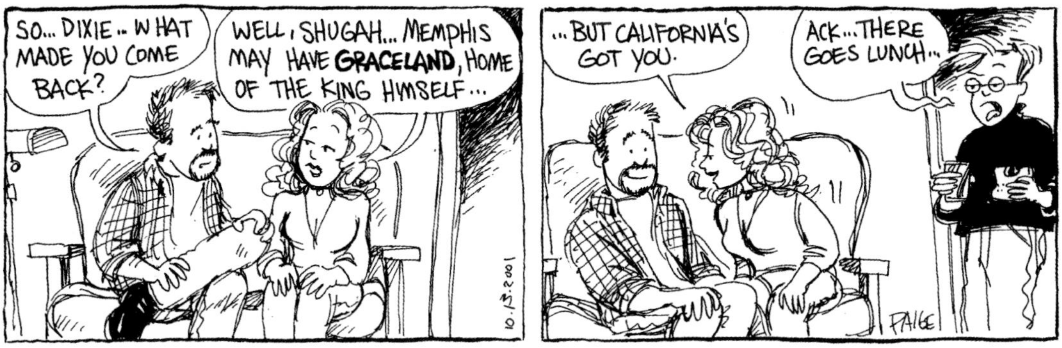
SO... DIXIE.. WHAT MADE YOU COME BACK?
WELL, SHUGAH... MEMPHIS MAY HAVE **GRACELAND**, HOME OF THE KING HIMSELF...
10·13·2001
...BUT CALIFORNIA'S GOT YOU.
ACK... THERE GOES LUNCH...
PAIGE

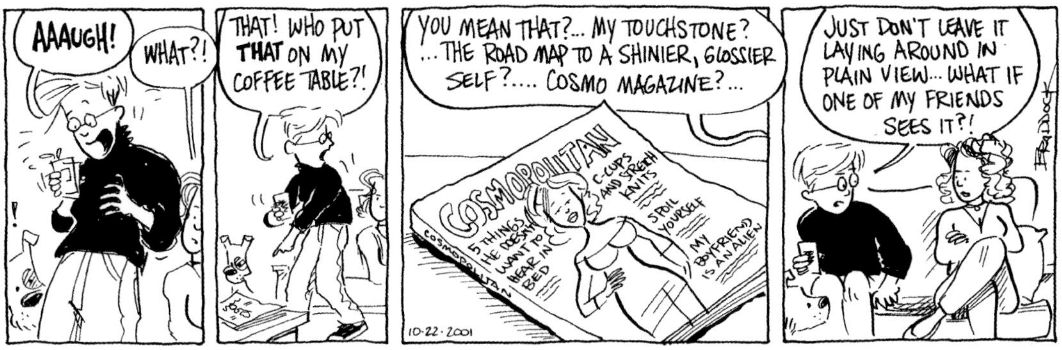
AAAUGH!
WHAT?!
THAT! WHO PUT **THAT** ON MY COFFEE TABLE?!
YOU MEAN THAT?... MY TOUCHSTONE? ...THE ROAD MAP TO A SHINIER, GLOSSIER SELF?.... COSMO MAGAZINE?...
COSMOPOLITAN
C-CUPS AND STRETCH KNITS
5 THINGS HE DOESN'T WANT TO HEAR IN BED
SPOIL YOURSELF
MY BOYFRIEND IS AN ALIEN
COSMOPOLITAN
10·22·2001
JUST DON'T LEAVE IT LAYING AROUND IN PLAIN VIEW... WHAT IF ONE OF MY FRIENDS SEES IT?!

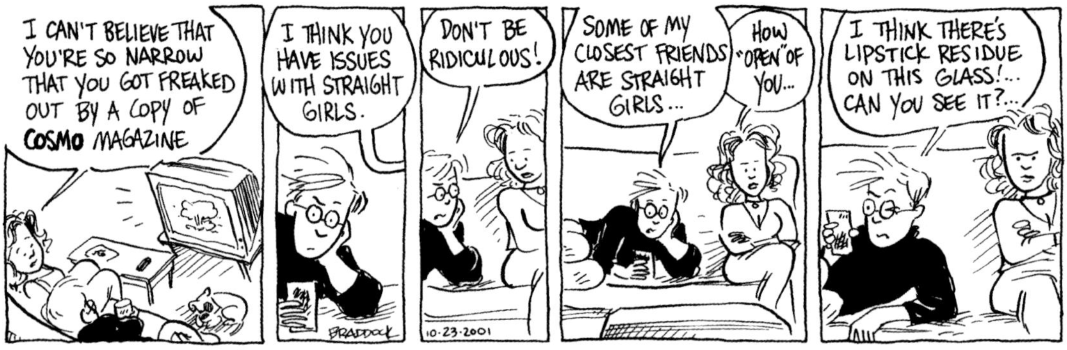
I CAN'T BELIEVE THAT YOU'RE SO NARROW THAT YOU GOT FREAKED OUT BY A COPY OF **COSMO** MAGAZINE
I THINK YOU HAVE ISSUES WITH STRAIGHT GIRLS.
BRADDOCK
DON'T BE RIDICULOUS!
10-23-2001
SOME OF MY CLOSEST FRIENDS ARE STRAIGHT GIRLS...
HOW "OPEN" OF YOU...
I THINK THERE'S LIPSTICK RESIDUE ON THIS GLASS!... CAN YOU SEE IT?...

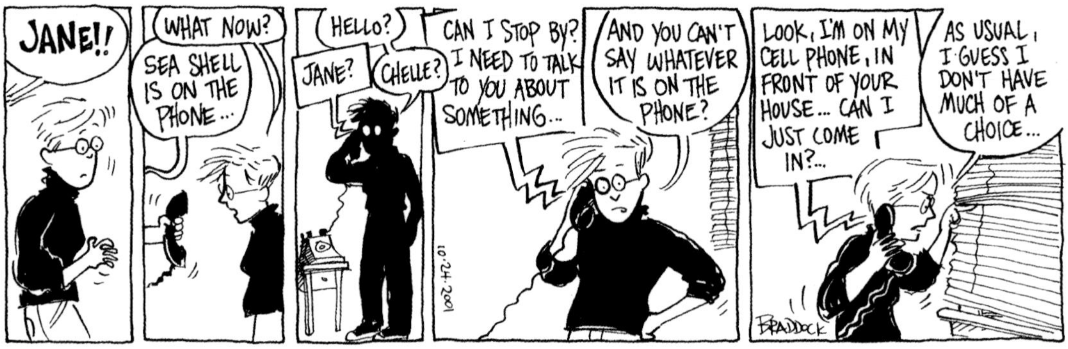
JANE!!
WHAT NOW?
SEA SHELL IS ON THE PHONE...
HELLO?
JANE?
CHELLE?
10-24-2001
CAN I STOP BY? I NEED TO TALK TO YOU ABOUT SOMETHING...
AND YOU CAN'T SAY WHATEVER IT IS ON THE PHONE?
LOOK, I'M ON MY CELL PHONE, IN FRONT OF YOUR HOUSE... CAN I JUST COME IN?...
AS USUAL, I GUESS I DON'T HAVE MUCH OF A CHOICE...
BRADDOCK

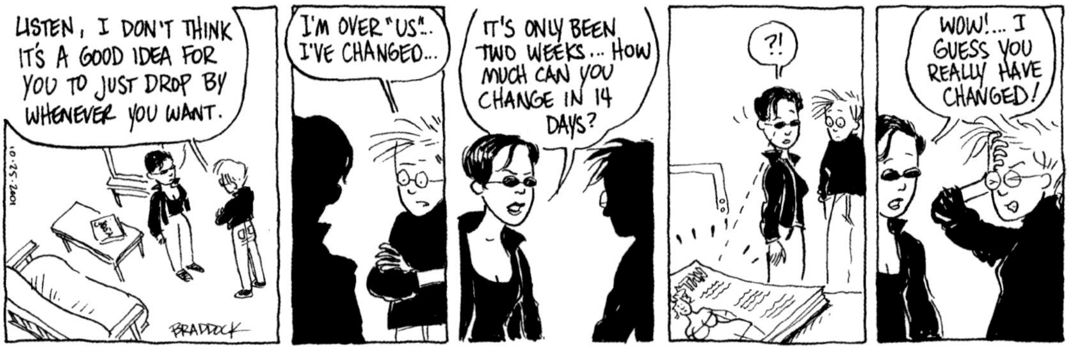
LISTEN, I DON'T THINK IT'S A GOOD IDEA FOR YOU TO JUST DROP BY WHENEVER YOU WANT.
10-25-2001
BRADDOCK
I'M OVER "US"... I'VE CHANGED...
IT'S ONLY BEEN TWO WEEKS... HOW MUCH CAN YOU CHANGE IN 14 DAYS?
?!
WOW!... I GUESS YOU REALLY HAVE CHANGED!

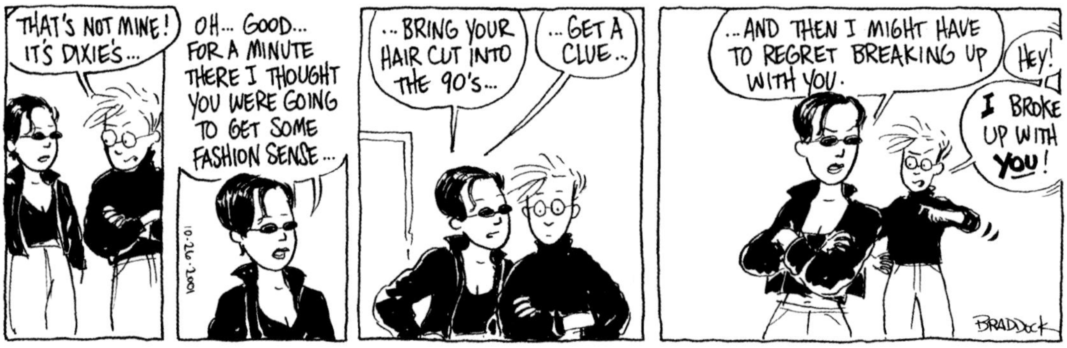
THAT'S NOT MINE! IT'S DIXIE'S...
OH... GOOD... FOR A MINUTE THERE I THOUGHT YOU WERE GOING TO GET SOME FASHION SENSE...
10-26-2001
...BRING YOUR HAIR CUT INTO THE 90'S...
...GET A CLUE...
...AND THEN I MIGHT HAVE TO REGRET BREAKING UP WITH YOU.
HEY!
I BROKE UP WITH **YOU**!
BRADDOCK

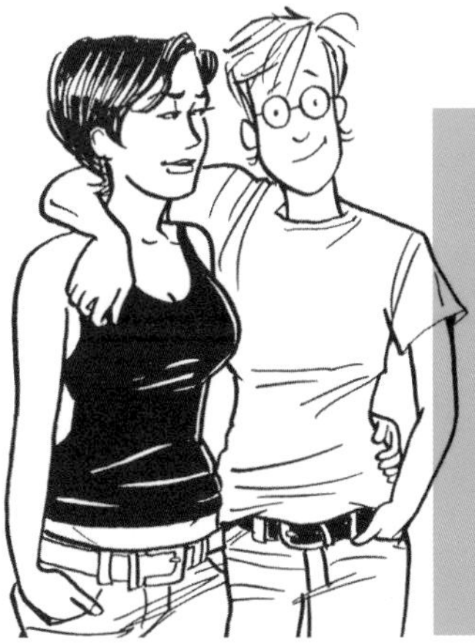

"*Jane's World* remains a warm, hilarious voice in queer cartooning, a strip whose pioneering feat was to assure its readers, gay or straight, that the love of found family is universally glorious and goofy in nearly equal measure."

SHANNON WATTERS, Editor, *Lumberjanes*

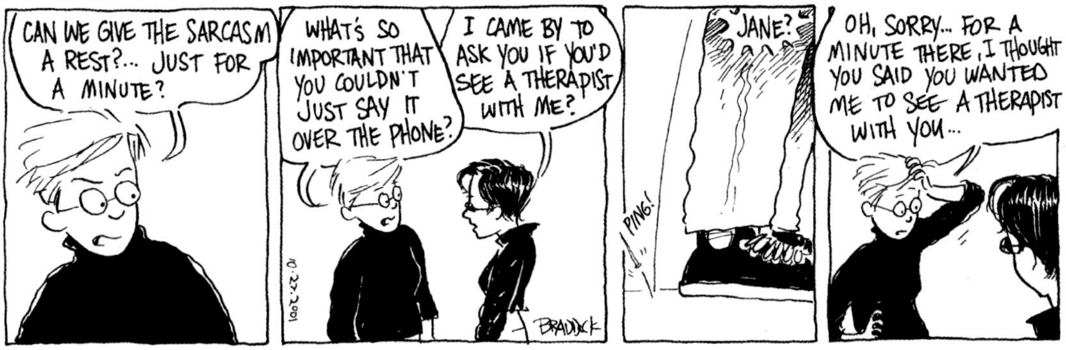
CAN WE GIVE THE SARCASM A REST?... JUST FOR A MINUTE?
WHAT'S SO IMPORTANT THAT YOU COULDN'T JUST SAY IT OVER THE PHONE?
I CAME BY TO ASK YOU IF YOU'D SEE A THERAPIST WITH ME?
BRADDCK
JANE?
PING!
OH, SORRY... FOR A MINUTE THERE, I THOUGHT YOU SAID YOU WANTED ME TO SEE A THERAPIST WITH YOU...

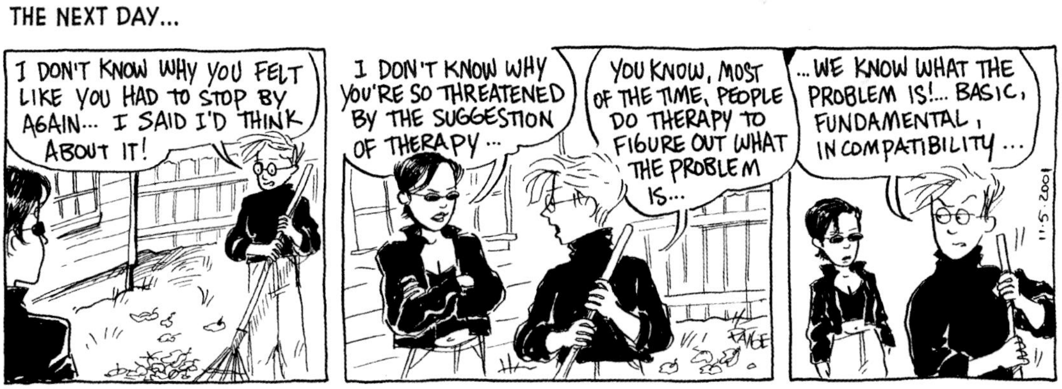
THE NEXT DAY...
I DON'T KNOW WHY YOU FELT LIKE YOU HAD TO STOP BY AGAIN... I SAID I'D THINK ABOUT IT!
I DON'T KNOW WHY YOU'RE SO THREATENED BY THE SUGGESTION OF THERAPY...
YOU KNOW, MOST OF THE TIME, PEOPLE DO THERAPY TO FIGURE OUT WHAT THE PROBLEM IS...
PAIGE
...WE KNOW WHAT THE PROBLEM IS!... BASIC, FUNDAMENTAL, INCOMPATIBILITY...
11-5-2001

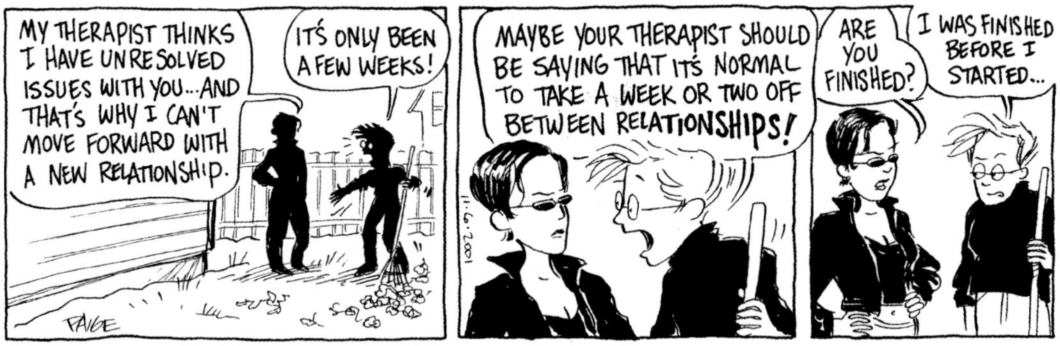
MY THERAPIST THINKS I HAVE UNRESOLVED ISSUES WITH YOU... AND THAT'S WHY I CAN'T MOVE FORWARD WITH A NEW RELATIONSHIP.
IT'S ONLY BEEN A FEW WEEKS!
PAIGE
MAYBE YOUR THERAPIST SHOULD BE SAYING THAT IT'S NORMAL TO TAKE A WEEK OR TWO OFF BETWEEN RELATIONSHIPS!
11-6-2001
ARE YOU FINISHED?
I WAS FINISHED BEFORE I STARTED...

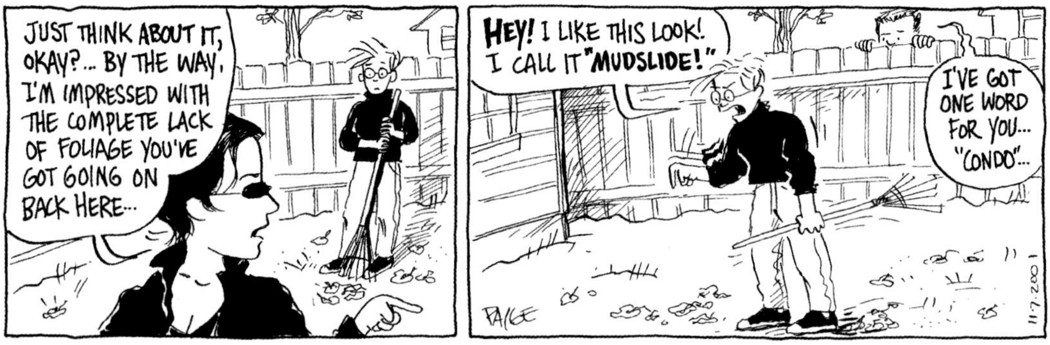
JUST THINK ABOUT IT, OKAY?... BY THE WAY, I'M IMPRESSED WITH THE COMPLETE LACK OF FOLIAGE YOU'VE GOT GOING ON BACK HERE...
HEY! I LIKE THIS LOOK! I CALL IT "MUDSLIDE!"
I'VE GOT ONE WORD FOR YOU... "CONDO"...
PAIGE
11·7·2001

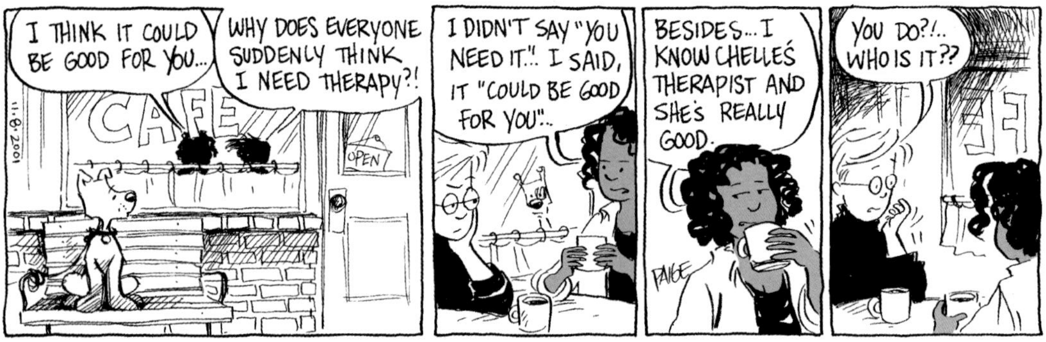
11·8·2001
I THINK IT COULD BE GOOD FOR YOU...
WHY DOES EVERYONE SUDDENLY THINK I NEED THERAPY?!
CAFE
OPEN
I DIDN'T SAY "YOU NEED IT."! I SAID, IT "COULD BE GOOD FOR YOU"..
BESIDES... I KNOW CHELLE'S THERAPIST AND SHE'S REALLY GOOD.
PAIGE
YOU DO?!.. WHO IS IT??

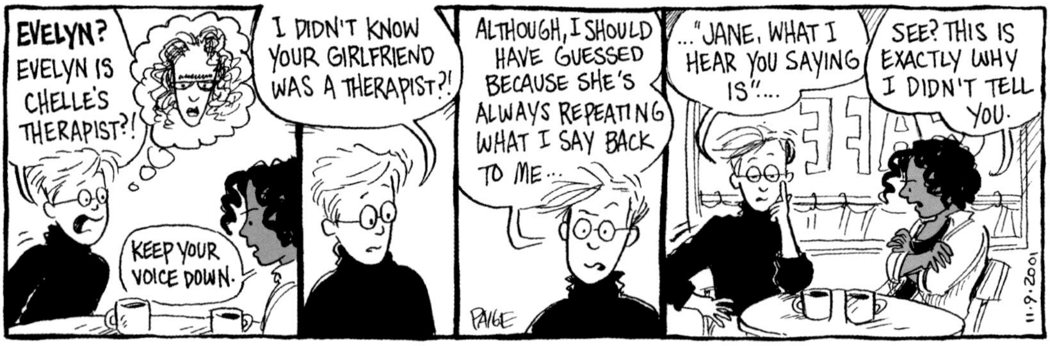
EVELYN? EVELYN IS CHELLE'S THERAPIST?!
KEEP YOUR VOICE DOWN.
I DIDN'T KNOW YOUR GIRLFRIEND WAS A THERAPIST?!
ALTHOUGH, I SHOULD HAVE GUESSED BECAUSE SHE'S ALWAYS REPEATING WHAT I SAY BACK TO ME...
PAIGE
..."JANE, WHAT I HEAR YOU SAYING IS"...
SEE? THIS IS EXACTLY WHY I DIDN'T TELL YOU.
11·9·2001

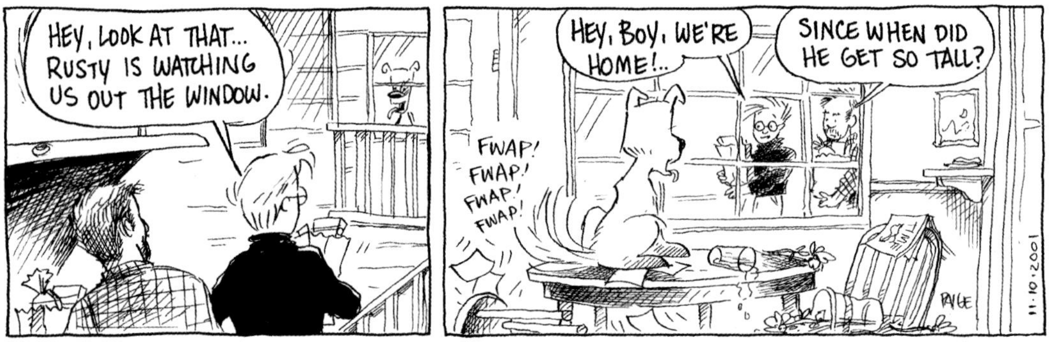
HEY, LOOK AT THAT... RUSTY IS WATCHING US OUT THE WINDOW.
HEY, BOY, WE'RE HOME!..
SINCE WHEN DID HE GET SO TALL?
FWAP! FWAP! FWAP! FWAP!
PAIGE
11·10·2001

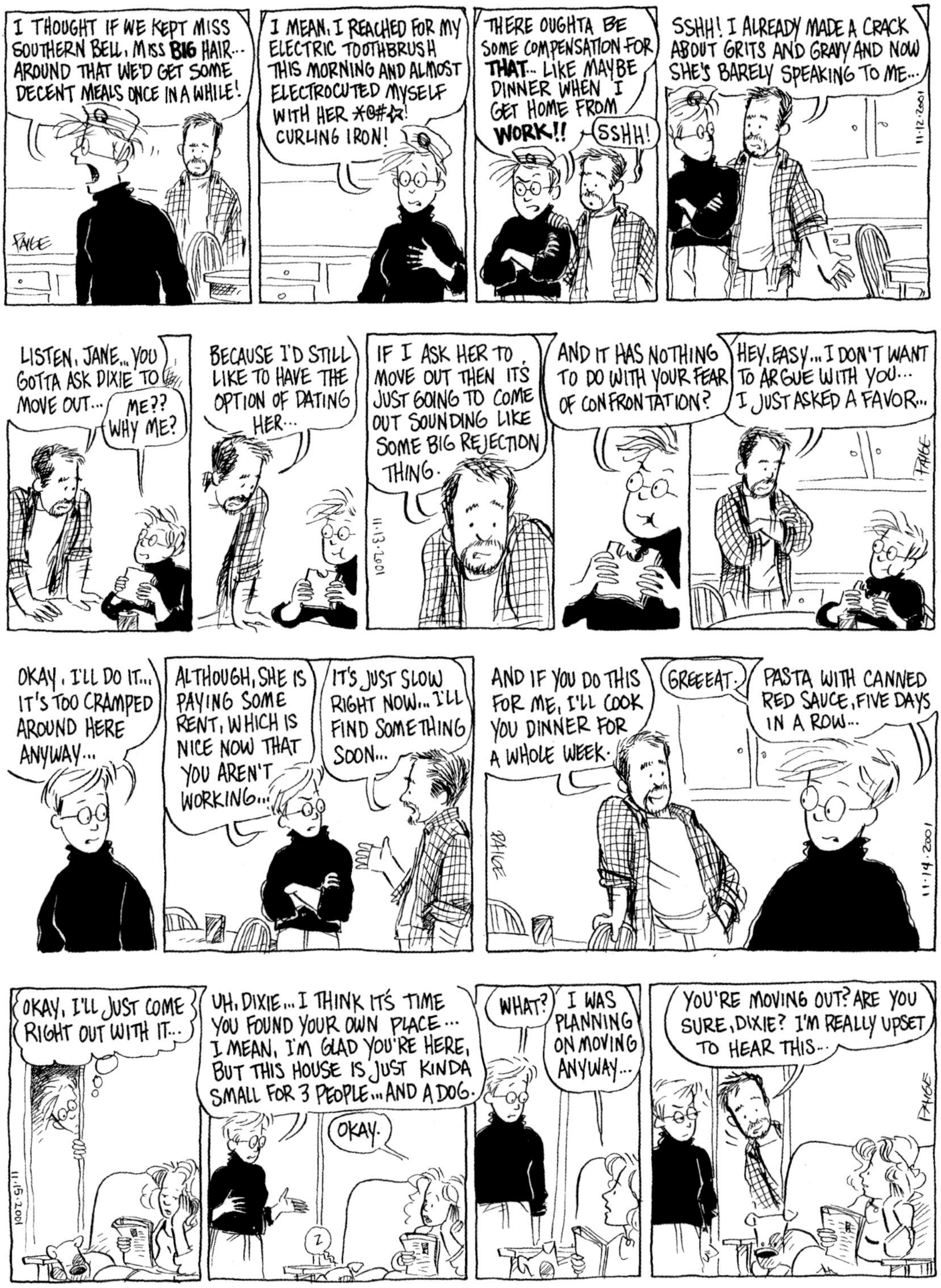
I THOUGHT IF WE KEPT MISS SOUTHERN BELL, MISS **BIG** HAIR... AROUND THAT WE'D GET SOME DECENT MEALS ONCE IN A WHILE!
PAIGE
I MEAN, I REACHED FOR MY ELECTRIC TOOTHBRUSH THIS MORNING AND ALMOST ELECTROCUTED MYSELF WITH HER *@#☆! CURLING IRON!
THERE OUGHTA BE SOME COMPENSATION FOR **THAT**... LIKE MAYBE DINNER WHEN I GET HOME FROM **WORK!!**
SSHH!
SSHH! I ALREADY MADE A CRACK ABOUT GRITS AND GRAVY AND NOW SHE'S BARELY SPEAKING TO ME...
11-12-2001
LISTEN, JANE... YOU GOTTA ASK DIXIE TO MOVE OUT...
ME?? WHY ME?
BECAUSE I'D STILL LIKE TO HAVE THE OPTION OF DATING HER...
IF I ASK HER TO MOVE OUT THEN IT'S JUST GOING TO COME OUT SOUNDING LIKE SOME BIG REJECTION THING.
11-13-2001
AND IT HAS NOTHING TO DO WITH YOUR FEAR OF CONFRONTATION?
HEY, EASY... I DON'T WANT TO ARGUE WITH YOU... I JUST ASKED A FAVOR...
PAIGE
OKAY. I'LL DO IT... IT'S TOO CRAMPED AROUND HERE ANYWAY...
ALTHOUGH, SHE IS PAYING SOME RENT, WHICH IS NICE NOW THAT YOU AREN'T WORKING...
IT'S JUST SLOW RIGHT NOW... I'LL FIND SOMETHING SOON...
AND IF YOU DO THIS FOR ME, I'LL COOK YOU DINNER FOR A WHOLE WEEK.
PAIGE
GREEEAT.
PASTA WITH CANNED RED SAUCE, FIVE DAYS IN A ROW...
11-14-2001
OKAY, I'LL JUST COME RIGHT OUT WITH IT...
11-15-2001
UH, DIXIE... I THINK IT'S TIME YOU FOUND YOUR OWN PLACE... I MEAN, I'M GLAD YOU'RE HERE, BUT THIS HOUSE IS JUST KINDA SMALL FOR 3 PEOPLE... AND A DOG.
OKAY.
WHAT?
I WAS PLANNING ON MOVING ANYWAY...
YOU'RE MOVING OUT? ARE YOU SURE, DIXIE? I'M REALLY UPSET TO HEAR THIS...
PAIGE

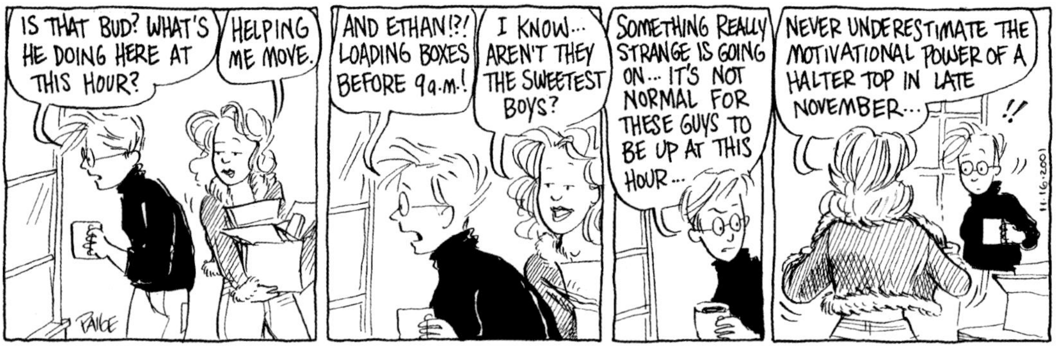
IS THAT BUD? WHAT'S HE DOING HERE AT THIS HOUR?
HELPING ME MOVE.
PAIGE
AND ETHAN!?! LOADING BOXES BEFORE 9a.m.!
I KNOW... AREN'T THEY THE SWEETEST BOYS?
SOMETHING REALLY STRANGE IS GOING ON... IT'S NOT NORMAL FOR THESE GUYS TO BE UP AT THIS HOUR...
NEVER UNDERESTIMATE THE MOTIVATIONAL POWER OF A HALTER TOP IN LATE NOVEMBER...
!!
11·16·2001

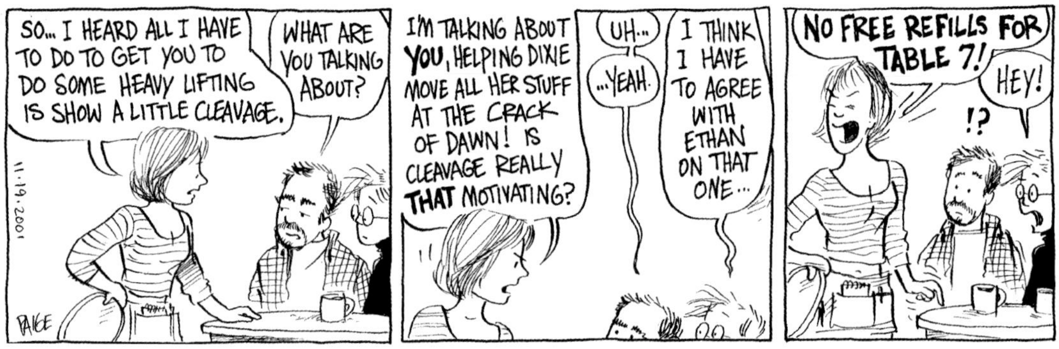
SO... I HEARD ALL I HAVE TO DO TO GET YOU TO DO SOME HEAVY LIFTING IS SHOW A LITTLE CLEAVAGE.
WHAT ARE YOU TALKING ABOUT?
11·19·2001
PAIGE
I'M TALKING ABOUT YOU, HELPING DIXIE MOVE ALL HER STUFF AT THE CRACK OF DAWN! IS CLEAVAGE REALLY THAT MOTIVATING?
UH...
...YEAH.
I THINK I HAVE TO AGREE WITH ETHAN ON THAT ONE...
NO FREE REFILLS FOR TABLE 7!
HEY!
!?

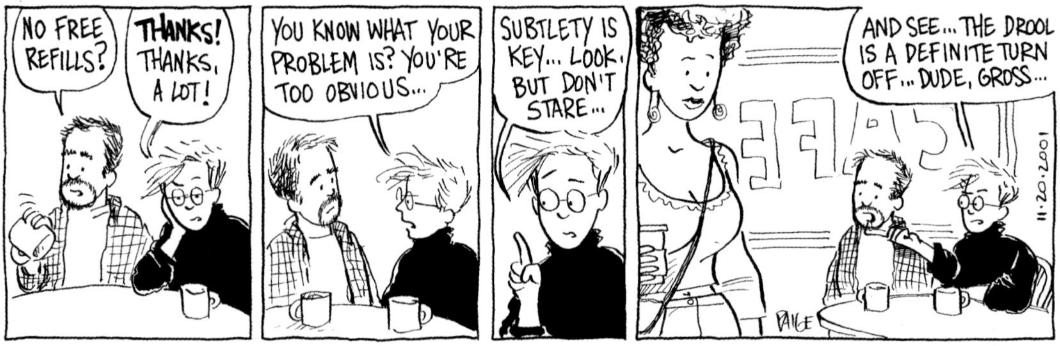
NO FREE REFILLS?
THANKS! THANKS, A LOT!
YOU KNOW WHAT YOUR PROBLEM IS? YOU'RE TOO OBVIOUS...
SUBTLETY IS KEY... LOOK, BUT DON'T STARE...
AND SEE... THE DROOL IS A DEFINITE TURN OFF... DUDE, GROSS...
11·20·2001
PAIGE

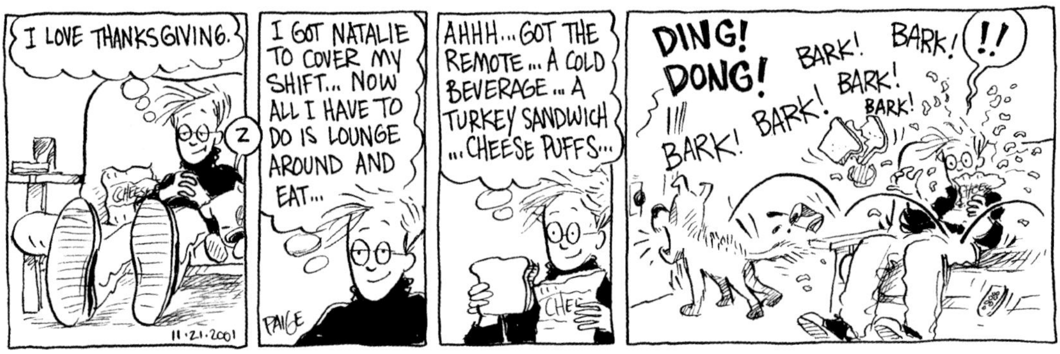
I LOVE THANKSGIVING.
Z
11·21·2001
I GOT NATALIE TO COVER MY SHIFT... NOW ALL I HAVE TO DO IS LOUNGE AROUND AND EAT...
PAIGE
AHHH... GOT THE REMOTE... A COLD BEVERAGE... A TURKEY SANDWICH ...CHEESE PUFFS...
DING! DONG!
BARK! BARK!
!!
BARK! BARK! BARK! BARK! BARK!

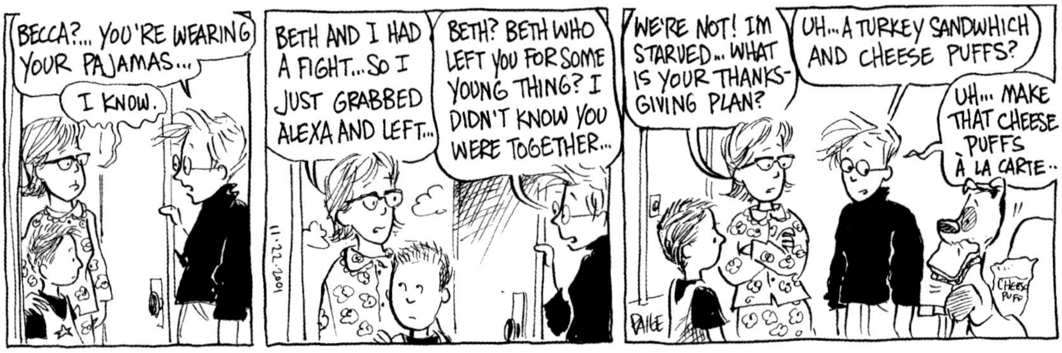
BECCA?... YOU'RE WEARING YOUR PAJAMAS...
I KNOW.
BETH AND I HAD A FIGHT... SO I JUST GRABBED ALEXA AND LEFT...
BETH? BETH WHO LEFT YOU FOR SOME YOUNG THING? I DIDN'T KNOW YOU WERE TOGETHER...
11·22·2001
WE'RE NOT! I'M STARVED... WHAT IS YOUR THANKSGIVING PLAN?
UH... A TURKEY SANDWHICH AND CHEESE PUFFS?
UH... MAKE THAT CHEESE PUFFS À LA CARTE..
PAIGE

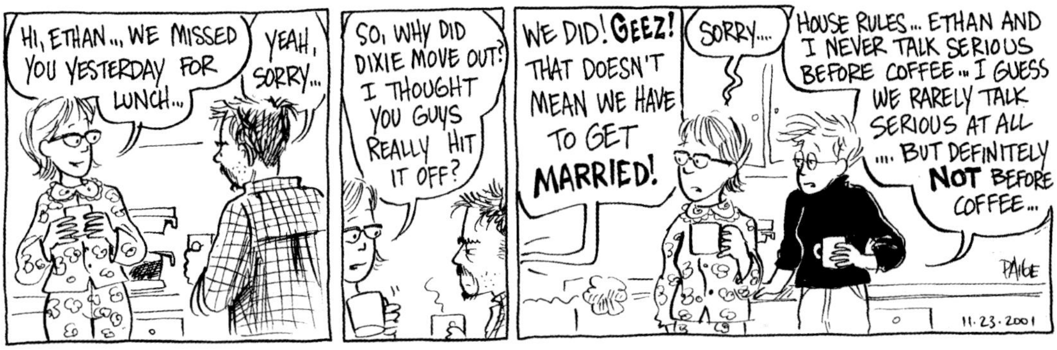
HI, ETHAN... WE MISSED YOU YESTERDAY FOR LUNCH...
YEAH, SORRY...
SO, WHY DID DIXIE MOVE OUT? I THOUGHT YOU GUYS REALLY HIT IT OFF?
WE DID! GEEZ! THAT DOESN'T MEAN WE HAVE TO GET MARRIED!
SORRY...
HOUSE RULES... ETHAN AND I NEVER TALK SERIOUS BEFORE COFFEE... I GUESS WE RARELY TALK SERIOUS AT ALL ... BUT DEFINITELY NOT BEFORE COFFEE...
PAIGE
11·23·2001

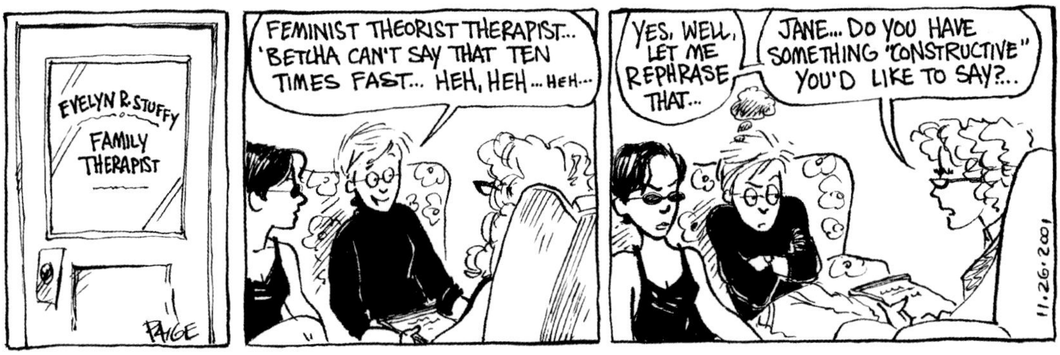
EVELYN R. STUFFY
FAMILY THERAPIST
PAIGE
FEMINIST THEORIST THERAPIST... 'BETCHA CAN'T SAY THAT TEN TIMES FAST... HEH, HEH... HEH...
YES, WELL, LET ME REPHRASE THAT...
JANE... DO YOU HAVE SOMETHING "CONSTRUCTIVE" YOU'D LIKE TO SAY?..
11·26·2001

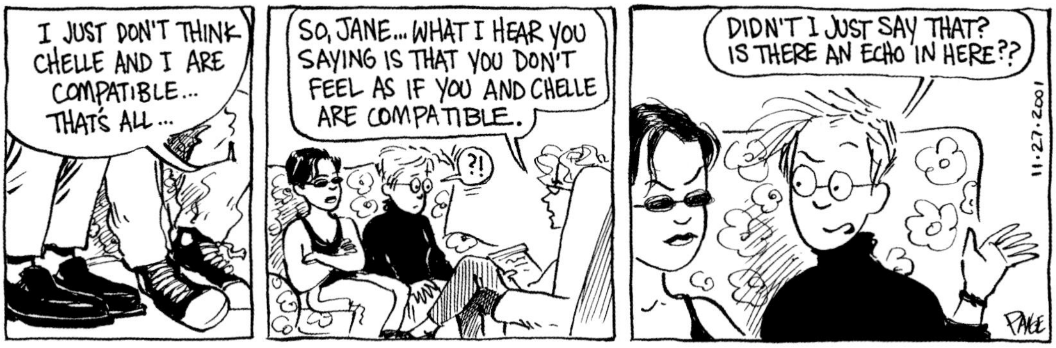
I JUST DON'T THINK CHELLE AND I ARE COMPATIBLE... THAT'S ALL...
SO, JANE... WHAT I HEAR YOU SAYING IS THAT YOU DON'T FEEL AS IF YOU AND CHELLE ARE COMPATIBLE.
?!
DIDN'T I JUST SAY THAT? IS THERE AN ECHO IN HERE??
11·27·2001
PAIGE

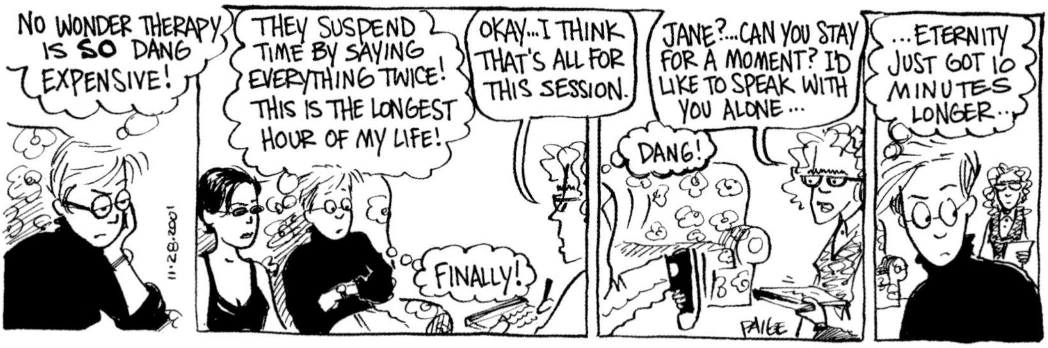
NO WONDER THERAPY IS SO DANG EXPENSIVE!
THEY SUSPEND TIME BY SAYING EVERYTHING TWICE! THIS IS THE LONGEST HOUR OF MY LIFE!
11·28·2001
OKAY...I THINK THAT'S ALL FOR THIS SESSION.
FINALLY!
JANE?...CAN YOU STAY FOR A MOMENT? I'D LIKE TO SPEAK WITH YOU ALONE...
DANG!
PAIGE
...ETERNITY JUST GOT 10 MINUTES LONGER...

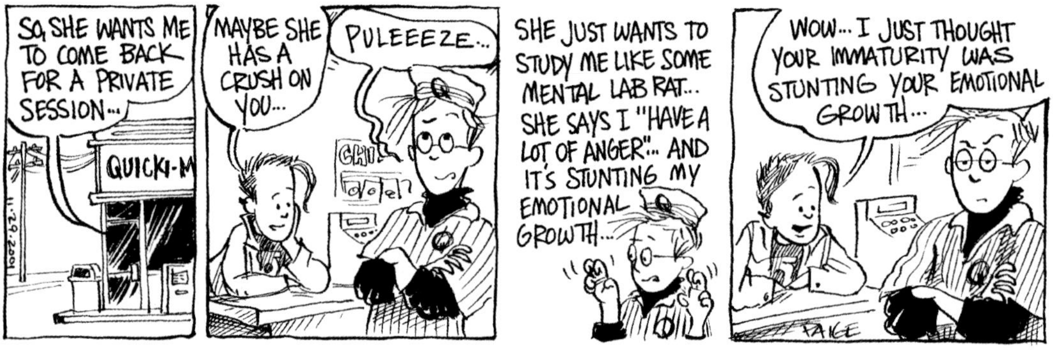
SO, SHE WANTS ME TO COME BACK FOR A PRIVATE SESSION...
QUICKI-M
11·29·2001
MAYBE SHE HAS A CRUSH ON YOU...
PULEEEZE...
SHE JUST WANTS TO STUDY ME LIKE SOME MENTAL LAB RAT... SHE SAYS I "HAVE A LOT OF ANGER"... AND IT'S STUNTING MY EMOTIONAL GROWTH...
WOW... I JUST THOUGHT YOUR IMMATURITY WAS STUNTING YOUR EMOTIONAL GROWTH...
PAIGE

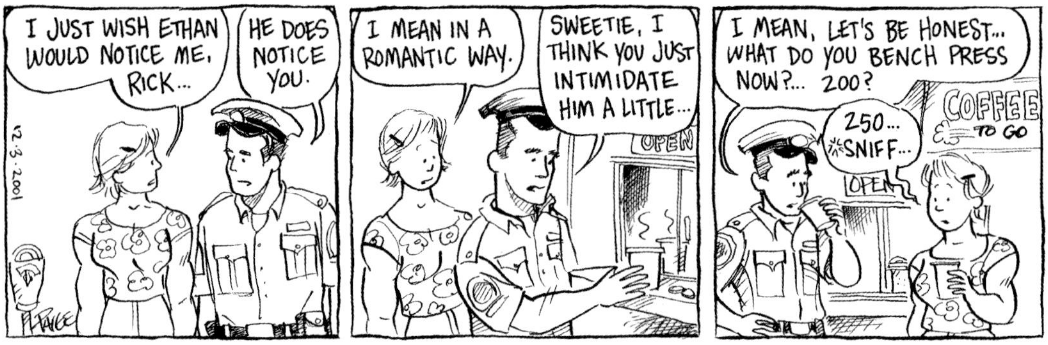
I JUST WISH ETHAN WOULD NOTICE ME, RICK...
HE DOES NOTICE YOU.
12·3·2001
PAIGE
I MEAN IN A ROMANTIC WAY.
SWEETIE, I THINK YOU JUST INTIMIDATE HIM A LITTLE...
OPEN
I MEAN, LET'S BE HONEST... WHAT DO YOU BENCH PRESS NOW?... 200?
250... SNIFF...
COFFEE TO GO
OPEN

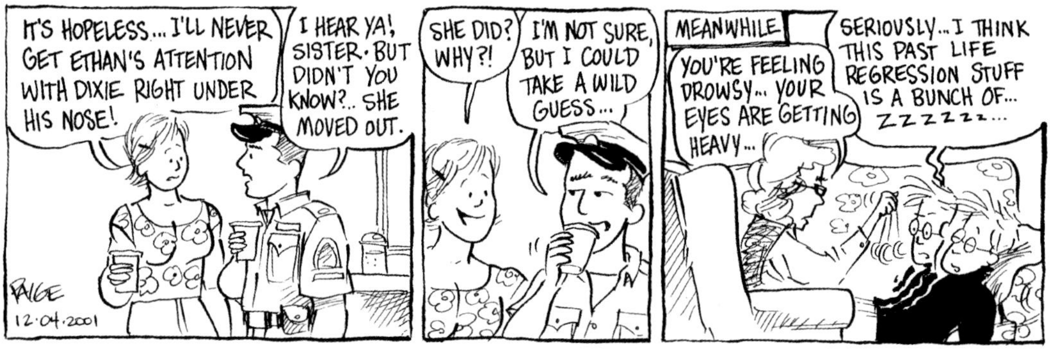
IT'S HOPELESS... I'LL NEVER GET ETHAN'S ATTENTION WITH DIXIE RIGHT UNDER HIS NOSE!
I HEAR YA, SISTER. BUT DIDN'T YOU KNOW?.. SHE MOVED OUT.
PAIGE
12·04·2001
SHE DID? WHY?!
I'M NOT SURE, BUT I COULD TAKE A WILD GUESS...
MEANWHILE
YOU'RE FEELING DROWSY... YOUR EYES ARE GETTING HEAVY...
SERIOUSLY...I THINK THIS PAST LIFE REGRESSION STUFF IS A BUNCH OF... ZZZZZZ...

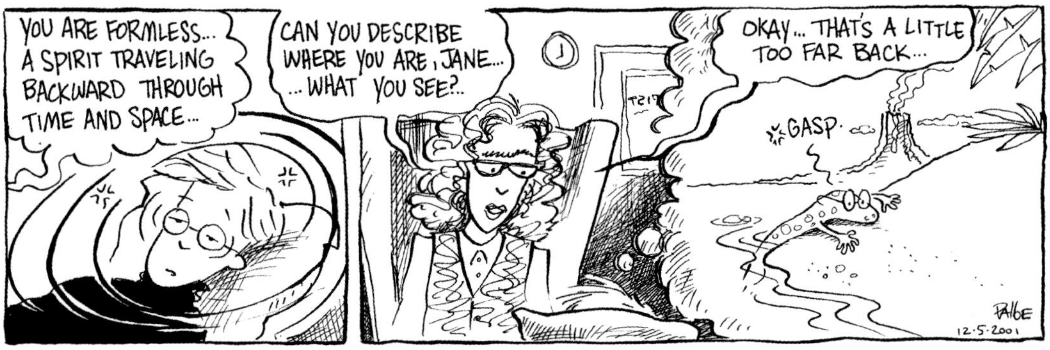
YOU ARE FORMLESS... A SPIRIT TRAVELING BACKWARD THROUGH TIME AND SPACE...
CAN YOU DESCRIBE WHERE YOU ARE, JANE... ...WHAT YOU SEE?..
OKAY... THAT'S A LITTLE TOO FAR BACK...
GASP
PAIGE
12.5.2001

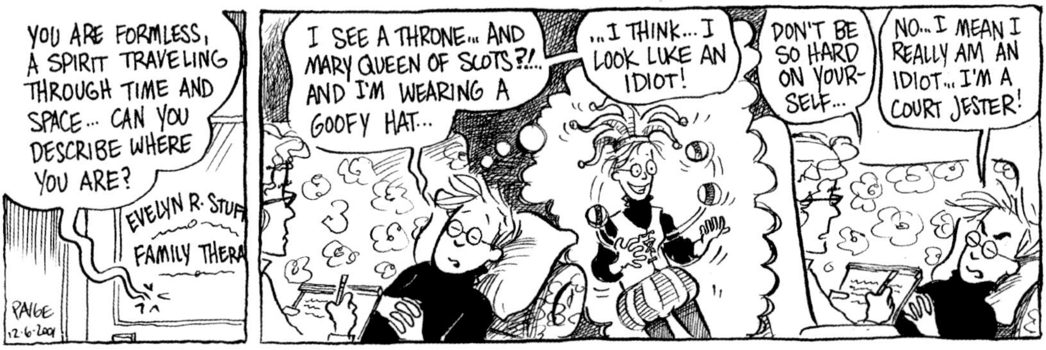
YOU ARE FORMLESS, A SPIRIT TRAVELING THROUGH TIME AND SPACE... CAN YOU DESCRIBE WHERE YOU ARE?
EVELYN R. STUF
FAMILY THERA
PAIGE
12.6.2001
I SEE A THRONE... AND MARY QUEEN OF SCOTS?!... AND I'M WEARING A GOOFY HAT...
...I THINK... I LOOK LIKE AN IDIOT!
DON'T BE SO HARD ON YOURSELF...
NO... I MEAN I REALLY AM AN IDIOT... I'M A COURT JESTER!

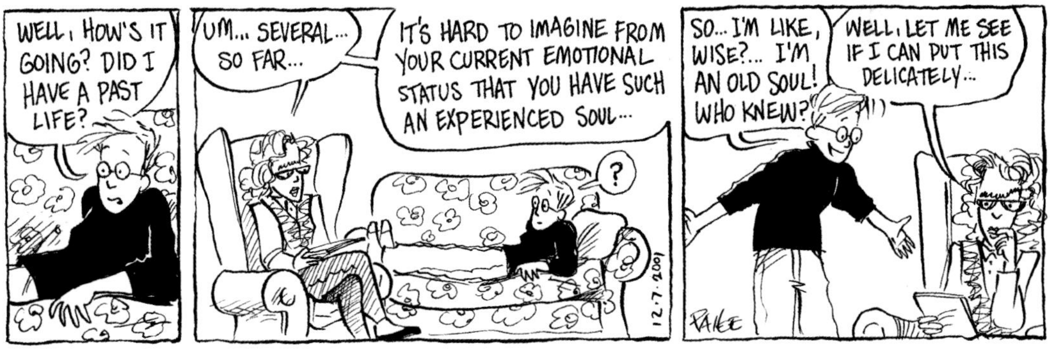
WELL, HOW'S IT GOING? DID I HAVE A PAST LIFE?
UM... SEVERAL... SO FAR...
IT'S HARD TO IMAGINE FROM YOUR CURRENT EMOTIONAL STATUS THAT YOU HAVE SUCH AN EXPERIENCED SOUL...
?
12.7.2001
SO... I'M LIKE, WISE?... I'M AN OLD SOUL! WHO KNEW?
WELL, LET ME SEE IF I CAN PUT THIS DELICATELY...
PAIGE

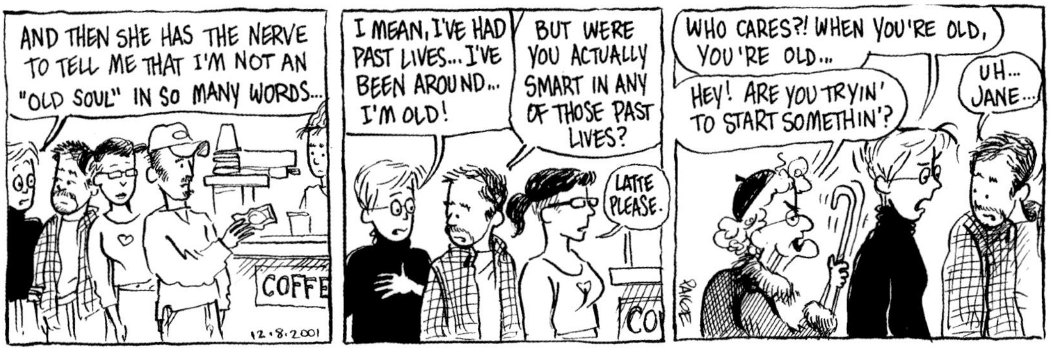
AND THEN SHE HAS THE NERVE TO TELL ME THAT I'M NOT AN "OLD SOUL" IN SO MANY WORDS...
COFFE
12.8.2001
I MEAN, I'VE HAD PAST LIVES... I'VE BEEN AROUND... I'M OLD!
BUT WERE YOU ACTUALLY SMART IN ANY OF THOSE PAST LIVES?
LATTE PLEASE.
CO
WHO CARES?! WHEN YOU'RE OLD, YOU'RE OLD...
HEY! ARE YOU TRYIN' TO START SOMETHIN'?
UH... JANE...
PAIGE

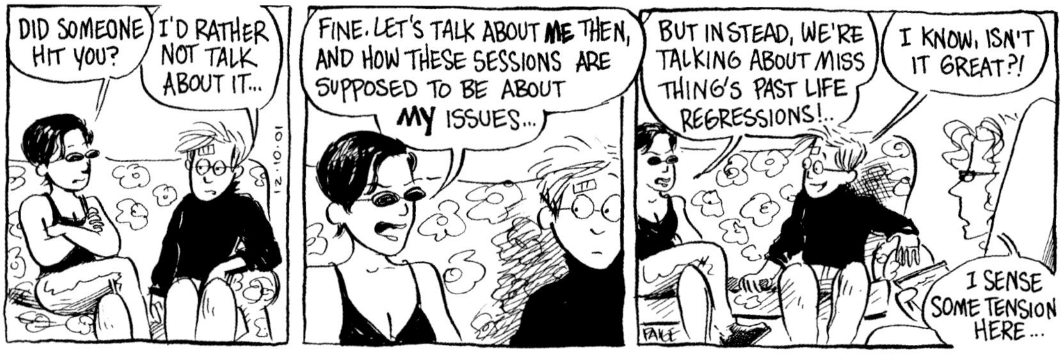
DID SOMEONE HIT YOU?
I'D RATHER NOT TALK ABOUT IT...
12·10·01
FINE. LET'S TALK ABOUT ME THEN, AND HOW THESE SESSIONS ARE SUPPOSED TO BE ABOUT MY ISSUES...
BUT INSTEAD, WE'RE TALKING ABOUT MISS THING'S PAST LIFE REGRESSIONS!..
I KNOW, ISN'T IT GREAT?!
I SENSE SOME TENSION HERE...
PAIGE

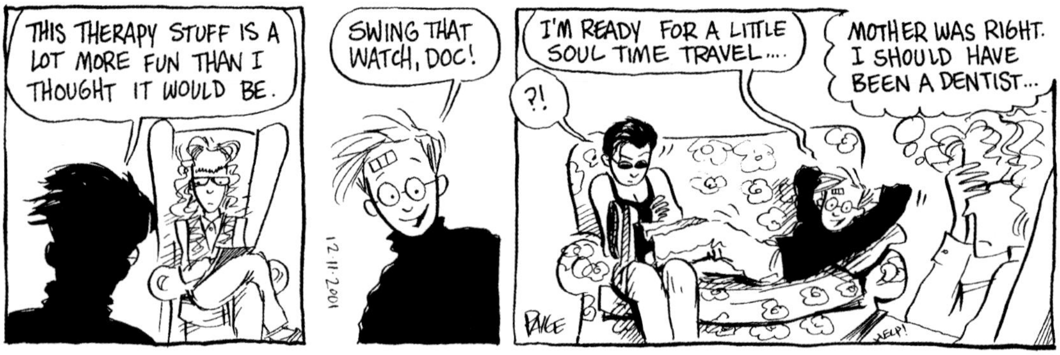
THIS THERAPY STUFF IS A LOT MORE FUN THAN I THOUGHT IT WOULD BE.
SWING THAT WATCH, DOC!
12·11·2001
I'M READY FOR A LITTLE SOUL TIME TRAVEL....
?!
MOTHER WAS RIGHT. I SHOULD HAVE BEEN A DENTIST...
HELP!
PAIGE

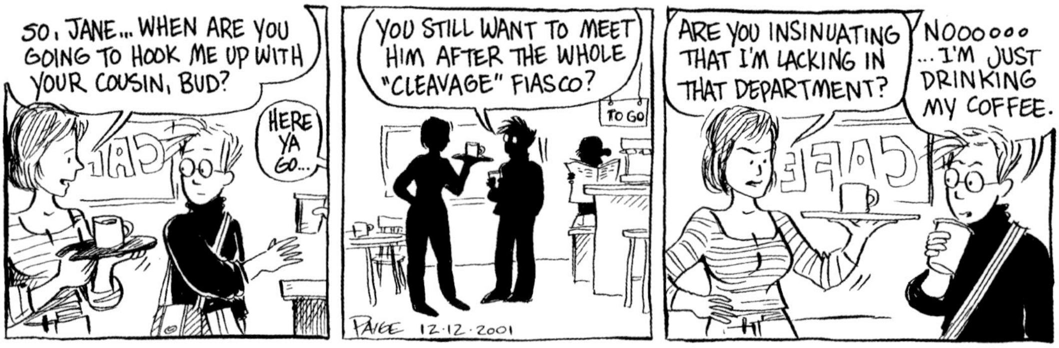
SO, JANE... WHEN ARE YOU GOING TO HOOK ME UP WITH YOUR COUSIN, BUD?
HERE YA GO...
YOU STILL WANT TO MEET HIM AFTER THE WHOLE "CLEAVAGE" FIASCO?
TO GO
PAIGE 12·12·2001
ARE YOU INSINUATING THAT I'M LACKING IN THAT DEPARTMENT?
NOOOOOO ... I'M JUST DRINKING MY COFFEE.
CAFE

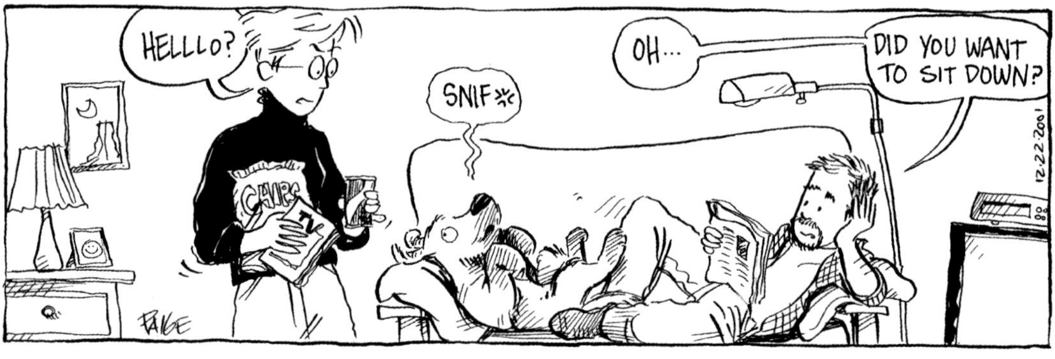
HELLLO?
SNIF
OH...
DID YOU WANT TO SIT DOWN?
12·22·2001
PAIGE

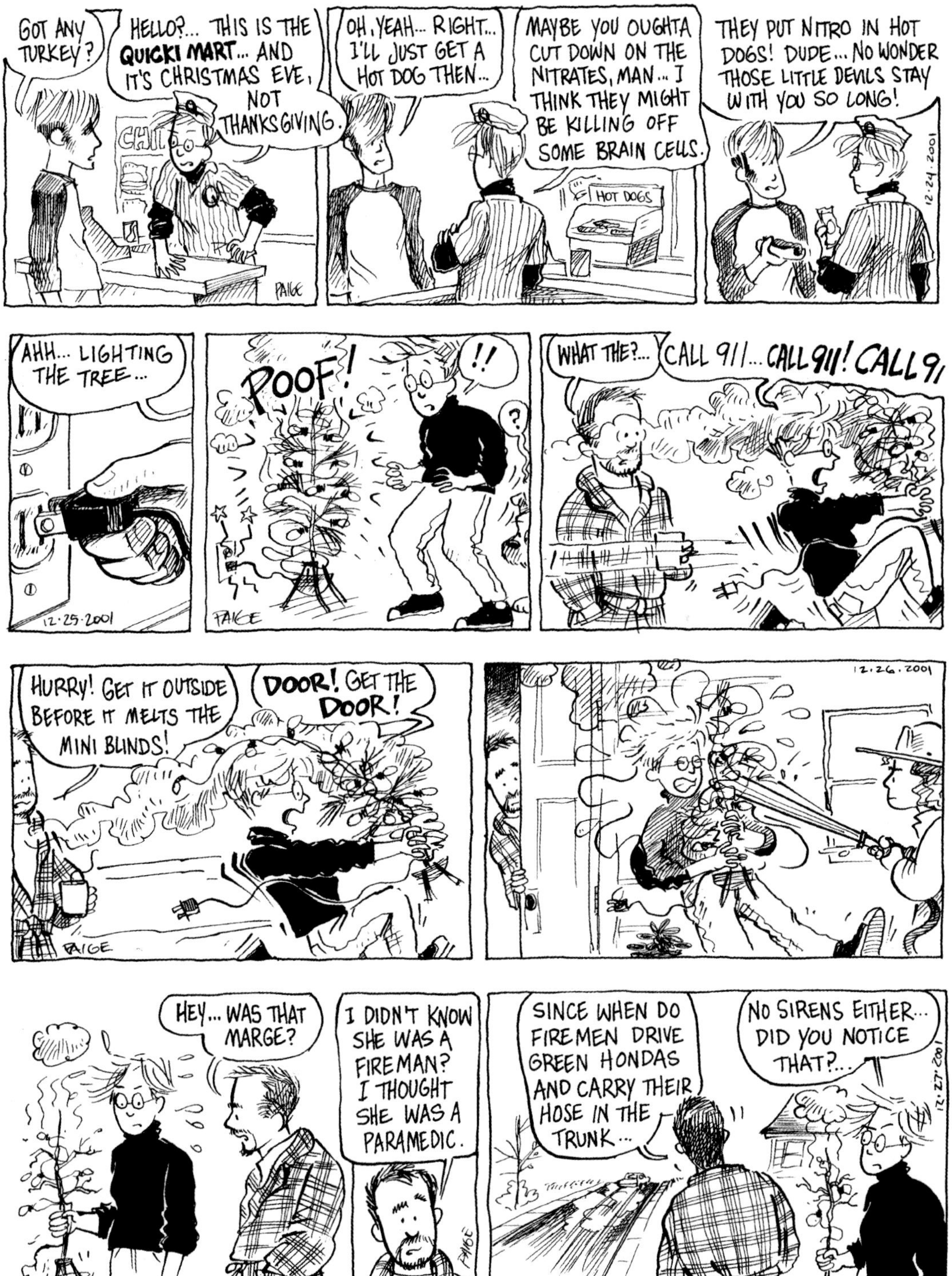
GOT ANY TURKEY?
HELLO?... THIS IS THE QUICKI MART... AND IT'S CHRISTMAS EVE, NOT THANKSGIVING.
PAIGE
OH, YEAH... RIGHT... I'LL JUST GET A HOT DOG THEN...
MAYBE YOU OUGHTA CUT DOWN ON THE NITRATES, MAN... I THINK THEY MIGHT BE KILLING OFF SOME BRAIN CELLS.
HOT DOGS
THEY PUT NITRO IN HOT DOGS! DUDE... NO WONDER THOSE LITTLE DEVILS STAY WITH YOU SO LONG!
12·24·2001
AHH... LIGHTING THE TREE...
12·25·2001
POOF!
!!
?
PAIGE
WHAT THE?...
CALL 911... CALL 911! CALL 9
HURRY! GET IT OUTSIDE BEFORE IT MELTS THE MINI BLINDS!
DOOR! GET THE DOOR!
PAIGE
12·26·2001
HEY... WAS THAT MARGE?
I DIDN'T KNOW SHE WAS A FIREMAN? I THOUGHT SHE WAS A PARAMEDIC.
PAIGE
SINCE WHEN DO FIREMEN DRIVE GREEN HONDAS AND CARRY THEIR HOSE IN THE TRUNK...
NO SIRENS EITHER... DID YOU NOTICE THAT?...
12·27·2001

SHE'S A **FAKE?!**
WELL, MARGE IS WHAT WE CALL DOWN AT THE STATION...
...A "WANNA BE".
REAL FIREMAN
12.28.2001
PAIGE
SHE GETS LOCATIONS USING A POLICE SCANNER...LUCKILY, THERE WAS NO HARM DONE...
NO HARM?!... I THINK I'M SUFFERING FROM BLUNT FORCE HOSE TRAUMA!!
THERE'S NO NEED TO GET GRAPHIC MISS...

YOU KNOW, THEY SAY THAT YOUR NEW YEAR'S EVE EXPERIENCE SETS THE TONE FOR THE WHOLE YEAR.
I KNOW, THAT'S WHY I SPIKED THE SLUSHI MACHINE.
SLUSHI
HOT DOGS
BOURBON AND BLUE RASPBERRY ...**WOO HOO!**
HEY! I'M GONNA HAVE TO REPORT THIS TO THE MANAGER!
12.31.2001
OH, WAIT... I **AM** THE MANAGER.
...AND I DON'T CARE...
PAIGE

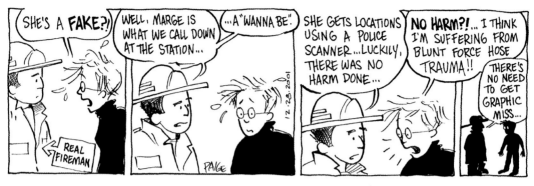

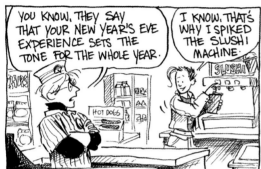

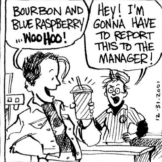

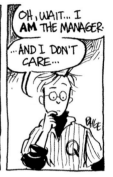

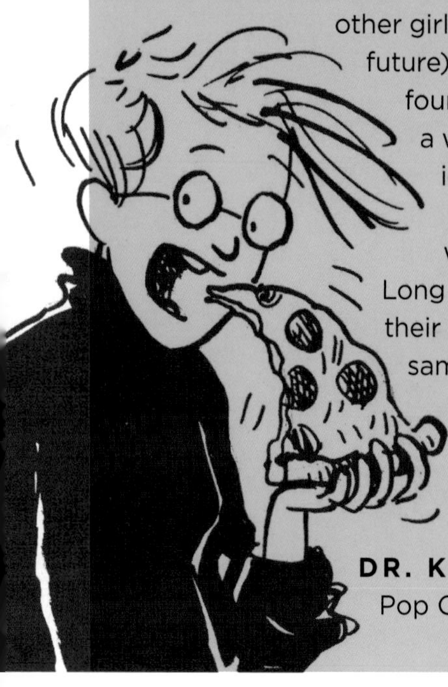

"The first time I saw a copy of *Jane's World* I was in a locally owned bookstore in Columbus, Ohio, and I happened to be pretty nervous about my upcoming engagement to a man. I had snuck away from my family to visit the area of Columbus where I felt safest, where I could be myself (someone who had a nervous suspicion she might have secret crushes on other girls despite her conservative upbringing and supposed future). When I opened up the pages of *Jane's World* I found a world populated by people and their stories, a world where sexual orientation played a part in identifying the characters but did not holistically define them. I found men and women who struggled with the same personal and public issues that I did. Long story short: I fell in love with the characters and their stories in *Jane's World*, and slowly but surely those same characters and their stories also helped me fall in love with myself. I am more than thrilled to see an anniversary edition of *Jane's World* being published for an entirely new generation of readers and their stories."

DR. KATIE MONNIN, Director of Education, Pop Culture Classroom

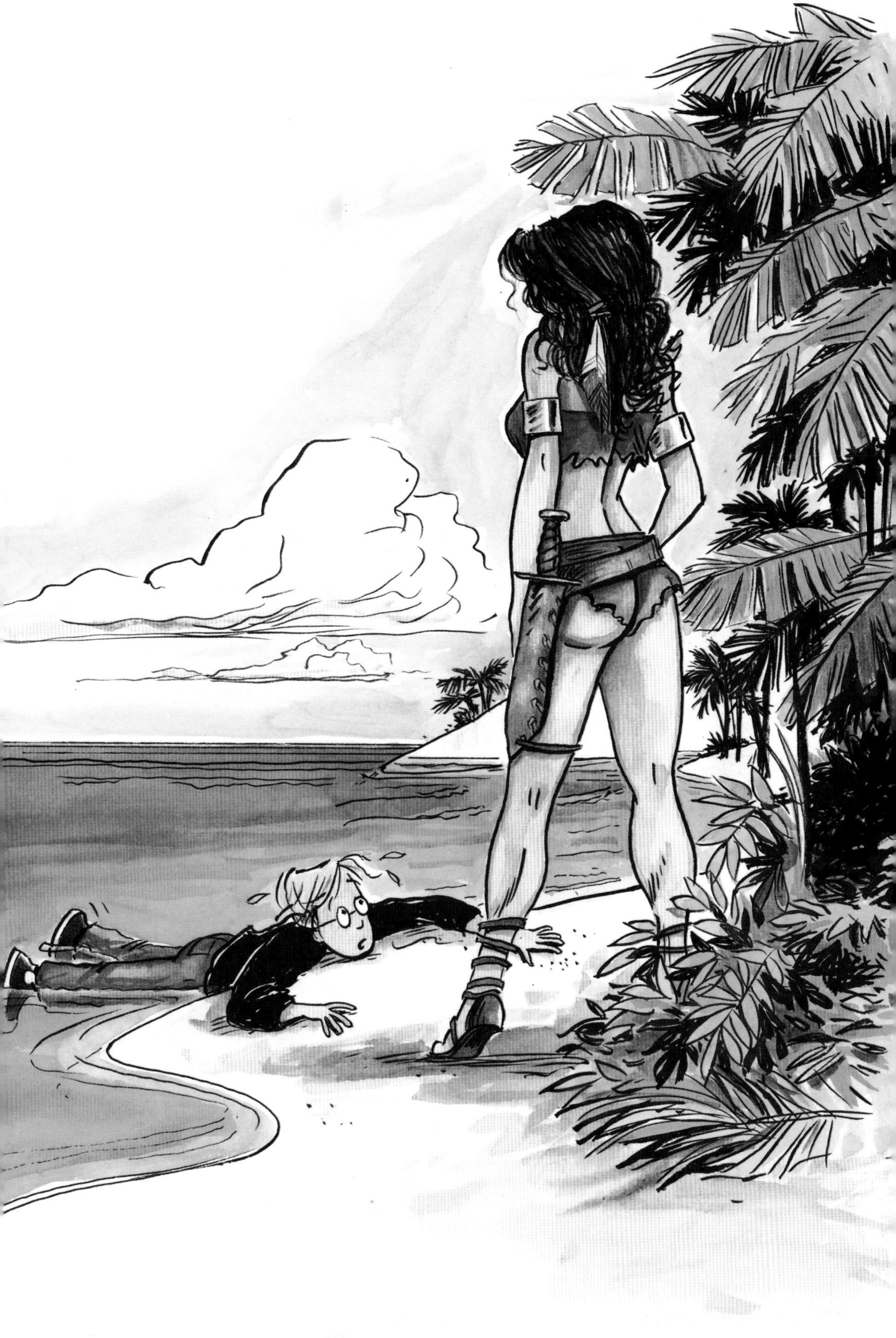

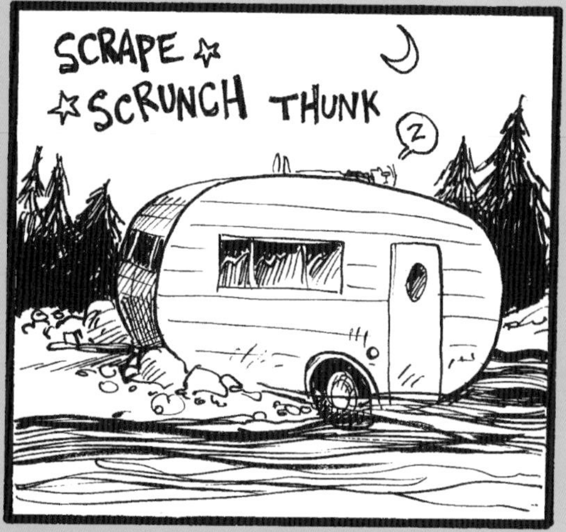
SCRAPE
SCRUNCH THUNK
Z

The Great Trailer Escape

Jane's vintage Mustang dies and she talks Ethan into flying to Texas to pick up a Jeep she purchased on eBay. While she's away she makes the mistake of asking Dorothy, a known cat person, to watch her dog, Rusty. That doesn't go so well. But that's not really what this chapter is about. This chapter is about friendship, about risking it all for the sake of a friend...

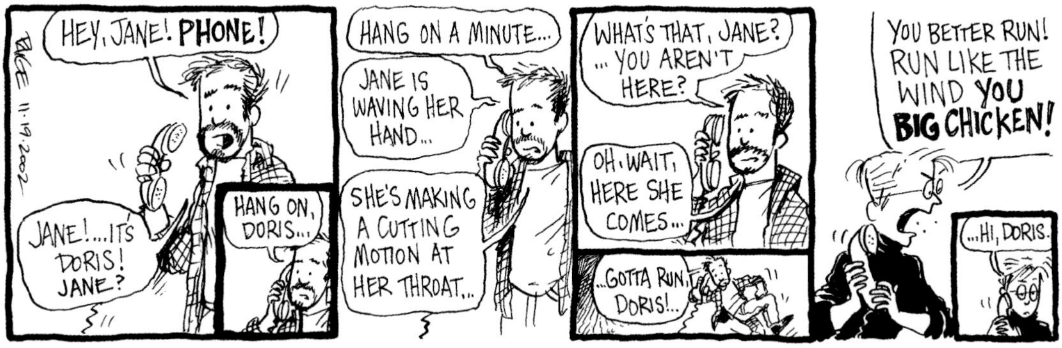
PAIGE 11.19.2002
HEY, JANE! PHONE!
JANE!...IT'S DORIS! JANE?
HANG ON, DORIS...
HANG ON A MINUTE...
JANE IS WAVING HER HAND...
SHE'S MAKING A CUTTING MOTION AT HER THROAT...
WHAT'S THAT, JANE? ... YOU AREN'T HERE?
OH, WAIT, HERE SHE COMES...
...GOTTA RUN, DORIS!..
YOU BETTER RUN! RUN LIKE THE WIND YOU BIG CHICKEN!
...HI, DORIS.

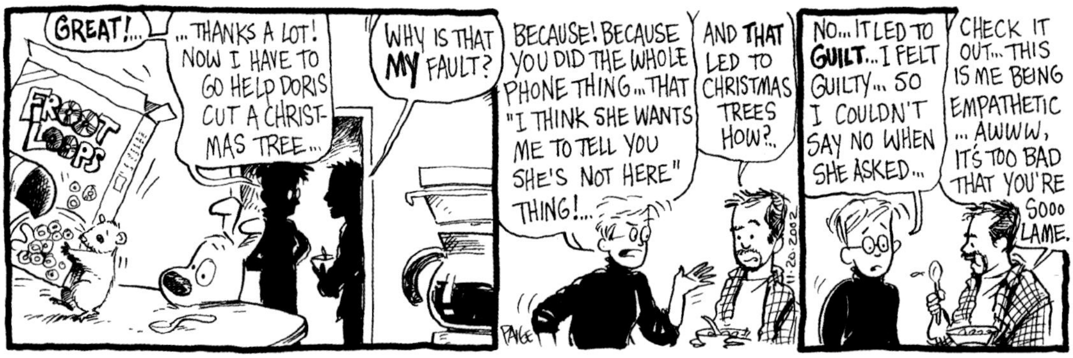
GREAT!...
...THANKS A LOT! NOW I HAVE TO GO HELP DORIS CUT A CHRISTMAS TREE...
FROOT LOOPS
WHY IS THAT MY FAULT?
BECAUSE! BECAUSE YOU DID THE WHOLE PHONE THING... THAT "I THINK SHE WANTS ME TO TELL YOU SHE'S NOT HERE" THING!...
AND THAT LED TO CHRISTMAS TREES HOW?..
PAIGE 11.20.2002
NO... IT LED TO GUILT... I FELT GUILTY... SO I COULDN'T SAY NO WHEN SHE ASKED...
CHECK IT OUT... THIS IS ME BEING EMPATHETIC ... AWWW, IT'S TOO BAD THAT YOU'RE SOOO LAME.

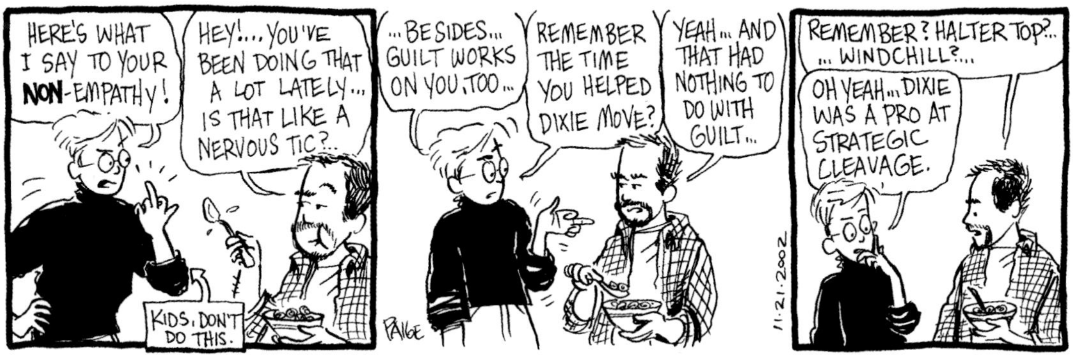
HERE'S WHAT I SAY TO YOUR NON-EMPATHY!
HEY!... YOU'VE BEEN DOING THAT A LOT LATELY... IS THAT LIKE A NERVOUS TIC?..
KIDS, DON'T DO THIS.
...BESIDES... GUILT WORKS ON YOU, TOO...
REMEMBER THE TIME YOU HELPED DIXIE MOVE?
YEAH... AND THAT HAD NOTHING TO DO WITH GUILT...
PAIGE
REMEMBER? HALTER TOP?.. ... WINDCHILL?...
OH YEAH... DIXIE WAS A PRO AT STRATEGIC CLEAVAGE.
11.21.2002

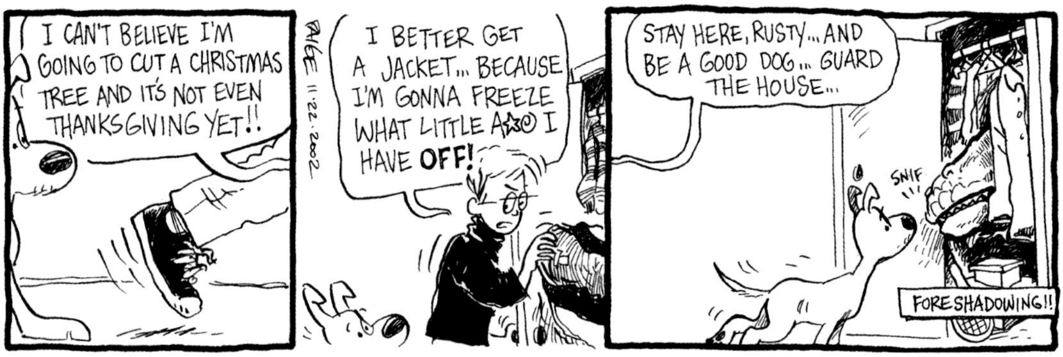
I CAN'T BELIEVE I'M GOING TO CUT A CHRISTMAS TREE AND IT'S NOT EVEN THANKSGIVING YET!!
PAIGE 11.22.2002
I BETTER GET A JACKET... BECAUSE I'M GONNA FREEZE WHAT LITTLE A☆© I HAVE OFF!
STAY HERE, RUSTY... AND BE A GOOD DOG... GUARD THE HOUSE...
SNIF
FORESHADOWING!!

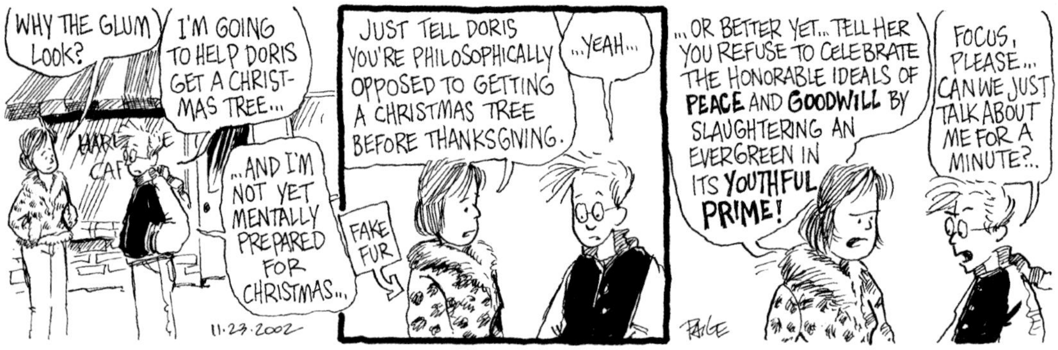
WHY THE GLUM LOOK?
I'M GOING TO HELP DORIS GET A CHRIST-MAS TREE...
...AND I'M NOT YET MENTALLY PREPARED FOR CHRISTMAS...
11·23·2002
JUST TELL DORIS YOU'RE PHILOSOPHICALLY OPPOSED TO GETTING A CHRISTMAS TREE BEFORE THANKSGIVING.
...YEAH...
FAKE FUR
...OR BETTER YET... TELL HER YOU REFUSE TO CELEBRATE THE HONORABLE IDEALS OF PEACE AND GOODWILL BY SLAUGHTERING AN EVERGREEN IN ITS YOUTHFUL PRIME!
FOCUS, PLEASE... CAN WE JUST TALK ABOUT ME FOR A MINUTE?..
PAIGE

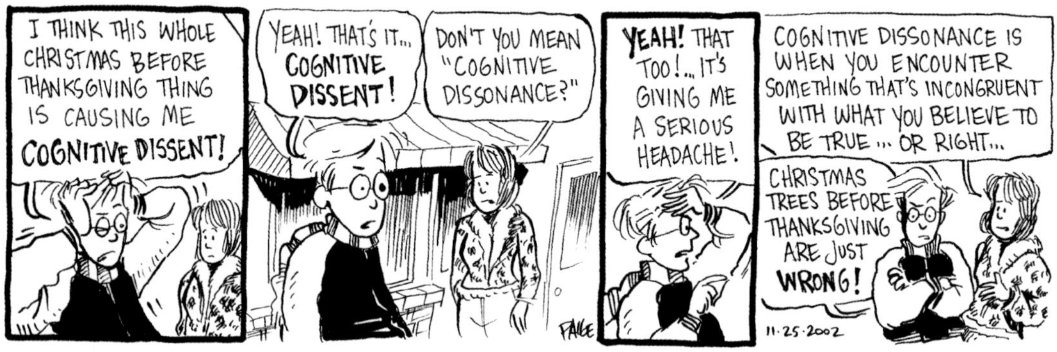
I THINK THIS WHOLE CHRISTMAS BEFORE THANKSGIVING THING IS CAUSING ME COGNITIVE DISSENT!
YEAH! THAT'S IT... COGNITIVE DISSENT!
DON'T YOU MEAN "COGNITIVE DISSONANCE?"
PAIGE
YEAH! THAT TOO!... IT'S GIVING ME A SERIOUS HEADACHE!
COGNITIVE DISSONANCE IS WHEN YOU ENCOUNTER SOMETHING THAT'S INCONGRUENT WITH WHAT YOU BELIEVE TO BE TRUE... OR RIGHT...
CHRISTMAS TREES BEFORE THANKSGIVING ARE JUST WRONG!
11·25·2002

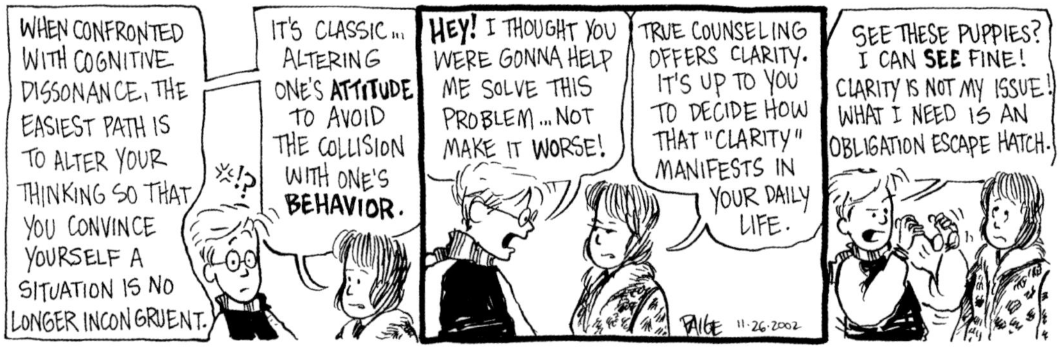
WHEN CONFRONTED WITH COGNITIVE DISSONANCE, THE EASIEST PATH IS TO ALTER YOUR THINKING SO THAT YOU CONVINCE YOURSELF A SITUATION IS NO LONGER INCONGRUENT.
!?
IT'S CLASSIC... ALTERING ONE'S ATTITUDE TO AVOID THE COLLISION WITH ONE'S BEHAVIOR.
HEY! I THOUGHT YOU WERE GONNA HELP ME SOLVE THIS PROBLEM... NOT MAKE IT WORSE!
TRUE COUNSELING OFFERS CLARITY. IT'S UP TO YOU TO DECIDE HOW THAT "CLARITY" MANIFESTS IN YOUR DAILY LIFE.
PAIGE 11·26·2002
SEE THESE PUPPIES? I CAN SEE FINE! CLARITY IS NOT MY ISSUE! WHAT I NEED IS AN OBLIGATION ESCAPE HATCH.

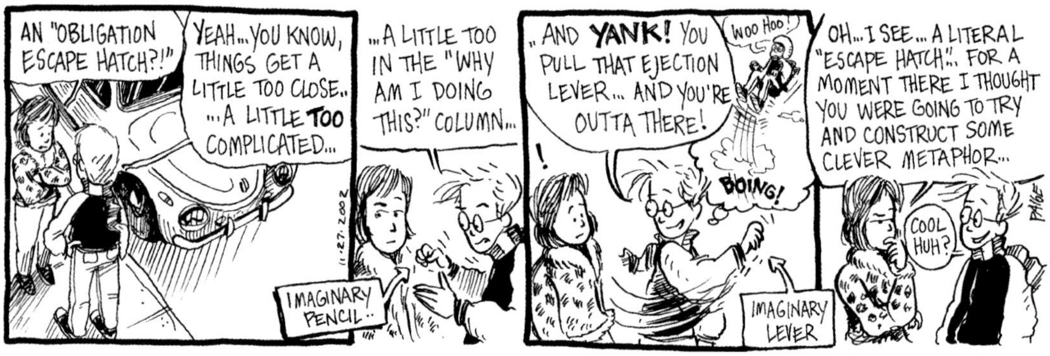
AN "OBLIGATION ESCAPE HATCH?!"
YEAH... YOU KNOW, THINGS GET A LITTLE TOO CLOSE... ...A LITTLE TOO COMPLICATED...
11·27·2002
...A LITTLE TOO IN THE "WHY AM I DOING THIS?" COLUMN...
IMAGINARY PENCIL..
...AND YANK! YOU PULL THAT EJECTION LEVER... AND YOU'RE OUTTA THERE!
WOO HOO!
!
BOING!
IMAGINARY LEVER
OH... I SEE... A LITERAL "ESCAPE HATCH"... FOR A MOMENT THERE I THOUGHT YOU WERE GOING TO TRY AND CONSTRUCT SOME CLEVER METAPHOR...
COOL HUH?
PAIGE

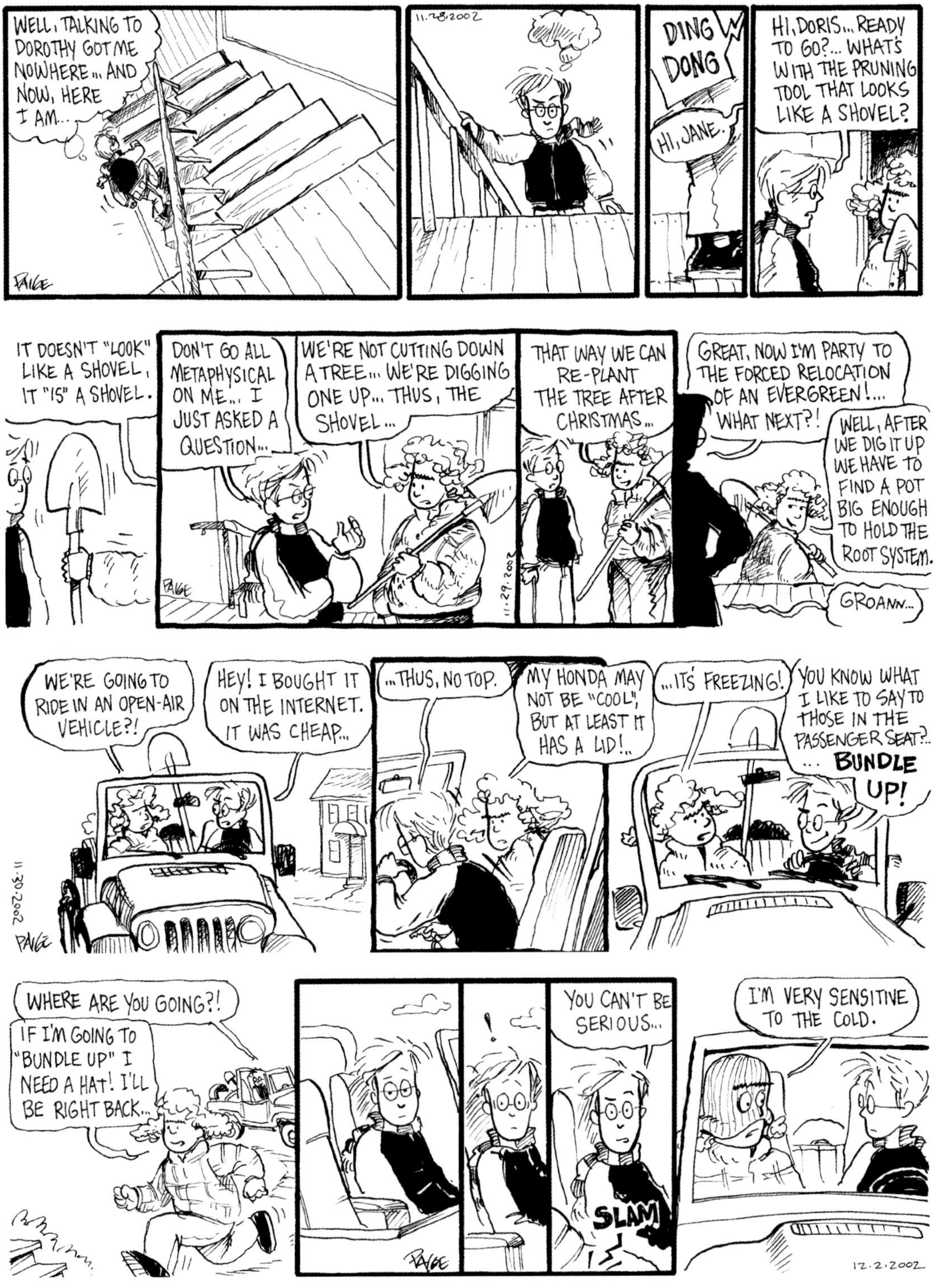
WELL, TALKING TO DOROTHY GOT ME NOWHERE... AND NOW, HERE I AM...
PAIGE
11.28.2002
DING DONG
HI, JANE.
HI, DORIS... READY TO GO?... WHAT'S WITH THE PRUNING TOOL THAT LOOKS LIKE A SHOVEL?
IT DOESN'T "LOOK" LIKE A SHOVEL, IT "IS" A SHOVEL.
DON'T GO ALL METAPHYSICAL ON ME... I JUST ASKED A QUESTION...
WE'RE NOT CUTTING DOWN A TREE... WE'RE DIGGING ONE UP... THUS, THE SHOVEL...
PAIGE
11.29.2002
THAT WAY WE CAN RE-PLANT THE TREE AFTER CHRISTMAS...
GREAT, NOW I'M PARTY TO THE FORCED RELOCATION OF AN EVERGREEN!... WHAT NEXT?!
WELL, AFTER WE DIG IT UP WE HAVE TO FIND A POT BIG ENOUGH TO HOLD THE ROOT SYSTEM.
GROANN...
WE'RE GOING TO RIDE IN AN OPEN-AIR VEHICLE?!
HEY! I BOUGHT IT ON THE INTERNET. IT WAS CHEAP...
11.30.2002
PAIGE
...THUS, NO TOP.
MY HONDA MAY NOT BE "COOL", BUT AT LEAST IT HAS A LID!...
...IT'S FREEZING!
YOU KNOW WHAT I LIKE TO SAY TO THOSE IN THE PASSENGER SEAT?... ... BUNDLE UP!
WHERE ARE YOU GOING?!
IF I'M GOING TO "BUNDLE UP" I NEED A HAT! I'LL BE RIGHT BACK...
!
YOU CAN'T BE SERIOUS...
SLAM
PAIGE
I'M VERY SENSITIVE TO THE COLD.
12.2.2002

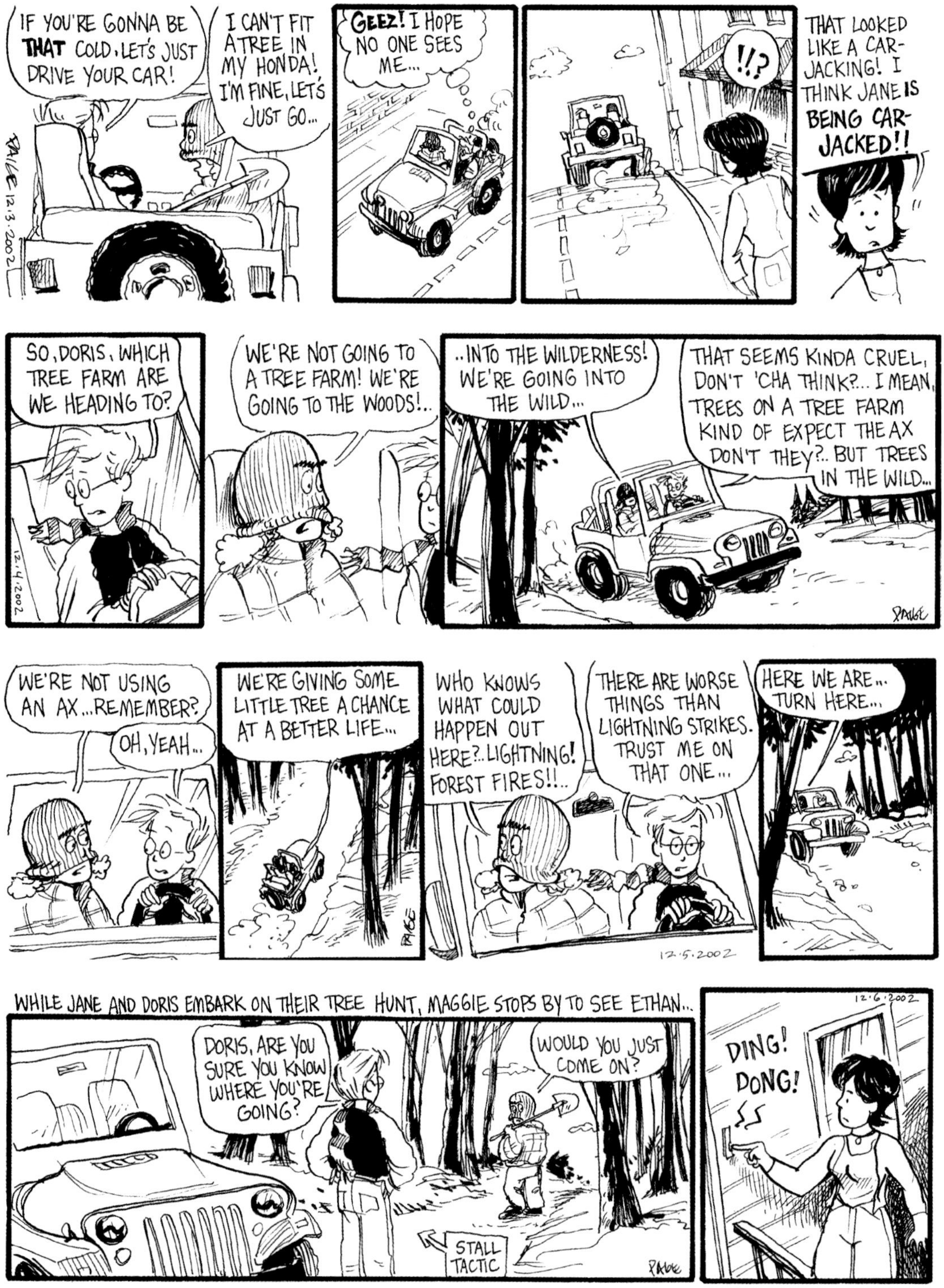
IF YOU'RE GONNA BE **THAT** COLD, LET'S JUST DRIVE YOUR CAR!
I CAN'T FIT A TREE IN MY HONDA! I'M FINE, LET'S JUST GO...
PAIGE 12.3.2002
GEEZ! I HOPE NO ONE SEES ME...
!!?
THAT LOOKED LIKE A CAR-JACKING! I THINK JANE **IS BEING CAR-JACKED!!**
SO, DORIS, WHICH TREE FARM ARE WE HEADING TO?
12.4.2002
WE'RE NOT GOING TO A TREE FARM! WE'RE GOING TO THE WOODS!..
..INTO THE WILDERNESS! WE'RE GOING INTO THE WILD...
THAT SEEMS KINDA CRUEL, DON'T 'CHA THINK?... I MEAN, TREES ON A TREE FARM KIND OF EXPECT THE AX DON'T THEY?.. BUT TREES IN THE WILD...
PAIGE
WE'RE NOT USING AN AX...REMEMBER?
OH, YEAH...
WE'RE GIVING SOME LITTLE TREE A CHANCE AT A BETTER LIFE...
PAIGE
WHO KNOWS WHAT COULD HAPPEN OUT HERE?.. LIGHTNING! FOREST FIRES!!..
THERE ARE WORSE THINGS THAN LIGHTNING STRIKES. TRUST ME ON THAT ONE...
12.5.2002
HERE WE ARE... TURN HERE...
WHILE JANE AND DORIS EMBARK ON THEIR TREE HUNT, MAGGIE STOPS BY TO SEE ETHAN...
DORIS, ARE YOU SURE YOU KNOW WHERE YOU'RE GOING?
WOULD YOU JUST COME ON?
STALL TACTIC
PAIGE
12.6.2002
DING! DONG!

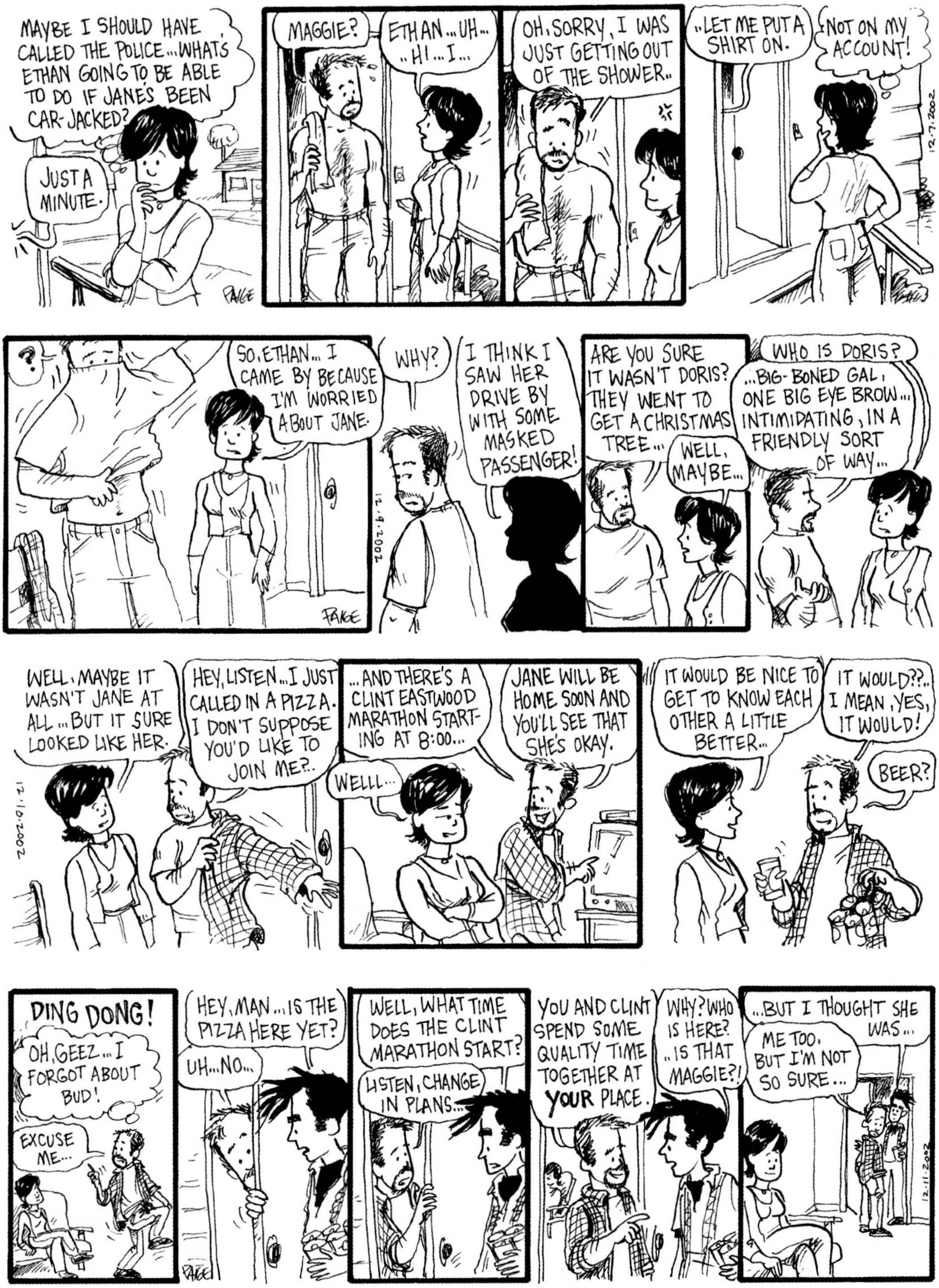

MAYBE I SHOULD HAVE CALLED THE POLICE... WHAT'S ETHAN GOING TO BE ABLE TO DO IF JANE'S BEEN CAR-JACKED?
JUST A MINUTE.
MAGGIE?
ETHAN... UH... ..HI... I...
OH, SORRY, I WAS JUST GETTING OUT OF THE SHOWER..
..LET ME PUT A SHIRT ON.
NOT ON MY ACCOUNT!
?
SO, ETHAN... I CAME BY BECAUSE I'M WORRIED ABOUT JANE.
WHY?
I THINK I SAW HER DRIVE BY WITH SOME MASKED PASSENGER!
ARE YOU SURE IT WASN'T DORIS? THEY WENT TO GET A CHRISTMAS TREE...
WELL, MAYBE...
WHO IS DORIS?
...BIG-BONED GAL, ONE BIG EYE BROW... INTIMIDATING, IN A FRIENDLY SORT OF WAY...
WELL, MAYBE IT WASN'T JANE AT ALL... BUT IT SURE LOOKED LIKE HER.
HEY, LISTEN... I JUST CALLED IN A PIZZA. I DON'T SUPPOSE YOU'D LIKE TO JOIN ME?..
...AND THERE'S A CLINT EASTWOOD MARATHON STARTING AT 8:00...
WELLL...
JANE WILL BE HOME SOON AND YOU'LL SEE THAT SHE'S OKAY.
IT WOULD BE NICE TO GET TO KNOW EACH OTHER A LITTLE BETTER...
IT WOULD?.. I MEAN, YES, IT WOULD!
BEER?
DING DONG!
OH, GEEZ... I FORGOT ABOUT BUD!
EXCUSE ME...
HEY, MAN... IS THE PIZZA HERE YET?
UH... NO...
WELL, WHAT TIME DOES THE CLINT MARATHON START?
LISTEN, CHANGE IN PLANS...
YOU AND CLINT SPEND SOME QUALITY TIME TOGETHER AT YOUR PLACE.
WHY? WHO IS HERE? ..IS THAT MAGGIE?!
...BUT I THOUGHT SHE WAS...
ME TOO, BUT I'M NOT SO SURE...

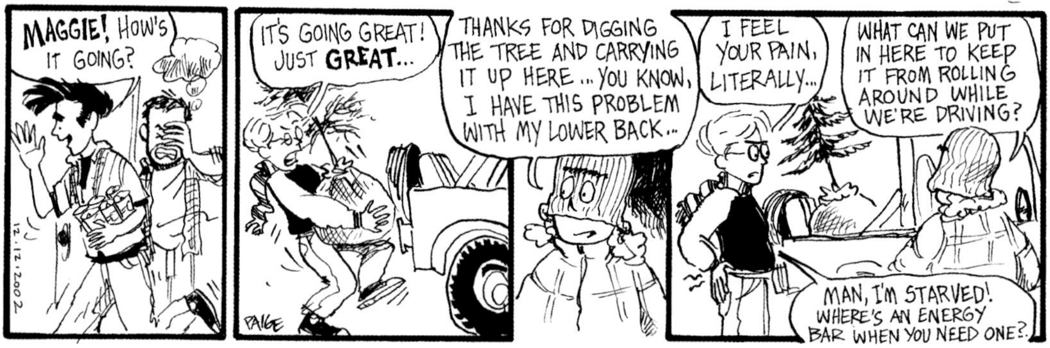
MAGGIE! HOW'S IT GOING?
12·12·2002
IT'S GOING GREAT! JUST GREAT...
PAIGE
THANKS FOR DIGGING THE TREE AND CARRYING IT UP HERE... YOU KNOW, I HAVE THIS PROBLEM WITH MY LOWER BACK...
I FEEL YOUR PAIN, LITERALLY...
WHAT CAN WE PUT IN HERE TO KEEP IT FROM ROLLING AROUND WHILE WE'RE DRIVING?
MAN, I'M STARVED! WHERE'S AN ENERGY BAR WHEN YOU NEED ONE?

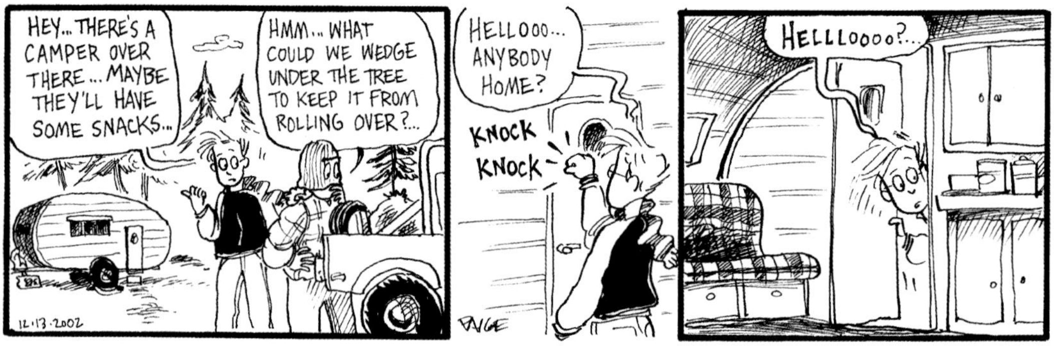
HEY... THERE'S A CAMPER OVER THERE... MAYBE THEY'LL HAVE SOME SNACKS...
HMM... WHAT COULD WE WEDGE UNDER THE TREE TO KEEP IT FROM ROLLING OVER?...
12·13·2002
HELLOOO... ANYBODY HOME?
KNOCK KNOCK
PAIGE
HELLLOOOO?...

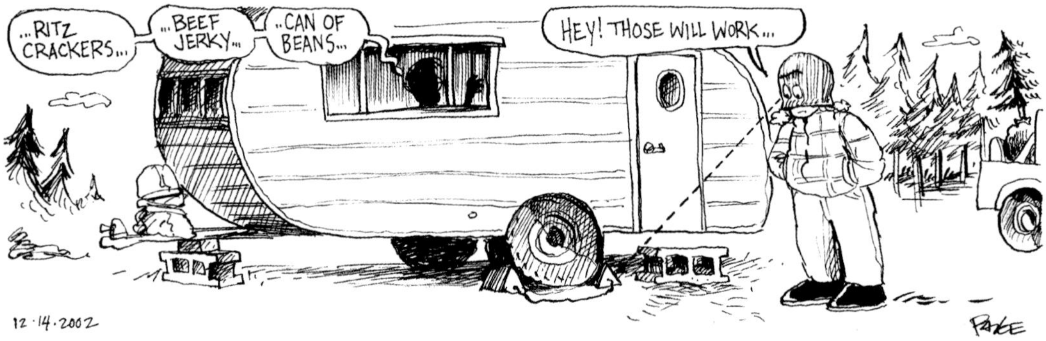
...RITZ CRACKERS...
...BEEF JERKY...
...CAN OF BEANS...
HEY! THOSE WILL WORK...
12·14·2002
PAIGE

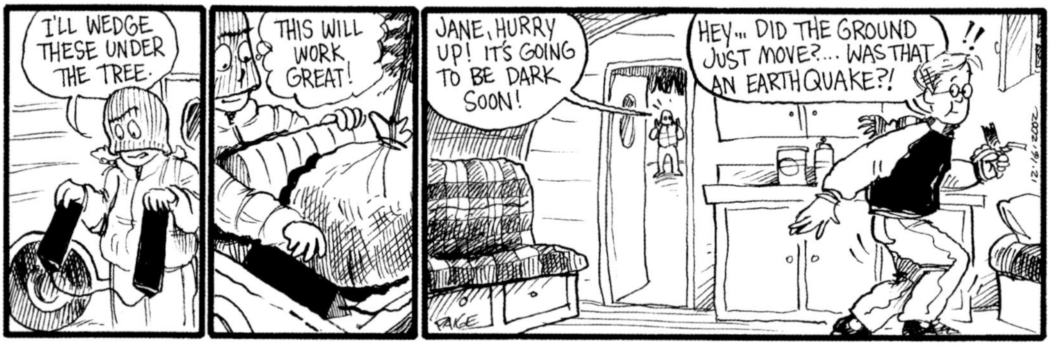
I'LL WEDGE THESE UNDER THE TREE.
THIS WILL WORK GREAT!
JANE, HURRY UP! IT'S GOING TO BE DARK SOON!
PAIGE
HEY... DID THE GROUND JUST MOVE?... WAS THAT AN EARTHQUAKE?!
!!
12·16·2002

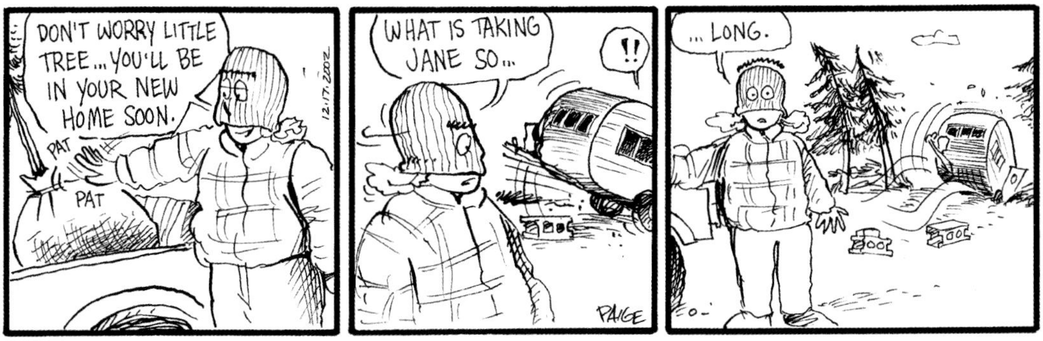
DON'T WORRY LITTLE TREE... YOU'LL BE IN YOUR NEW HOME SOON.
PAT
PAT
12.17.2002
WHAT IS TAKING JANE SO...
!!
PAIGE
... LONG.

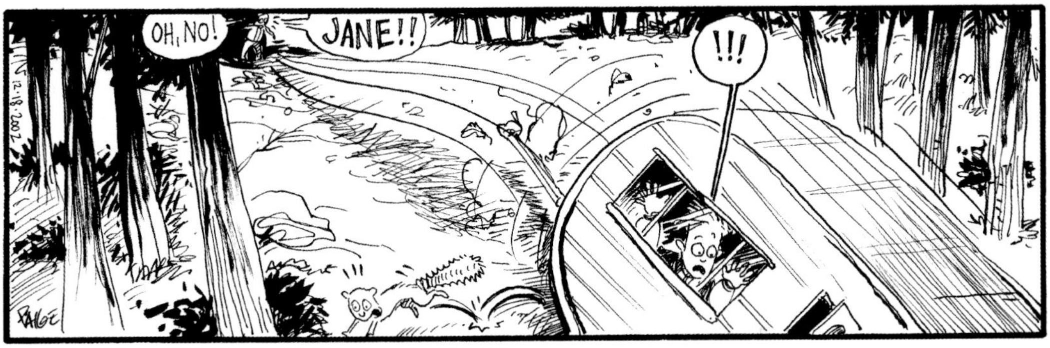
12.18.2002
OH, NO!
JANE!!
!!!
PAIGE

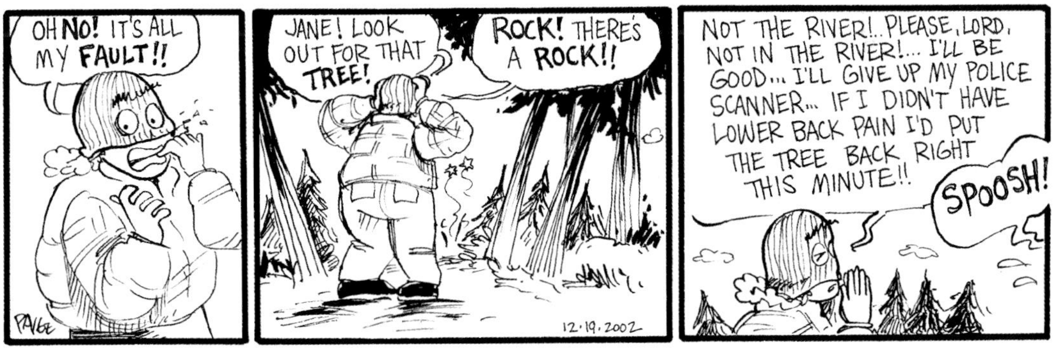
OH NO! IT'S ALL MY FAULT!!
PAIGE
JANE! LOOK OUT FOR THAT TREE!
ROCK! THERE'S A ROCK!!
12.19.2002
NOT THE RIVER!.. PLEASE, LORD, NOT IN THE RIVER!... I'LL BE GOOD... I'LL GIVE UP MY POLICE SCANNER... IF I DIDN'T HAVE LOWER BACK PAIN I'D PUT THE TREE BACK RIGHT THIS MINUTE!!
SPOOSH!

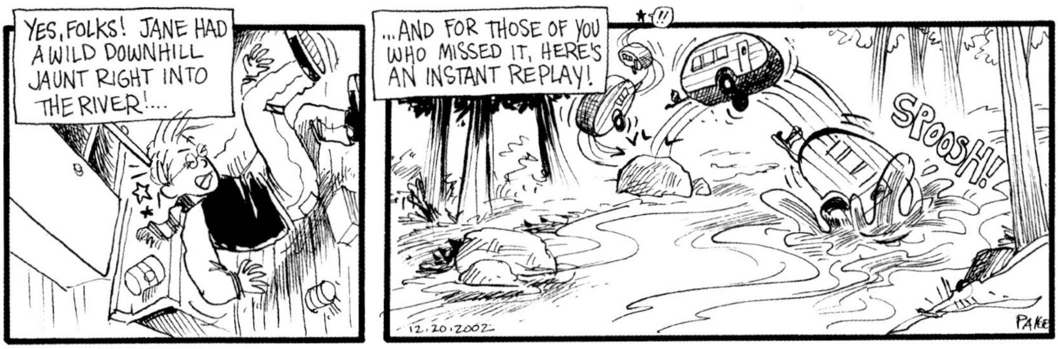
YES, FOLKS! JANE HAD A WILD DOWNHILL JAUNT RIGHT INTO THE RIVER!...
...AND FOR THOSE OF YOU WHO MISSED IT, HERE'S AN INSTANT REPLAY!
!!
SPOOSH!
12.20.2002
PAIGE

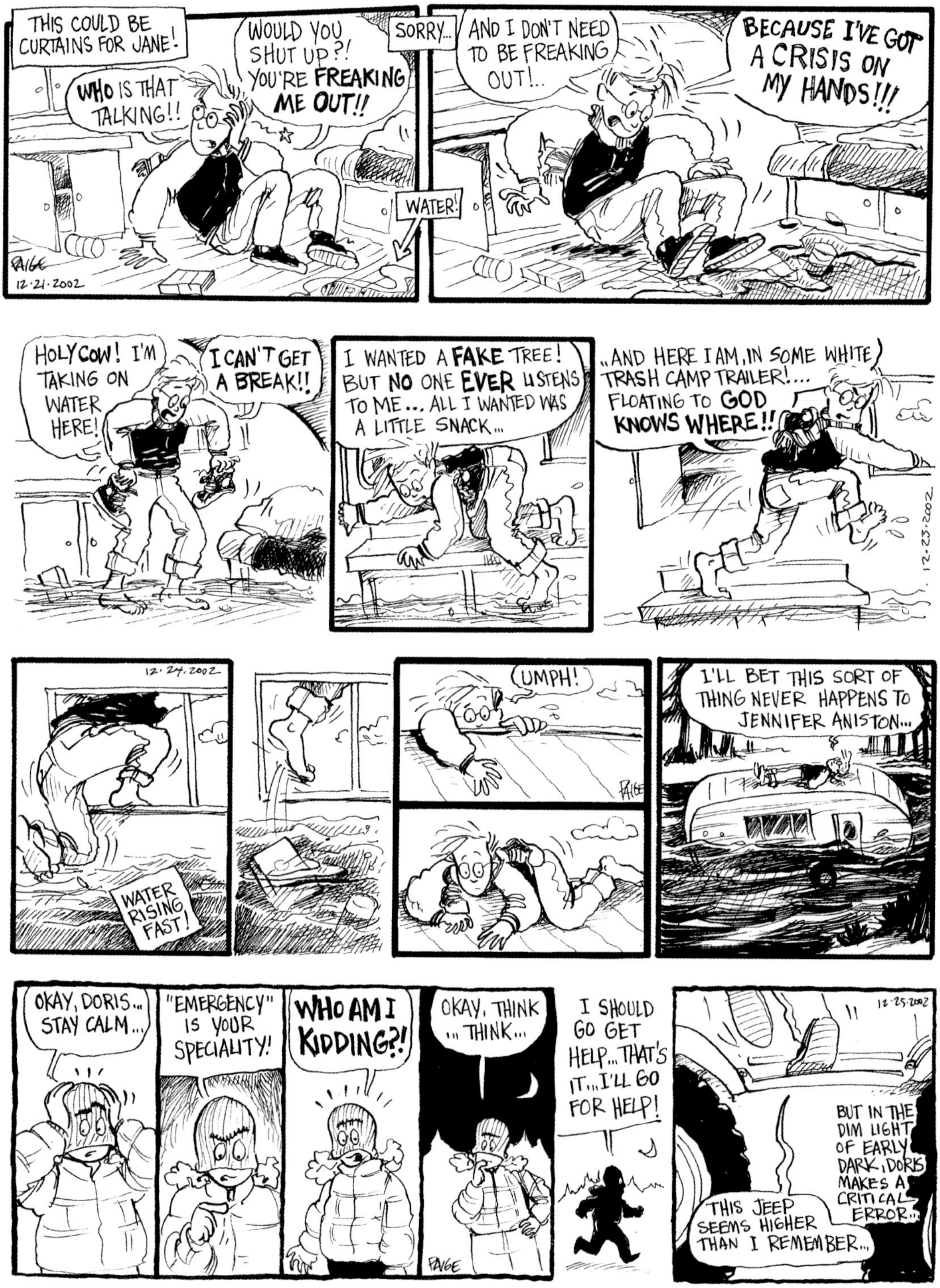
THIS COULD BE CURTAINS FOR JANE!
WHO IS THAT TALKING!!
WOULD YOU SHUT UP?! YOU'RE FREAKING ME OUT!!
WATER!
PAIGE
12·21·2002
SORRY...
AND I DON'T NEED TO BE FREAKING OUT!..
BECAUSE I'VE GOT A CRISIS ON MY HANDS!!!
HOLY COW! I'M TAKING ON WATER HERE!
I CAN'T GET A BREAK!!
I WANTED A FAKE TREE! BUT NO ONE EVER LISTENS TO ME... ALL I WANTED WAS A LITTLE SNACK...
..AND HERE I AM, IN SOME WHITE TRASH CAMP TRAILER!... FLOATING TO GOD KNOWS WHERE!!
12·23·2002
12·24·2002
WATER RISING FAST!
UMPH!
PAIGE
I'LL BET THIS SORT OF THING NEVER HAPPENS TO JENNIFER ANISTON...
OKAY, DORIS... STAY CALM...
"EMERGENCY" IS YOUR SPECIALITY!
WHO AM I KIDDING?!
OKAY, THINK ... THINK...
PAIGE
I SHOULD GO GET HELP... THAT'S IT... I'LL GO FOR HELP!
12·25·2002
BUT IN THE DIM LIGHT OF EARLY DARK, DORIS MAKES A CRITICAL ERROR...
THIS JEEP SEEMS HIGHER THAN I REMEMBER...

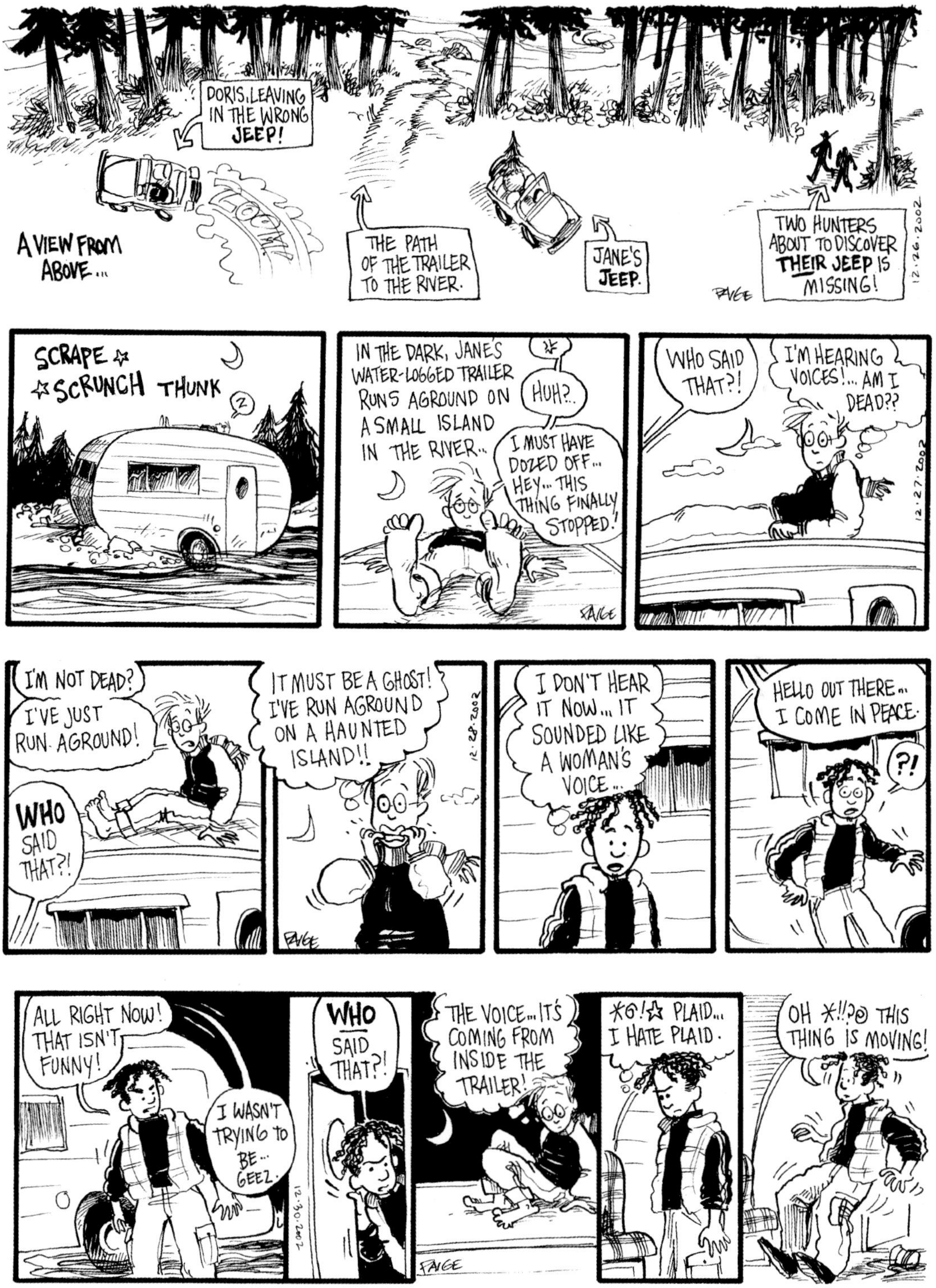
DORIS, LEAVING IN THE WRONG **JEEP!**
ZOOM!
A VIEW FROM ABOVE...
THE PATH OF THE TRAILER TO THE RIVER.
JANE'S **JEEP**.
TWO HUNTERS ABOUT TO DISCOVER **THEIR JEEP** IS MISSING!
PAIGE
12·26·2002
SCRAPE ☆ ☆ SCRUNCH THUNK
Z
IN THE DARK, JANE'S WATER-LOGGED TRAILER RUNS AGROUND ON A SMALL ISLAND IN THE RIVER...
HUH?..
I MUST HAVE DOZED OFF... HEY... THIS THING FINALLY STOPPED!
PAIGE
WHO SAID THAT?!
I'M HEARING VOICES!... AM I DEAD??
12·27·2002
I'M NOT DEAD?
I'VE JUST RUN AGROUND!
WHO SAID THAT?!
IT MUST BE A GHOST! I'VE RUN AGROUND ON A HAUNTED ISLAND!!
12·28·2002
PAIGE
I DON'T HEAR IT NOW... IT SOUNDED LIKE A WOMAN'S VOICE...
HELLO OUT THERE... I COME IN PEACE.
?!
ALL RIGHT NOW! THAT ISN'T FUNNY!
I WASN'T TRYING TO BE... GEEZ.
WHO SAID THAT?!
12·30·2002
THE VOICE... IT'S COMING FROM INSIDE THE TRAILER!
PAIGE
*G!☆ PLAID... I HATE PLAID.
OH *!!?@ THIS THING IS MOVING!

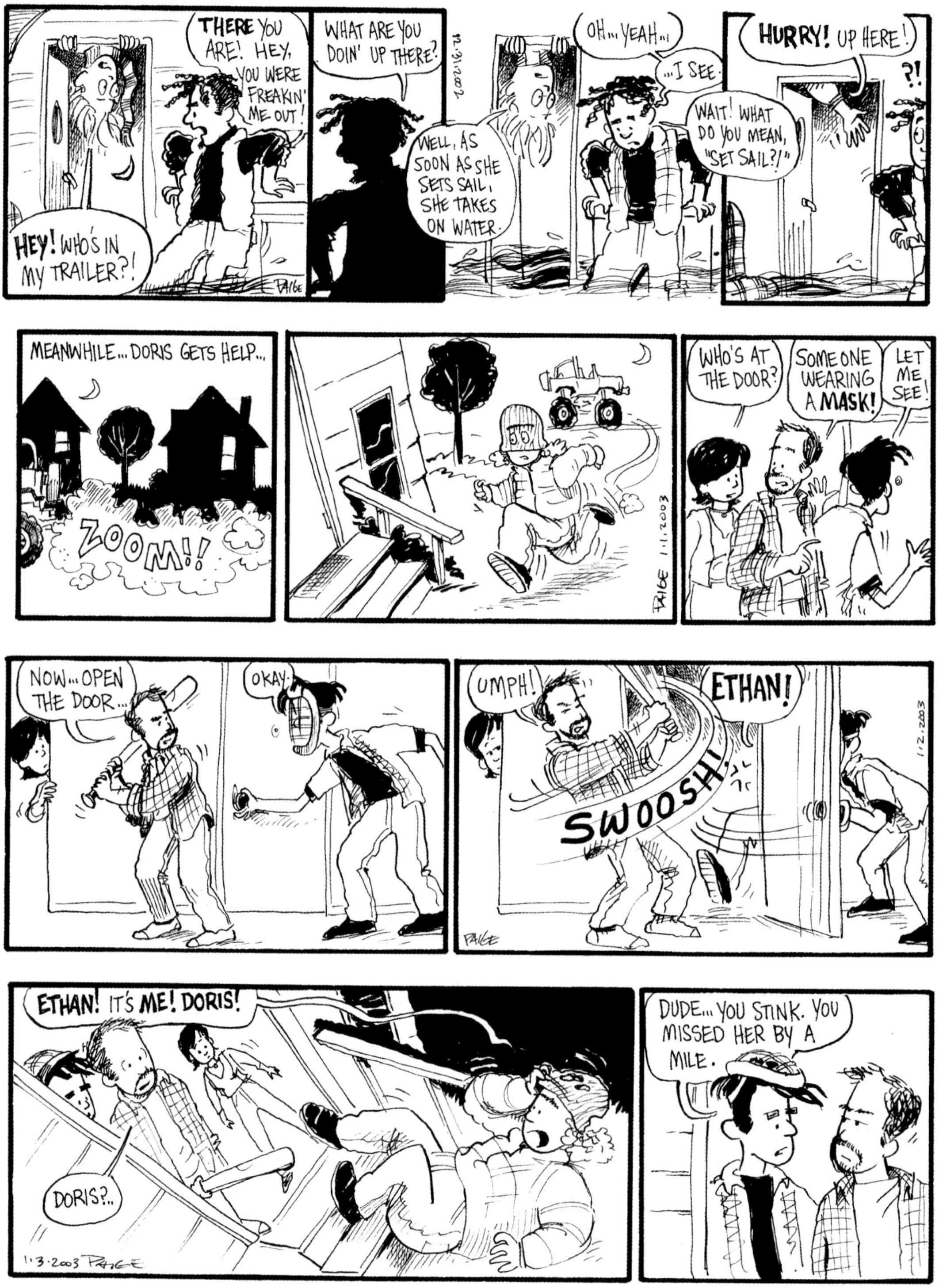
THERE YOU ARE! HEY, YOU WERE FREAKIN' ME OUT!
HEY! WHO'S IN MY TRAILER?!
PAIGE
WHAT ARE YOU DOIN' UP THERE?
12.31.2002
WELL, AS SOON AS SHE SETS SAIL, SHE TAKES ON WATER.
OH... YEAH...
...I SEE.
HURRY! UP HERE!
?!
WAIT! WHAT DO YOU MEAN, "SET SAIL?!"
MEANWHILE... DORIS GETS HELP...
ZOOM!!
1.1.2003
PAIGE
WHO'S AT THE DOOR?
SOME ONE WEARING A MASK!
LET ME SEE!
NOW... OPEN THE DOOR...
OKAY.
UMPH!
ETHAN!
SWOOSH!
1.2.2003
PAIGE
ETHAN! IT'S ME! DORIS!
DORIS?..
1.3.2003 PAIGE
DUDE... YOU STINK. YOU MISSED HER BY A MILE.

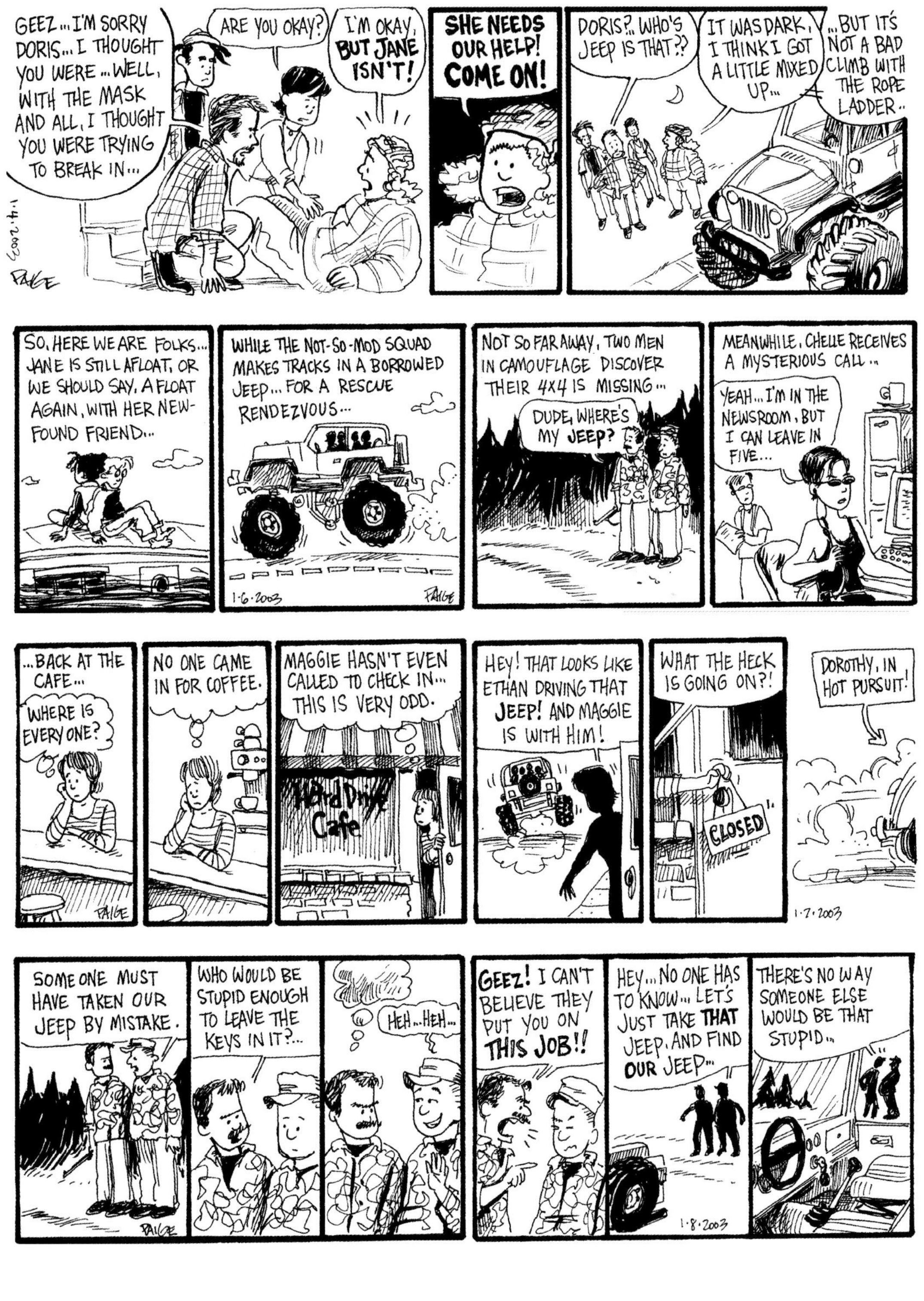

GEEZ... I'M SORRY DORIS... I THOUGHT YOU WERE... WELL, WITH THE MASK AND ALL, I THOUGHT YOU WERE TRYING TO BREAK IN...
ARE YOU OKAY?
I'M OKAY, BUT JANE ISN'T!
1.4.2003
PAIGE
SHE NEEDS OUR HELP! COME ON!
DORIS?... WHO'S JEEP IS THAT??
IT WAS DARK, I THINK I GOT A LITTLE MIXED UP...
...BUT IT'S NOT A BAD CLIMB WITH THE ROPE LADDER...
SO, HERE WE ARE FOLKS... JANE IS STILL AFLOAT, OR WE SHOULD SAY, AFLOAT AGAIN, WITH HER NEW-FOUND FRIEND...
WHILE THE NOT-SO-MOD SQUAD MAKES TRACKS IN A BORROWED JEEP... FOR A RESCUE RENDEZVOUS...
1.6.2003
PAIGE
NOT SO FAR AWAY, TWO MEN IN CAMOUFLAGE DISCOVER THEIR 4X4 IS MISSING...
DUDE, WHERE'S MY JEEP?
MEANWHILE, CHELLE RECEIVES A MYSTERIOUS CALL...
YEAH... I'M IN THE NEWSROOM, BUT I CAN LEAVE IN FIVE...
...BACK AT THE CAFE...
WHERE IS EVERYONE?
PAIGE
NO ONE CAME IN FOR COFFEE.
MAGGIE HASN'T EVEN CALLED TO CHECK IN... THIS IS VERY ODD.
Hard Drive Cafe
HEY! THAT LOOKS LIKE ETHAN DRIVING THAT JEEP! AND MAGGIE IS WITH HIM!
WHAT THE HECK IS GOING ON?!
CLOSED
DOROTHY, IN HOT PURSUIT!
1.7.2003
SOMEONE MUST HAVE TAKEN OUR JEEP BY MISTAKE.
WHO WOULD BE STUPID ENOUGH TO LEAVE THE KEYS IN IT?...
PAIGE
HEH... HEH...
GEEZ! I CAN'T BELIEVE THEY PUT YOU ON THIS JOB!!
HEY... NO ONE HAS TO KNOW... LET'S JUST TAKE THAT JEEP, AND FIND OUR JEEP...
1.8.2003
THERE'S NO WAY SOMEONE ELSE WOULD BE THAT STUPID...

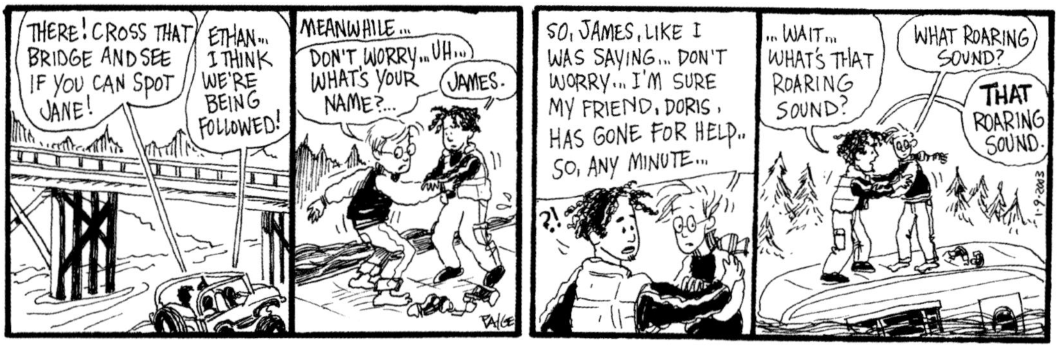
THERE! CROSS THAT BRIDGE AND SEE IF YOU CAN SPOT JANE!
ETHAN... I THINK WE'RE BEING FOLLOWED!
MEANWHILE...
DON'T WORRY... UH... WHAT'S YOUR NAME?...
JAMES.
SO, JAMES, LIKE I WAS SAYING... DON'T WORRY... I'M SURE MY FRIEND, DORIS, HAS GONE FOR HELP.. SO, ANY MINUTE...
?!
...WAIT... WHAT'S THAT ROARING SOUND?
WHAT ROARING SOUND?
THAT ROARING SOUND.
1-9-2003
PAIGE

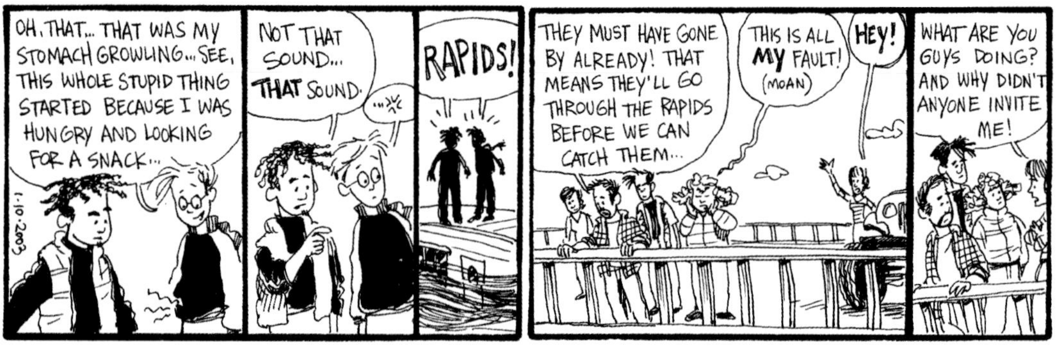
OH, THAT... THAT WAS MY STOMACH GROWLING... SEE, THIS WHOLE STUPID THING STARTED BECAUSE I WAS HUNGRY AND LOOKING FOR A SNACK...
1-10-2003
NOT THAT SOUND... THAT SOUND.
RAPIDS!
THEY MUST HAVE GONE BY ALREADY! THAT MEANS THEY'LL GO THROUGH THE RAPIDS BEFORE WE CAN CATCH THEM...
THIS IS ALL MY FAULT! (MOAN)
HEY!
WHAT ARE YOU GUYS DOING? AND WHY DIDN'T ANYONE INVITE ME!

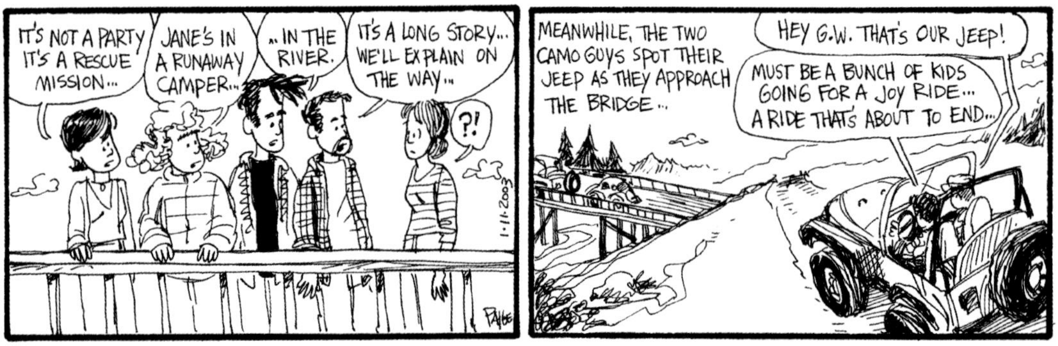
IT'S NOT A PARTY IT'S A RESCUE MISSION...
JANE'S IN A RUNAWAY CAMPER...
...IN THE RIVER.
IT'S A LONG STORY... WE'LL EXPLAIN ON THE WAY...
?!
1-11-2003
PAIGE
MEANWHILE, THE TWO CAMO GUYS SPOT THEIR JEEP AS THEY APPROACH THE BRIDGE...
HEY G.W. THAT'S OUR JEEP!
MUST BE A BUNCH OF KIDS GOING FOR A JOY RIDE... A RIDE THAT'S ABOUT TO END...

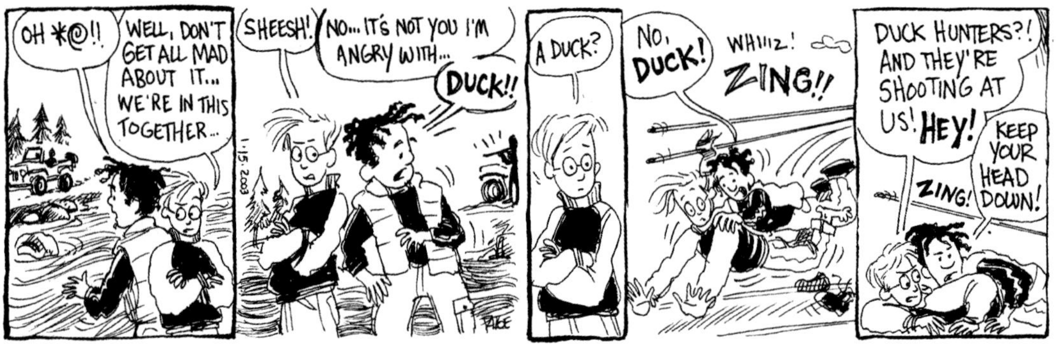
OH *@!!
WELL, DON'T GET ALL MAD ABOUT IT... WE'RE IN THIS TOGETHER...
1-15-2003
SHEESH!
NO... IT'S NOT YOU I'M ANGRY WITH...
DUCK!!
PAIGE
A DUCK?
NO, DUCK!
WHIIZ!
ZING!!
DUCK HUNTERS?! AND THEY'RE SHOOTING AT US! HEY!
KEEP YOUR HEAD DOWN!
ZING!

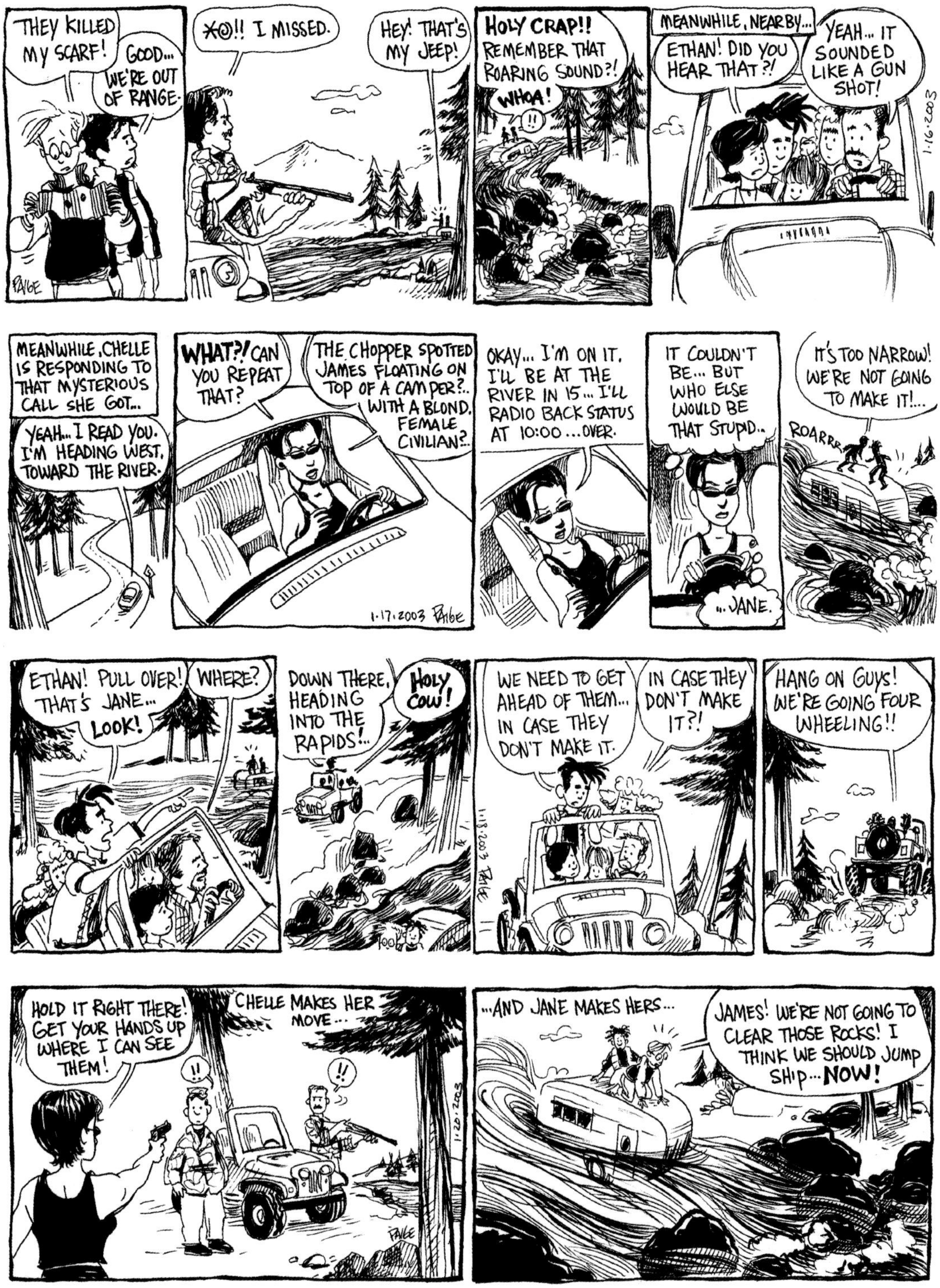
THEY KILLED MY SCARF!
GOOD... WE'RE OUT OF RANGE.
PAIGE
*@!! I MISSED.
HEY! THAT'S MY JEEP!
HOLY CRAP!! REMEMBER THAT ROARING SOUND?!
WHOA!
!!
MEANWHILE, NEARBY...
ETHAN! DID YOU HEAR THAT?!
YEAH... IT SOUNDED LIKE A GUN SHOT!
1.16.2003
MEANWHILE, CHELLE IS RESPONDING TO THAT MYSTERIOUS CALL SHE GOT...
YEAH... I READ YOU. I'M HEADING WEST, TOWARD THE RIVER.
WHAT?! CAN YOU REPEAT THAT?
THE CHOPPER SPOTTED JAMES FLOATING ON TOP OF A CAMPER?.. WITH A BLOND, FEMALE CIVILIAN?..
1.17.2003 PAIGE
OKAY... I'M ON IT. I'LL BE AT THE RIVER IN 15... I'LL RADIO BACK STATUS AT 10:00... OVER.
IT COULDN'T BE... BUT WHO ELSE WOULD BE THAT STUPID..
...JANE.
IT'S TOO NARROW! WE'RE NOT GOING TO MAKE IT!...
ROARRR
ETHAN! PULL OVER! THAT'S JANE... LOOK!
WHERE?
DOWN THERE, HEADING INTO THE RAPIDS!..
HOLY COW!
1.18.2003 PAIGE
WE NEED TO GET AHEAD OF THEM... IN CASE THEY DON'T MAKE IT.
IN CASE THEY DON'T MAKE IT?!
HANG ON GUYS! WE'RE GOING FOUR WHEELING!!
HOLD IT RIGHT THERE! GET YOUR HANDS UP WHERE I CAN SEE THEM!
CHELLE MAKES HER MOVE...
!!
!!
1.20.2003
PAIGE
...AND JANE MAKES HERS...
JAMES! WE'RE NOT GOING TO CLEAR THOSE ROCKS! I THINK WE SHOULD JUMP SHIP... NOW!

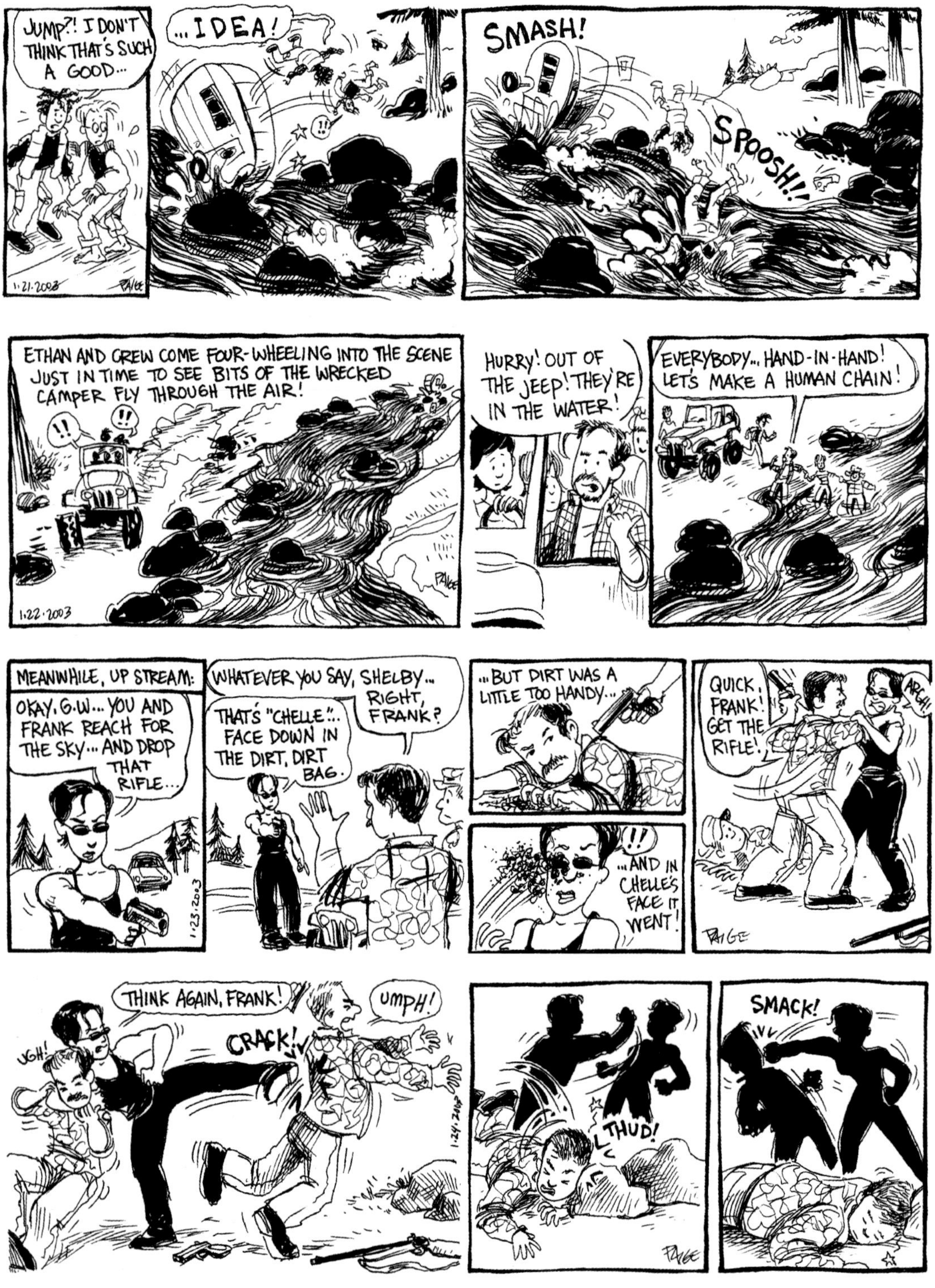
JUMP?! I DON'T THINK THAT'S SUCH A GOOD...
...IDEA!
!!
1.21.2003
SMASH!
SPOOSH!!
ETHAN AND CREW COME FOUR-WHEELING INTO THE SCENE JUST IN TIME TO SEE BITS OF THE WRECKED CAMPER FLY THROUGH THE AIR!
!!
!!
1.22.2003
HURRY! OUT OF THE JEEP! THEY'RE IN THE WATER!
EVERYBODY... HAND-IN-HAND! LET'S MAKE A HUMAN CHAIN!
MEANWHILE, UP STREAM:
OKAY, G.W... YOU AND FRANK REACH FOR THE SKY... AND DROP THAT RIFLE...
1.23.2003
WHATEVER YOU SAY, SHELBY... RIGHT, FRANK?
THAT'S "CHELLE"... FACE DOWN IN THE DIRT, DIRT BAG.
...BUT DIRT WAS A LITTLE TOO HANDY...
!!
...AND IN CHELLE'S FACE IT WENT!
QUICK, FRANK! GET THE RIFLE!
ARGH!
THINK AGAIN, FRANK!
UMPH!
UGH!
CRACK!
1.24.2003
THUD!
SMACK!

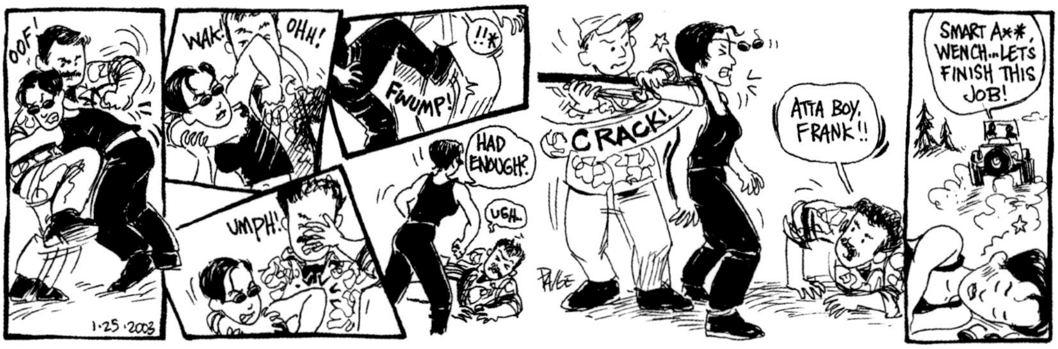
OOF!
1·25·2003
WAK!
OHH!
UMPH!
!!*
FWUMP!
HAD ENOUGH?
UGH.
CRACK!
PAIGE
ATTA BOY, FRANK!!
SMART A**, WENCH... LETS FINISH THIS JOB!

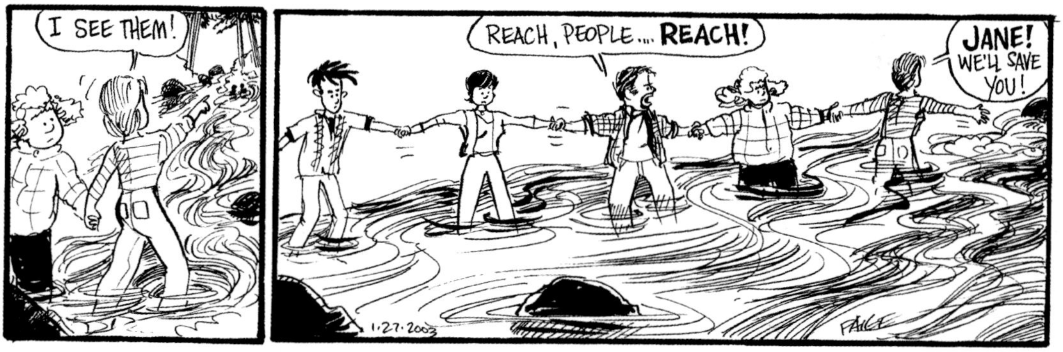
I SEE THEM!
REACH, PEOPLE.... REACH!
JANE! WE'LL SAVE YOU!
1·27·2003
PAIGE

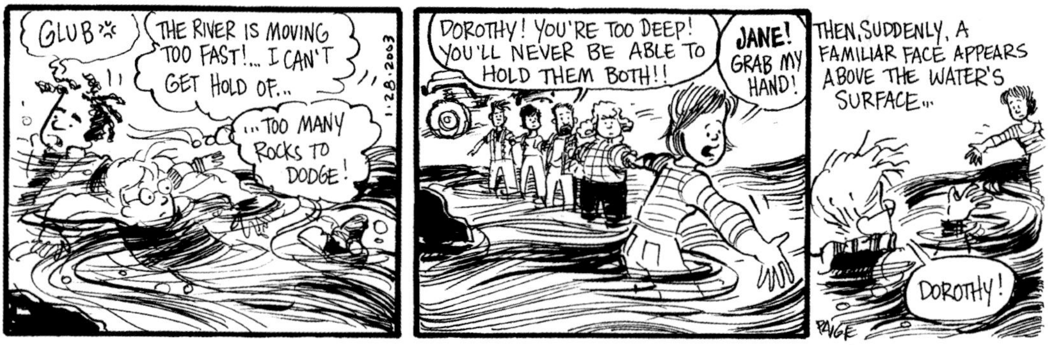
GLUB
THE RIVER IS MOVING TOO FAST!... I CAN'T GET HOLD OF...
...TOO MANY ROCKS TO DODGE!
1·28·2003
DOROTHY! YOU'RE TOO DEEP! YOU'LL NEVER BE ABLE TO HOLD THEM BOTH!!
JANE! GRAB MY HAND!
THEN, SUDDENLY, A FAMILIAR FACE APPEARS ABOVE THE WATER'S SURFACE...
DOROTHY!
PAIGE

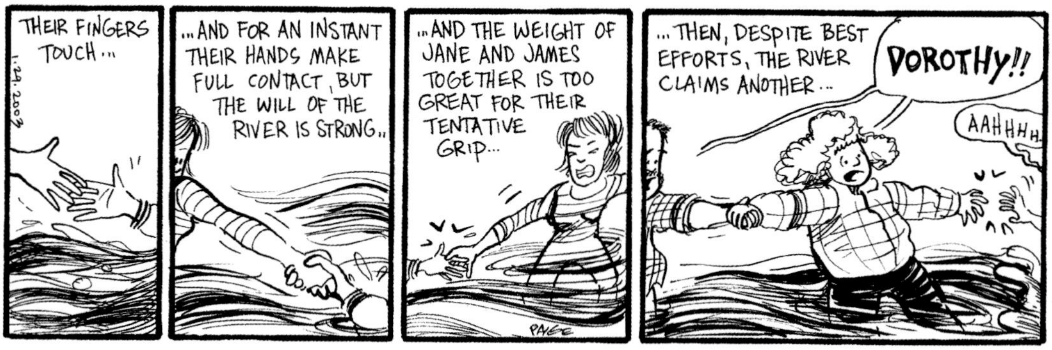
THEIR FINGERS TOUCH...
1·29·2003
...AND FOR AN INSTANT THEIR HANDS MAKE FULL CONTACT, BUT THE WILL OF THE RIVER IS STRONG..
...AND THE WEIGHT OF JANE AND JAMES TOGETHER IS TOO GREAT FOR THEIR TENTATIVE GRIP...
PAIGE
...THEN, DESPITE BEST EFFORTS, THE RIVER CLAIMS ANOTHER...
DOROTHY!!
AAHHHH

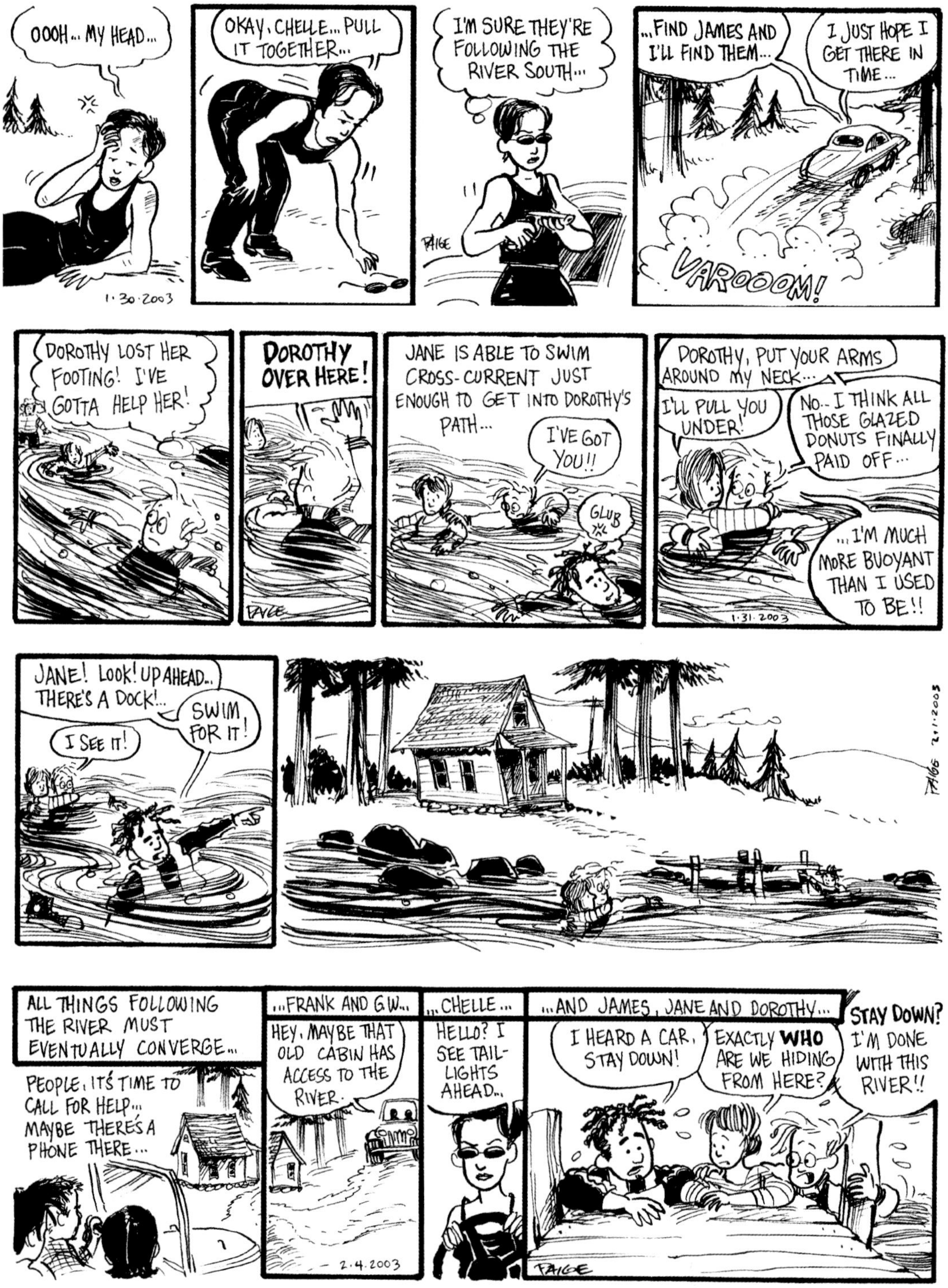
OOOH... MY HEAD...
1·30·2003
OKAY, CHELLE... PULL IT TOGETHER...
I'M SURE THEY'RE FOLLOWING THE RIVER SOUTH...
PAIGE
...FIND JAMES AND I'LL FIND THEM...
I JUST HOPE I GET THERE IN TIME...
VAROOOM!
DOROTHY LOST HER FOOTING! I'VE GOTTA HELP HER!
DOROTHY OVER HERE!
PAIGE
JANE IS ABLE TO SWIM CROSS-CURRENT JUST ENOUGH TO GET INTO DOROTHY'S PATH...
I'VE GOT YOU!!
GLUB
DOROTHY, PUT YOUR ARMS AROUND MY NECK...
I'LL PULL YOU UNDER!
NO.. I THINK ALL THOSE GLAZED DONUTS FINALLY PAID OFF...
...I'M MUCH MORE BUOYANT THAN I USED TO BE!!
1·31·2003
JANE! LOOK! UP AHEAD.. THERE'S A DOCK!...
SWIM FOR IT!
I SEE IT!
PAIGE 2·1·2003
ALL THINGS FOLLOWING THE RIVER MUST EVENTUALLY CONVERGE...
PEOPLE, IT'S TIME TO CALL FOR HELP... MAYBE THERE'S A PHONE THERE...
...FRANK AND G.W...
HEY, MAYBE THAT OLD CABIN HAS ACCESS TO THE RIVER.
2·4·2003
...CHELLE...
HELLO? I SEE TAIL-LIGHTS AHEAD..
...AND JAMES, JANE AND DOROTHY...
I HEARD A CAR, STAY DOWN!
EXACTLY WHO ARE WE HIDING FROM HERE?
STAY DOWN? I'M DONE WITH THIS RIVER!!
PAIGE

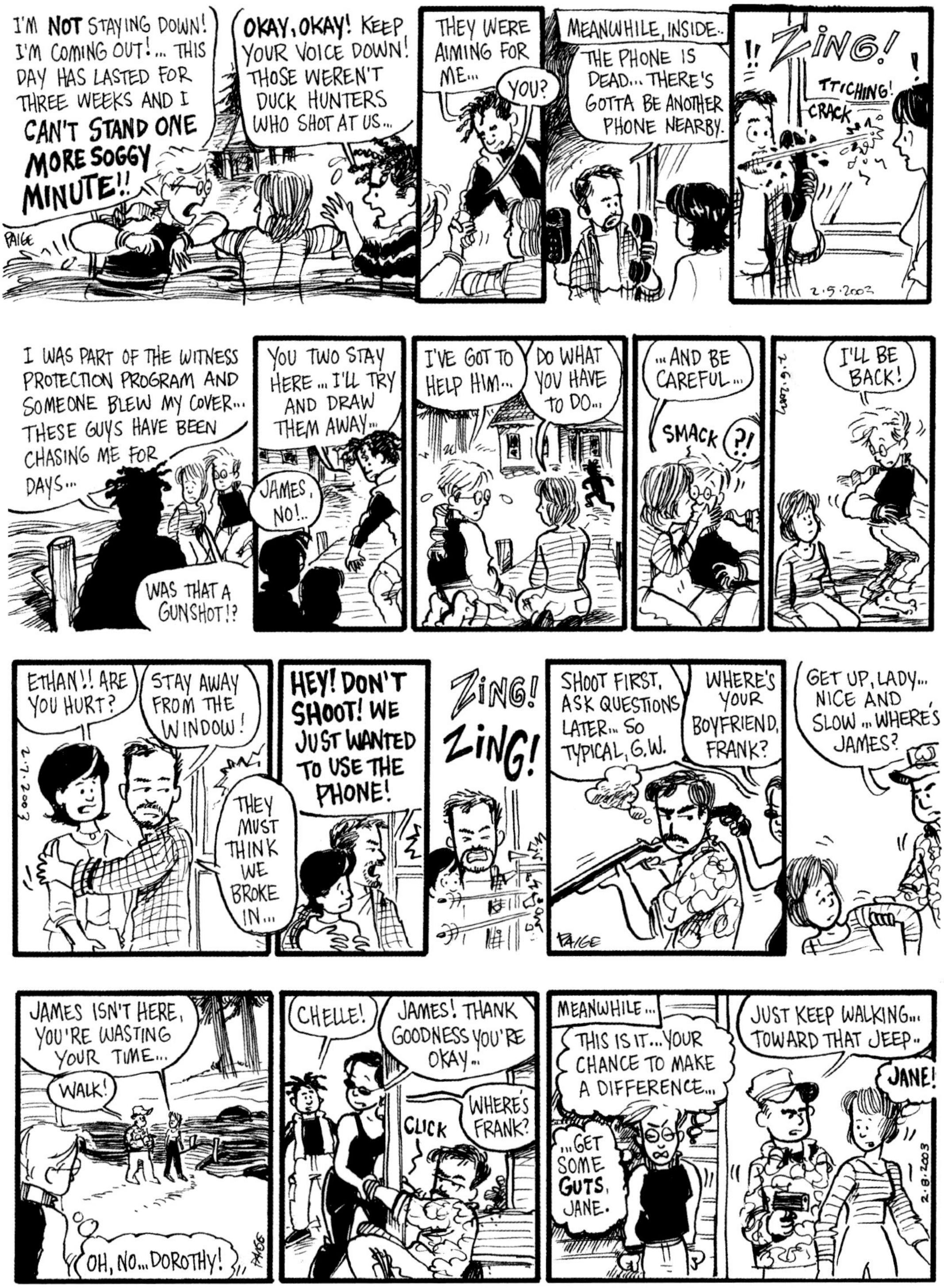
I'M NOT STAYING DOWN! I'M COMING OUT!... THIS DAY HAS LASTED FOR THREE WEEKS AND I CAN'T STAND ONE MORE SOGGY MINUTE!!
OKAY, OKAY! KEEP YOUR VOICE DOWN! THOSE WEREN'T DUCK HUNTERS WHO SHOT AT US...
PAIGE
THEY WERE AIMING FOR ME...
YOU?
MEANWHILE, INSIDE..
THE PHONE IS DEAD... THERE'S GOTTA BE ANOTHER PHONE NEARBY.
ZING!
TTICHING!
CRACK
2.5.2003
I WAS PART OF THE WITNESS PROTECTION PROGRAM AND SOMEONE BLEW MY COVER... THESE GUYS HAVE BEEN CHASING ME FOR DAYS...
WAS THAT A GUNSHOT!?
YOU TWO STAY HERE... I'LL TRY AND DRAW THEM AWAY...
JAMES, NO!..
I'VE GOT TO HELP HIM...
DO WHAT YOU HAVE TO DO...
...AND BE CAREFUL...
SMACK
?!
2.6.2003
I'LL BE BACK!
ETHAN!! ARE YOU HURT?
STAY AWAY FROM THE WINDOW!
THEY MUST THINK WE BROKE IN...
2.7.2003
HEY! DON'T SHOOT! WE JUST WANTED TO USE THE PHONE!
ZING!
ZING!
SHOOT FIRST, ASK QUESTIONS LATER... SO TYPICAL, G.W.
WHERE'S YOUR BOYFRIEND, FRANK?
PAIGE
GET UP, LADY... NICE AND SLOW... WHERE'S JAMES?
JAMES ISN'T HERE, YOU'RE WASTING YOUR TIME...
WALK!
OH, NO... DOROTHY!
PAIGE
CHELLE!
JAMES! THANK GOODNESS YOU'RE OKAY..
WHERE'S FRANK?
CLICK
MEANWHILE...
THIS IS IT... YOUR CHANCE TO MAKE A DIFFERENCE...
...GET SOME GUTS, JANE.
JUST KEEP WALKING... TOWARD THAT JEEP..
JANE!
2.8.2003

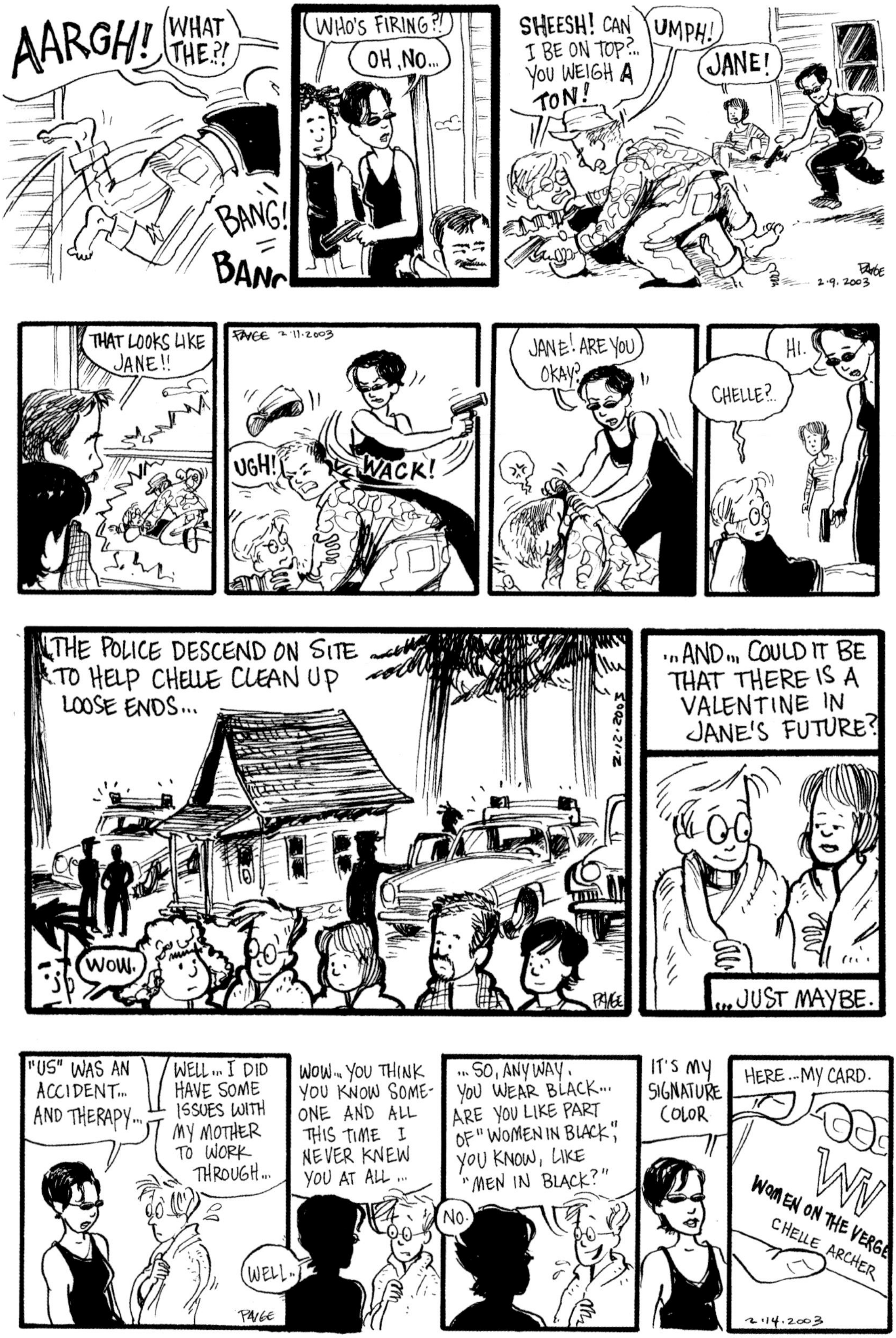
AARGH!
WHAT THE?!
BANG!
BANG
WHO'S FIRING?!
OH, NO...
SHEESH! CAN I BE ON TOP?... YOU WEIGH A TON!
UMPH!
JANE!
PAIGE 2.9.2003
THAT LOOKS LIKE JANE!!
PAIGE 2.11.2003
UGH!
WACK!
JANE! ARE YOU OKAY?
HI.
CHELLE?..
THE POLICE DESCEND ON SITE TO HELP CHELLE CLEAN UP LOOSE ENDS...
WOW.
PAIGE
...AND... COULD IT BE THAT THERE IS A VALENTINE IN JANE'S FUTURE?
...JUST MAYBE.
"US" WAS AN ACCIDENT... AND THERAPY...
WELL... I DID HAVE SOME ISSUES WITH MY MOTHER TO WORK THROUGH...
PAIGE
WELL..
WOW... YOU THINK YOU KNOW SOMEONE AND ALL THIS TIME I NEVER KNEW YOU AT ALL...
...SO, ANYWAY, YOU WEAR BLACK... ARE YOU LIKE PART OF "WOMEN IN BLACK," YOU KNOW, LIKE "MEN IN BLACK?"
NO.
IT'S MY SIGNATURE COLOR
HERE...MY CARD.
WOMEN ON THE VERGE
CHELLE ARCHER
2.14.2003

WOMEN ON THE VERGE OF WHAT?
ON THE VERGE OF WHATEVER IT TAKES TO GET THE JOB DONE.
SHE'S WEARING A TOWEL
COOOOL...
HEY, SO NOW THAT WE KNOW, CAN WE HELP YOU SOLVE CASES AND STUFF?..
?!
PAIGE
...LIKE THE WAY BUFFY'S PALS HELP HER SLAY VAMPIRES... I MEAN, NOW THAT THEY KNOW HER SECRET IDENTITY THEY'RE LIKE HER POSSE... CAN WE...
NO.
2·15·2003

HAVE YOU SEEN MY ROOM?!
PAIGE
GRANTED, IT WAS A LONG 24 HOURS, BUT YOU'D THINK RUSTY HAD A MONTH TO REDECORATE!
2·17·2003
NO
RUSTY
RUS

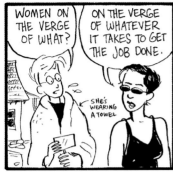

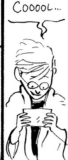

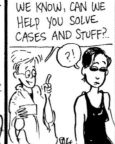

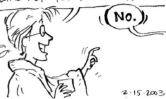

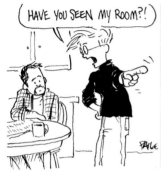

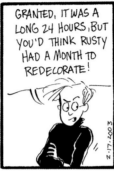

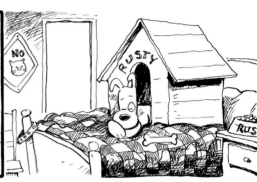

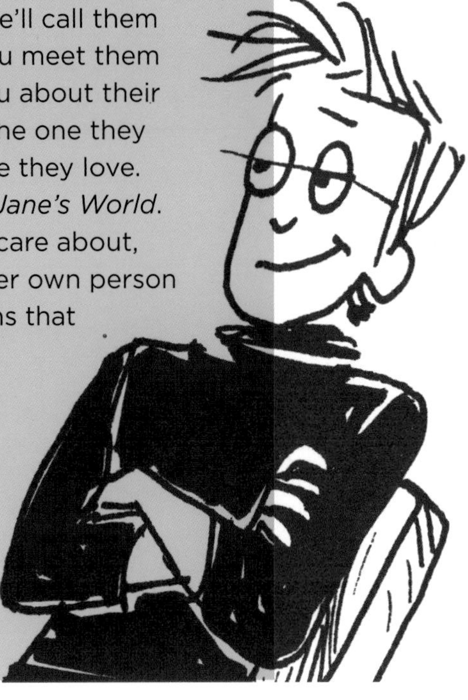

"I met Paige and Jane many years ago at cartoonist event in San Antonio, Texas. Paige was a charming bundle of energy and enthusiasm. Not a minute passed before she told me about Jane. Most non-cartooning people—we'll call them muggles—will let you know early on after you meet them if they have a life partner. Cartoonists tell you about their character, the original one they've created, the one they are pouring their heart and time into, the one they love. I liked Paige the person, so I began reading *Jane's World*. Since then it's a bit like having two friends I care about, because Jane is like Paige but Jane is also her own person with her own friends and lovers and decisions that perhaps should have been considered more carefully. Reading *Jane* over the years has brought me a lot of happiness and that's the best gift you can give anyone. Besides donuts, of course. So, for the smiles alone, I will always be in Paige and Jane's debt."

TERRY MOORE, *Strangers in Paradise, Rachel Rising, Motor Girl*

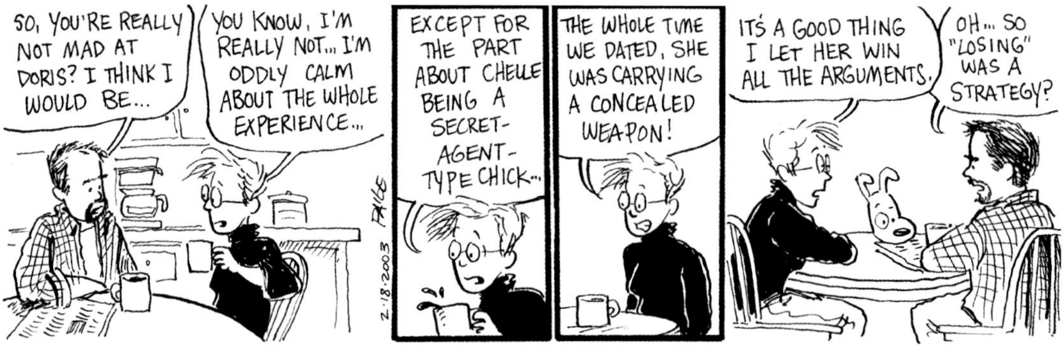
SO, YOU'RE REALLY NOT MAD AT DORIS? I THINK I WOULD BE...
YOU KNOW, I'M REALLY NOT... I'M ODDLY CALM ABOUT THE WHOLE EXPERIENCE...
EXCEPT FOR THE PART ABOUT CHELLE BEING A SECRET-AGENT-TYPE CHICK...
THE WHOLE TIME WE DATED, SHE WAS CARRYING A CONCEALED WEAPON!
IT'S A GOOD THING I LET HER WIN ALL THE ARGUMENTS.
OH... SO "LOSING" WAS A STRATEGY?
PAIGE
2.18.2003

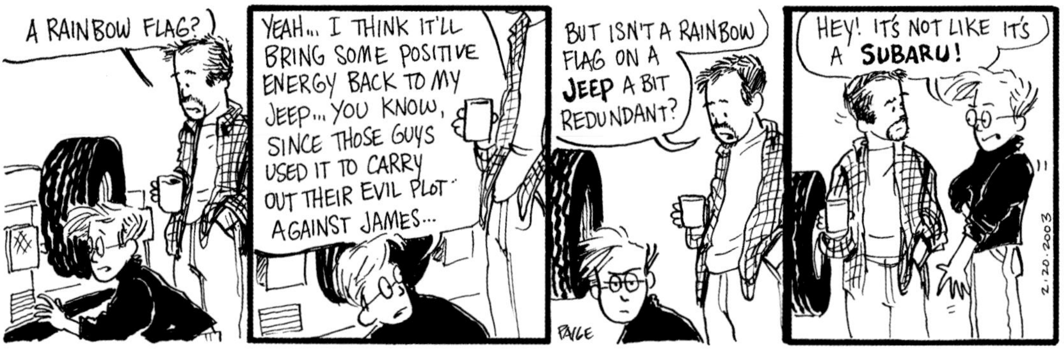
A RAINBOW FLAG?
YEAH... I THINK IT'LL BRING SOME POSITIVE ENERGY BACK TO MY JEEP... YOU KNOW, SINCE THOSE GUYS USED IT TO CARRY OUT THEIR EVIL PLOT AGAINST JAMES...
BUT ISN'T A RAINBOW FLAG ON A JEEP A BIT REDUNDANT?
HEY! IT'S NOT LIKE IT'S A SUBARU!
PAIGE
2.20.2003

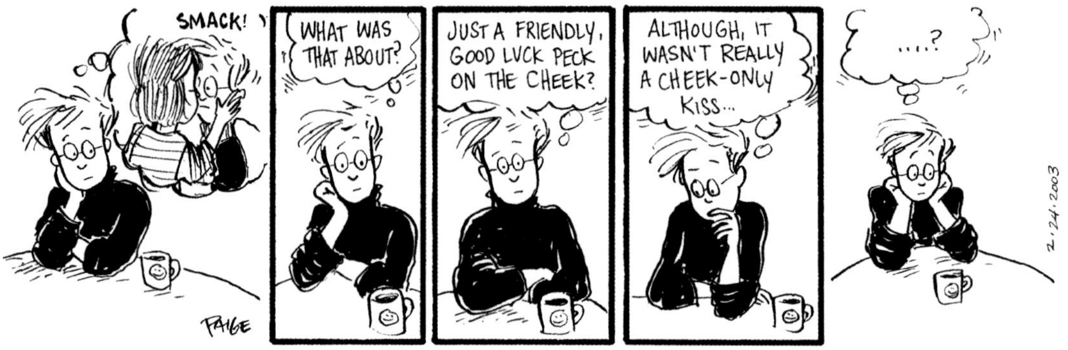
SMACK!
PAIGE
WHAT WAS THAT ABOUT?
JUST A FRIENDLY, GOOD LUCK PECK ON THE CHEEK?
ALTHOUGH, IT WASN'T REALLY A CHEEK-ONLY KISS...
....?
2.24.2003

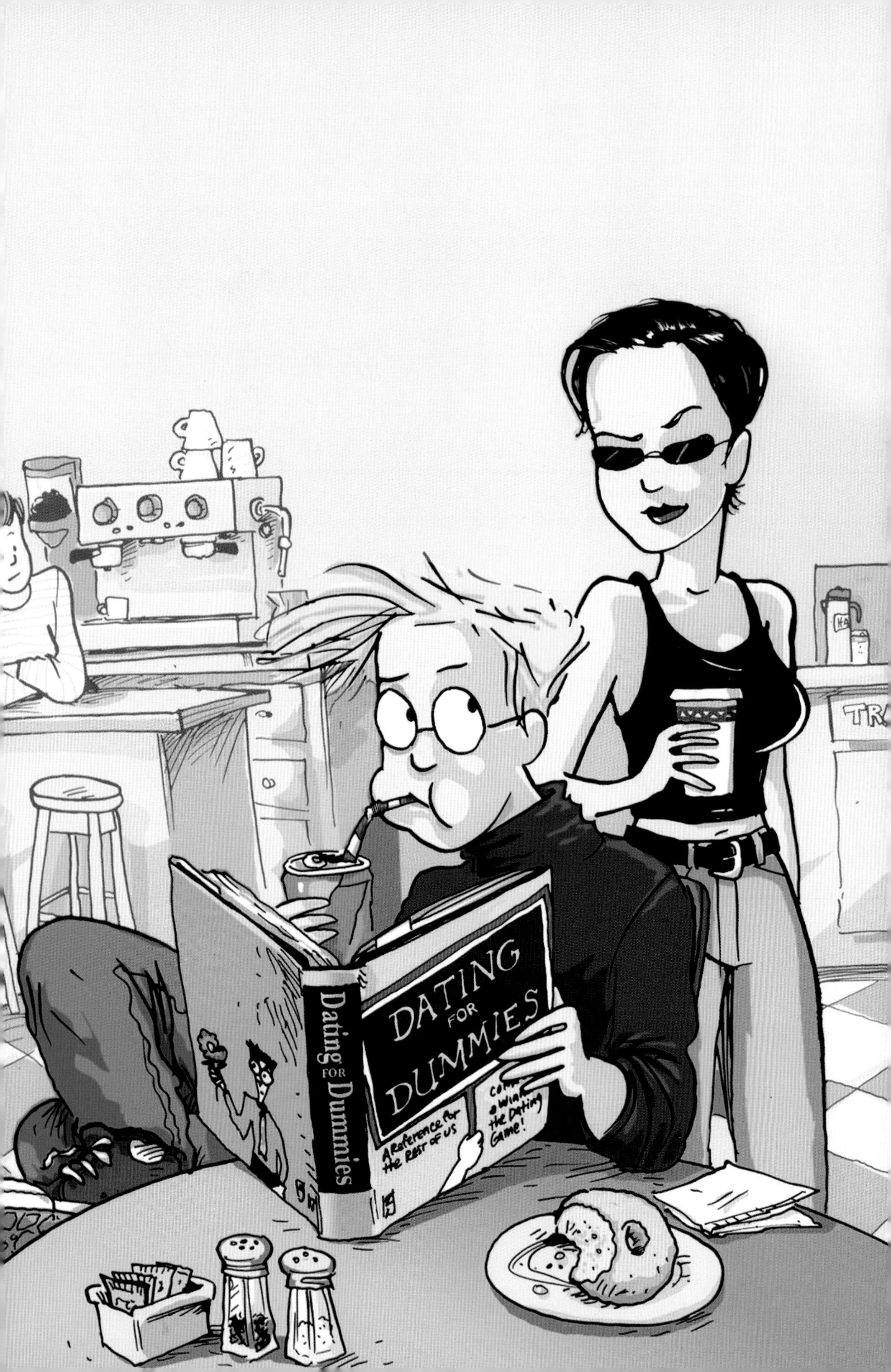
DATING FOR DUMMIES
Dating FOR Dummies
A Reference for the Rest of US
the Dating Game!

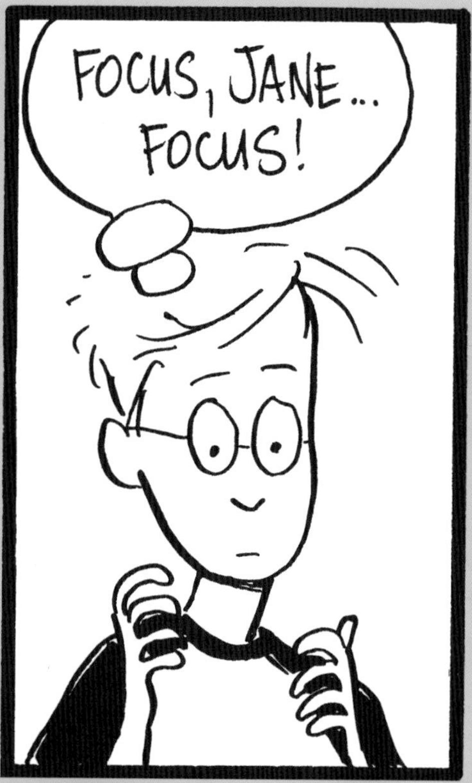
FOCUS, JANE...
FOCUS!

When Girls Collide (Boobapalooza)

Jane's cousin Bud lobbies to rename the comic due to recent character enhancements. Then Dorothy arranges for Jane to meet with a life coach. Because there are more things in Jane's life that need "fixing" than just her wardrobe.

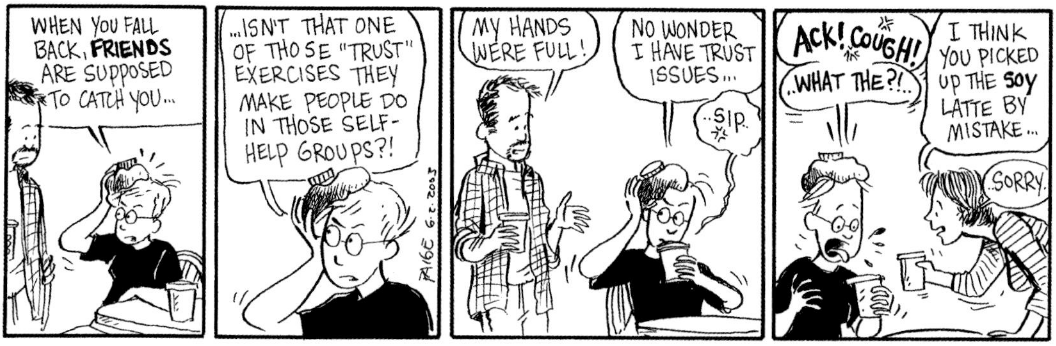
WHEN YOU FALL BACK, **FRIENDS** ARE SUPPOSED TO CATCH YOU...
...ISN'T THAT ONE OF THOSE "TRUST" EXERCISES THEY MAKE PEOPLE DO IN THOSE SELF-HELP GROUPS?!
PAIGE 6.2.2003
MY HANDS WERE FULL!
NO WONDER I HAVE TRUST ISSUES...
..SIP..
ACK! COUGH!
..WHAT THE?!..
I THINK YOU PICKED UP THE **SOY** LATTE BY MISTAKE...
..SORRY.

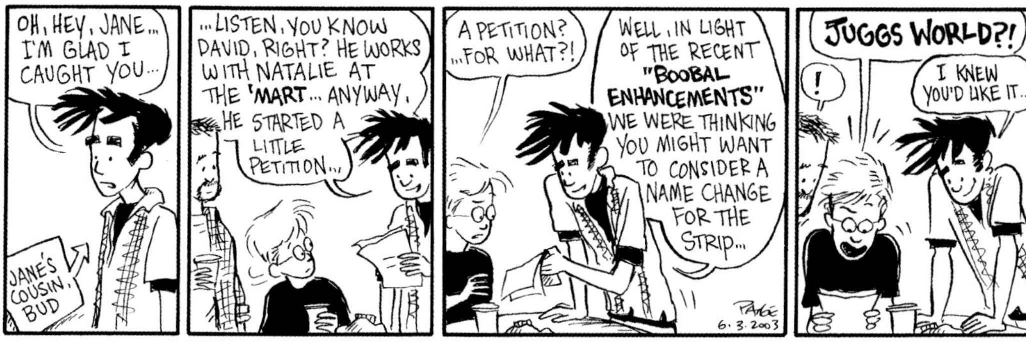
OH, HEY, JANE... I'M GLAD I CAUGHT YOU...
JANE'S COUSIN, BUD
...LISTEN, YOU KNOW DAVID, RIGHT? HE WORKS WITH NATALIE AT THE **'MART**... ANYWAY, HE STARTED A LITTLE PETITION...
A PETITION? ...FOR WHAT?!
WELL, IN LIGHT OF THE RECENT **"BOOBAL ENHANCEMENTS"** WE WERE THINKING YOU MIGHT WANT TO CONSIDER A NAME CHANGE FOR THE STRIP...
PAIGE 6.3.2003
JUGGS WORLD?!
!
I KNEW YOU'D LIKE IT...

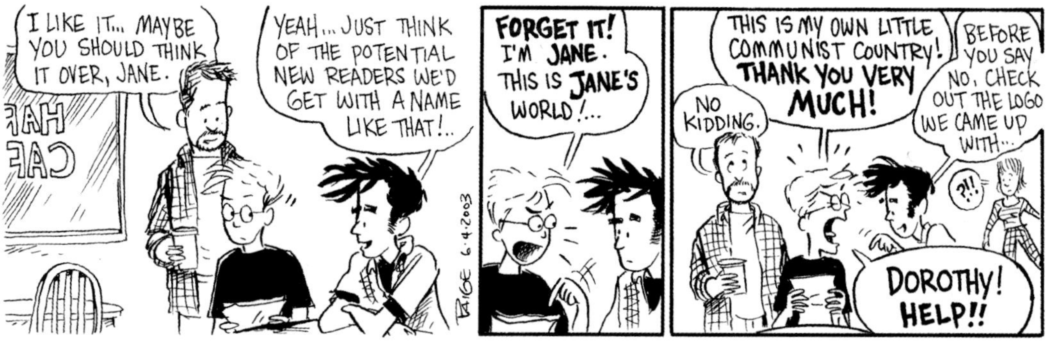
I LIKE IT... MAYBE YOU SHOULD THINK IT OVER, JANE.
YEAH... JUST THINK OF THE POTENTIAL NEW READERS WE'D GET WITH A NAME LIKE THAT!..
PAIGE 6.4.2003
FORGET IT! I'M **JANE**. THIS IS **JANE'S** WORLD!...
NO KIDDING.
THIS IS MY OWN LITTLE COMMUNIST COUNTRY! **THANK YOU VERY MUCH!**
BEFORE YOU SAY NO, CHECK OUT THE LOGO WE CAME UP WITH...
?!!
DOROTHY! HELP!!

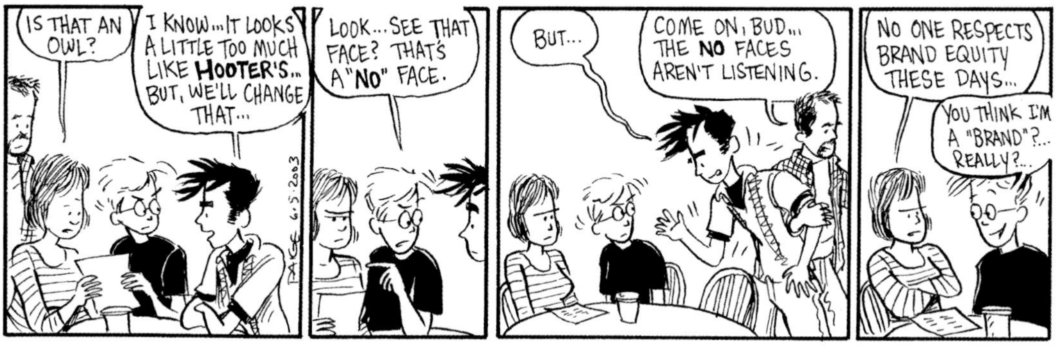
IS THAT AN OWL?
I KNOW... IT LOOKS A LITTLE TOO MUCH LIKE **HOOTER'S**.. BUT, WE'LL CHANGE THAT...
PAIGE 6.5.2003
LOOK... SEE THAT FACE? THAT'S A "**NO**" FACE.
BUT...
COME ON, BUD... THE **NO** FACES AREN'T LISTENING.
NO ONE RESPECTS BRAND EQUITY THESE DAYS...
YOU THINK I'M A "BRAND"?... REALLY?...

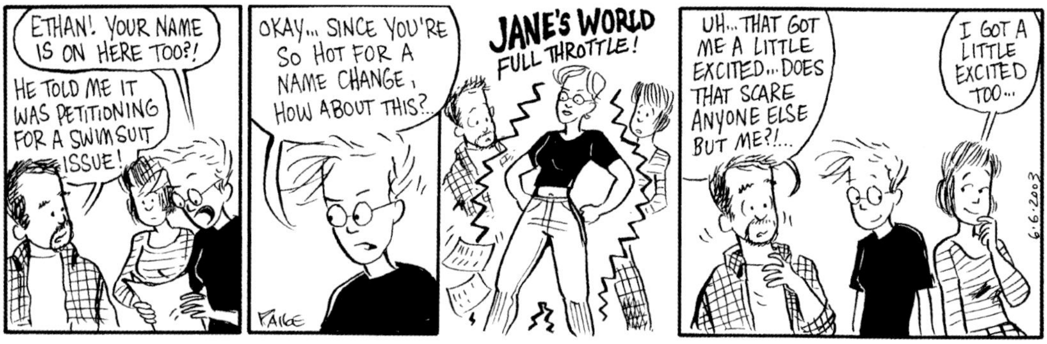
ETHAN! YOUR NAME IS ON HERE TOO?!
HE TOLD ME IT WAS PETITIONING FOR A SWIMSUIT ISSUE!
OKAY... SINCE YOU'RE SO HOT FOR A NAME CHANGE, HOW ABOUT THIS?..
PAIGE
JANE'S WORLD FULL THROTTLE!
UH... THAT GOT ME A LITTLE EXCITED... DOES THAT SCARE ANYONE ELSE BUT ME?!...
I GOT A LITTLE EXCITED TOO...
6.6.2003

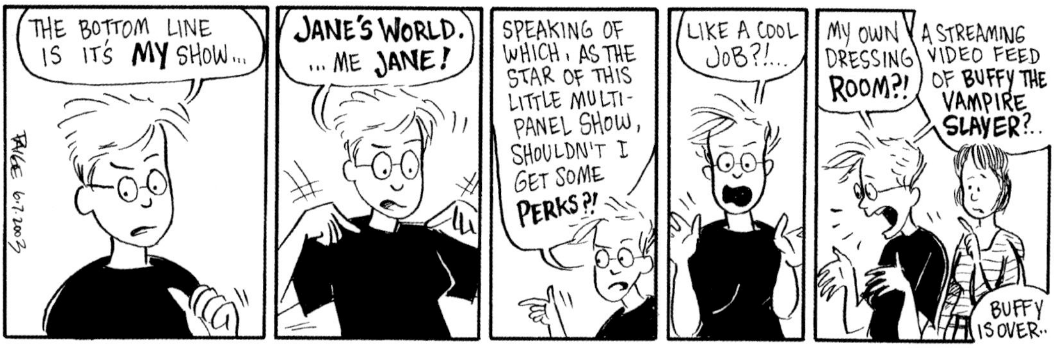
THE BOTTOM LINE IS IT'S MY SHOW...
PAIGE 6.7.2003
JANE'S WORLD. ... ME JANE!
SPEAKING OF WHICH, AS THE STAR OF THIS LITTLE MULTI-PANEL SHOW, SHOULDN'T I GET SOME PERKS?!
LIKE A COOL JOB?!...
MY OWN DRESSING ROOM?!
A STREAMING VIDEO FEED OF BUFFY THE VAMPIRE SLAYER?..
BUFFY IS OVER..

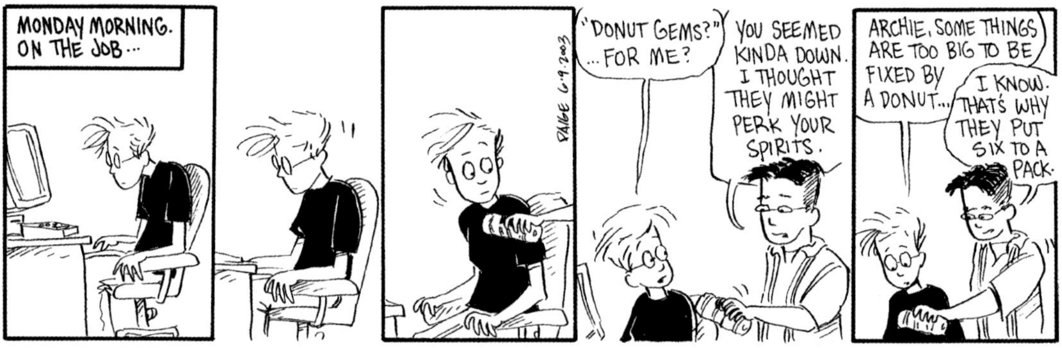
MONDAY MORNING. ON THE JOB...
PAIGE 6.9.2003
"DONUT GEMS?" ...FOR ME?
YOU SEEMED KINDA DOWN. I THOUGHT THEY MIGHT PERK YOUR SPIRITS.
ARCHIE, SOME THINGS ARE TOO BIG TO BE FIXED BY A DONUT...
I KNOW. THAT'S WHY THEY PUT SIX TO A PACK.

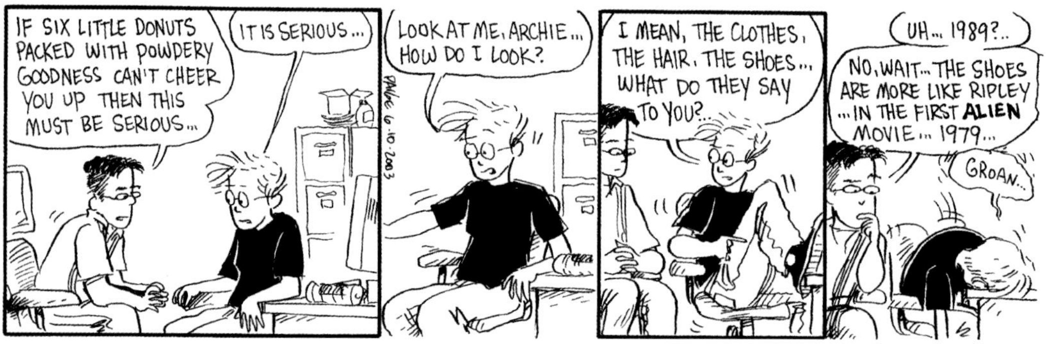
IF SIX LITTLE DONUTS PACKED WITH POWDERY GOODNESS CAN'T CHEER YOU UP THEN THIS MUST BE SERIOUS...
IT IS SERIOUS...
LOOK AT ME, ARCHIE... HOW DO I LOOK?
PAIGE 6.10.2003
I MEAN, THE CLOTHES, THE HAIR, THE SHOES... WHAT DO THEY SAY TO YOU?..
UH... 1989?..
NO, WAIT... THE SHOES ARE MORE LIKE RIPLEY ...IN THE FIRST ALIEN MOVIE... 1979...
GROAN...

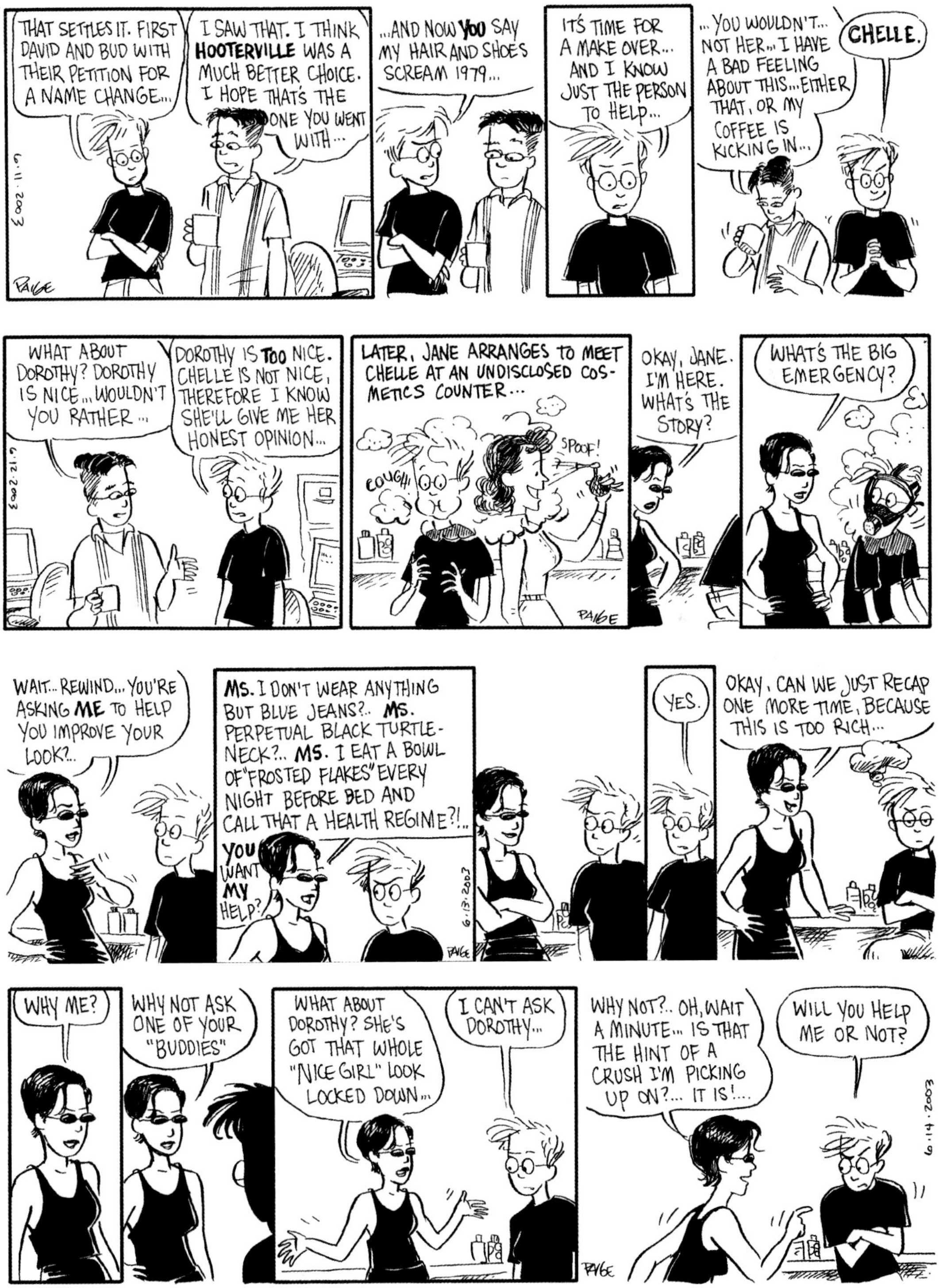
THAT SETTLES IT. FIRST DAVID AND BUD WITH THEIR PETITION FOR A NAME CHANGE...
I SAW THAT. I THINK HOOTERVILLE WAS A MUCH BETTER CHOICE. I HOPE THAT'S THE ONE YOU WENT WITH...
6.11.2003
PAIGE
...AND NOW YOU SAY MY HAIR AND SHOES SCREAM 1979...
IT'S TIME FOR A MAKE OVER... AND I KNOW JUST THE PERSON TO HELP...
...YOU WOULDN'T... NOT HER... I HAVE A BAD FEELING ABOUT THIS... EITHER THAT, OR MY COFFEE IS KICKING IN...
CHELLE.
WHAT ABOUT DOROTHY? DOROTHY IS NICE... WOULDN'T YOU RATHER...
DOROTHY IS TOO NICE. CHELLE IS NOT NICE, THEREFORE I KNOW SHE'LL GIVE ME HER HONEST OPINION...
6.12.2003
LATER, JANE ARRANGES TO MEET CHELLE AT AN UNDISCLOSED COSMETICS COUNTER...
COUGH!
SPOOF!
PAIGE
OKAY, JANE. I'M HERE. WHAT'S THE STORY?
WHAT'S THE BIG EMERGENCY?
WAIT... REWIND... YOU'RE ASKING ME TO HELP YOU IMPROVE YOUR LOOK?..
MS. I DON'T WEAR ANYTHING BUT BLUE JEANS?.. MS. PERPETUAL BLACK TURTLE-NECK?.. MS. I EAT A BOWL OF "FROSTED FLAKES" EVERY NIGHT BEFORE BED AND CALL THAT A HEALTH REGIME?!..
YOU WANT MY HELP?
6.13.2003
PAIGE
YES.
OKAY, CAN WE JUST RECAP ONE MORE TIME, BECAUSE THIS IS TOO RICH...
WHY ME?
WHY NOT ASK ONE OF YOUR "BUDDIES"
WHAT ABOUT DOROTHY? SHE'S GOT THAT WHOLE "NICE GIRL" LOOK LOCKED DOWN...
I CAN'T ASK DOROTHY...
PAIGE
WHY NOT?.. OH, WAIT A MINUTE... IS THAT THE HINT OF A CRUSH I'M PICKING UP ON?... IT IS!...
WILL YOU HELP ME OR NOT?
6.14.2003

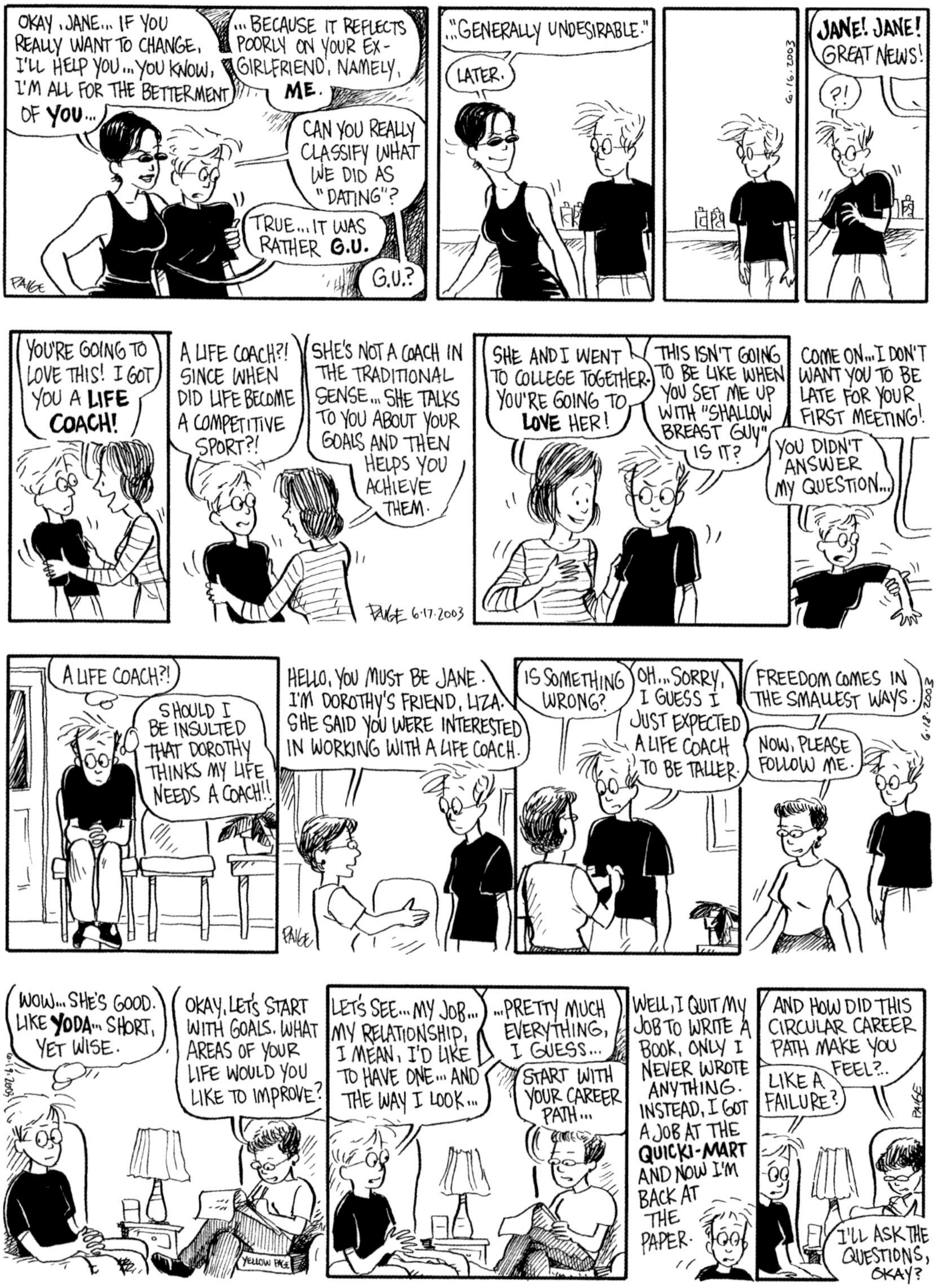
OKAY, JANE... IF YOU REALLY WANT TO CHANGE, I'LL HELP YOU... YOU KNOW, I'M ALL FOR THE BETTERMENT OF YOU...
...BECAUSE IT REFLECTS POORLY ON YOUR EX-GIRLFRIEND, NAMELY, ME.
CAN YOU REALLY CLASSIFY WHAT WE DID AS "DATING"?
TRUE... IT WAS RATHER G.U.
G.U.?
..."GENERALLY UNDESIRABLE."
LATER.
6.16.2003
JANE! JANE! GREAT NEWS!
?!
YOU'RE GOING TO LOVE THIS! I GOT YOU A LIFE COACH!
A LIFE COACH?! SINCE WHEN DID LIFE BECOME A COMPETITIVE SPORT?!
SHE'S NOT A COACH IN THE TRADITIONAL SENSE... SHE TALKS TO YOU ABOUT YOUR GOALS AND THEN HELPS YOU ACHIEVE THEM.
6.17.2003
SHE AND I WENT TO COLLEGE TOGETHER. YOU'RE GOING TO LOVE HER!
THIS ISN'T GOING TO BE LIKE WHEN YOU SET ME UP WITH "SHALLOW BREAST GUY" IS IT?
COME ON... I DON'T WANT YOU TO BE LATE FOR YOUR FIRST MEETING!
YOU DIDN'T ANSWER MY QUESTION...
A LIFE COACH?!
SHOULD I BE INSULTED THAT DOROTHY THINKS MY LIFE NEEDS A COACH!!
HELLO, YOU MUST BE JANE. I'M DOROTHY'S FRIEND, LIZA. SHE SAID YOU WERE INTERESTED IN WORKING WITH A LIFE COACH.
IS SOMETHING WRONG?
OH... SORRY, I GUESS I JUST EXPECTED A LIFE COACH TO BE TALLER.
FREEDOM COMES IN THE SMALLEST WAYS.
NOW, PLEASE FOLLOW ME.
6.18.2003
WOW... SHE'S GOOD. LIKE YODA... SHORT, YET WISE.
6.19.2003
OKAY, LET'S START WITH GOALS. WHAT AREAS OF YOUR LIFE WOULD YOU LIKE TO IMPROVE?
YELLOW PAGE
LET'S SEE... MY JOB... MY RELATIONSHIP, I MEAN, I'D LIKE TO HAVE ONE... AND THE WAY I LOOK...
...PRETTY MUCH EVERYTHING, I GUESS...
START WITH YOUR CAREER PATH...
WELL, I QUIT MY JOB TO WRITE A BOOK, ONLY I NEVER WROTE ANYTHING. INSTEAD, I GOT A JOB AT THE QUICKI-MART AND NOW I'M BACK AT THE PAPER.
AND HOW DID THIS CIRCULAR CAREER PATH MAKE YOU FEEL?..
LIKE A FAILURE?
I'LL ASK THE QUESTIONS, OKAY?

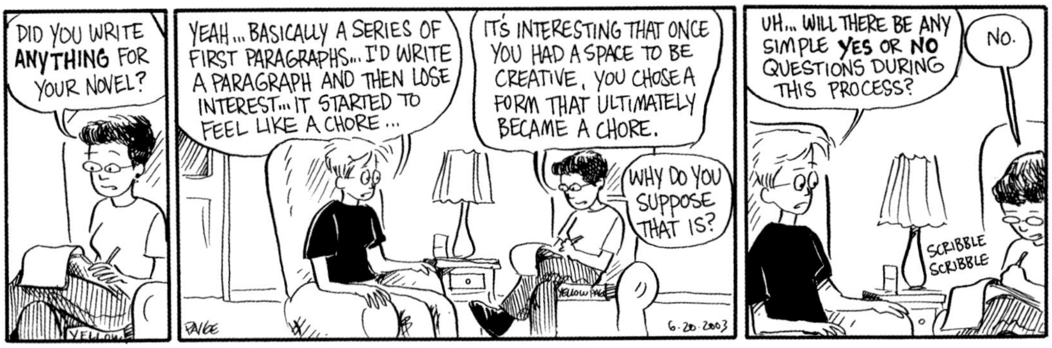
DID YOU WRITE ANYTHING FOR YOUR NOVEL?
YELLOW
YEAH... BASICALLY A SERIES OF FIRST PARAGRAPHS... I'D WRITE A PARAGRAPH AND THEN LOSE INTEREST... IT STARTED TO FEEL LIKE A CHORE...
IT'S INTERESTING THAT ONCE YOU HAD A SPACE TO BE CREATIVE, YOU CHOSE A FORM THAT ULTIMATELY BECAME A CHORE.
WHY DO YOU SUPPOSE THAT IS?
PAIGE
6·20·2003
UH... WILL THERE BE ANY SIMPLE YES OR NO QUESTIONS DURING THIS PROCESS?
NO.
SCRIBBLE SCRIBBLE

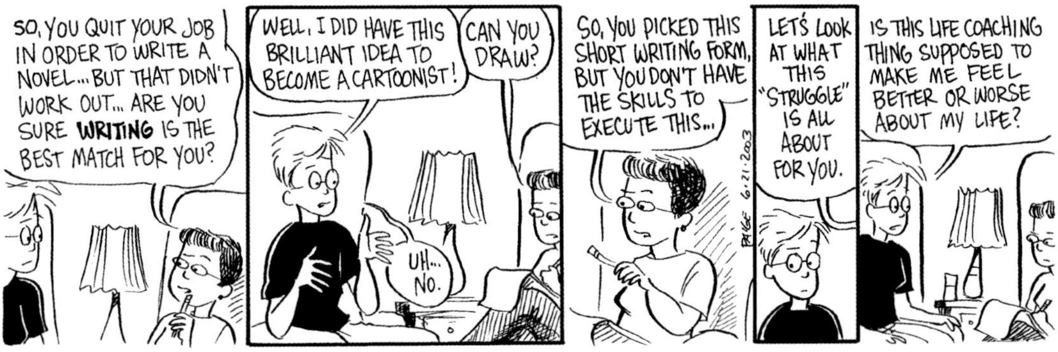
SO, YOU QUIT YOUR JOB IN ORDER TO WRITE A NOVEL... BUT THAT DIDN'T WORK OUT... ARE YOU SURE WRITING IS THE BEST MATCH FOR YOU?
WELL, I DID HAVE THIS BRILLIANT IDEA TO BECOME A CARTOONIST!
CAN YOU DRAW?
UH... NO.
SO, YOU PICKED THIS SHORT WRITING FORM, BUT YOU DON'T HAVE THE SKILLS TO EXECUTE THIS...
6·21·2003
PAIGE
LET'S LOOK AT WHAT THIS "STRUGGLE" IS ALL ABOUT FOR YOU.
IS THIS LIFE COACHING THING SUPPOSED TO MAKE ME FEEL BETTER OR WORSE ABOUT MY LIFE?

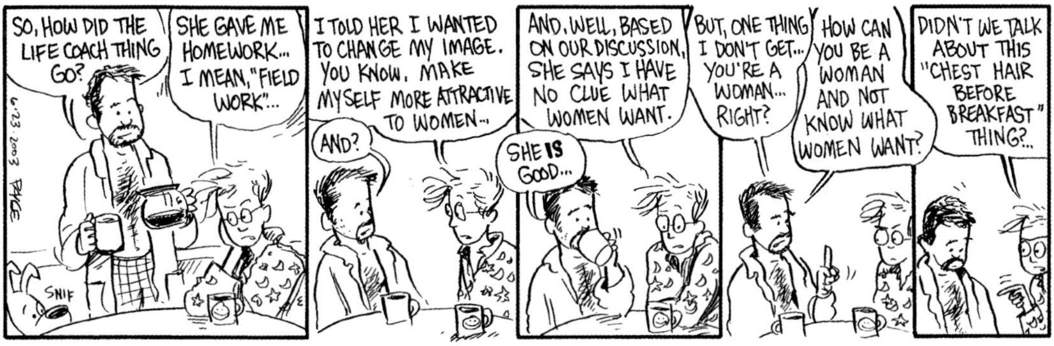
SO, HOW DID THE LIFE COACH THING GO?
SHE GAVE ME HOMEWORK... I MEAN, "FIELD WORK"...
6·23·2003
PAIGE
SNIF
I TOLD HER I WANTED TO CHANGE MY IMAGE. YOU KNOW, MAKE MYSELF MORE ATTRACTIVE TO WOMEN...
AND?
AND, WELL, BASED ON OUR DISCUSSION, SHE SAYS I HAVE NO CLUE WHAT WOMEN WANT.
SHE IS GOOD...
BUT, ONE THING I DON'T GET... YOU'RE A WOMAN... RIGHT?
HOW CAN YOU BE A WOMAN AND NOT KNOW WHAT WOMEN WANT?
DIDN'T WE TALK ABOUT THIS "CHEST HAIR BEFORE BREAKFAST" THING?...

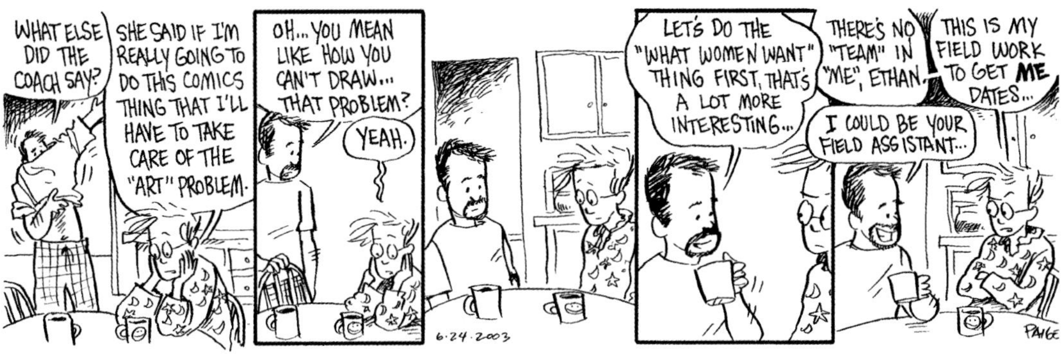
WHAT ELSE DID THE COACH SAY?
SHE SAID IF I'M REALLY GOING TO DO THIS COMICS THING THAT I'LL HAVE TO TAKE CARE OF THE "ART" PROBLEM.
OH... YOU MEAN LIKE HOW YOU CAN'T DRAW... THAT PROBLEM?
YEAH.
6·24·2003
LET'S DO THE "WHAT WOMEN WANT" THING FIRST, THAT'S A LOT MORE INTERESTING...
I COULD BE YOUR FIELD ASSISTANT...
THERE'S NO "TEAM" IN "ME", ETHAN.
THIS IS MY FIELD WORK TO GET ME DATES...
PAIGE

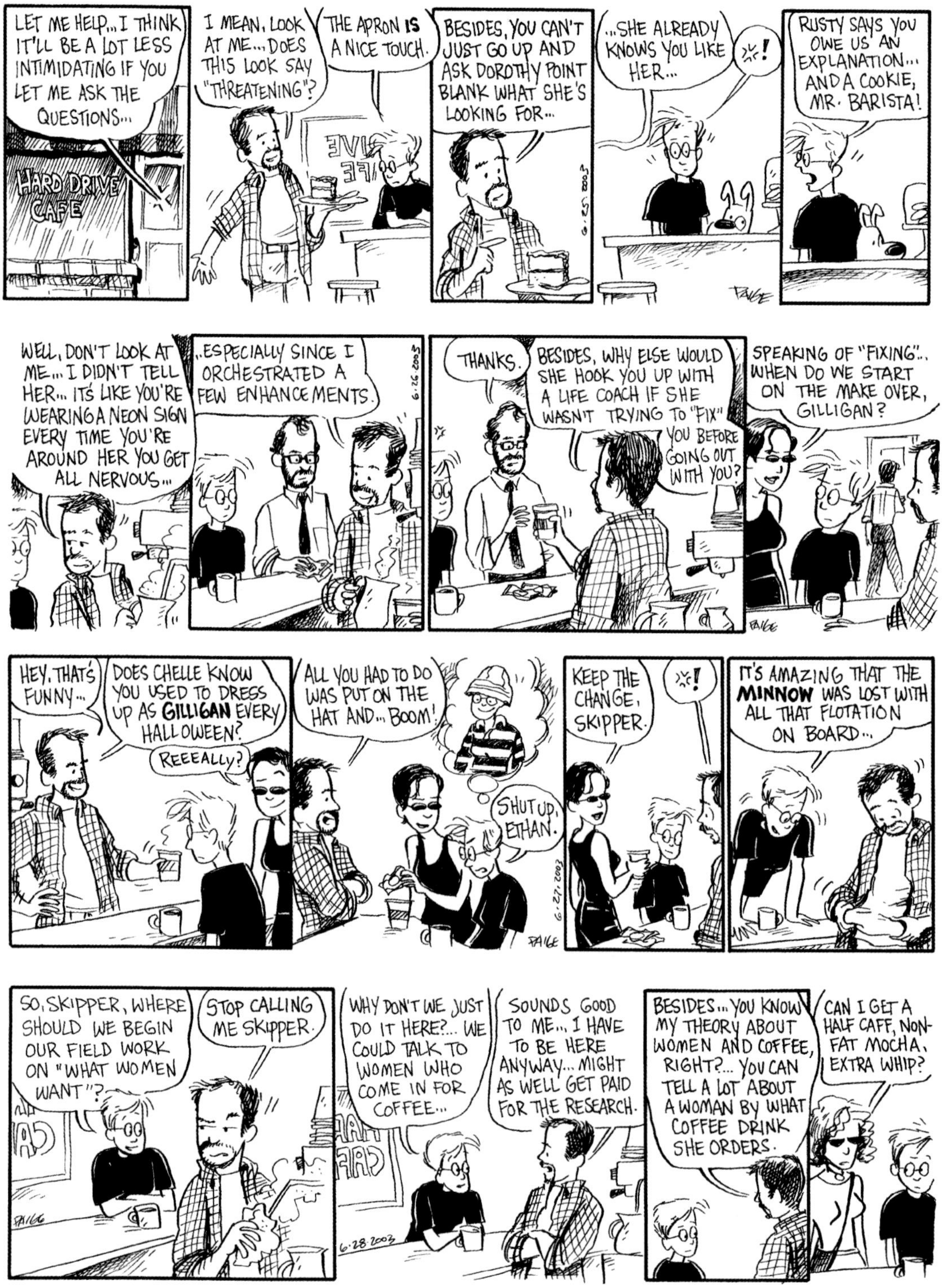
LET ME HELP... I THINK IT'LL BE A LOT LESS INTIMIDATING IF YOU LET ME ASK THE QUESTIONS...
HARD DRIVE CAFE
I MEAN, LOOK AT ME... DOES THIS LOOK SAY "THREATENING"?
THE APRON IS A NICE TOUCH.
BESIDES, YOU CAN'T JUST GO UP AND ASK DOROTHY POINT BLANK WHAT SHE'S LOOKING FOR...
6-25-2003
...SHE ALREADY KNOWS YOU LIKE HER...
!
RUSTY SAYS YOU OWE US AN EXPLANATION... AND A COOKIE, MR. BARISTA!
PAIGE
WELL, DON'T LOOK AT ME... I DIDN'T TELL HER... IT'S LIKE YOU'RE WEARING A NEON SIGN EVERY TIME YOU'RE AROUND HER YOU GET ALL NERVOUS...
..ESPECIALLY SINCE I ORCHESTRATED A FEW ENHANCEMENTS.
6-26-2003
THANKS.
BESIDES, WHY ELSE WOULD SHE HOOK YOU UP WITH A LIFE COACH IF SHE WASN'T TRYING TO "FIX" YOU BEFORE GOING OUT WITH YOU?
SPEAKING OF "FIXING".. WHEN DO WE START ON THE MAKE OVER, GILLIGAN?
PAIGE
HEY, THAT'S FUNNY...
DOES CHELLE KNOW YOU USED TO DRESS UP AS GILLIGAN EVERY HALLOWEEN?
REEEALLY?
ALL YOU HAD TO DO WAS PUT ON THE HAT AND... BOOM!
SHUT UP, ETHAN.
6-27-2003
PAIGE
KEEP THE CHANGE, SKIPPER.
!
IT'S AMAZING THAT THE MINNOW WAS LOST WITH ALL THAT FLOTATION ON BOARD...
SO, SKIPPER, WHERE SHOULD WE BEGIN OUR FIELD WORK ON "WHAT WOMEN WANT"?
STOP CALLING ME SKIPPER.
PAIGE
WHY DON'T WE JUST DO IT HERE?... WE COULD TALK TO WOMEN WHO COME IN FOR COFFEE...
6-28-2003
SOUNDS GOOD TO ME... I HAVE TO BE HERE ANYWAY... MIGHT AS WELL GET PAID FOR THE RESEARCH.
BESIDES... YOU KNOW MY THEORY ABOUT WOMEN AND COFFEE, RIGHT?... YOU CAN TELL A LOT ABOUT A WOMAN BY WHAT COFFEE DRINK SHE ORDERS.
CAN I GET A HALF CAFF, NON-FAT MOCHA, EXTRA WHIP?

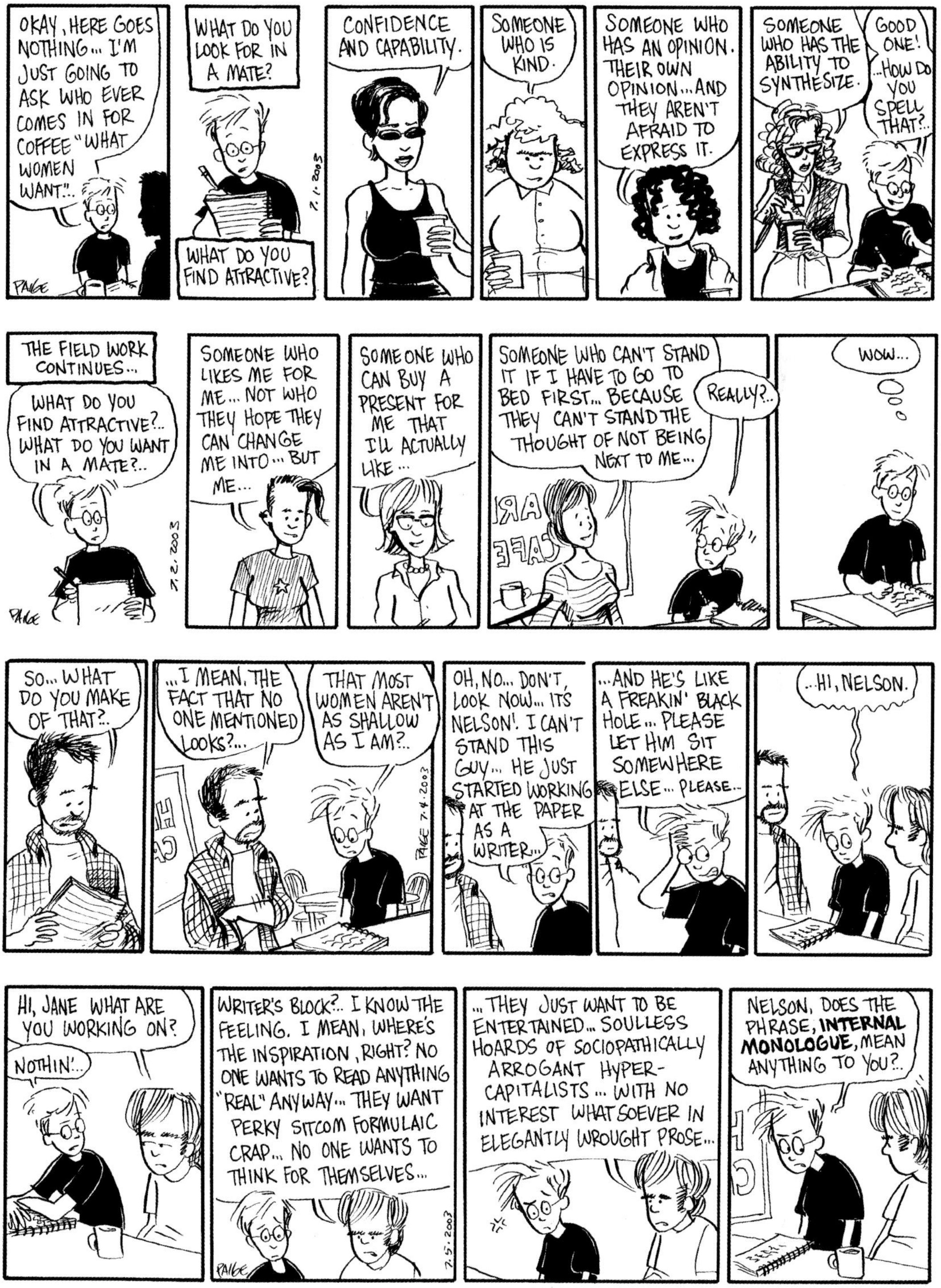

OKAY, HERE GOES NOTHING... I'M JUST GOING TO ASK WHO EVER COMES IN FOR COFFEE "WHAT WOMEN WANT."..
WHAT DO YOU LOOK FOR IN A MATE?
WHAT DO YOU FIND ATTRACTIVE?
7.1.2003
CONFIDENCE AND CAPABILITY.
SOMEONE WHO IS KIND.
SOMEONE WHO HAS AN OPINION. THEIR OWN OPINION... AND THEY AREN'T AFRAID TO EXPRESS IT.
SOMEONE WHO HAS THE ABILITY TO SYNTHESIZE.
GOOD ONE! ...HOW DO YOU SPELL THAT?..
THE FIELD WORK CONTINUES...
WHAT DO YOU FIND ATTRACTIVE?.. WHAT DO YOU WANT IN A MATE?..
7.2.2003
SOMEONE WHO LIKES ME FOR ME... NOT WHO THEY HOPE THEY CAN CHANGE ME INTO... BUT ME...
SOMEONE WHO CAN BUY A PRESENT FOR ME THAT I'LL ACTUALLY LIKE...
SOMEONE WHO CAN'T STAND IT IF I HAVE TO GO TO BED FIRST... BECAUSE THEY CAN'T STAND THE THOUGHT OF NOT BEING NEXT TO ME...
REALLY?..
WOW...
SO... WHAT DO YOU MAKE OF THAT?..
...I MEAN, THE FACT THAT NO ONE MENTIONED LOOKS?...
THAT MOST WOMEN AREN'T AS SHALLOW AS I AM?..
7.4.2003
OH, NO... DON'T LOOK NOW... IT'S NELSON! I CAN'T STAND THIS GUY... HE JUST STARTED WORKING AT THE PAPER AS A WRITER...
...AND HE'S LIKE A FREAKIN' BLACK HOLE... PLEASE LET HIM SIT SOMEWHERE ELSE... PLEASE..
...HI, NELSON.
HI, JANE WHAT ARE YOU WORKING ON?
NOTHIN'...
WRITER'S BLOCK?.. I KNOW THE FEELING. I MEAN, WHERE'S THE INSPIRATION, RIGHT? NO ONE WANTS TO READ ANYTHING "REAL" ANYWAY... THEY WANT PERKY SITCOM FORMULAIC CRAP... NO ONE WANTS TO THINK FOR THEMSELVES...
7.5.2003
...THEY JUST WANT TO BE ENTERTAINED... SOULLESS HOARDS OF SOCIOPATHICALLY ARROGANT HYPER-CAPITALISTS... WITH NO INTEREST WHATSOEVER IN ELEGANTLY WROUGHT PROSE...
NELSON, DOES THE PHRASE, **INTERNAL MONOLOGUE**, MEAN ANYTHING TO YOU?..

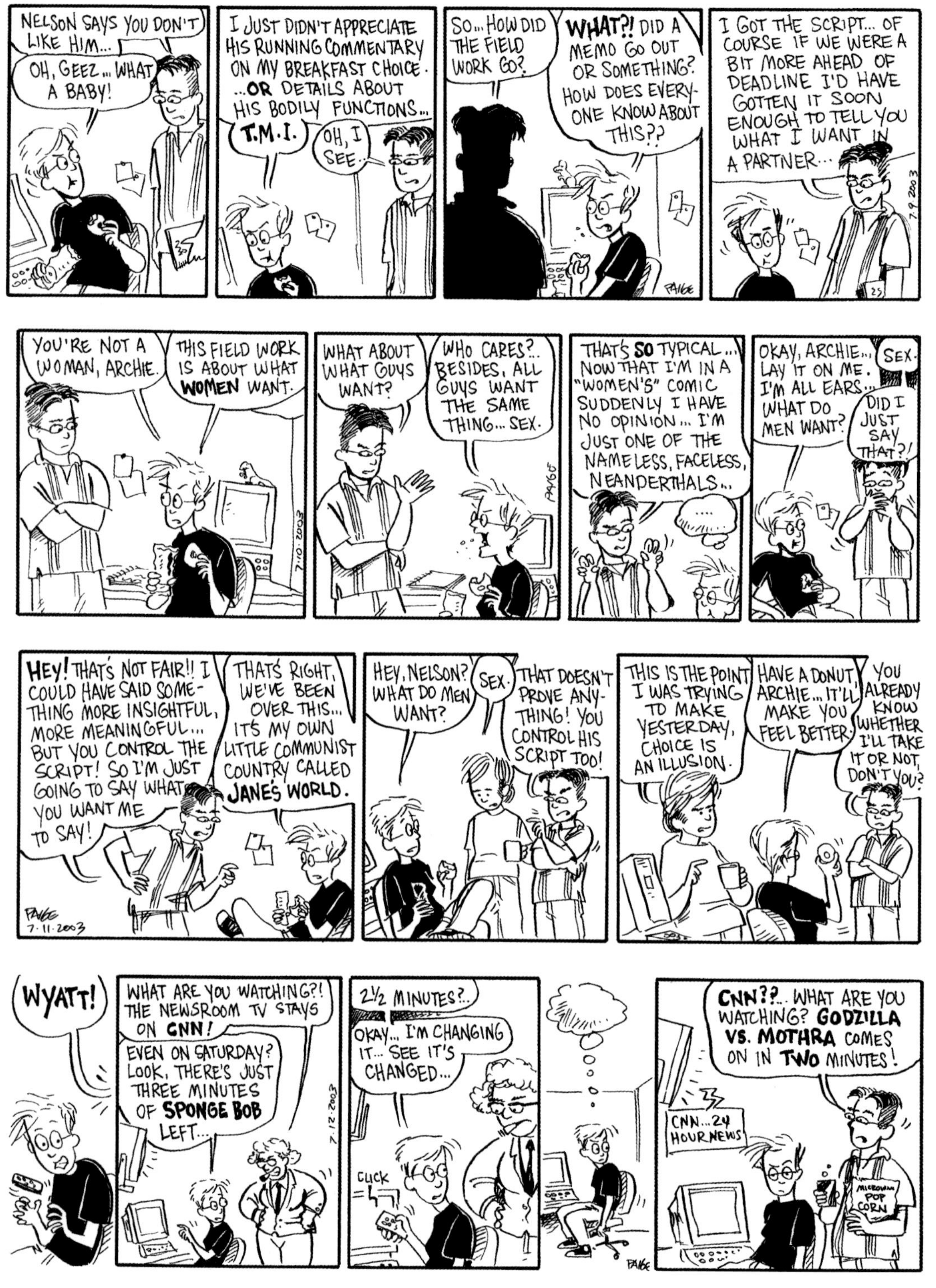

NELSON SAYS YOU DON'T LIKE HIM...
OH, GEEZ... WHAT A BABY!
I JUST DIDN'T APPRECIATE HIS RUNNING COMMENTARY ON MY BREAKFAST CHOICE. ...OR DETAILS ABOUT HIS BODILY FUNCTIONS...
T.M.I.
OH, I SEE...
SO... HOW DID THE FIELD WORK GO?
WHAT?! DID A MEMO GO OUT OR SOMETHING? HOW DOES EVERYONE KNOW ABOUT THIS??
PAIGE
I GOT THE SCRIPT... OF COURSE IF WE WERE A BIT MORE AHEAD OF DEADLINE I'D HAVE GOTTEN IT SOON ENOUGH TO TELL YOU WHAT I WANT IN A PARTNER...
7.9.2003
YOU'RE NOT A WOMAN, ARCHIE.
THIS FIELD WORK IS ABOUT WHAT WOMEN WANT.
7.10.2003
WHAT ABOUT WHAT GUYS WANT?
WHO CARES?.. BESIDES, ALL GUYS WANT THE SAME THING... SEX.
PAIGE
THAT'S SO TYPICAL... NOW THAT I'M IN A "WOMEN'S" COMIC SUDDENLY I HAVE NO OPINION... I'M JUST ONE OF THE NAMELESS, FACELESS, NEANDERTHALS...
.....
OKAY, ARCHIE... LAY IT ON ME. I'M ALL EARS... WHAT DO MEN WANT?
SEX.
DID I JUST SAY THAT?!
HEY! THAT'S NOT FAIR!! I COULD HAVE SAID SOMETHING MORE INSIGHTFUL, MORE MEANINGFUL... BUT YOU CONTROL THE SCRIPT! SO I'M JUST GOING TO SAY WHAT YOU WANT ME TO SAY!
THAT'S RIGHT, WE'VE BEEN OVER THIS... IT'S MY OWN LITTLE COMMUNIST COUNTRY CALLED JANE'S WORLD.
PAIGE
7.11.2003
HEY, NELSON? WHAT DO MEN WANT?
SEX.
THAT DOESN'T PROVE ANYTHING! YOU CONTROL HIS SCRIPT TOO!
THIS IS THE POINT I WAS TRYING TO MAKE YESTERDAY, CHOICE IS AN ILLUSION.
HAVE A DONUT, ARCHIE... IT'LL MAKE YOU FEEL BETTER.
YOU ALREADY KNOW WHETHER I'LL TAKE IT OR NOT, DON'T YOU?
WYATT!
WHAT ARE YOU WATCHING?! THE NEWSROOM TV STAYS ON CNN!
EVEN ON SATURDAY? LOOK, THERE'S JUST THREE MINUTES OF SPONGE BOB LEFT...
7.12.2003
2½ MINUTES?..
OKAY... I'M CHANGING IT... SEE IT'S CHANGED...
CLICK
PAIGE
CNN??.. WHAT ARE YOU WATCHING? GODZILLA VS. MOTHRA COMES ON IN TWO MINUTES!
CNN... 24 HOUR NEWS
MICROWAVE POP CORN

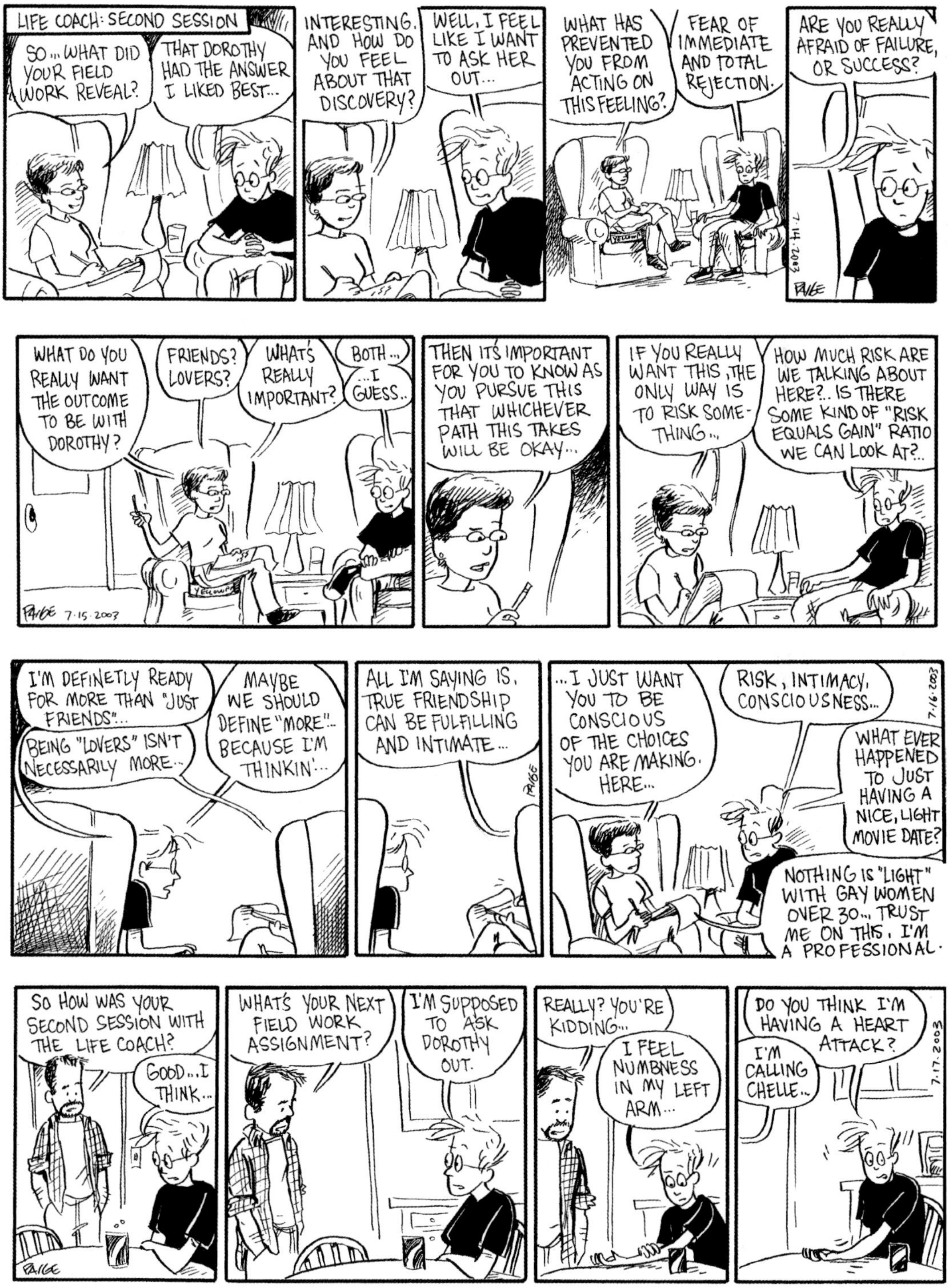
LIFE COACH: SECOND SESSION
SO... WHAT DID YOUR FIELD WORK REVEAL?
THAT DOROTHY HAD THE ANSWER I LIKED BEST...
INTERESTING. AND HOW DO YOU FEEL ABOUT THAT DISCOVERY?
WELL, I FEEL LIKE I WANT TO ASK HER OUT...
WHAT HAS PREVENTED YOU FROM ACTING ON THIS FEELING?
FEAR OF IMMEDIATE AND TOTAL REJECTION.
ARE YOU REALLY AFRAID OF FAILURE, OR SUCCESS?
7·14·2003
PAIGE
WHAT DO YOU REALLY WANT THE OUTCOME TO BE WITH DOROTHY?
FRIENDS? LOVERS?
WHAT'S REALLY IMPORTANT?
BOTH... ...I GUESS..
PAIGE 7·15·2003
THEN IT'S IMPORTANT FOR YOU TO KNOW AS YOU PURSUE THIS THAT WHICHEVER PATH THIS TAKES WILL BE OKAY...
IF YOU REALLY WANT THIS, THE ONLY WAY IS TO RISK SOMETHING...
HOW MUCH RISK ARE WE TALKING ABOUT HERE?.. IS THERE SOME KIND OF "RISK EQUALS GAIN" RATIO WE CAN LOOK AT?..
I'M DEFINETLY READY FOR MORE THAN "JUST FRIENDS"...
BEING "LOVERS" ISN'T NECESSARILY MORE...
MAYBE WE SHOULD DEFINE "MORE"... BECAUSE I'M THINKIN'...
ALL I'M SAYING IS, TRUE FRIENDSHIP CAN BE FULFILLING AND INTIMATE...
PAIGE
...I JUST WANT YOU TO BE CONSCIOUS OF THE CHOICES YOU ARE MAKING HERE...
RISK, INTIMACY, CONSCIOUSNESS...
7·16·2003
WHAT EVER HAPPENED TO JUST HAVING A NICE, LIGHT MOVIE DATE?
NOTHING IS "LIGHT" WITH GAY WOMEN OVER 30... TRUST ME ON THIS. I'M A PROFESSIONAL.
SO HOW WAS YOUR SECOND SESSION WITH THE LIFE COACH?
GOOD... I THINK...
PAIGE
WHAT'S YOUR NEXT FIELD WORK ASSIGNMENT?
I'M SUPPOSED TO ASK DOROTHY OUT.
REALLY? YOU'RE KIDDING...
I FEEL NUMBNESS IN MY LEFT ARM...
DO YOU THINK I'M HAVING A HEART ATTACK?
I'M CALLING CHELLE...
7·17·2003

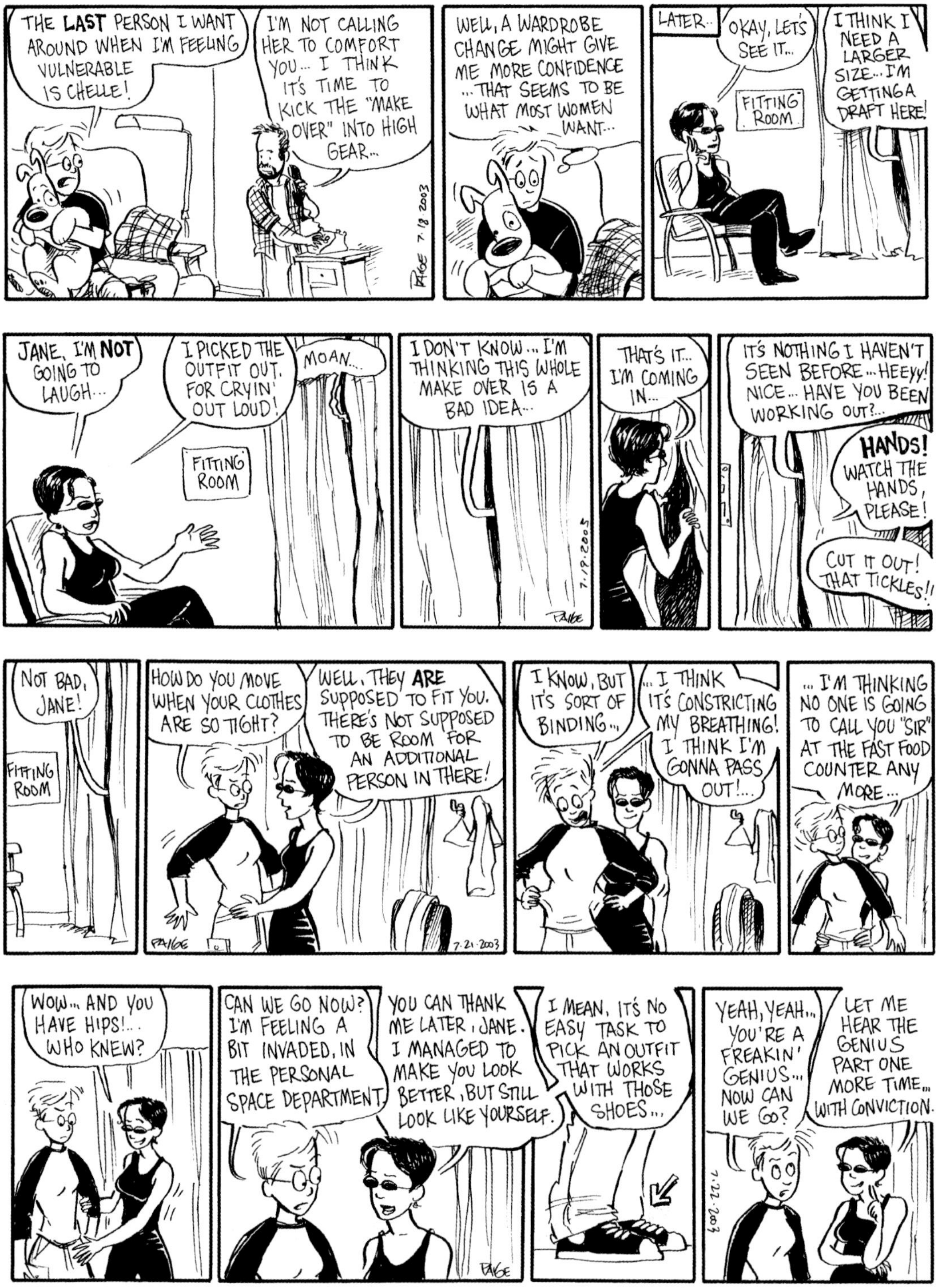
THE **LAST** PERSON I WANT AROUND WHEN I'M FEELING VULNERABLE IS CHELLE!
I'M NOT CALLING HER TO COMFORT YOU... I THINK IT'S TIME TO KICK THE "MAKE OVER" INTO HIGH GEAR...
7.18.2003
PAIGE
WELL, A WARDROBE CHANGE MIGHT GIVE ME MORE CONFIDENCE ...THAT SEEMS TO BE WHAT MOST WOMEN WANT...
LATER..
OKAY, LET'S SEE IT...
FITTING ROOM
I THINK I NEED A LARGER SIZE... I'M GETTING A DRAFT HERE!
JANE, I'M **NOT** GOING TO LAUGH...
I PICKED THE OUTFIT OUT, FOR CRYIN' OUT LOUD!
MOAN...
FITTING ROOM
I DON'T KNOW... I'M THINKING THIS WHOLE MAKE OVER IS A BAD IDEA...
7.19.2003
PAIGE
THAT'S IT... I'M COMING IN...
IT'S NOTHING I HAVEN'T SEEN BEFORE... HEEYY! NICE... HAVE YOU BEEN WORKING OUT?...
HANDS! WATCH THE HANDS, PLEASE!
CUT IT OUT! THAT TICKLES!!
NOT BAD, JANE!
FITTING ROOM
PAIGE
HOW DO YOU MOVE WHEN YOUR CLOTHES ARE SO TIGHT?
WELL, THEY **ARE** SUPPOSED TO FIT YOU. THERE'S NOT SUPPOSED TO BE ROOM FOR AN ADDITIONAL PERSON IN THERE!
7.21.2003
I KNOW, BUT IT'S SORT OF BINDING...
... I THINK IT'S CONSTRICTING MY BREATHING! I THINK I'M GONNA PASS OUT!...
... I'M THINKING NO ONE IS GOING TO CALL YOU "SIR" AT THE FAST FOOD COUNTER ANY MORE...
WOW... AND YOU HAVE HIPS!... WHO KNEW?
CAN WE GO NOW? I'M FEELING A BIT INVADED, IN THE PERSONAL SPACE DEPARTMENT.
YOU CAN THANK ME LATER, JANE. I MANAGED TO MAKE YOU LOOK BETTER, BUT STILL LOOK LIKE YOURSELF.
PAIGE
I MEAN, IT'S NO EASY TASK TO PICK AN OUTFIT THAT WORKS WITH THOSE SHOES...
YEAH, YEAH... YOU'RE A FREAKIN' GENIUS... NOW CAN WE GO?
7.22.2003
LET ME HEAR THE GENIUS PART ONE MORE TIME... WITH CONVICTION.

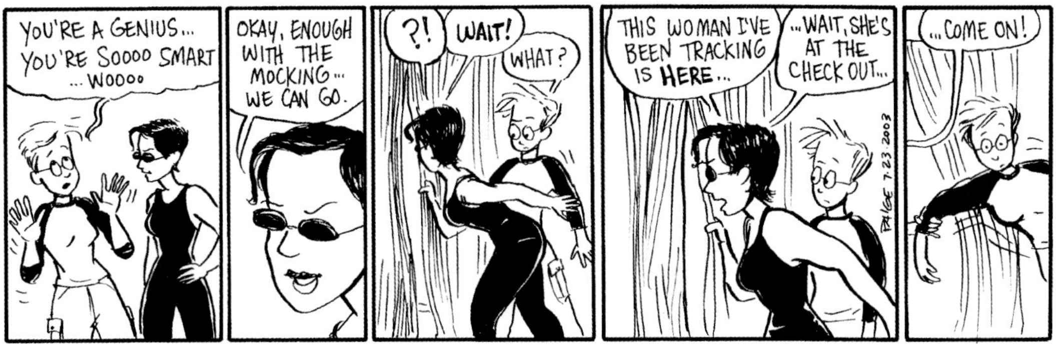
YOU'RE A GENIUS... YOU'RE SOOOO SMART ...WOOOO
OKAY, ENOUGH WITH THE MOCKING... WE CAN GO.
?!
WAIT!
WHAT?
THIS WOMAN I'VE BEEN TRACKING IS HERE...
...WAIT, SHE'S AT THE CHECK OUT...
PAIGE 7.23.2003
...COME ON!

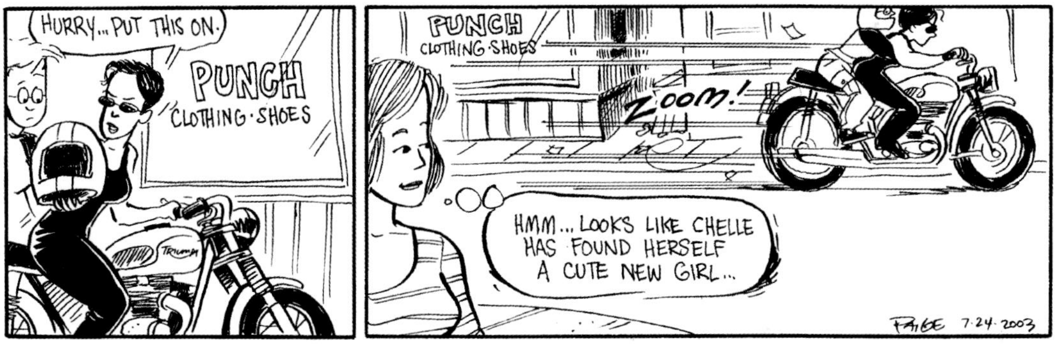
HURRY...PUT THIS ON.
PUNCH CLOTHING·SHOES
PUNCH CLOTHING·SHOES
ZOOM!
HMM... LOOKS LIKE CHELLE HAS FOUND HERSELF A CUTE NEW GIRL...
PAIGE 7·24·2003

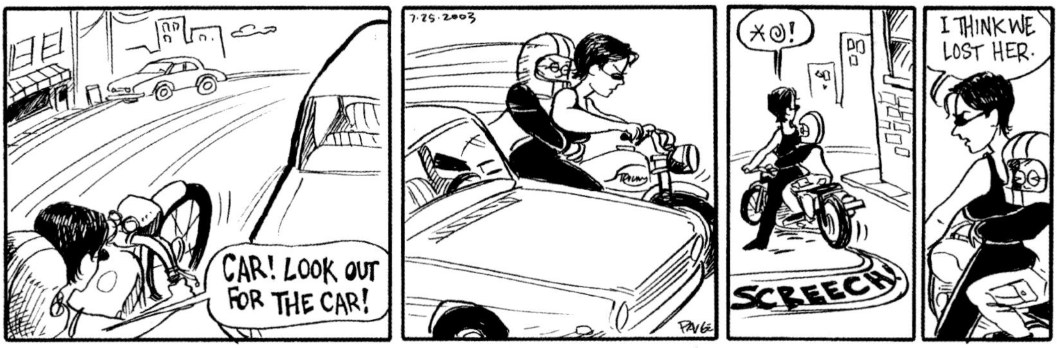
CAR! LOOK OUT FOR THE CAR!
7.25.2003
PAIGE
*@!
SCREECH
I THINK WE LOST HER.

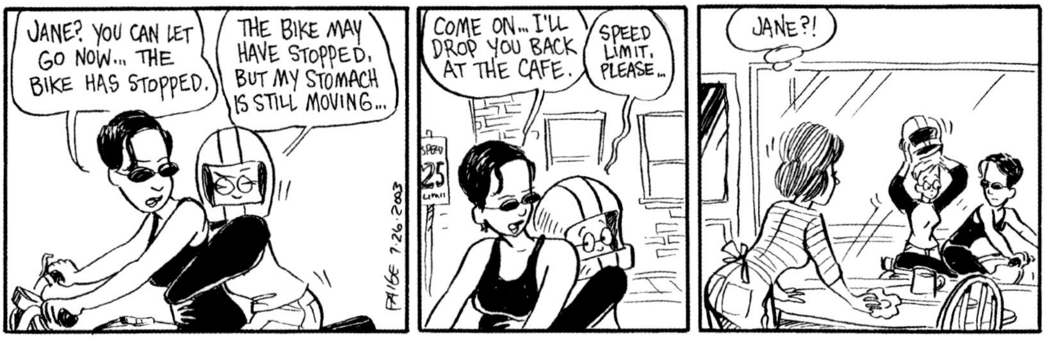
JANE? YOU CAN LET GO NOW... THE BIKE HAS STOPPED.
THE BIKE MAY HAVE STOPPED, BUT MY STOMACH IS STILL MOVING...
PAIGE 7.26.2003
COME ON... I'LL DROP YOU BACK AT THE CAFE.
SPEED LIMIT, PLEASE...
SPEED 25 LIMIT
JANE?!

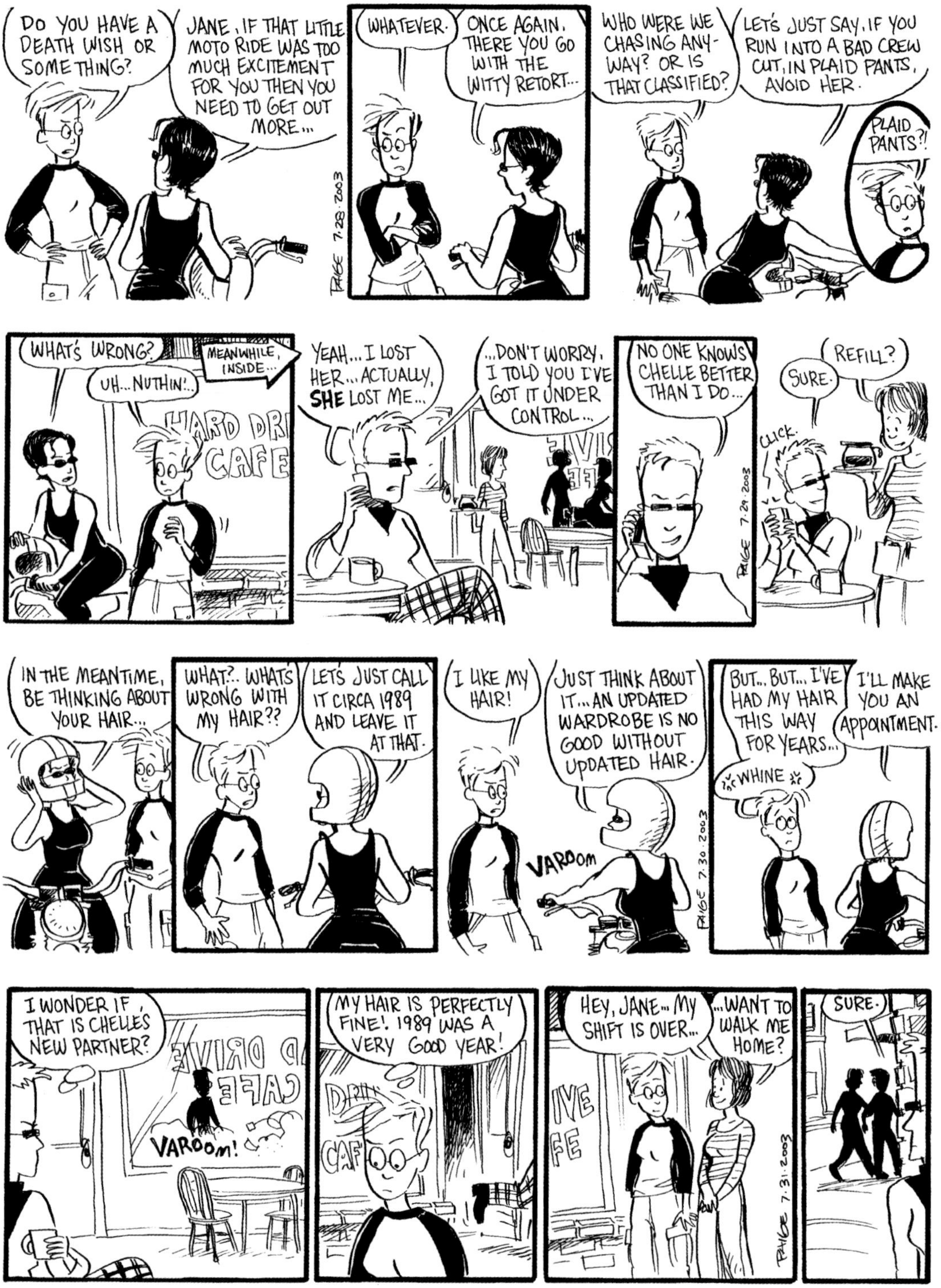
DO YOU HAVE A DEATH WISH OR SOMETHING?
JANE, IF THAT LITTLE MOTO RIDE WAS TOO MUCH EXCITEMENT FOR YOU THEN YOU NEED TO GET OUT MORE...
PAIGE 7.28.2003
WHATEVER.
ONCE AGAIN, THERE YOU GO WITH THE WITTY RETORT...
WHO WERE WE CHASING ANY-WAY? OR IS THAT CLASSIFIED?
LET'S JUST SAY, IF YOU RUN INTO A BAD CREW CUT, IN PLAID PANTS, AVOID HER.
PLAID PANTS?!
WHAT'S WRONG?
UH... NUTHIN'...
MEANWHILE, INSIDE...
HARD DRI
CAFE
YEAH... I LOST HER... ACTUALLY, SHE LOST ME...
...DON'T WORRY, I TOLD YOU I'VE GOT IT UNDER CONTROL...
NO ONE KNOWS CHELLE BETTER THAN I DO...
PAIGE 7.29.2003
CLICK.
SURE.
REFILL?
IN THE MEANTIME, BE THINKING ABOUT YOUR HAIR...
WHAT?.. WHAT'S WRONG WITH MY HAIR??
LET'S JUST CALL IT CIRCA 1989 AND LEAVE IT AT THAT.
I LIKE MY HAIR!
JUST THINK ABOUT IT... AN UPDATED WARDROBE IS NO GOOD WITHOUT UPDATED HAIR.
VAROOM
PAIGE 7.30.2003
BUT... BUT... I'VE HAD MY HAIR THIS WAY FOR YEARS...
WHINE
I'LL MAKE YOU AN APPOINTMENT.
I WONDER IF THAT IS CHELLE'S NEW PARTNER?
VAROOM!
MY HAIR IS PERFECTLY FINE! 1989 WAS A VERY GOOD YEAR!
HEY, JANE... MY SHIFT IS OVER...
...WANT TO WALK ME HOME?
PAIGE 7.31.2003
SURE.

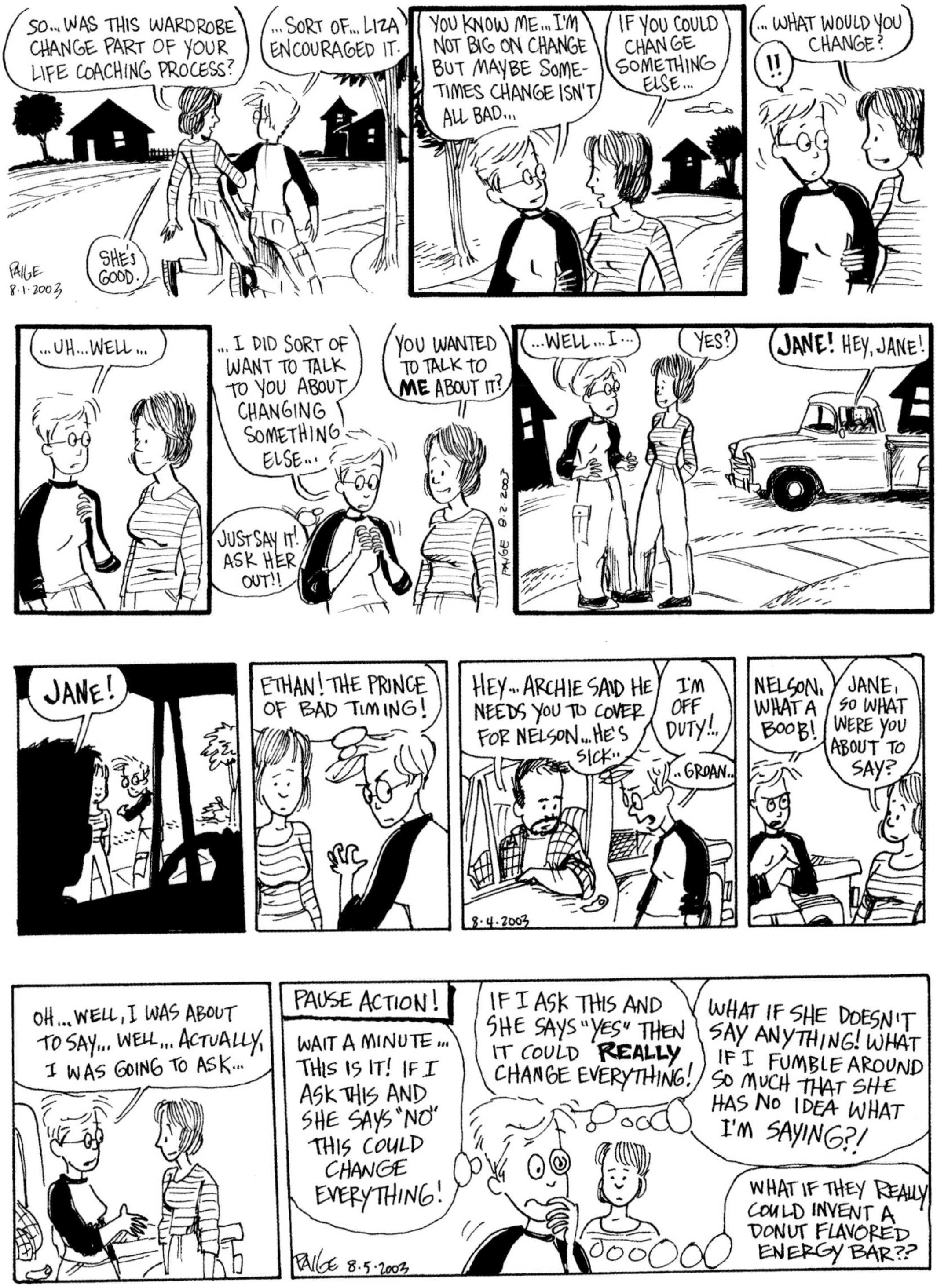
SO... WAS THIS WARDROBE CHANGE PART OF YOUR LIFE COACHING PROCESS?
...SORT OF... LIZA ENCOURAGED IT.
SHE'S GOOD.
PAIGE 8·1·2003
YOU KNOW ME... I'M NOT BIG ON CHANGE BUT MAYBE SOMETIMES CHANGE ISN'T ALL BAD...
IF YOU COULD CHANGE SOMETHING ELSE...
...WHAT WOULD YOU CHANGE?
!!
...UH...WELL...
...I DID SORT OF WANT TO TALK TO YOU ABOUT CHANGING SOMETHING ELSE...
YOU WANTED TO TALK TO **ME** ABOUT IT?
JUST SAY IT! ASK HER OUT!!
PAIGE 8·2·2003
...WELL...I...
YES?
JANE! HEY, JANE!
JANE!
ETHAN! THE PRINCE OF BAD TIMING!
HEY... ARCHIE SAID HE NEEDS YOU TO COVER FOR NELSON... HE'S SICK...
I'M OFF DUTY!..
..GROAN..
8·4·2003
NELSON, WHAT A BOOB!
JANE, SO WHAT WERE YOU ABOUT TO SAY?
OH...WELL, I WAS ABOUT TO SAY... WELL... ACTUALLY, I WAS GOING TO ASK...
PAUSE ACTION!
WAIT A MINUTE... THIS IS IT! IF I ASK THIS AND SHE SAYS "NO" THIS COULD CHANGE EVERYTHING!
IF I ASK THIS AND SHE SAYS "YES" THEN IT COULD **REALLY** CHANGE EVERYTHING!
WHAT IF SHE DOESN'T SAY ANYTHING! WHAT IF I FUMBLE AROUND SO MUCH THAT SHE HAS NO IDEA WHAT I'M SAYING?!
WHAT IF THEY REALLY COULD INVENT A DONUT FLAVORED ENERGY BAR??
PAIGE 8·5·2003

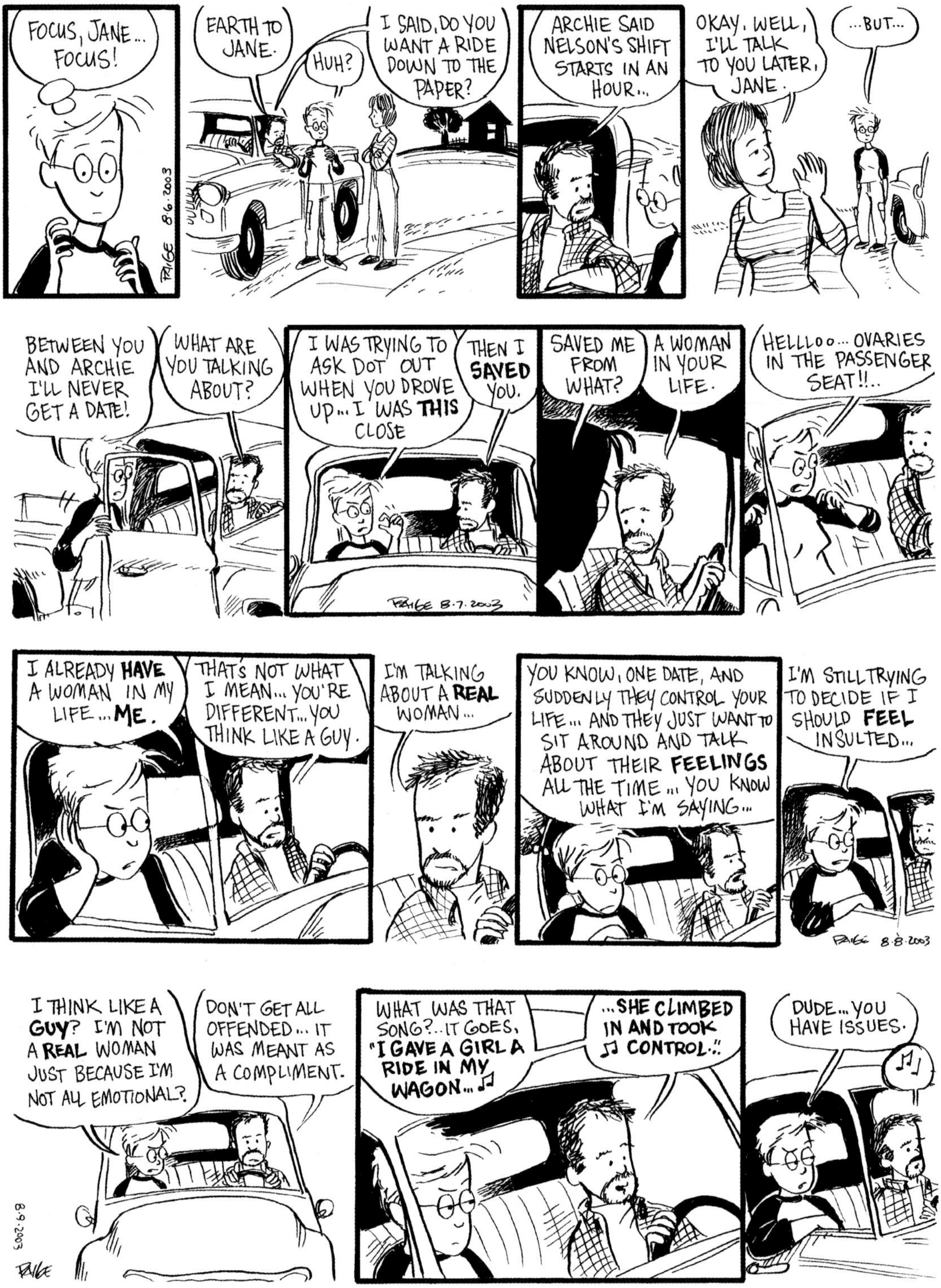
FOCUS, JANE... FOCUS!
PAIGE 8.6.2003
EARTH TO JANE.
HUH?
I SAID, DO YOU WANT A RIDE DOWN TO THE PAPER?
ARCHIE SAID NELSON'S SHIFT STARTS IN AN HOUR...
OKAY. WELL, I'LL TALK TO YOU LATER, JANE.
...BUT...
BETWEEN YOU AND ARCHIE I'LL NEVER GET A DATE!
WHAT ARE YOU TALKING ABOUT?
I WAS TRYING TO ASK DOT OUT WHEN YOU DROVE UP... I WAS THIS CLOSE
THEN I SAVED YOU.
PAIGE 8.7.2003
SAVED ME FROM WHAT?
A WOMAN IN YOUR LIFE.
HELLLOO... OVARIES IN THE PASSENGER SEAT!!...
I ALREADY HAVE A WOMAN IN MY LIFE... ME.
THAT'S NOT WHAT I MEAN... YOU'RE DIFFERENT... YOU THINK LIKE A GUY.
I'M TALKING ABOUT A REAL WOMAN...
YOU KNOW, ONE DATE, AND SUDDENLY THEY CONTROL YOUR LIFE... AND THEY JUST WANT TO SIT AROUND AND TALK ABOUT THEIR FEELINGS ALL THE TIME... YOU KNOW WHAT I'M SAYING...
I'M STILL TRYING TO DECIDE IF I SHOULD FEEL INSULTED...
PAIGE 8.8.2003
I THINK LIKE A GUY? I'M NOT A REAL WOMAN JUST BECAUSE I'M NOT ALL EMOTIONAL?
DON'T GET ALL OFFENDED... IT WAS MEANT AS A COMPLIMENT.
8.9.2003
PAIGE
WHAT WAS THAT SONG?.. IT GOES, "I GAVE A GIRL A RIDE IN MY WAGON... ♫
...SHE CLIMBED IN AND TOOK ♫ CONTROL."
DUDE... YOU HAVE ISSUES.

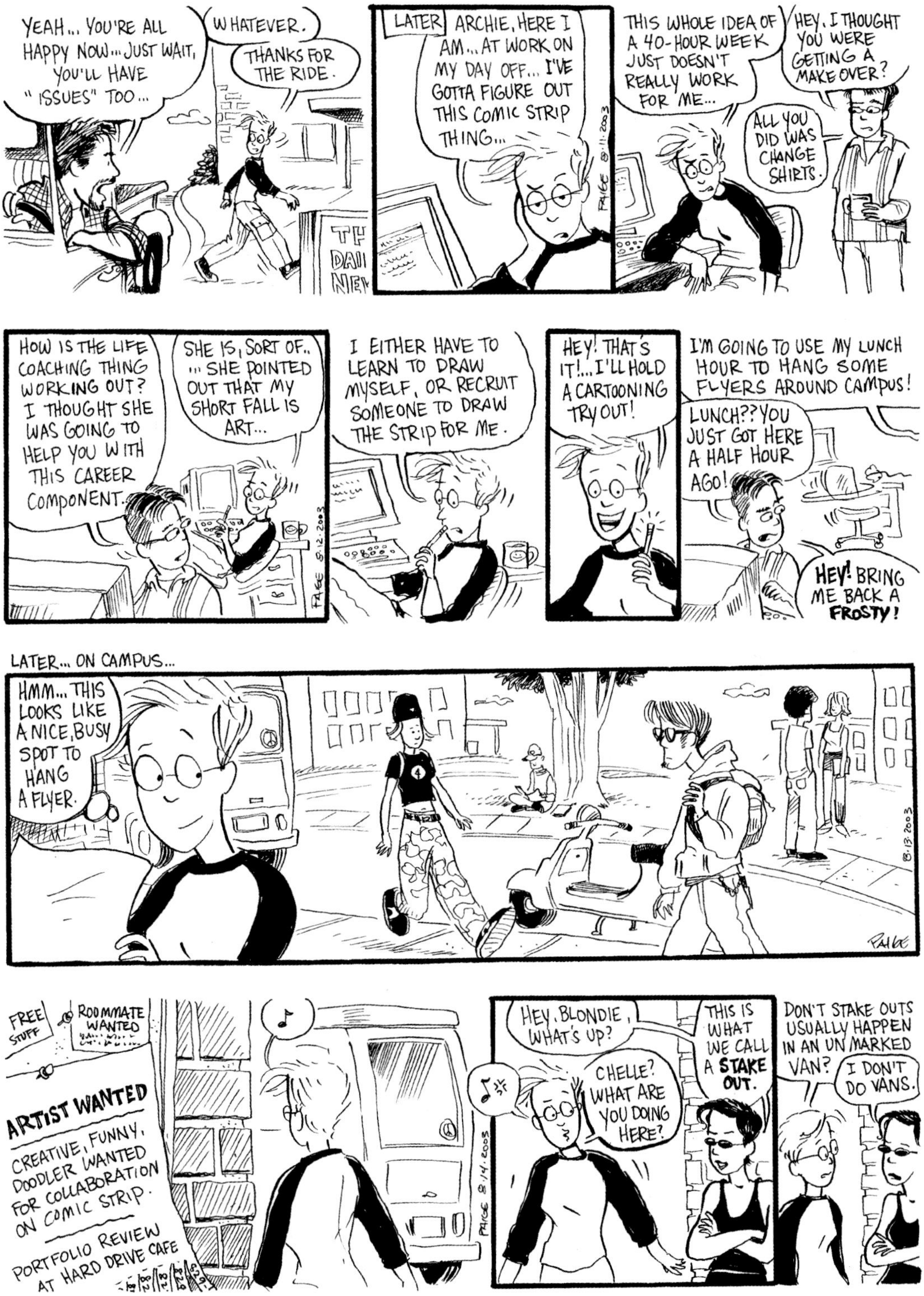
YEAH... YOU'RE ALL HAPPY NOW... JUST WAIT, YOU'LL HAVE "ISSUES" TOO...
WHATEVER.
THANKS FOR THE RIDE.
LATER
ARCHIE, HERE I AM... AT WORK ON MY DAY OFF... I'VE GOTTA FIGURE OUT THIS COMIC STRIP THING...
THIS WHOLE IDEA OF A 40-HOUR WEEK JUST DOESN'T REALLY WORK FOR ME...
HEY, I THOUGHT YOU WERE GETTING A MAKE OVER?
ALL YOU DID WAS CHANGE SHIRTS.
PAIGE 8.11.2003
HOW IS THE LIFE COACHING THING WORKING OUT? I THOUGHT SHE WAS GOING TO HELP YOU WITH THIS CAREER COMPONENT...
SHE IS, SORT OF.. ...SHE POINTED OUT THAT MY SHORT FALL IS ART...
I EITHER HAVE TO LEARN TO DRAW MYSELF, OR RECRUIT SOMEONE TO DRAW THE STRIP FOR ME.
HEY! THAT'S IT!... I'LL HOLD A CARTOONING TRYOUT!
I'M GOING TO USE MY LUNCH HOUR TO HANG SOME FLYERS AROUND CAMPUS!
LUNCH?? YOU JUST GOT HERE A HALF HOUR AGO!
HEY! BRING ME BACK A FROSTY!
PAIGE 8.12.2003
LATER... ON CAMPUS...
HMM... THIS LOOKS LIKE A NICE, BUSY SPOT TO HANG A FLYER.
8.13.2003
PAIGE
FREE STUFF
ROOMMATE WANTED
ARTIST WANTED
CREATIVE, FUNNY, DOODLER WANTED FOR COLLABORATION ON COMIC STRIP.
PORTFOLIO REVIEW AT HARD DRIVE CAFE
PAIGE 8.14.2003
HEY, BLONDIE, WHAT'S UP?
CHELLE? WHAT ARE YOU DOING HERE?
THIS IS WHAT WE CALL A STAKE OUT.
DON'T STAKE OUTS USUALLY HAPPEN IN AN UNMARKED VAN?
I DON'T DO VANS.

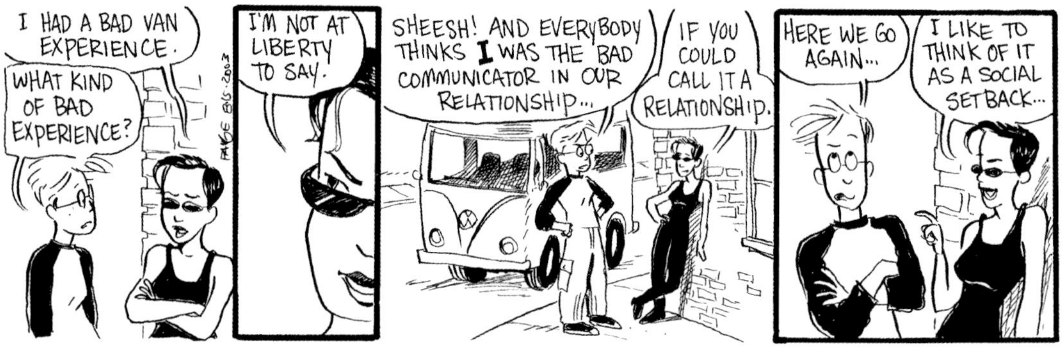
I HAD A BAD VAN EXPERIENCE.
WHAT KIND OF BAD EXPERIENCE?
I'M NOT AT LIBERTY TO SAY.
SHEESH! AND EVERYBODY THINKS **I** WAS THE BAD COMMUNICATOR IN OUR RELATIONSHIP...
IF YOU COULD CALL IT A RELATIONSHIP.
HERE WE GO AGAIN...
I LIKE TO THINK OF IT AS A SOCIAL SETBACK...

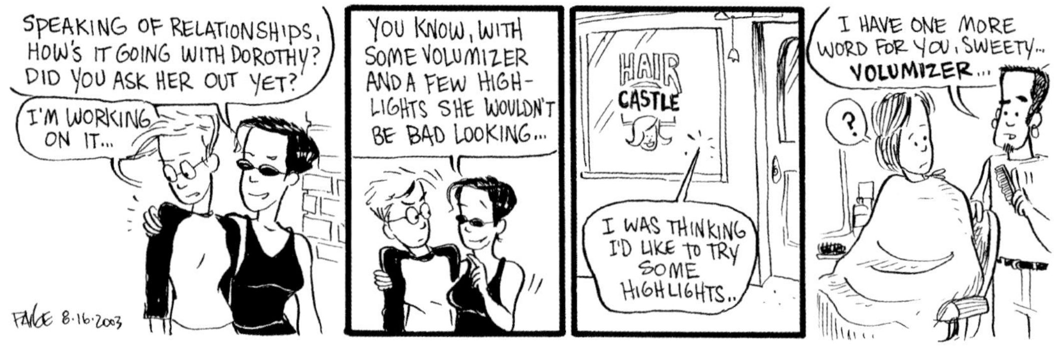
SPEAKING OF RELATIONSHIPS, HOW'S IT GOING WITH DOROTHY? DID YOU ASK HER OUT YET?
I'M WORKING ON IT...
FAIGE 8.16.2003
YOU KNOW, WITH SOME VOLUMIZER AND A FEW HIGHLIGHTS SHE WOULDN'T BE BAD LOOKING...
HAIR CASTLE
I WAS THINKING I'D LIKE TO TRY SOME HIGHLIGHTS...
I HAVE ONE MORE WORD FOR YOU, SWEETY... **VOLUMIZER**...
?

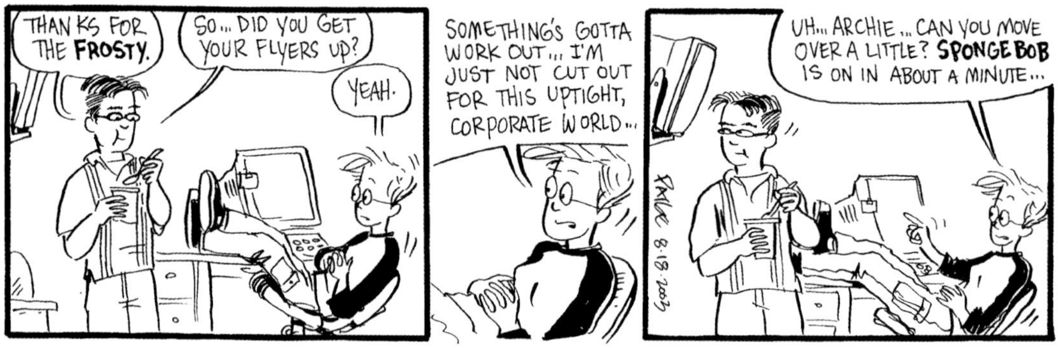
THANKS FOR THE **FROSTY**.
SO... DID YOU GET YOUR FLYERS UP?
YEAH.
SOMETHING'S GOTTA WORK OUT... I'M JUST NOT CUT OUT FOR THIS UPTIGHT, CORPORATE WORLD...
UH... ARCHIE... CAN YOU MOVE OVER A LITTLE? **SPONGEBOB** IS ON IN ABOUT A MINUTE...

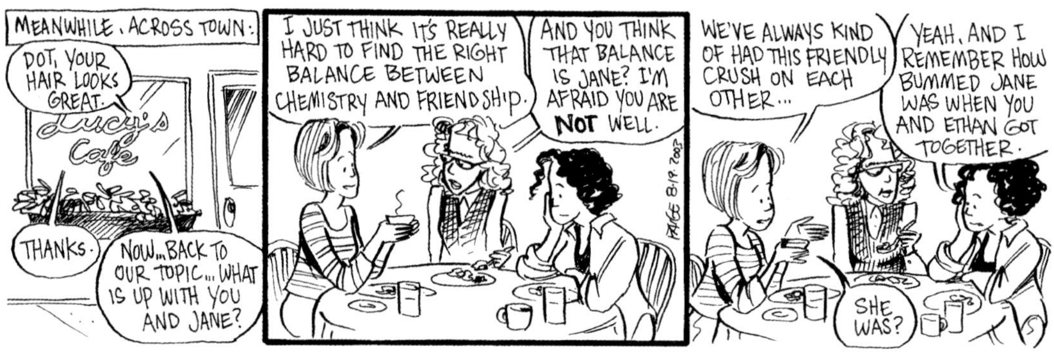
MEANWHILE, ACROSS TOWN:
DOT, YOUR HAIR LOOKS GREAT.
Lucy's Cafe
THANKS.
NOW... BACK TO OUR TOPIC... WHAT IS UP WITH YOU AND JANE?
I JUST THINK IT'S REALLY HARD TO FIND THE RIGHT BALANCE BETWEEN CHEMISTRY AND FRIENDSHIP.
AND YOU THINK THAT BALANCE IS JANE? I'M AFRAID YOU ARE **NOT** WELL.
WE'VE ALWAYS KIND OF HAD THIS FRIENDLY CRUSH ON EACH OTHER...
YEAH, AND I REMEMBER HOW BUMMED JANE WAS WHEN YOU AND ETHAN GOT TOGETHER.
SHE WAS?

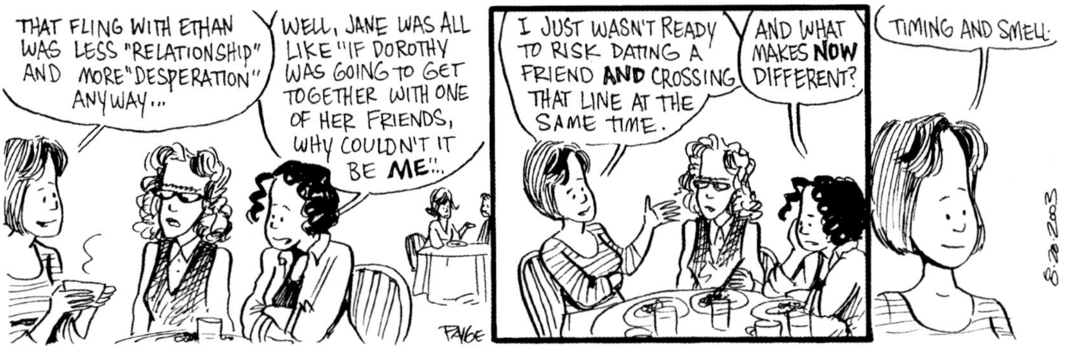
THAT FLING WITH ETHAN WAS LESS "RELATIONSHIP" AND MORE "DESPERATION" ANYWAY...
WELL, JANE WAS ALL LIKE "IF DOROTHY WAS GOING TO GET TOGETHER WITH ONE OF HER FRIENDS, WHY COULDN'T IT BE **ME**!"...
PAIGE
I JUST WASN'T READY TO RISK DATING A FRIEND **AND** CROSSING THAT LINE AT THE SAME TIME.
AND WHAT MAKES **NOW** DIFFERENT?
TIMING AND SMELL.
8.20.2003

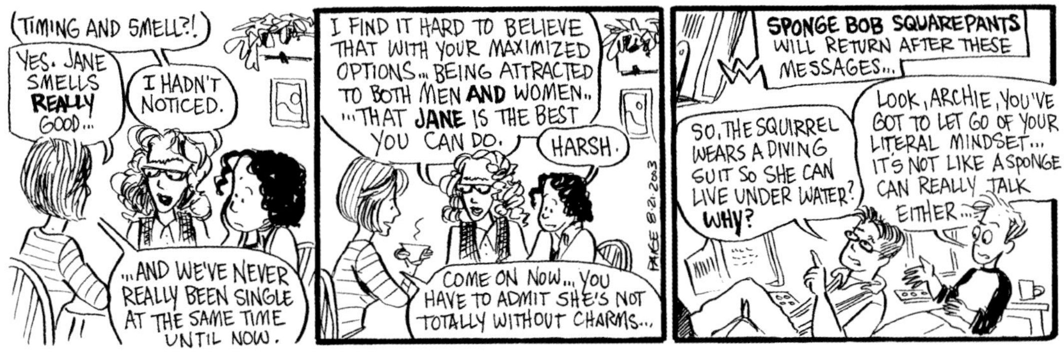
(TIMING AND SMELL?!)
YES. JANE SMELLS **REALLY** GOOD...
I HADN'T NOTICED.
...AND WE'VE NEVER REALLY BEEN SINGLE AT THE SAME TIME UNTIL NOW.
I FIND IT HARD TO BELIEVE THAT WITH YOUR MAXIMIZED OPTIONS... BEING ATTRACTED TO BOTH MEN **AND** WOMEN... ...THAT **JANE** IS THE BEST YOU CAN DO.
HARSH.
COME ON NOW... YOU HAVE TO ADMIT SHE'S NOT TOTALLY WITHOUT CHARMS...
PAIGE 8.21.2003
SPONGE BOB SQUAREPANTS WILL RETURN AFTER THESE MESSAGES...
SO, THE SQUIRREL WEARS A DIVING SUIT SO SHE CAN LIVE UNDER WATER? **WHY**?
LOOK, ARCHIE, YOU'VE GOT TO LET GO OF YOUR LITERAL MINDSET... IT'S NOT LIKE A SPONGE CAN REALLY TALK EITHER...

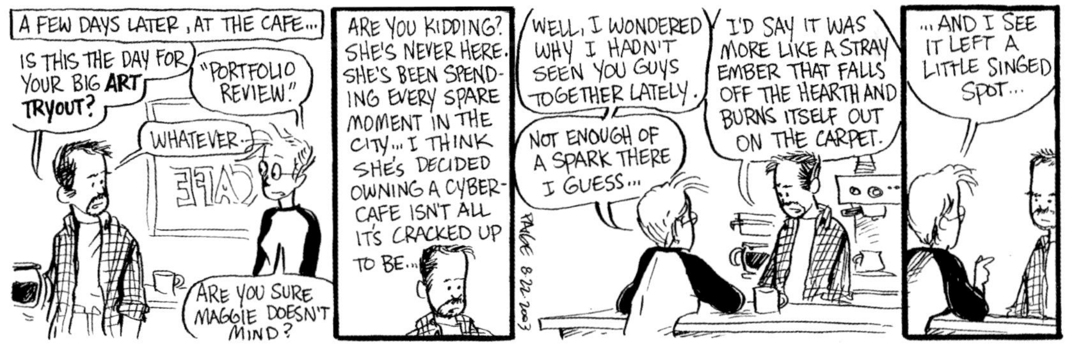
A FEW DAYS LATER, AT THE CAFE...
IS THIS THE DAY FOR YOUR BIG **ART TRYOUT**?
"PORTFOLIO REVIEW."
WHATEVER.
CAFE
ARE YOU SURE MAGGIE DOESN'T MIND?
ARE YOU KIDDING? SHE'S NEVER HERE. SHE'S BEEN SPENDING EVERY SPARE MOMENT IN THE CITY... I THINK SHE'S DECIDED OWNING A CYBER-CAFE ISN'T ALL IT'S CRACKED UP TO BE...
PAIGE 8.22.2003
WELL, I WONDERED WHY I HADN'T SEEN YOU GUYS TOGETHER LATELY.
NOT ENOUGH OF A SPARK THERE I GUESS...
I'D SAY IT WAS MORE LIKE A STRAY EMBER THAT FALLS OFF THE HEARTH AND BURNS ITSELF OUT ON THE CARPET.
...AND I SEE IT LEFT A LITTLE SINGED SPOT...

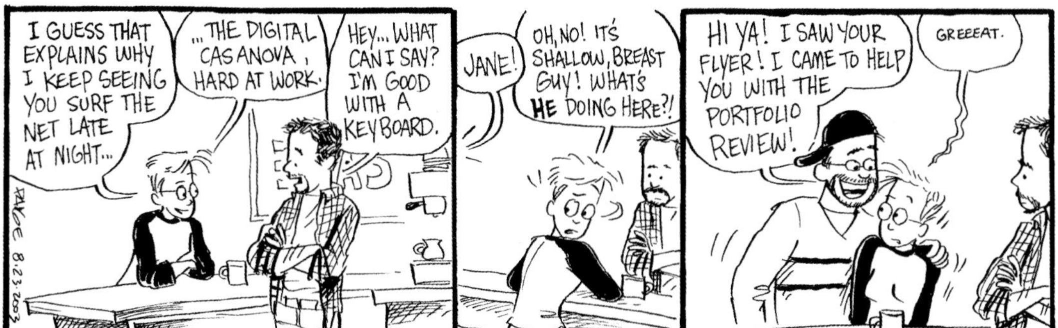
I GUESS THAT EXPLAINS WHY I KEEP SEEING YOU SURF THE NET LATE AT NIGHT...
...THE DIGITAL CASANOVA, HARD AT WORK.
HEY... WHAT CAN I SAY? I'M GOOD WITH A KEYBOARD.
PAIGE 8.23.2003
JANE!
OH, NO! IT'S SHALLOW, BREAST GUY! WHAT'S **HE** DOING HERE?!
HI YA! I SAW YOUR FLYER! I CAME TO HELP YOU WITH THE PORTFOLIO REVIEW!
GREEEAT.

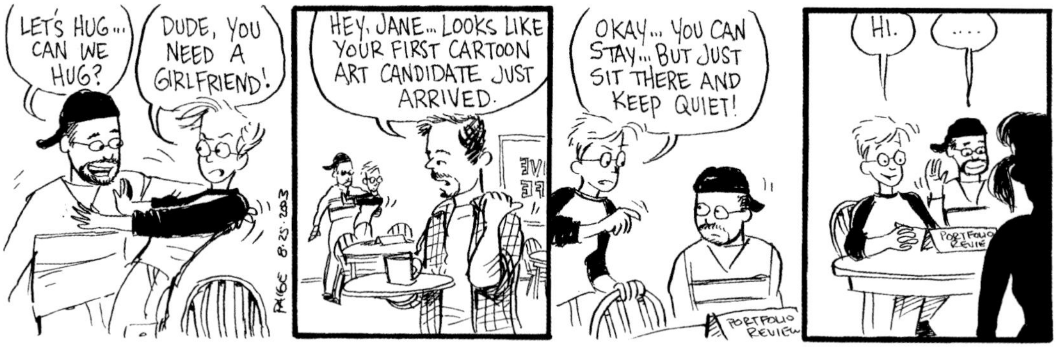
LET'S HUG... CAN WE HUG?
DUDE, YOU NEED A GIRLFRIEND!
PAIGE 8·25·2003
HEY, JANE... LOOKS LIKE YOUR FIRST CARTOON ART CANDIDATE JUST ARRIVED.
OKAY... YOU CAN STAY... BUT JUST SIT THERE AND KEEP QUIET!
PORTFOLIO REVIEW
HI.
....
PORTFOLIO REVIEW

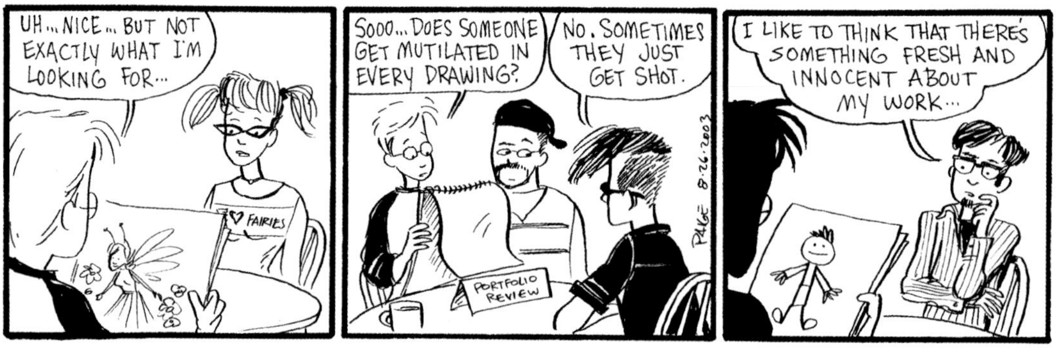
UH... NICE... BUT NOT EXACTLY WHAT I'M LOOKING FOR...
♥ FAIRIES
SOOO... DOES SOMEONE GET MUTILATED IN EVERY DRAWING?
NO. SOMETIMES THEY JUST GET SHOT.
PORTFOLIO REVIEW
PAIGE 8·26·2003
I LIKE TO THINK THAT THERE'S SOMETHING FRESH AND INNOCENT ABOUT MY WORK...

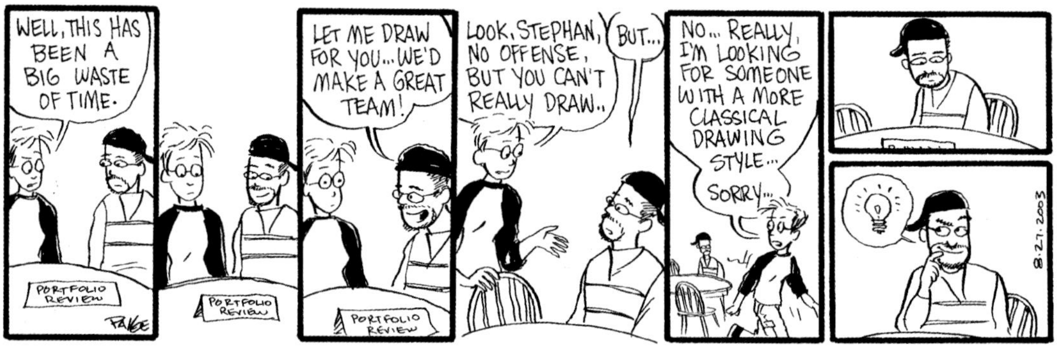
WELL, THIS HAS BEEN A BIG WASTE OF TIME.
PORTFOLIO REVIEW
PAIGE
PORTFOLIO REVIEW
LET ME DRAW FOR YOU... WE'D MAKE A GREAT TEAM!
PORTFOLIO REVIEW
LOOK, STEPHAN, NO OFFENSE, BUT YOU CAN'T REALLY DRAW..
BUT...
NO... REALLY, I'M LOOKING FOR SOMEONE WITH A MORE CLASSICAL DRAWING STYLE...
SORRY...
8·27·2003

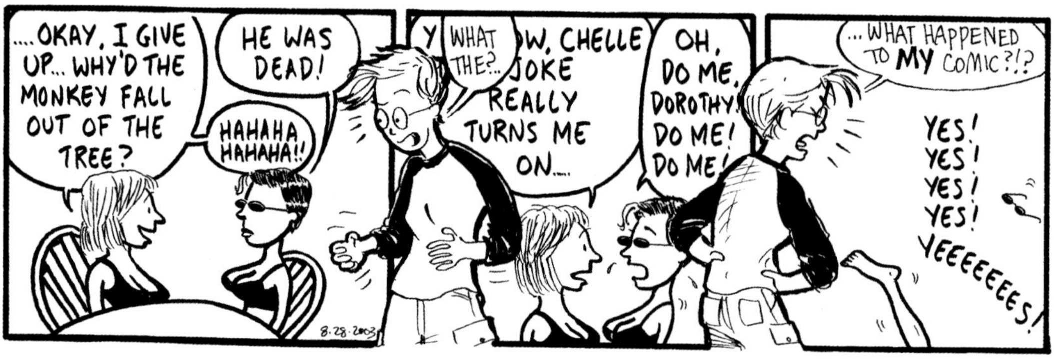
....OKAY, I GIVE UP... WHY'D THE MONKEY FALL OUT OF THE TREE?
HE WAS DEAD!
HAHAHA HAHAHA!!
8·28·2003
Y
WHAT THE?..
W, CHELLE
JOKE REALLY TURNS ME ON....
OH, DO ME, DOROTHY! DO ME! DO ME!
...WHAT HAPPENED TO MY COMIC?!?
YES! YES! YES! YES! YEEEEEEES!

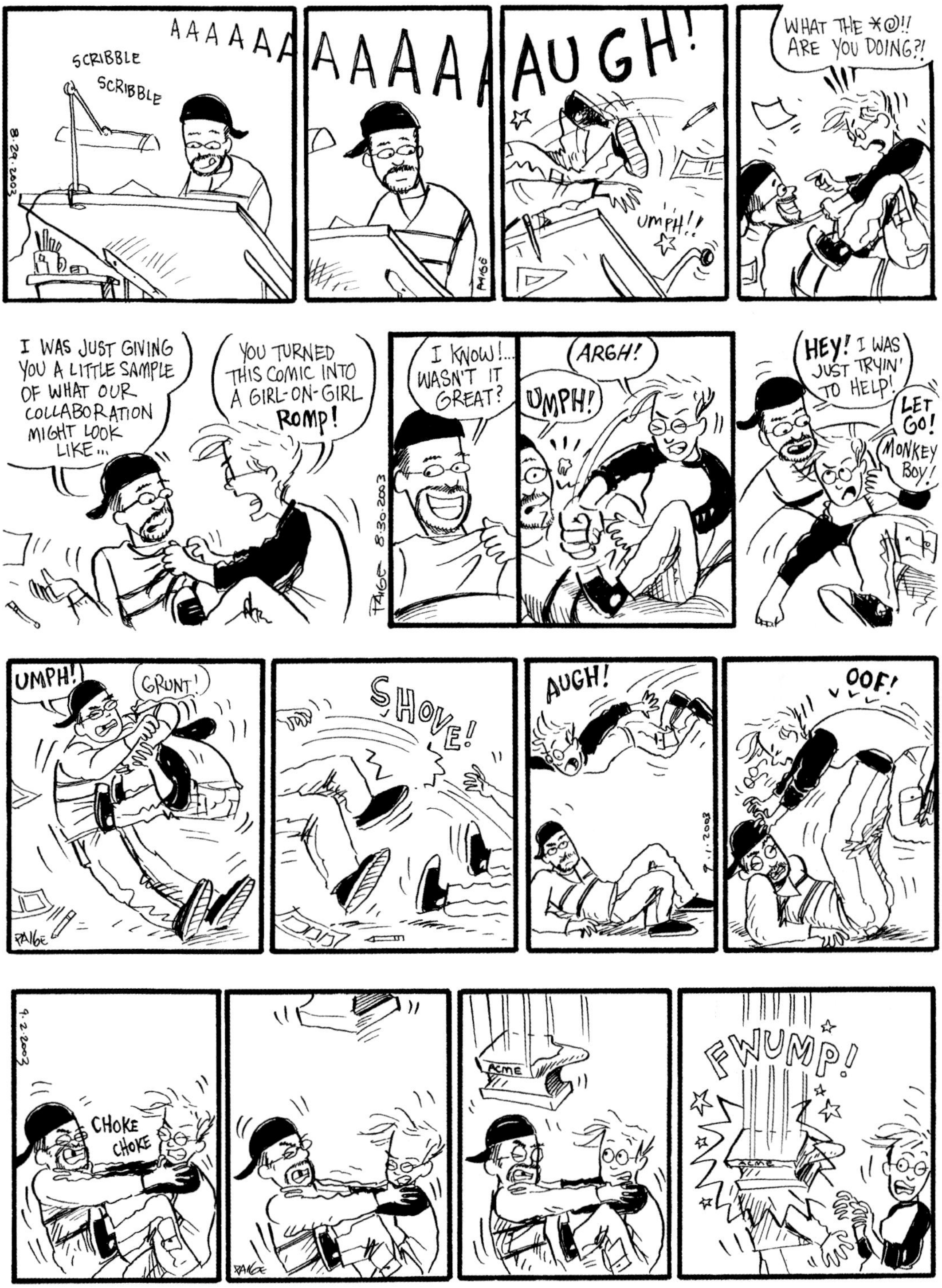
8.29.2003
SCRIBBLE
SCRIBBLE
AAAAAAAAAAAAUGH!
PAIGE
UMPH!!
WHAT THE *@!! ARE YOU DOING?!
I WAS JUST GIVING YOU A LITTLE SAMPLE OF WHAT OUR COLLABORATION MIGHT LOOK LIKE...
YOU TURNED THIS COMIC INTO A GIRL-ON-GIRL ROMP!
PAIGE
8.30.2003
I KNOW!... WASN'T IT GREAT?
ARGH!
UMPH!
HEY! I WAS JUST TRYIN' TO HELP!
LET GO!
MONKEY BOY!
UMPH!
GRUNT!
PAIGE
SHOVE!
AUGH!
9.1.2003
OOF!
9.2.2003
CHOKE
CHOKE
PAIGE
ACME
FWUMP!
ACME

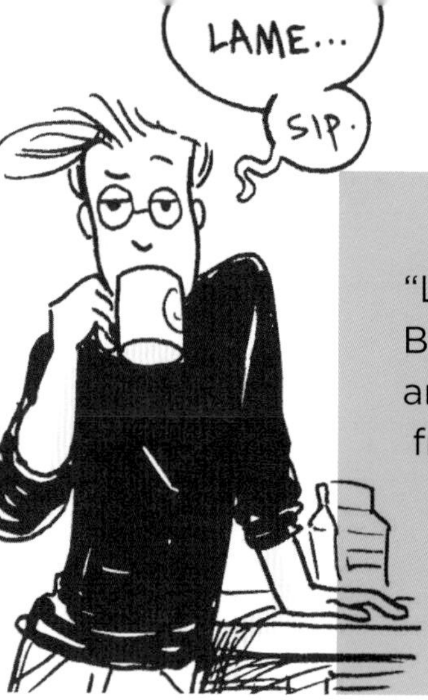

LAME...
SIP.

“Like an underhanded literary squirrel, Paige Braddock writes down everything you say and stores it away for future use...if you are a friend or acquaintance of Paige, and you have something of a rather private, or intimate nature to say to her...keep it to yourself.”

STEPHAN PASTIS, *Pearls Before Swine*

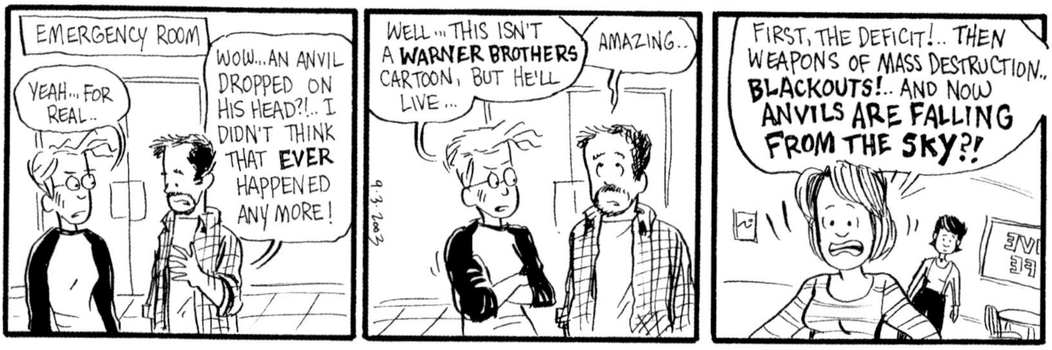

EMERGENCY ROOM
YEAH... FOR REAL..
WOW... AN ANVIL DROPPED ON HIS HEAD?!.. I DIDN'T THINK THAT EVER HAPPENED ANY MORE!
WELL... THIS ISN'T A WARNER BROTHERS CARTOON, BUT HE'LL LIVE...
AMAZING..
9.3.2003
FIRST, THE DEFICIT!.. THEN WEAPONS OF MASS DESTRUCTION.. BLACKOUTS!.. AND NOW ANVILS ARE FALLING FROM THE SKY?!

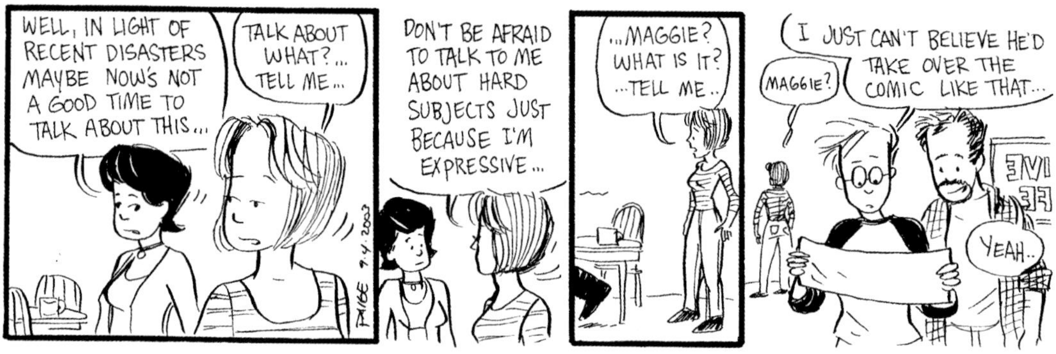

WELL, IN LIGHT OF RECENT DISASTERS MAYBE NOW'S NOT A GOOD TIME TO TALK ABOUT THIS...
TALK ABOUT WHAT?... TELL ME...
PAIGE 9.4.2003
DON'T BE AFRAID TO TALK TO ME ABOUT HARD SUBJECTS JUST BECAUSE I'M EXPRESSIVE...
...MAGGIE? WHAT IS IT? ...TELL ME..
I JUST CAN'T BELIEVE HE'D TAKE OVER THE COMIC LIKE THAT...
MAGGIE?
YEAH..

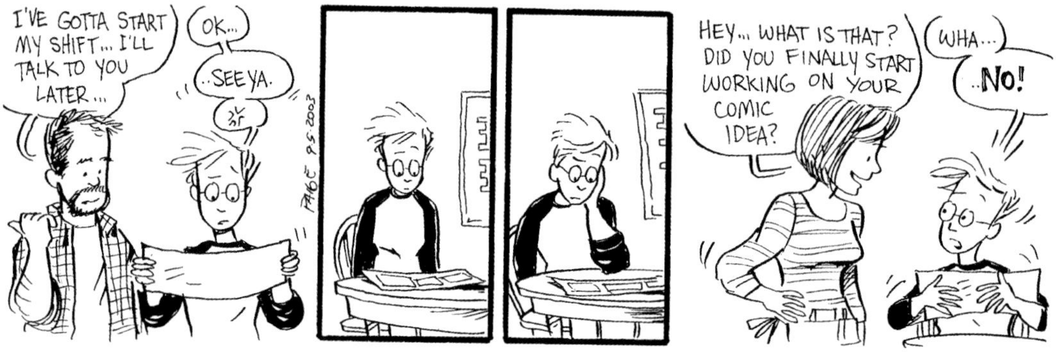

I'VE GOTTA START MY SHIFT... I'LL TALK TO YOU LATER...
OK...
..SEE YA.
PAIGE 9.5.2003
HEY... WHAT IS THAT? DID YOU FINALLY START WORKING ON YOUR COMIC IDEA?
WHA...
..NO!

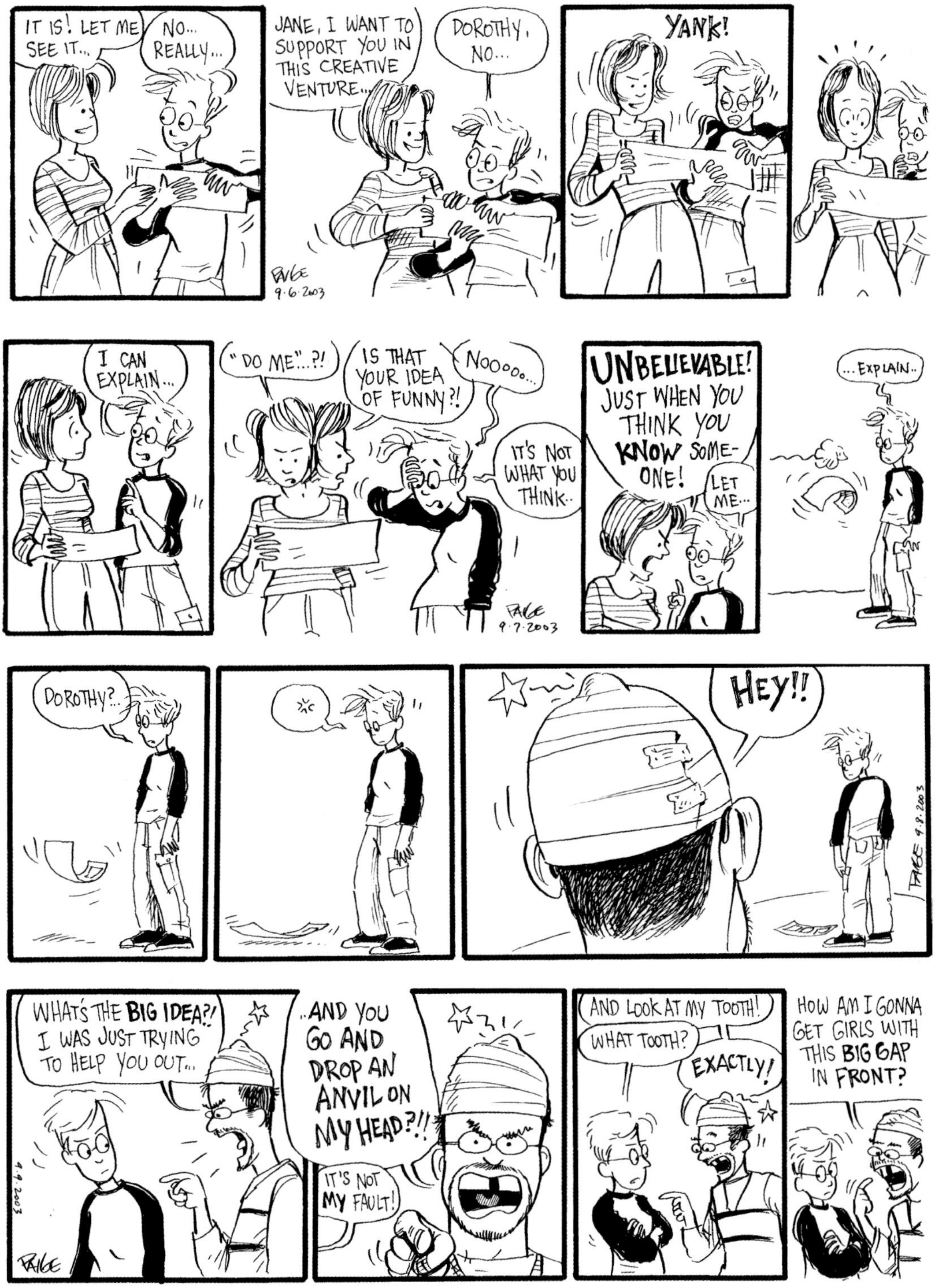
IT IS! LET ME SEE IT...
NO... REALLY...
JANE, I WANT TO SUPPORT YOU IN THIS CREATIVE VENTURE...
DOROTHY, NO...
PAIGE 9·6·2003
YANK!
I CAN EXPLAIN...
"DO ME"...?!
IS THAT YOUR IDEA OF FUNNY?!
NOooo...
IT'S NOT WHAT YOU THINK..
PAIGE 9·7·2003
UNBELIEVABLE! JUST WHEN YOU THINK YOU KNOW SOME-ONE!
LET ME...
...EXPLAIN..
DOROTHY?..
HEY!!
PAIGE 9·8·2003
WHAT'S THE BIG IDEA?! I WAS JUST TRYING TO HELP YOU OUT...
9·9·2003
PAIGE
..AND YOU GO AND DROP AN ANVIL ON MY HEAD?!!
IT'S NOT MY FAULT!
AND LOOK AT MY TOOTH!
WHAT TOOTH?
EXACTLY!
HOW AM I GONNA GET GIRLS WITH THIS BIG GAP IN FRONT?

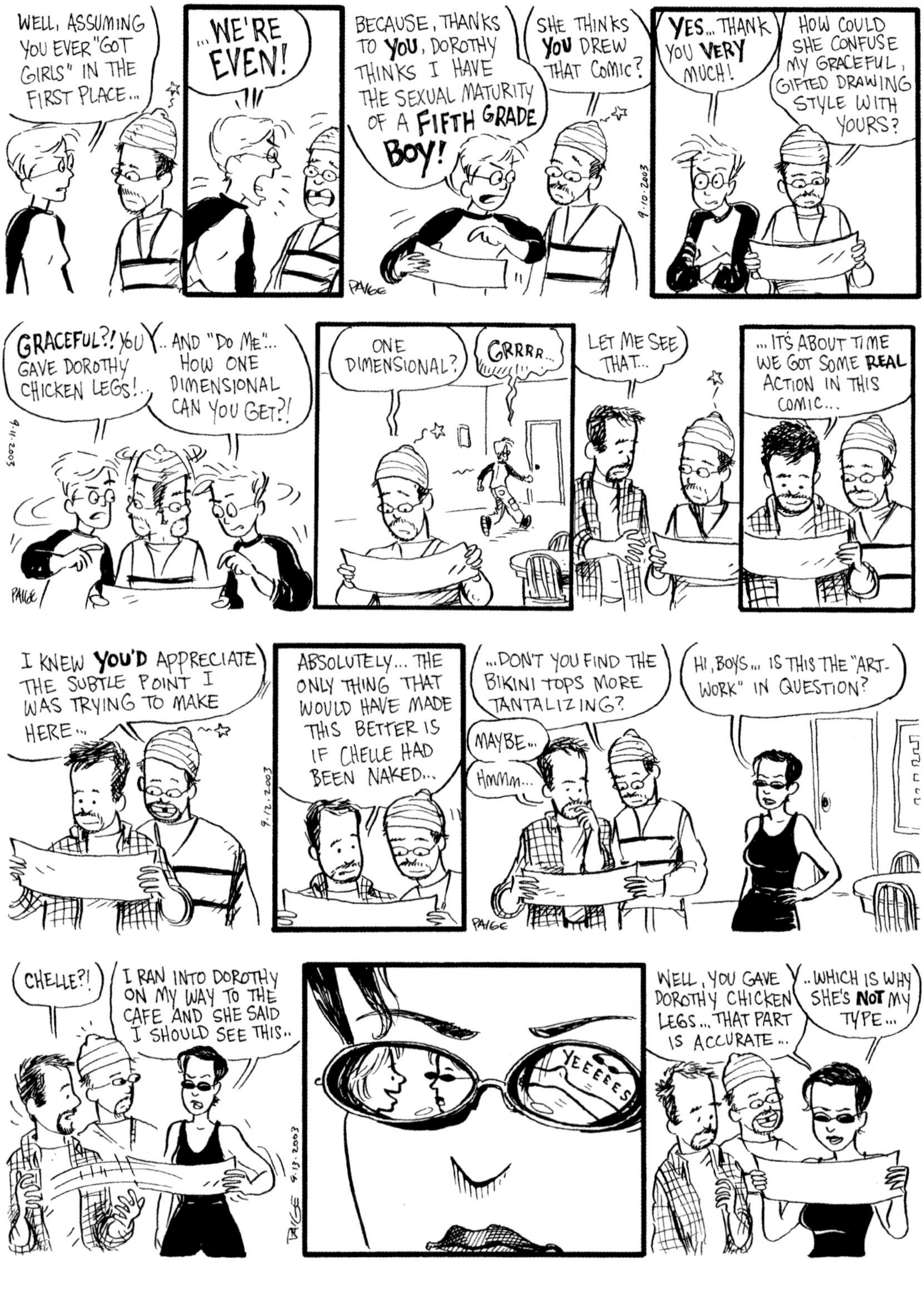

WELL, ASSUMING YOU EVER "GOT GIRLS" IN THE FIRST PLACE...
...WE'RE EVEN!
BECAUSE, THANKS TO **YOU**, DOROTHY THINKS I HAVE THE SEXUAL MATURITY OF A **FIFTH GRADE BOY!**
SHE THINKS **YOU** DREW THAT COMIC?
9.10.2003
PAIGE
YES... THANK YOU **VERY** MUCH!
HOW COULD SHE CONFUSE MY GRACEFUL, GIFTED DRAWING STYLE WITH YOURS?
GRACEFUL?! YOU GAVE DOROTHY CHICKEN LEGS!..
.. AND "DO ME"... HOW ONE DIMENSIONAL CAN YOU GET?!
9.11.2003
PAIGE
ONE DIMENSIONAL?
GRRRR...
LET ME SEE THAT...
... IT'S ABOUT TIME WE GOT SOME **REAL** ACTION IN THIS COMIC...
I KNEW **YOU'D** APPRECIATE THE SUBTLE POINT I WAS TRYING TO MAKE HERE...
ABSOLUTELY... THE ONLY THING THAT WOULD HAVE MADE THIS BETTER IS IF CHELLE HAD BEEN NAKED...
9.12.2003
...DON'T YOU FIND THE BIKINI TOPS MORE TANTALIZING?
MAYBE...
HMMM...
PAIGE
HI, BOYS... IS THIS THE "ART-WORK" IN QUESTION?
CHELLE?!
I RAN INTO DOROTHY ON MY WAY TO THE CAFE AND SHE SAID I SHOULD SEE THIS..
9.13.2003
PAIGE
YEEEEES
WELL, YOU GAVE DOROTHY CHICKEN LEGS... THAT PART IS ACCURATE...
..WHICH IS WHY SHE'S **NOT** MY TYPE...

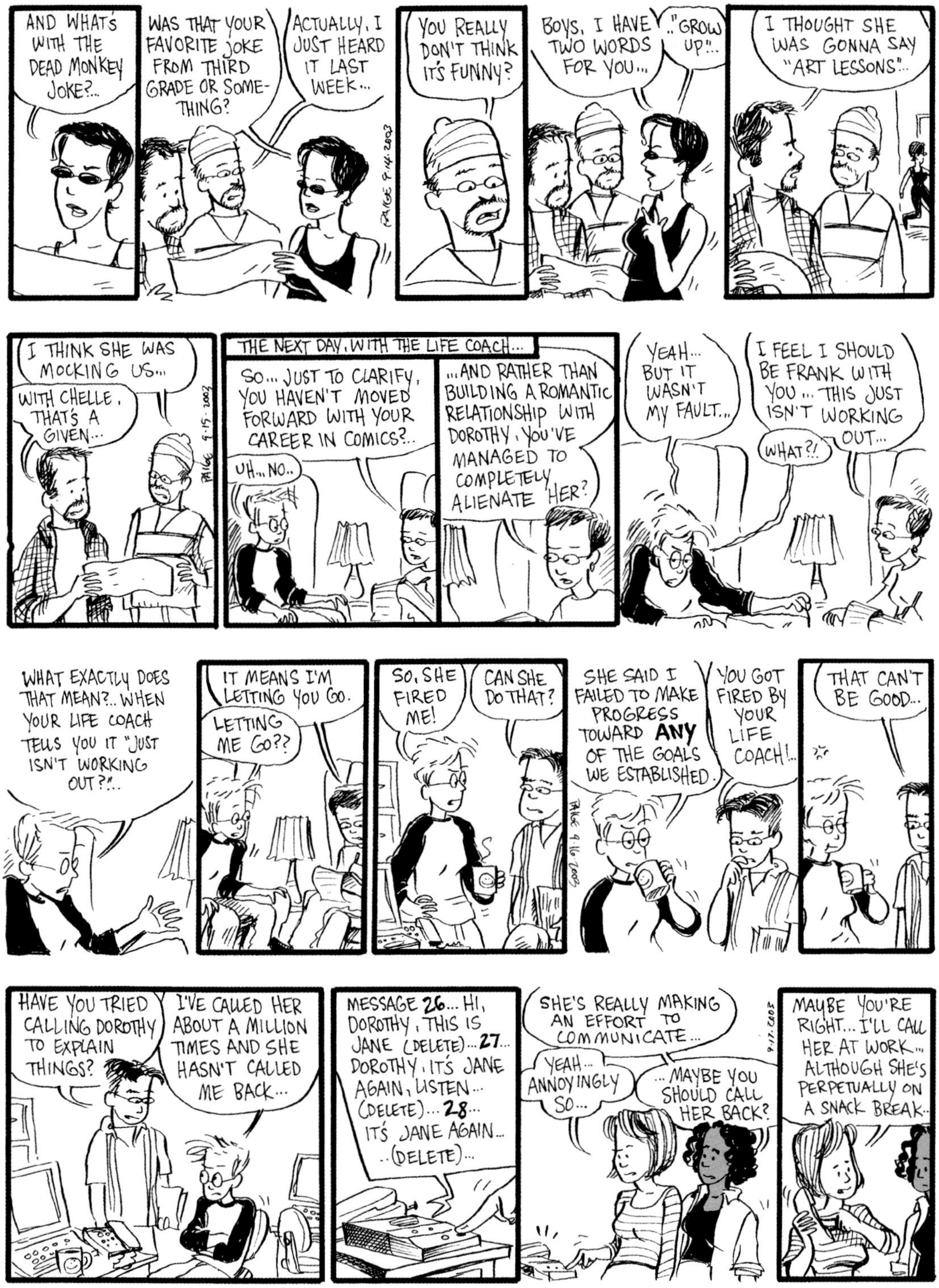
AND WHAT'S WITH THE DEAD MONKEY JOKE?..
WAS THAT YOUR FAVORITE JOKE FROM THIRD GRADE OR SOME-THING?
ACTUALLY, I JUST HEARD IT LAST WEEK...
PAIGE 9.14.2003
YOU REALLY DON'T THINK IT'S FUNNY?
BOYS, I HAVE TWO WORDS FOR YOU...
.."GROW UP!"...
I THOUGHT SHE WAS GONNA SAY "ART LESSONS"...
I THINK SHE WAS MOCKING US...
WITH CHELLE, THAT'S A GIVEN...
PAIGE 9.15.2003
THE NEXT DAY, WITH THE LIFE COACH...
SO... JUST TO CLARIFY, YOU HAVEN'T MOVED FORWARD WITH YOUR CAREER IN COMICS?..
UH... NO..
...AND RATHER THAN BUILDING A ROMANTIC RELATIONSHIP WITH DOROTHY, YOU'VE MANAGED TO COMPLETELY ALIENATE HER?
YEAH... BUT IT WASN'T MY FAULT...
I FEEL I SHOULD BE FRANK WITH YOU... THIS JUST ISN'T WORKING OUT...
WHAT?!
WHAT EXACTLY DOES THAT MEAN?.. WHEN YOUR LIFE COACH TELLS YOU IT "JUST ISN'T WORKING OUT?"...
IT MEANS I'M LETTING YOU GO.
LETTING ME GO??
SO, SHE FIRED ME!
CAN SHE DO THAT?
PAIGE 9.16.2003
SHE SAID I FAILED TO MAKE PROGRESS TOWARD ANY OF THE GOALS WE ESTABLISHED.
YOU GOT FIRED BY YOUR LIFE COACH!..
THAT CAN'T BE GOOD...
HAVE YOU TRIED CALLING DOROTHY TO EXPLAIN THINGS?
I'VE CALLED HER ABOUT A MILLION TIMES AND SHE HASN'T CALLED ME BACK...
MESSAGE 26... HI, DOROTHY, THIS IS JANE (DELETE)... 27... DOROTHY, IT'S JANE AGAIN, LISTEN... (DELETE)... 28... IT'S JANE AGAIN... ..(DELETE)...
SHE'S REALLY MAKING AN EFFORT TO COMMUNICATE...
YEAH... ANNOYINGLY SO...
...MAYBE YOU SHOULD CALL HER BACK?
9.17.2003
MAYBE YOU'RE RIGHT... I'LL CALL HER AT WORK... ALTHOUGH SHE'S PERPETUALLY ON A SNACK BREAK..

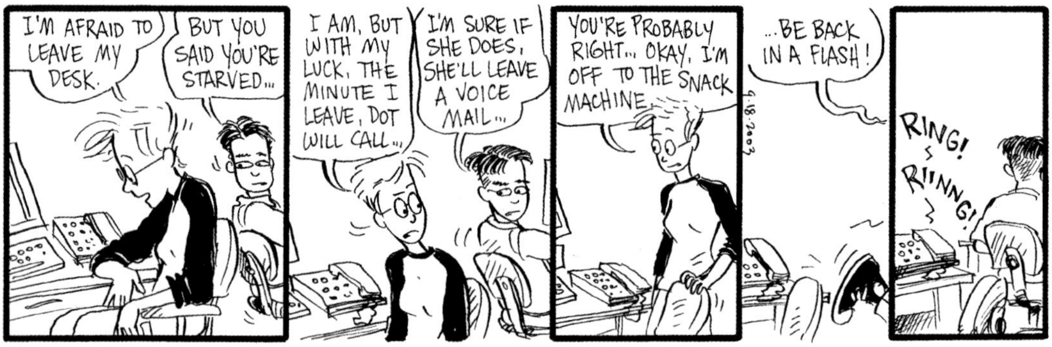
I'M AFRAID TO LEAVE MY DESK.
BUT YOU SAID YOU'RE STARVED...
I AM, BUT WITH MY LUCK, THE MINUTE I LEAVE, DOT WILL CALL...
I'M SURE IF SHE DOES, SHE'LL LEAVE A VOICE MAIL...
YOU'RE PROBABLY RIGHT... OKAY, I'M OFF TO THE SNACK MACHINE.
9.18.2003
...BE BACK IN A FLASH!
RING!
RIINNG!

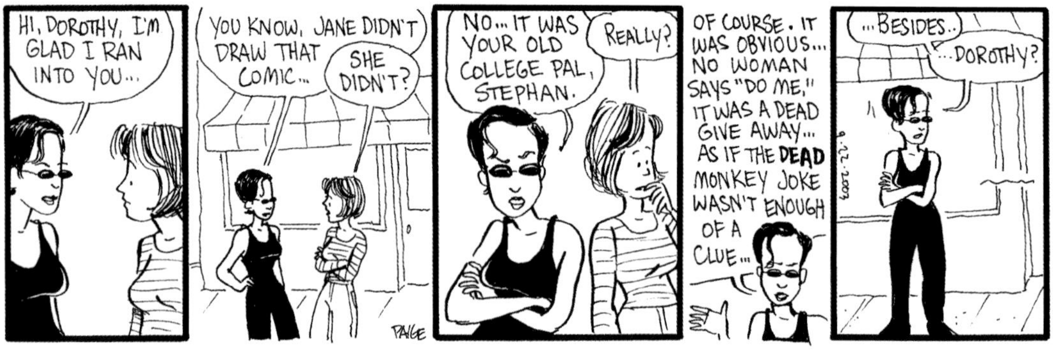
HI, DOROTHY, I'M GLAD I RAN INTO YOU...
YOU KNOW, JANE DIDN'T DRAW THAT COMIC...
SHE DIDN'T?
NO... IT WAS YOUR OLD COLLEGE PAL, STEPHAN.
REALLY?
PAIGE
OF COURSE. IT WAS OBVIOUS... NO WOMAN SAYS "DO ME," IT WAS A DEAD GIVE AWAY... AS IF THE DEAD MONKEY JOKE WASN'T ENOUGH OF A CLUE...
9.22.2003
...BESIDES..
...DOROTHY?

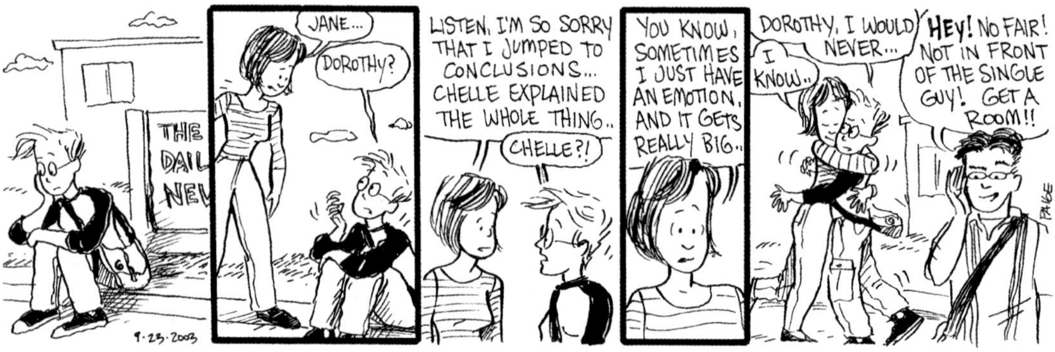
THE DAIL NEW
9.23.2003
JANE...
DOROTHY?
LISTEN, I'M SO SORRY THAT I JUMPED TO CONCLUSIONS... CHELLE EXPLAINED THE WHOLE THING..
CHELLE?!
YOU KNOW, SOMETIMES I JUST HAVE AN EMOTION, AND IT GETS REALLY BIG..
DOROTHY, I WOULD NEVER...
I KNOW..
HEY! NO FAIR! NOT IN FRONT OF THE SINGLE GUY! GET A ROOM!!
PAIGE

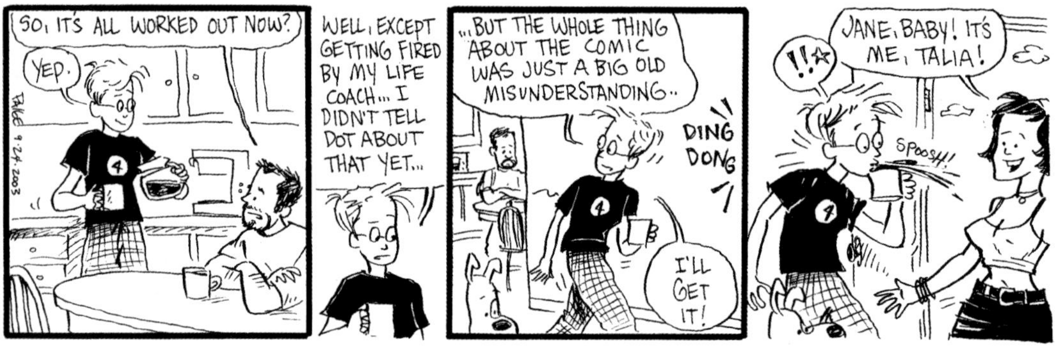
SO, IT'S ALL WORKED OUT NOW?
YEP.
PAIGE 9.24.2003
WELL, EXCEPT GETTING FIRED BY MY LIFE COACH... I DIDN'T TELL DOT ABOUT THAT YET...
...BUT THE WHOLE THING ABOUT THE COMIC WAS JUST A BIG OLD MISUNDERSTANDING..
DING DONG
I'LL GET IT!
JANE, BABY! IT'S ME, TALIA!
!!☆
SPOOSH!

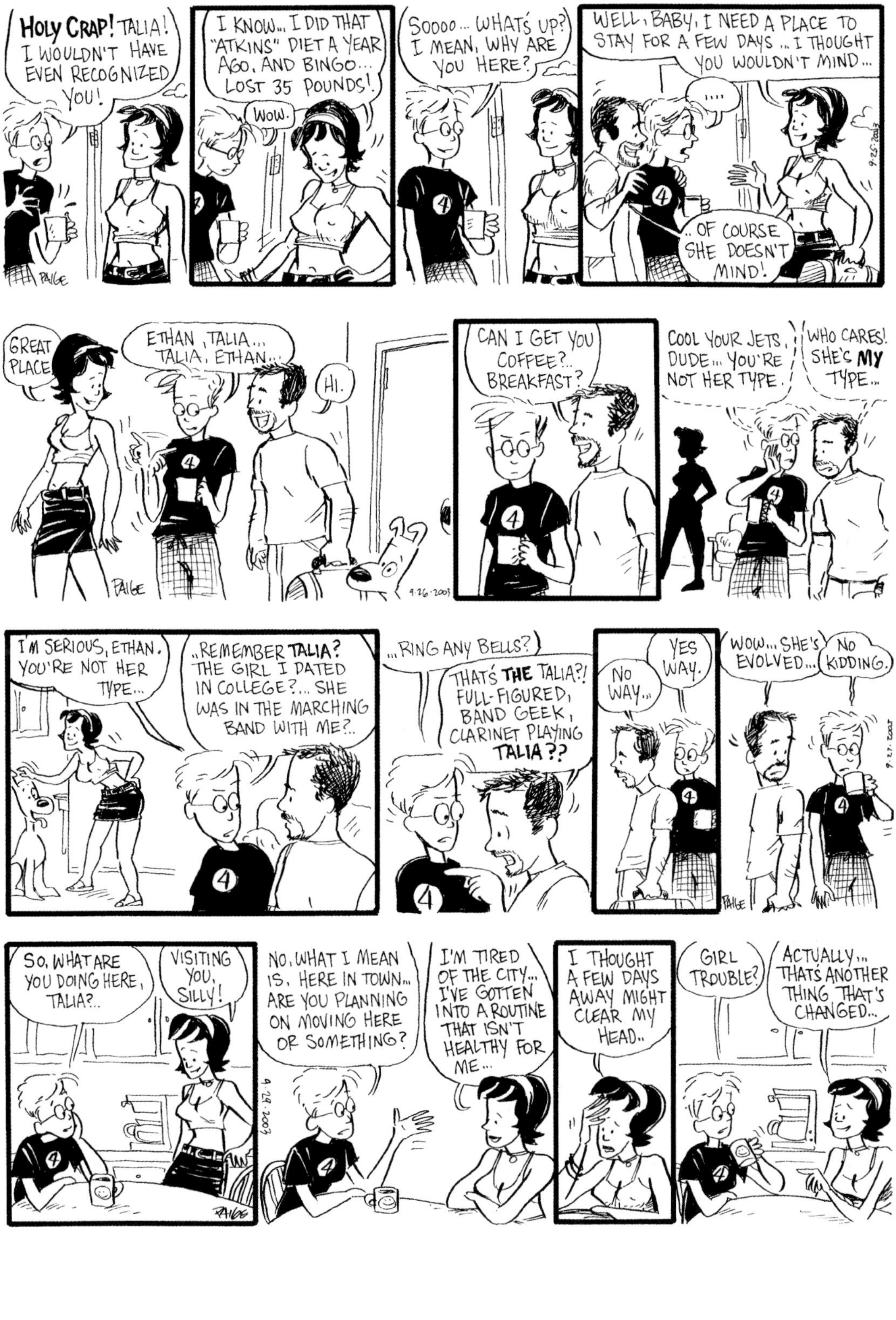
HOLY CRAP! TALIA! I WOULDN'T HAVE EVEN RECOGNIZED YOU!
PAIGE
I KNOW... I DID THAT "ATKINS" DIET A YEAR AGO, AND BINGO... LOST 35 POUNDS!
WOW.
SOOOO... WHAT'S UP? I MEAN, WHY ARE YOU HERE?
WELL, BABY, I NEED A PLACE TO STAY FOR A FEW DAYS ... I THOUGHT YOU WOULDN'T MIND...
....
..OF COURSE SHE DOESN'T MIND!
9-25-2003
GREAT PLACE
ETHAN, TALIA... TALIA, ETHAN...
HI.
PAIGE
9-26-2003
CAN I GET YOU COFFEE?.. BREAKFAST?
COOL YOUR JETS, DUDE... YOU'RE NOT HER TYPE.
WHO CARES! SHE'S MY TYPE...
I'M SERIOUS, ETHAN. YOU'RE NOT HER TYPE...
..REMEMBER TALIA? THE GIRL I DATED IN COLLEGE?... SHE WAS IN THE MARCHING BAND WITH ME?..
...RING ANY BELLS?
THAT'S THE TALIA?! FULL-FIGURED, BAND GEEK, CLARINET PLAYING TALIA??
NO WAY...
YES WAY.
WOW... SHE'S EVOLVED...
NO KIDDING.
9-27-2003
PAIGE
SO, WHAT ARE YOU DOING HERE, TALIA?..
VISITING YOU, SILLY!
PAIGE
9-29-2003
NO, WHAT I MEAN IS, HERE IN TOWN... ARE YOU PLANNING ON MOVING HERE OR SOMETHING?
I'M TIRED OF THE CITY... I'VE GOTTEN INTO A ROUTINE THAT ISN'T HEALTHY FOR ME...
I THOUGHT A FEW DAYS AWAY MIGHT CLEAR MY HEAD..
GIRL TROUBLE?
ACTUALLY... THAT'S ANOTHER THING THAT'S CHANGED...

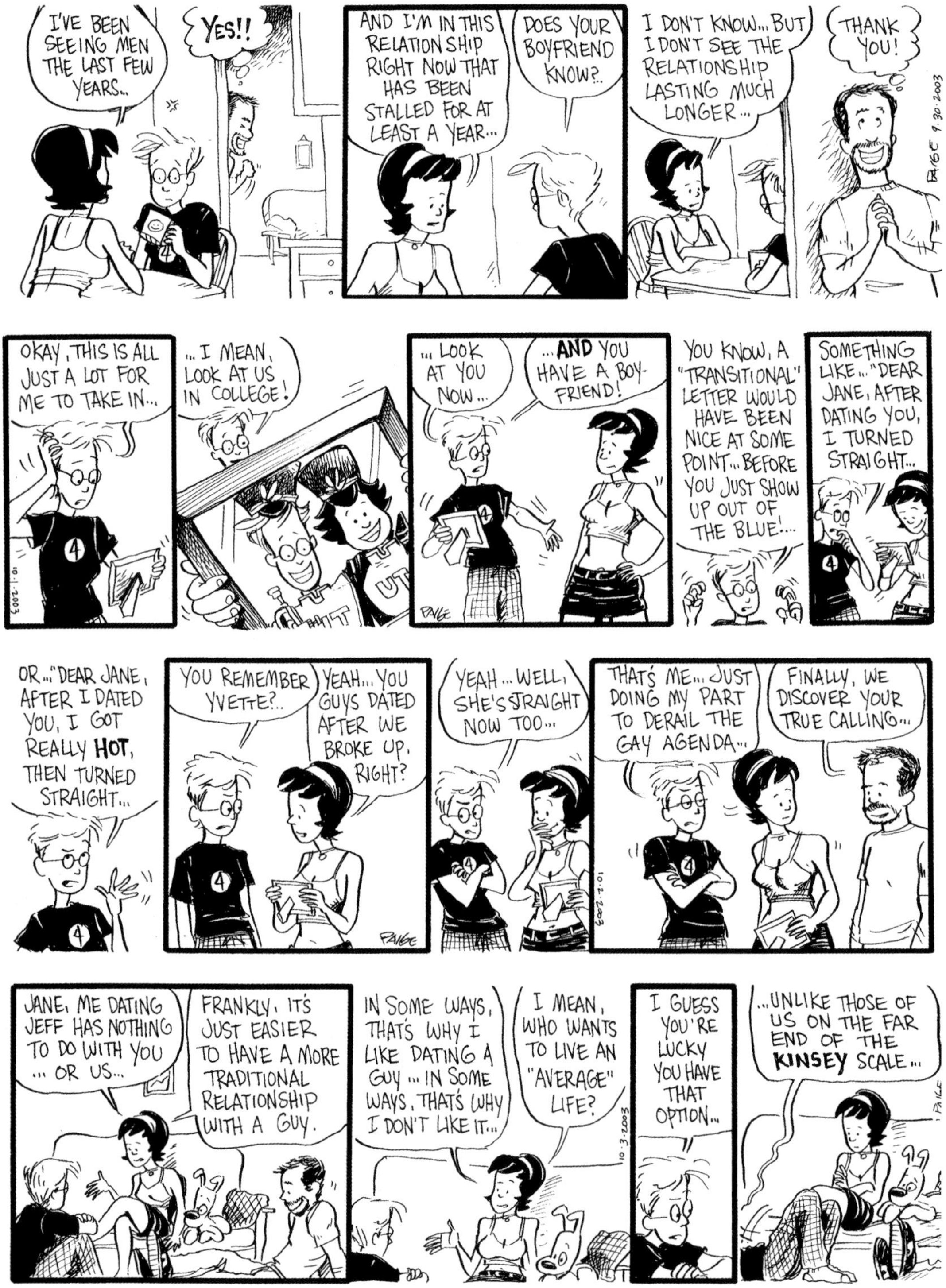
I'VE BEEN SEEING MEN THE LAST FEW YEARS..
YES!!
AND I'M IN THIS RELATIONSHIP RIGHT NOW THAT HAS BEEN STALLED FOR AT LEAST A YEAR...
DOES YOUR BOYFRIEND KNOW?..
I DON'T KNOW... BUT I DON'T SEE THE RELATIONSHIP LASTING MUCH LONGER...
THANK YOU!
PAIGE 9.30.2003
OKAY, THIS IS ALL JUST A LOT FOR ME TO TAKE IN...
... I MEAN, LOOK AT US IN COLLEGE!
10.1.2003
... LOOK AT YOU NOW...
... AND YOU HAVE A BOY-FRIEND!
PAIGE
YOU KNOW, A "TRANSITIONAL" LETTER WOULD HAVE BEEN NICE AT SOME POINT... BEFORE YOU JUST SHOW UP OUT OF THE BLUE!...
SOMETHING LIKE..."DEAR JANE, AFTER DATING YOU, I TURNED STRAIGHT...
OR..."DEAR JANE, AFTER I DATED YOU, I GOT REALLY HOT, THEN TURNED STRAIGHT...
YOU REMEMBER YVETTE?..
YEAH... YOU GUYS DATED AFTER WE BROKE UP, RIGHT?
PAIGE
YEAH ... WELL, SHE'S STRAIGHT NOW TOO...
10.2.2003
THAT'S ME... JUST DOING MY PART TO DERAIL THE GAY AGENDA...
FINALLY, WE DISCOVER YOUR TRUE CALLING...
JANE, ME DATING JEFF HAS NOTHING TO DO WITH YOU ... OR US...
FRANKLY, IT'S JUST EASIER TO HAVE A MORE TRADITIONAL RELATIONSHIP WITH A GUY.
IN SOME WAYS, THAT'S WHY I LIKE DATING A GUY ... IN SOME WAYS, THAT'S WHY I DON'T LIKE IT...
I MEAN, WHO WANTS TO LIVE AN "AVERAGE" LIFE?
10.3.2003
I GUESS YOU'RE LUCKY YOU HAVE THAT OPTION...
...UNLIKE THOSE OF US ON THE FAR END OF THE KINSEY SCALE...
PAIGE

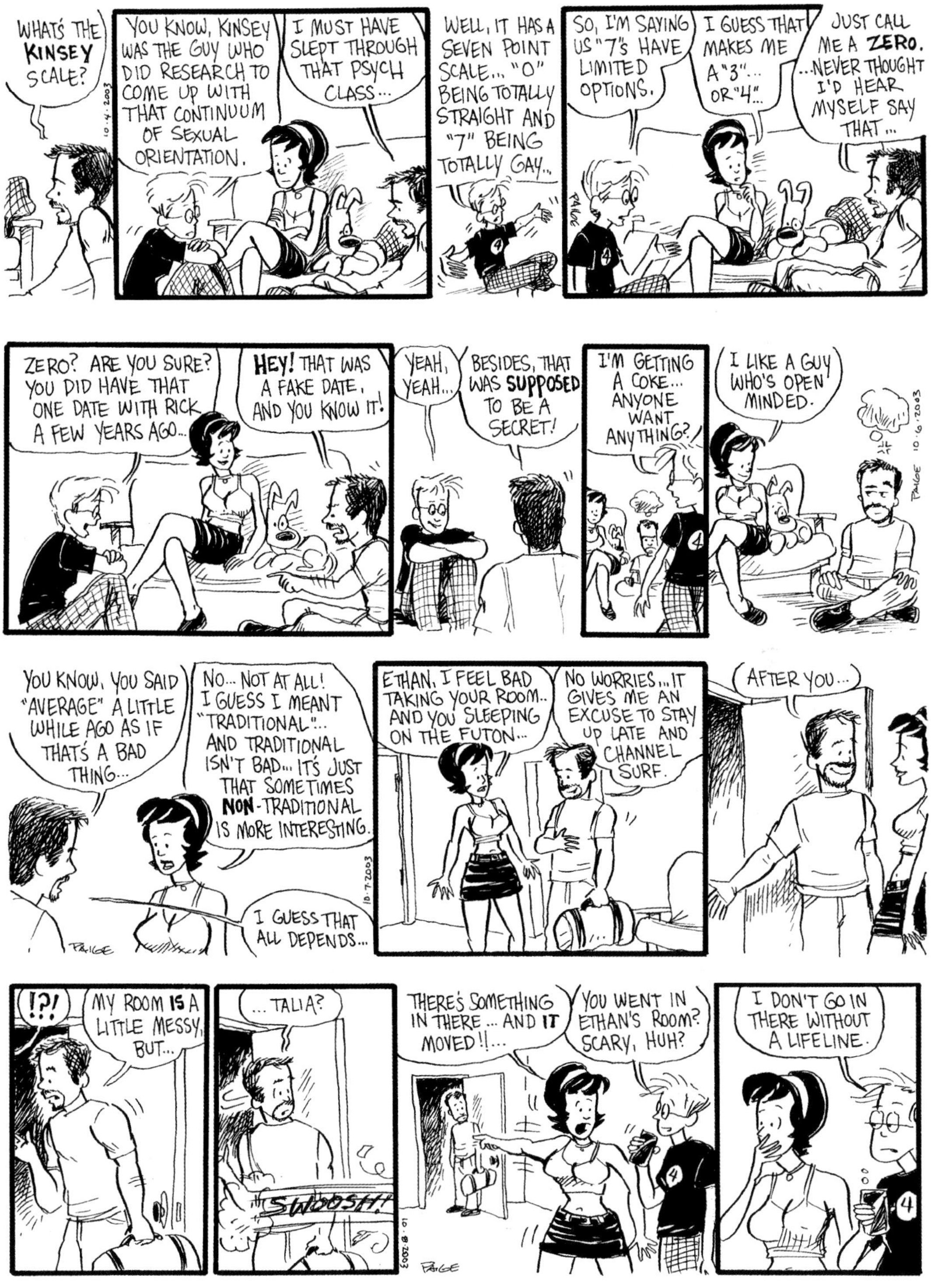
WHAT'S THE KINSEY SCALE?
10.4.2003
YOU KNOW, KINSEY WAS THE GUY WHO DID RESEARCH TO COME UP WITH THAT CONTINUUM OF SEXUAL ORIENTATION.
I MUST HAVE SLEPT THROUGH THAT PSYCH CLASS...
WELL, IT HAS A SEVEN POINT SCALE... "0" BEING TOTALLY STRAIGHT AND "7" BEING TOTALLY GAY...
PAIGE
SO, I'M SAYING US "7"s HAVE LIMITED OPTIONS.
I GUESS THAT MAKES ME A "3"... OR "4"...
JUST CALL ME A ZERO. ...NEVER THOUGHT I'D HEAR MYSELF SAY THAT...
ZERO? ARE YOU SURE? YOU DID HAVE THAT ONE DATE WITH RICK A FEW YEARS AGO...
HEY! THAT WAS A FAKE DATE, AND YOU KNOW IT!
YEAH, YEAH...
BESIDES, THAT WAS SUPPOSED TO BE A SECRET!
I'M GETTING A COKE... ANYONE WANT ANYTHING?
I LIKE A GUY WHO'S OPEN MINDED.
10.6.2003
PAIGE
YOU KNOW, YOU SAID "AVERAGE" A LITTLE WHILE AGO AS IF THAT'S A BAD THING...
NO... NOT AT ALL! I GUESS I MEANT "TRADITIONAL"... AND TRADITIONAL ISN'T BAD... IT'S JUST THAT SOMETIMES NON-TRADITIONAL IS MORE INTERESTING.
I GUESS THAT ALL DEPENDS...
10.7.2003
PAIGE
ETHAN, I FEEL BAD TAKING YOUR ROOM.. AND YOU SLEEPING ON THE FUTON...
NO WORRIES... IT GIVES ME AN EXCUSE TO STAY UP LATE AND CHANNEL SURF.
AFTER YOU...
!?!
MY ROOM IS A LITTLE MESSY, BUT...
... TALIA?
SWOOSH!
10.8.2003
THERE'S SOMETHING IN THERE ... AND IT MOVED!!...
YOU WENT IN ETHAN'S ROOM? SCARY, HUH?
PAIGE
I DON'T GO IN THERE WITHOUT A LIFELINE.

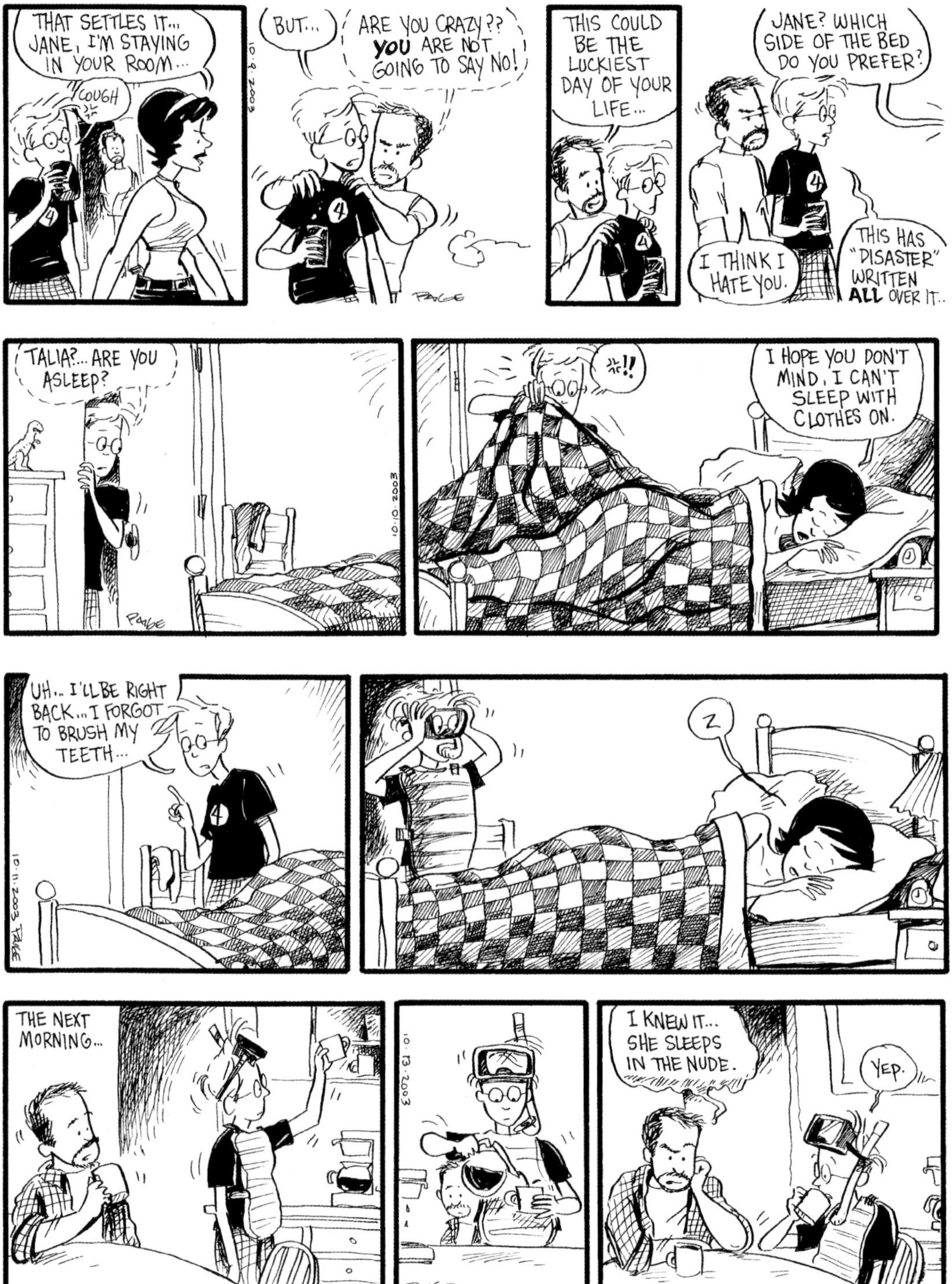
THAT SETTLES IT... JANE, I'M STAYING IN YOUR ROOM...
COUGH
10.8.2003
BUT...
ARE YOU CRAZY?? YOU ARE NOT GOING TO SAY NO!
PAGE
THIS COULD BE THE LUCKIEST DAY OF YOUR LIFE...
JANE? WHICH SIDE OF THE BED DO YOU PREFER?
I THINK I HATE YOU.
THIS HAS "DISASTER" WRITTEN ALL OVER IT..
TALIA?... ARE YOU ASLEEP?
10.10.2003
PAGE
!!
I HOPE YOU DON'T MIND, I CAN'T SLEEP WITH CLOTHES ON.
UH.. I'LL BE RIGHT BACK... I FORGOT TO BRUSH MY TEETH...
10.11.2003
PAGE
Z
THE NEXT MORNING...
10.13.2003
PAGE
I KNEW IT... SHE SLEEPS IN THE NUDE.
YEP.

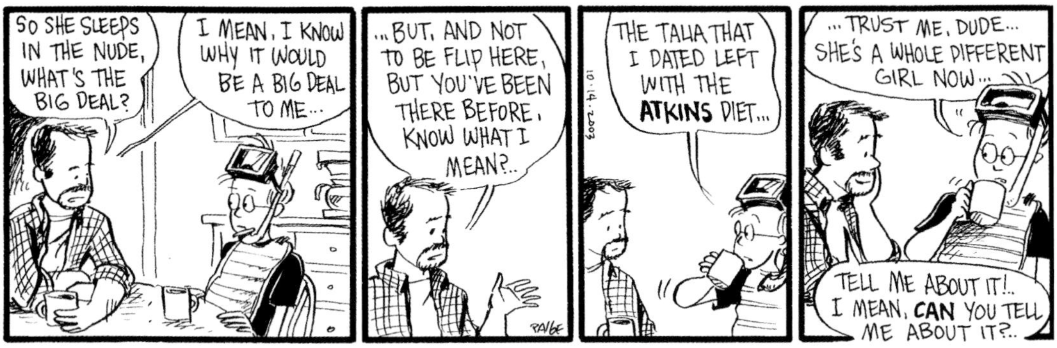
SO SHE SLEEPS IN THE NUDE, WHAT'S THE BIG DEAL?
I MEAN, I KNOW WHY IT WOULD BE A BIG DEAL TO ME...
...BUT, AND NOT TO BE FLIP HERE, BUT YOU'VE BEEN THERE BEFORE, KNOW WHAT I MEAN?..
PAIGE
10·14·2003
THE TALIA THAT I DATED LEFT WITH THE ATKINS DIET...
...TRUST ME, DUDE... SHE'S A WHOLE DIFFERENT GIRL NOW...
TELL ME ABOUT IT!.. I MEAN, CAN YOU TELL ME ABOUT IT?..

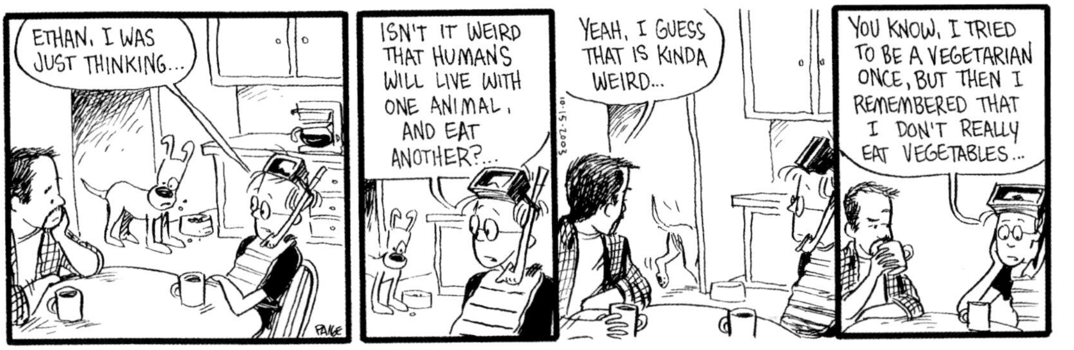
ETHAN, I WAS JUST THINKING...
PAIGE
ISN'T IT WEIRD THAT HUMANS WILL LIVE WITH ONE ANIMAL, AND EAT ANOTHER?...
10·15·2003
YEAH, I GUESS THAT IS KINDA WEIRD...
YOU KNOW, I TRIED TO BE A VEGETARIAN ONCE, BUT THEN I REMEMBERED THAT I DON'T REALLY EAT VEGETABLES...

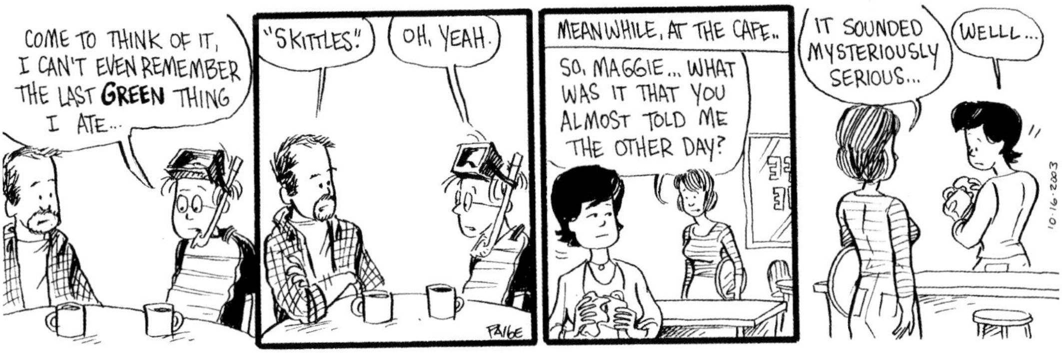
COME TO THINK OF IT, I CAN'T EVEN REMEMBER THE LAST GREEN THING I ATE...
"SKITTLES."
OH, YEAH.
PAIGE
MEANWHILE, AT THE CAFE..
SO, MAGGIE... WHAT WAS IT THAT YOU ALMOST TOLD ME THE OTHER DAY?
IT SOUNDED MYSTERIOUSLY SERIOUS...
WELLL...
10·16·2003

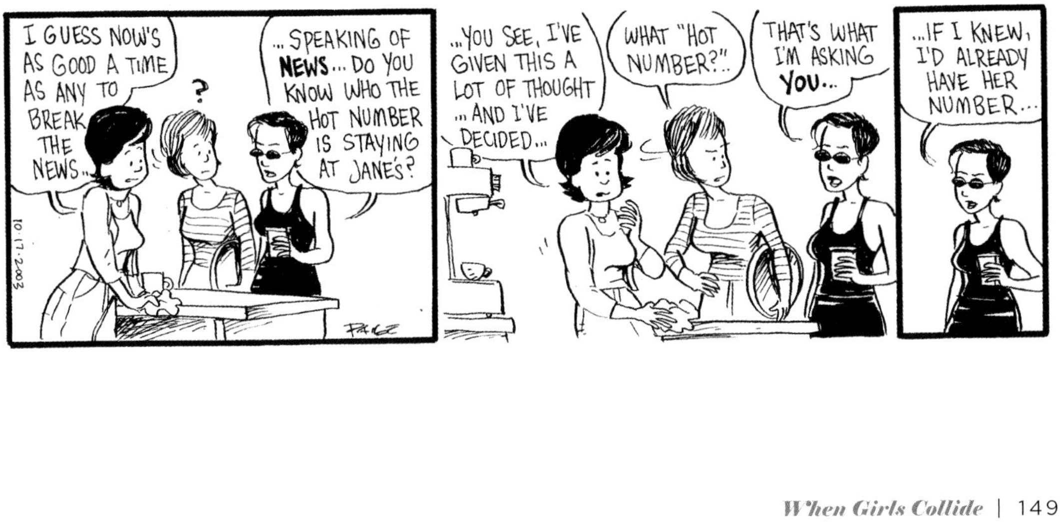
I GUESS NOW'S AS GOOD A TIME AS ANY TO BREAK THE NEWS...
?
...SPEAKING OF NEWS... DO YOU KNOW WHO THE HOT NUMBER IS STAYING AT JANE'S?
10·17·2003
PAIGE
...YOU SEE, I'VE GIVEN THIS A LOT OF THOUGHT ...AND I'VE DECIDED...
WHAT "HOT NUMBER?"..
THAT'S WHAT I'M ASKING YOU...
...IF I KNEW, I'D ALREADY HAVE HER NUMBER...

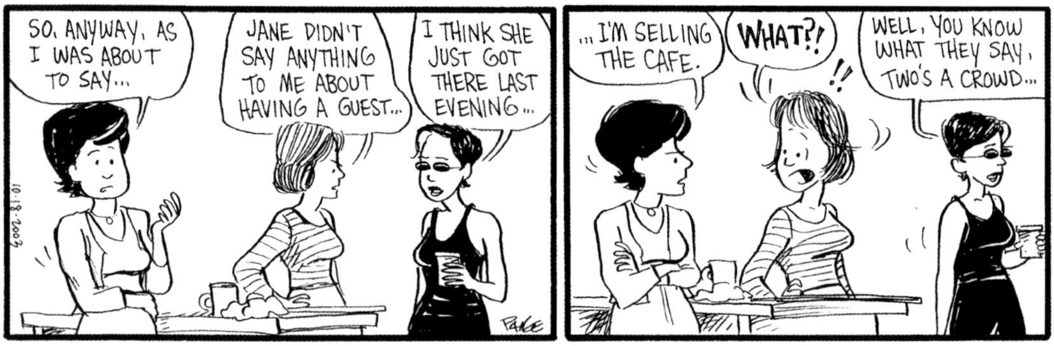
SO, ANYWAY, AS I WAS ABOUT TO SAY...
JANE DIDN'T SAY ANYTHING TO ME ABOUT HAVING A GUEST...
I THINK SHE JUST GOT THERE LAST EVENING...
10·18·2003
PAIGE
...I'M SELLING THE CAFE.
WHAT?!
!!
WELL, YOU KNOW WHAT THEY SAY, TWO'S A CROWD...

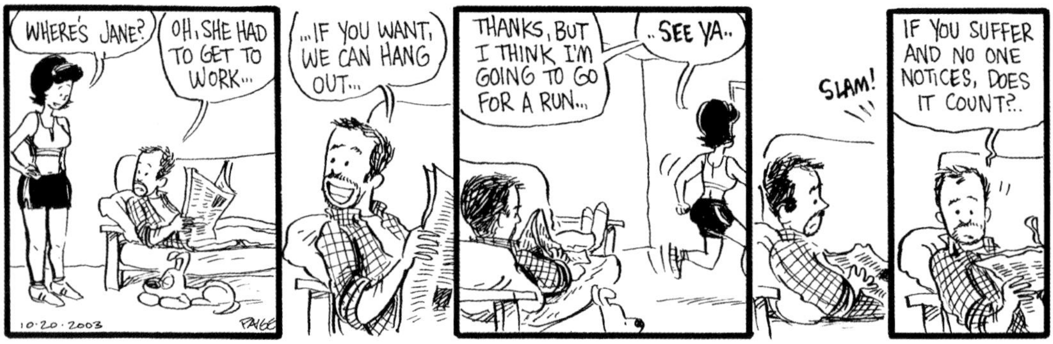
WHERE'S JANE?
OH, SHE HAD TO GET TO WORK...
10·20·2003
PAIGE
...IF YOU WANT, WE CAN HANG OUT...
THANKS, BUT I THINK I'M GOING TO GO FOR A RUN...
..SEE YA..
SLAM!
IF YOU SUFFER AND NO ONE NOTICES, DOES IT COUNT?..

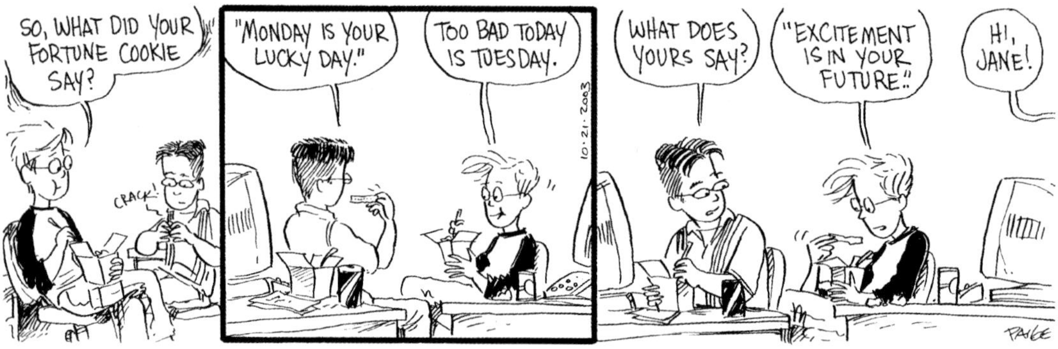
SO, WHAT DID YOUR FORTUNE COOKIE SAY?
CRACK!
"MONDAY IS YOUR LUCKY DAY."
TOO BAD TODAY IS TUESDAY.
10·21·2003
WHAT DOES YOURS SAY?
"EXCITEMENT IS IN YOUR FUTURE."
HI, JANE!
PAIGE

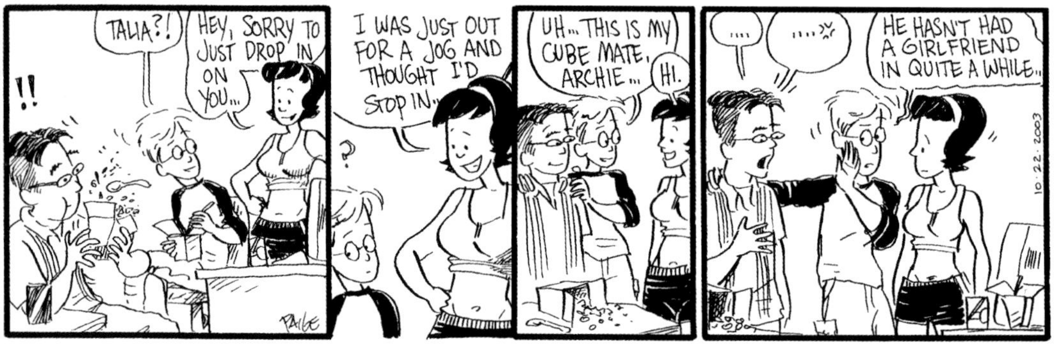
!!
TALIA?!
HEY, SORRY TO JUST DROP IN ON YOU...
PAIGE
I WAS JUST OUT FOR A JOG AND THOUGHT I'D STOP IN.
?
UH... THIS IS MY CUBE MATE, ARCHIE...
HI.
....
.....
HE HASN'T HAD A GIRLFRIEND IN QUITE A WHILE...
10·22·2003

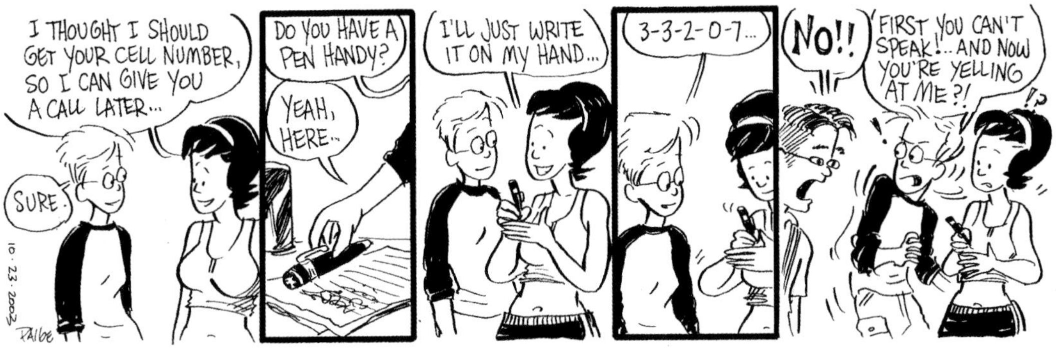
I THOUGHT I SHOULD GET YOUR CELL NUMBER, SO I CAN GIVE YOU A CALL LATER...
SURE.
10.23.2003
PAIGE
DO YOU HAVE A PEN HANDY?
YEAH, HERE...
I'LL JUST WRITE IT ON MY HAND...
3-3-2-0-7...
NO!!
FIRST YOU CAN'T SPEAK!...AND NOW YOU'RE YELLING AT ME?!

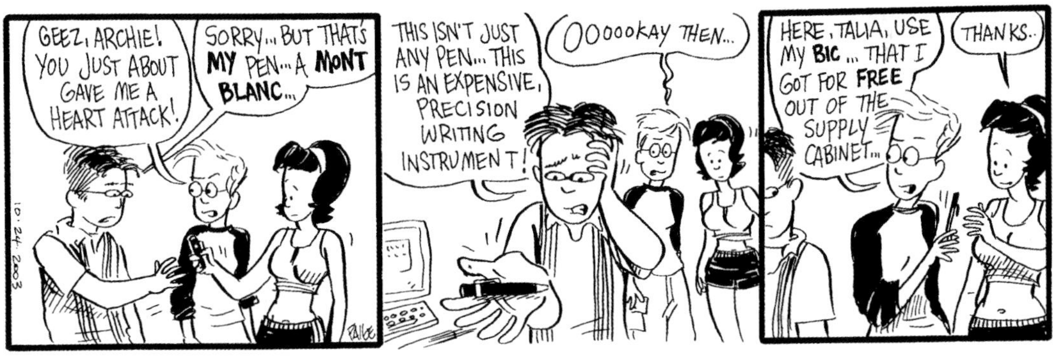
GEEZ, ARCHIE! YOU JUST ABOUT GAVE ME A HEART ATTACK!
SORRY... BUT THAT'S MY PEN... A MONT BLANC...
10.24.2003
PAIGE
THIS ISN'T JUST ANY PEN... THIS IS AN EXPENSIVE, PRECISION WRITING INSTRUMENT!
OOOOOKAY THEN...
HERE, TALIA, USE MY BIC... THAT I GOT FOR FREE OUT OF THE SUPPLY CABINET...
THANKS..

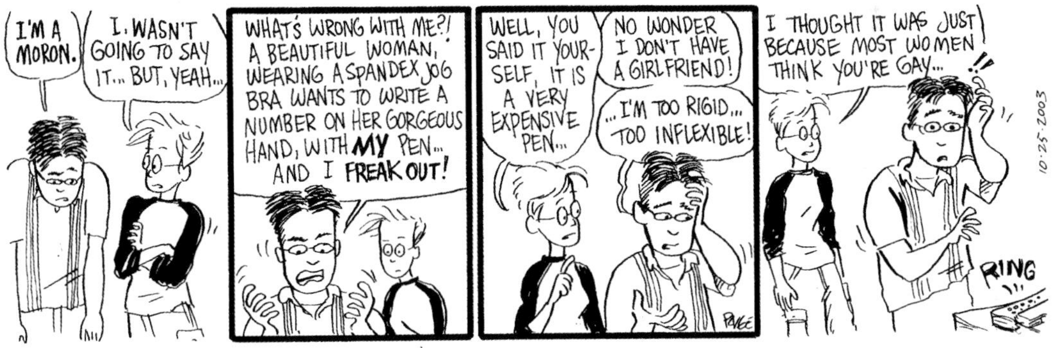
I'M A MORON.
I. WASN'T GOING TO SAY IT... BUT, YEAH...
WHAT'S WRONG WITH ME?! A BEAUTIFUL WOMAN, WEARING A SPANDEX JOG BRA WANTS TO WRITE A NUMBER ON HER GORGEOUS HAND, WITH MY PEN... AND I FREAK OUT!
WELL, YOU SAID IT YOURSELF, IT IS A VERY EXPENSIVE PEN...
NO WONDER I DON'T HAVE A GIRLFRIEND!
...I'M TOO RIGID... TOO INFLEXIBLE!
PAIGE
I THOUGHT IT WAS JUST BECAUSE MOST WOMEN THINK YOU'RE GAY...
10.25.2003
RING

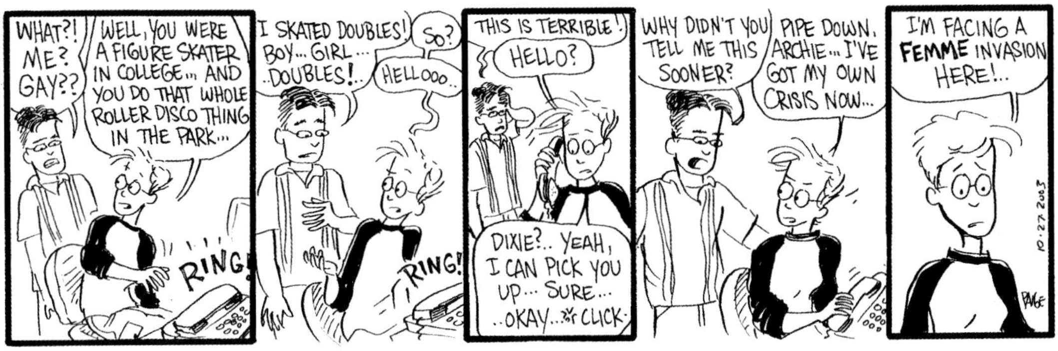
WHAT?! ME? GAY??
WELL, YOU WERE A FIGURE SKATER IN COLLEGE... AND YOU DO THAT WHOLE ROLLER DISCO THING IN THE PARK...
RING!
I SKATED DOUBLES! BOY... GIRL... ...DOUBLES!..
SO?
HELLOOO...
RING!
THIS IS TERRIBLE!
HELLO?
DIXIE?.. YEAH, I CAN PICK YOU UP... SURE... ..OKAY.. CLICK.
WHY DIDN'T YOU TELL ME THIS SOONER?
PIPE DOWN, ARCHIE... I'VE GOT MY OWN CRISIS NOW...
I'M FACING A FEMME INVASION HERE!..
10.27.2003
PAIGE

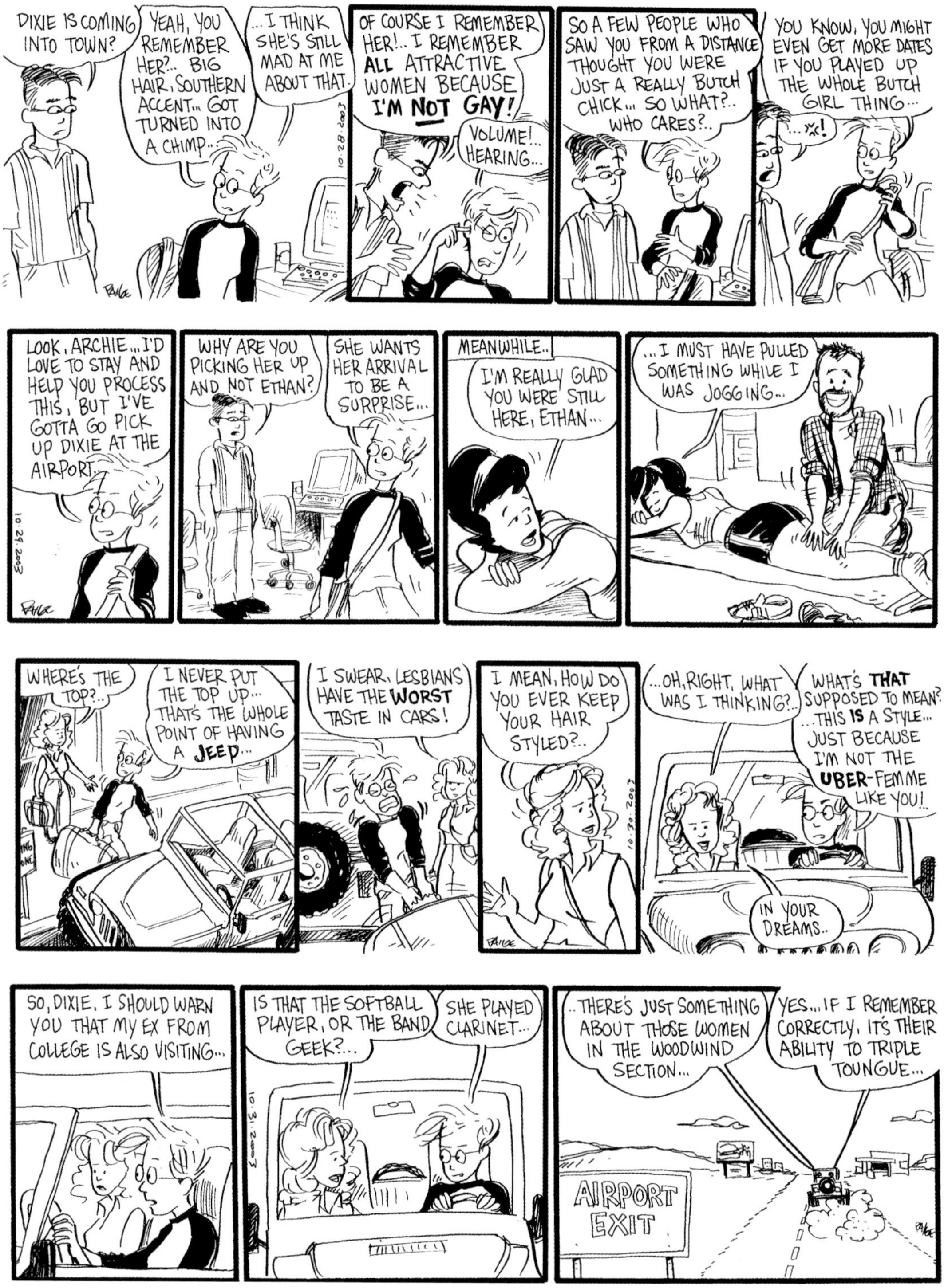
DIXIE IS COMING INTO TOWN?
YEAH, YOU REMEMBER HER?.. BIG HAIR, SOUTHERN ACCENT... GOT TURNED INTO A CHIMP..
...I THINK SHE'S STILL MAD AT ME ABOUT THAT.
10.28.2003
OF COURSE I REMEMBER HER!.. I REMEMBER **ALL** ATTRACTIVE WOMEN BECAUSE **I'M NOT GAY!**
VOLUME!.. HEARING...
SO A FEW PEOPLE WHO SAW YOU FROM A DISTANCE THOUGHT YOU WERE JUST A REALLY BUTCH CHICK... SO WHAT?.. WHO CARES?..
YOU KNOW, YOU MIGHT EVEN GET MORE DATES IF YOU PLAYED UP THE WHOLE BUTCH GIRL THING...
...※!
PAIGE
LOOK, ARCHIE...I'D LOVE TO STAY AND HELP YOU PROCESS THIS, BUT I'VE GOTTA GO PICK UP DIXIE AT THE AIRPORT...
10.29.2003
WHY ARE YOU PICKING HER UP AND NOT ETHAN?
SHE WANTS HER ARRIVAL TO BE A SURPRISE...
MEANWHILE..
I'M REALLY GLAD YOU WERE STILL HERE, ETHAN...
...I MUST HAVE PULLED SOMETHING WHILE I WAS JOGGING...
PAIGE
WHERE'S THE TOP?..
I NEVER PUT THE TOP UP... THAT'S THE WHOLE POINT OF HAVING A **JEEP**...
I SWEAR, LESBIANS HAVE THE **WORST** TASTE IN CARS!
I MEAN, HOW DO YOU EVER KEEP YOUR HAIR STYLED?..
10.30.2003
...OH, RIGHT, WHAT WAS I THINKING?..
WHAT'S **THAT** SUPPOSED TO MEAN?.. ...THIS **IS** A STYLE... JUST BECAUSE I'M NOT THE **UBER**-FEMME LIKE YOU!..
IN YOUR DREAMS..
PAIGE
SO, DIXIE, I SHOULD WARN YOU THAT MY EX FROM COLLEGE IS ALSO VISITING...
10.31.2003
IS THAT THE SOFTBALL PLAYER, OR THE BAND GEEK?...
SHE PLAYED CLARINET...
..THERE'S JUST SOMETHING ABOUT THOSE WOMEN IN THE WOODWIND SECTION...
YES...IF I REMEMBER CORRECTLY, IT'S THEIR ABILITY TO TRIPLE TOUNGUE...
AIRPORT EXIT
PAIGE

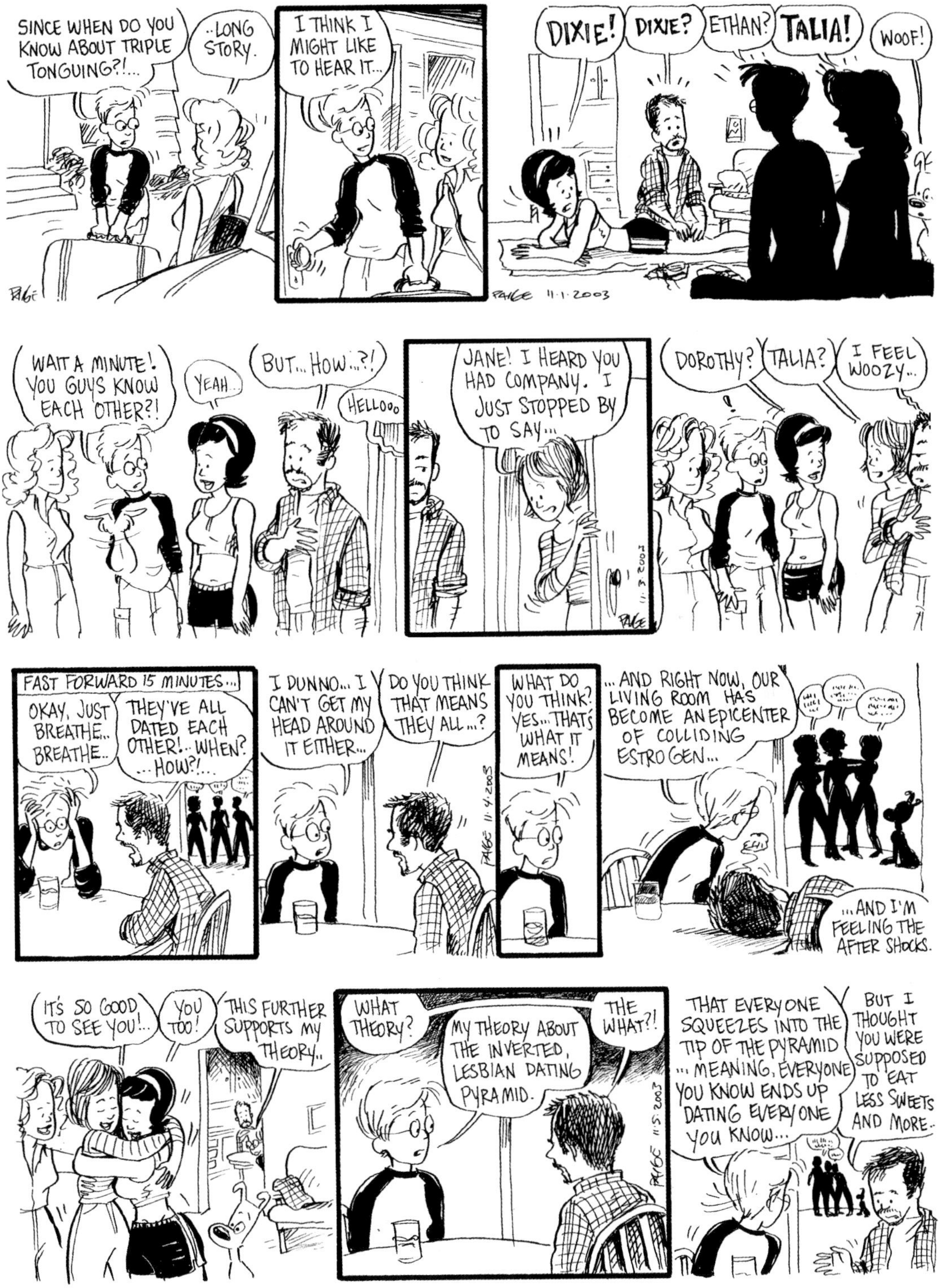
SINCE WHEN DO YOU KNOW ABOUT TRIPLE TONGUING?!...
..LONG STORY.
I THINK I MIGHT LIKE TO HEAR IT...
DIXIE!
DIXIE?
ETHAN?
TALIA!
WOOF!
PAIGE 11.1.2003
WAIT A MINUTE! YOU GUYS KNOW EACH OTHER?!
YEAH..
BUT... HOW...?!
HELLOOO
JANE! I HEARD YOU HAD COMPANY. I JUST STOPPED BY TO SAY...
DOROTHY?
TALIA?
I FEEL WOOZY...
FAST FORWARD 15 MINUTES...
OKAY, JUST BREATHE... BREATHE..
THEY'VE ALL DATED EACH OTHER!.. WHEN? ...HOW?!...
I DUNNO... I CAN'T GET MY HEAD AROUND IT EITHER...
DO YOU THINK THAT MEANS THEY ALL...?
PAIGE 11.4.2003
WHAT DO YOU THINK? YES...THAT'S WHAT IT MEANS!
...AND RIGHT NOW, OUR LIVING ROOM HAS BECOME AN EPICENTER OF COLLIDING ESTROGEN...
...AND I'M FEELING THE AFTER SHOCKS.
IT'S SO GOOD TO SEE YOU!...
YOU TOO!
THIS FURTHER SUPPORTS MY THEORY..
WHAT THEORY?
MY THEORY ABOUT THE INVERTED, LESBIAN DATING PYRAMID.
THE WHAT?!
PAIGE 11.5.2003
THAT EVERYONE SQUEEZES INTO THE TIP OF THE PYRAMID ...MEANING, EVERYONE YOU KNOW ENDS UP DATING EVERYONE YOU KNOW...
BUT I THOUGHT YOU WERE SUPPOSED TO EAT LESS SWEETS AND MORE..

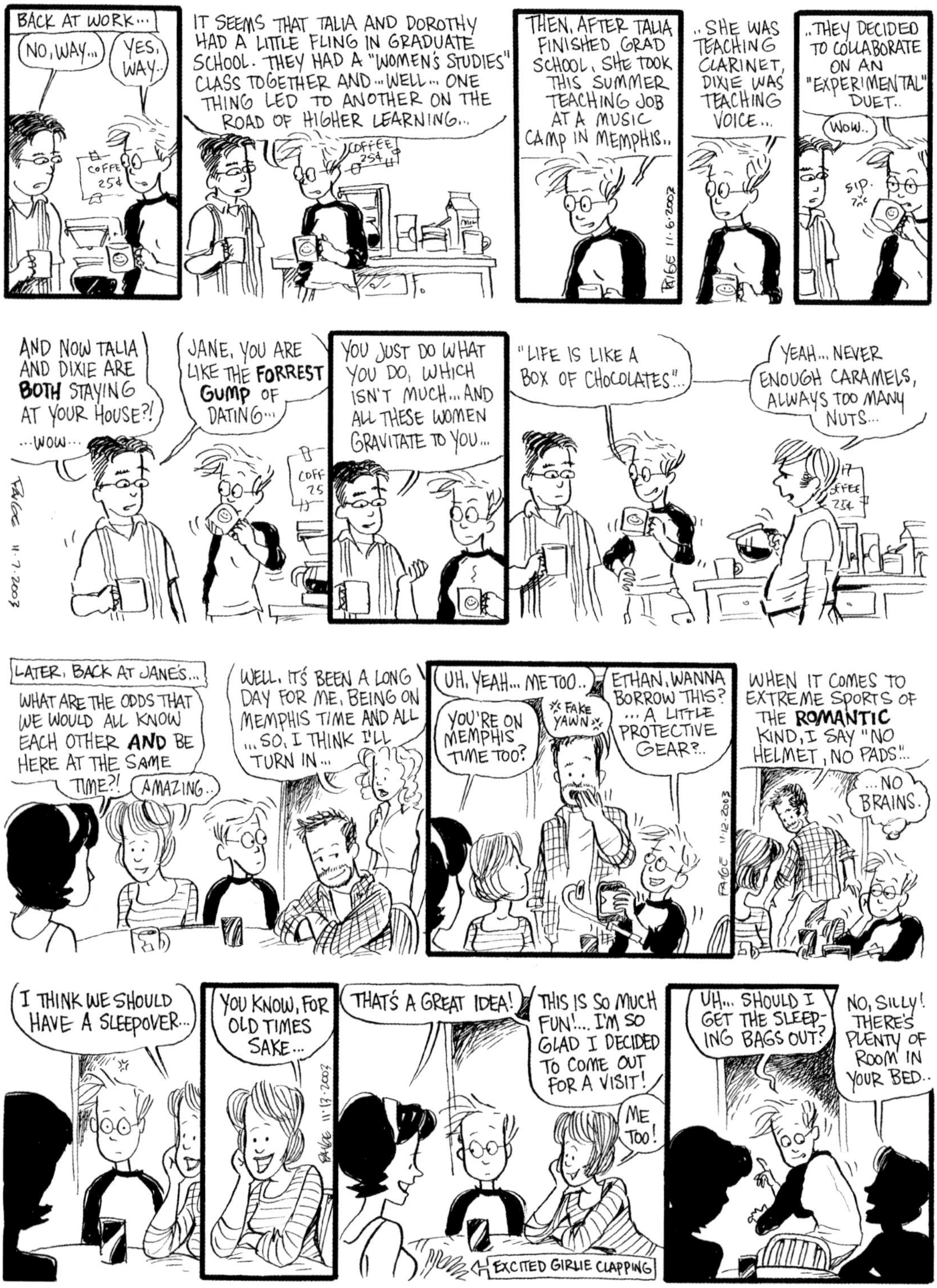
BACK AT WORK...
NO, WAY...
YES, WAY..
COFFEE 25¢
IT SEEMS THAT TALIA AND DOROTHY HAD A LITTLE FLING IN GRADUATE SCHOOL. THEY HAD A "WOMEN'S STUDIES" CLASS TOGETHER AND...WELL... ONE THING LED TO ANOTHER ON THE ROAD OF HIGHER LEARNING...
COFFEE 25¢
THEN, AFTER TALIA FINISHED GRAD SCHOOL, SHE TOOK THIS SUMMER TEACHING JOB AT A MUSIC CAMP IN MEMPHIS..
PAIGE 11·6·2003
..SHE WAS TEACHING CLARINET, DIXIE WAS TEACHING VOICE...
..THEY DECIDED TO COLLABORATE ON AN "EXPERIMENTAL" DUET..
WOW..
SIP.
AND NOW TALIA AND DIXIE ARE BOTH STAYING AT YOUR HOUSE?! ...WOW...
PAIGE 11·7·2003
JANE, YOU ARE LIKE THE FORREST GUMP OF DATING...
COFFEE 25
YOU JUST DO WHAT YOU DO, WHICH ISN'T MUCH... AND ALL THESE WOMEN GRAVITATE TO YOU...
"LIFE IS LIKE A BOX OF CHOCOLATES"...
YEAH... NEVER ENOUGH CARAMELS, ALWAYS TOO MANY NUTS...
COFFEE 25¢
LATER, BACK AT JANE'S...
WHAT ARE THE ODDS THAT WE WOULD ALL KNOW EACH OTHER AND BE HERE AT THE SAME TIME?!
AMAZING..
WELL, IT'S BEEN A LONG DAY FOR ME, BEING ON MEMPHIS TIME AND ALL ...SO, I THINK I'LL TURN IN...
UH, YEAH... ME TOO..
YOU'RE ON MEMPHIS TIME TOO?
FAKE YAWN
ETHAN, WANNA BORROW THIS? ...A LITTLE PROTECTIVE GEAR?..
PAIGE 11·12·2003
WHEN IT COMES TO EXTREME SPORTS OF THE ROMANTIC KIND, I SAY "NO HELMET, NO PADS"...
...NO BRAINS.
I THINK WE SHOULD HAVE A SLEEPOVER...
YOU KNOW, FOR OLD TIMES SAKE...
PAIGE 11·13·2003
THAT'S A GREAT IDEA!
THIS IS SO MUCH FUN!... I'M SO GLAD I DECIDED TO COME OUT FOR A VISIT!
ME TOO!
EXCITED GIRLIE CLAPPING
UH... SHOULD I GET THE SLEEPING BAGS OUT?
NO, SILLY! THERE'S PLENTY OF ROOM IN YOUR BED..

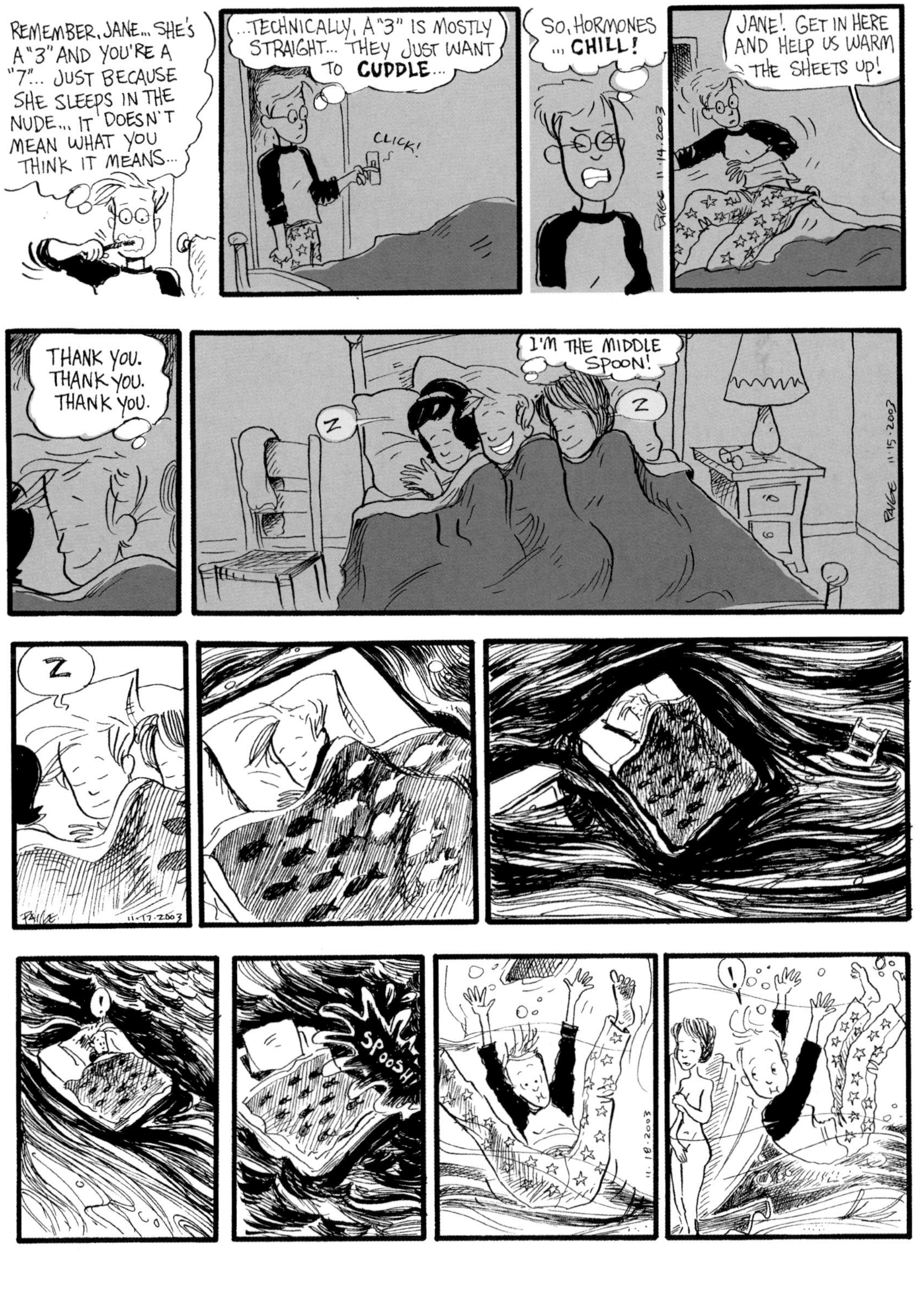
REMEMBER, JANE... SHE'S A "3" AND YOU'RE A "7"... JUST BECAUSE SHE SLEEPS IN THE NUDE... IT DOESN'T MEAN WHAT YOU THINK IT MEANS...
...TECHNICALLY, A "3" IS MOSTLY STRAIGHT... THEY JUST WANT TO CUDDLE...
CLICK!
SO, HORMONES ...CHILL!
PAIGE 11·14·2003
JANE! GET IN HERE AND HELP US WARM THE SHEETS UP!
THANK YOU. THANK YOU. THANK YOU.
I'M THE MIDDLE SPOON!
Z
Z
PAIGE 11·15·2003
Z
PAIGE 11·17·2003
!
SPOOSH!
11·18·2003
!

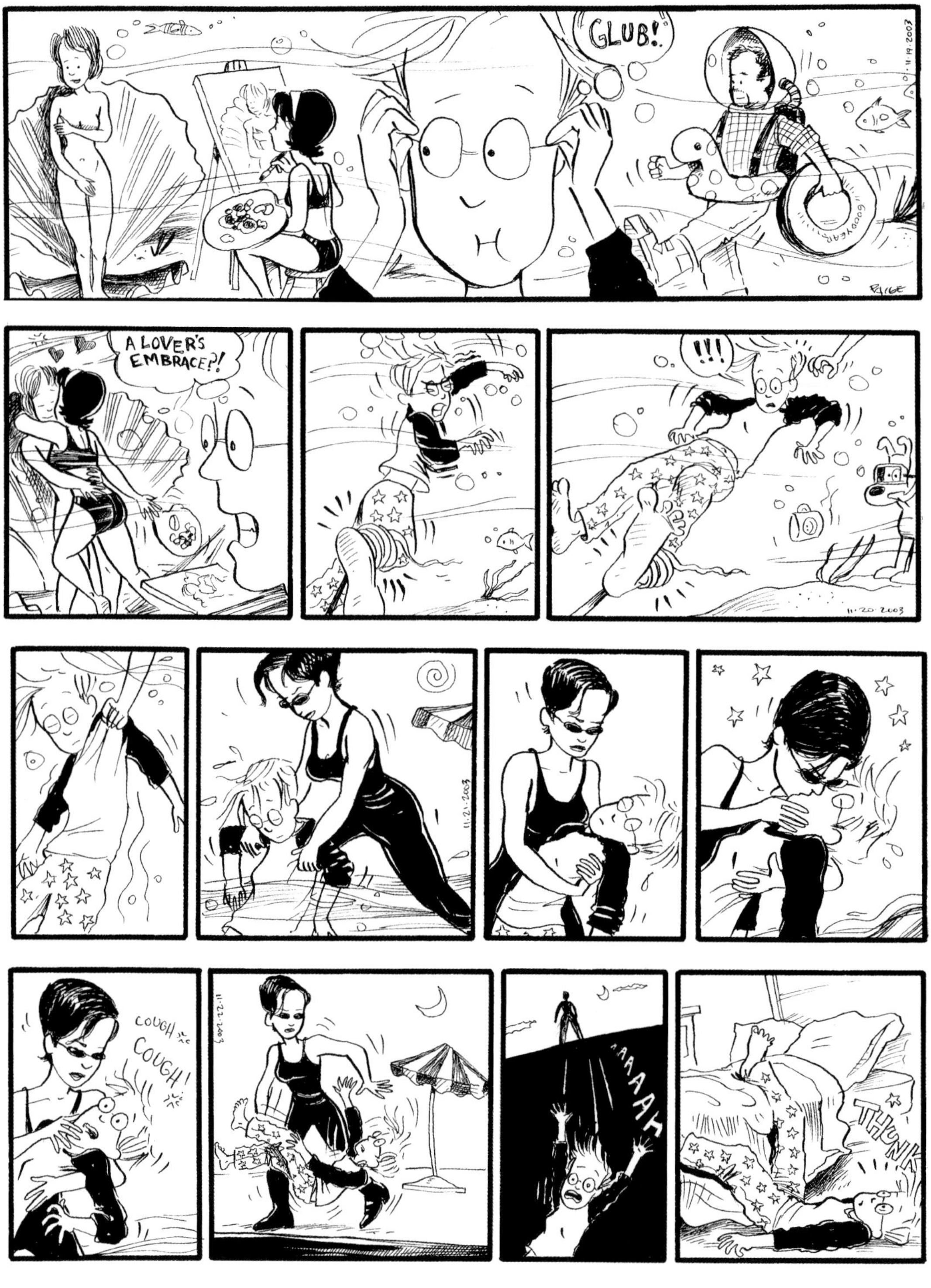
GLUB!
11.19.2003
GOODYEAR
PAIGE
A LOVER'S EMBRACE?!
!!!
11.20.2003
11.21.2003
COUGH
COUGH!
11.22.2003
AAAAAAH
THUNK

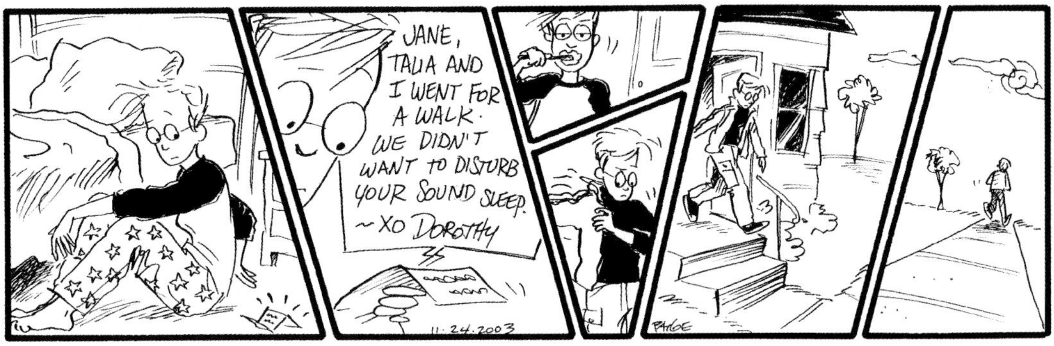

JANE, TALIA AND I WENT FOR A WALK. WE DIDN'T WANT TO DISTURB YOUR SOUND SLEEP. ~XO DOROTHY
11.24.2003
PAIGE

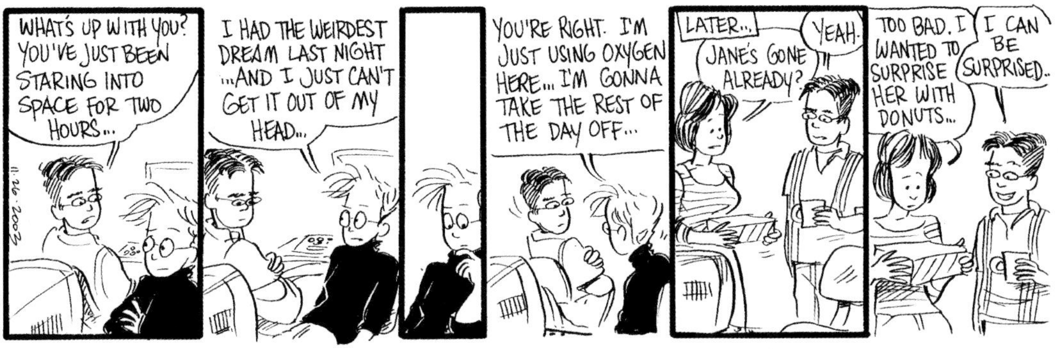

WHAT'S UP WITH YOU? YOU'VE JUST BEEN STARING INTO SPACE FOR TWO HOURS...
11.26.2003
I HAD THE WEIRDEST DREAM LAST NIGHT ...AND I JUST CAN'T GET IT OUT OF MY HEAD...
YOU'RE RIGHT. I'M JUST USING OXYGEN HERE... I'M GONNA TAKE THE REST OF THE DAY OFF...
LATER...
JANE'S GONE ALREADY?
YEAH.
TOO BAD. I WANTED TO SURPRISE HER WITH DONUTS...
I CAN BE SURPRISED..

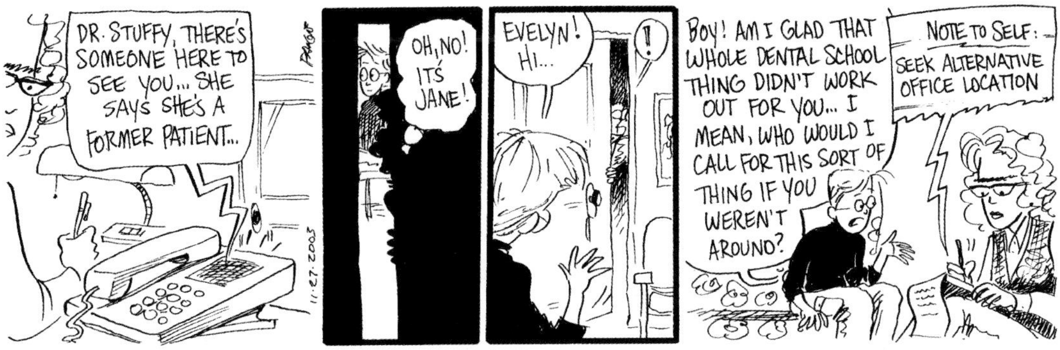

DR. STUFFY, THERE'S SOMEONE HERE TO SEE YOU... SHE SAYS SHE'S A FORMER PATIENT...
PAIGE
11.27.2003
OH, NO! IT'S JANE!
EVELYN! HI...
!
BOY! AM I GLAD THAT WHOLE DENTAL SCHOOL THING DIDN'T WORK OUT FOR YOU... I MEAN, WHO WOULD I CALL FOR THIS SORT OF THING IF YOU WEREN'T AROUND?
NOTE TO SELF: SEEK ALTERNATIVE OFFICE LOCATION

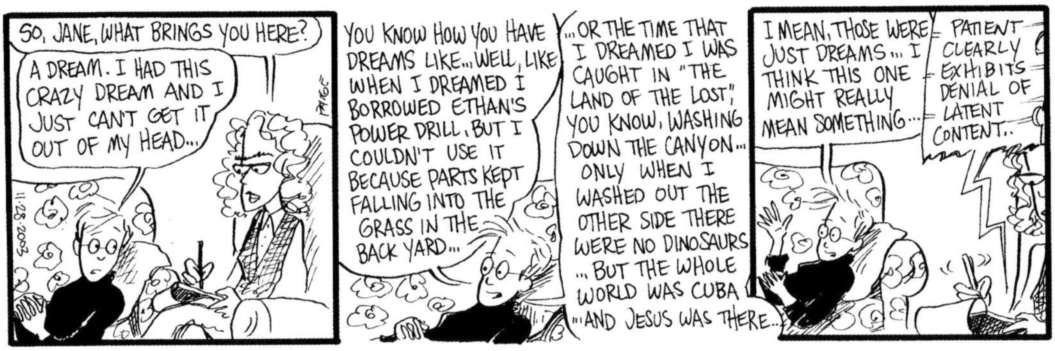

SO, JANE, WHAT BRINGS YOU HERE?
A DREAM. I HAD THIS CRAZY DREAM AND I JUST CAN'T GET IT OUT OF MY HEAD...
PAIGE
11.28.2003
YOU KNOW HOW YOU HAVE DREAMS LIKE... WELL, LIKE WHEN I DREAMED I BORROWED ETHAN'S POWER DRILL, BUT I COULDN'T USE IT BECAUSE PARTS KEPT FALLING INTO THE GRASS IN THE BACK YARD...
...OR THE TIME THAT I DREAMED I WAS CAUGHT IN "THE LAND OF THE LOST", YOU KNOW, WASHING DOWN THE CANYON... ONLY WHEN I WASHED OUT THE OTHER SIDE THERE WERE NO DINOSAURS ... BUT THE WHOLE WORLD WAS CUBA ...AND JESUS WAS THERE...
I MEAN, THOSE WERE JUST DREAMS... I THINK THIS ONE MIGHT REALLY MEAN SOMETHING...
PATIENT CLEARLY EXHIBITS DENIAL OF LATENT CONTENT..

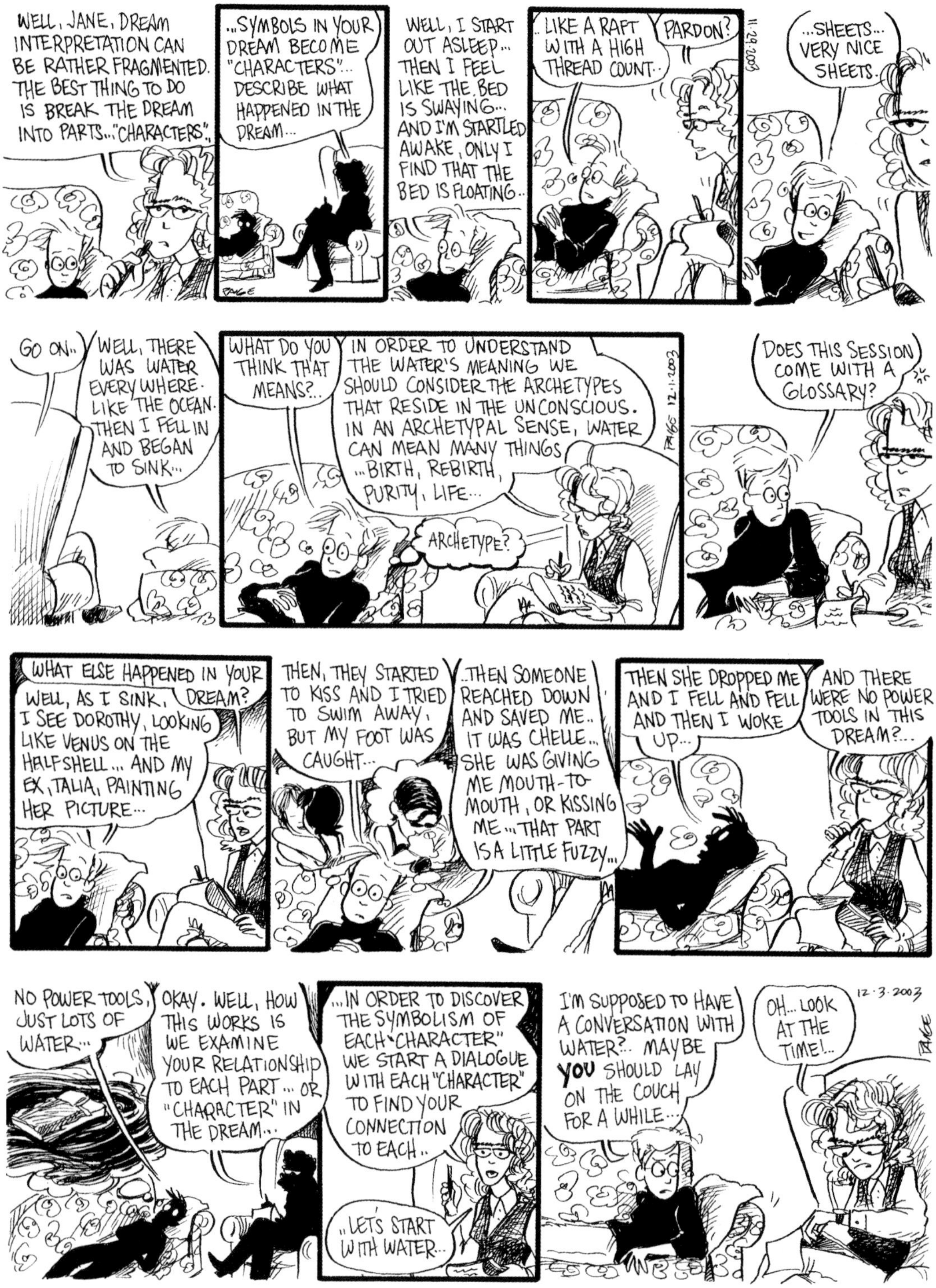
WELL, JANE, DREAM INTERPRETATION CAN BE RATHER FRAGMENTED. THE BEST THING TO DO IS BREAK THE DREAM INTO PARTS..."CHARACTERS".
...SYMBOLS IN YOUR DREAM BECOME "CHARACTERS"... DESCRIBE WHAT HAPPENED IN THE DREAM...
PAIGE
WELL, I START OUT ASLEEP... THEN I FEEL LIKE THE BED IS SWAYING... AND I'M STARTLED AWAKE, ONLY I FIND THAT THE BED IS FLOATING...
..LIKE A RAFT WITH A HIGH THREAD COUNT..
PARDON?
11-29-2003
...SHEETS... VERY NICE SHEETS...
GO ON..
WELL, THERE WAS WATER EVERYWHERE. LIKE THE OCEAN. THEN I FELL IN AND BEGAN TO SINK...
WHAT DO YOU THINK THAT MEANS?...
IN ORDER TO UNDERSTAND THE WATER'S MEANING WE SHOULD CONSIDER THE ARCHETYPES THAT RESIDE IN THE UNCONSCIOUS. IN AN ARCHETYPAL SENSE, WATER CAN MEAN MANY THINGS ...BIRTH, REBIRTH, PURITY, LIFE...
ARCHETYPE?
PAIGE 12-1-2003
DOES THIS SESSION COME WITH A GLOSSARY?
WHAT ELSE HAPPENED IN YOUR DREAM?
WELL, AS I SINK, I SEE DOROTHY, LOOKING LIKE VENUS ON THE HALFSHELL... AND MY EX, TALIA, PAINTING HER PICTURE...
THEN, THEY STARTED TO KISS AND I TRIED TO SWIM AWAY, BUT MY FOOT WAS CAUGHT...
..THEN SOMEONE REACHED DOWN AND SAVED ME.. IT WAS CHELLE... SHE WAS GIVING ME MOUTH-TO-MOUTH, OR KISSING ME... THAT PART IS A LITTLE FUZZY...
THEN SHE DROPPED ME AND I FELL AND FELL AND THEN I WOKE UP...
AND THERE WERE NO POWER TOOLS IN THIS DREAM?...
NO POWER TOOLS, JUST LOTS OF WATER...
OKAY. WELL, HOW THIS WORKS IS WE EXAMINE YOUR RELATIONSHIP TO EACH PART... OR "CHARACTER" IN THE DREAM...
...IN ORDER TO DISCOVER THE SYMBOLISM OF EACH "CHARACTER" WE START A DIALOGUE WITH EACH "CHARACTER" TO FIND YOUR CONNECTION TO EACH..
..LET'S START WITH WATER...
I'M SUPPOSED TO HAVE A CONVERSATION WITH WATER?.. MAYBE YOU SHOULD LAY ON THE COUCH FOR A WHILE...
OH... LOOK AT THE TIME!..
12-3-2003
PAIGE

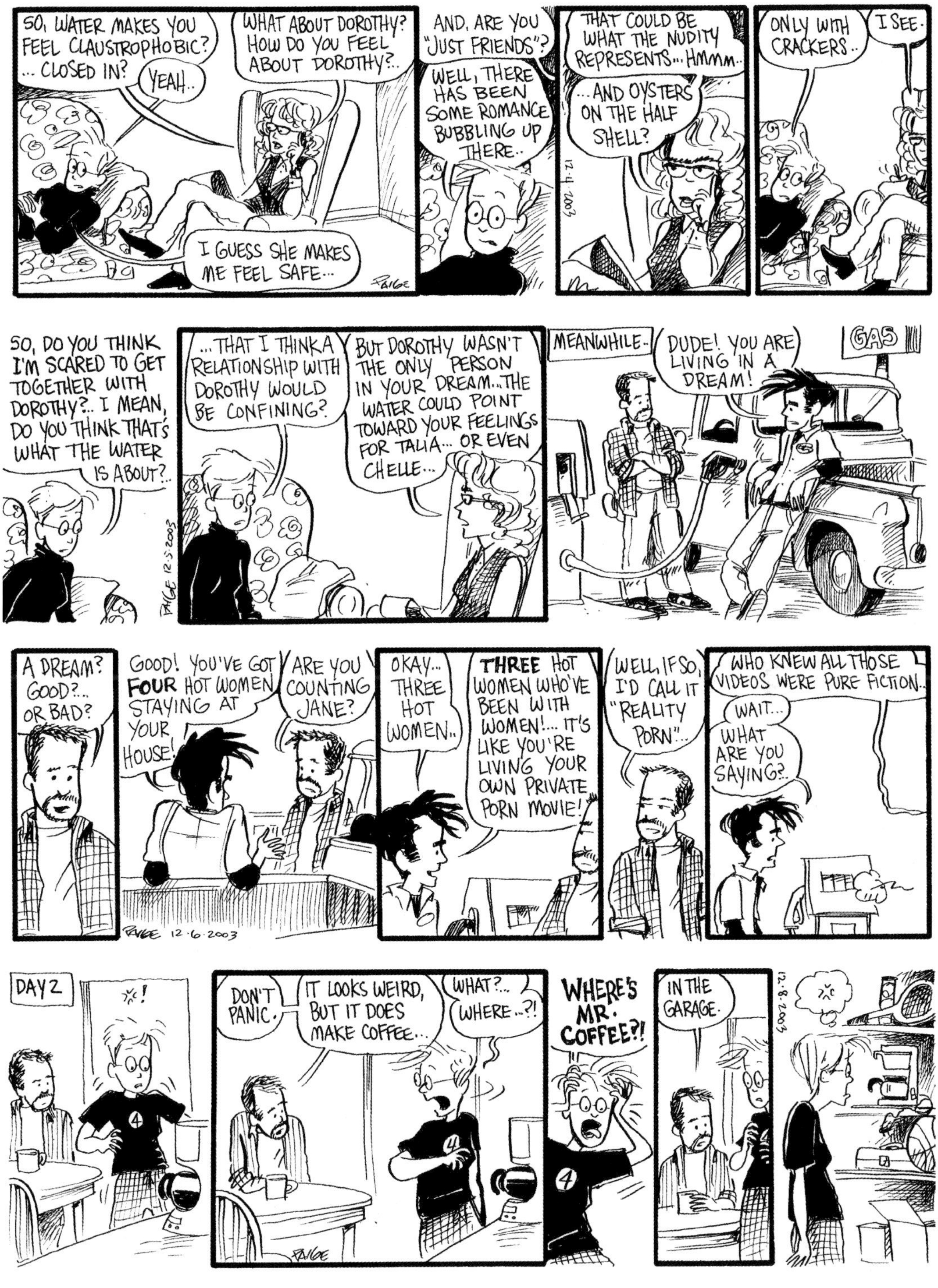
SO, WATER MAKES YOU FEEL CLAUSTROPHOBIC? ... CLOSED IN?
YEAH..
WHAT ABOUT DOROTHY? HOW DO YOU FEEL ABOUT DOROTHY?..
I GUESS SHE MAKES ME FEEL SAFE...
PAIGE
AND, ARE YOU "JUST FRIENDS"?
WELL, THERE HAS BEEN SOME ROMANCE BUBBLING UP THERE..
THAT COULD BE WHAT THE NUDITY REPRESENTS... HMMM..
12·4·2003
...AND OYSTERS ON THE HALF SHELL?
ONLY WITH CRACKERS..
I SEE.
SO, DO YOU THINK **I'M** SCARED TO GET TOGETHER WITH DOROTHY?.. I MEAN, DO YOU THINK THAT'S WHAT THE WATER IS ABOUT?..
PAIGE 12·5·2003
...THAT I THINK A RELATIONSHIP WITH DOROTHY WOULD BE CONFINING?
BUT DOROTHY WASN'T THE ONLY PERSON IN YOUR DREAM... THE WATER COULD POINT TOWARD YOUR FEELINGS FOR TALIA... OR EVEN CHELLE...
MEANWHILE..
DUDE! YOU ARE LIVING IN A DREAM!
GAS
A DREAM? GOOD?.. OR BAD?
GOOD! YOU'VE GOT **FOUR** HOT WOMEN STAYING AT YOUR HOUSE!
ARE YOU COUNTING JANE?
PAIGE 12·6·2003
OKAY... THREE HOT WOMEN..
THREE HOT WOMEN WHO'VE BEEN WITH WOMEN!... IT'S LIKE YOU'RE LIVING YOUR OWN PRIVATE PORN MOVIE!
WELL, IF SO, I'D CALL IT "REALITY PORN"...
WHO KNEW ALL THOSE VIDEOS WERE PURE FICTION..
WAIT...
WHAT ARE YOU SAYING?..
DAY 2
DON'T PANIC.
IT LOOKS WEIRD, BUT IT DOES MAKE COFFEE...
WHAT?... WHERE...?!
PAIGE
WHERE'S MR. COFFEE?!
IN THE GARAGE.
12·8·2003

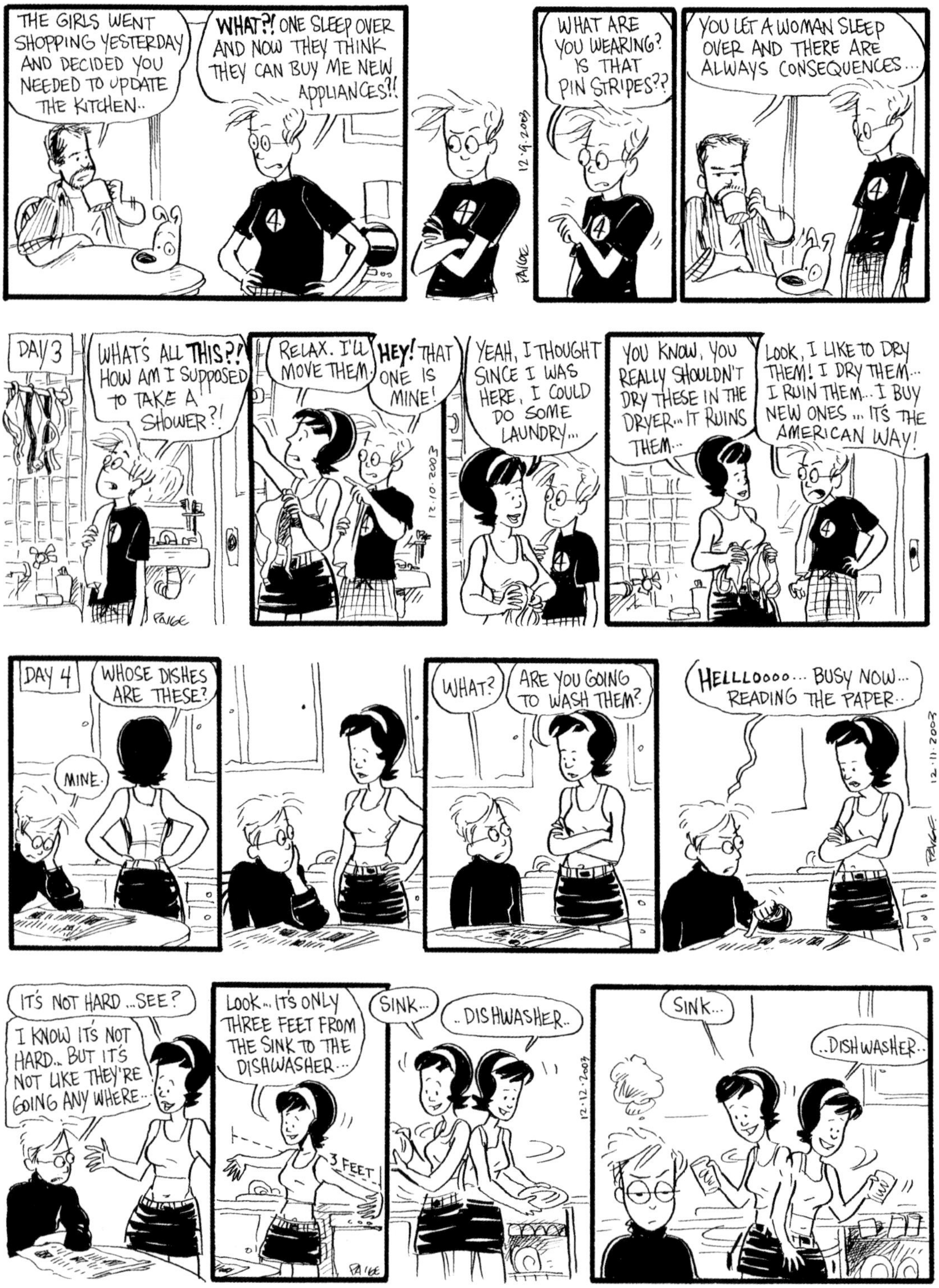
THE GIRLS WENT SHOPPING YESTERDAY AND DECIDED YOU NEEDED TO UPDATE THE KITCHEN..
WHAT?! ONE SLEEP OVER AND NOW THEY THINK THEY CAN BUY ME NEW APPLIANCES?!
12.9.2003
PAIGE
WHAT ARE YOU WEARING? IS THAT PIN STRIPES??
YOU LET A WOMAN SLEEP OVER AND THERE ARE ALWAYS CONSEQUENCES...
DAY 3
WHAT'S ALL THIS?! HOW AM I SUPPOSED TO TAKE A SHOWER?!
PAIGE
RELAX. I'LL MOVE THEM.
HEY! THAT ONE IS MINE!
12.10.2003
YEAH, I THOUGHT SINCE I WAS HERE, I COULD DO SOME LAUNDRY...
YOU KNOW, YOU REALLY SHOULDN'T DRY THESE IN THE DRYER... IT RUINS THEM...
LOOK, I LIKE TO DRY THEM! I DRY THEM... I RUIN THEM... I BUY NEW ONES ... IT'S THE AMERICAN WAY!
DAY 4
WHOSE DISHES ARE THESE?
MINE.
WHAT?
ARE YOU GOING TO WASH THEM?
HELLLOOOO... BUSY NOW... READING THE PAPER..
12.11.2003
PAIGE
IT'S NOT HARD ...SEE?
I KNOW IT'S NOT HARD.. BUT IT'S NOT LIKE THEY'RE GOING ANY WHERE...
LOOK.. IT'S ONLY THREE FEET FROM THE SINK TO THE DISHWASHER...
3 FEET
PAIGE
SINK...
.. DISHWASHER..
12.12.2003
SINK...
..DISHWASHER..

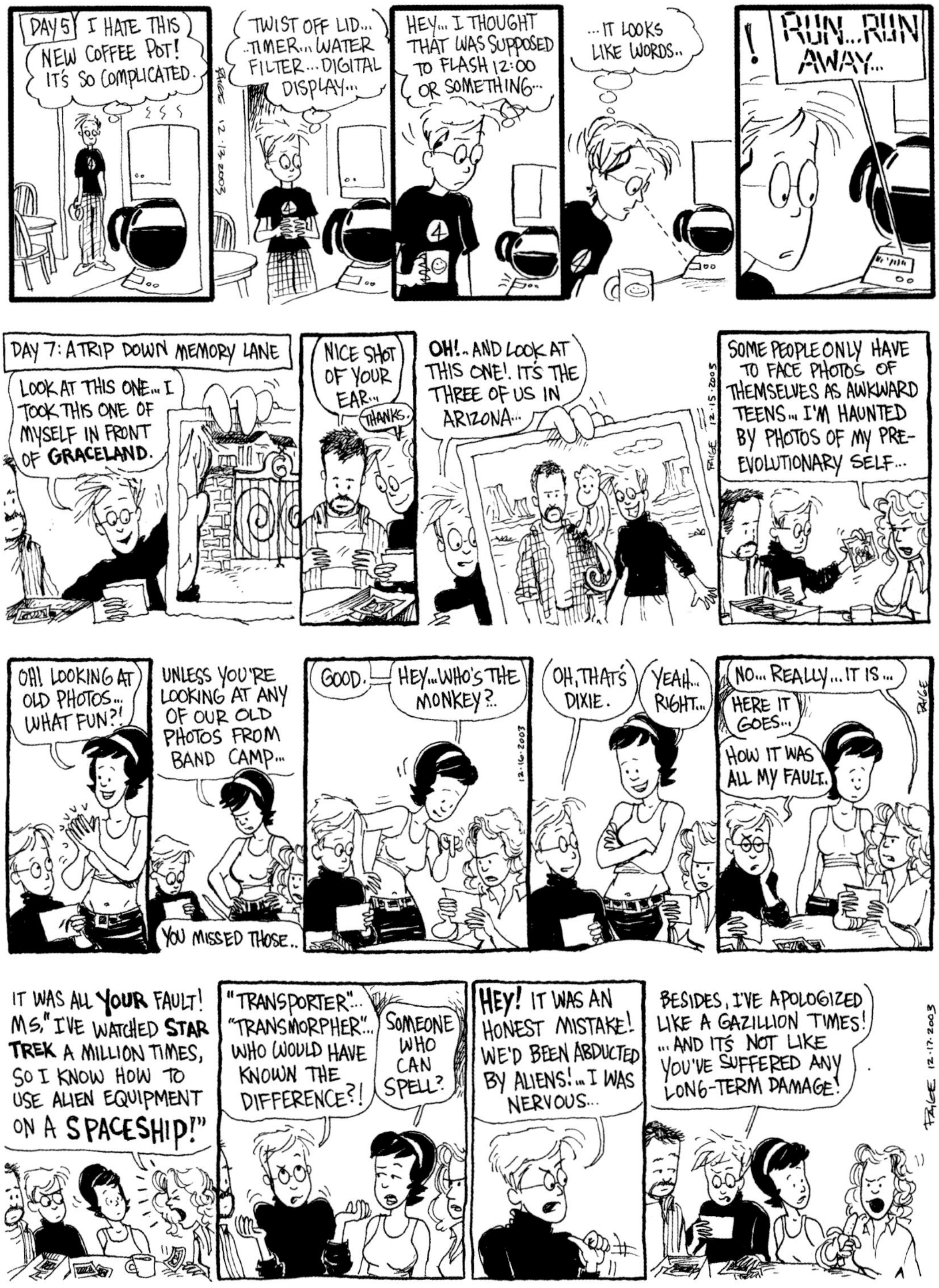
DAY 5
I HATE THIS NEW COFFEE POT! IT'S SO COMPLICATED.
PAIGE 12·13·2003
TWIST OFF LID... TIMER... WATER FILTER... DIGITAL DISPLAY...
HEY... I THOUGHT THAT WAS SUPPOSED TO FLASH 12:00 OR SOMETHING...
...IT LOOKS LIKE WORDS..
!
RUN...RUN AWAY...
DAY 7: A TRIP DOWN MEMORY LANE
LOOK AT THIS ONE... I TOOK THIS ONE OF MYSELF IN FRONT OF GRACELAND.
NICE SHOT OF YOUR EAR...
THANKS.
OH!.. AND LOOK AT THIS ONE! IT'S THE THREE OF US IN ARIZONA...
PAIGE 12·15·2003
SOME PEOPLE ONLY HAVE TO FACE PHOTOS OF THEMSELVES AS AWKWARD TEENS... I'M HAUNTED BY PHOTOS OF MY PRE-EVOLUTIONARY SELF...
OH! LOOKING AT OLD PHOTOS... WHAT FUN?!
UNLESS YOU'RE LOOKING AT ANY OF OUR OLD PHOTOS FROM BAND CAMP...
YOU MISSED THOSE..
GOOD.
HEY...WHO'S THE MONKEY?..
12·16·2003
OH, THAT'S DIXIE.
YEAH... RIGHT...
NO... REALLY... IT IS...
PAIGE
HERE IT GOES...
HOW IT WAS ALL MY FAULT..
IT WAS ALL YOUR FAULT! MS. "I'VE WATCHED STAR TREK A MILLION TIMES, SO I KNOW HOW TO USE ALIEN EQUIPMENT ON A SPACESHIP!"
"TRANSPORTER"... "TRANSMORPHER"... WHO WOULD HAVE KNOWN THE DIFFERENCE?!
SOMEONE WHO CAN SPELL?
HEY! IT WAS AN HONEST MISTAKE! WE'D BEEN ABDUCTED BY ALIENS!... I WAS NERVOUS...
BESIDES, I'VE APOLOGIZED LIKE A GAZILLION TIMES! ...AND IT'S NOT LIKE YOU'VE SUFFERED ANY LONG-TERM DAMAGE!
12·17·2003
PAIGE

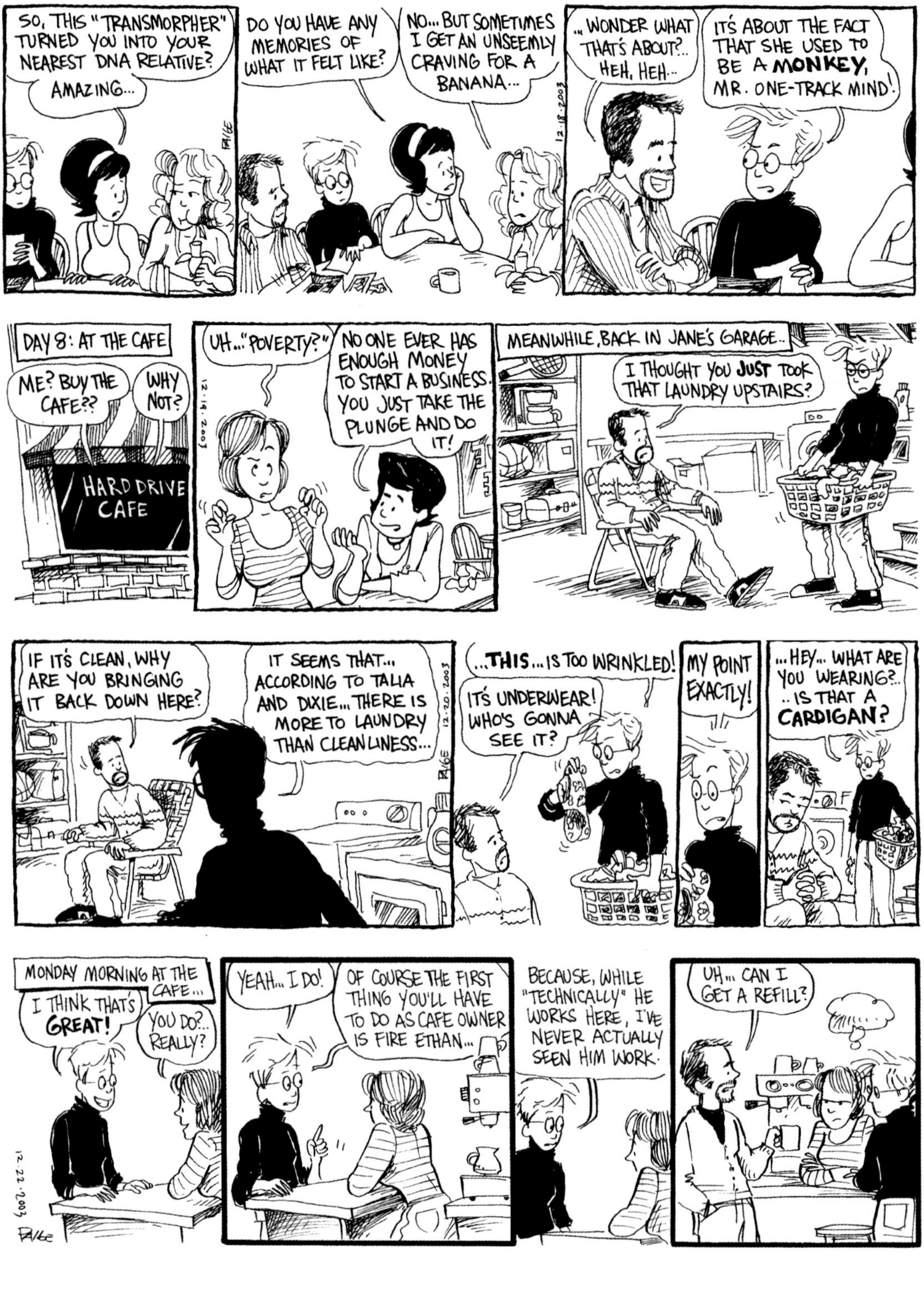

SO, THIS "TRANSMORPHER" TURNED YOU INTO YOUR NEAREST DNA RELATIVE?
AMAZING...
DO YOU HAVE ANY MEMORIES OF WHAT IT FELT LIKE?
NO... BUT SOMETIMES I GET AN UNSEEMLY CRAVING FOR A BANANA...
12.18.2003
... WONDER WHAT THAT'S ABOUT?.. HEH, HEH...
IT'S ABOUT THE FACT THAT SHE USED TO BE A **MONKEY**, MR. ONE-TRACK MIND!
DAY 8: AT THE CAFE
ME? BUY THE CAFE??
WHY NOT?
HARD DRIVE CAFE
12.19.2003
UH... "POVERTY?"
NO ONE EVER HAS ENOUGH MONEY TO START A BUSINESS. YOU JUST TAKE THE PLUNGE AND DO IT!
MEANWHILE, BACK IN JANE'S GARAGE..
I THOUGHT YOU **JUST** TOOK THAT LAUNDRY UPSTAIRS?
IF IT'S CLEAN, WHY ARE YOU BRINGING IT BACK DOWN HERE?
IT SEEMS THAT... ACCORDING TO TALIA AND DIXIE... THERE IS MORE TO LAUNDRY THAN CLEANLINESS...
12.20.2003
...**THIS**... IS TOO WRINKLED!
IT'S UNDERWEAR! WHO'S GONNA SEE IT?
MY POINT EXACTLY!
...HEY... WHAT ARE YOU WEARING?.. ..IS THAT A **CARDIGAN**?
MONDAY MORNING AT THE CAFE...
I THINK THAT'S **GREAT**!
YOU DO?.. REALLY?
12.22.2003
YEAH... I DO!
OF COURSE THE FIRST THING YOU'LL HAVE TO DO AS CAFE OWNER IS FIRE ETHAN...
BECAUSE, WHILE "TECHNICALLY" HE WORKS HERE, I'VE NEVER ACTUALLY SEEN HIM WORK.
UH... CAN I GET A REFILL?

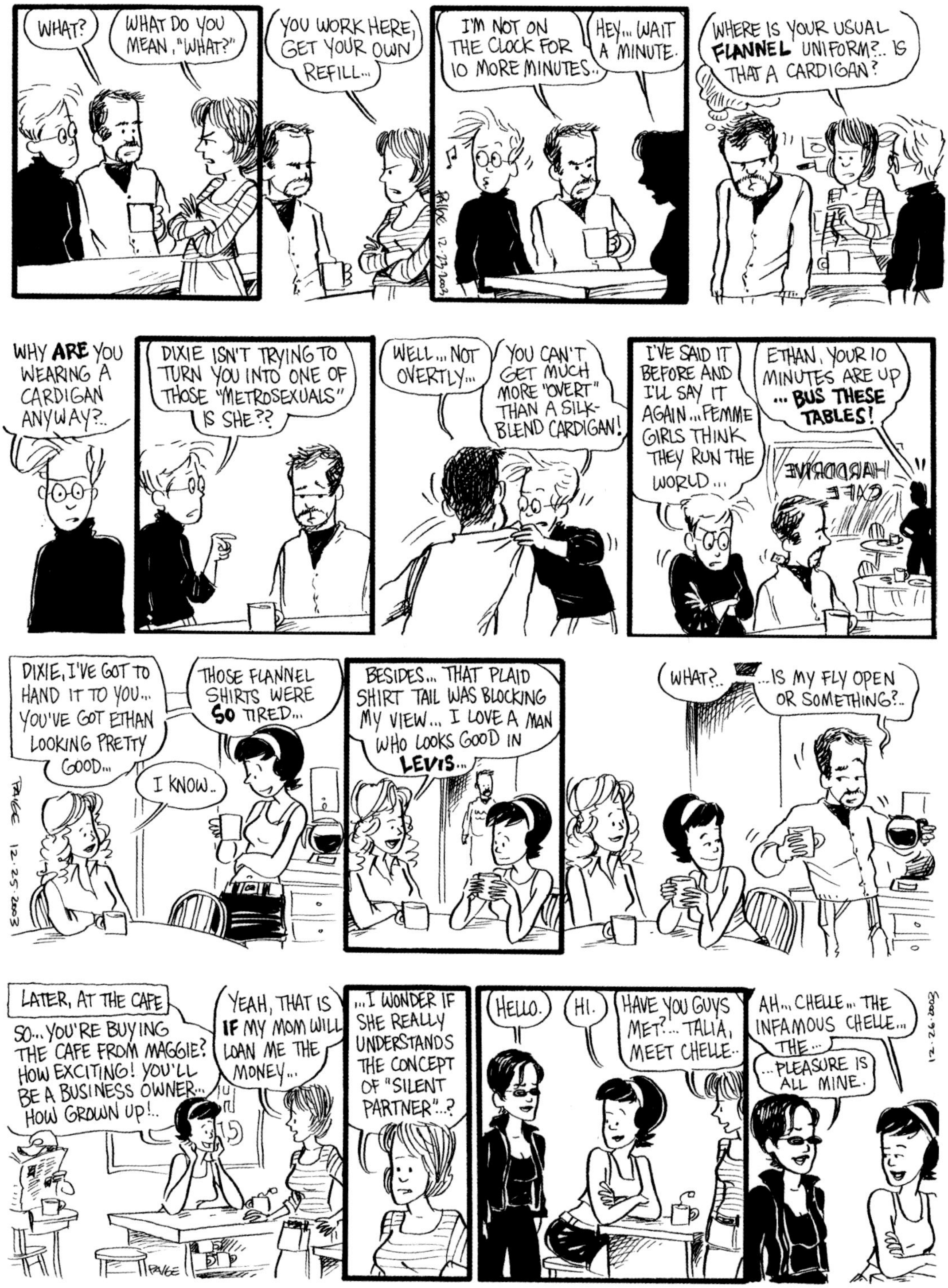
WHAT?
WHAT DO YOU MEAN, "WHAT?"
YOU WORK HERE, GET YOUR OWN REFILL...
12·27·2003
I'M NOT ON THE CLOCK FOR 10 MORE MINUTES...
HEY... WAIT A MINUTE.
WHERE IS YOUR USUAL **FLANNEL** UNIFORM?.. IS THAT A CARDIGAN?
WHY **ARE** YOU WEARING A CARDIGAN ANYWAY?..
DIXIE ISN'T TRYING TO TURN YOU INTO ONE OF THOSE "METROSEXUALS" IS SHE??
WELL... NOT OVERTLY...
YOU CAN'T GET MUCH MORE "OVERT" THAN A SILK-BLEND CARDIGAN!
I'VE SAID IT BEFORE AND I'LL SAY IT AGAIN... FEMME GIRLS THINK THEY RUN THE WORLD...
ETHAN, YOUR 10 MINUTES ARE UP **... BUS THESE TABLES!**
DIXIE, I'VE GOT TO HAND IT TO YOU... YOU'VE GOT ETHAN LOOKING PRETTY GOOD...
THOSE FLANNEL SHIRTS WERE **SO** TIRED...
I KNOW..
12·25·2003
BESIDES... THAT PLAID SHIRT TAIL WAS BLOCKING MY VIEW... I LOVE A MAN WHO LOOKS GOOD IN **LEVIS**...
WHAT?.. ...IS MY FLY OPEN OR SOMETHING?..
LATER, AT THE CAFE
SO... YOU'RE BUYING THE CAFE FROM MAGGIE? HOW EXCITING! YOU'LL BE A BUSINESS OWNER... HOW GROWN UP!..
YEAH, THAT IS **IF** MY MOM WILL LOAN ME THE MONEY...
...I WONDER IF SHE REALLY UNDERSTANDS THE CONCEPT OF "SILENT PARTNER"..?
HELLO.
HI.
HAVE YOU GUYS MET?... TALIA, MEET CHELLE..
AH... CHELLE... THE INFAMOUS CHELLE... THE...
...PLEASURE IS ALL MINE.
12·26·2003

Road Trip

There's nothing like a long drive to the desert with your ex to force you to face bad patterns in your life. The dry climate and soul-searching under the stars offer Jane a moment of clarity about her younger self.

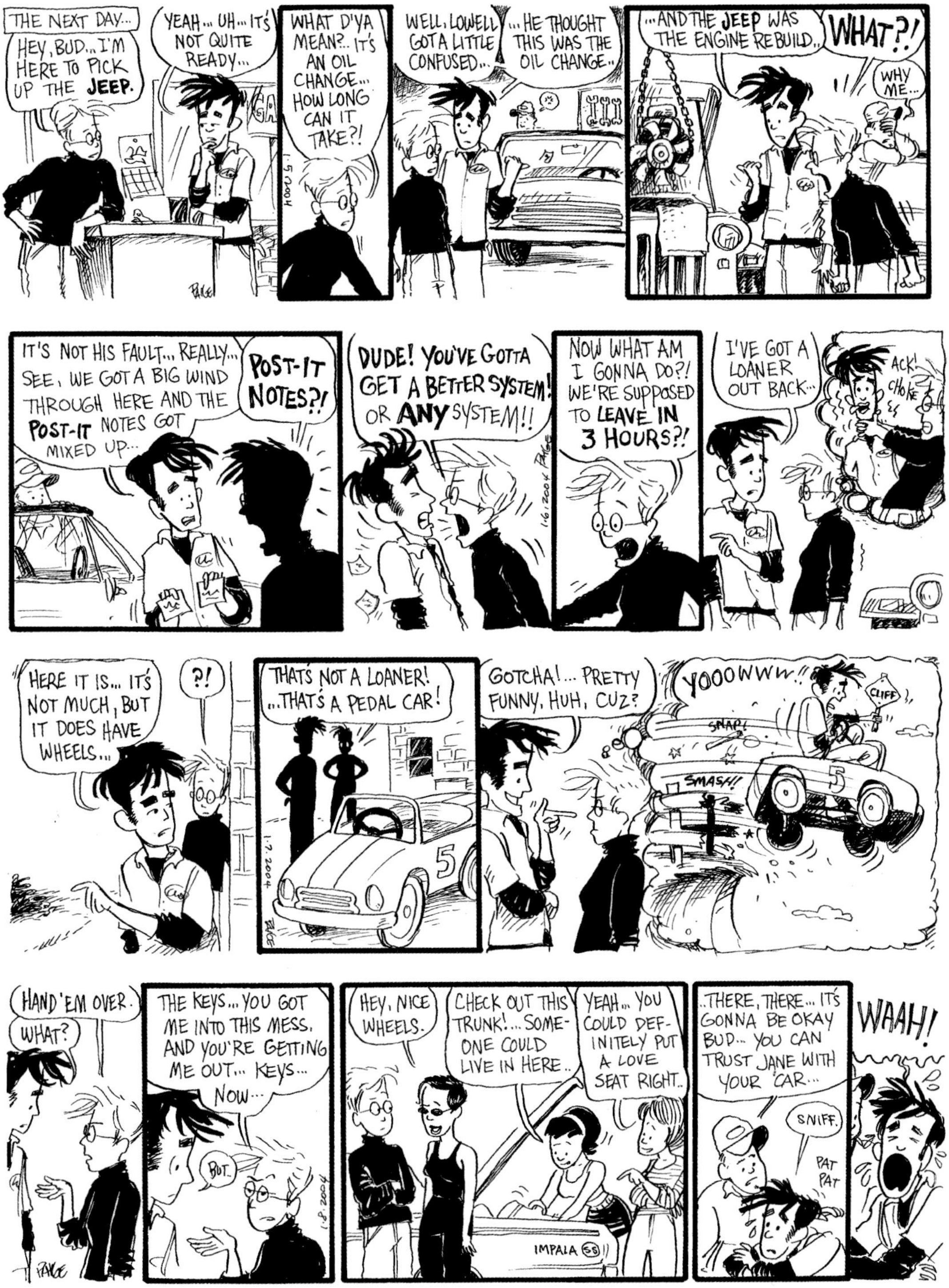
THE NEXT DAY...
HEY, BUD... I'M HERE TO PICK UP THE JEEP.
YEAH... UH... IT'S NOT QUITE READY...
PAIGE
WHAT D'YA MEAN?.. IT'S AN OIL CHANGE... HOW LONG CAN IT TAKE?!
1.5.2004
WELL, LOWELL GOT A LITTLE CONFUSED...
...HE THOUGHT THIS WAS THE OIL CHANGE...
...AND THE JEEP WAS THE ENGINE REBUILD...
WHAT?!
WHY ME...
IT'S NOT HIS FAULT... REALLY... SEE, WE GOT A BIG WIND THROUGH HERE AND THE POST-IT NOTES GOT MIXED UP...
POST-IT NOTES?!
DUDE! YOU'VE GOTTA GET A BETTER SYSTEM! OR ANY SYSTEM!!
PAIGE
1.6.2004
NOW WHAT AM I GONNA DO?! WE'RE SUPPOSED TO LEAVE IN 3 HOURS?!
I'VE GOT A LOANER OUT BACK...
ACK! CHOKE
HERE IT IS... IT'S NOT MUCH, BUT IT DOES HAVE WHEELS...
?!
THAT'S NOT A LOANER! ...THAT'S A PEDAL CAR!
1.7.2004
PAIGE
GOTCHA!... PRETTY FUNNY, HUH, CUZ?
YOOOWWW!!
CLIFF
SNAP!
SMASH!!
HAND 'EM OVER.
WHAT?
PAIGE
THE KEYS... YOU GOT ME INTO THIS MESS, AND YOU'RE GETTING ME OUT... KEYS... NOW...
BUT..
1.8.2004
HEY, NICE WHEELS.
CHECK OUT THIS TRUNK!... SOME-ONE COULD LIVE IN HERE..
YEAH... YOU COULD DEF-INITELY PUT A LOVE SEAT RIGHT..
IMPALA
..THERE, THERE... IT'S GONNA BE OKAY BUD... YOU CAN TRUST JANE WITH YOUR CAR...
SNIFF.
PAT PAT
WAAH!

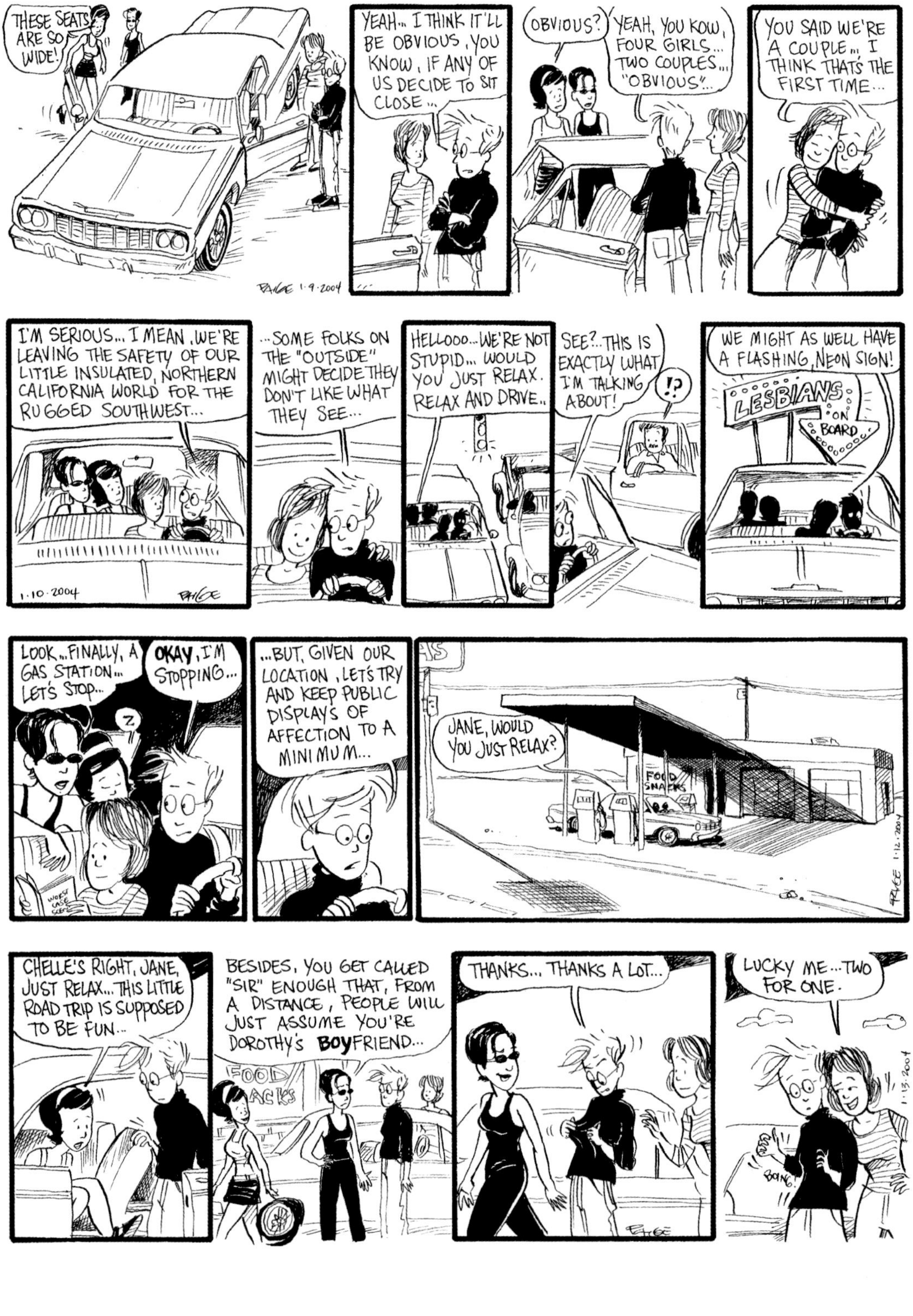
THESE SEATS ARE SO WIDE!
YEAH... I THINK IT'LL BE OBVIOUS, YOU KNOW, IF ANY OF US DECIDE TO SIT CLOSE...
OBVIOUS?
YEAH, YOU KOW, FOUR GIRLS... TWO COUPLES... "OBVIOUS"...
YOU SAID WE'RE A COUPLE... I THINK THAT'S THE FIRST TIME...
PAIGE 1·9·2004
I'M SERIOUS... I MEAN, WE'RE LEAVING THE SAFETY OF OUR LITTLE INSULATED, NORTHERN CALIFORNIA WORLD FOR THE RUGGED SOUTHWEST...
...SOME FOLKS ON THE "OUTSIDE" MIGHT DECIDE THEY DON'T LIKE WHAT THEY SEE...
HELLOOO... WE'RE NOT STUPID... WOULD YOU JUST RELAX. RELAX AND DRIVE..
SEE?... THIS IS EXACTLY WHAT I'M TALKING ABOUT!
!?
WE MIGHT AS WELL HAVE A FLASHING, NEON SIGN!
LESBIANS ON BOARD
1·10·2004 PAIGE
LOOK... FINALLY, A GAS STATION... LET'S STOP...
Z
OKAY, I'M STOPPING...
...BUT, GIVEN OUR LOCATION, LET'S TRY AND KEEP PUBLIC DISPLAYS OF AFFECTION TO A MINIMUM...
JANE, WOULD YOU JUST RELAX?
FOOD SNACKS
PAIGE 1·12·2004
CHELLE'S RIGHT, JANE, JUST RELAX... THIS LITTLE ROAD TRIP IS SUPPOSED TO BE FUN...
BESIDES, YOU GET CALLED "SIR" ENOUGH THAT, FROM A DISTANCE, PEOPLE WILL JUST ASSUME YOU'RE DOROTHY'S BOYFRIEND...
THANKS... THANKS A LOT...
LUCKY ME... TWO FOR ONE.
BOING!
1·13·2004
PAIGE

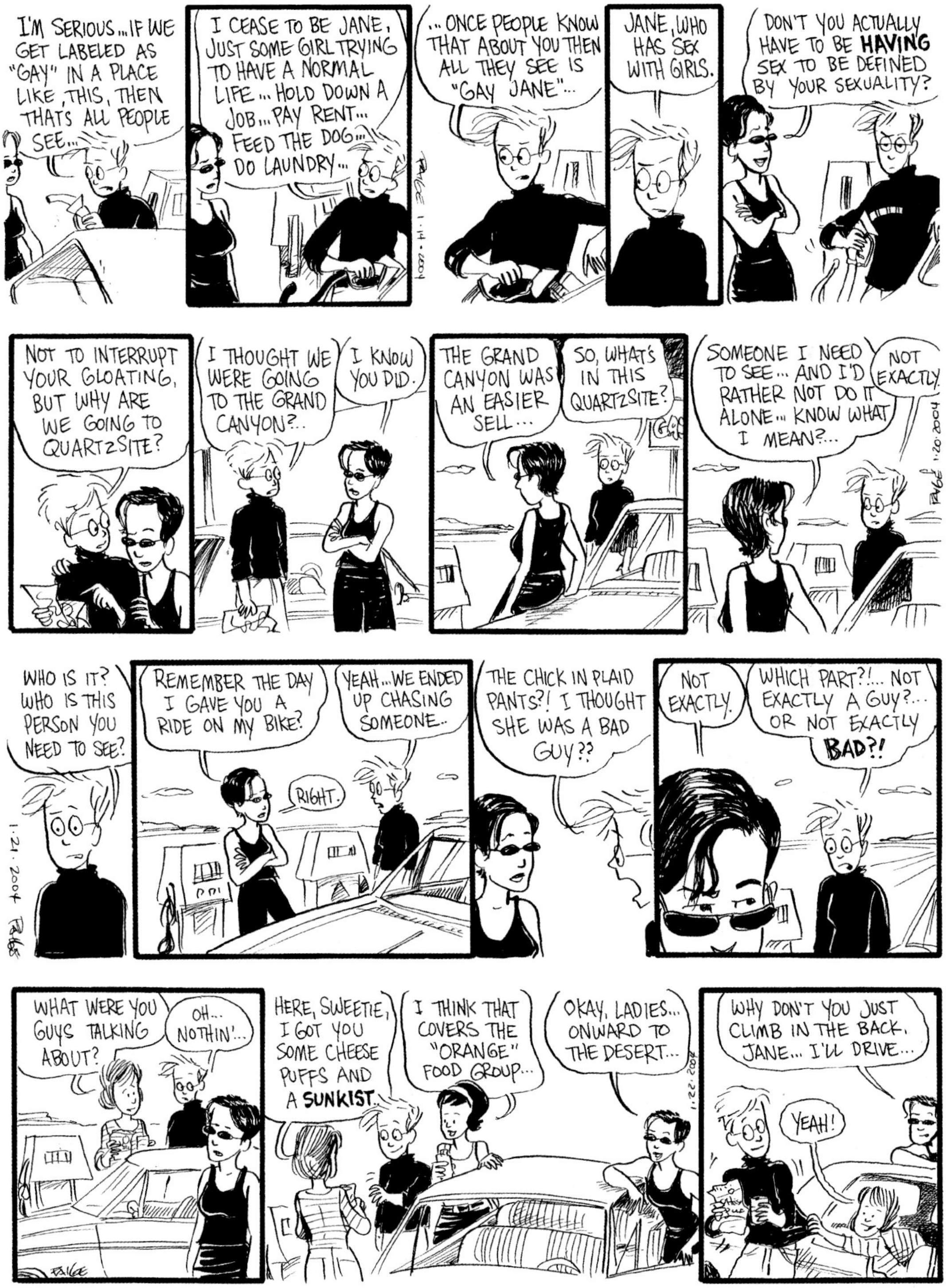
I'M SERIOUS... IF WE GET LABELED AS "GAY" IN A PLACE LIKE, THIS, THEN THAT'S ALL PEOPLE SEE...
I CEASE TO BE JANE, JUST SOME GIRL TRYING TO HAVE A NORMAL LIFE... HOLD DOWN A JOB... PAY RENT... FEED THE DOG... DO LAUNDRY...
PAIGE 1·14·2004
...ONCE PEOPLE KNOW THAT ABOUT YOU THEN ALL THEY SEE IS "GAY JANE"...
JANE, WHO HAS SEX WITH GIRLS.
DON'T YOU ACTUALLY HAVE TO BE **HAVING** SEX TO BE DEFINED BY YOUR SEXUALITY?
NOT TO INTERRUPT YOUR GLOATING, BUT WHY ARE WE GOING TO QUARTZSITE?
I THOUGHT WE WERE GOING TO THE GRAND CANYON?...
I KNOW YOU DID.
THE GRAND CANYON WAS AN EASIER SELL...
SO, WHAT'S IN THIS QUARTZSITE?
SOMEONE I NEED TO SEE... AND I'D RATHER NOT DO IT ALONE... KNOW WHAT I MEAN?...
NOT EXACTLY.
PAIGE 1·20·2004
WHO IS IT? WHO IS THIS PERSON YOU NEED TO SEE?
1·21·2004 PAIGE
REMEMBER THE DAY I GAVE YOU A RIDE ON MY BIKE?
YEAH... WE ENDED UP CHASING SOMEONE..
RIGHT.
THE CHICK IN PLAID PANTS?! I THOUGHT SHE WAS A BAD GUY??
NOT EXACTLY.
WHICH PART?!... NOT EXACTLY A GUY?... OR NOT EXACTLY **BAD?!**
WHAT WERE YOU GUYS TALKING ABOUT?
OH... NOTHIN'...
PAIGE
HERE, SWEETIE, I GOT YOU SOME CHEESE PUFFS AND A **SUNKIST**.
I THINK THAT COVERS THE "ORANGE" FOOD GROUP...
OKAY, LADIES... ONWARD TO THE DESERT...
1·22·2004
WHY DON'T YOU JUST CLIMB IN THE BACK, JANE... I'LL DRIVE...
YEAH!

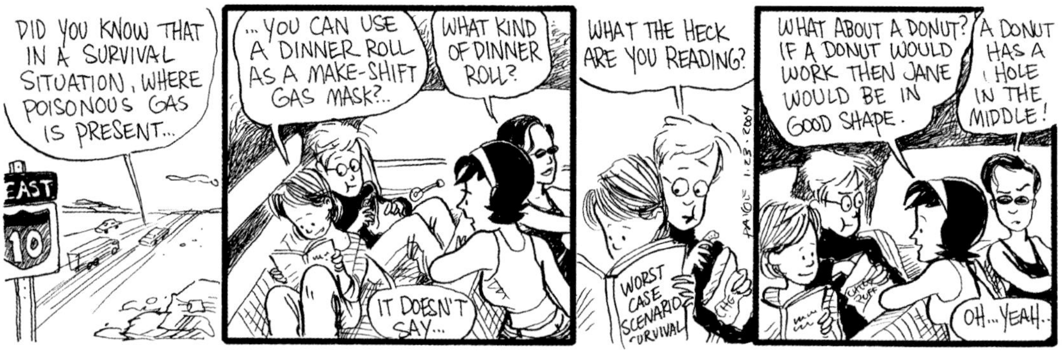
EAST
10
DID YOU KNOW THAT IN A SURVIVAL SITUATION, WHERE POISONOUS GAS IS PRESENT...
...YOU CAN USE A DINNER ROLL AS A MAKE-SHIFT GAS MASK?...
WHAT KIND OF DINNER ROLL?
IT DOESN'T SAY...
WHAT THE HECK ARE YOU READING?
WORST CASE SCENARIO SURVIVAL
1·23·2004
WHAT ABOUT A DONUT? IF A DONUT WOULD WORK THEN JANE WOULD BE IN GOOD SHAPE.
A DONUT HAS A HOLE IN THE MIDDLE!
OH...YEAH...

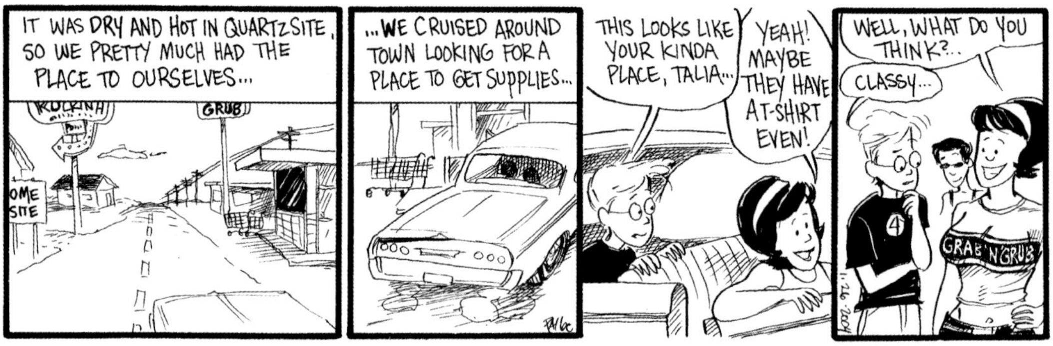
IT WAS DRY AND HOT IN QUARTZSITE, SO WE PRETTY MUCH HAD THE PLACE TO OURSELVES...
GRUB
...WE CRUISED AROUND TOWN LOOKING FOR A PLACE TO GET SUPPLIES...
THIS LOOKS LIKE YOUR KINDA PLACE, TALIA...
YEAH! MAYBE THEY HAVE A T-SHIRT EVEN!
WELL, WHAT DO YOU THINK?...
CLASSY...
GRAB 'N' GRUB

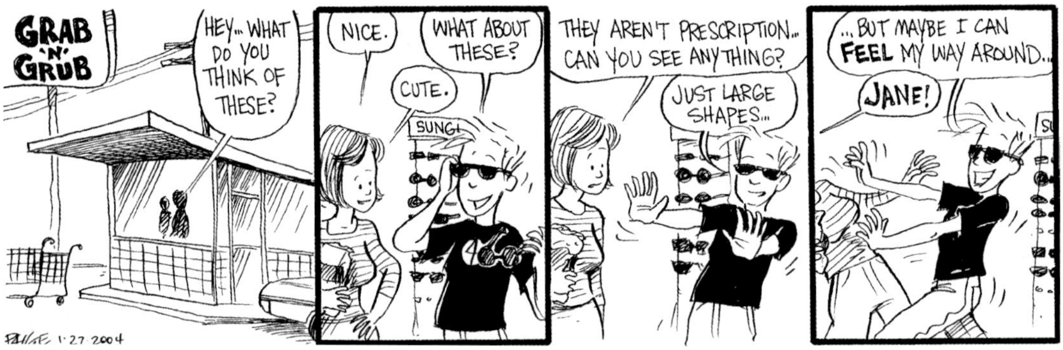
GRAB 'N' GRUB
HEY... WHAT DO YOU THINK OF THESE?
PAIGE 1·27·2004
NICE.
WHAT ABOUT THESE?
CUTE.
SUNG
THEY AREN'T PRESCRIPTION... CAN YOU SEE ANYTHING?
JUST LARGE SHAPES...
...BUT MAYBE I CAN FEEL MY WAY AROUND...
JANE!

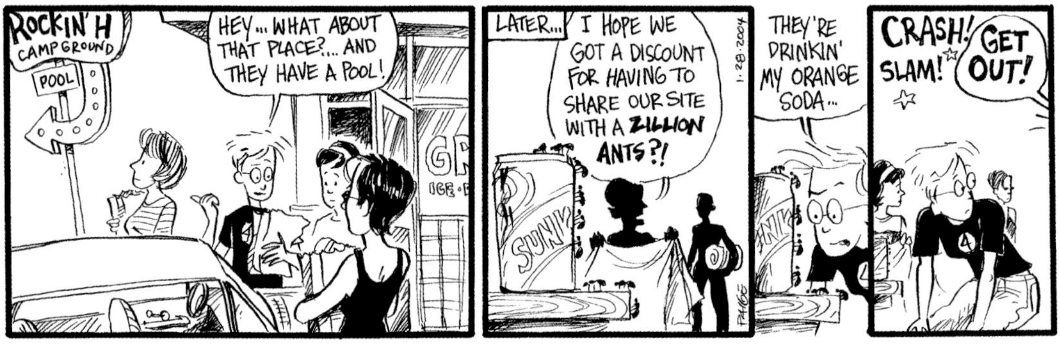
ROCKIN' H CAMPGROUND
POOL
HEY... WHAT ABOUT THAT PLACE?... AND THEY HAVE A POOL!
LATER...
I HOPE WE GOT A DISCOUNT FOR HAVING TO SHARE OUR SITE WITH A ZILLION ANTS?!
1·28·2004
THEY'RE DRINKIN' MY ORANGE SODA...
CRASH!
SLAM!
GET OUT!

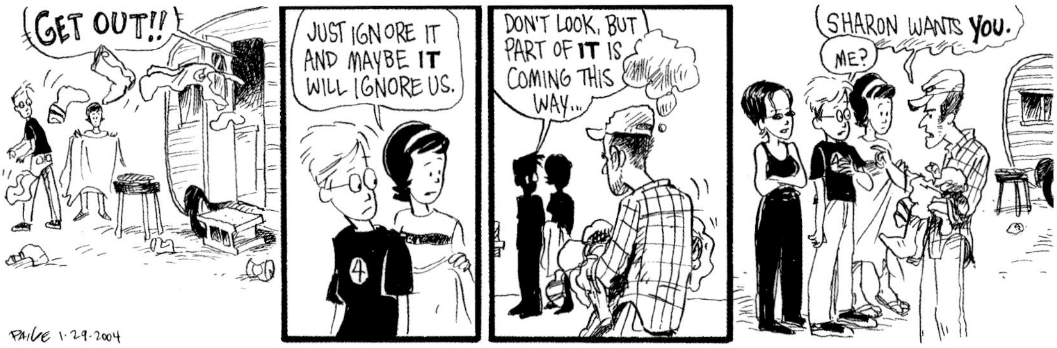
GET OUT!!
JUST IGNORE IT AND MAYBE IT WILL IGNORE US.
DON'T LOOK, BUT PART OF IT IS COMING THIS WAY...
SHARON WANTS YOU.
ME?
PAIGE 1·29·2004

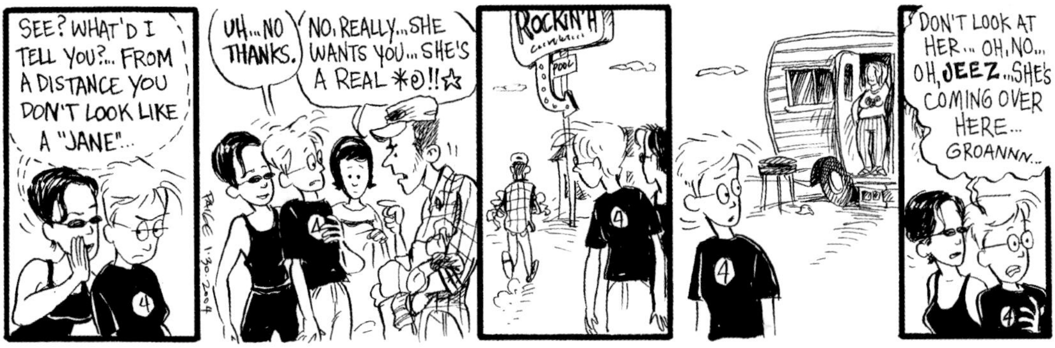
SEE? WHAT'D I TELL YOU?... FROM A DISTANCE YOU DON'T LOOK LIKE A "JANE"...
UH... NO THANKS.
NO, REALLY... SHE WANTS YOU... SHE'S A REAL *@!!☆
PAIGE 1·30·2004
ROCKIN' H
POOL
DON'T LOOK AT HER... OH, NO... OH, JEEZ... SHE'S COMING OVER HERE... GROANNN...

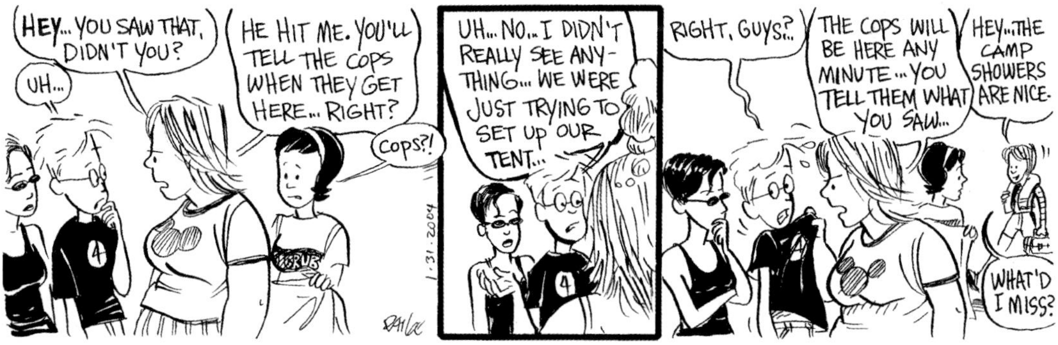
HEY... YOU SAW THAT, DIDN'T YOU?
UH...
HE HIT ME. YOU'LL TELL THE COPS WHEN THEY GET HERE... RIGHT?
COPS?!
1·31·2004 PAIGE
UH... NO... I DIDN'T REALLY SEE ANYTHING... WE WERE JUST TRYING TO SET UP OUR TENT...
RIGHT, GUYS?...
THE COPS WILL BE HERE ANY MINUTE... YOU TELL THEM WHAT YOU SAW...
HEY... THE CAMP SHOWERS ARE NICE.
WHAT'D I MISS?

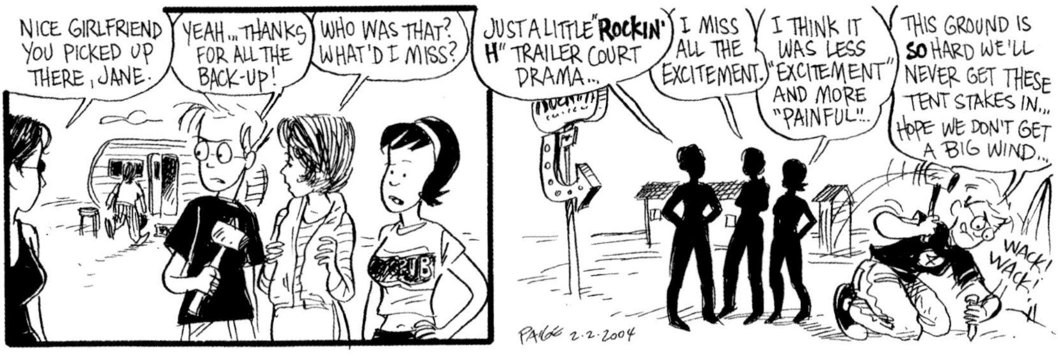
NICE GIRLFRIEND YOU PICKED UP THERE, JANE.
YEAH... THANKS FOR ALL THE BACK-UP!
WHO WAS THAT? WHAT'D I MISS?
JUST A LITTLE "ROCKIN' H" TRAILER COURT DRAMA...
I MISS ALL THE EXCITEMENT.
I THINK IT WAS LESS "EXCITEMENT" AND MORE "PAINFUL"!..
THIS GROUND IS SO HARD WE'LL NEVER GET THESE TENT STAKES IN... HOPE WE DON'T GET A BIG WIND...
WACK! WACK!
PAIGE 2·2·2004

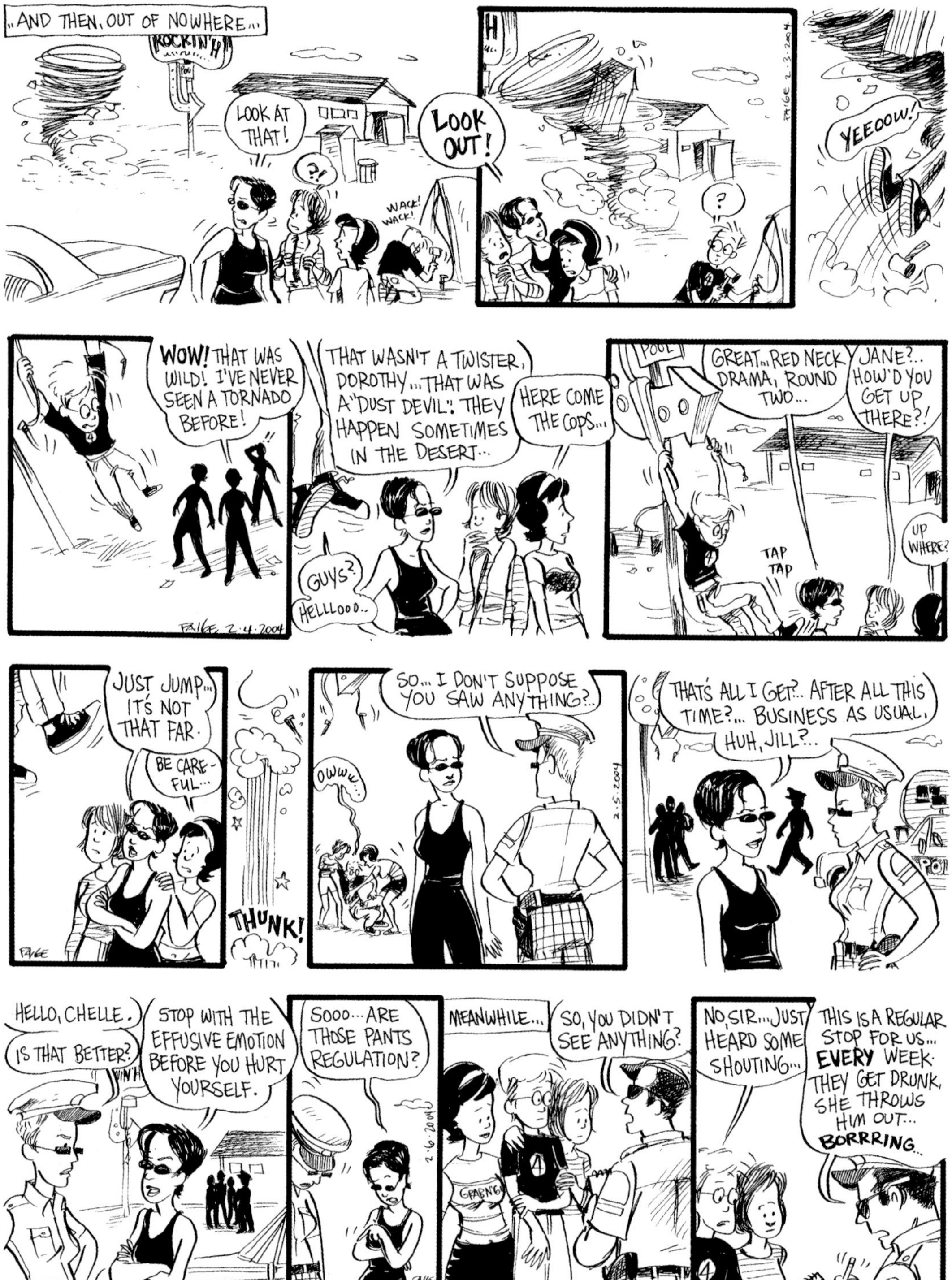
...AND THEN, OUT OF NOWHERE...
ROCKIN' H
LOOK AT THAT!
?!
WACK! WACK!
LOOK OUT!
?
YEEOOW!
WOW! THAT WAS WILD! I'VE NEVER SEEN A TORNADO BEFORE!
THAT WASN'T A TWISTER, DOROTHY... THAT WAS A "DUST DEVIL". THEY HAPPEN SOMETIMES IN THE DESERT...
HERE COME THE COPS...
GUYS?
HELLLOOO..
POOL
GREAT... RED NECK DRAMA, ROUND TWO...
JANE?... HOW'D YOU GET UP THERE?!
TAP TAP
UP WHERE?
JUST JUMP... IT'S NOT THAT FAR.
BE CARE-FUL...
THUNK!
SO... I DON'T SUPPOSE YOU SAW ANYTHING?..
OWWW...
THAT'S ALL I GET?.. AFTER ALL THIS TIME?... BUSINESS AS USUAL, HUH, JILL?...
HELLO, CHELLE.
IS THAT BETTER?
STOP WITH THE EFFUSIVE EMOTION BEFORE YOU HURT YOURSELF.
SOOO... ARE THOSE PANTS REGULATION?
MEANWHILE...
SO, YOU DIDN'T SEE ANYTHING?
NO, SIR... JUST HEARD SOME SHOUTING...
THIS IS A REGULAR STOP FOR US... EVERY WEEK. THEY GET DRUNK, SHE THROWS HIM OUT... BORRRING...

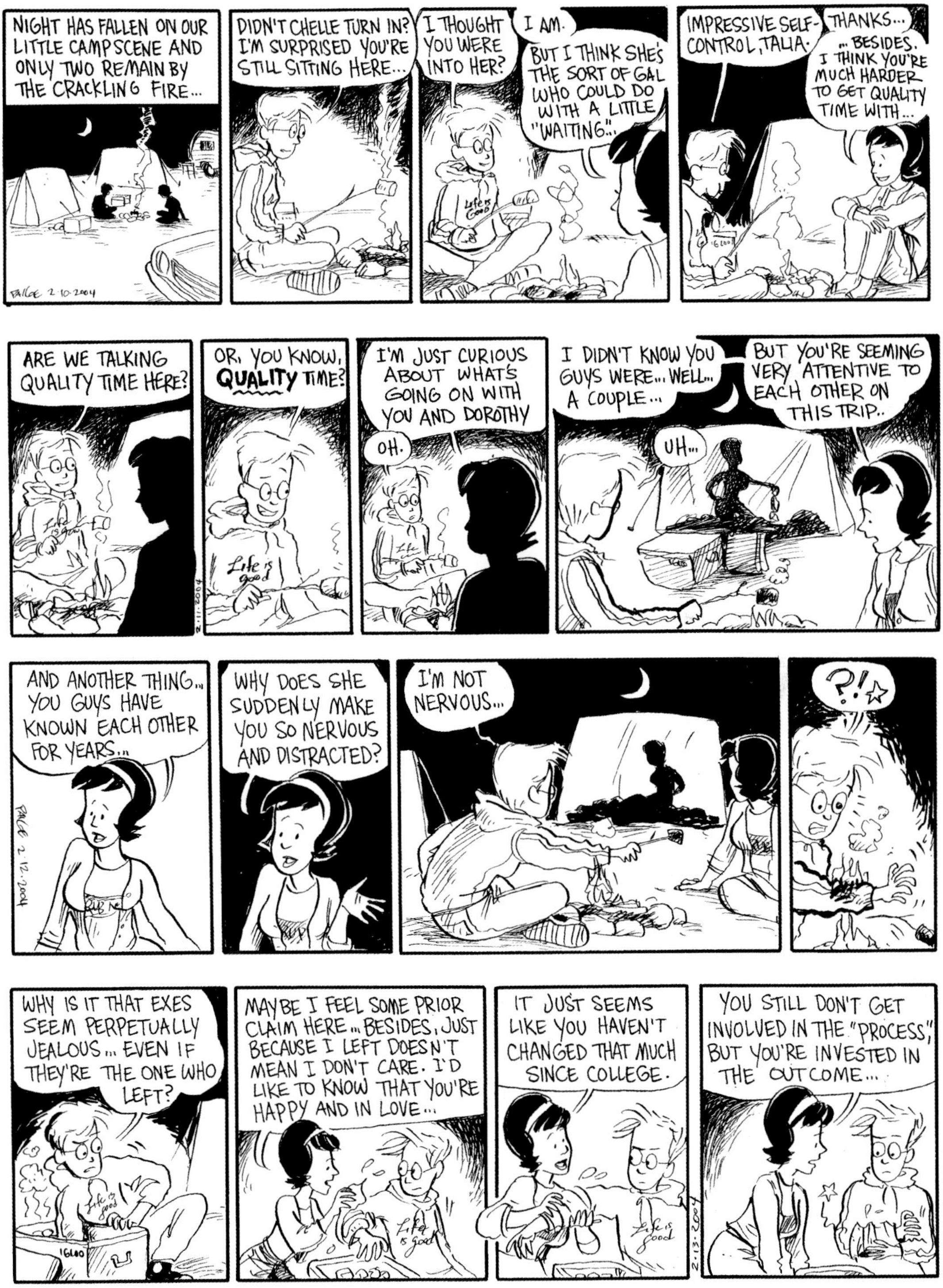
NIGHT HAS FALLEN ON OUR LITTLE CAMPSCENE AND ONLY TWO REMAIN BY THE CRACKLING FIRE...
PAIGE 2-10-2004
DIDN'T CHELLE TURN IN? I'M SURPRISED YOU'RE STILL SITTING HERE...
I THOUGHT YOU WERE INTO HER?
I AM.
BUT I THINK SHE'S THE SORT OF GAL WHO COULD DO WITH A LITTLE "WAITING."
IMPRESSIVE SELF-CONTROL, TALIA.
THANKS...
... BESIDES, I THINK YOU'RE MUCH HARDER TO GET QUALITY TIME WITH...
ARE WE TALKING QUALITY TIME HERE?
OR, YOU KNOW, QUALITY TIME?
2-11-2004
I'M JUST CURIOUS ABOUT WHAT'S GOING ON WITH YOU AND DOROTHY
OH.
I DIDN'T KNOW YOU GUYS WERE... WELL... A COUPLE...
BUT YOU'RE SEEMING VERY ATTENTIVE TO EACH OTHER ON THIS TRIP..
UH...
AND ANOTHER THING... YOU GUYS HAVE KNOWN EACH OTHER FOR YEARS...
PAIGE 2-12-2004
WHY DOES SHE SUDDENLY MAKE YOU SO NERVOUS AND DISTRACTED?
I'M NOT NERVOUS...
?!☆
WHY IS IT THAT EXES SEEM PERPETUALLY JEALOUS... EVEN IF THEY'RE THE ONE WHO LEFT?
MAYBE I FEEL SOME PRIOR CLAIM HERE... BESIDES, JUST BECAUSE I LEFT DOESN'T MEAN I DON'T CARE. I'D LIKE TO KNOW THAT YOU'RE HAPPY AND IN LOVE...
IT JUST SEEMS LIKE YOU HAVEN'T CHANGED THAT MUCH SINCE COLLEGE.
2-13-2004
YOU STILL DON'T GET INVOLVED IN THE "PROCESS", BUT YOU'RE INVESTED IN THE OUTCOME...

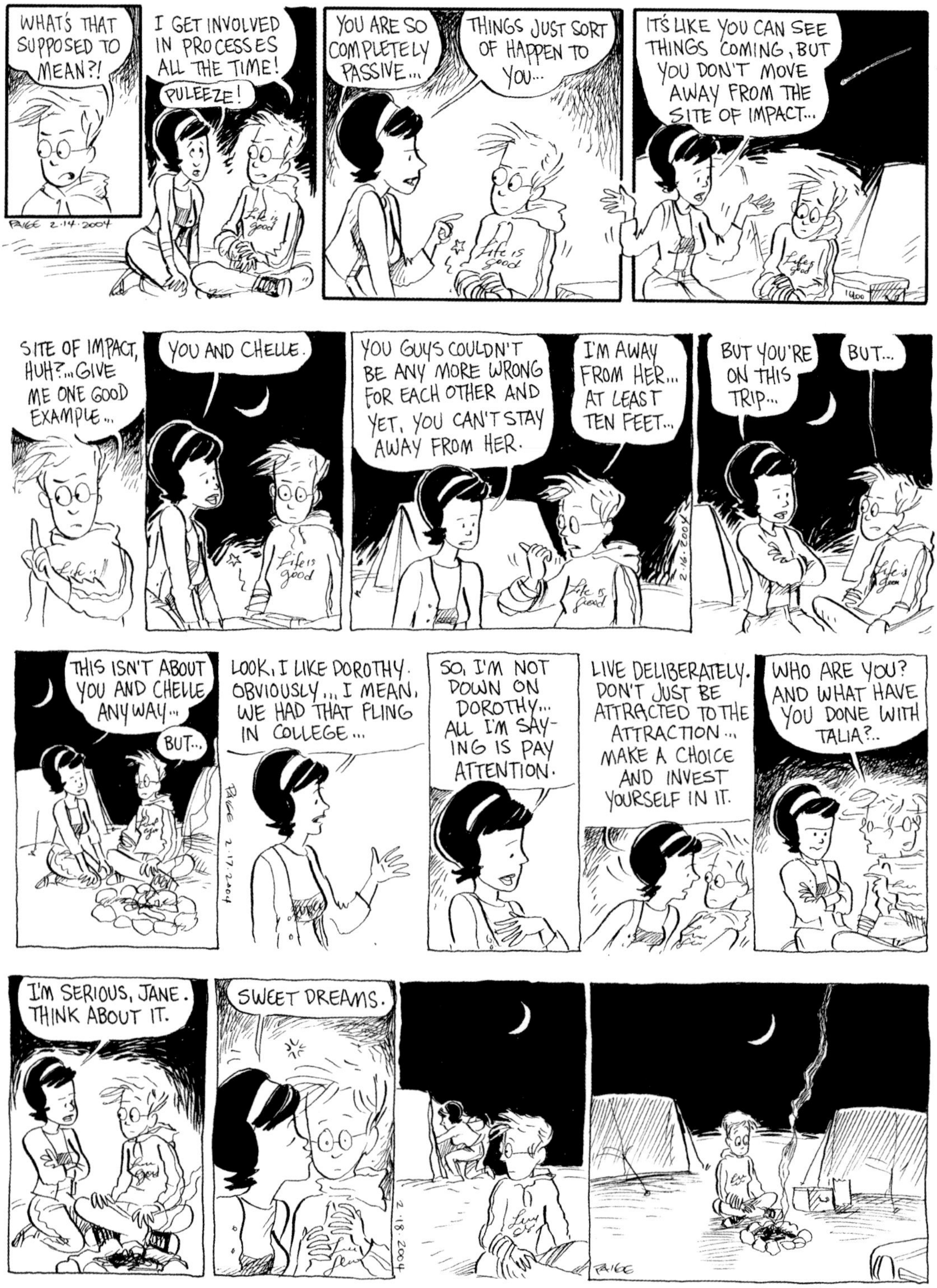
WHAT'S THAT SUPPOSED TO MEAN?!
I GET INVOLVED IN PROCESSES ALL THE TIME!
PULEEZE!
PAIGE 2·14·2004
Life is good
YOU ARE SO COMPLETELY PASSIVE...
THINGS JUST SORT OF HAPPEN TO YOU...
Life is good
IT'S LIKE YOU CAN SEE THINGS COMING, BUT YOU DON'T MOVE AWAY FROM THE SITE OF IMPACT...
Life is good
SITE OF IMPACT, HUH?...GIVE ME ONE GOOD EXAMPLE...
YOU AND CHELLE.
Life is good
YOU GUYS COULDN'T BE ANY MORE WRONG FOR EACH OTHER AND YET, YOU CAN'T STAY AWAY FROM HER.
I'M AWAY FROM HER... AT LEAST TEN FEET...
Life is good
2·16·2004
BUT YOU'RE ON THIS TRIP...
BUT...
THIS ISN'T ABOUT YOU AND CHELLE ANYWAY...
BUT...
LOOK, I LIKE DOROTHY. OBVIOUSLY... I MEAN, WE HAD THAT FLING IN COLLEGE...
PAIGE 2·17·2004
SO, I'M NOT DOWN ON DOROTHY... ALL I'M SAYING IS PAY ATTENTION.
LIVE DELIBERATELY. DON'T JUST BE ATTRACTED TO THE ATTRACTION... MAKE A CHOICE AND INVEST YOURSELF IN IT.
WHO ARE YOU? AND WHAT HAVE YOU DONE WITH TALIA?..
I'M SERIOUS, JANE. THINK ABOUT IT.
SWEET DREAMS.
2·18·2004
PAIGE

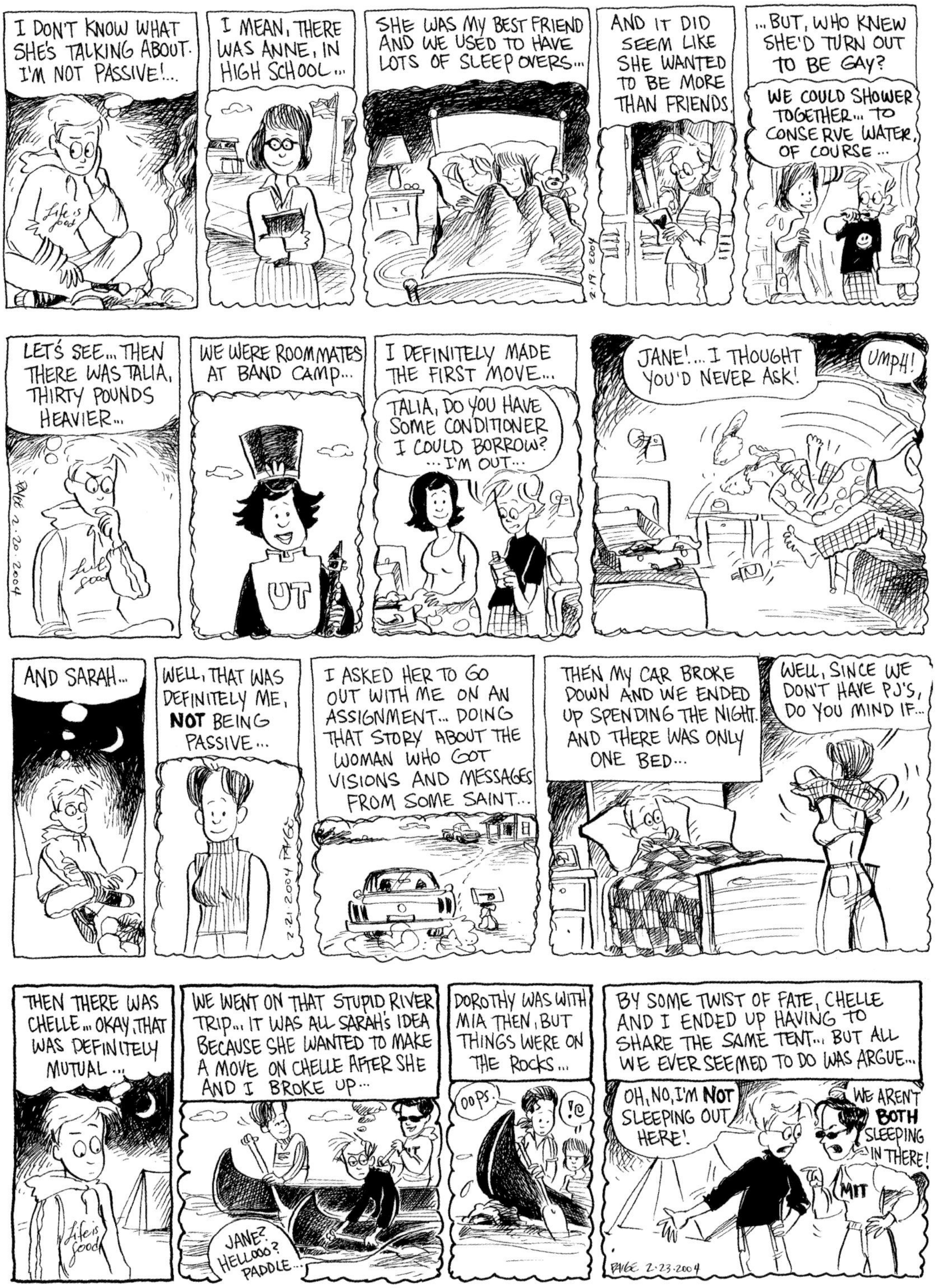
I DON'T KNOW WHAT SHE'S TALKING ABOUT. I'M NOT PASSIVE!...
Life is good
I MEAN, THERE WAS ANNE, IN HIGH SCHOOL...
SHE WAS MY BEST FRIEND AND WE USED TO HAVE LOTS OF SLEEP OVERS...
AND IT DID SEEM LIKE SHE WANTED TO BE MORE THAN FRIENDS.
2.19.2004
...BUT, WHO KNEW SHE'D TURN OUT TO BE GAY?
WE COULD SHOWER TOGETHER... TO CONSERVE WATER, OF COURSE...
LET'S SEE... THEN THERE WAS TALIA, THIRTY POUNDS HEAVIER...
PAIGE 2.20.2004
WE WERE ROOMMATES AT BAND CAMP...
UT
I DEFINITELY MADE THE FIRST MOVE...
TALIA, DO YOU HAVE SOME CONDITIONER I COULD BORROW? ...I'M OUT...
JANE!... I THOUGHT YOU'D NEVER ASK!
UMPH!
AND SARAH...
WELL, THAT WAS DEFINITELY ME, **NOT** BEING PASSIVE...
2.21.2004 PAIGE
I ASKED HER TO GO OUT WITH ME ON AN ASSIGNMENT... DOING THAT STORY ABOUT THE WOMAN WHO GOT VISIONS AND MESSAGES FROM SOME SAINT...
THEN MY CAR BROKE DOWN AND WE ENDED UP SPENDING THE NIGHT. AND THERE WAS ONLY ONE BED...
WELL, SINCE WE DON'T HAVE PJ'S, DO YOU MIND IF...
THEN THERE WAS CHELLE... OKAY, THAT WAS DEFINITELY MUTUAL...
Life is good
WE WENT ON THAT STUPID RIVER TRIP... IT WAS ALL SARAH'S IDEA BECAUSE SHE WANTED TO MAKE A MOVE ON CHELLE AFTER SHE AND I BROKE UP...
JANE? HELLOOO? PADDLE...
DOROTHY WAS WITH MIA THEN, BUT THINGS WERE ON THE ROCKS...
OOPS!
!@
BY SOME TWIST OF FATE, CHELLE AND I ENDED UP HAVING TO SHARE THE SAME TENT... BUT ALL WE EVER SEEMED TO DO WAS ARGUE...
OH, NO, I'M **NOT** SLEEPING OUT HERE!
WE AREN'T **BOTH** SLEEPING IN THERE!
MIT
PAIGE 2.23.2004

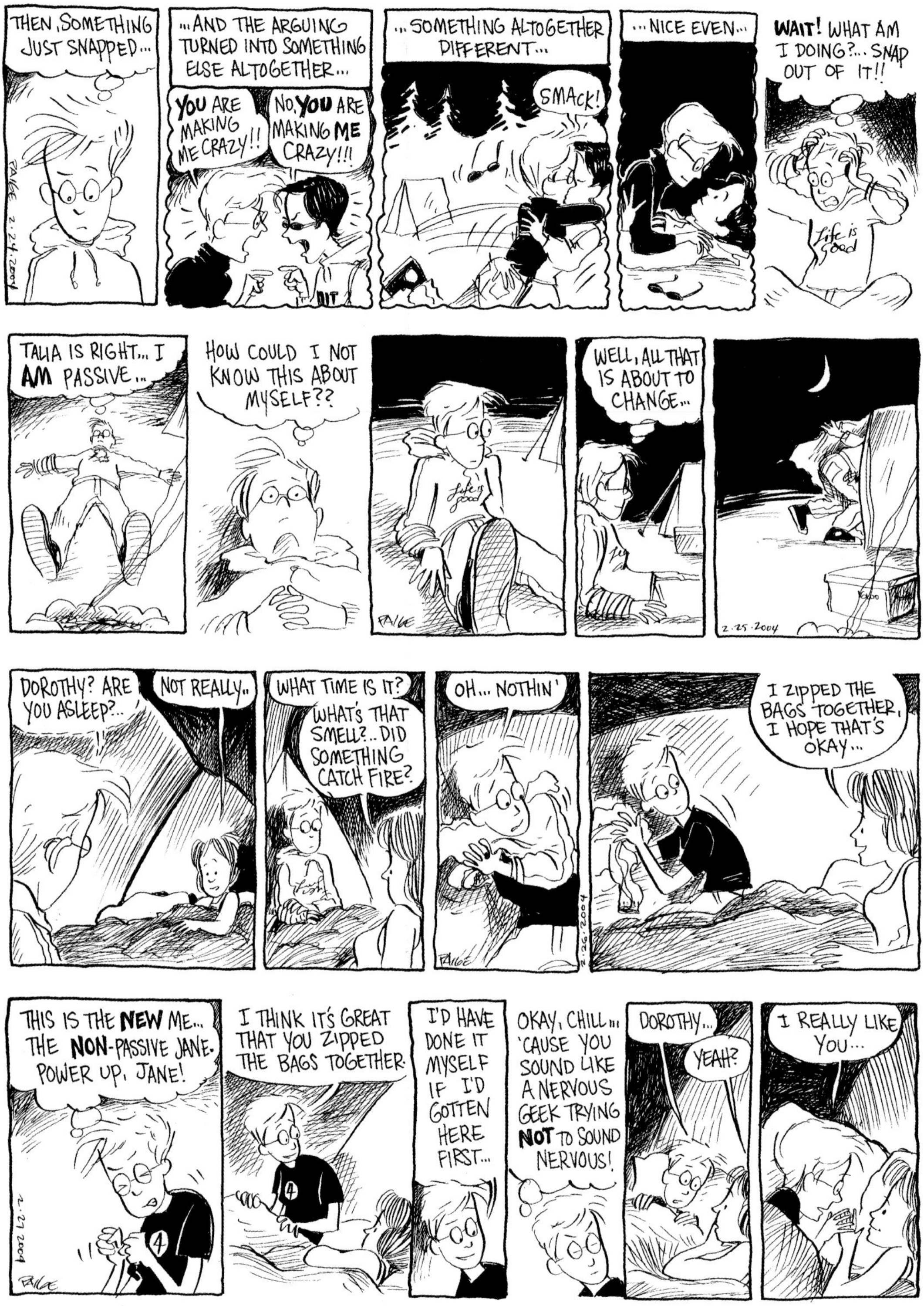

THEN, SOMETHING JUST SNAPPED...
PAIGE 2.24.2004
...AND THE ARGUING TURNED INTO SOMETHING ELSE ALTOGETHER...
YOU ARE MAKING ME CRAZY!!
NO, **YOU** ARE MAKING **ME** CRAZY!!!
...SOMETHING ALTOGETHER DIFFERENT...
SMACK!
...NICE EVEN...
WAIT! WHAT AM I DOING?... SNAP OUT OF IT!!
Life is Good
TALIA IS RIGHT... I **AM** PASSIVE...
HOW COULD I NOT KNOW THIS ABOUT MYSELF??
PAIGE
WELL, ALL THAT IS ABOUT TO CHANGE...
2.25.2004
DOROTHY? ARE YOU ASLEEP?..
NOT REALLY..
WHAT TIME IS IT?
WHAT'S THAT SMELL?.. DID SOMETHING CATCH FIRE?
OH... NOTHIN'
PAIGE 2.26.2004
I ZIPPED THE BAGS TOGETHER, I HOPE THAT'S OKAY...
THIS IS THE **NEW** ME... THE **NON**-PASSIVE JANE. POWER UP, JANE!
2.27.2004 PAIGE
I THINK IT'S GREAT THAT YOU ZIPPED THE BAGS TOGETHER.
I'D HAVE DONE IT MYSELF IF I'D GOTTEN HERE FIRST...
OKAY, CHILL... 'CAUSE YOU SOUND LIKE A NERVOUS GEEK TRYING **NOT** TO SOUND NERVOUS!
DOROTHY...
YEAH?
I REALLY LIKE YOU...

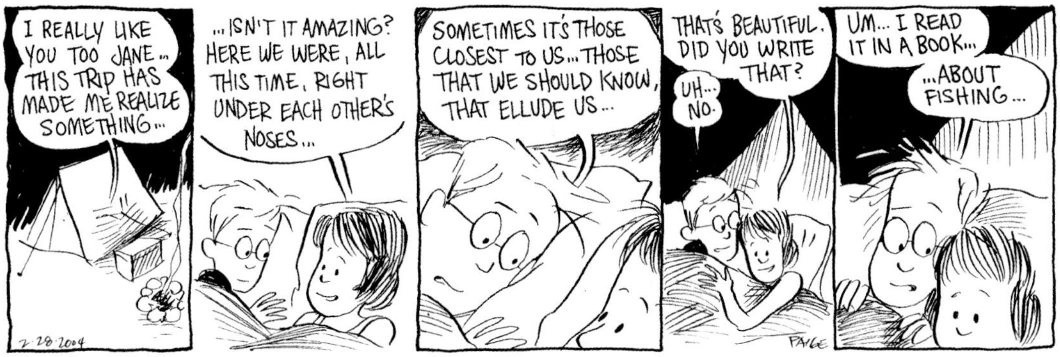
I REALLY LIKE YOU TOO JANE... THIS TRIP HAS MADE ME REALIZE SOMETHING...
2·28·2004
...ISN'T IT AMAZING? HERE WE WERE, ALL THIS TIME, RIGHT UNDER EACH OTHER'S NOSES...
SOMETIMES IT'S THOSE CLOSEST TO US... THOSE THAT WE SHOULD KNOW, THAT ELLUDE US...
THAT'S BEAUTIFUL. DID YOU WRITE THAT?
UH... NO.
UM... I READ IT IN A BOOK...
...ABOUT FISHING...
PAIGE

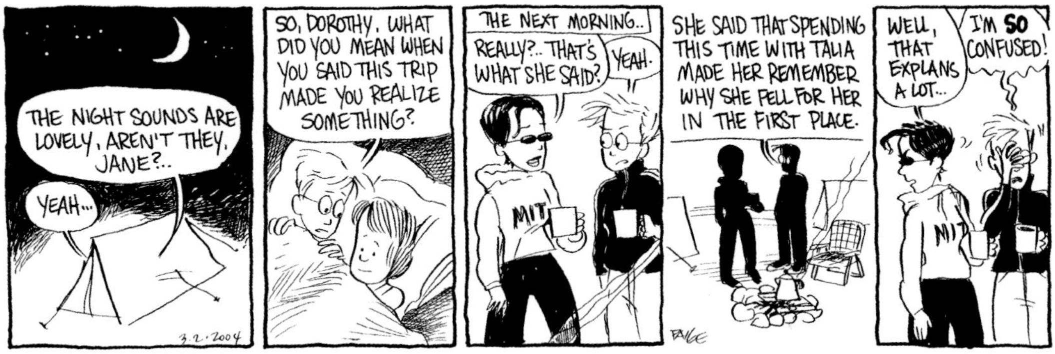
THE NIGHT SOUNDS ARE LOVELY, AREN'T THEY, JANE?..
YEAH...
3·2·2004
SO, DOROTHY, WHAT DID YOU MEAN WHEN YOU SAID THIS TRIP MADE YOU REALIZE SOMETHING?
THE NEXT MORNING..
REALLY?.. THAT'S WHAT SHE SAID?
YEAH.
MIT
SHE SAID THAT SPENDING THIS TIME WITH TALIA MADE HER REMEMBER WHY SHE FELL FOR HER IN THE FIRST PLACE.
PAIGE
WELL, THAT EXPLAINS A LOT...
I'M **SO** CONFUSED!
MIT

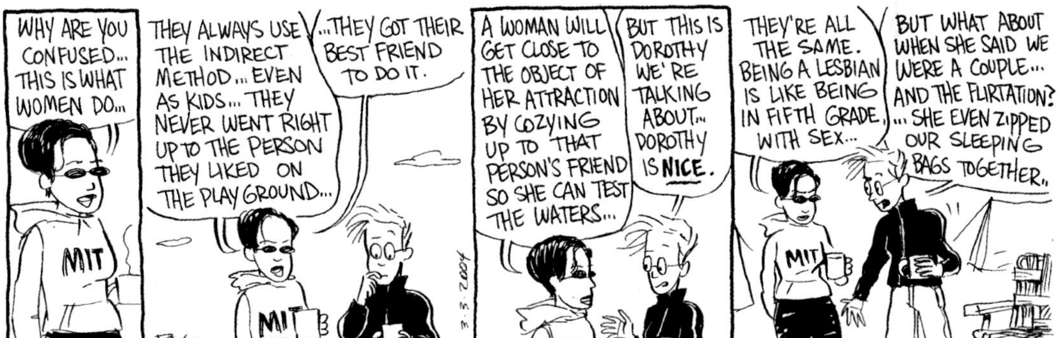
WHY ARE YOU CONFUSED... THIS IS WHAT WOMEN DO...
MIT
PAIGE
THEY ALWAYS USE THE INDIRECT METHOD... EVEN AS KIDS... THEY NEVER WENT RIGHT UP TO THE PERSON THEY LIKED ON THE PLAYGROUND...
...THEY GOT THEIR BEST FRIEND TO DO IT.
MIT
3·3·2004
A WOMAN WILL GET CLOSE TO THE OBJECT OF HER ATTRACTION BY COZYING UP TO THAT PERSON'S FRIEND SO SHE CAN TEST THE WATERS...
BUT THIS IS DOROTHY WE'RE TALKING ABOUT... DOROTHY IS **NICE**.
THEY'RE ALL THE SAME. BEING A LESBIAN IS LIKE BEING IN FIFTH GRADE, WITH SEX...
BUT WHAT ABOUT WHEN SHE SAID WE WERE A COUPLE... AND THE FLIRTATION? ...SHE EVEN ZIPPED OUR SLEEPING BAGS TOGETHER..
MIT

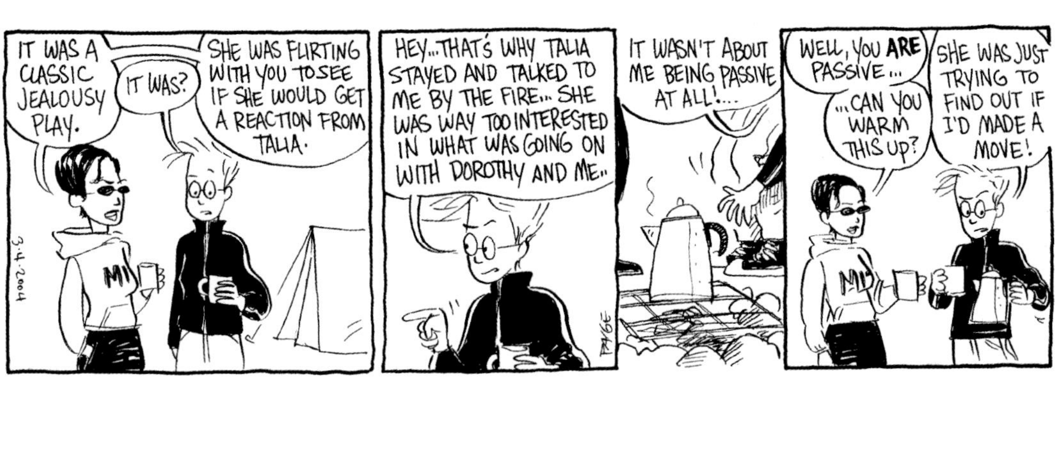
IT WAS A CLASSIC JEALOUSY PLAY.
IT WAS?
SHE WAS FLIRTING WITH YOU TO SEE IF SHE WOULD GET A REACTION FROM TALIA.
3·4·2004
MIT
HEY... THAT'S WHY TALIA STAYED AND TALKED TO ME BY THE FIRE... SHE WAS WAY TOO INTERESTED IN WHAT WAS GOING ON WITH DOROTHY AND ME..
PAIGE
IT WASN'T ABOUT ME BEING PASSIVE AT ALL!...
WELL, YOU **ARE** PASSIVE...
...CAN YOU WARM THIS UP?
SHE WAS JUST TRYING TO FIND OUT IF I'D MADE A MOVE!
MIT

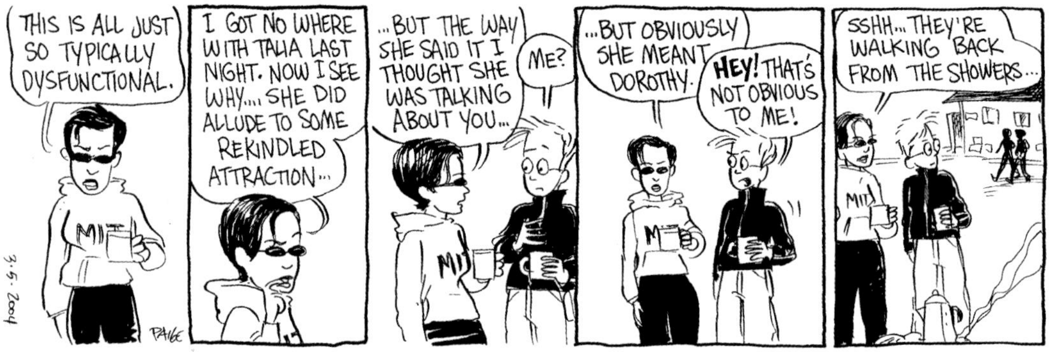
THIS IS ALL JUST SO TYPICALLY DYSFUNCTIONAL.
3.6.2004
PAIGE
I GOT NO WHERE WITH TALIA LAST NIGHT. NOW I SEE WHY.... SHE DID ALLUDE TO SOME REKINDLED ATTRACTION...
...BUT THE WAY SHE SAID IT I THOUGHT SHE WAS TALKING ABOUT YOU...
ME?
...BUT OBVIOUSLY SHE MEANT DOROTHY.
HEY! THAT'S NOT OBVIOUS TO ME!
SSHH... THEY'RE WALKING BACK FROM THE SHOWERS...

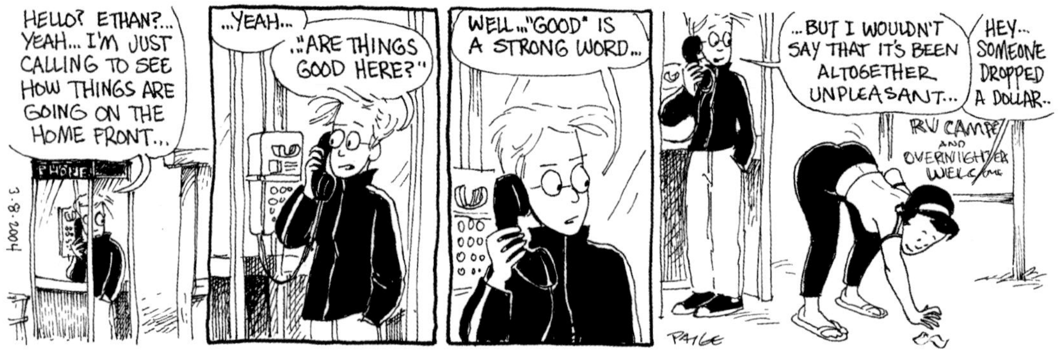
HELLO? ETHAN?... YEAH... I'M JUST CALLING TO SEE HOW THINGS ARE GOING ON THE HOME FRONT...
PHONE
3.8.2004
...YEAH...
..."ARE THINGS GOOD HERE?"
WELL..."GOOD" IS A STRONG WORD...
...BUT I WOULDN'T SAY THAT IT'S BEEN ALTOGETHER UNPLEASANT...
HEY... SOMEONE DROPPED A DOLLAR..
RV CAMPS
AND
PAIGE

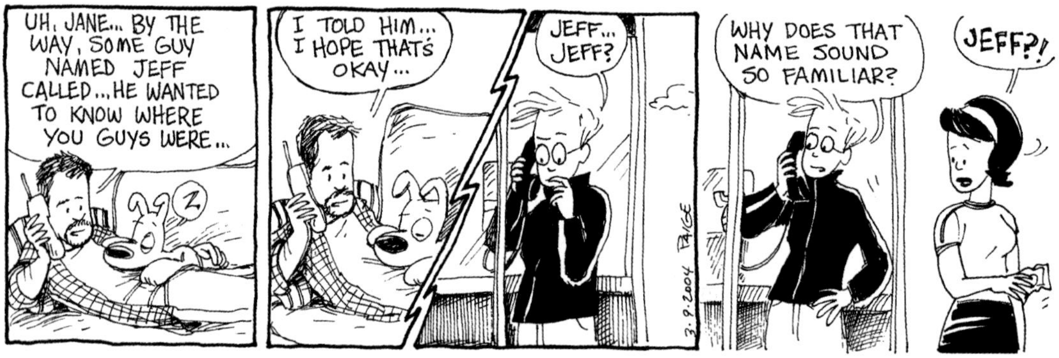
UH, JANE... BY THE WAY, SOME GUY NAMED JEFF CALLED...HE WANTED TO KNOW WHERE YOU GUYS WERE...
Z
I TOLD HIM... I HOPE THAT'S OKAY...
JEFF... JEFF?
3.9.2004 PAIGE
WHY DOES THAT NAME SOUND SO FAMILIAR?
JEFF?!

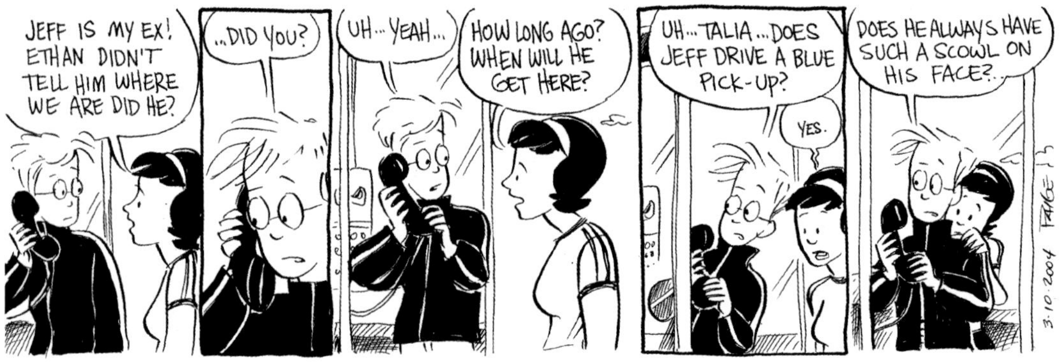
JEFF IS MY EX! ETHAN DIDN'T TELL HIM WHERE WE ARE DID HE?
...DID YOU?
UH... YEAH...
HOW LONG AGO? WHEN WILL HE GET HERE?
UH... TALIA... DOES JEFF DRIVE A BLUE PICK-UP?
YES.
DOES HE ALWAYS HAVE SUCH A SCOWL ON HIS FACE?...
3.10.2004 PAIGE

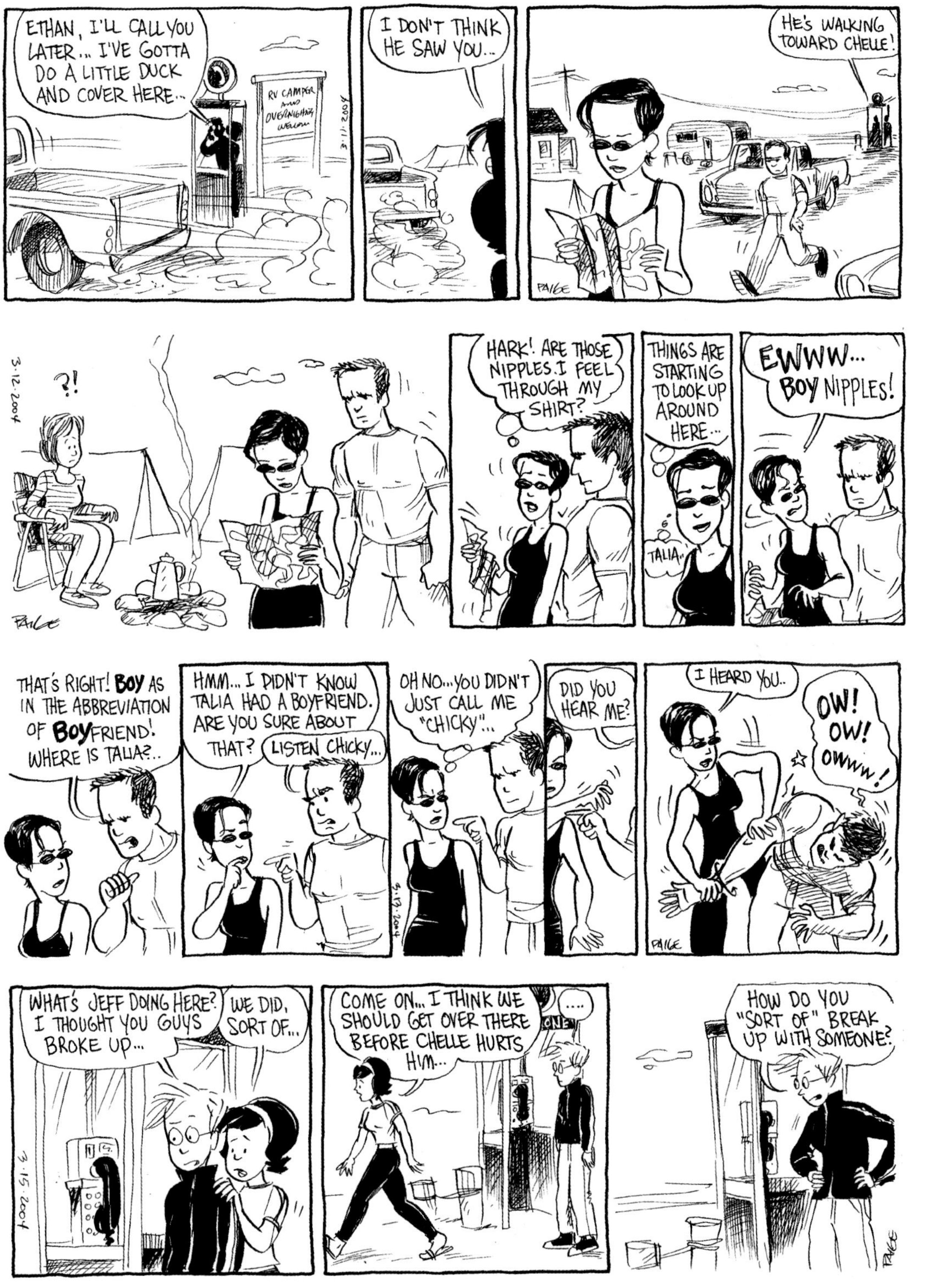
ETHAN, I'LL CALL YOU LATER... I'VE GOTTA DO A LITTLE DUCK AND COVER HERE...
RV CAMPER AND OVERNIGHTERS WELCOME
3.11.2004
I DON'T THINK HE SAW YOU...
HE'S WALKING TOWARD CHELLE!
PAIGE
3.12.2004
?!
PAIGE
HARK! ARE THOSE NIPPLES I FEEL THROUGH MY SHIRT?
THINGS ARE STARTING TO LOOK UP AROUND HERE...
TALIA..
EWWW... BOY NIPPLES!
THAT'S RIGHT! BOY AS IN THE ABBREVIATION OF BOYFRIEND! WHERE IS TALIA?..
HMM... I DIDN'T KNOW TALIA HAD A BOYFRIEND. ARE YOU SURE ABOUT THAT?
LISTEN CHICKY...
OH NO... YOU DIDN'T JUST CALL ME "CHICKY"...
3.13.2004
DID YOU HEAR ME?
I HEARD YOU..
OW! OW! OWWW!
PAIGE
WHAT'S JEFF DOING HERE? I THOUGHT YOU GUYS BROKE UP...
WE DID, SORT OF...
3.15.2004
COME ON... I THINK WE SHOULD GET OVER THERE BEFORE CHELLE HURTS HIM...
....
HOW DO YOU "SORT OF" BREAK UP WITH SOMEONE?
PAIGE

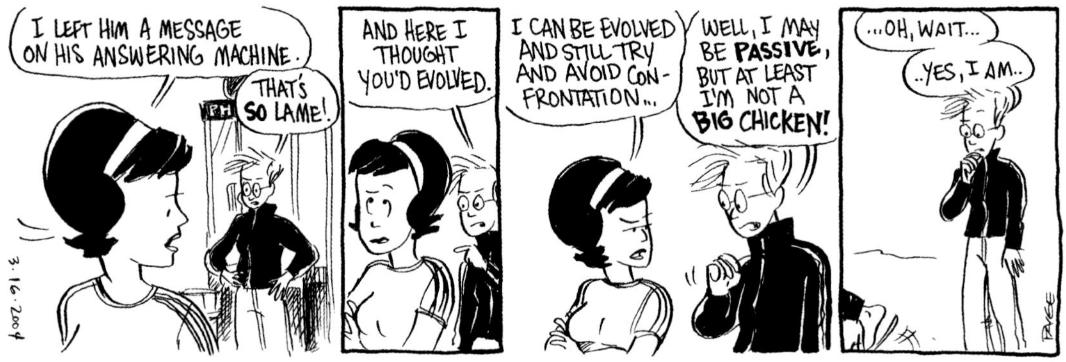
I LEFT HIM A MESSAGE ON HIS ANSWERING MACHINE.
THAT'S SO LAME!
AND HERE I THOUGHT YOU'D EVOLVED.
I CAN BE EVOLVED AND STILL TRY AND AVOID CON-FRONTATION...
WELL, I MAY BE PASSIVE, BUT AT LEAST I'M NOT A BIG CHICKEN!
...OH, WAIT...
..YES, I AM..
3·16·2004

“ ”

“There was a hotel room. At a conference. Tequila was involved—the expensive, silver kind. What do three lesbians do when it gets to that point in the night? Scratch that. What do three lesbians *who have girlfriends at home* do when it gets to that time of the night? They arm wrestle. Or two of them do—one takes pictures on her flip phone. Biceps bulged. Teeth were clenched. Noises came from deep in their throats. Their conjoined fist shook as one arm tried desperately to lower itself onto the other....Who won that night? We all did. Watching Alison Bechdel and Paige Braddock duke it out—the two cartoonists who best capture lesbian desire in the comics—I realized I was not simply a fan of *Jane's World*. I was inside a double-page spread.”

HILARY PRICE,
Rhymes with Orange

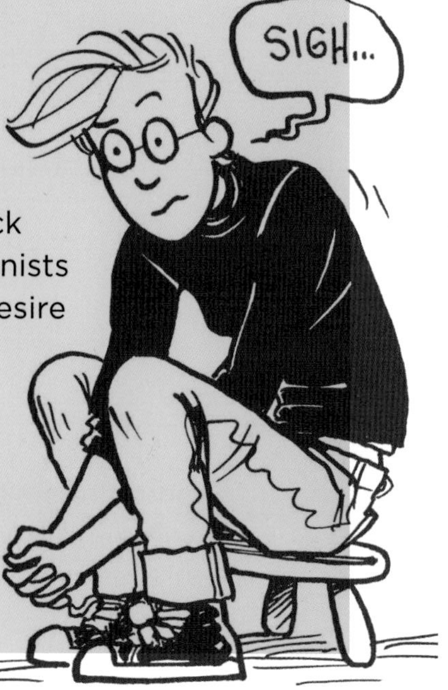
SIGH...

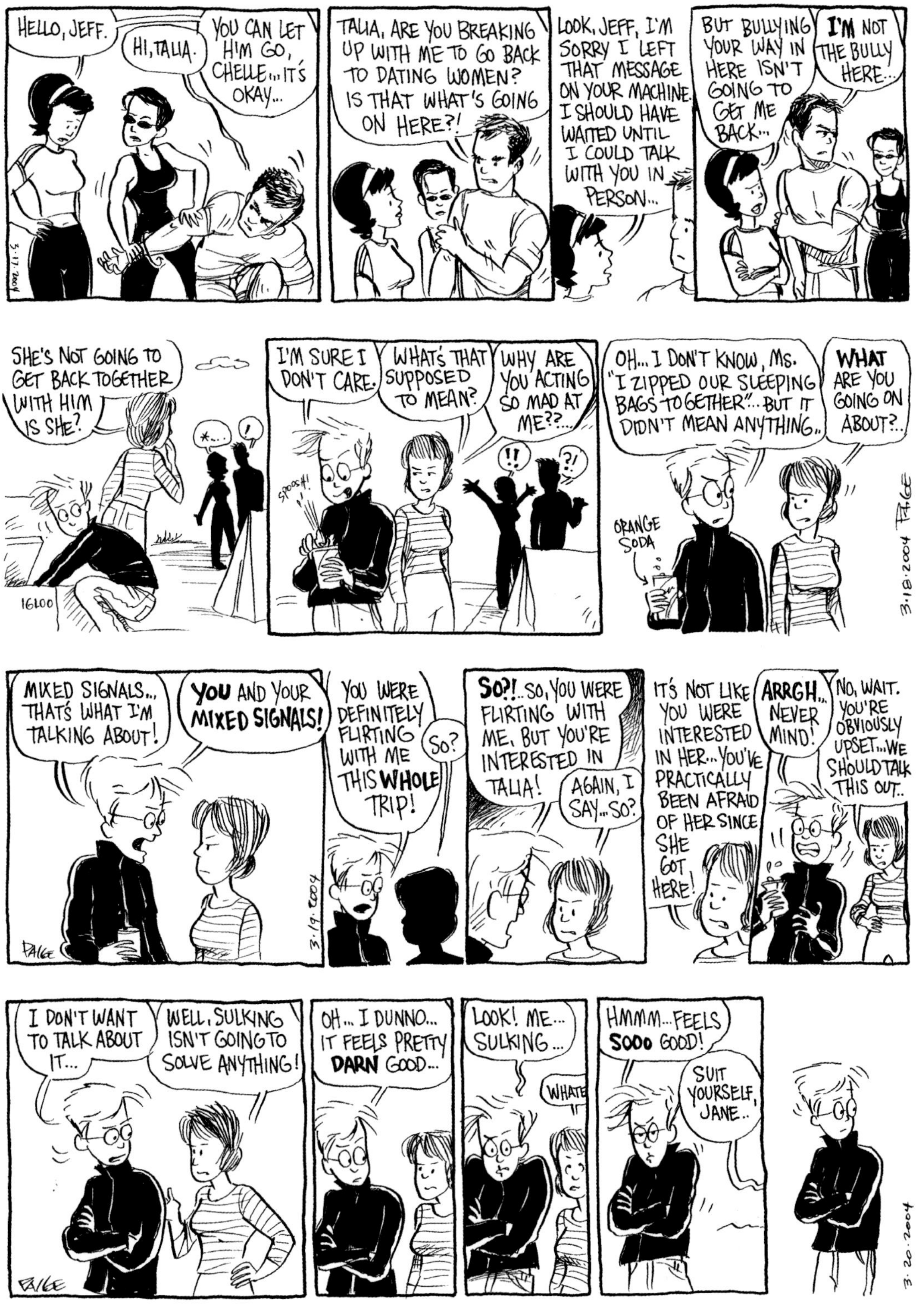
HELLO, JEFF.
HI, TALIA.
YOU CAN LET HIM GO, CHELLE... IT'S OKAY...
3.17.2004
TALIA, ARE YOU BREAKING UP WITH ME TO GO BACK TO DATING WOMEN? IS THAT WHAT'S GOING ON HERE?!
LOOK, JEFF, I'M SORRY I LEFT THAT MESSAGE ON YOUR MACHINE. I SHOULD HAVE WAITED UNTIL I COULD TALK WITH YOU IN PERSON...
BUT BULLYING YOUR WAY IN HERE ISN'T GOING TO GET ME BACK...
I'M NOT THE BULLY HERE...
SHE'S NOT GOING TO GET BACK TOGETHER WITH HIM IS SHE?
IGLOO
I'M SURE I DON'T CARE.
WHAT'S THAT SUPPOSED TO MEAN?
WHY ARE YOU ACTING SO MAD AT ME??...
SPOOSH!
!!
?!
OH... I DON'T KNOW, MS. "I ZIPPED OUR SLEEPING BAGS TOGETHER"... BUT IT DIDN'T MEAN ANYTHING..
WHAT ARE YOU GOING ON ABOUT?..
ORANGE SODA
PAIGE
3.18.2004
MIXED SIGNALS... THAT'S WHAT I'M TALKING ABOUT!
YOU AND YOUR MIXED SIGNALS!
PAIGE
YOU WERE DEFINITELY FLIRTING WITH ME THIS WHOLE TRIP!
SO?
3.19.2004
SO?!..SO, YOU WERE FLIRTING WITH ME, BUT YOU'RE INTERESTED IN TALIA!
AGAIN, I SAY... SO?
IT'S NOT LIKE YOU WERE INTERESTED IN HER... YOU'VE PRACTICALLY BEEN AFRAID OF HER SINCE SHE GOT HERE!
ARRGH.. NEVER MIND!
NO, WAIT. YOU'RE OBVIOUSLY UPSET... WE SHOULD TALK THIS OUT..
I DON'T WANT TO TALK ABOUT IT...
WELL, SULKING ISN'T GOING TO SOLVE ANYTHING!
PAIGE
OH... I DUNNO... IT FEELS PRETTY DARN GOOD...
LOOK! ME... SULKING...
WHATE
HMMM... FEELS SOOO GOOD!
SUIT YOURSELF, JANE..
3.20.2004

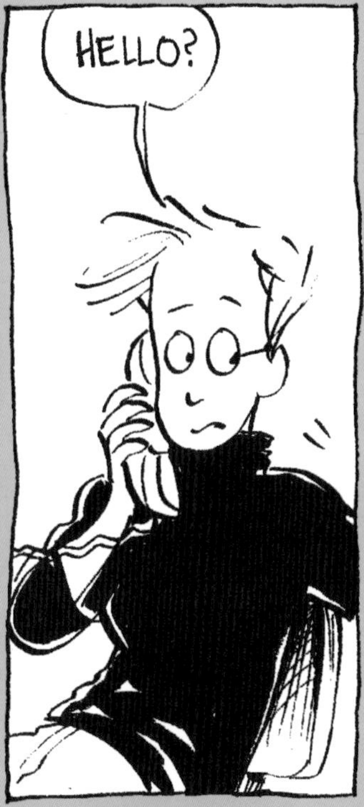
HELLO?

Mock Meatballs

Jane finally gets her job at the newspaper back, only to have her living situation upended by Dixie's bad money management. Ethan finds a solution, but Jane isn't too happy about it.

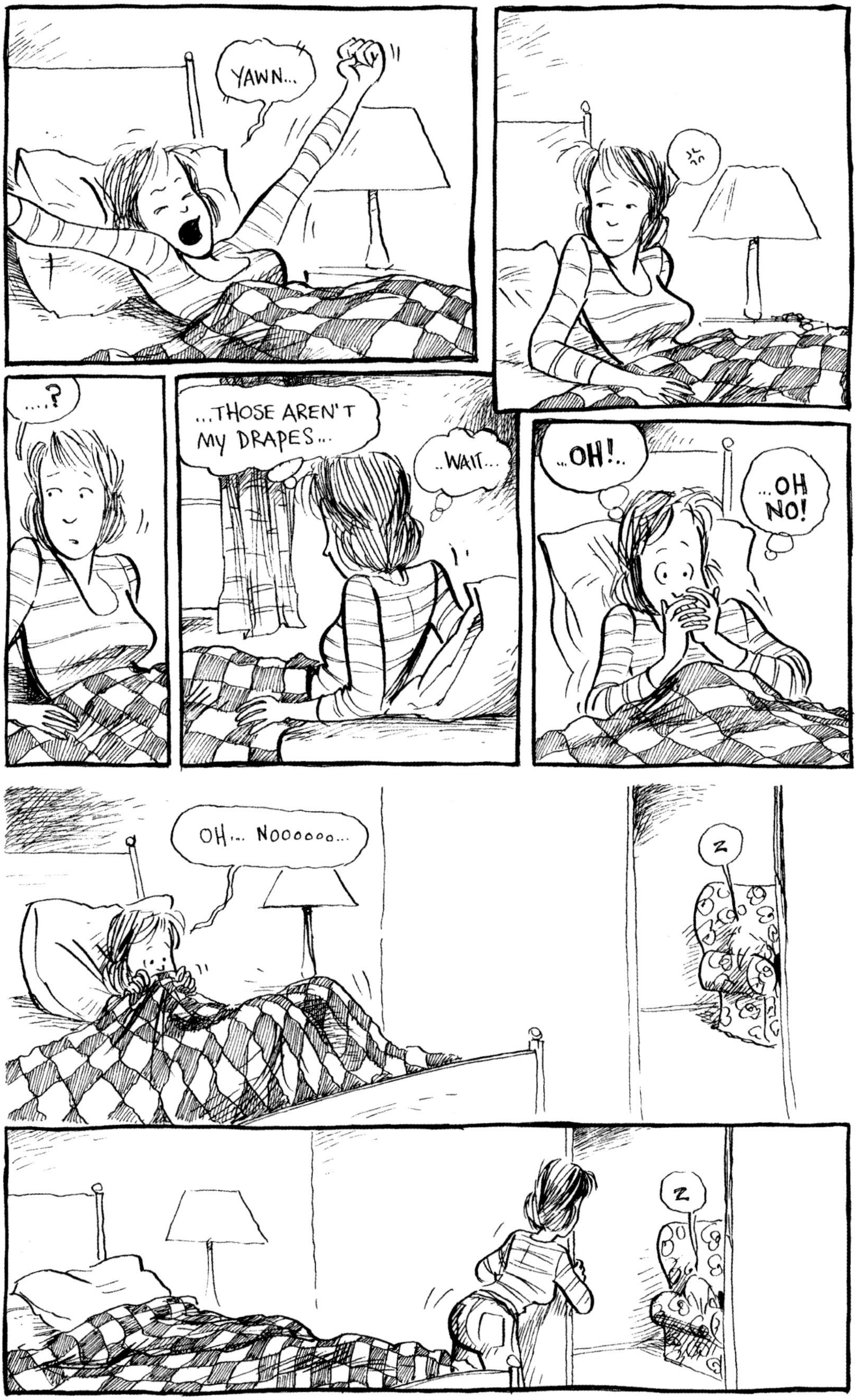
YAWN...
....?
...THOSE AREN'T MY DRAPES...
...WAIT...
...OH!...
...OH NO!
OH... NOOoooo...
Z
Z

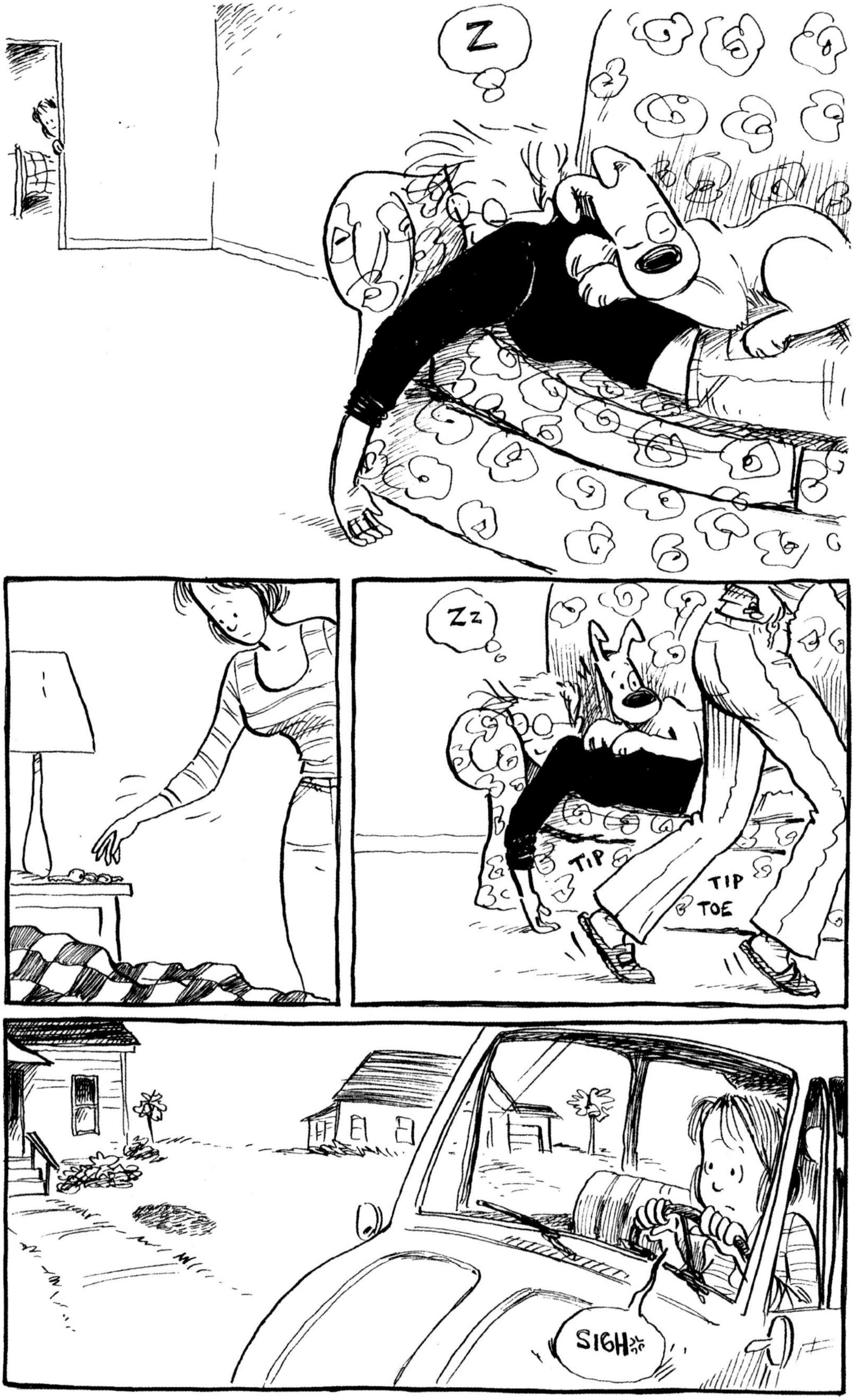
Z
Zz
TIP
TIP
TOE
SIGH

SHORTLY...

MOM...

"...LET IT GO..."

WELL, IF I HADN'T BEEN ASLEEP I'D HAVE BEEN WORRIED SICK!

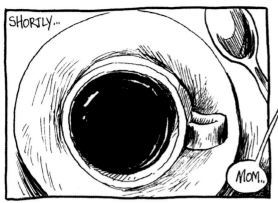

I HAD A LITTLE TOO MUCH TO DRINK... JANE THOUGHT I SHOULDN'T DRIVE ...END OF STORY...

JANE SLEPT ON THE COUCH... IT WAS NO BIG DEAL ...: NOTHING HAPPENED...

"...SO CAN WE JUST STOP TALKING ABOUT IT??..."

WHO'S TALKING? I'M NOT TALKING...

WHY ARE YOU SO DEFENSIVE?

ASIDE FROM HER FENG SHUI ILLITERACY JANE'S A GOOD CATCH...

MOMMM...

MEANWHILE ...

I WOKE UP AND SHE WAS GONE... WITHOUT A WORD...

AND I HAD TO GET ETHAN TO GIVE ME A RIDE BACK TO THE CAFE TO GET MY **JEEP**...

I'M SURE SHE DOESN'T EVEN REMEMBER WHAT HAPPENED...

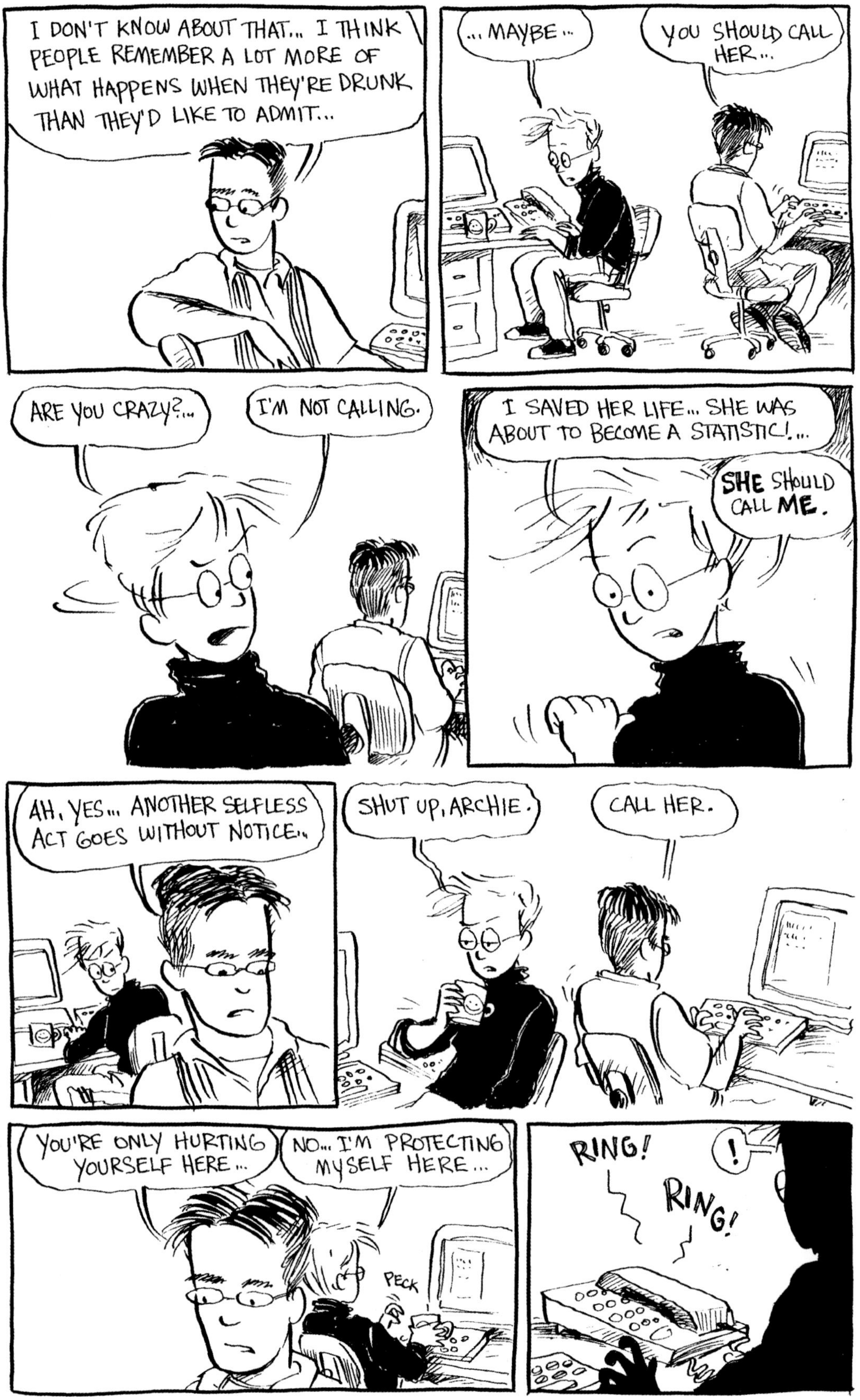
I DON'T KNOW ABOUT THAT... I THINK PEOPLE REMEMBER A LOT MORE OF WHAT HAPPENS WHEN THEY'RE DRUNK THAN THEY'D LIKE TO ADMIT...
...MAYBE...
YOU SHOULD CALL HER...
ARE YOU CRAZY?...
I'M NOT CALLING.
I SAVED HER LIFE... SHE WAS ABOUT TO BECOME A STATISTIC!...
SHE SHOULD CALL ME.
AH, YES... ANOTHER SELFLESS ACT GOES WITHOUT NOTICE...
SHUT UP, ARCHIE.
CALL HER.
YOU'RE ONLY HURTING YOURSELF HERE...
NO... I'M PROTECTING MYSELF HERE...
PECK
RING!
RING!
!

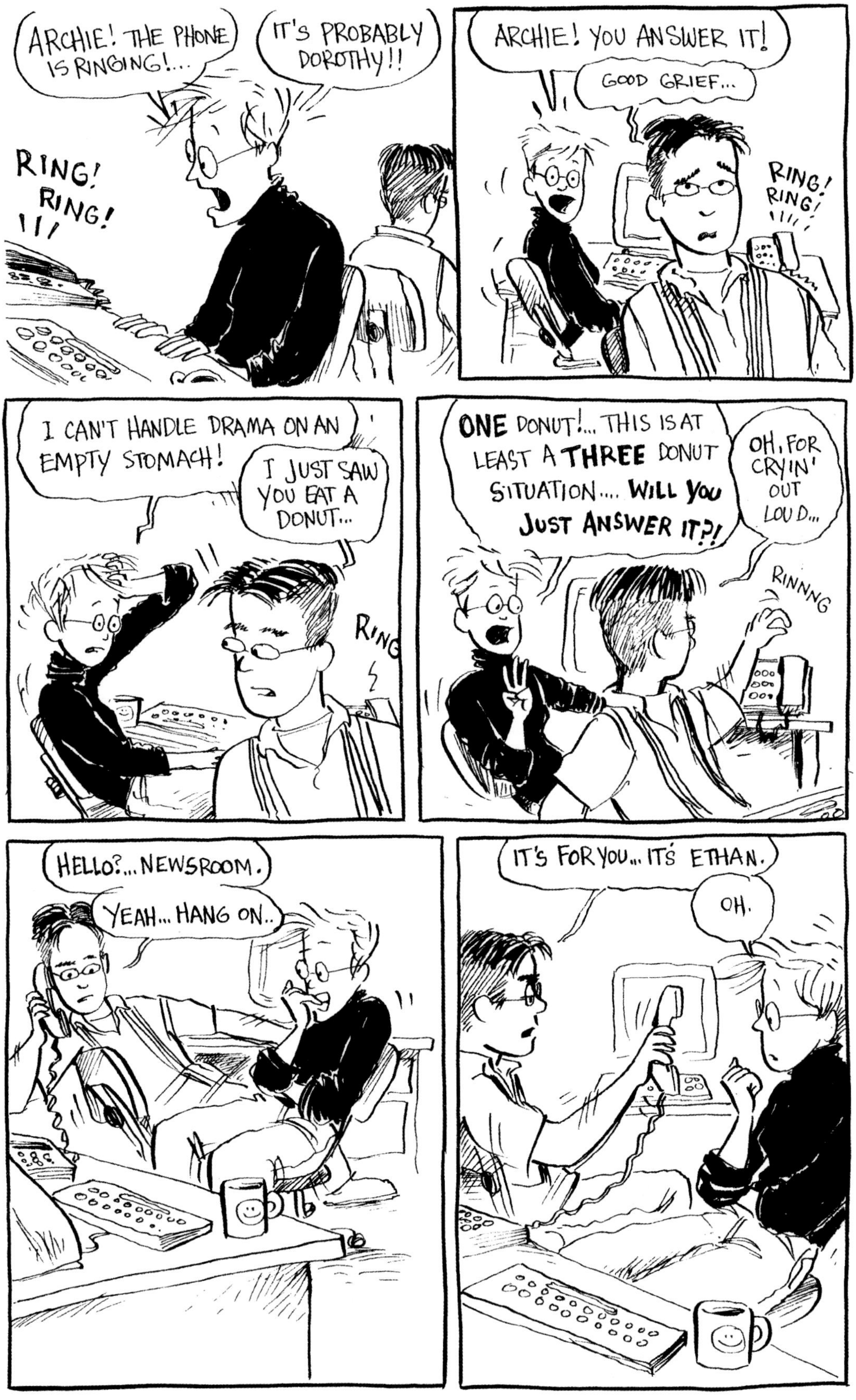
ARCHIE! THE PHONE IS RINGING!...
IT'S PROBABLY DOROTHY!!
RING! RING!
ARCHIE! YOU ANSWER IT!
GOOD GRIEF...
RING! RING!
I CAN'T HANDLE DRAMA ON AN EMPTY STOMACH!
I JUST SAW YOU EAT A DONUT...
RING
ONE DONUT!... THIS IS AT LEAST A THREE DONUT SITUATION.... WILL YOU JUST ANSWER IT?!
OH, FOR CRYIN' OUT LOUD...
RINNNG
HELLO?... NEWSROOM.
YEAH... HANG ON..
IT'S FOR YOU... IT'S ETHAN.
OH.

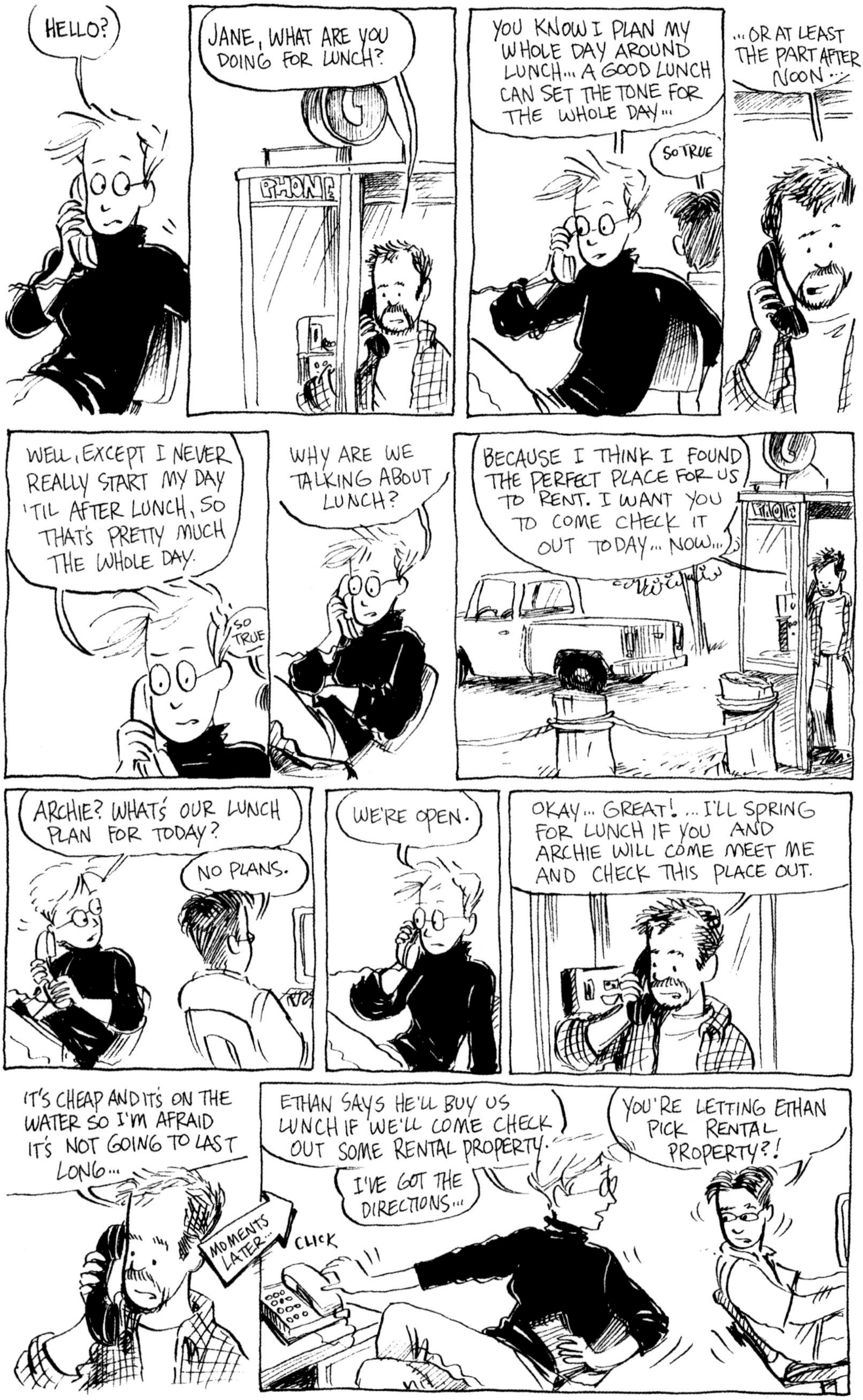
HELLO?
JANE, WHAT ARE YOU DOING FOR LUNCH?
PHONE
YOU KNOW I PLAN MY WHOLE DAY AROUND LUNCH... A GOOD LUNCH CAN SET THE TONE FOR THE WHOLE DAY...
SO TRUE
...OR AT LEAST THE PART AFTER NOON...
WELL, EXCEPT I NEVER REALLY START MY DAY 'TIL AFTER LUNCH, SO THAT'S PRETTY MUCH THE WHOLE DAY.
SO TRUE
WHY ARE WE TALKING ABOUT LUNCH?
BECAUSE I THINK I FOUND THE PERFECT PLACE FOR US TO RENT. I WANT YOU TO COME CHECK IT OUT TODAY... NOW...
ARCHIE? WHAT'S OUR LUNCH PLAN FOR TODAY?
NO PLANS.
WE'RE OPEN.
OKAY... GREAT! ...I'LL SPRING FOR LUNCH IF YOU AND ARCHIE WILL COME MEET ME AND CHECK THIS PLACE OUT.
IT'S CHEAP AND IT'S ON THE WATER SO I'M AFRAID IT'S NOT GOING TO LAST LONG...
MOMENTS LATER...
CLICK
I'VE GOT THE DIRECTIONS...
ETHAN SAYS HE'LL BUY US LUNCH IF WE'LL COME CHECK OUT SOME RENTAL PROPERTY.
YOU'RE LETTING ETHAN PICK RENTAL PROPERTY?!

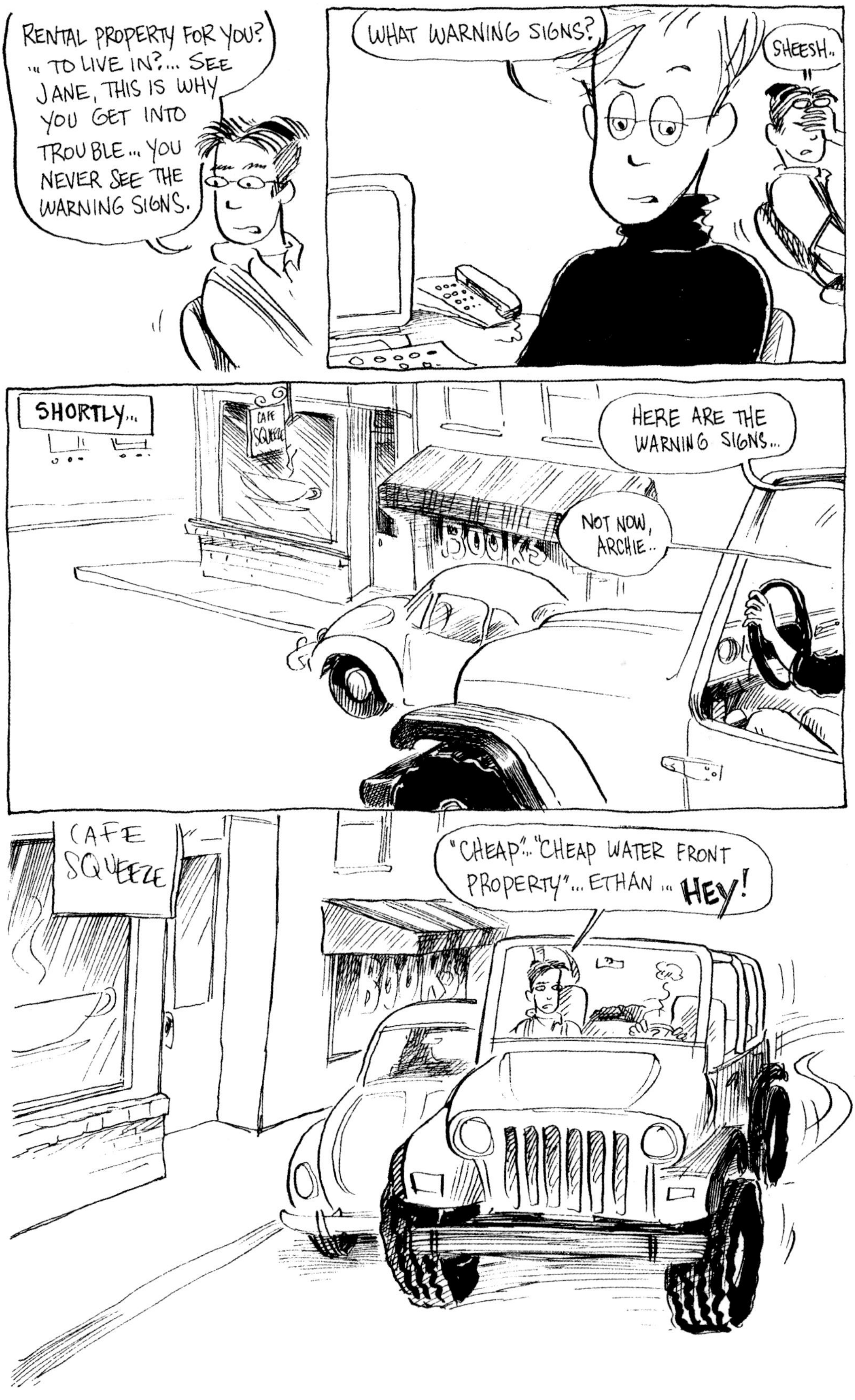
RENTAL PROPERTY FOR YOU? ... TO LIVE IN?... SEE JANE, THIS IS WHY YOU GET INTO TROUBLE... YOU NEVER SEE THE WARNING SIGNS.
WHAT WARNING SIGNS?
SHEESH..
SHORTLY...
CAFE SQUEEZE
HERE ARE THE WARNING SIGNS...
NOT NOW, ARCHIE..
BOOKS
CAFE SQUEEZE
"CHEAP".."CHEAP WATER FRONT PROPERTY"... ETHAN ... HEY!

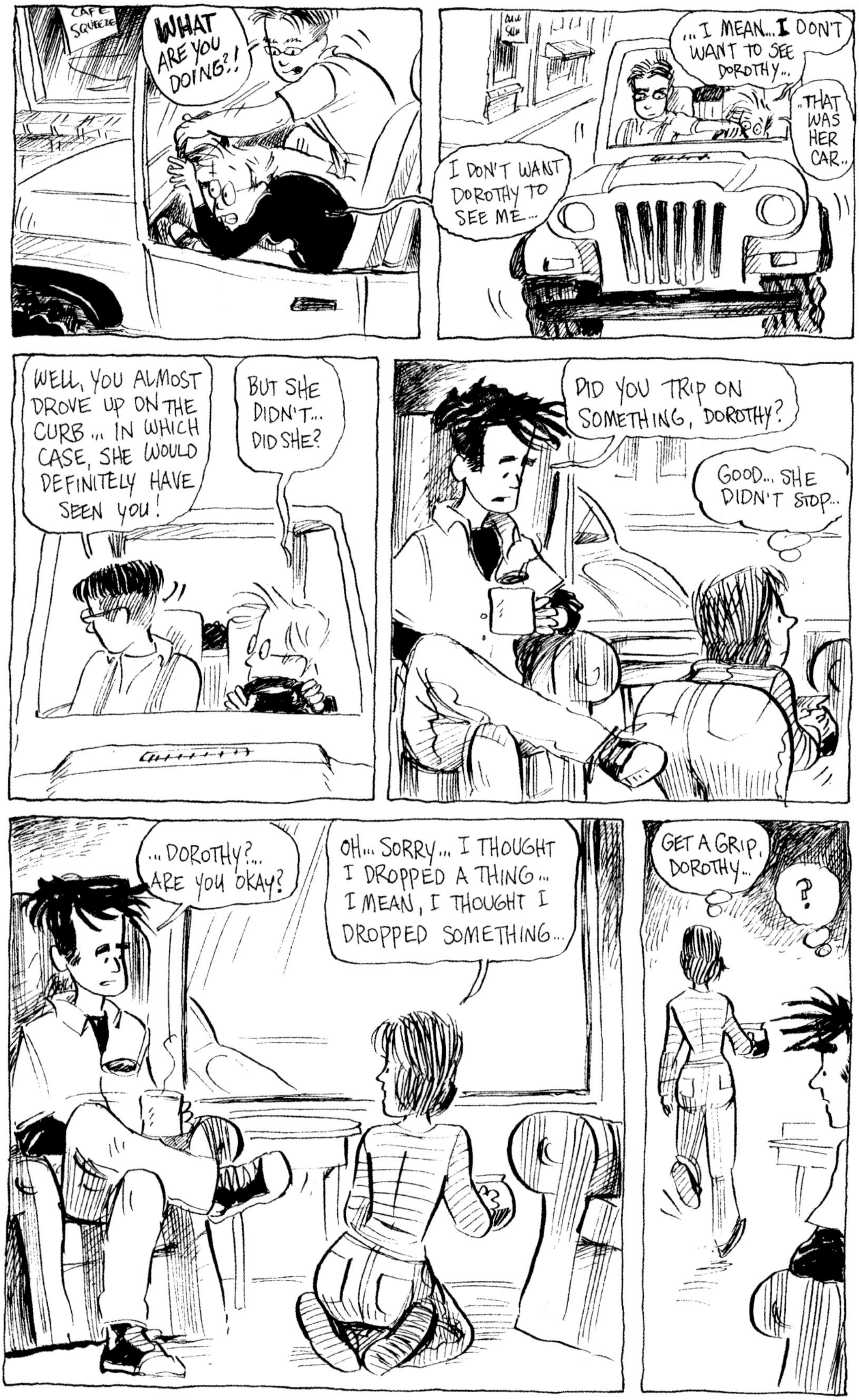
CAFE SQUEEZE
WHAT ARE YOU DOING?!
I DON'T WANT DOROTHY TO SEE ME...
...I MEAN... I DON'T WANT TO SEE DOROTHY...
..THAT WAS HER CAR..
WELL, YOU ALMOST DROVE UP ON THE CURB... IN WHICH CASE, SHE WOULD DEFINITELY HAVE SEEN YOU!
BUT SHE DIDN'T... DID SHE?
DID YOU TRIP ON SOMETHING, DOROTHY?
GOOD... SHE DIDN'T STOP...
...DOROTHY?... ARE YOU OKAY?
OH... SORRY... I THOUGHT I DROPPED A THING... I MEAN, I THOUGHT I DROPPED SOMETHING...
GET A GRIP, DOROTHY...
?

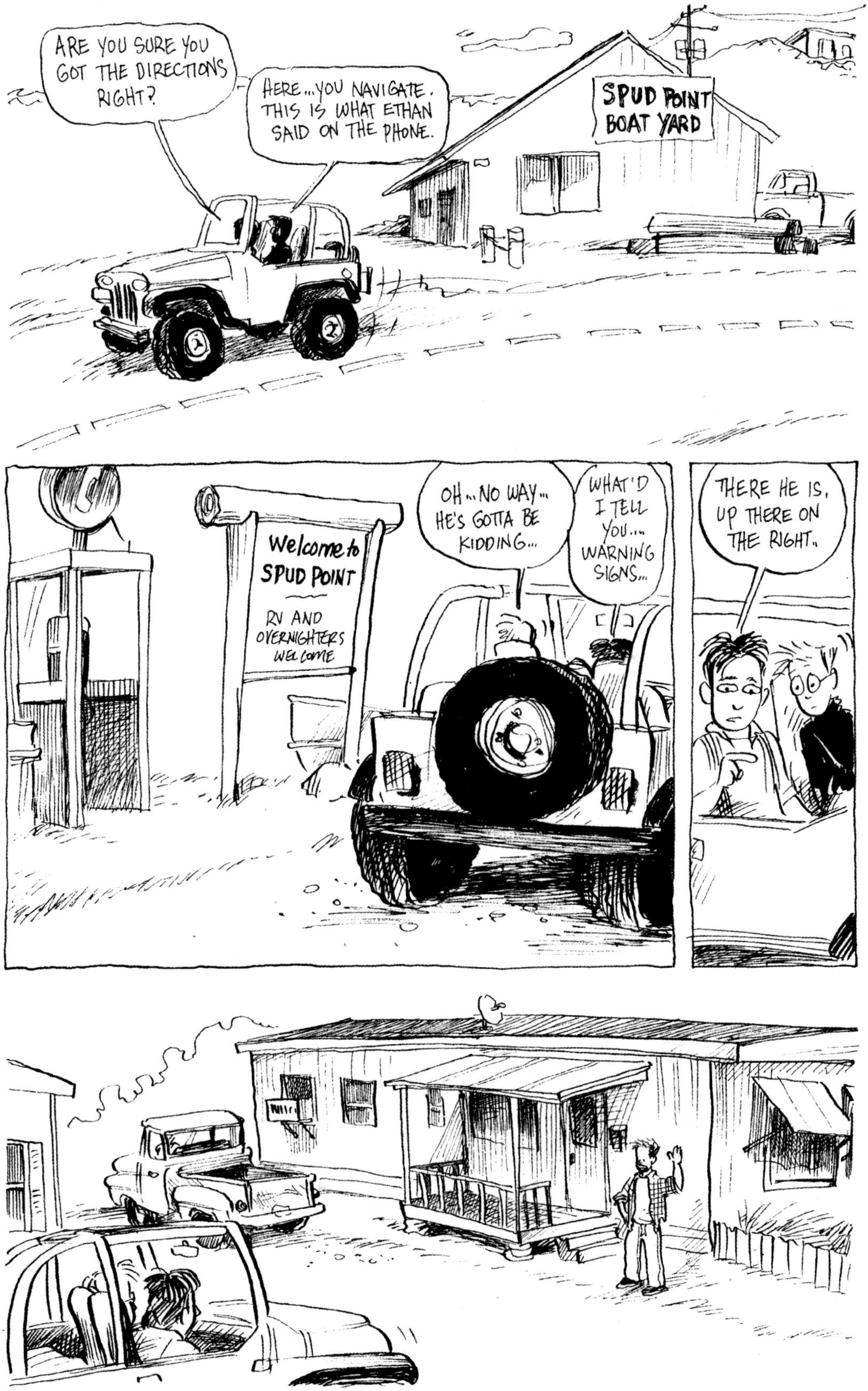
ARE YOU SURE YOU GOT THE DIRECTIONS RIGHT?
HERE...YOU NAVIGATE. THIS IS WHAT ETHAN SAID ON THE PHONE.
SPUD POINT BOAT YARD
Welcome to SPUD POINT
RV AND OVERNIGHTERS WELCOME
OH...NO WAY... HE'S GOTTA BE KIDDING...
WHAT'D I TELL YOU.... WARNING SIGNS...
THERE HE IS, UP THERE ON THE RIGHT..

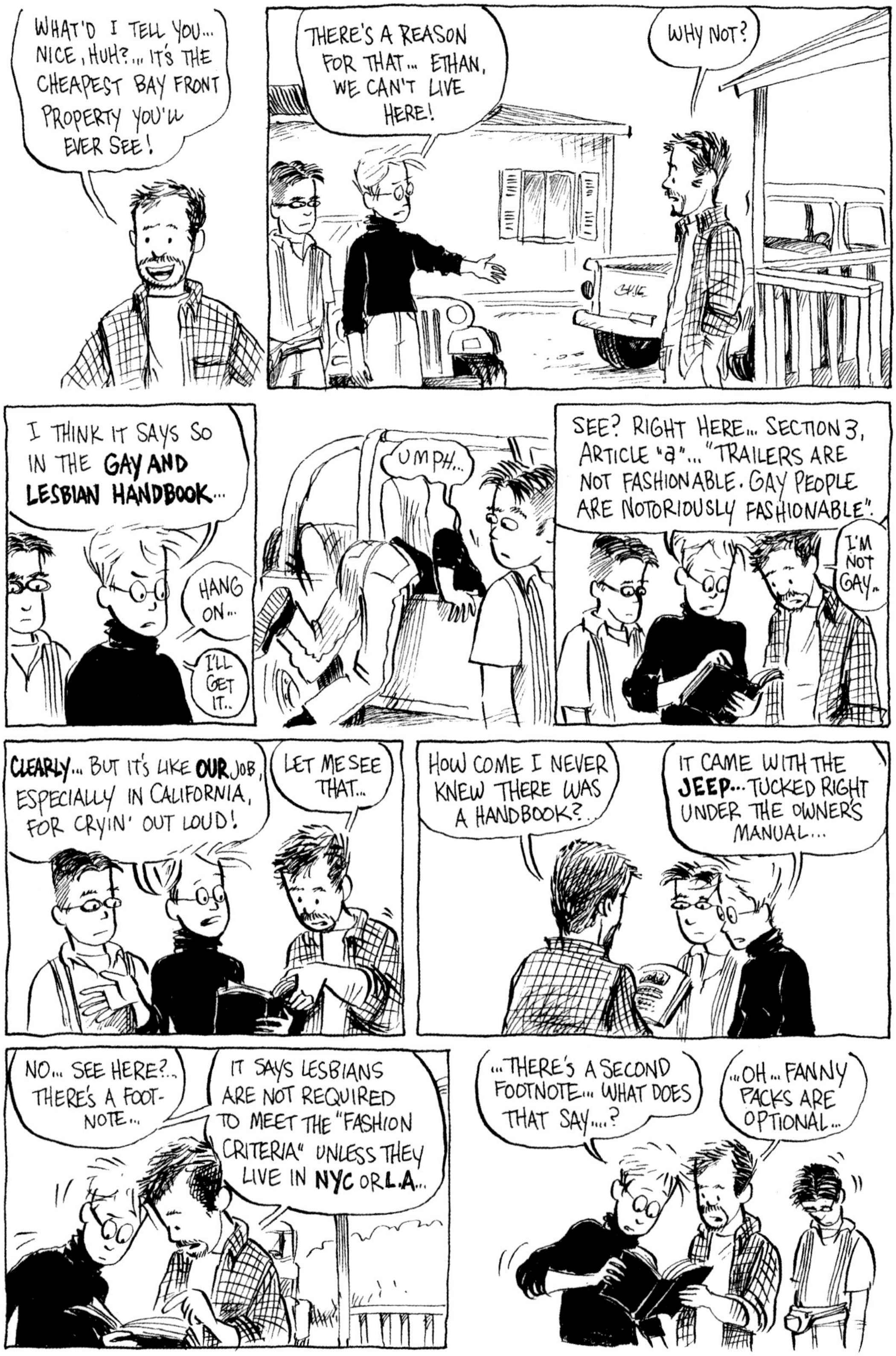
WHAT'D I TELL YOU... NICE, HUH?... IT'S THE CHEAPEST BAY FRONT PROPERTY YOU'LL EVER SEE!
THERE'S A REASON FOR THAT... ETHAN, WE CAN'T LIVE HERE!
WHY NOT?
I THINK IT SAYS SO IN THE GAY AND LESBIAN HANDBOOK...
HANG ON...
I'LL GET IT..
UMPH...
SEE? RIGHT HERE... SECTION 3, ARTICLE "a"... "TRAILERS ARE NOT FASHIONABLE. GAY PEOPLE ARE NOTORIOUSLY FASHIONABLE".
I'M NOT GAY..
CLEARLY... BUT IT'S LIKE OUR JOB, ESPECIALLY IN CALIFORNIA, FOR CRYIN' OUT LOUD!
LET ME SEE THAT...
HOW COME I NEVER KNEW THERE WAS A HANDBOOK?
IT CAME WITH THE JEEP... TUCKED RIGHT UNDER THE OWNER'S MANUAL...
NO... SEE HERE?.. THERE'S A FOOT-NOTE...
IT SAYS LESBIANS ARE NOT REQUIRED TO MEET THE "FASHION CRITERIA" UNLESS THEY LIVE IN NYC OR L.A...
...THERE'S A SECOND FOOTNOTE... WHAT DOES THAT SAY....?
...OH... FANNY PACKS ARE OPTIONAL...

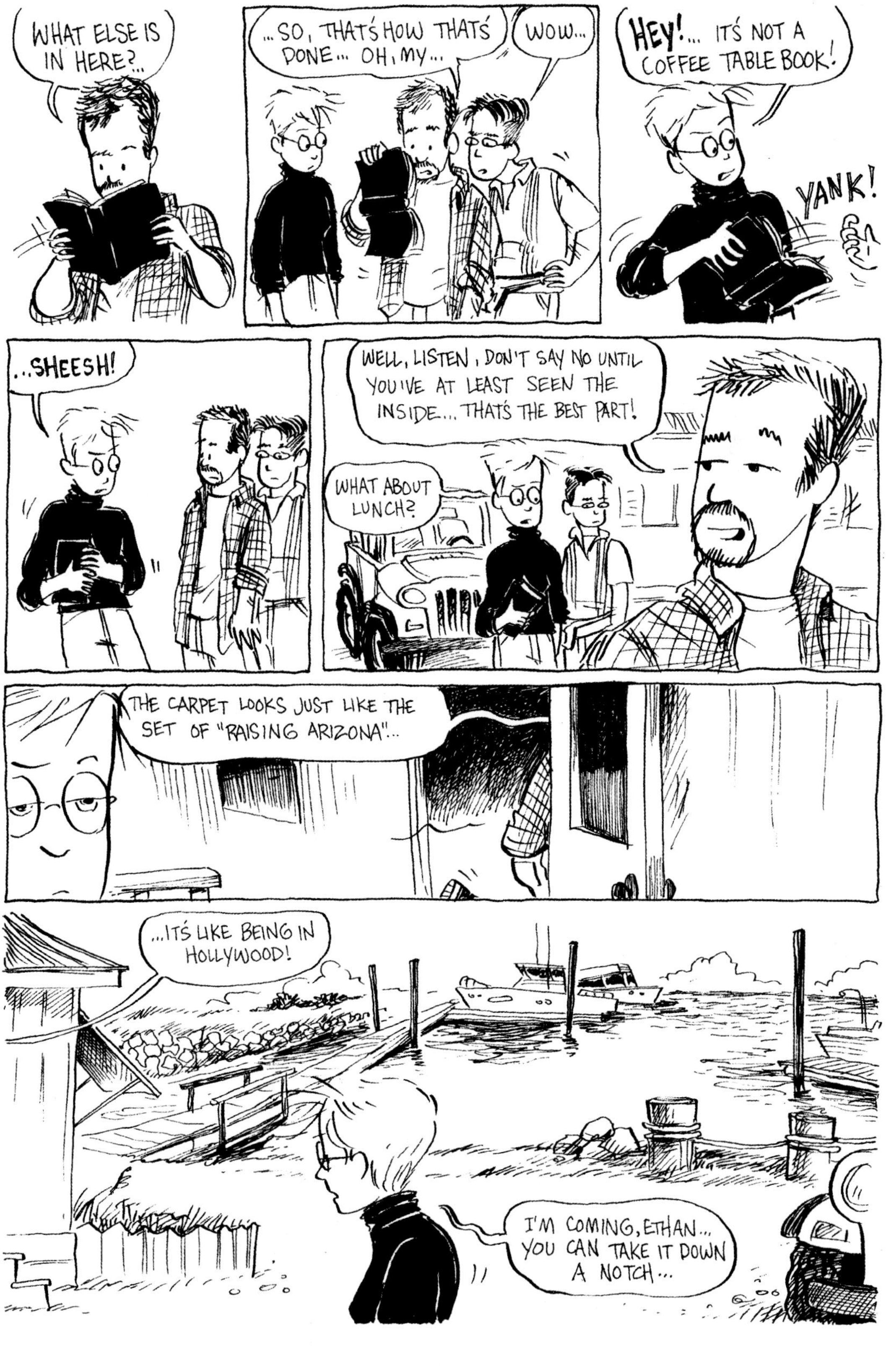
WHAT ELSE IS IN HERE?..
...SO, THAT'S HOW THAT'S DONE... OH, MY...
WOW...
HEY!... IT'S NOT A COFFEE TABLE BOOK!
YANK!
...SHEESH!
WELL, LISTEN, DON'T SAY NO UNTIL YOU'VE AT LEAST SEEN THE INSIDE... THAT'S THE BEST PART!
WHAT ABOUT LUNCH?
THE CARPET LOOKS JUST LIKE THE SET OF "RAISING ARIZONA"...
...IT'S LIKE BEING IN HOLLYWOOD!
I'M COMING, ETHAN... YOU CAN TAKE IT DOWN A NOTCH...

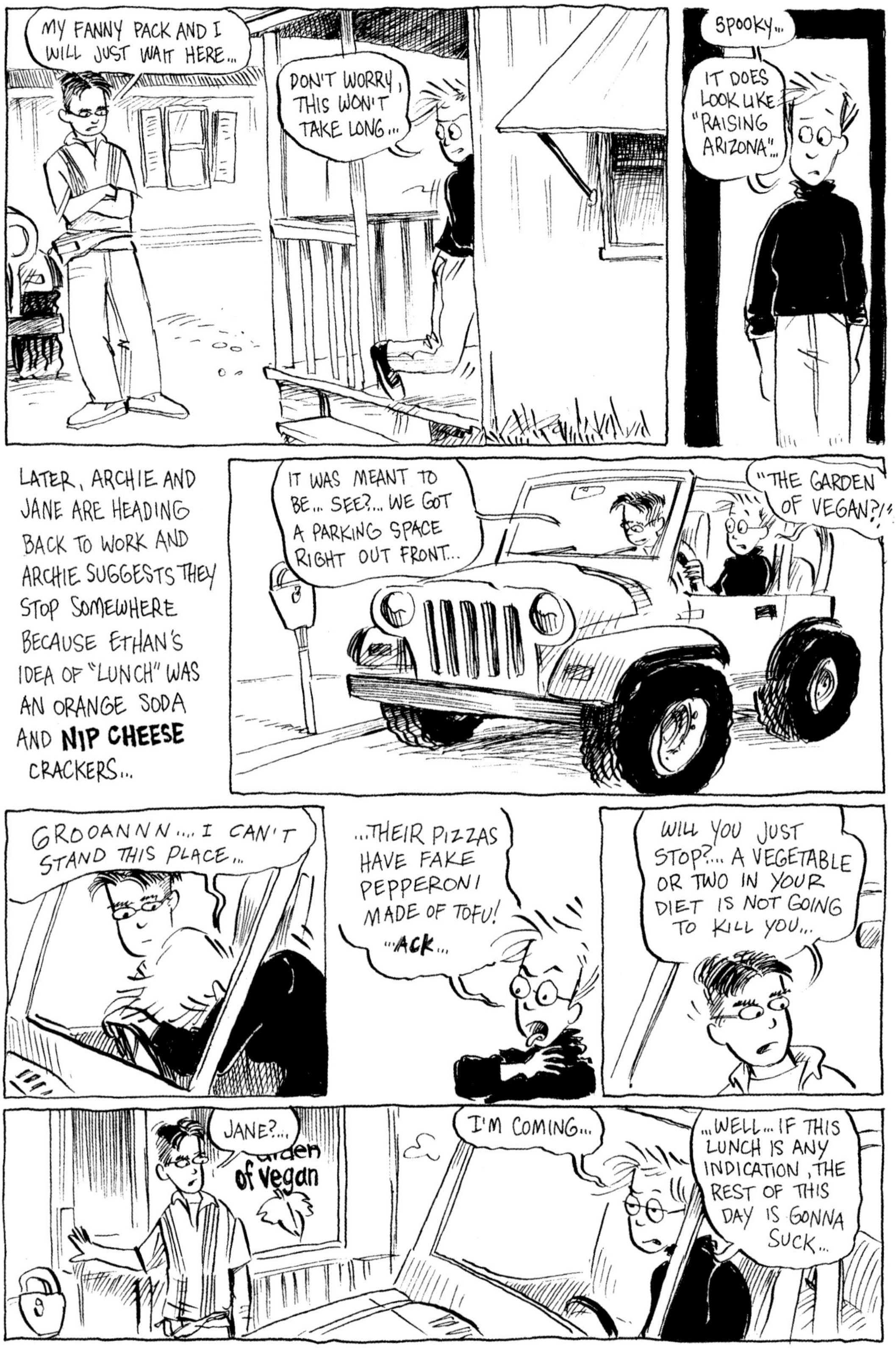
MY FANNY PACK AND I WILL JUST WAIT HERE...
DON'T WORRY, THIS WON'T TAKE LONG...
SPOOKY...
IT DOES LOOK LIKE "RAISING ARIZONA"...
LATER, ARCHIE AND JANE ARE HEADING BACK TO WORK AND ARCHIE SUGGESTS THEY STOP SOMEWHERE BECAUSE ETHAN'S IDEA OF "LUNCH" WAS AN ORANGE SODA AND NIP CHEESE CRACKERS...
IT WAS MEANT TO BE... SEE?... WE GOT A PARKING SPACE RIGHT OUT FRONT...
"THE GARDEN OF VEGAN?!"
GROOANNN.... I CAN'T STAND THIS PLACE...
...THEIR PIZZAS HAVE FAKE PEPPERONI MADE OF TOFU! ...ACK...
WILL YOU JUST STOP?... A VEGETABLE OR TWO IN YOUR DIET IS NOT GOING TO KILL YOU...
JANE?...
of vegan
I'M COMING...
...WELL... IF THIS LUNCH IS ANY INDICATION, THE REST OF THIS DAY IS GONNA SUCK...

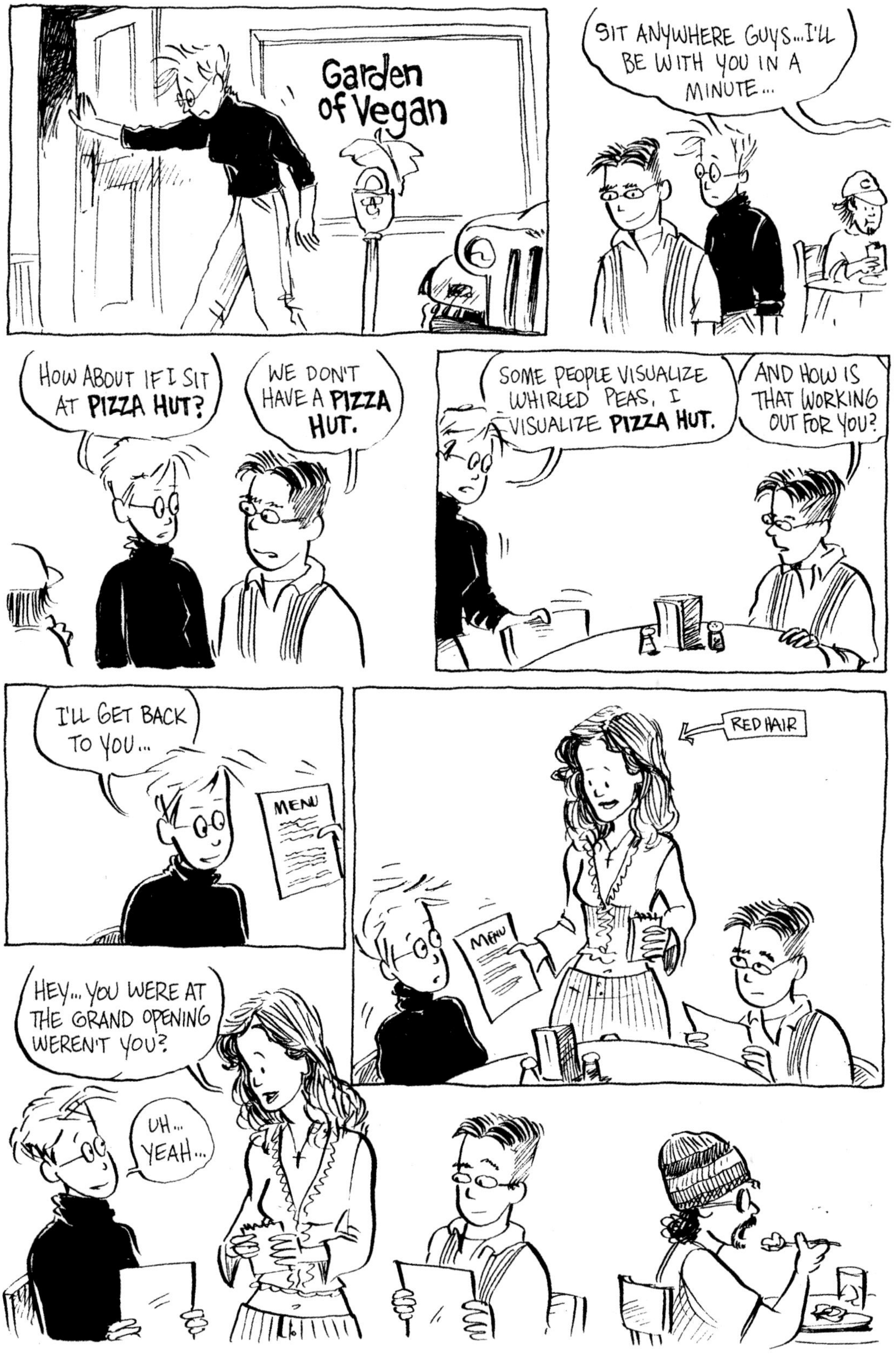
Garden of Vegan
SIT ANYWHERE GUYS...I'LL BE WITH YOU IN A MINUTE...
HOW ABOUT IF I SIT AT PIZZA HUT?
WE DON'T HAVE A PIZZA HUT.
SOME PEOPLE VISUALIZE WHIRLED PEAS, I VISUALIZE PIZZA HUT.
AND HOW IS THAT WORKING OUT FOR YOU?
I'LL GET BACK TO YOU...
MENU
RED HAIR
MENU
HEY... YOU WERE AT THE GRAND OPENING WEREN'T YOU?
UH... YEAH...

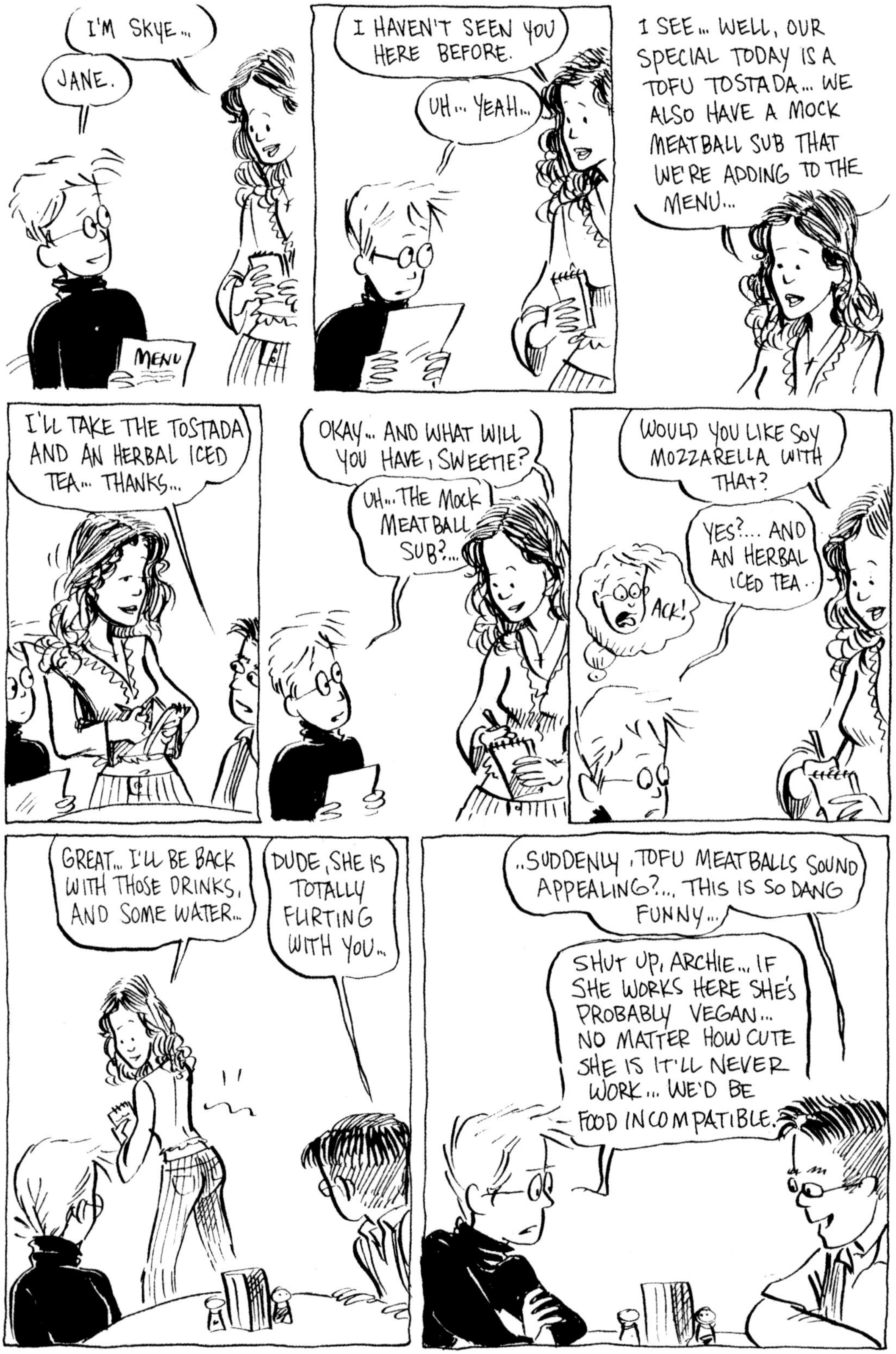
I'M SKYE...
JANE.
I HAVEN'T SEEN YOU HERE BEFORE.
UH... YEAH...
I SEE... WELL, OUR SPECIAL TODAY IS A TOFU TOSTADA... WE ALSO HAVE A MOCK MEATBALL SUB THAT WE'RE ADDING TO THE MENU...
MENU
I'LL TAKE THE TOSTADA AND AN HERBAL ICED TEA... THANKS...
OKAY... AND WHAT WILL YOU HAVE, SWEETIE?
UH... THE MOCK MEATBALL SUB?...
WOULD YOU LIKE SOY MOZZARELLA WITH THAT?
YES?... AND AN HERBAL ICED TEA...
ACK!
GREAT... I'LL BE BACK WITH THOSE DRINKS, AND SOME WATER...
DUDE, SHE IS TOTALLY FLIRTING WITH YOU...
..SUDDENLY, TOFU MEATBALLS SOUND APPEALING?... THIS IS SO DANG FUNNY...
SHUT UP, ARCHIE... IF SHE WORKS HERE SHE'S PROBABLY VEGAN... NO MATTER HOW CUTE SHE IS IT'LL NEVER WORK... WE'D BE FOOD INCOMPATIBLE.

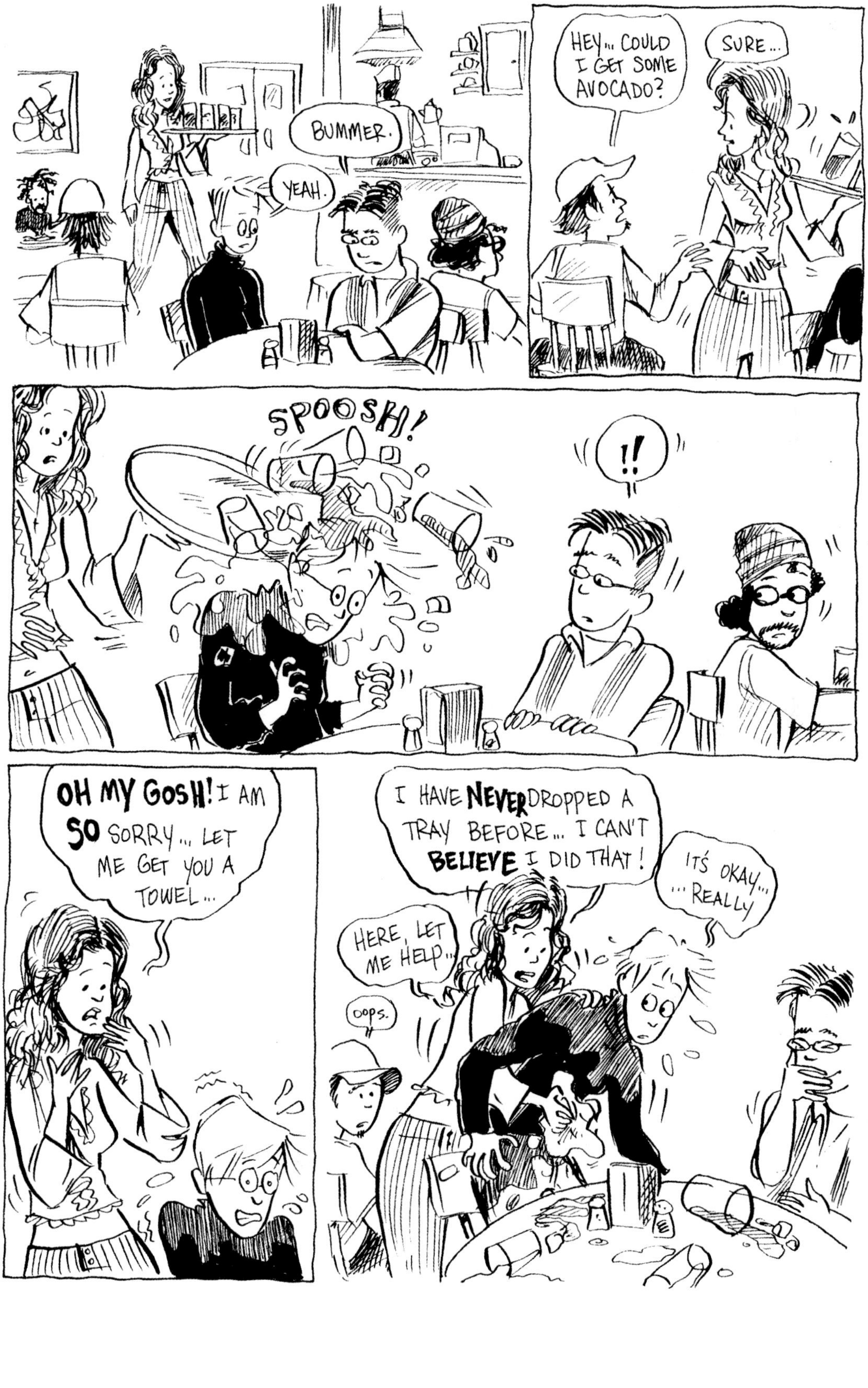
BUMMER.
YEAH.
HEY... COULD I GET SOME AVOCADO?
SURE...
SPOOSH!
!!
OH MY GOSH! I AM SO SORRY... LET ME GET YOU A TOWEL...
I HAVE NEVER DROPPED A TRAY BEFORE... I CAN'T BELIEVE I DID THAT!
IT'S OKAY... ...REALLY
HERE, LET ME HELP...
OOPS.

Quest for Love

Jane is on a quest for love, but will she succeed?
Knowing Jane, probably not. But the journey is
nonetheless filled with romantic misadventures,
misunderstandings, and general quixotic mayhem. Jane
is sent out to cover a mountain bike race, which of course
ends in disaster. The entire cast of new loves and exes
collides in this bike race turned wilderness adventure.

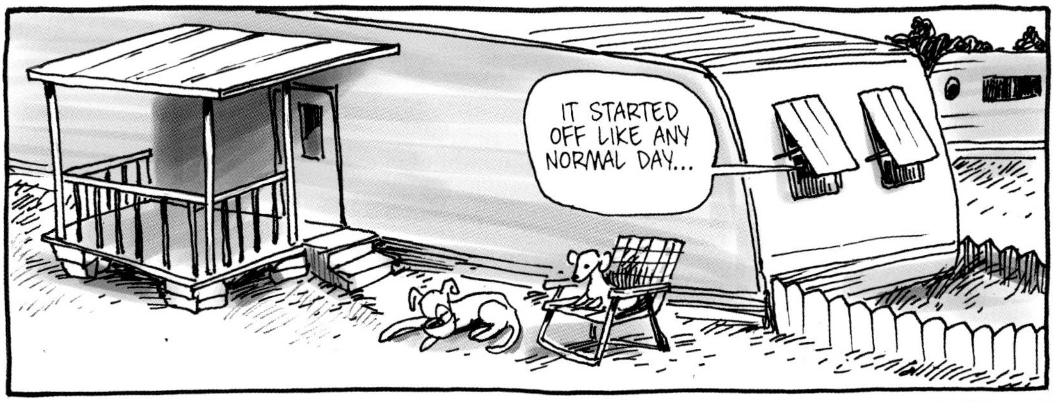
IT STARTED OFF LIKE ANY NORMAL DAY...

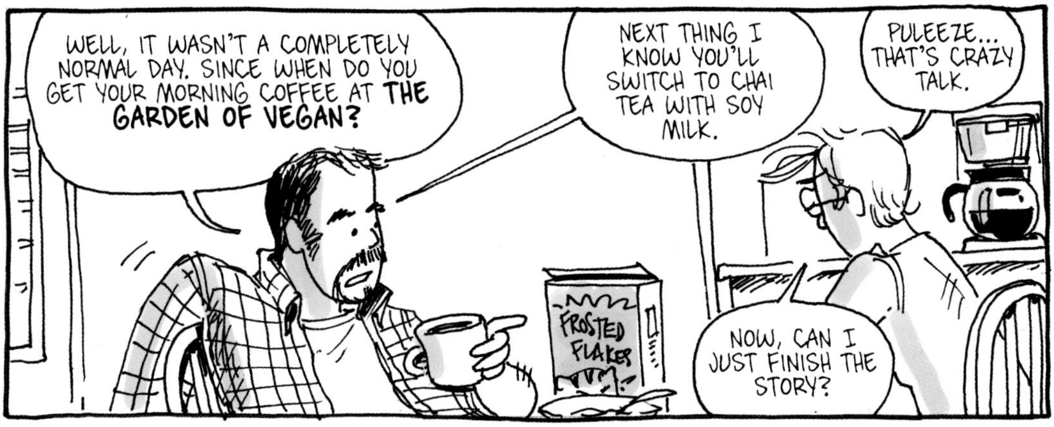
WELL, IT WASN'T A COMPLETELY NORMAL DAY. SINCE WHEN DO YOU GET YOUR MORNING COFFEE AT **THE GARDEN OF VEGAN?**
NEXT THING I KNOW YOU'LL SWITCH TO CHAI TEA WITH SOY MILK.
FROSTED FLAKES
PULEEZE... THAT'S CRAZY TALK.
NOW, CAN I JUST FINISH THE STORY?

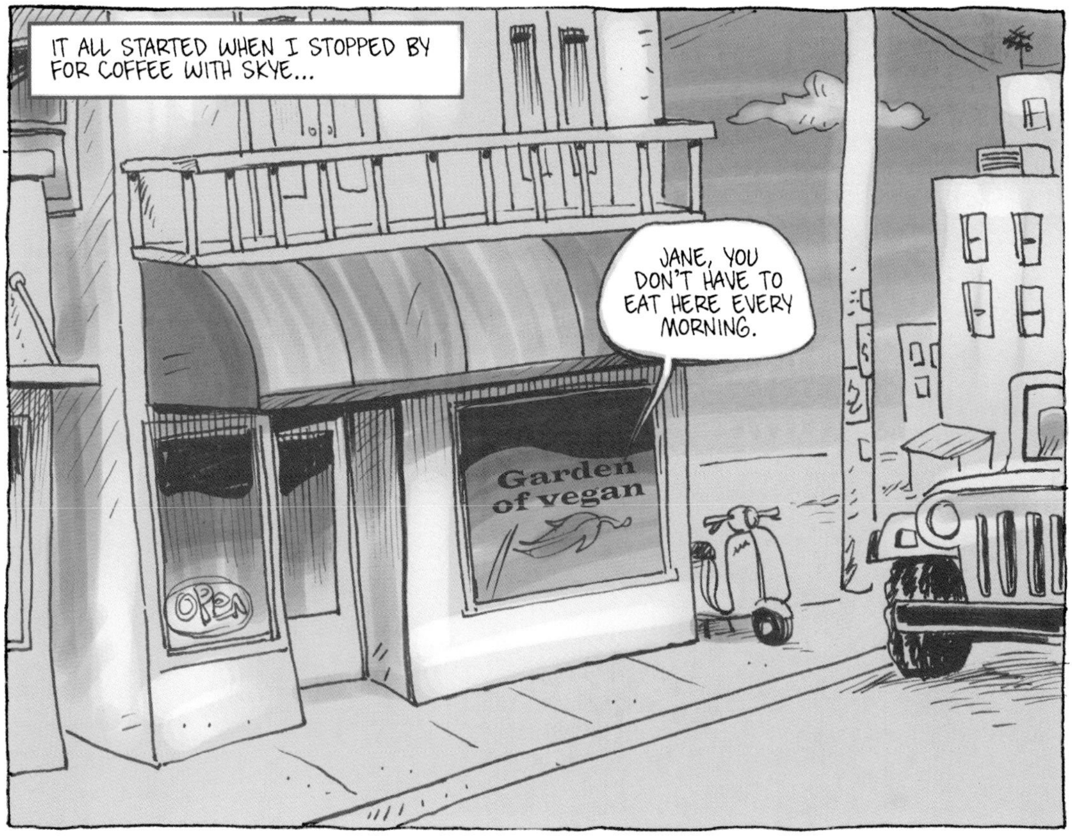
IT ALL STARTED WHEN I STOPPED BY FOR COFFEE WITH SKYE...
JANE, YOU DON'T HAVE TO EAT HERE EVERY MORNING.
Garden of vegan
OPEN

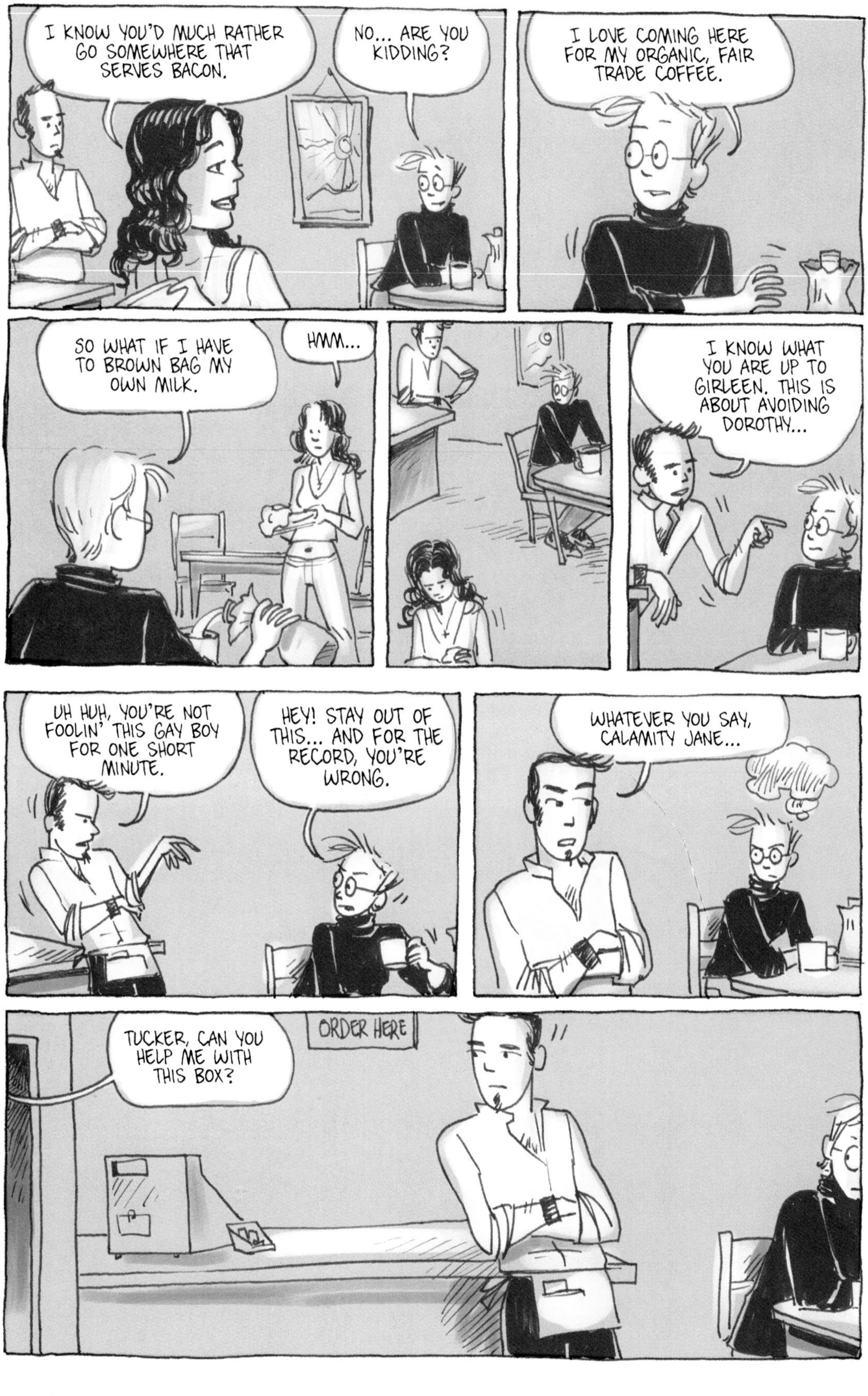
I KNOW YOU'D MUCH RATHER GO SOMEWHERE THAT SERVES BACON.
NO... ARE YOU KIDDING?
I LOVE COMING HERE FOR MY ORGANIC, FAIR TRADE COFFEE.
SO WHAT IF I HAVE TO BROWN BAG MY OWN MILK.
HMM...
I KNOW WHAT YOU ARE UP TO GIRLEEN. THIS IS ABOUT AVOIDING DOROTHY...
UH HUH, YOU'RE NOT FOOLIN' THIS GAY BOY FOR ONE SHORT MINUTE.
HEY! STAY OUT OF THIS... AND FOR THE RECORD, YOU'RE WRONG.
WHATEVER YOU SAY, CALAMITY JANE...
TUCKER, CAN YOU HELP ME WITH THIS BOX?
ORDER HERE

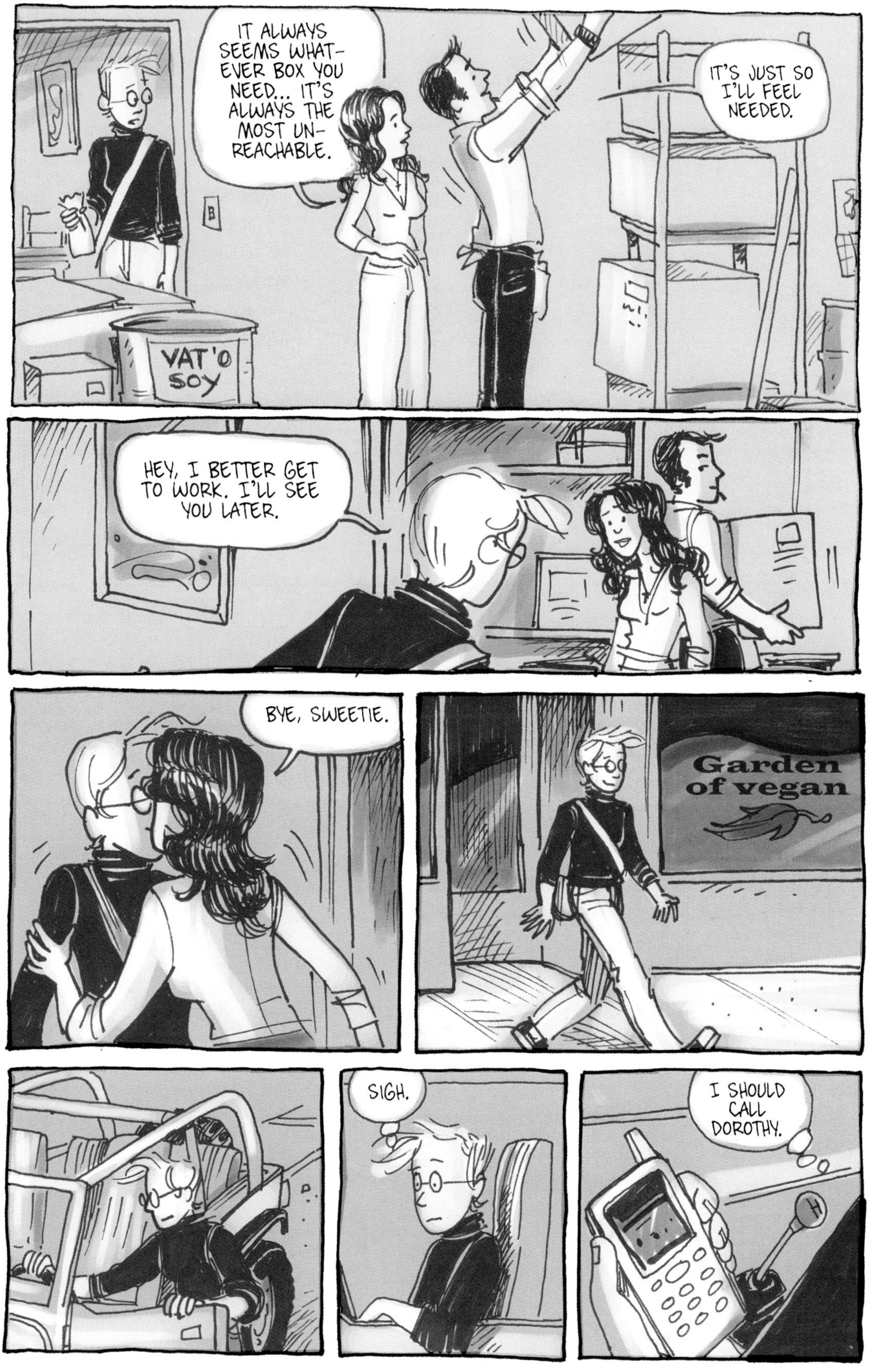
IT ALWAYS SEEMS WHAT-EVER BOX YOU NEED... IT'S ALWAYS THE MOST UN-REACHABLE.
IT'S JUST SO I'LL FEEL NEEDED.
VAT'O SOY
HEY, I BETTER GET TO WORK. I'LL SEE YOU LATER.
BYE, SWEETIE.
Garden of vegan
SIGH.
I SHOULD CALL DOROTHY.

BUT THEN SHE CALLED ME FIRST...

RRING

HELLO?

YEAH... I COULD COME BY AFTER WORK... I SUPPOSE WE DO NEED TO TALK... BUT... BUT OKAY... YOU CLOSE UP AT 10:00?

I'LL SEE YOU AT 10:00.

AS STORIES GO, I'VE GOTTA SAY THIS ONE IS PRETTY BORING.

I HAD TO SET THE SCENE... I'M GETTING TO THE **DISASTER** PART.

FROSTED FLAKES

WELL, I HOPE THERE'S AT LEAST A HOT MAKE OUT SESSION PRIOR TO THE "DISASTER."

JUST WAIT...

FROSTED FLAKE

SO I GET TO THE COFFEE SHOP RIGHT AFTER IT CLOSES.

10:02 PM

CAFE

DOROTHY?

SHE WAS SITTING ON THE SOFA... I SAT DOWN AND WE STARTED TO TALK...

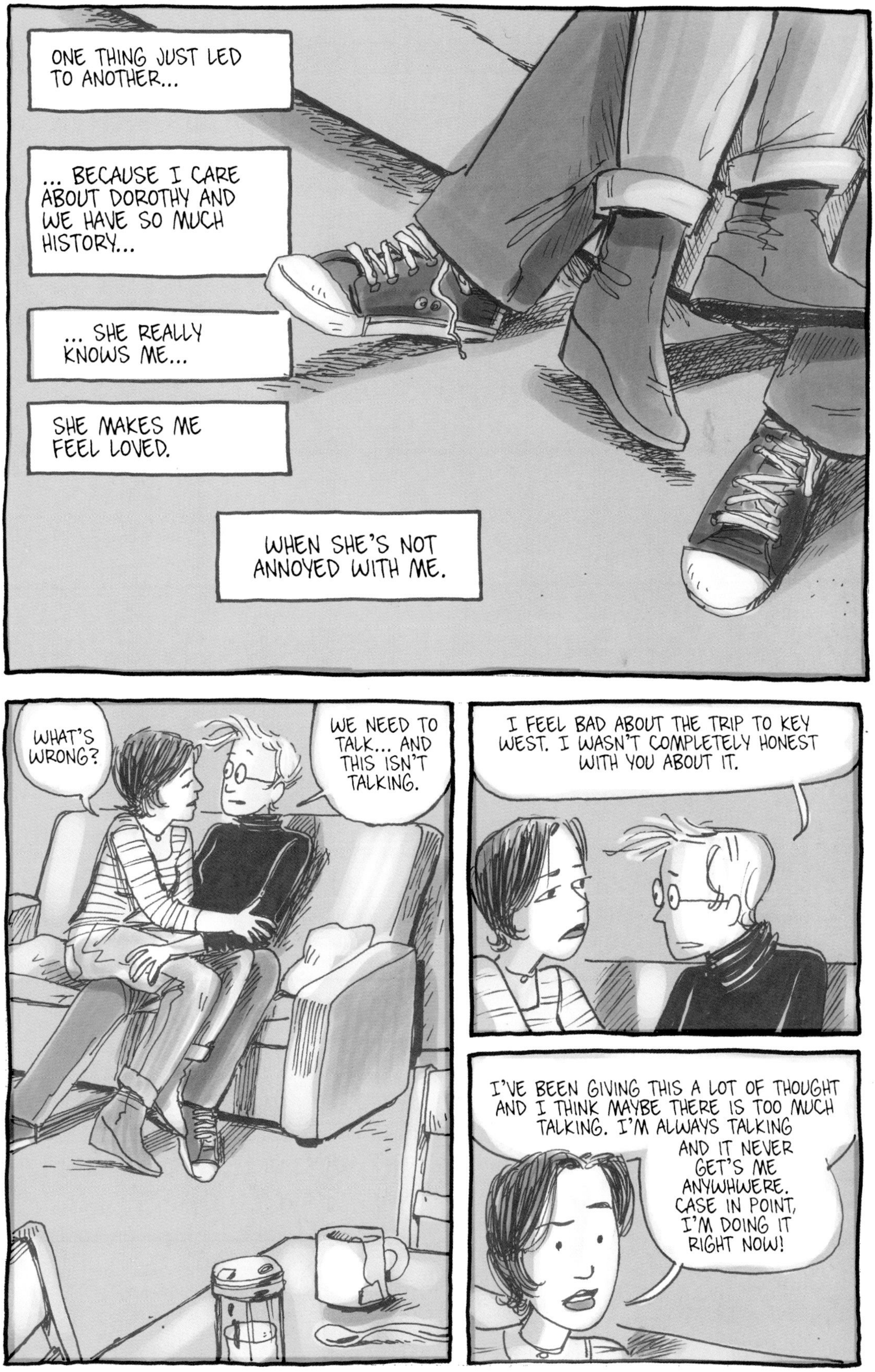
ONE THING JUST LED TO ANOTHER...
... BECAUSE I CARE ABOUT DOROTHY AND WE HAVE SO MUCH HISTORY...
... SHE REALLY KNOWS ME...
SHE MAKES ME FEEL LOVED.
WHEN SHE'S NOT ANNOYED WITH ME.
WHAT'S WRONG?
WE NEED TO TALK... AND THIS ISN'T TALKING.
I FEEL BAD ABOUT THE TRIP TO KEY WEST. I WASN'T COMPLETELY HONEST WITH YOU ABOUT IT.
I'VE BEEN GIVING THIS A LOT OF THOUGHT AND I THINK MAYBE THERE IS TOO MUCH TALKING. I'M ALWAYS TALKING AND IT NEVER GET'S ME ANYWHWERE. CASE IN POINT, I'M DOING IT RIGHT NOW!

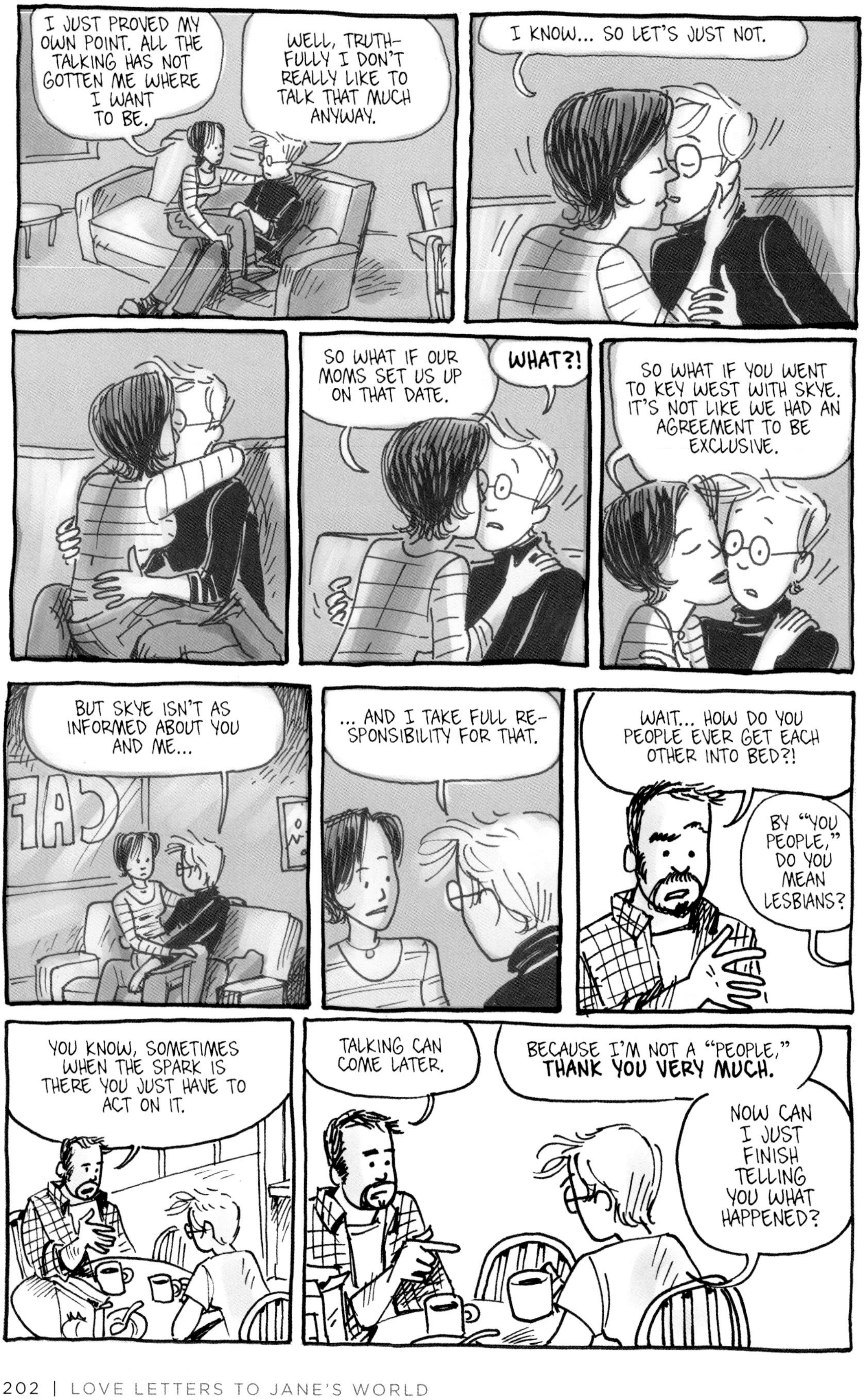
I JUST PROVED MY OWN POINT. ALL THE TALKING HAS NOT GOTTEN ME WHERE I WANT TO BE.
WELL, TRUTHFULLY I DON'T REALLY LIKE TO TALK THAT MUCH ANYWAY.
I KNOW... SO LET'S JUST NOT.
SO WHAT IF OUR MOMS SET US UP ON THAT DATE.
WHAT?!
SO WHAT IF YOU WENT TO KEY WEST WITH SKYE. IT'S NOT LIKE WE HAD AN AGREEMENT TO BE EXCLUSIVE.
BUT SKYE ISN'T AS INFORMED ABOUT YOU AND ME...
... AND I TAKE FULL RESPONSIBILITY FOR THAT.
WAIT... HOW DO YOU PEOPLE EVER GET EACH OTHER INTO BED?!
BY "YOU PEOPLE," DO YOU MEAN LESBIANS?
YOU KNOW, SOMETIMES WHEN THE SPARK IS THERE YOU JUST HAVE TO ACT ON IT.
TALKING CAN COME LATER.
BECAUSE I'M NOT A "PEOPLE," THANK YOU VERY MUCH.
NOW CAN I JUST FINISH TELLING YOU WHAT HAPPENED?

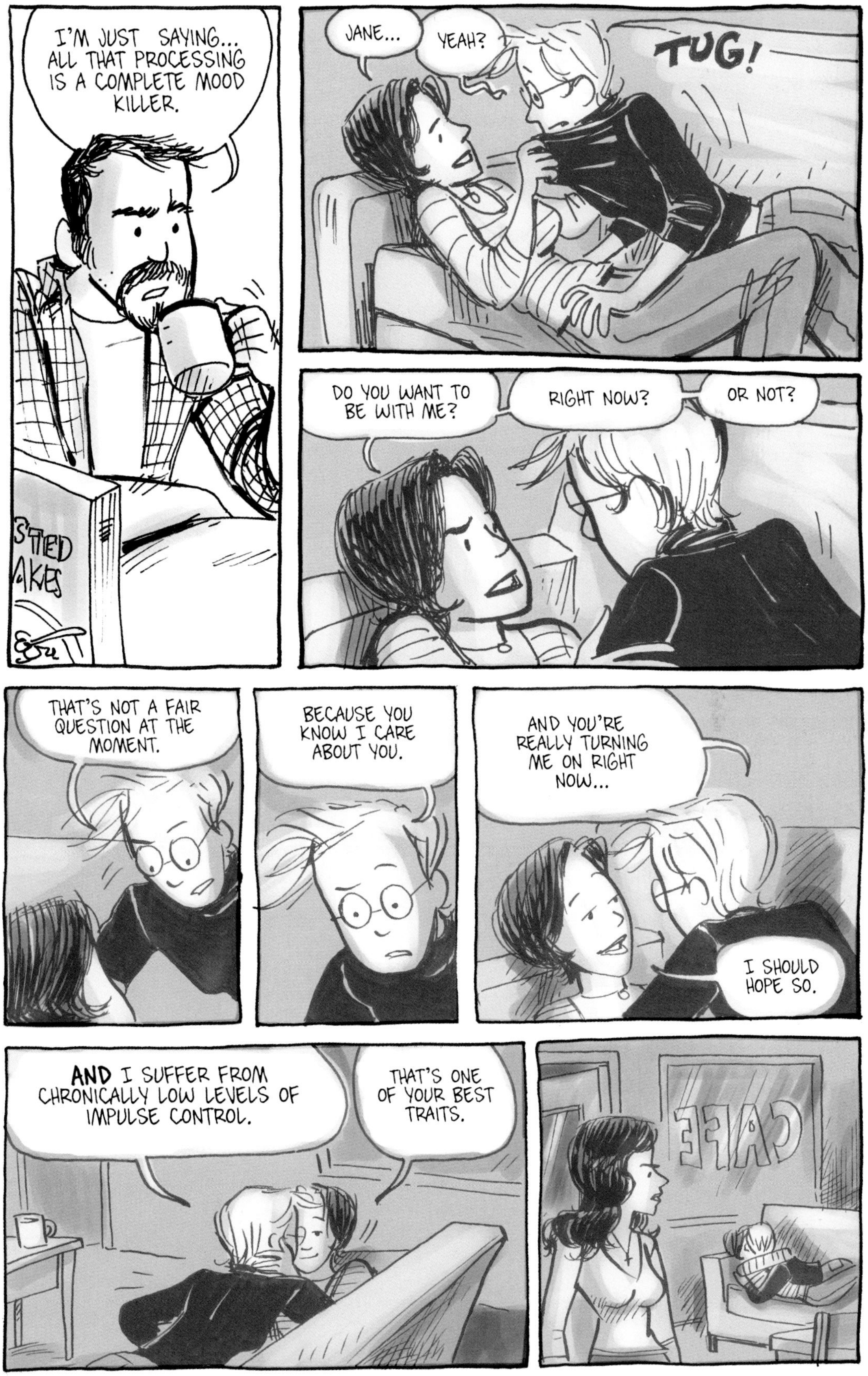
I'M JUST SAYING... ALL THAT PROCESSING IS A COMPLETE MOOD KILLER.
JANE...
YEAH?
TUG!
DO YOU WANT TO BE WITH ME?
RIGHT NOW?
OR NOT?
THAT'S NOT A FAIR QUESTION AT THE MOMENT.
BECAUSE YOU KNOW I CARE ABOUT YOU.
AND YOU'RE REALLY TURNING ME ON RIGHT NOW...
I SHOULD HOPE SO.
AND I SUFFER FROM CHRONICALLY LOW LEVELS OF IMPULSE CONTROL.
THAT'S ONE OF YOUR BEST TRAITS.

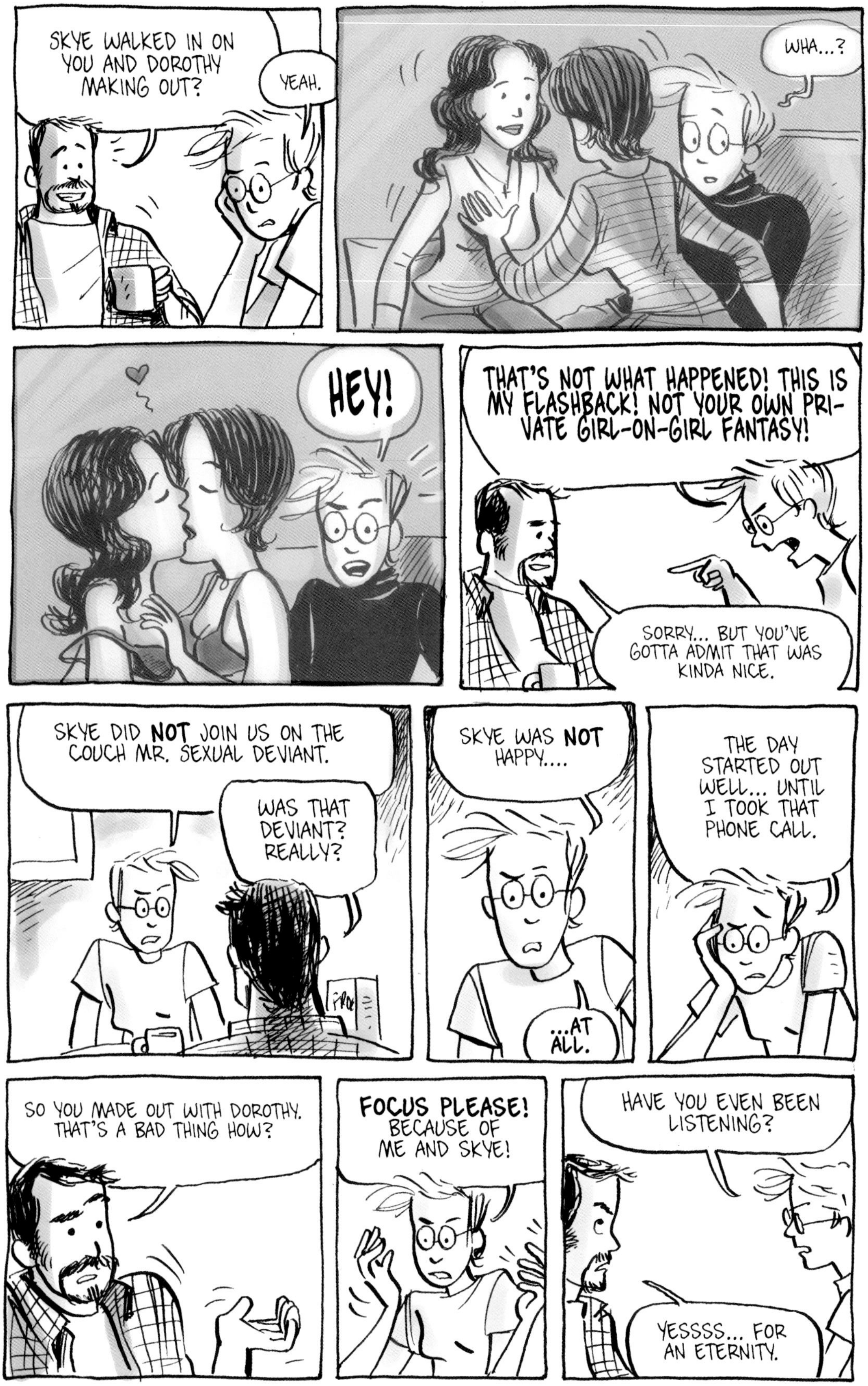
SKYE WALKED IN ON YOU AND DOROTHY MAKING OUT?
YEAH.
WHA...?
HEY!
THAT'S NOT WHAT HAPPENED! THIS IS MY FLASHBACK! NOT YOUR OWN PRIVATE GIRL-ON-GIRL FANTASY!
SORRY... BUT YOU'VE GOTTA ADMIT THAT WAS KINDA NICE.
SKYE DID **NOT** JOIN US ON THE COUCH MR. SEXUAL DEVIANT.
WAS THAT DEVIANT? REALLY?
SKYE WAS **NOT** HAPPY....
...AT ALL.
THE DAY STARTED OUT WELL... UNTIL I TOOK THAT PHONE CALL.
SO YOU MADE OUT WITH DOROTHY. THAT'S A BAD THING HOW?
FOCUS PLEASE! BECAUSE OF ME AND SKYE!
HAVE YOU EVEN BEEN LISTENING?
YESSSS... FOR AN ETERNITY.

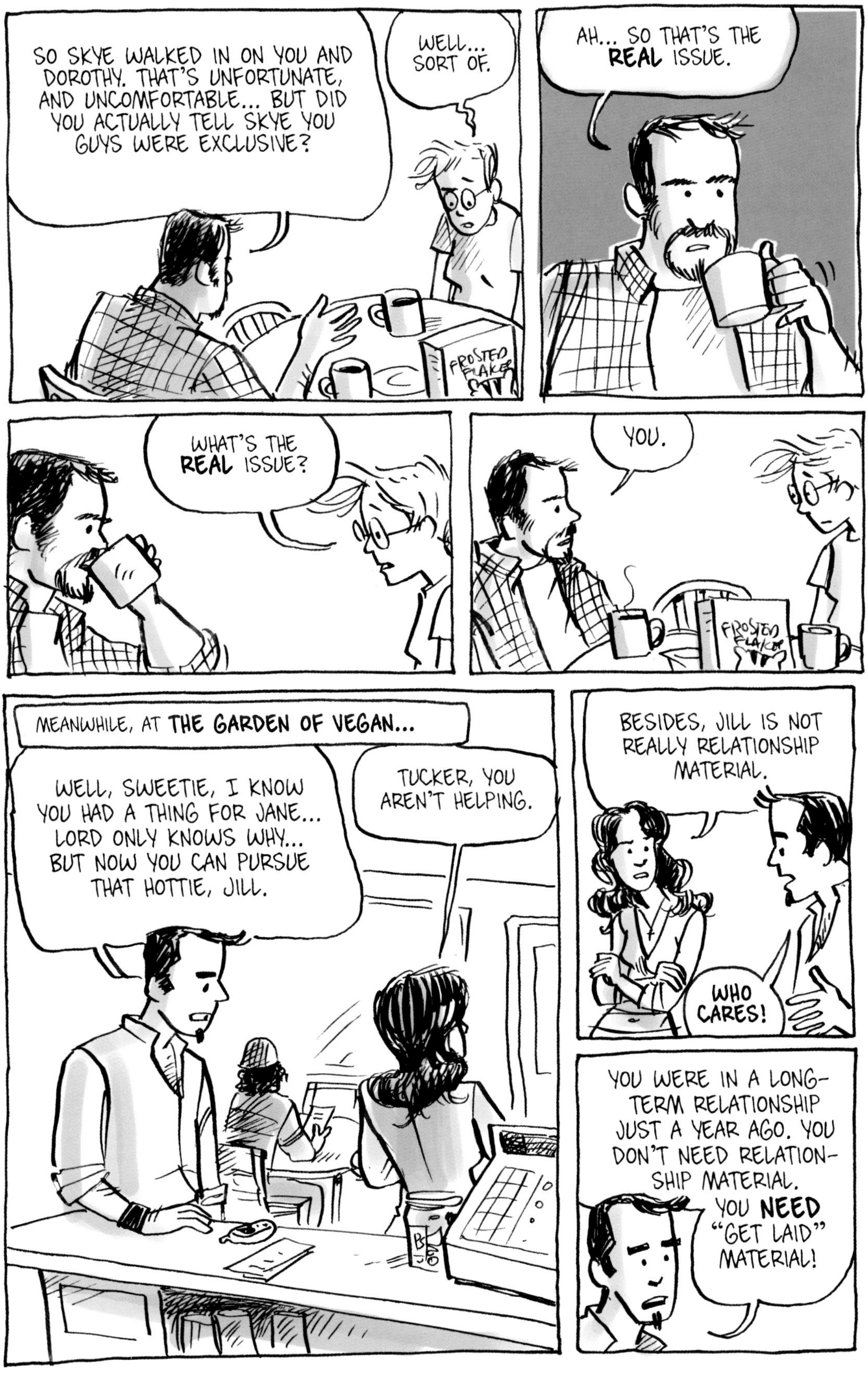
SO SKYE WALKED IN ON YOU AND DOROTHY. THAT'S UNFORTUNATE, AND UNCOMFORTABLE... BUT DID YOU ACTUALLY TELL SKYE YOU GUYS WERE EXCLUSIVE?
WELL... SORT OF.
FROSTED FLAKES
AH... SO THAT'S THE **REAL** ISSUE.
WHAT'S THE **REAL** ISSUE?
YOU.
FROSTED FLAKES
MEANWHILE, AT **THE GARDEN OF VEGAN...**
WELL, SWEETIE, I KNOW YOU HAD A THING FOR JANE... LORD ONLY KNOWS WHY... BUT NOW YOU CAN PURSUE THAT HOTTIE, JILL.
TUCKER, YOU AREN'T HELPING.
BESIDES, JILL IS NOT REALLY RELATIONSHIP MATERIAL.
WHO CARES!
YOU WERE IN A LONG-TERM RELATIONSHIP JUST A YEAR AGO. YOU DON'T NEED RELATIONSHIP MATERIAL.
YOU **NEED** "GET LAID" MATERIAL!

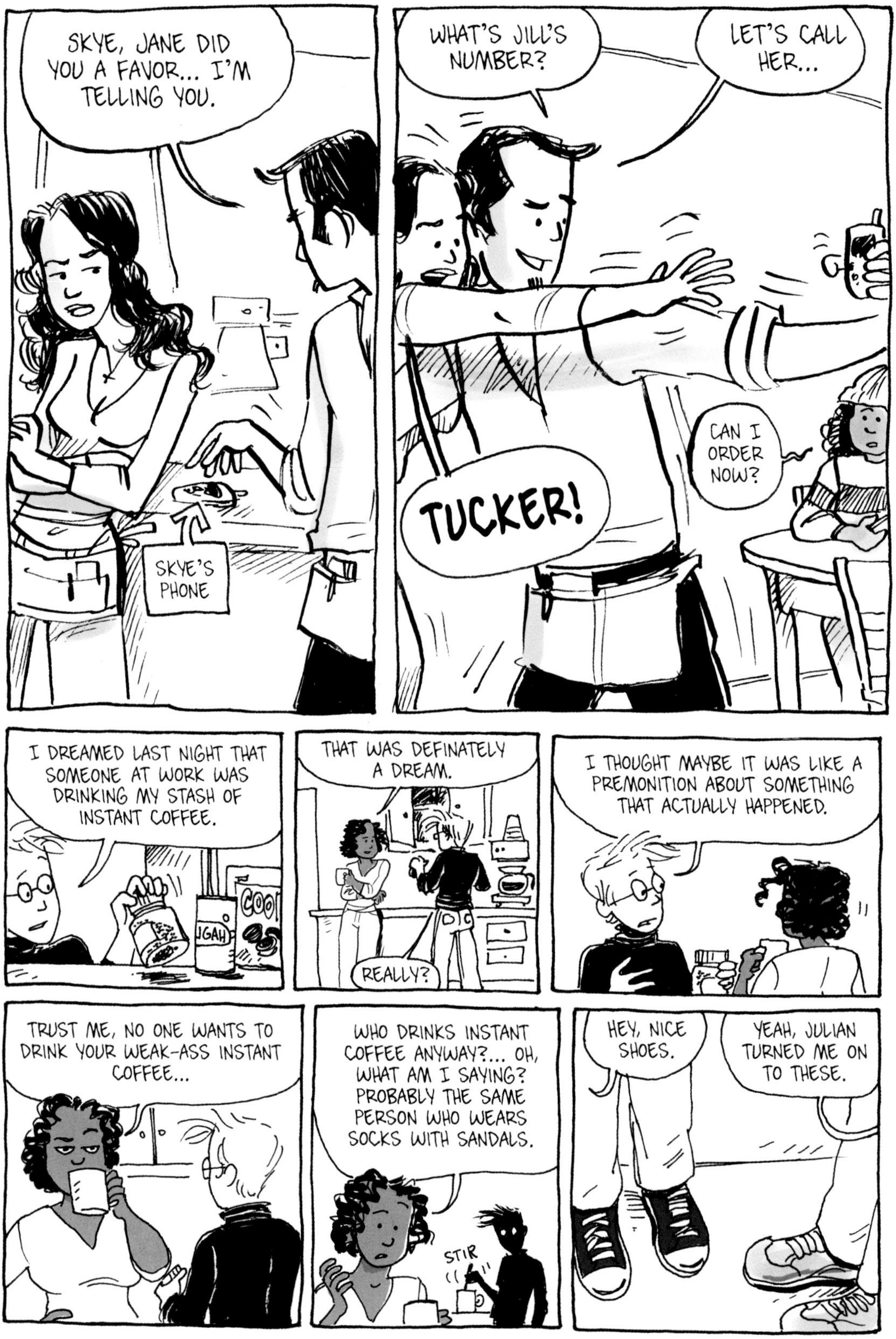

SKYE, JANE DID YOU A FAVOR... I'M TELLING YOU.
SKYE'S PHONE
WHAT'S JILL'S NUMBER?
LET'S CALL HER...
TUCKER!
CAN I ORDER NOW?
I DREAMED LAST NIGHT THAT SOMEONE AT WORK WAS DRINKING MY STASH OF INSTANT COFFEE.
JGAH
COO
THAT WAS DEFINATELY A DREAM.
REALLY?
I THOUGHT MAYBE IT WAS LIKE A PREMONITION ABOUT SOMETHING THAT ACTUALLY HAPPENED.
TRUST ME, NO ONE WANTS TO DRINK YOUR WEAK-ASS INSTANT COFFEE...
WHO DRINKS INSTANT COFFEE ANYWAY?... OH, WHAT AM I SAYING? PROBABLY THE SAME PERSON WHO WEARS SOCKS WITH SANDALS.
STIR
HEY, NICE SHOES.
YEAH, JULIAN TURNED ME ON TO THESE.

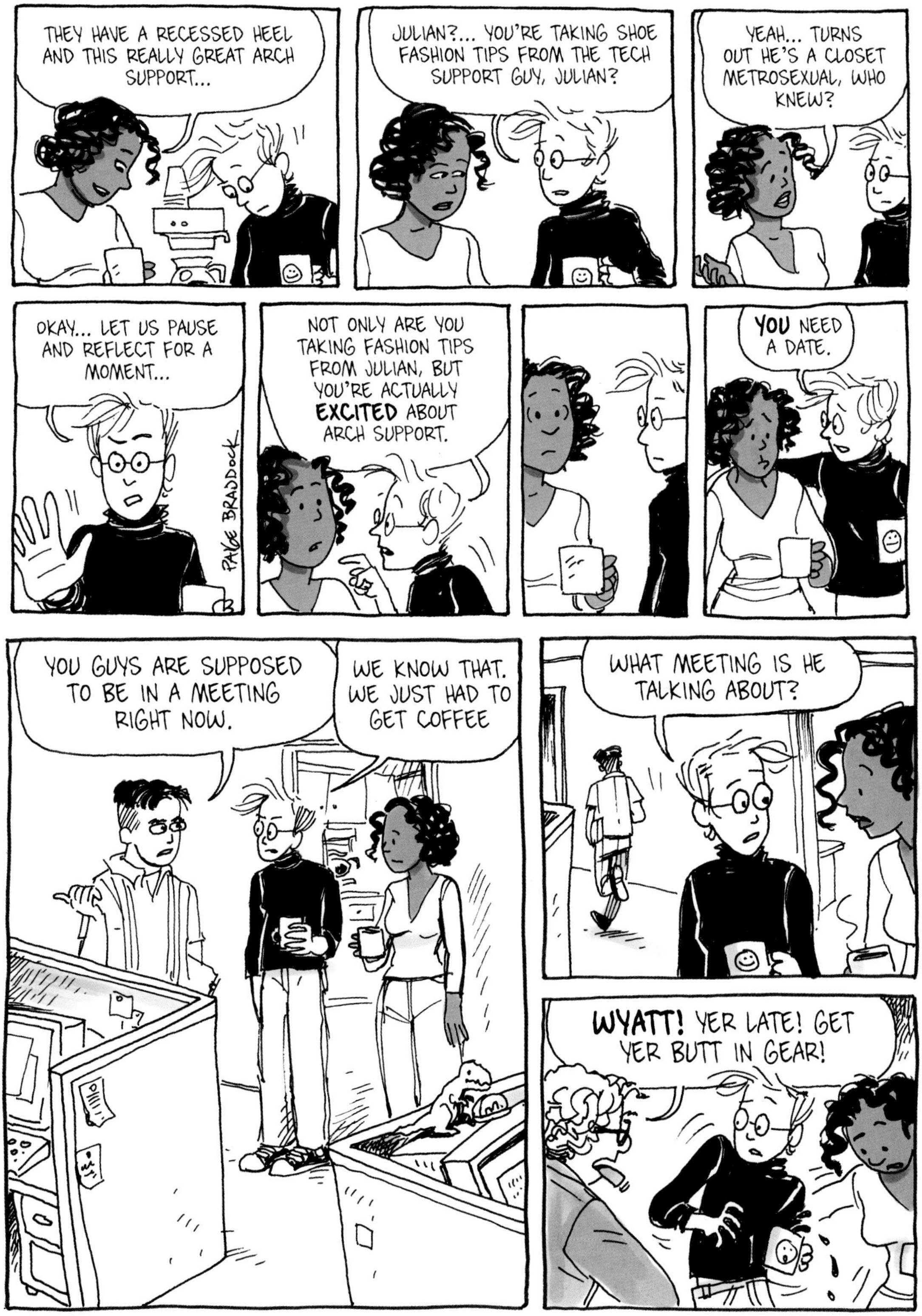
THEY HAVE A RECESSED HEEL AND THIS REALLY GREAT ARCH SUPPORT...
JULIAN?... YOU'RE TAKING SHOE FASHION TIPS FROM THE TECH SUPPORT GUY, JULIAN?
YEAH... TURNS OUT HE'S A CLOSET METROSEXUAL, WHO KNEW?
OKAY... LET US PAUSE AND REFLECT FOR A MOMENT...
PAIGE BRADDOCK
NOT ONLY ARE YOU TAKING FASHION TIPS FROM JULIAN, BUT YOU'RE ACTUALLY **EXCITED** ABOUT ARCH SUPPORT.
YOU NEED A DATE.
YOU GUYS ARE SUPPOSED TO BE IN A MEETING RIGHT NOW.
WE KNOW THAT. WE JUST HAD TO GET COFFEE
WHAT MEETING IS HE TALKING ABOUT?
WYATT! YER LATE! GET YER BUTT IN GEAR!

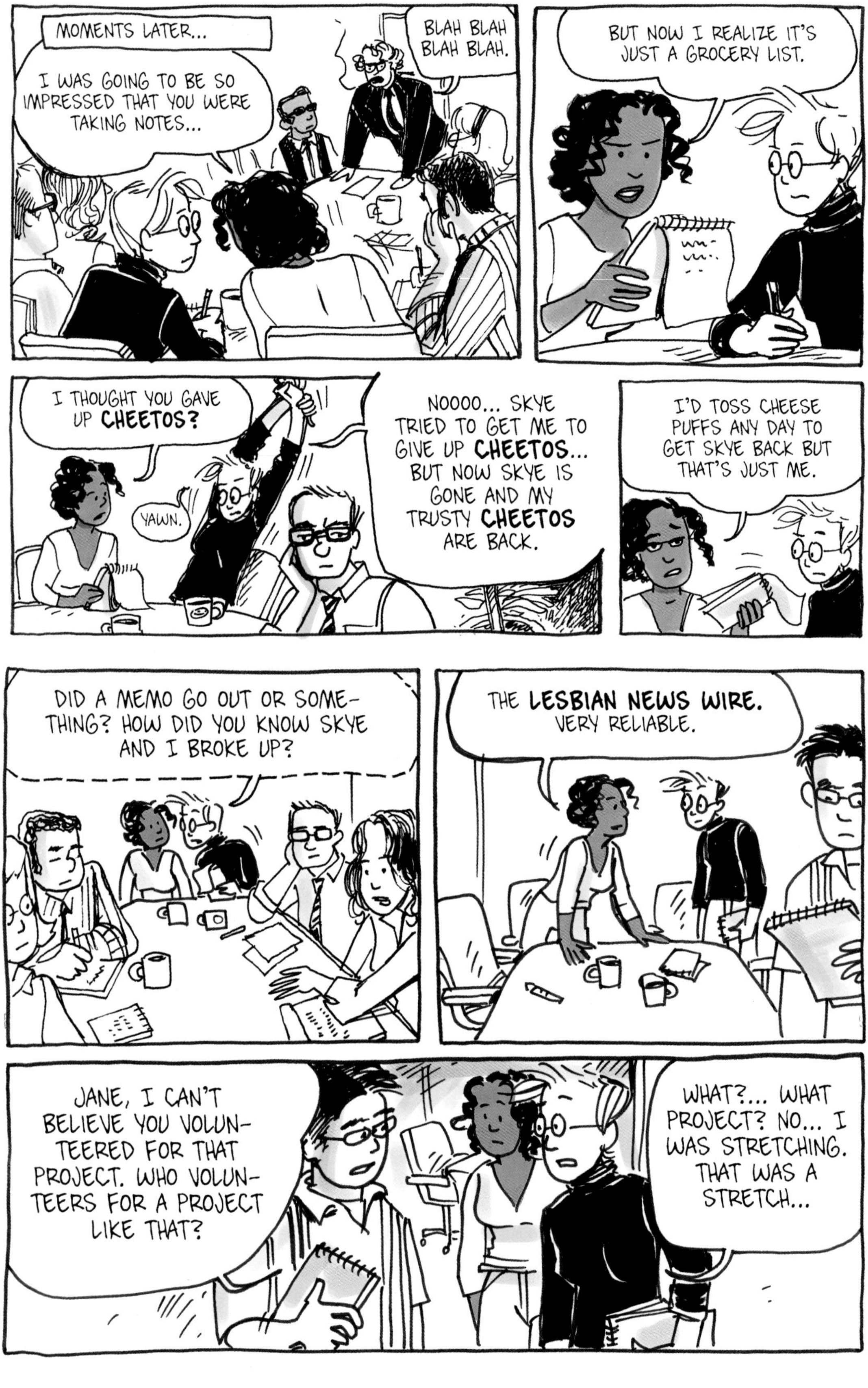
MOMENTS LATER...
I WAS GOING TO BE SO IMPRESSED THAT YOU WERE TAKING NOTES...
BLAH BLAH BLAH BLAH.
BUT NOW I REALIZE IT'S JUST A GROCERY LIST.
I THOUGHT YOU GAVE UP CHEETOS?
YAWN.
NOOOO... SKYE TRIED TO GET ME TO GIVE UP CHEETOS... BUT NOW SKYE IS GONE AND MY TRUSTY CHEETOS ARE BACK.
I'D TOSS CHEESE PUFFS ANY DAY TO GET SKYE BACK BUT THAT'S JUST ME.
DID A MEMO GO OUT OR SOMETHING? HOW DID YOU KNOW SKYE AND I BROKE UP?
THE LESBIAN NEWS WIRE. VERY RELIABLE.
JANE, I CAN'T BELIEVE YOU VOLUNTEERED FOR THAT PROJECT. WHO VOLUNTEERS FOR A PROJECT LIKE THAT?
WHAT?.... WHAT PROJECT? NO... I WAS STRETCHING. THAT WAS A STRETCH...

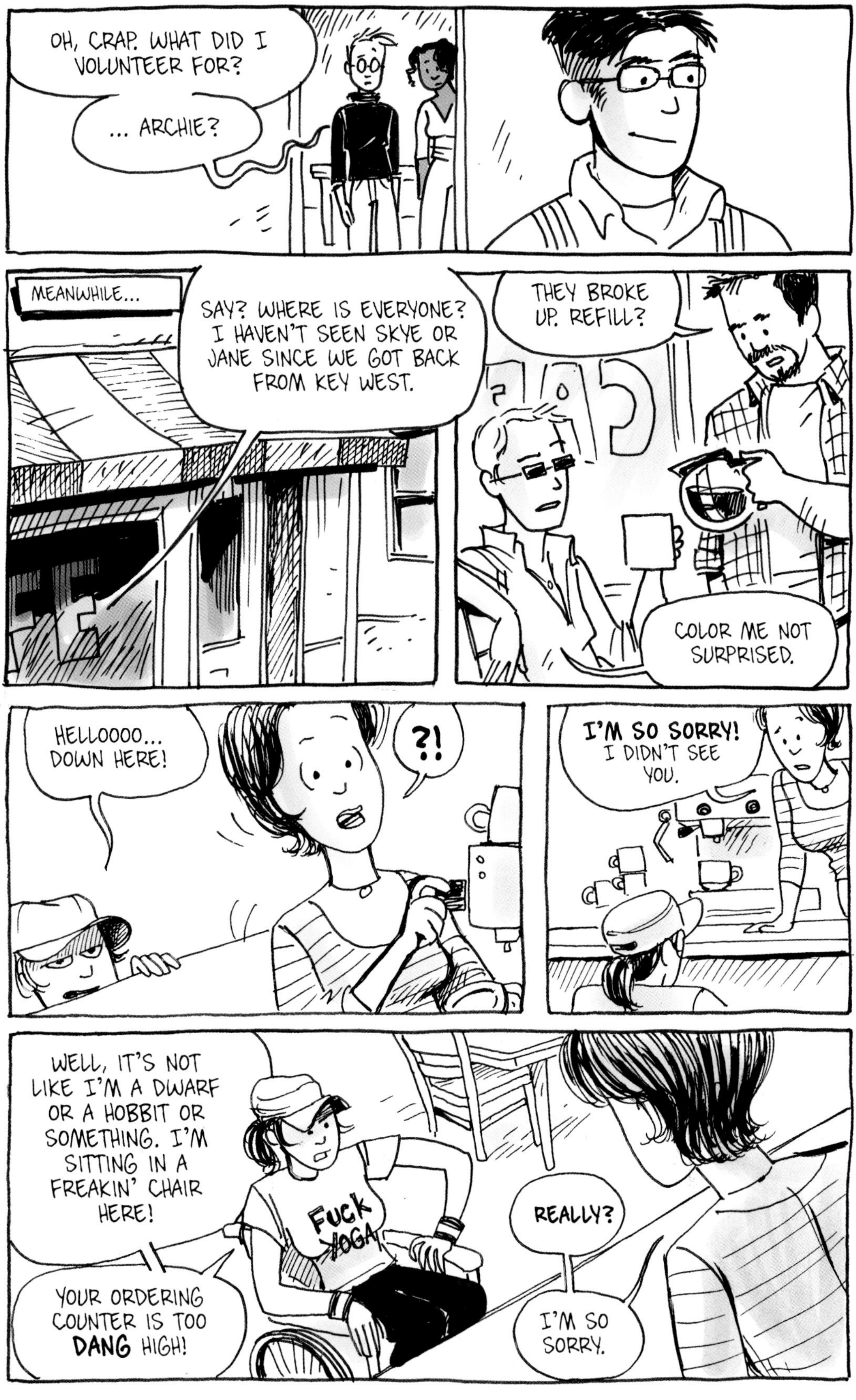
OH, CRAP. WHAT DID I VOLUNTEER FOR?
... ARCHIE?
MEANWHILE...
SAY? WHERE IS EVERYONE? I HAVEN'T SEEN SKYE OR JANE SINCE WE GOT BACK FROM KEY WEST.
THEY BROKE UP. REFILL?
COLOR ME NOT SURPRISED.
HELLOOOO... DOWN HERE!
?!
I'M SO SORRY! I DIDN'T SEE YOU.
WELL, IT'S NOT LIKE I'M A DWARF OR A HOBBIT OR SOMETHING. I'M SITTING IN A FREAKIN' CHAIR HERE!
YOUR ORDERING COUNTER IS TOO DANG HIGH!
FUCK YOGA
REALLY?
I'M SO SORRY.

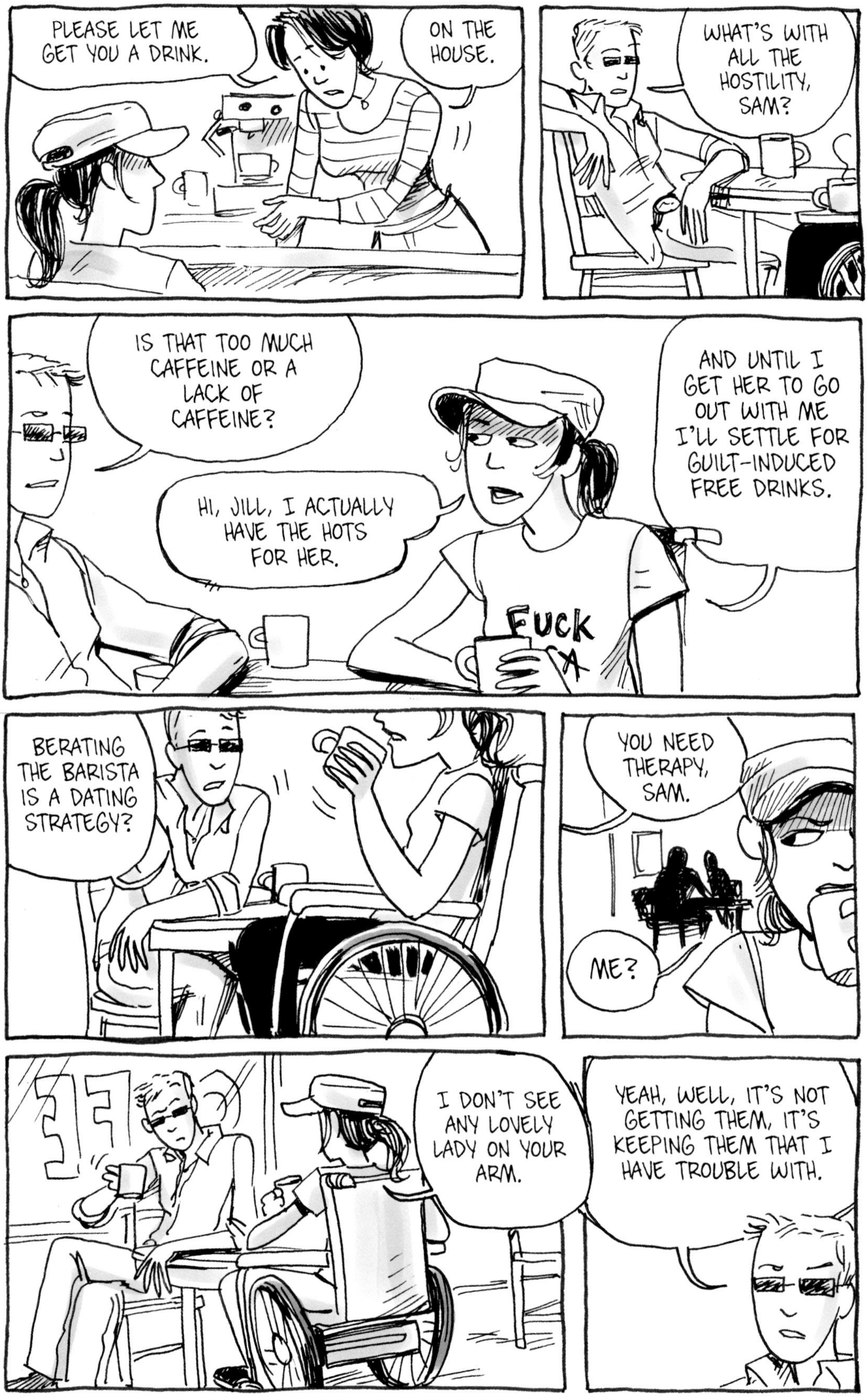
PLEASE LET ME GET YOU A DRINK.
ON THE HOUSE.
WHAT'S WITH ALL THE HOSTILITY, SAM?
IS THAT TOO MUCH CAFFEINE OR A LACK OF CAFFEINE?
HI, JILL, I ACTUALLY HAVE THE HOTS FOR HER.
AND UNTIL I GET HER TO GO OUT WITH ME I'LL SETTLE FOR GUILT-INDUCED FREE DRINKS.
FUCK
BERATING THE BARISTA IS A DATING STRATEGY?
YOU NEED THERAPY, SAM.
ME?
I DON'T SEE ANY LOVELY LADY ON YOUR ARM.
YEAH, WELL, IT'S NOT GETTING THEM, IT'S KEEPING THEM THAT I HAVE TROUBLE WITH.

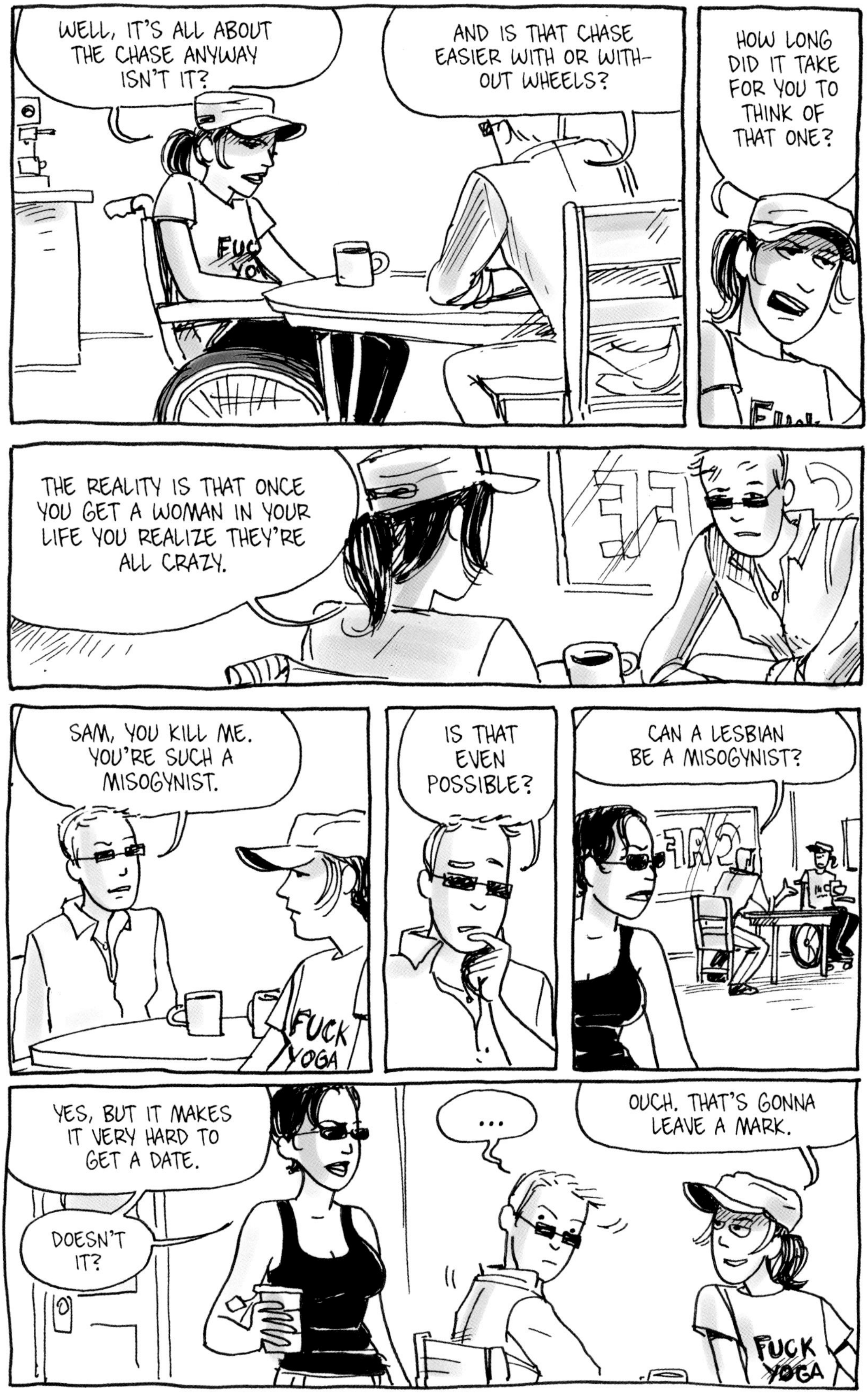
WELL, IT'S ALL ABOUT THE CHASE ANYWAY ISN'T IT?
AND IS THAT CHASE EASIER WITH OR WITH-OUT WHEELS?
HOW LONG DID IT TAKE FOR YOU TO THINK OF THAT ONE?
FUCK YOGA
THE REALITY IS THAT ONCE YOU GET A WOMAN IN YOUR LIFE YOU REALIZE THEY'RE ALL CRAZY.
SAM, YOU KILL ME. YOU'RE SUCH A MISOGYNIST.
FUCK YOGA
IS THAT EVEN POSSIBLE?
CAN A LESBIAN BE A MISOGYNIST?
YES, BUT IT MAKES IT VERY HARD TO GET A DATE.
DOESN'T IT?
...
OUCH. THAT'S GONNA LEAVE A MARK.
FUCK YOGA

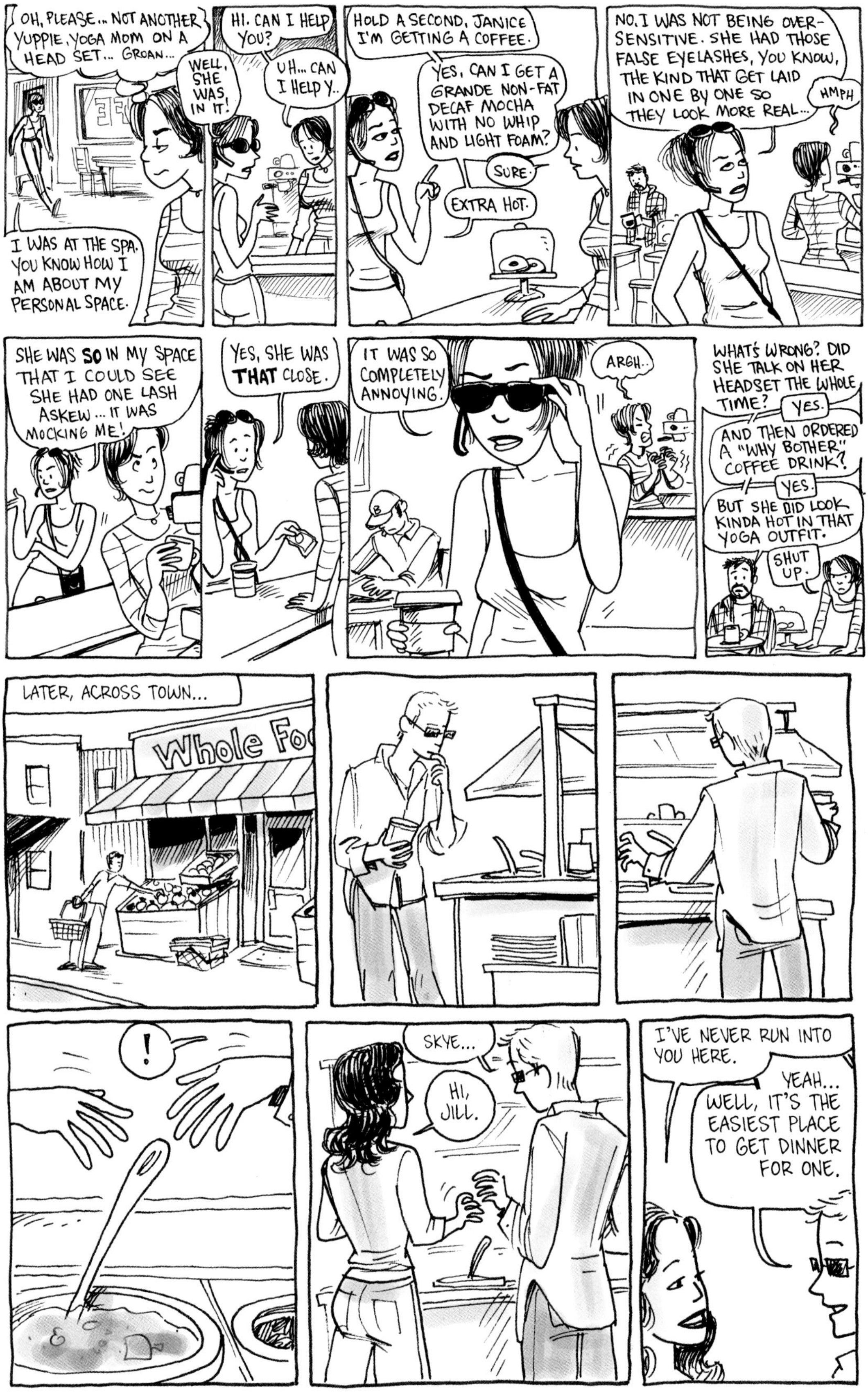
OH, PLEASE... NOT ANOTHER YUPPIE, YOGA MOM ON A HEAD SET... GROAN...
WELL, SHE WAS IN IT!
I WAS AT THE SPA. YOU KNOW HOW I AM ABOUT MY PERSONAL SPACE.
HI. CAN I HELP YOU?
UH... CAN I HELP Y..
HOLD A SECOND, JANICE I'M GETTING A COFFEE.
YES, CAN I GET A GRANDE NON-FAT DECAF MOCHA WITH NO WHIP AND LIGHT FOAM?
SURE.
EXTRA HOT.
NO, I WAS NOT BEING OVER-SENSITIVE. SHE HAD THOSE FALSE EYELASHES, YOU KNOW, THE KIND THAT GET LAID IN ONE BY ONE SO THEY LOOK MORE REAL...
HMPH
SHE WAS SO IN MY SPACE THAT I COULD SEE SHE HAD ONE LASH ASKEW... IT WAS MOCKING ME!
YES, SHE WAS THAT CLOSE.
IT WAS SO COMPLETELY ANNOYING.
ARGH..
WHAT'S WRONG? DID SHE TALK ON HER HEADSET THE WHOLE TIME?
YES.
AND THEN ORDERED A "WHY BOTHER" COFFEE DRINK?
YES.
BUT SHE DID LOOK KINDA HOT IN THAT YOGA OUTFIT.
SHUT UP.
LATER, ACROSS TOWN...
Whole Fo
!
SKYE...
HI, JILL.
I'VE NEVER RUN INTO YOU HERE.
YEAH... WELL, IT'S THE EASIEST PLACE TO GET DINNER FOR ONE.

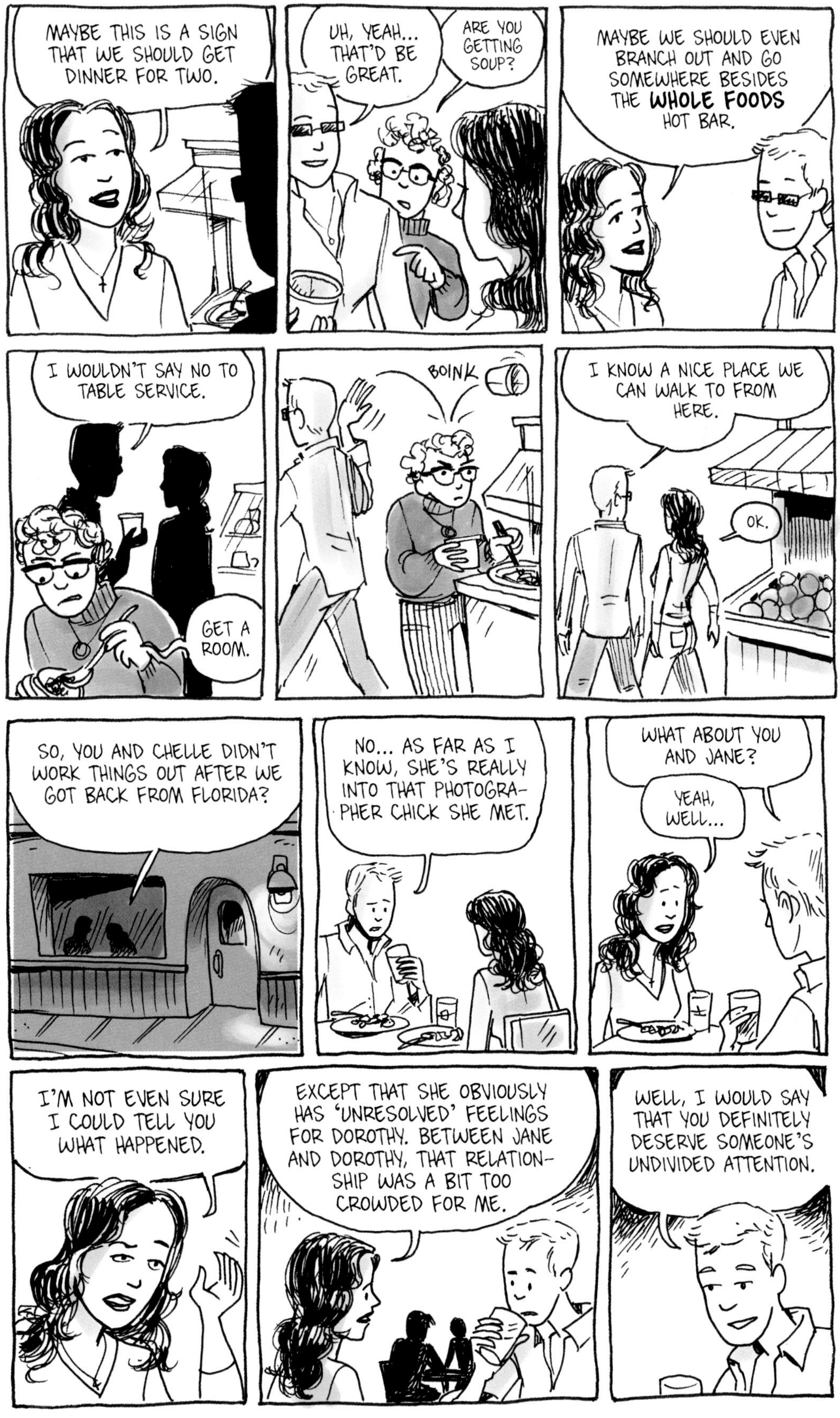
MAYBE THIS IS A SIGN THAT WE SHOULD GET DINNER FOR TWO.
UH, YEAH... THAT'D BE GREAT.
ARE YOU GETTING SOUP?
MAYBE WE SHOULD EVEN BRANCH OUT AND GO SOMEWHERE BESIDES THE **WHOLE FOODS** HOT BAR.
I WOULDN'T SAY NO TO TABLE SERVICE.
GET A ROOM.
BOINK
I KNOW A NICE PLACE WE CAN WALK TO FROM HERE.
OK.
SO, YOU AND CHELLE DIDN'T WORK THINGS OUT AFTER WE GOT BACK FROM FLORIDA?
NO... AS FAR AS I KNOW, SHE'S REALLY INTO THAT PHOTOGRA-PHER CHICK SHE MET.
WHAT ABOUT YOU AND JANE?
YEAH, WELL...
I'M NOT EVEN SURE I COULD TELL YOU WHAT HAPPENED.
EXCEPT THAT SHE OBVIOUSLY HAS 'UNRESOLVED' FEELINGS FOR DOROTHY. BETWEEN JANE AND DOROTHY, THAT RELATION-SHIP WAS A BIT TOO CROWDED FOR ME.
WELL, I WOULD SAY THAT YOU DEFINITELY DESERVE SOMEONE'S UNDIVIDED ATTENTION.

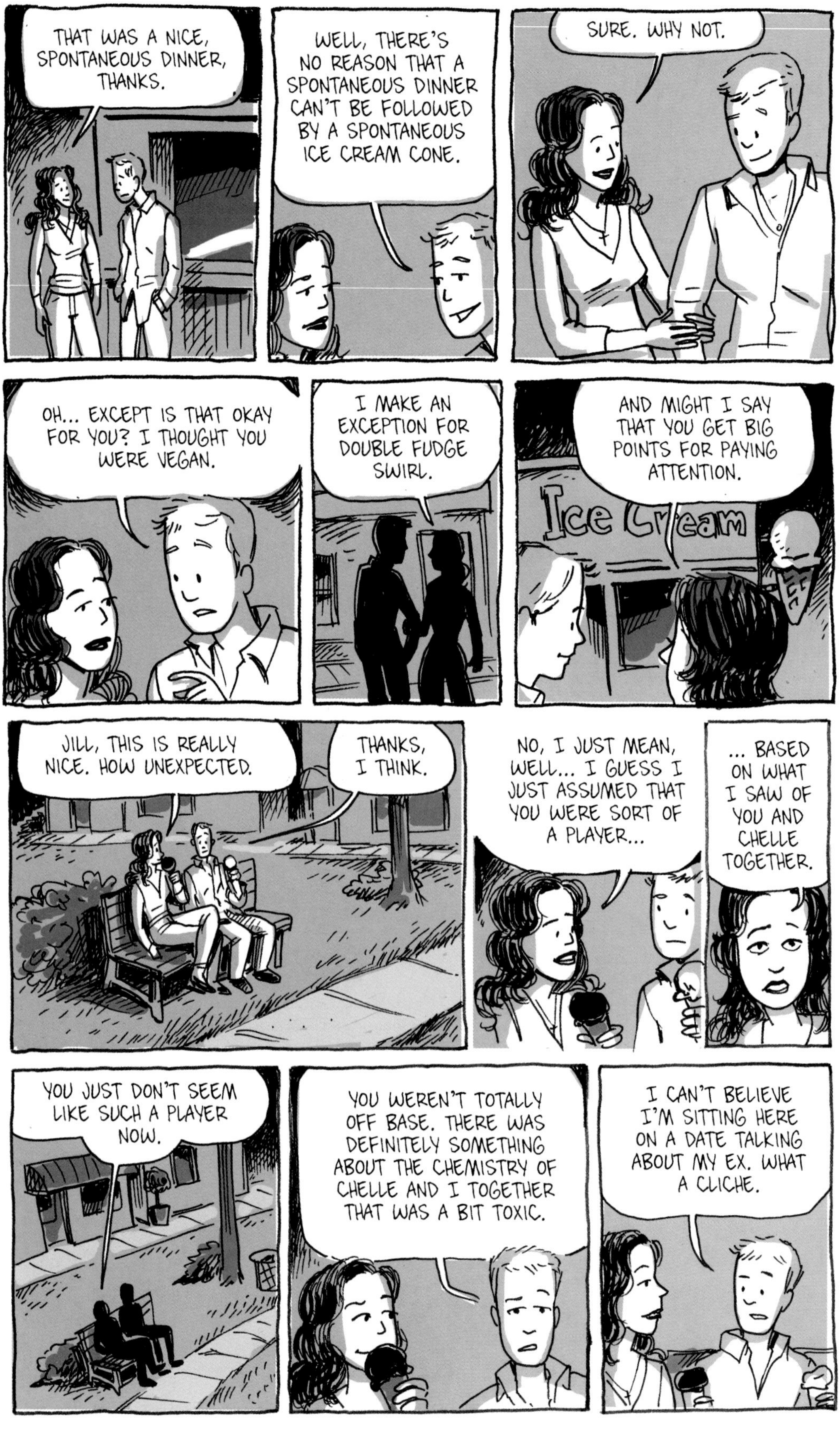
THAT WAS A NICE, SPONTANEOUS DINNER, THANKS.
WELL, THERE'S NO REASON THAT A SPONTANEOUS DINNER CAN'T BE FOLLOWED BY A SPONTANEOUS ICE CREAM CONE.
SURE. WHY NOT.
OH... EXCEPT IS THAT OKAY FOR YOU? I THOUGHT YOU WERE VEGAN.
I MAKE AN EXCEPTION FOR DOUBLE FUDGE SWIRL.
AND MIGHT I SAY THAT YOU GET BIG POINTS FOR PAYING ATTENTION.
Ice Cream
JILL, THIS IS REALLY NICE. HOW UNEXPECTED.
THANKS, I THINK.
NO, I JUST MEAN, WELL... I GUESS I JUST ASSUMED THAT YOU WERE SORT OF A PLAYER...
... BASED ON WHAT I SAW OF YOU AND CHELLE TOGETHER.
YOU JUST DON'T SEEM LIKE SUCH A PLAYER NOW.
YOU WEREN'T TOTALLY OFF BASE. THERE WAS DEFINITELY SOMETHING ABOUT THE CHEMISTRY OF CHELLE AND I TOGETHER THAT WAS A BIT TOXIC.
I CAN'T BELIEVE I'M SITTING HERE ON A DATE TALKING ABOUT MY EX. WHAT A CLICHE.

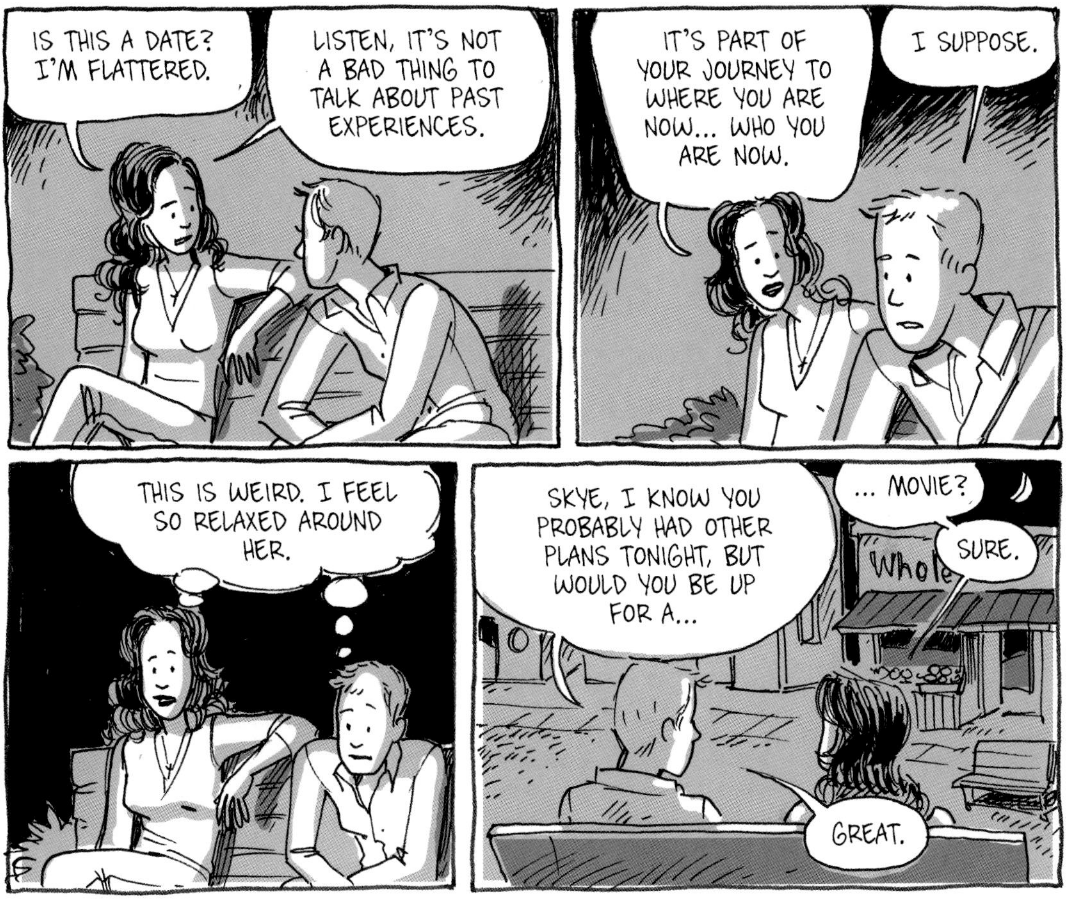
IS THIS A DATE? I'M FLATTERED.
LISTEN, IT'S NOT A BAD THING TO TALK ABOUT PAST EXPERIENCES.
IT'S PART OF YOUR JOURNEY TO WHERE YOU ARE NOW... WHO YOU ARE NOW.
I SUPPOSE.
THIS IS WEIRD. I FEEL SO RELAXED AROUND HER.
SKYE, I KNOW YOU PROBABLY HAD OTHER PLANS TONIGHT, BUT WOULD YOU BE UP FOR A...
... MOVIE?
SURE.
Whole
GREAT.

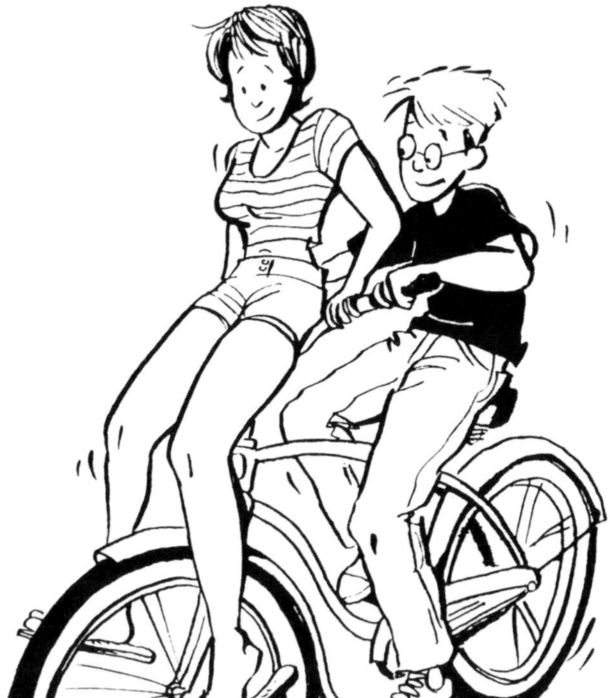

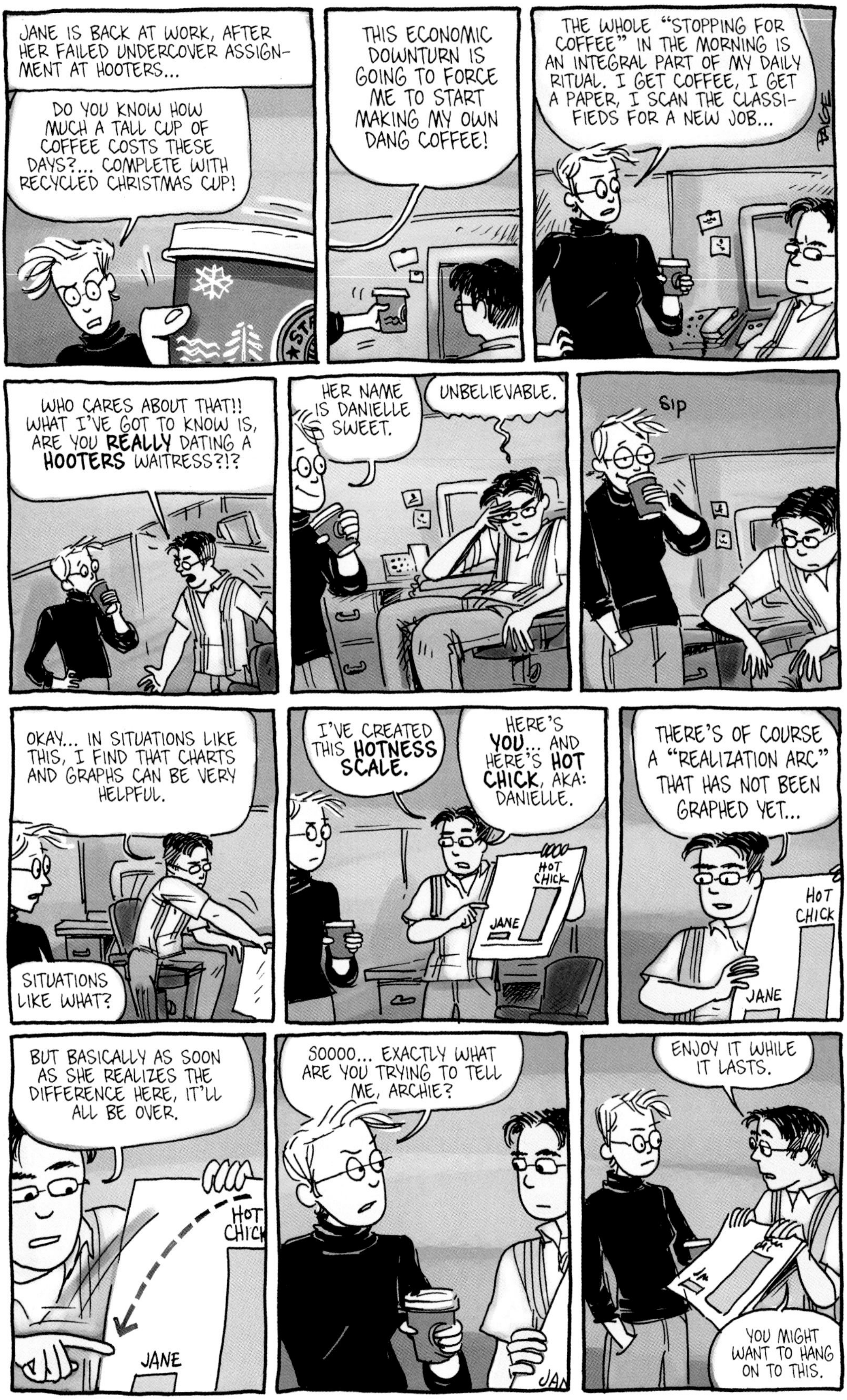
JANE IS BACK AT WORK, AFTER HER FAILED UNDERCOVER ASSIGNMENT AT HOOTERS...
DO YOU KNOW HOW MUCH A TALL CUP OF COFFEE COSTS THESE DAYS?... COMPLETE WITH RECYCLED CHRISTMAS CUP!
THIS ECONOMIC DOWNTURN IS GOING TO FORCE ME TO START MAKING MY OWN DANG COFFEE!
THE WHOLE "STOPPING FOR COFFEE" IN THE MORNING IS AN INTEGRAL PART OF MY DAILY RITUAL. I GET COFFEE, I GET A PAPER, I SCAN THE CLASSIFIEDS FOR A NEW JOB...
WHO CARES ABOUT THAT!! WHAT I'VE GOT TO KNOW IS, ARE YOU **REALLY** DATING A **HOOTERS** WAITRESS?!?
HER NAME IS DANIELLE SWEET.
UNBELIEVABLE.
SIP
OKAY... IN SITUATIONS LIKE THIS, I FIND THAT CHARTS AND GRAPHS CAN BE VERY HELPFUL.
SITUATIONS LIKE WHAT?
I'VE CREATED THIS **HOTNESS SCALE.**
HERE'S **YOU**... AND HERE'S **HOT CHICK**, AKA: DANIELLE.
HOT CHICK
JANE
THERE'S OF COURSE A "REALIZATION ARC" THAT HAS NOT BEEN GRAPHED YET...
HOT CHICK
JANE
BUT BASICALLY AS SOON AS SHE REALIZES THE DIFFERENCE HERE, IT'LL ALL BE OVER.
JANE
SOOOO... EXACTLY WHAT ARE YOU TRYING TO TELL ME, ARCHIE?
ENJOY IT WHILE IT LASTS.
YOU MIGHT WANT TO HANG ON TO THIS.

TWO WEEKS LATER, JANE FINALLY GETS ENOUGH NERVE TO GO SEE DOROTHY

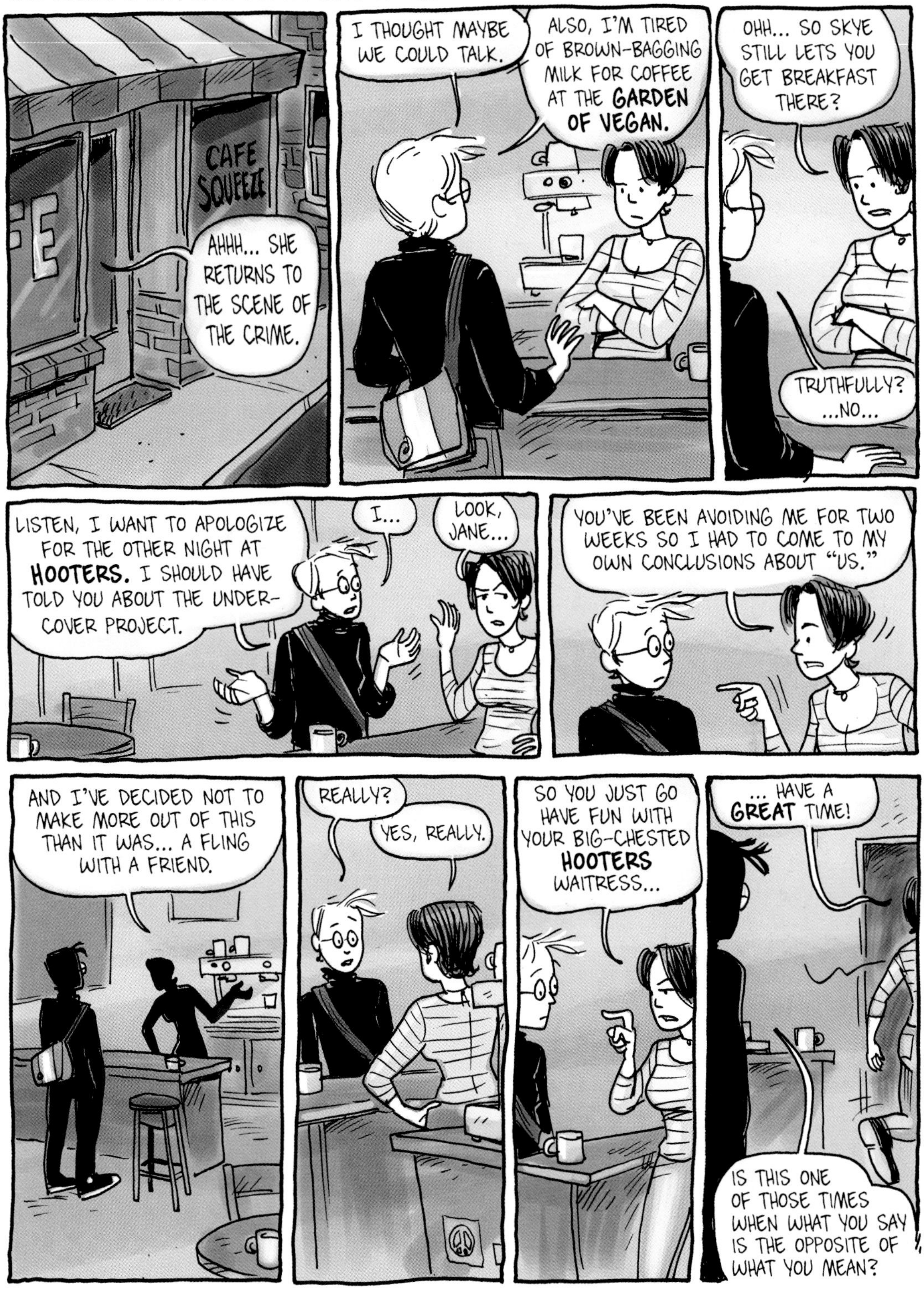
CAFE SQUEEZE
AHHH... SHE RETURNS TO THE SCENE OF THE CRIME.
I THOUGHT MAYBE WE COULD TALK.
ALSO, I'M TIRED OF BROWN-BAGGING MILK FOR COFFEE AT THE **GARDEN OF VEGAN.**
OHH... SO SKYE STILL LETS YOU GET BREAKFAST THERE?
TRUTHFULLY? ...NO...
LISTEN, I WANT TO APOLOGIZE FOR THE OTHER NIGHT AT **HOOTERS.** I SHOULD HAVE TOLD YOU ABOUT THE UNDER-COVER PROJECT.
I...
LOOK, JANE...
YOU'VE BEEN AVOIDING ME FOR TWO WEEKS SO I HAD TO COME TO MY OWN CONCLUSIONS ABOUT "US."
AND I'VE DECIDED NOT TO MAKE MORE OUT OF THIS THAN IT WAS... A FLING WITH A FRIEND.
REALLY?
YES, REALLY.
SO YOU JUST GO HAVE FUN WITH YOUR BIG-CHESTED **HOOTERS** WAITRESS...
... HAVE A **GREAT** TIME!
IS THIS ONE OF THOSE TIMES WHEN WHAT YOU SAY IS THE OPPOSITE OF WHAT YOU MEAN?

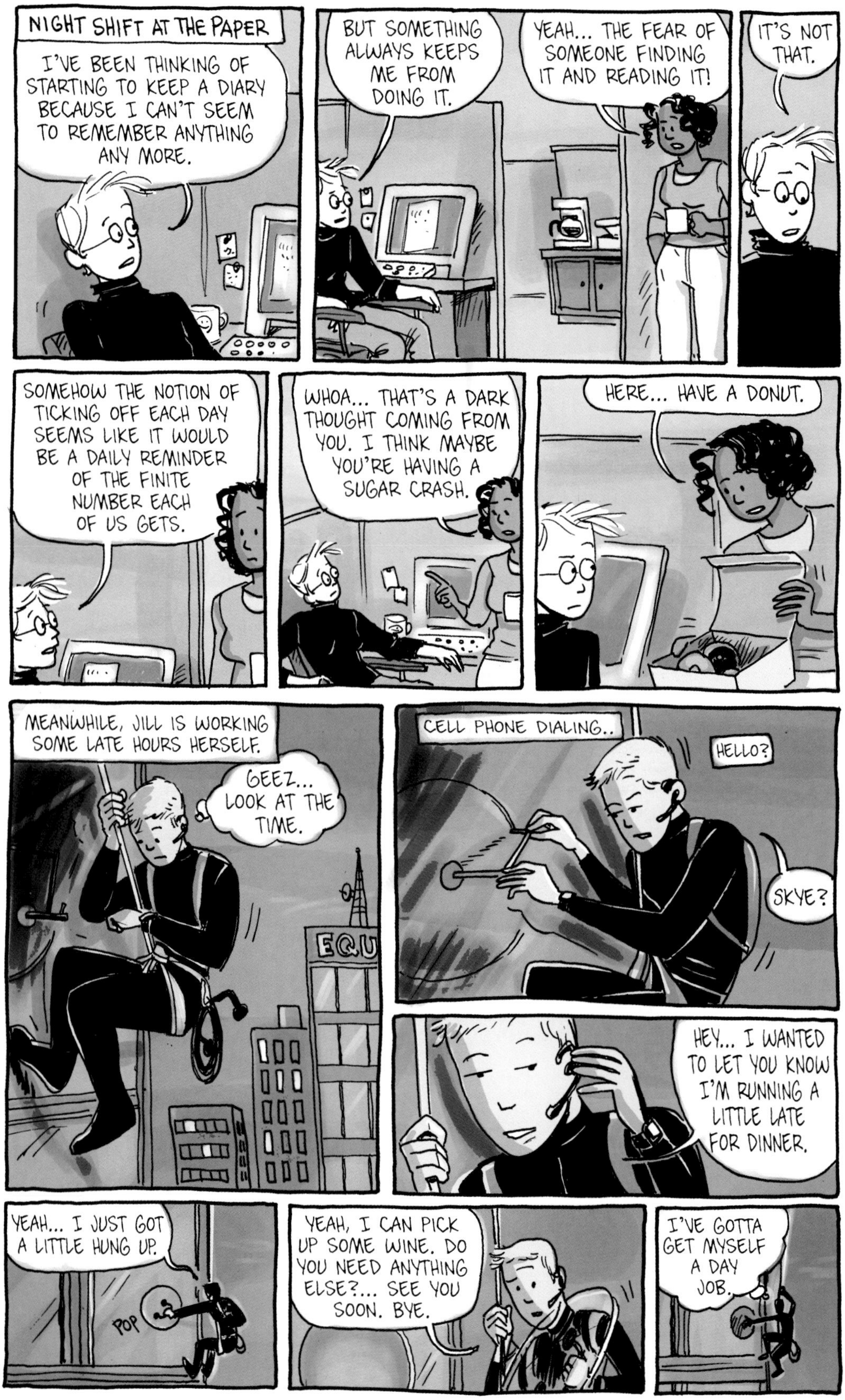
NIGHT SHIFT AT THE PAPER
I'VE BEEN THINKING OF STARTING TO KEEP A DIARY BECAUSE I CAN'T SEEM TO REMEMBER ANYTHING ANY MORE.
BUT SOMETHING ALWAYS KEEPS ME FROM DOING IT.
YEAH... THE FEAR OF SOMEONE FINDING IT AND READING IT!
IT'S NOT THAT.
SOMEHOW THE NOTION OF TICKING OFF EACH DAY SEEMS LIKE IT WOULD BE A DAILY REMINDER OF THE FINITE NUMBER EACH OF US GETS.
WHOA... THAT'S A DARK THOUGHT COMING FROM YOU. I THINK MAYBE YOU'RE HAVING A SUGAR CRASH.
HERE... HAVE A DONUT.
MEANWHILE, JILL IS WORKING SOME LATE HOURS HERSELF.
GEEZ... LOOK AT THE TIME.
EQU
CELL PHONE DIALING..
HELLO?
SKYE?
HEY... I WANTED TO LET YOU KNOW I'M RUNNING A LITTLE LATE FOR DINNER.
YEAH... I JUST GOT A LITTLE HUNG UP.
POP
YEAH, I CAN PICK UP SOME WINE. DO YOU NEED ANYTHING ELSE?... SEE YOU SOON. BYE.
I'VE GOTTA GET MYSELF A DAY JOB.

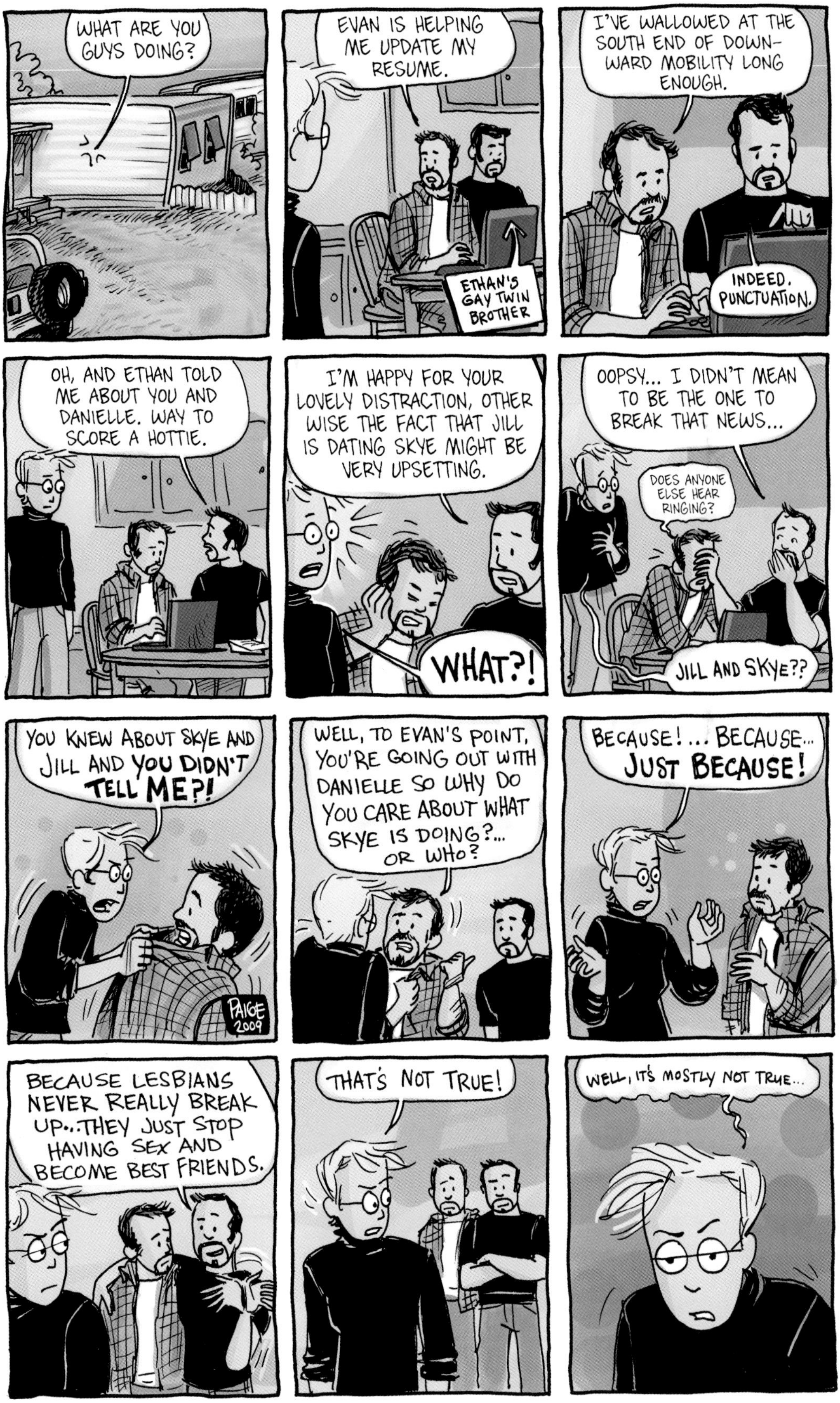
WHAT ARE YOU GUYS DOING?
EVAN IS HELPING ME UPDATE MY RESUME.
ETHAN'S GAY TWIN BROTHER
I'VE WALLOWED AT THE SOUTH END OF DOWNWARD MOBILITY LONG ENOUGH.
INDEED. PUNCTUATION.
OH, AND ETHAN TOLD ME ABOUT YOU AND DANIELLE. WAY TO SCORE A HOTTIE.
I'M HAPPY FOR YOUR LOVELY DISTRACTION, OTHER WISE THE FACT THAT JILL IS DATING SKYE MIGHT BE VERY UPSETTING.
WHAT?!
OOPSY... I DIDN'T MEAN TO BE THE ONE TO BREAK THAT NEWS...
DOES ANYONE ELSE HEAR RINGING?
JILL AND SKYE??
YOU KNEW ABOUT SKYE AND JILL AND YOU DIDN'T TELL ME?!
PAIGE 2009
WELL, TO EVAN'S POINT, YOU'RE GOING OUT WITH DANIELLE SO WHY DO YOU CARE ABOUT WHAT SKYE IS DOING?... OR WHO?
BECAUSE! ... BECAUSE... JUST BECAUSE!
BECAUSE LESBIANS NEVER REALLY BREAK UP..THEY JUST STOP HAVING SEX AND BECOME BEST FRIENDS.
THAT'S NOT TRUE!
WELL, IT'S MOSTLY NOT TRUE...

DORRIE, I THINK I NEED A SERIOUS WARDROBE UPGRADE...

I'M GOING TO MEET DANIELLE FOR A MOVIE AND I LOOK LIKE...

WELL, I LOOK LIKE ME.

YOU'LL BE IN THE THEATER. LOW LIGHTING WILL WORK IN YOUR FAVOR.

DORRIE, I'M SERIOUS!

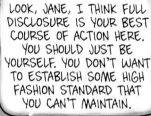

LOOK, JANE, I THINK FULL DISCLOSURE IS YOUR BEST COURSE OF ACTION HERE. YOU SHOULD JUST BE YOURSELF. YOU DON'T WANT TO ESTABLISH SOME HIGH FASHION STANDARD THAT YOU CAN'T MAINTAIN.

I WORE SOCKS WITH SANDALS **ONCE** AND NOW YOU'LL NEVER LET ME LIVE IT DOWN!

OH MY GOSH! IS THAT GUY WEARING A **HUGE** FANNY PACK??

DOUBLE FEATURE

UH...YEAH...I THINK HE IS.

HOW CAN ANYONE STILL WEAR ONE?!

I MEAN, THE JIG IS UP! WE KNOW THIS AS WELL AS WE KNOW THAT THE SUN RISES AND SETS.

FANNY PACKS AND MULLETS ARE **OVER**.

ARE YOU SURE? THERE MIGHT BE AN OCASSION WHEN A MULLET WORKS.

TICKETS

NOPE.

TWO PLEASE.

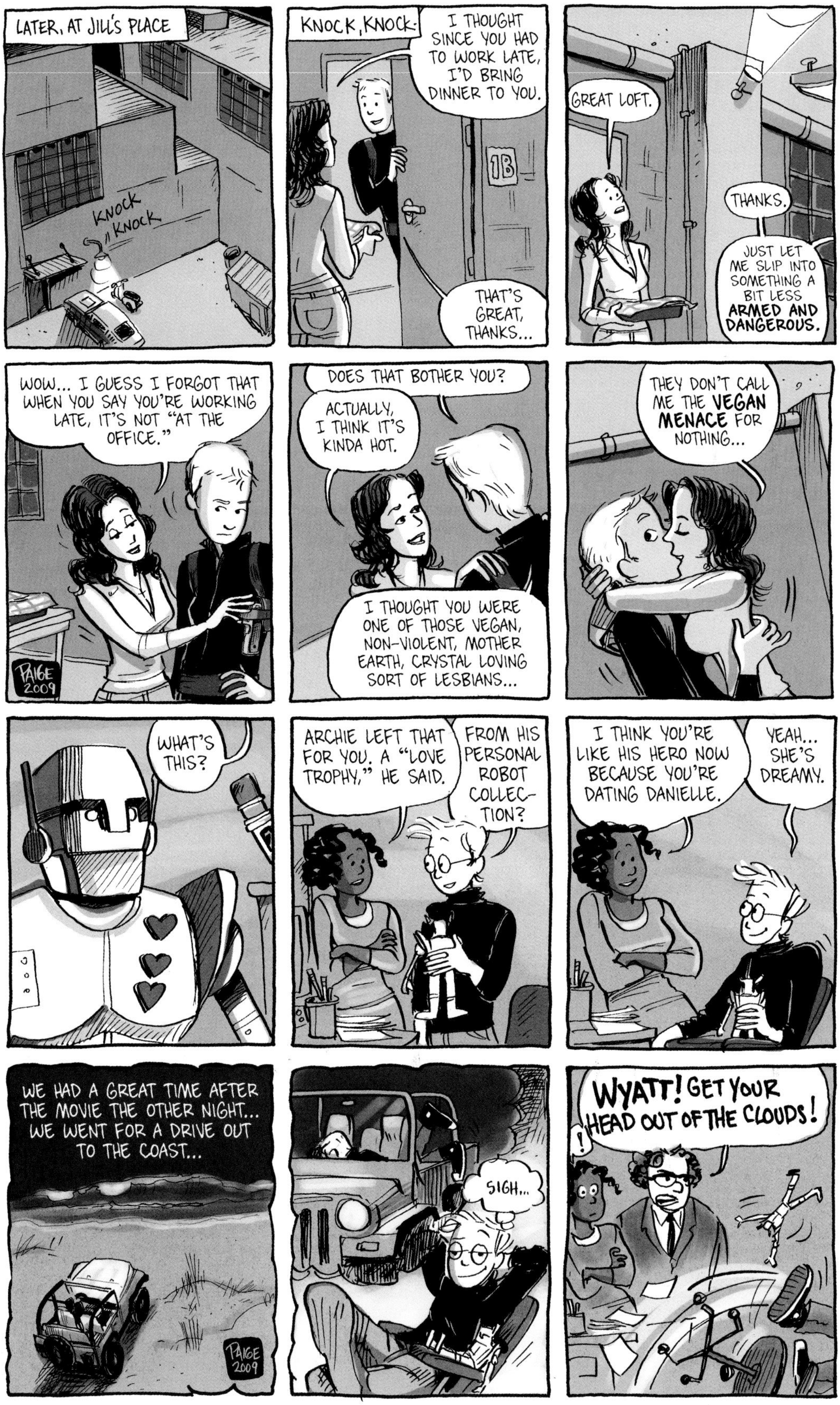

LATER, AT JILL'S PLACE
KNOCK KNOCK
KNOCK, KNOCK
I THOUGHT SINCE YOU HAD TO WORK LATE, I'D BRING DINNER TO YOU.
1B
THAT'S GREAT, THANKS...
GREAT LOFT.
THANKS.
JUST LET ME SLIP INTO SOMETHING A BIT LESS **ARMED AND DANGEROUS.**
WOW... I GUESS I FORGOT THAT WHEN YOU SAY YOU'RE WORKING LATE, IT'S NOT "AT THE OFFICE."
PAIGE 2009
DOES THAT BOTHER YOU?
ACTUALLY, I THINK IT'S KINDA HOT.
I THOUGHT YOU WERE ONE OF THOSE VEGAN, NON-VIOLENT, MOTHER EARTH, CRYSTAL LOVING SORT OF LESBIANS...
THEY DON'T CALL ME THE **VEGAN MENACE** FOR NOTHING...
WHAT'S THIS?
ARCHIE LEFT THAT FOR YOU. A "LOVE TROPHY," HE SAID.
FROM HIS PERSONAL ROBOT COLLECTION?
I THINK YOU'RE LIKE HIS HERO NOW BECAUSE YOU'RE DATING DANIELLE.
YEAH... SHE'S DREAMY.
WE HAD A GREAT TIME AFTER THE MOVIE THE OTHER NIGHT... WE WENT FOR A DRIVE OUT TO THE COAST...
PAIGE 2009
SIGH...
WYATT! GET YOUR HEAD OUT OF THE CLOUDS!
!

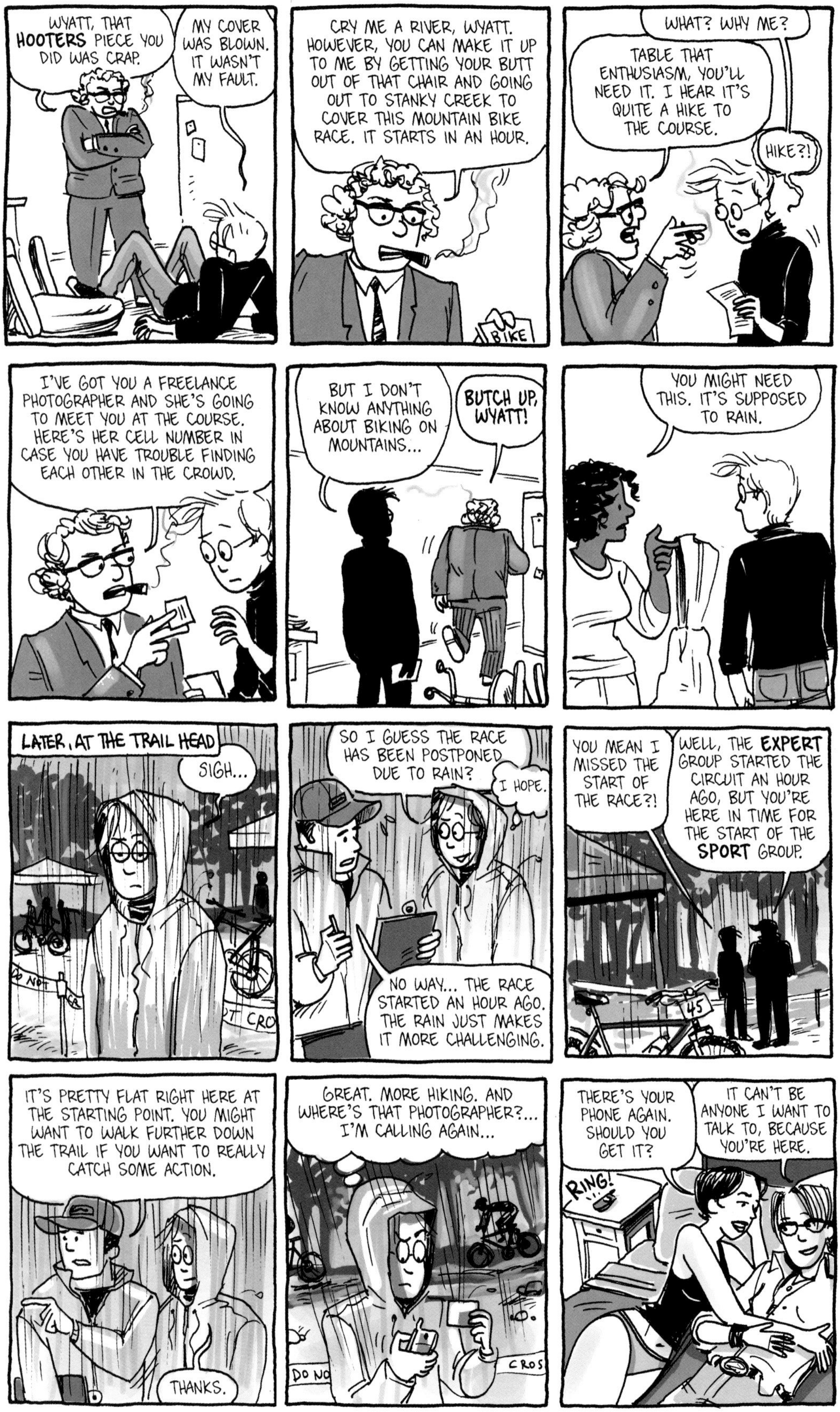
WYATT, THAT **HOOTERS** PIECE YOU DID WAS CRAP.
MY COVER WAS BLOWN. IT WASN'T MY FAULT.
CRY ME A RIVER, WYATT. HOWEVER, YOU CAN MAKE IT UP TO ME BY GETTING YOUR BUTT OUT OF THAT CHAIR AND GOING OUT TO STANKY CREEK TO COVER THIS MOUNTAIN BIKE RACE. IT STARTS IN AN HOUR.
BIKE
WHAT? WHY ME?
TABLE THAT ENTHUSIASM, YOU'LL NEED IT. I HEAR IT'S QUITE A HIKE TO THE COURSE.
HIKE?!
I'VE GOT YOU A FREELANCE PHOTOGRAPHER AND SHE'S GOING TO MEET YOU AT THE COURSE. HERE'S HER CELL NUMBER IN CASE YOU HAVE TROUBLE FINDING EACH OTHER IN THE CROWD.
BUT I DON'T KNOW ANYTHING ABOUT BIKING ON MOUNTAINS...
BUTCH UP, WYATT!
YOU MIGHT NEED THIS. IT'S SUPPOSED TO RAIN.
LATER, AT THE TRAIL HEAD
SIGH...
SO I GUESS THE RACE HAS BEEN POSTPONED DUE TO RAIN?
I HOPE.
NO WAY... THE RACE STARTED AN HOUR AGO. THE RAIN JUST MAKES IT MORE CHALLENGING.
YOU MEAN I MISSED THE START OF THE RACE?!
WELL, THE **EXPERT** GROUP STARTED THE CIRCUIT AN HOUR AGO, BUT YOU'RE HERE IN TIME FOR THE START OF THE **SPORT** GROUP.
45
IT'S PRETTY FLAT RIGHT HERE AT THE STARTING POINT. YOU MIGHT WANT TO WALK FURTHER DOWN THE TRAIL IF YOU WANT TO REALLY CATCH SOME ACTION.
THANKS.
GREAT. MORE HIKING. AND WHERE'S THAT PHOTOGRAPHER?... I'M CALLING AGAIN...
THERE'S YOUR PHONE AGAIN. SHOULD YOU GET IT?
IT CAN'T BE ANYONE I WANT TO TALK TO, BECAUSE YOU'RE HERE.
RING!

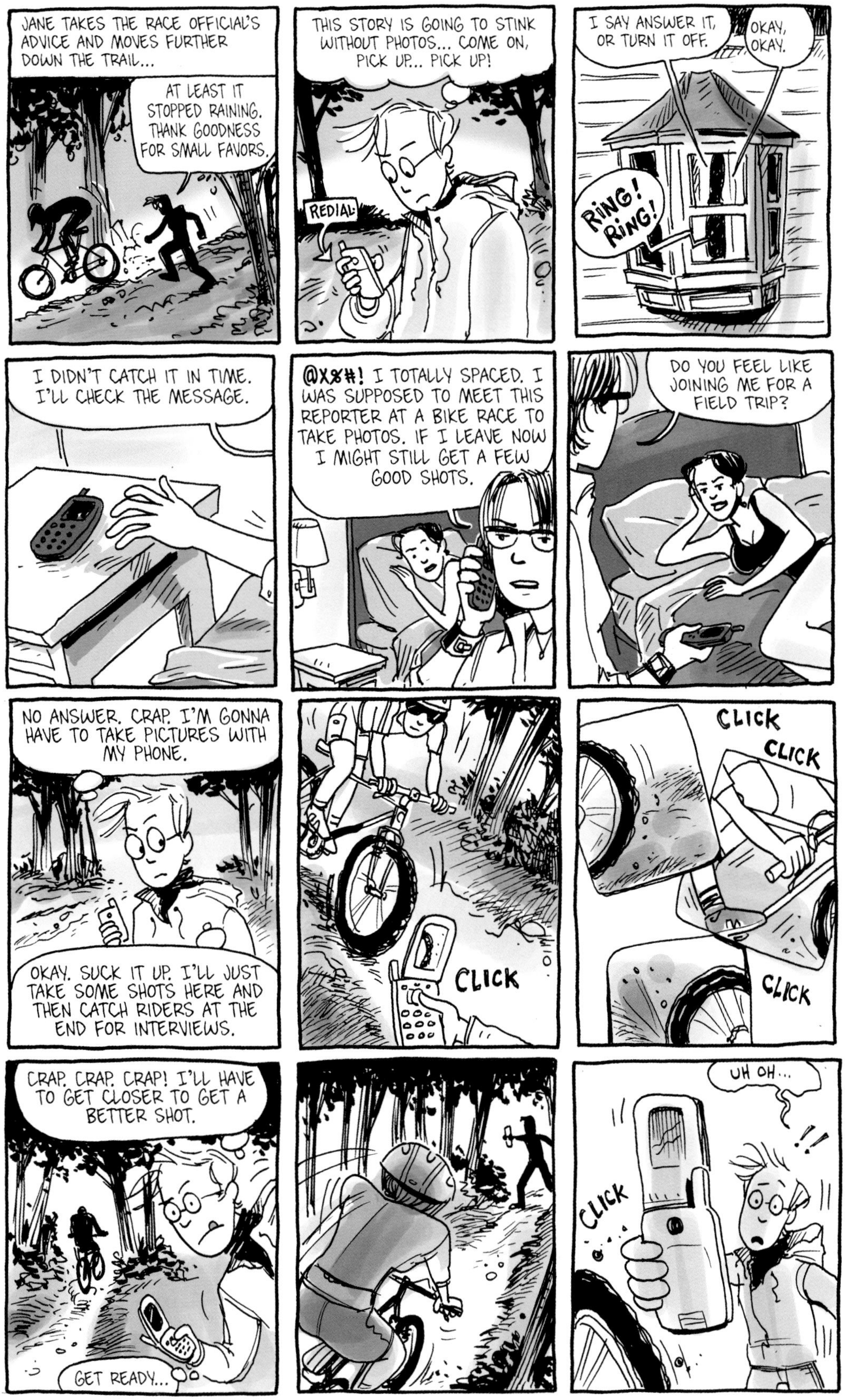
JANE TAKES THE RACE OFFICIAL'S ADVICE AND MOVES FURTHER DOWN THE TRAIL...
AT LEAST IT STOPPED RAINING. THANK GOODNESS FOR SMALL FAVORS.
THIS STORY IS GOING TO STINK WITHOUT PHOTOS... COME ON, PICK UP... PICK UP!
REDIAL
I SAY ANSWER IT, OR TURN IT OFF.
OKAY, OKAY.
RING! RING!
I DIDN'T CATCH IT IN TIME. I'LL CHECK THE MESSAGE.
@X&#! I TOTALLY SPACED. I WAS SUPPOSED TO MEET THIS REPORTER AT A BIKE RACE TO TAKE PHOTOS. IF I LEAVE NOW I MIGHT STILL GET A FEW GOOD SHOTS.
DO YOU FEEL LIKE JOINING ME FOR A FIELD TRIP?
NO ANSWER. CRAP. I'M GONNA HAVE TO TAKE PICTURES WITH MY PHONE.
OKAY. SUCK IT UP. I'LL JUST TAKE SOME SHOTS HERE AND THEN CATCH RIDERS AT THE END FOR INTERVIEWS.
CLICK
CLICK
CLICK
CLICK
CRAP. CRAP. CRAP! I'LL HAVE TO GET CLOSER TO GET A BETTER SHOT.
GET READY...
UH OH...
CLICK

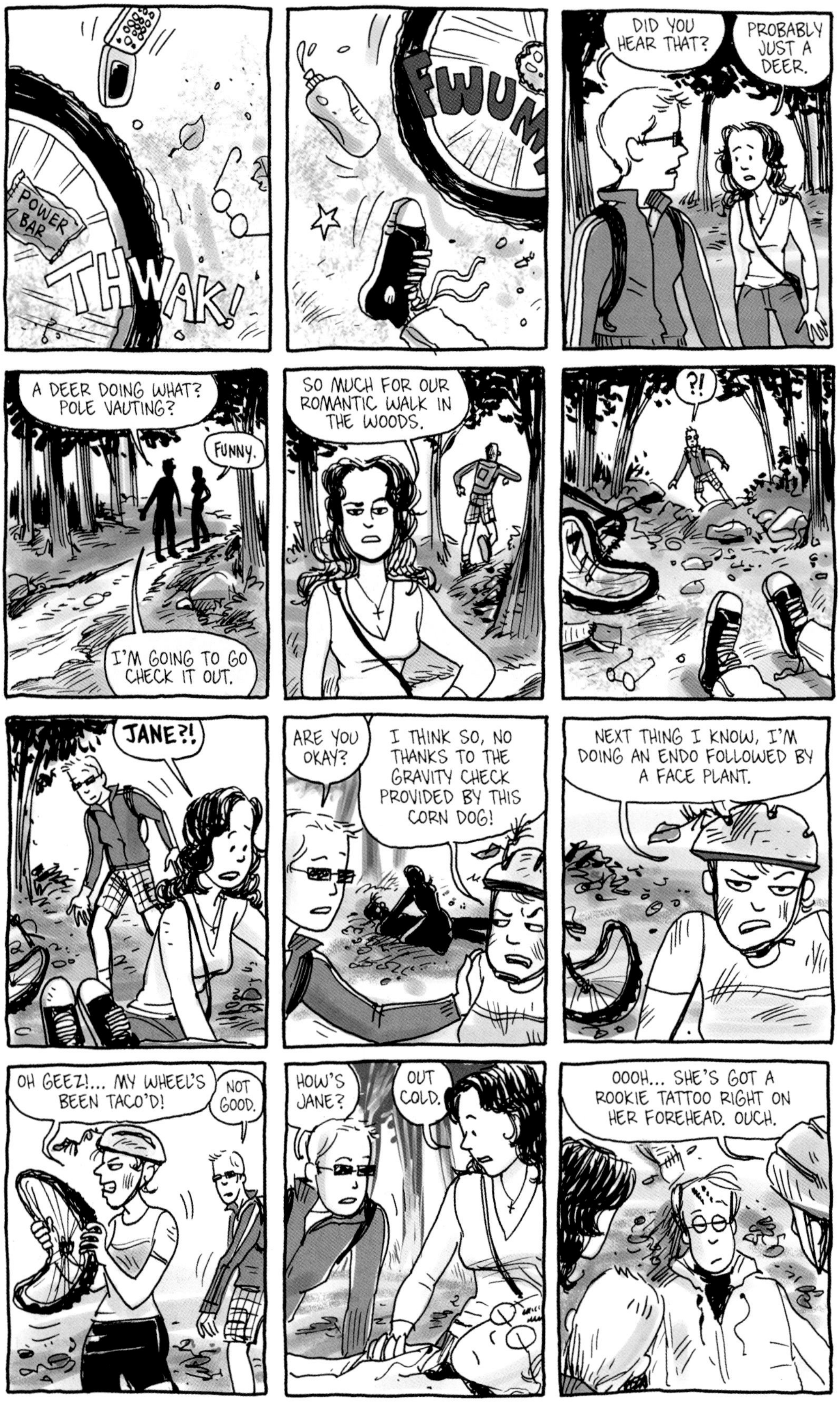
POWER BAR
THWAK!
FWUM
DID YOU HEAR THAT?
PROBABLY JUST A DEER.
A DEER DOING WHAT? POLE VAUTING?
FUNNY.
I'M GOING TO GO CHECK IT OUT.
SO MUCH FOR OUR ROMANTIC WALK IN THE WOODS.
?!
JANE?!
ARE YOU OKAY?
I THINK SO, NO THANKS TO THE GRAVITY CHECK PROVIDED BY THIS CORN DOG!
NEXT THING I KNOW, I'M DOING AN ENDO FOLLOWED BY A FACE PLANT.
OH GEEZ!... MY WHEEL'S BEEN TACO'D!
NOT GOOD.
HOW'S JANE?
OUT COLD.
OOOH... SHE'S GOT A ROOKIE TATTOO RIGHT ON HER FOREHEAD. OUCH.

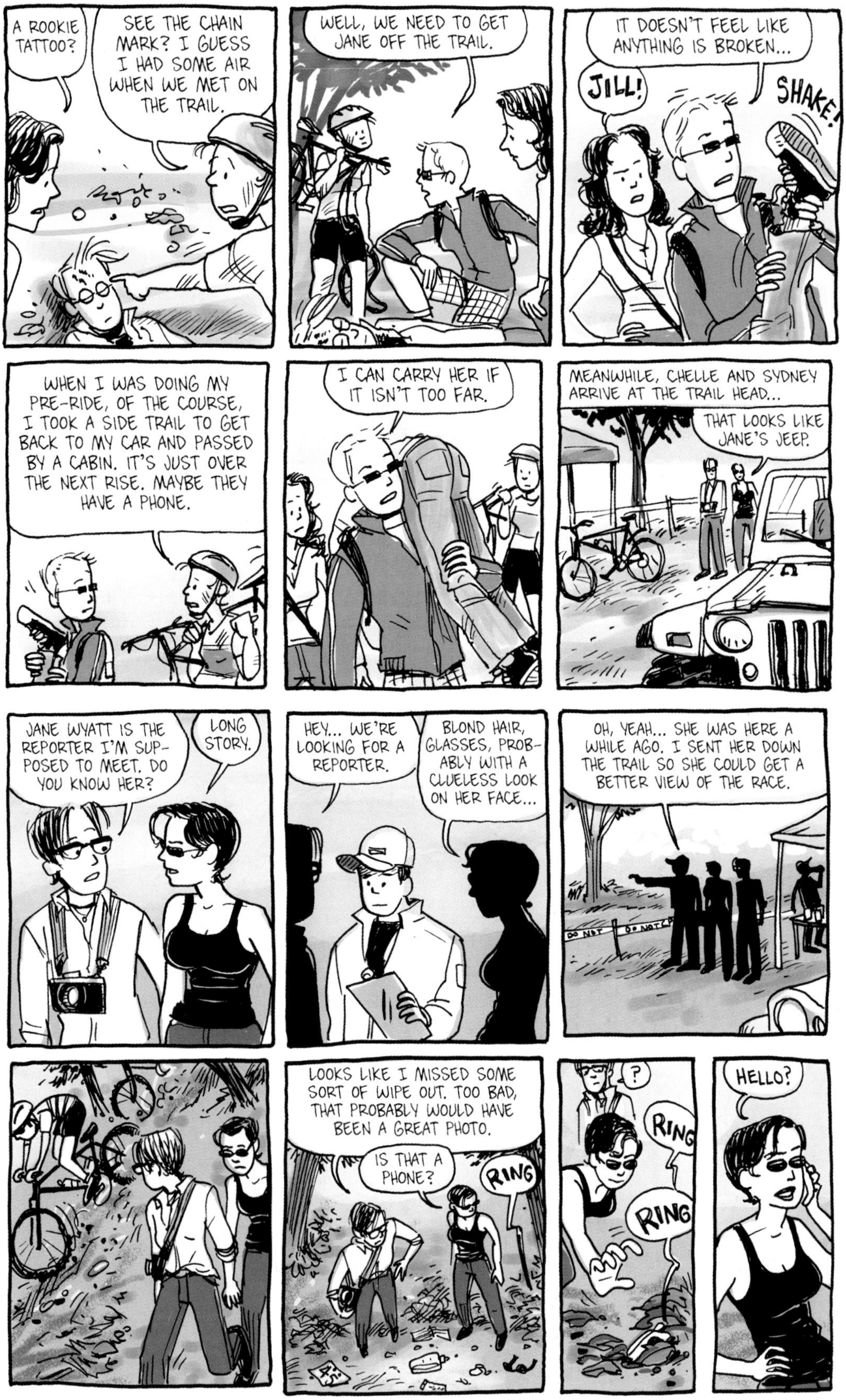
A ROOKIE TATTOO?
SEE THE CHAIN MARK? I GUESS I HAD SOME AIR WHEN WE MET ON THE TRAIL.
WELL, WE NEED TO GET JANE OFF THE TRAIL.
IT DOESN'T FEEL LIKE ANYTHING IS BROKEN...
JILL!
SHAKE!
WHEN I WAS DOING MY PRE-RIDE, OF THE COURSE, I TOOK A SIDE TRAIL TO GET BACK TO MY CAR AND PASSED BY A CABIN. IT'S JUST OVER THE NEXT RISE. MAYBE THEY HAVE A PHONE.
I CAN CARRY HER IF IT ISN'T TOO FAR.
MEANWHILE, CHELLE AND SYDNEY ARRIVE AT THE TRAIL HEAD...
THAT LOOKS LIKE JANE'S JEEP.
JANE WYATT IS THE REPORTER I'M SUPPOSED TO MEET. DO YOU KNOW HER?
LONG STORY.
HEY... WE'RE LOOKING FOR A REPORTER.
BLOND HAIR, GLASSES, PROBABLY WITH A CLUELESS LOOK ON HER FACE...
OH, YEAH... SHE WAS HERE A WHILE AGO. I SENT HER DOWN THE TRAIL SO SHE COULD GET A BETTER VIEW OF THE RACE.
LOOKS LIKE I MISSED SOME SORT OF WIPE OUT. TOO BAD, THAT PROBABLY WOULD HAVE BEEN A GREAT PHOTO.
IS THAT A PHONE?
RING
?
RING
RING
HELLO?

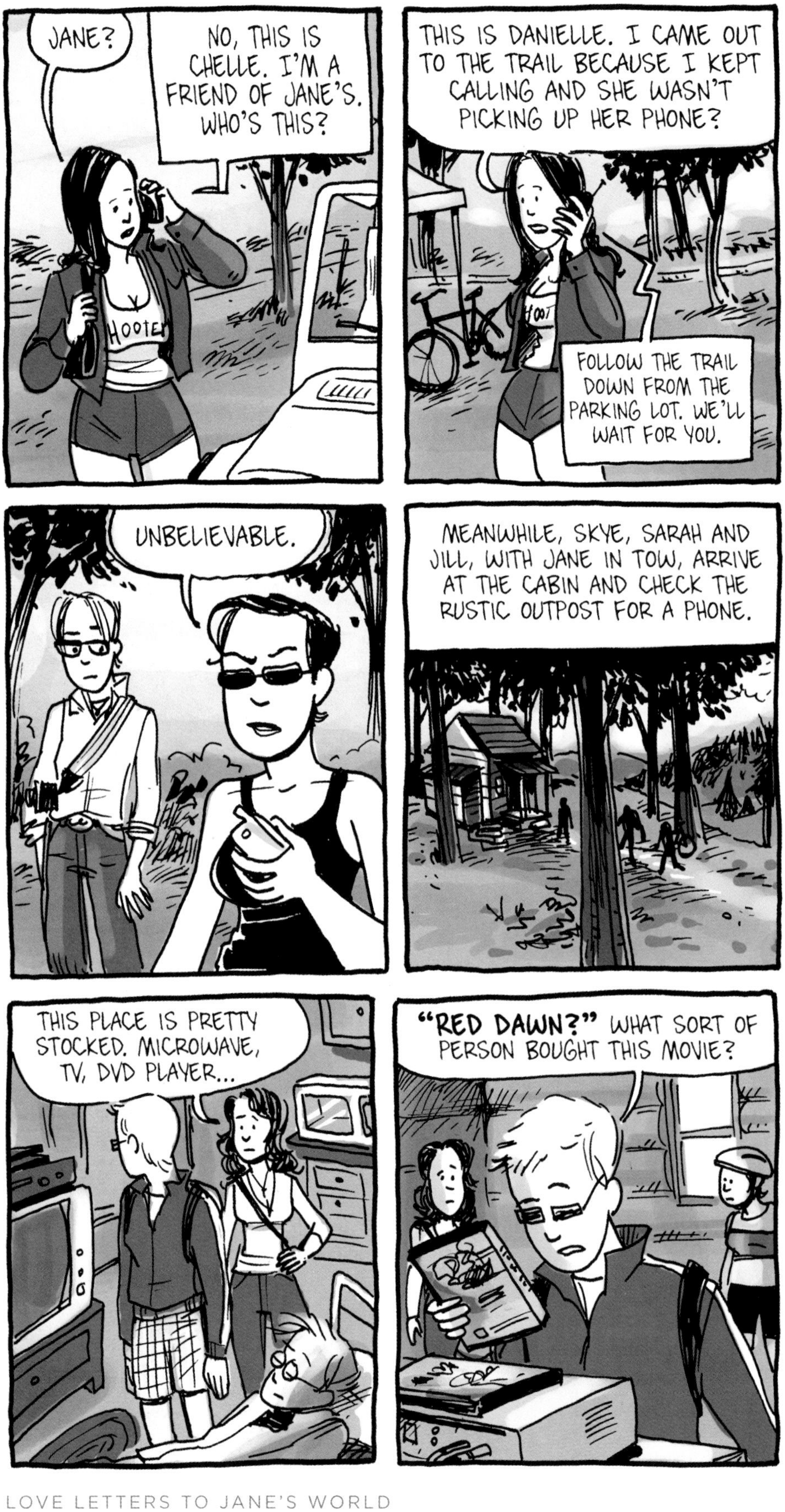
JANE?
NO, THIS IS CHELLE. I'M A FRIEND OF JANE'S. WHO'S THIS?
HOOTE
THIS IS DANIELLE. I CAME OUT TO THE TRAIL BECAUSE I KEPT CALLING AND SHE WASN'T PICKING UP HER PHONE?
HOOT
FOLLOW THE TRAIL DOWN FROM THE PARKING LOT. WE'LL WAIT FOR YOU.
UNBELIEVABLE.
MEANWHILE, SKYE, SARAH AND JILL, WITH JANE IN TOW, ARRIVE AT THE CABIN AND CHECK THE RUSTIC OUTPOST FOR A PHONE.
THIS PLACE IS PRETTY STOCKED. MICROWAVE, TV, DVD PLAYER...
"RED DAWN?" WHAT SORT OF PERSON BOUGHT THIS MOVIE?

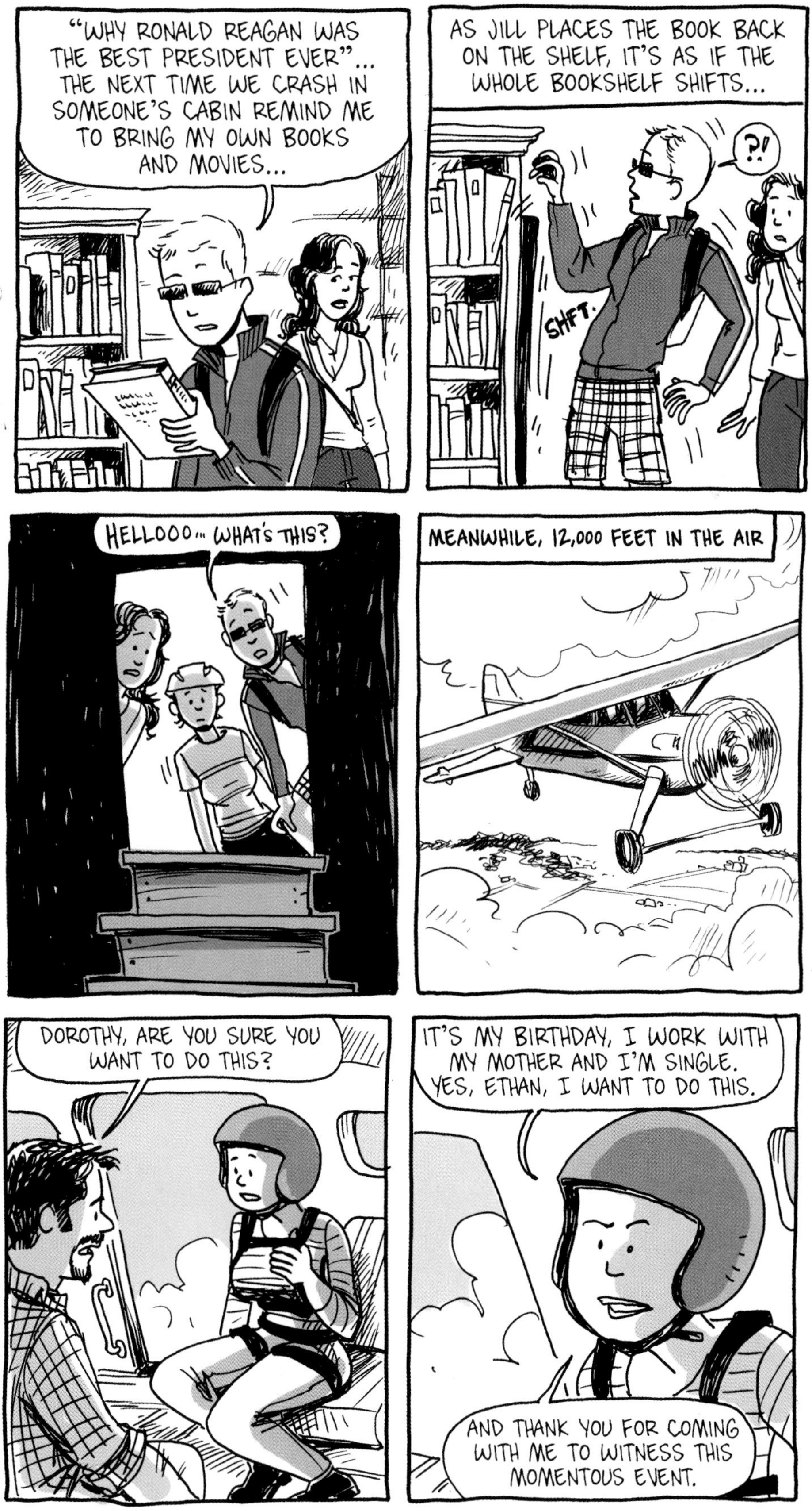

"WHY RONALD REAGAN WAS THE BEST PRESIDENT EVER"... THE NEXT TIME WE CRASH IN SOMEONE'S CABIN REMIND ME TO BRING MY OWN BOOKS AND MOVIES...
AS JILL PLACES THE BOOK BACK ON THE SHELF, IT'S AS IF THE WHOLE BOOKSHELF SHIFTS...
?!
SHFT.
HELLOOO... WHAT'S THIS?
MEANWHILE, 12,000 FEET IN THE AIR
DOROTHY, ARE YOU SURE YOU WANT TO DO THIS?
IT'S MY BIRTHDAY, I WORK WITH MY MOTHER AND I'M SINGLE. YES, ETHAN, I WANT TO DO THIS.
AND THANK YOU FOR COMING WITH ME TO WITNESS THIS MOMENTOUS EVENT.

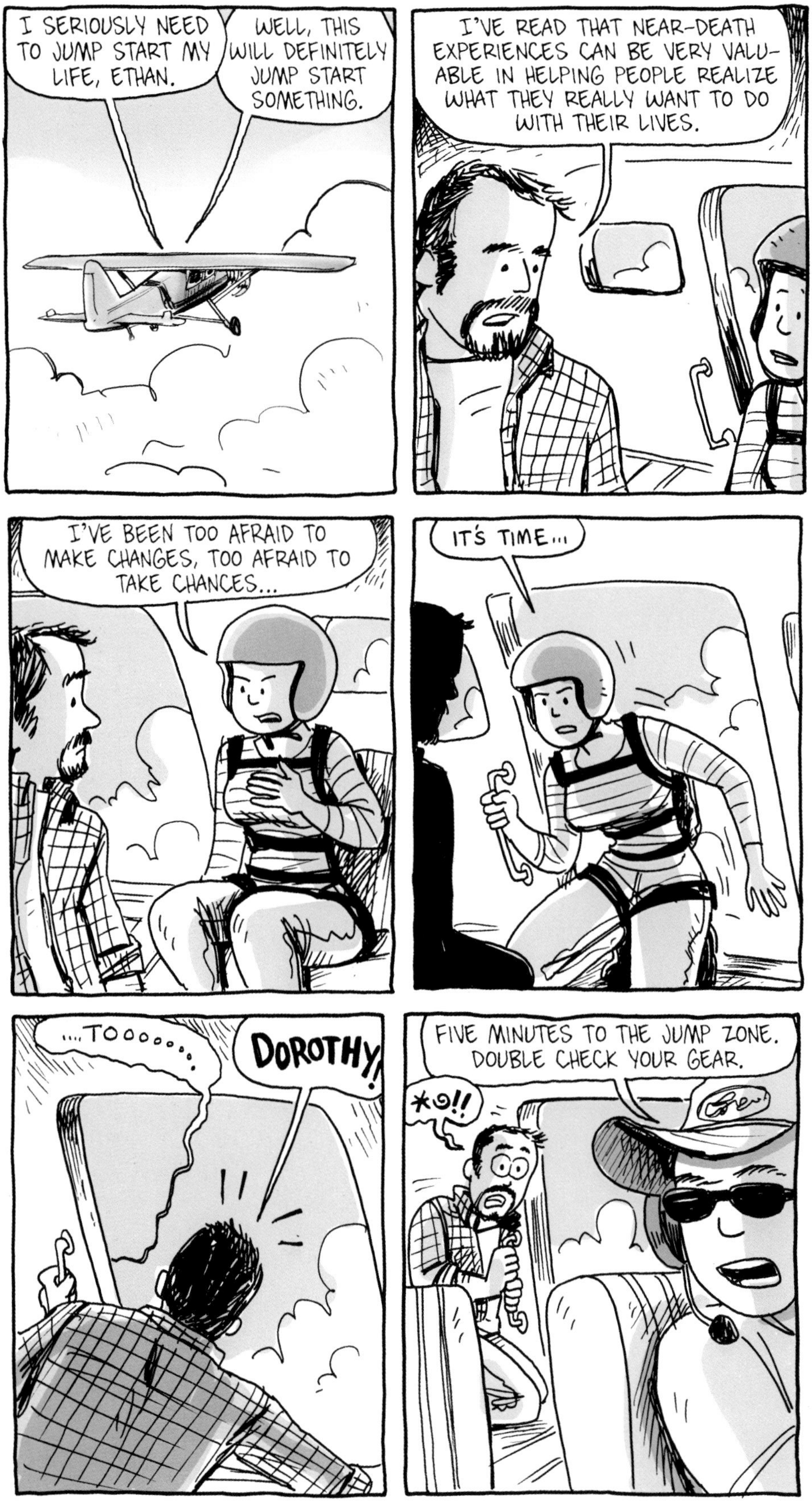
I SERIOUSLY NEED TO JUMP START MY LIFE, ETHAN.
WELL, THIS WILL DEFINITELY JUMP START SOMETHING.
I'VE READ THAT NEAR-DEATH EXPERIENCES CAN BE VERY VALUABLE IN HELPING PEOPLE REALIZE WHAT THEY REALLY WANT TO DO WITH THEIR LIVES.
I'VE BEEN TOO AFRAID TO MAKE CHANGES, TOO AFRAID TO TAKE CHANCES...
IT'S TIME...
....TOOooooo...
DOROTHY!
FIVE MINUTES TO THE JUMP ZONE. DOUBLE CHECK YOUR GEAR.
*@!!

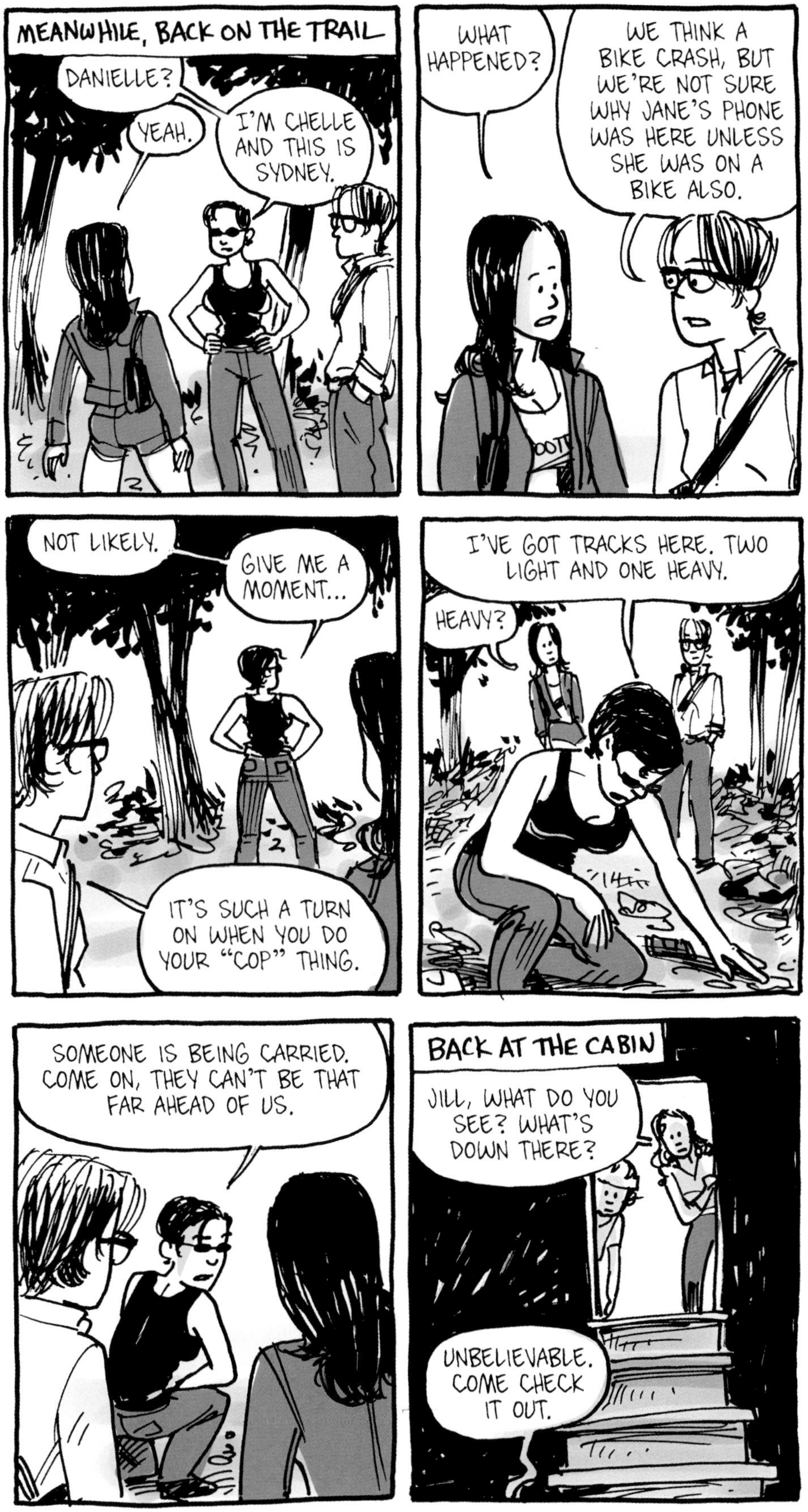
MEANWHILE, BACK ON THE TRAIL
DANIELLE?
YEAH.
I'M CHELLE AND THIS IS SYDNEY.
WHAT HAPPENED?
WE THINK A BIKE CRASH, BUT WE'RE NOT SURE WHY JANE'S PHONE WAS HERE UNLESS SHE WAS ON A BIKE ALSO.
NOT LIKELY.
GIVE ME A MOMENT...
IT'S SUCH A TURN ON WHEN YOU DO YOUR "COP" THING.
I'VE GOT TRACKS HERE. TWO LIGHT AND ONE HEAVY.
HEAVY?
SOMEONE IS BEING CARRIED. COME ON, THEY CAN'T BE THAT FAR AHEAD OF US.
BACK AT THE CABIN
JILL, WHAT DO YOU SEE? WHAT'S DOWN THERE?
UNBELIEVABLE. COME CHECK IT OUT.

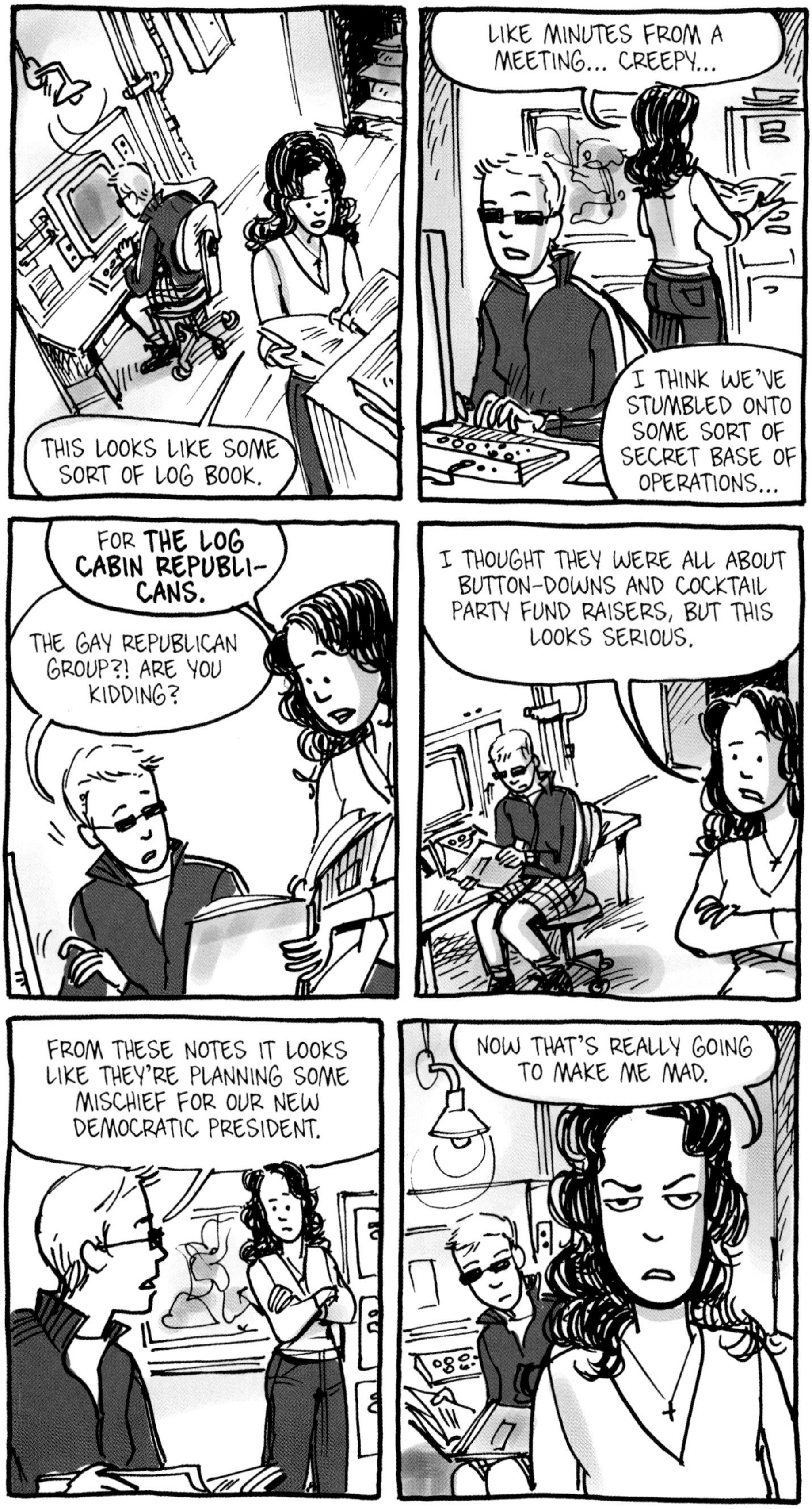
THIS LOOKS LIKE SOME SORT OF LOG BOOK.
LIKE MINUTES FROM A MEETING... CREEPY...
I THINK WE'VE STUMBLED ONTO SOME SORT OF SECRET BASE OF OPERATIONS...
FOR **THE LOG CABIN REPUBLICANS.**
THE GAY REPUBLICAN GROUP?! ARE YOU KIDDING?
I THOUGHT THEY WERE ALL ABOUT BUTTON-DOWNS AND COCKTAIL PARTY FUND RAISERS, BUT THIS LOOKS SERIOUS.
FROM THESE NOTES IT LOOKS LIKE THEY'RE PLANNING SOME MISCHIEF FOR OUR NEW DEMOCRATIC PRESIDENT.
NOW THAT'S REALLY GOING TO MAKE ME MAD.

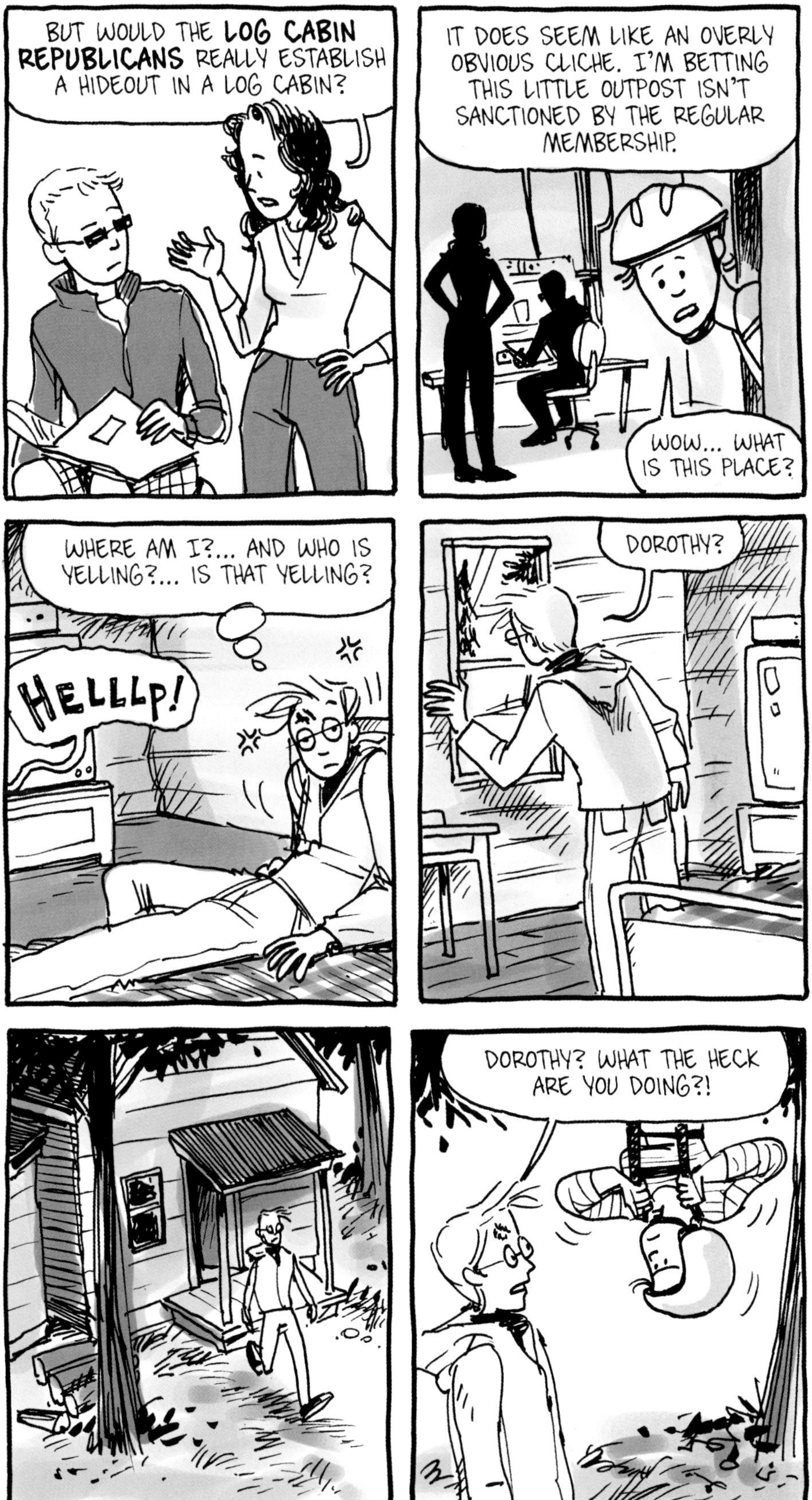
BUT WOULD THE **LOG CABIN REPUBLICANS** REALLY ESTABLISH A HIDEOUT IN A LOG CABIN?
IT DOES SEEM LIKE AN OVERLY OBVIOUS CLICHE. I'M BETTING THIS LITTLE OUTPOST ISN'T SANCTIONED BY THE REGULAR MEMBERSHIP.
WOW... WHAT IS THIS PLACE?
WHERE AM I?... AND WHO IS YELLING?... IS THAT YELLING?
HELLLP!
DOROTHY?
DOROTHY? WHAT THE HECK ARE YOU DOING?!

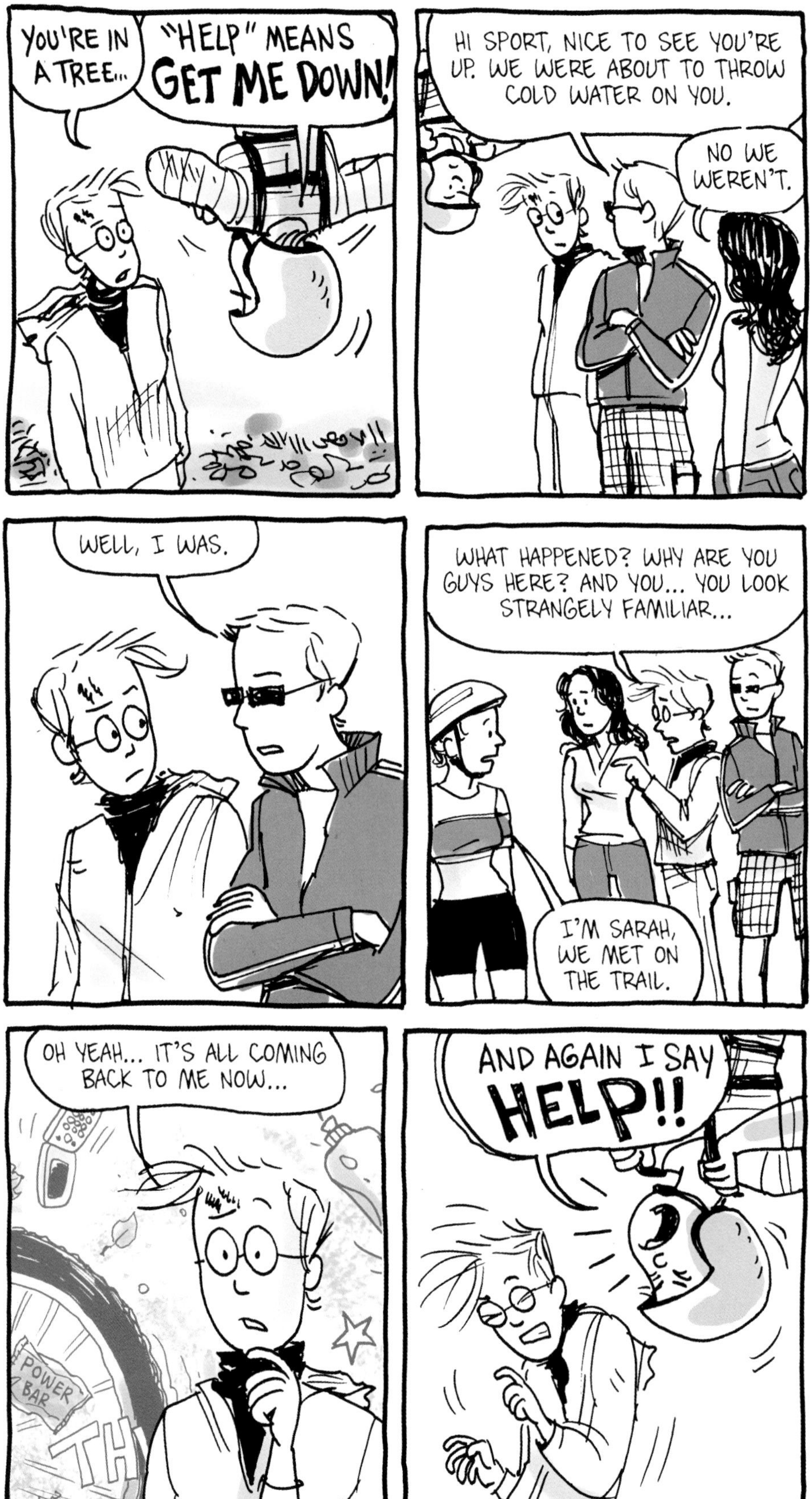
YOU'RE IN A TREE...
"HELP" MEANS GET ME DOWN!
HI SPORT, NICE TO SEE YOU'RE UP. WE WERE ABOUT TO THROW COLD WATER ON YOU.
NO WE WEREN'T.
WELL, I WAS.
WHAT HAPPENED? WHY ARE YOU GUYS HERE? AND YOU... YOU LOOK STRANGELY FAMILIAR...
I'M SARAH, WE MET ON THE TRAIL.
OH YEAH... IT'S ALL COMING BACK TO ME NOW...
POWER BAR
TH
AND AGAIN I SAY HELP!!

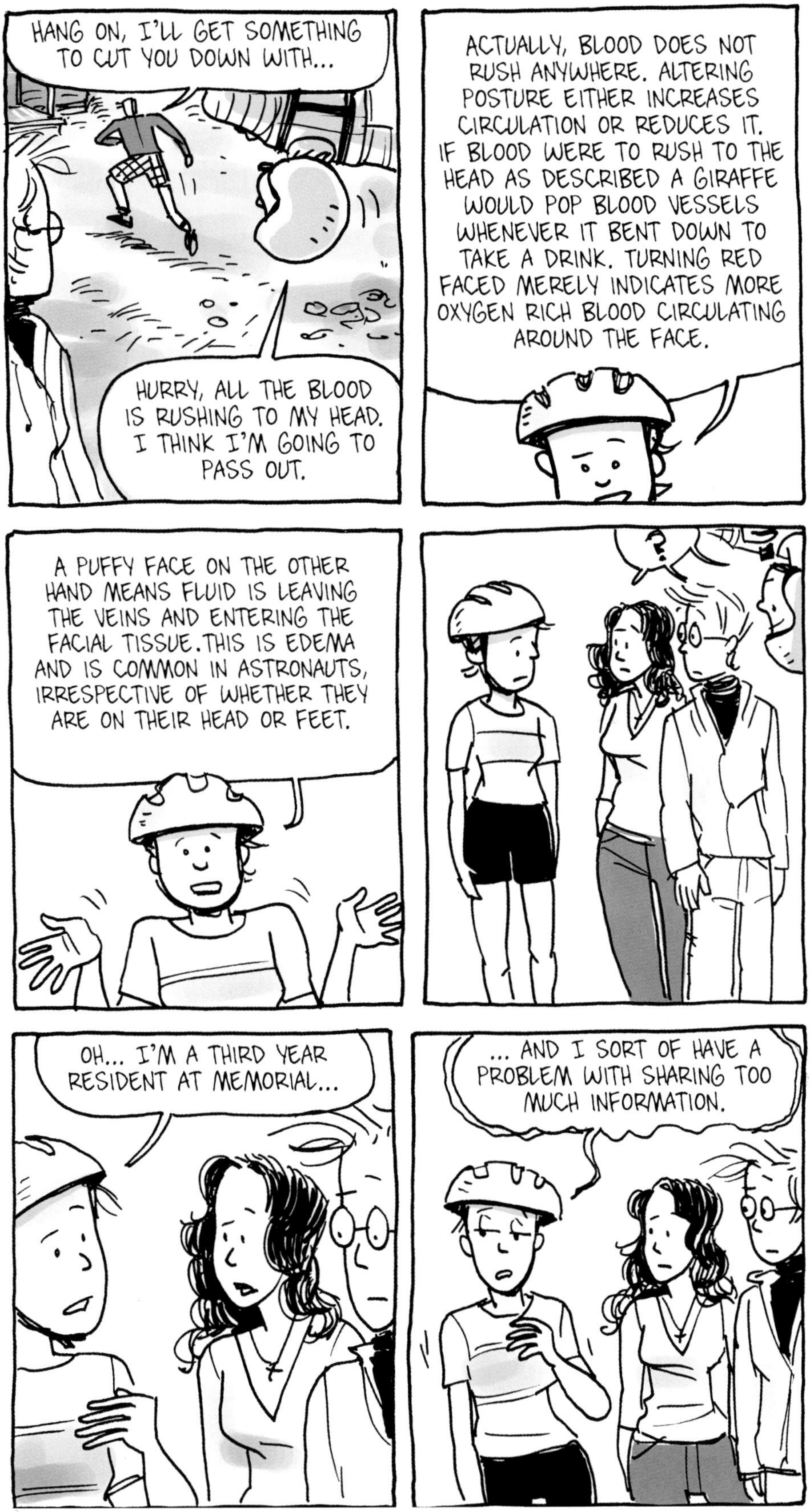
HANG ON, I'LL GET SOMETHING TO CUT YOU DOWN WITH...
HURRY, ALL THE BLOOD IS RUSHING TO MY HEAD. I THINK I'M GOING TO PASS OUT.
ACTUALLY, BLOOD DOES NOT RUSH ANYWHERE. ALTERING POSTURE EITHER INCREASES CIRCULATION OR REDUCES IT. IF BLOOD WERE TO RUSH TO THE HEAD AS DESCRIBED A GIRAFFE WOULD POP BLOOD VESSELS WHENEVER IT BENT DOWN TO TAKE A DRINK. TURNING RED FACED MERELY INDICATES MORE OXYGEN RICH BLOOD CIRCULATING AROUND THE FACE.
A PUFFY FACE ON THE OTHER HAND MEANS FLUID IS LEAVING THE VEINS AND ENTERING THE FACIAL TISSUE. THIS IS EDEMA AND IS COMMON IN ASTRONAUTS, IRRESPECTIVE OF WHETHER THEY ARE ON THEIR HEAD OR FEET.
?
OH... I'M A THIRD YEAR RESIDENT AT MEMORIAL...
... AND I SORT OF HAVE A PROBLEM WITH SHARING TOO MUCH INFORMATION.

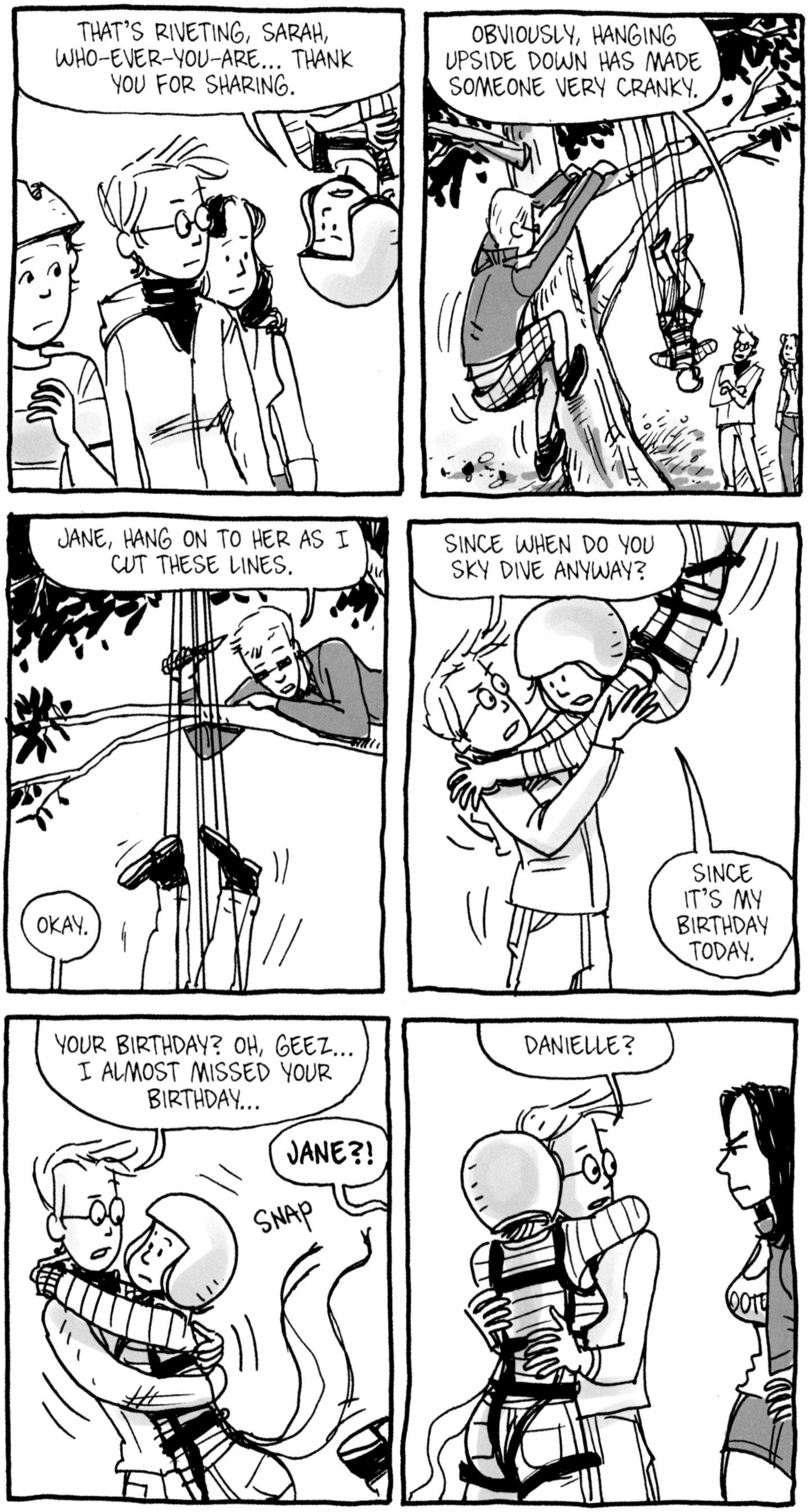
THAT'S RIVETING, SARAH, WHO-EVER-YOU-ARE... THANK YOU FOR SHARING.
OBVIOUSLY, HANGING UPSIDE DOWN HAS MADE SOMEONE VERY CRANKY.
JANE, HANG ON TO HER AS I CUT THESE LINES.
OKAY.
SINCE WHEN DO YOU SKY DIVE ANYWAY?
SINCE IT'S MY BIRTHDAY TODAY.
YOUR BIRTHDAY? OH, GEEZ... I ALMOST MISSED YOUR BIRTHDAY...
JANE?!
SNAP
DANIELLE?

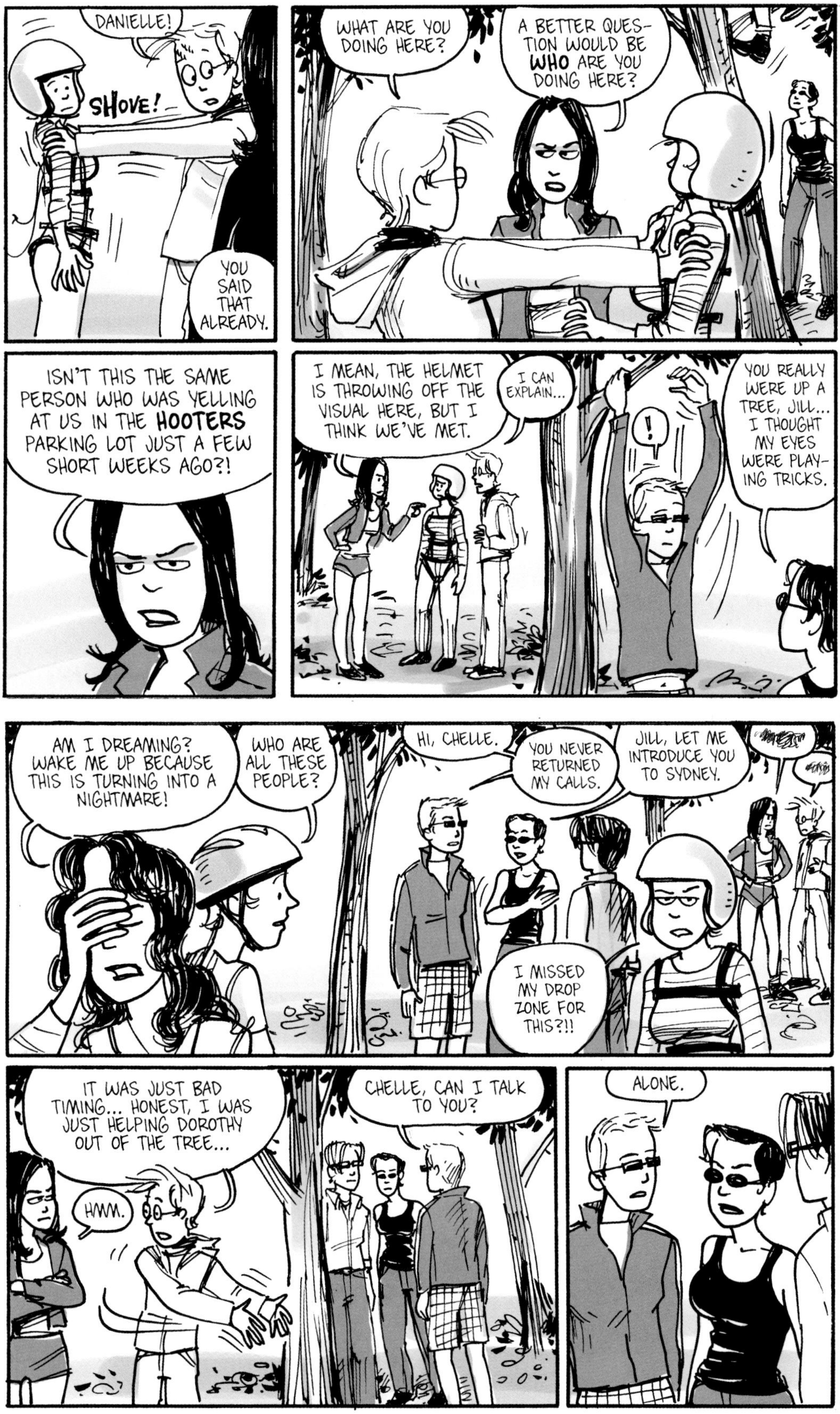
DANIELLE!
SHOVE!
YOU SAID THAT ALREADY.
WHAT ARE YOU DOING HERE?
A BETTER QUESTION WOULD BE WHO ARE YOU DOING HERE?
ISN'T THIS THE SAME PERSON WHO WAS YELLING AT US IN THE HOOTERS PARKING LOT JUST A FEW SHORT WEEKS AGO?!
I MEAN, THE HELMET IS THROWING OFF THE VISUAL HERE, BUT I THINK WE'VE MET.
I CAN EXPLAIN...
!
YOU REALLY WERE UP A TREE, JILL... I THOUGHT MY EYES WERE PLAYING TRICKS.
AM I DREAMING? WAKE ME UP BECAUSE THIS IS TURNING INTO A NIGHTMARE!
WHO ARE ALL THESE PEOPLE?
HI, CHELLE.
YOU NEVER RETURNED MY CALLS.
JILL, LET ME INTRODUCE YOU TO SYDNEY.
I MISSED MY DROP ZONE FOR THIS?!!
IT WAS JUST BAD TIMING... HONEST, I WAS JUST HELPING DOROTHY OUT OF THE TREE...
HMM.
CHELLE, CAN I TALK TO YOU?
ALONE.

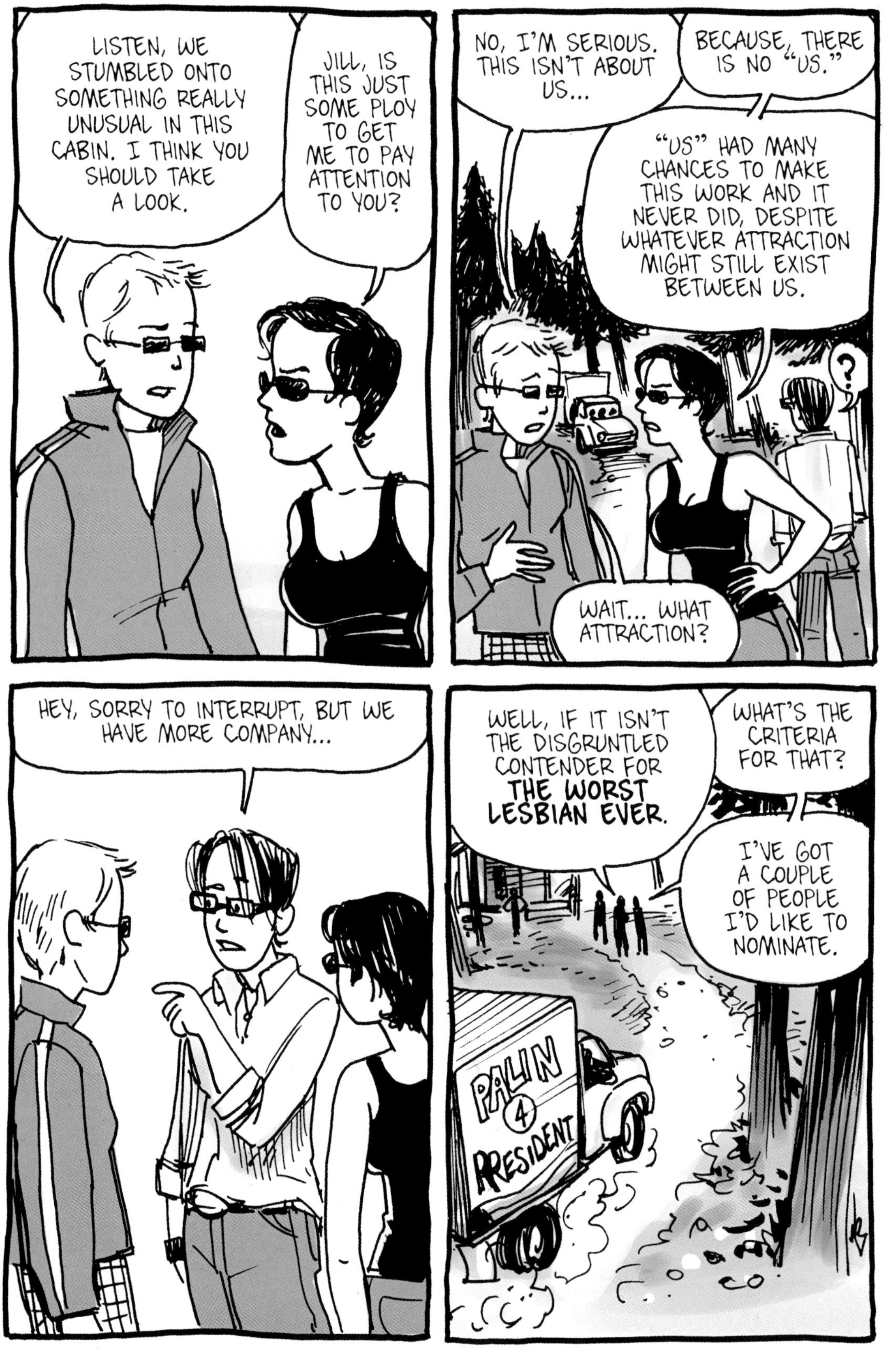
LISTEN, WE STUMBLED ONTO SOMETHING REALLY UNUSUAL IN THIS CABIN. I THINK YOU SHOULD TAKE A LOOK.
JILL, IS THIS JUST SOME PLOY TO GET ME TO PAY ATTENTION TO YOU?
NO, I'M SERIOUS. THIS ISN'T ABOUT US...
BECAUSE, THERE IS NO "US."
"US" HAD MANY CHANCES TO MAKE THIS WORK AND IT NEVER DID, DESPITE WHATEVER ATTRACTION MIGHT STILL EXIST BETWEEN US.
?
WAIT... WHAT ATTRACTION?
HEY, SORRY TO INTERRUPT, BUT WE HAVE MORE COMPANY...
WELL, IF IT ISN'T THE DISGRUNTLED CONTENDER FOR **THE WORST LESBIAN EVER**.
WHAT'S THE CRITERIA FOR THAT?
I'VE GOT A COUPLE OF PEOPLE I'D LIKE TO NOMINATE.
PALIN 4 PRESIDENT

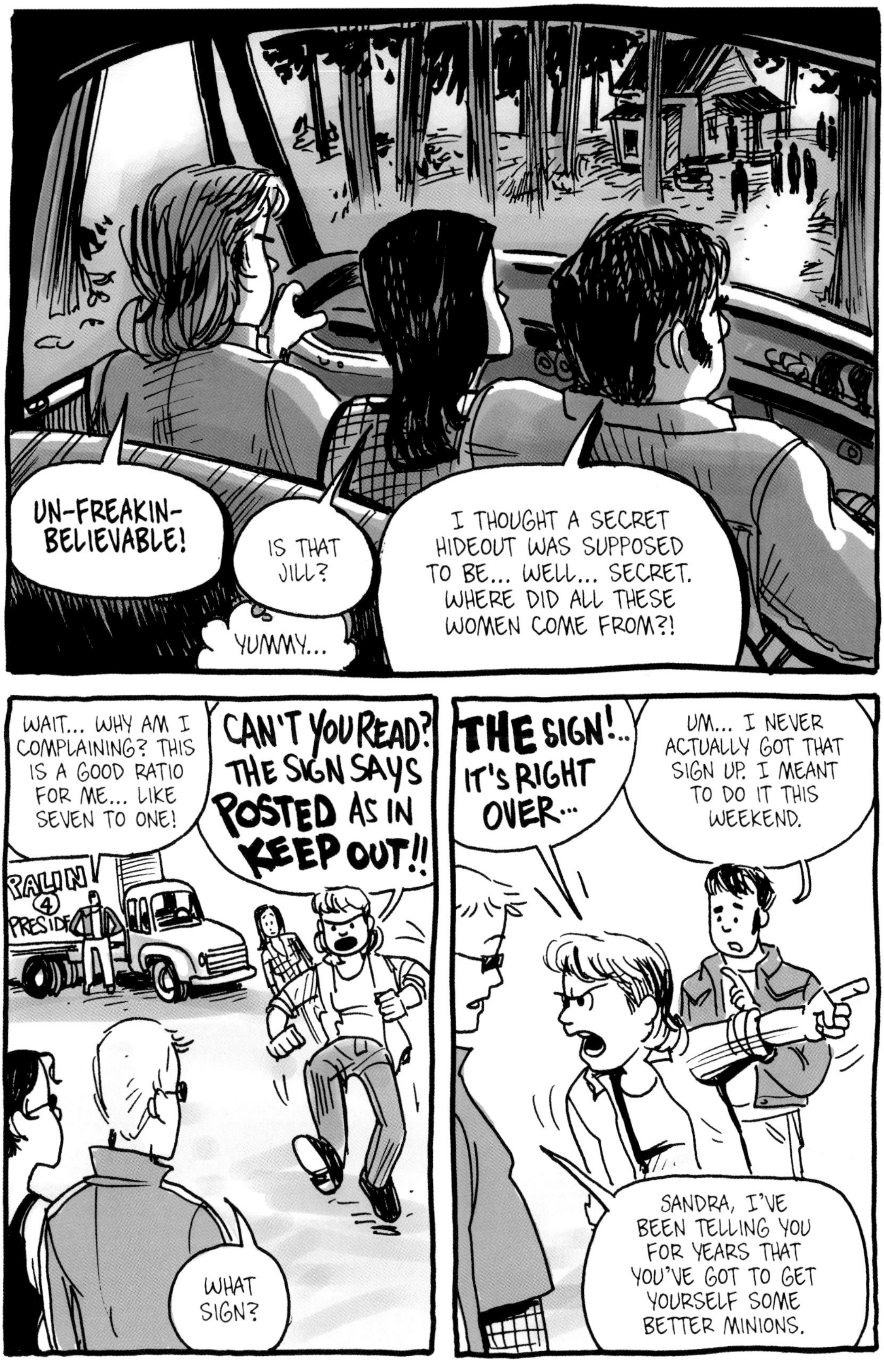
UN-FREAKIN-BELIEVABLE!
IS THAT JILL?
YUMMY...
I THOUGHT A SECRET HIDEOUT WAS SUPPOSED TO BE... WELL... SECRET. WHERE DID ALL THESE WOMEN COME FROM?!
WAIT... WHY AM I COMPLAINING? THIS IS A GOOD RATIO FOR ME... LIKE SEVEN TO ONE!
CAN'T YOU READ? THE SIGN SAYS POSTED AS IN KEEP OUT!!
PALIN 4 PRESIDE
WHAT SIGN?
THE SIGN!.. IT'S RIGHT OVER...
UM... I NEVER ACTUALLY GOT THAT SIGN UP. I MEANT TO DO IT THIS WEEKEND.
SANDRA, I'VE BEEN TELLING YOU FOR YEARS THAT YOU'VE GOT TO GET YOURSELF SOME BETTER MINIONS.

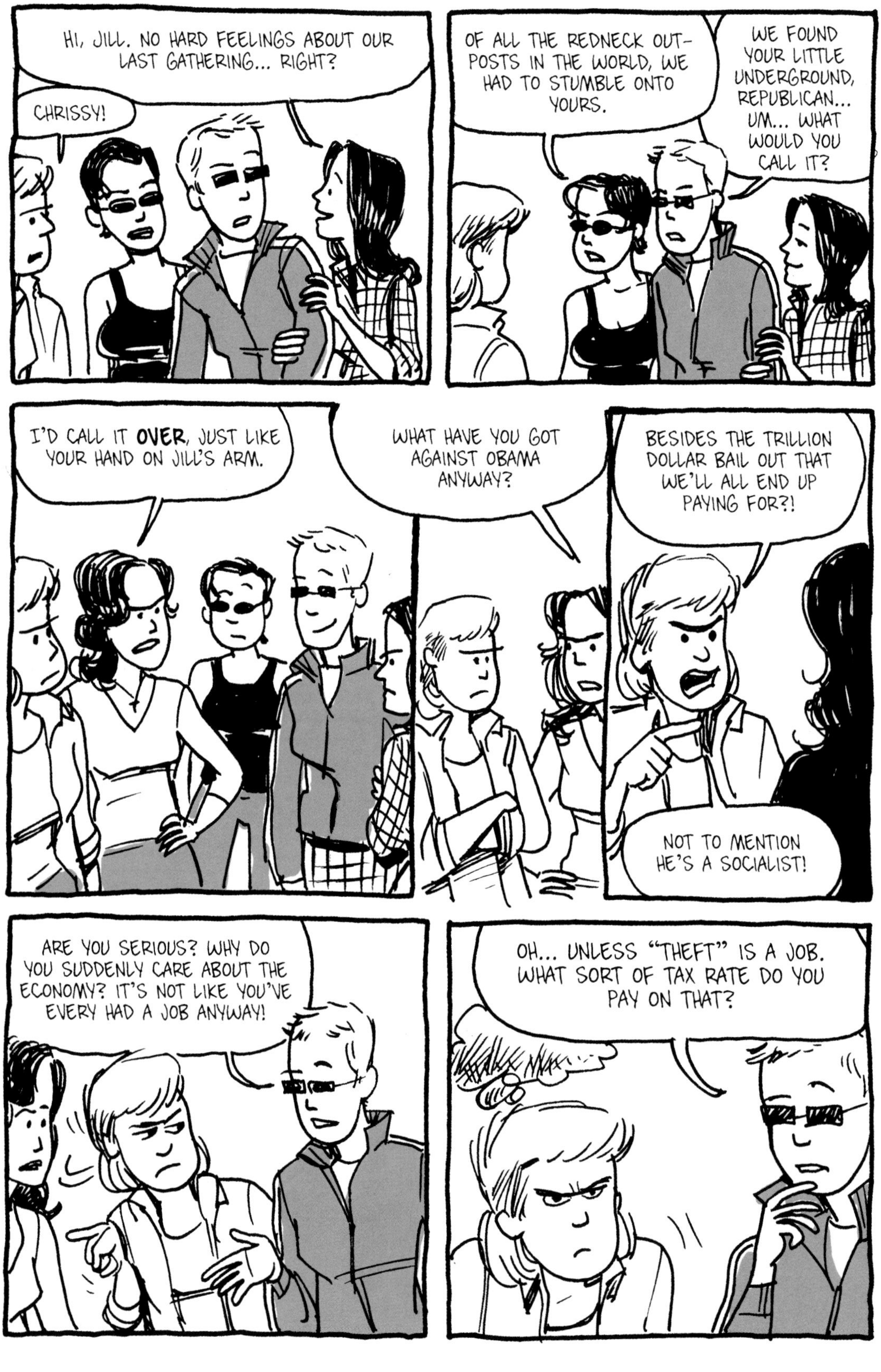
HI, JILL. NO HARD FEELINGS ABOUT OUR LAST GATHERING... RIGHT?
CHRISSY!
OF ALL THE REDNECK OUT-POSTS IN THE WORLD, WE HAD TO STUMBLE ONTO YOURS.
WE FOUND YOUR LITTLE UNDERGROUND, REPUBLICAN... UM... WHAT WOULD YOU CALL IT?
I'D CALL IT **OVER**, JUST LIKE YOUR HAND ON JILL'S ARM.
WHAT HAVE YOU GOT AGAINST OBAMA ANYWAY?
BESIDES THE TRILLION DOLLAR BAIL OUT THAT WE'LL ALL END UP PAYING FOR?!
NOT TO MENTION HE'S A SOCIALIST!
ARE YOU SERIOUS? WHY DO YOU SUDDENLY CARE ABOUT THE ECONOMY? IT'S NOT LIKE YOU'VE EVERY HAD A JOB ANYWAY!
OH... UNLESS "THEFT" IS A JOB. WHAT SORT OF TAX RATE DO YOU PAY ON THAT?

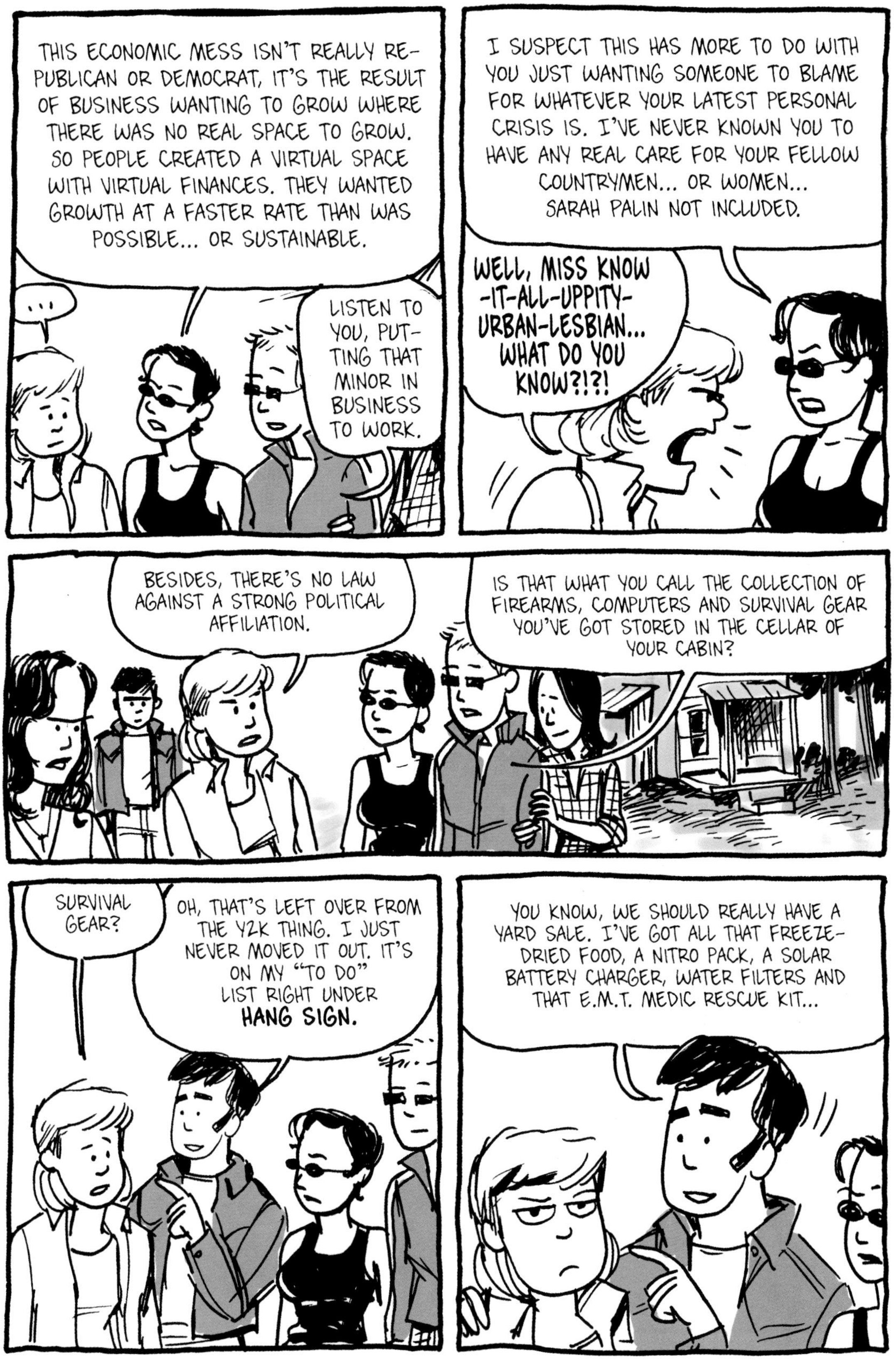
THIS ECONOMIC MESS ISN'T REALLY REPUBLICAN OR DEMOCRAT, IT'S THE RESULT OF BUSINESS WANTING TO GROW WHERE THERE WAS NO REAL SPACE TO GROW. SO PEOPLE CREATED A VIRTUAL SPACE WITH VIRTUAL FINANCES. THEY WANTED GROWTH AT A FASTER RATE THAN WAS POSSIBLE... OR SUSTAINABLE.
...
LISTEN TO YOU, PUTTING THAT MINOR IN BUSINESS TO WORK.
I SUSPECT THIS HAS MORE TO DO WITH YOU JUST WANTING SOMEONE TO BLAME FOR WHATEVER YOUR LATEST PERSONAL CRISIS IS. I'VE NEVER KNOWN YOU TO HAVE ANY REAL CARE FOR YOUR FELLOW COUNTRYMEN... OR WOMEN... SARAH PALIN NOT INCLUDED.
WELL, MISS KNOW-IT-ALL-UPPITY-URBAN-LESBIAN... WHAT DO YOU KNOW?!?!
BESIDES, THERE'S NO LAW AGAINST A STRONG POLITICAL AFFILIATION.
IS THAT WHAT YOU CALL THE COLLECTION OF FIREARMS, COMPUTERS AND SURVIVAL GEAR YOU'VE GOT STORED IN THE CELLAR OF YOUR CABIN?
SURVIVAL GEAR?
OH, THAT'S LEFT OVER FROM THE Y2K THING. I JUST NEVER MOVED IT OUT. IT'S ON MY "TO DO" LIST RIGHT UNDER HANG SIGN.
YOU KNOW, WE SHOULD REALLY HAVE A YARD SALE. I'VE GOT ALL THAT FREEZE-DRIED FOOD, A NITRO PACK, A SOLAR BATTERY CHARGER, WATER FILTERS AND THAT E.M.T. MEDIC RESCUE KIT...

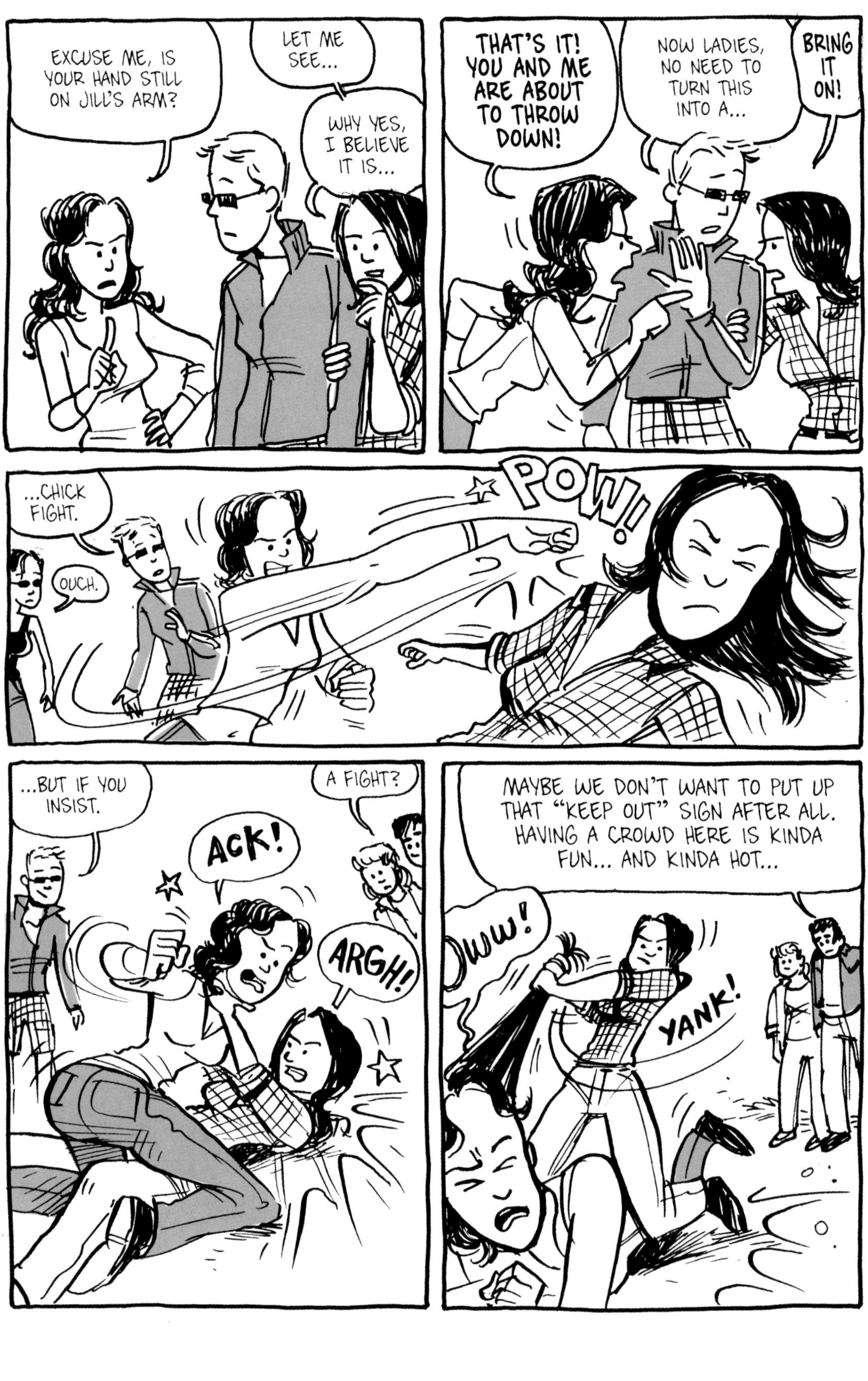
EXCUSE ME, IS YOUR HAND STILL ON JILL'S ARM?
LET ME SEE...
WHY YES, I BELIEVE IT IS...
THAT'S IT! YOU AND ME ARE ABOUT TO THROW DOWN!
NOW LADIES, NO NEED TO TURN THIS INTO A...
BRING IT ON!
...CHICK FIGHT.
OUCH.
POW!
...BUT IF YOU INSIST.
A FIGHT?
ACK!
ARGH!
MAYBE WE DON'T WANT TO PUT UP THAT "KEEP OUT" SIGN AFTER ALL. HAVING A CROWD HERE IS KINDA FUN... AND KINDA HOT...
OWW!
YANK!

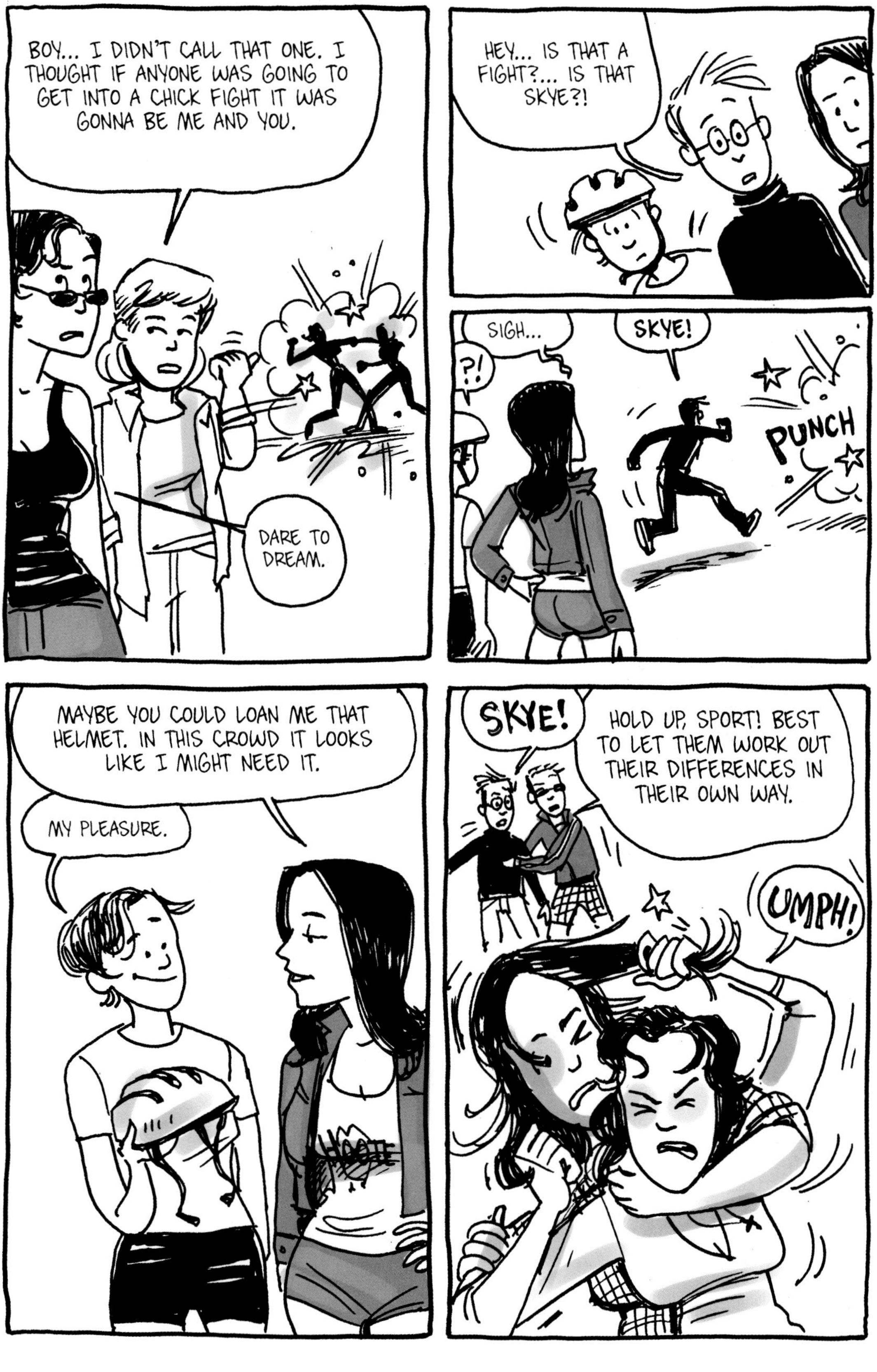
BOY... I DIDN'T CALL THAT ONE. I THOUGHT IF ANYONE WAS GOING TO GET INTO A CHICK FIGHT IT WAS GONNA BE ME AND YOU.
DARE TO DREAM.
HEY... IS THAT A FIGHT?... IS THAT SKYE?!
?!
SIGH...
SKYE!
PUNCH
MAYBE YOU COULD LOAN ME THAT HELMET. IN THIS CROWD IT LOOKS LIKE I MIGHT NEED IT.
MY PLEASURE.
SKYE!
HOLD UP, SPORT! BEST TO LET THEM WORK OUT THEIR DIFFERENCES IN THEIR OWN WAY.
UMPH!

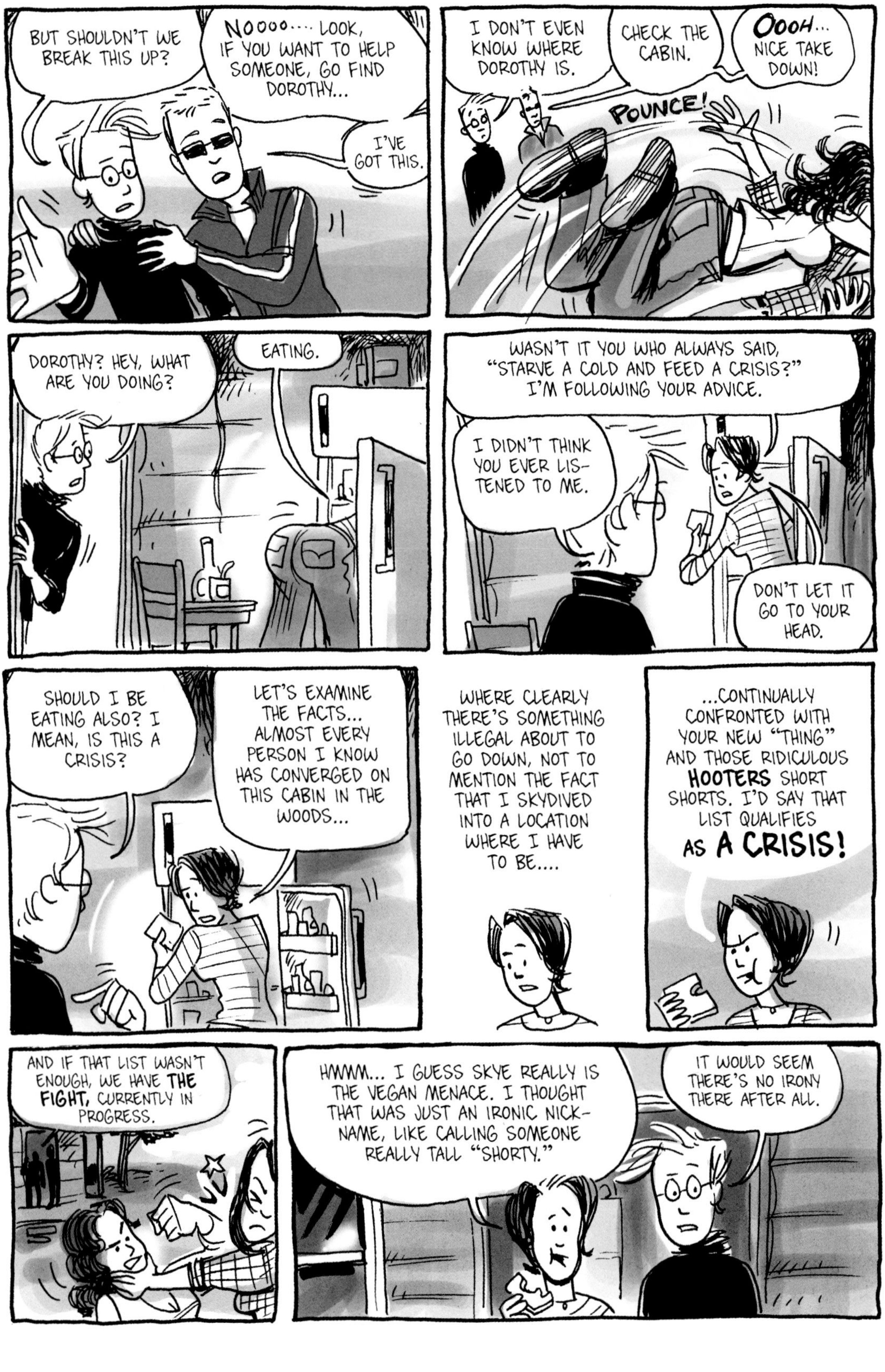
BUT SHOULDN'T WE BREAK THIS UP?
NOOOO.... LOOK, IF YOU WANT TO HELP SOMEONE, GO FIND DOROTHY...
I'VE GOT THIS.
I DON'T EVEN KNOW WHERE DOROTHY IS.
CHECK THE CABIN.
OOOH... NICE TAKE DOWN!
POUNCE!
DOROTHY? HEY, WHAT ARE YOU DOING?
EATING.
WASN'T IT YOU WHO ALWAYS SAID, "STARVE A COLD AND FEED A CRISIS?" I'M FOLLOWING YOUR ADVICE.
I DIDN'T THINK YOU EVER LIS-TENED TO ME.
DON'T LET IT GO TO YOUR HEAD.
SHOULD I BE EATING ALSO? I MEAN, IS THIS A CRISIS?
LET'S EXAMINE THE FACTS... ALMOST EVERY PERSON I KNOW HAS CONVERGED ON THIS CABIN IN THE WOODS...
WHERE CLEARLY THERE'S SOMETHING ILLEGAL ABOUT TO GO DOWN, NOT TO MENTION THE FACT THAT I SKYDIVED INTO A LOCATION WHERE I HAVE TO BE....
...CONTINUALLY CONFRONTED WITH YOUR NEW "THING" AND THOSE RIDICULOUS **HOOTERS** SHORT SHORTS. I'D SAY THAT LIST QUALIFIES **AS A CRISIS!**
AND IF THAT LIST WASN'T ENOUGH, WE HAVE **THE FIGHT,** CURRENTLY IN PROGRESS.
HMMM... I GUESS SKYE REALLY IS THE VEGAN MENACE. I THOUGHT THAT WAS JUST AN IRONIC NICK-NAME, LIKE CALLING SOMEONE REALLY TALL "SHORTY."
IT WOULD SEEM THERE'S NO IRONY THERE AFTER ALL.

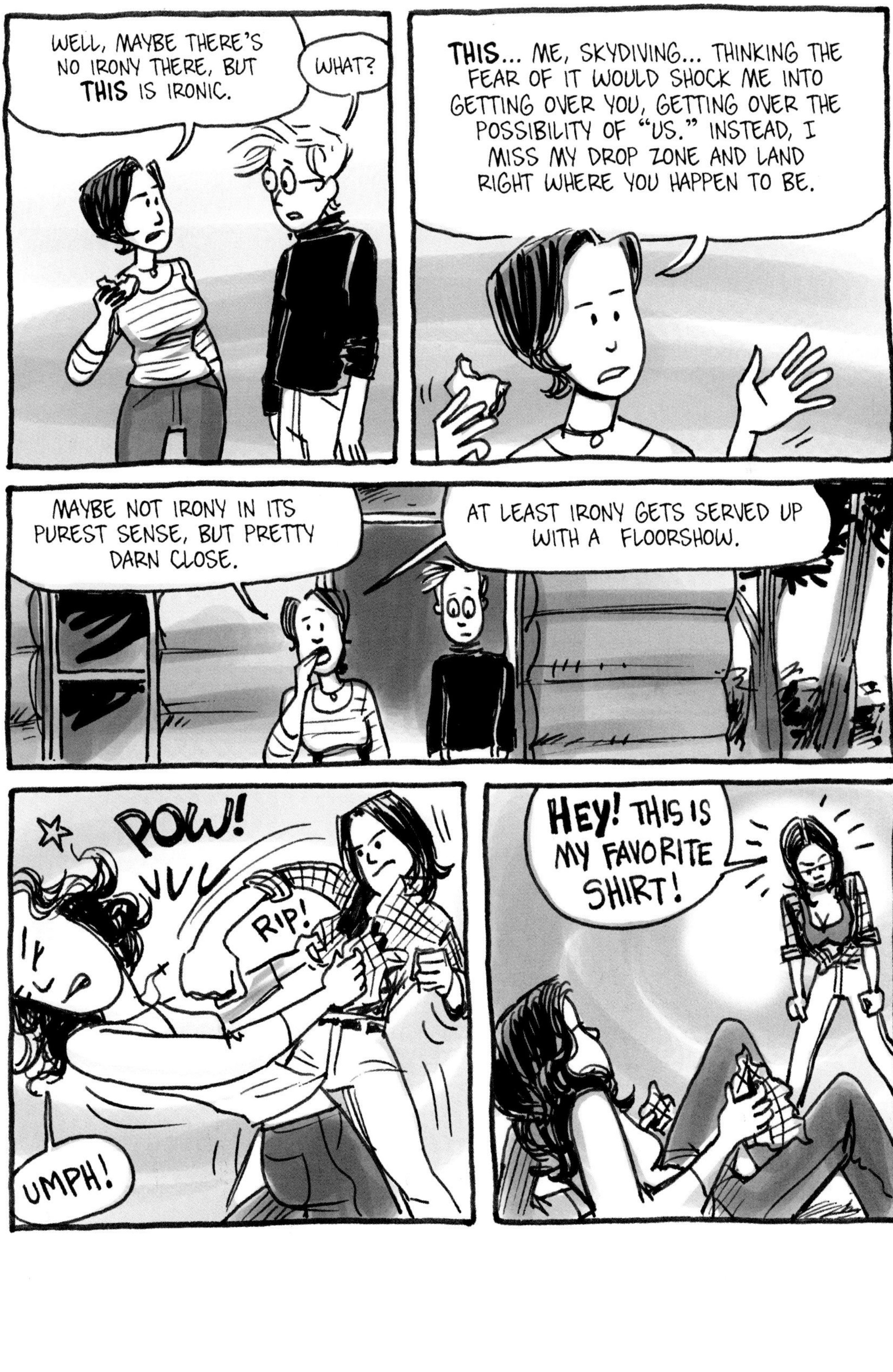
WELL, MAYBE THERE'S NO IRONY THERE, BUT THIS IS IRONIC.
WHAT?
THIS... ME, SKYDIVING... THINKING THE FEAR OF IT WOULD SHOCK ME INTO GETTING OVER YOU, GETTING OVER THE POSSIBILITY OF "US." INSTEAD, I MISS MY DROP ZONE AND LAND RIGHT WHERE YOU HAPPEN TO BE.
MAYBE NOT IRONY IN ITS PUREST SENSE, BUT PRETTY DARN CLOSE.
AT LEAST IRONY GETS SERVED UP WITH A FLOORSHOW.
POW!
RIP!
UMPH!
HEY! THIS IS MY FAVORITE SHIRT!

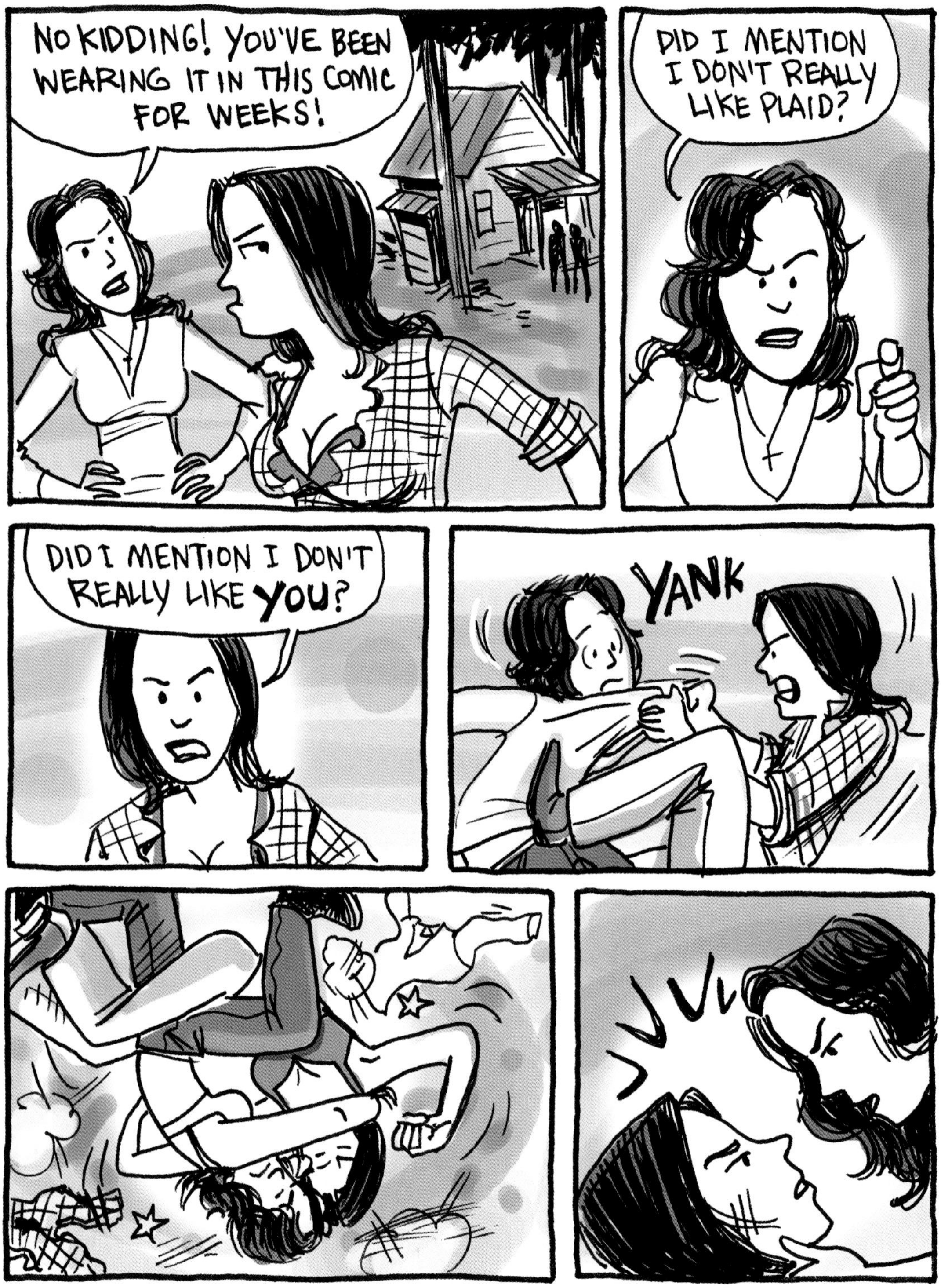
NO KIDDING! YOU'VE BEEN WEARING IT IN THIS COMIC FOR WEEKS!
DID I MENTION I DON'T REALLY LIKE PLAID?
DID I MENTION I DON'T REALLY LIKE YOU?
YANK

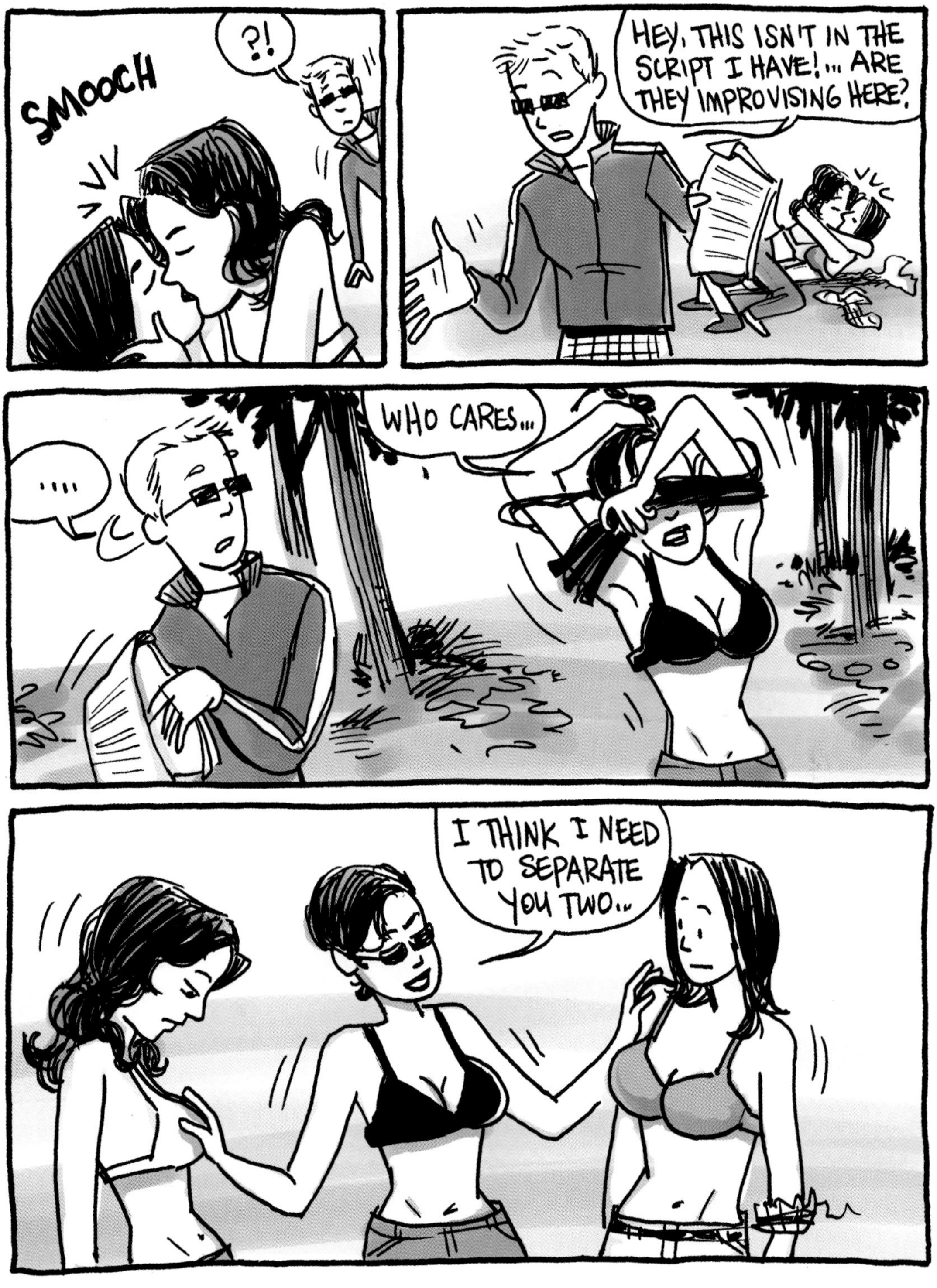
SMOOCH
?!
HEY, THIS ISN'T IN THE SCRIPT I HAVE!... ARE THEY IMPROVISING HERE?
.....
WHO CARES...
I THINK I NEED TO SEPARATE YOU TWO...

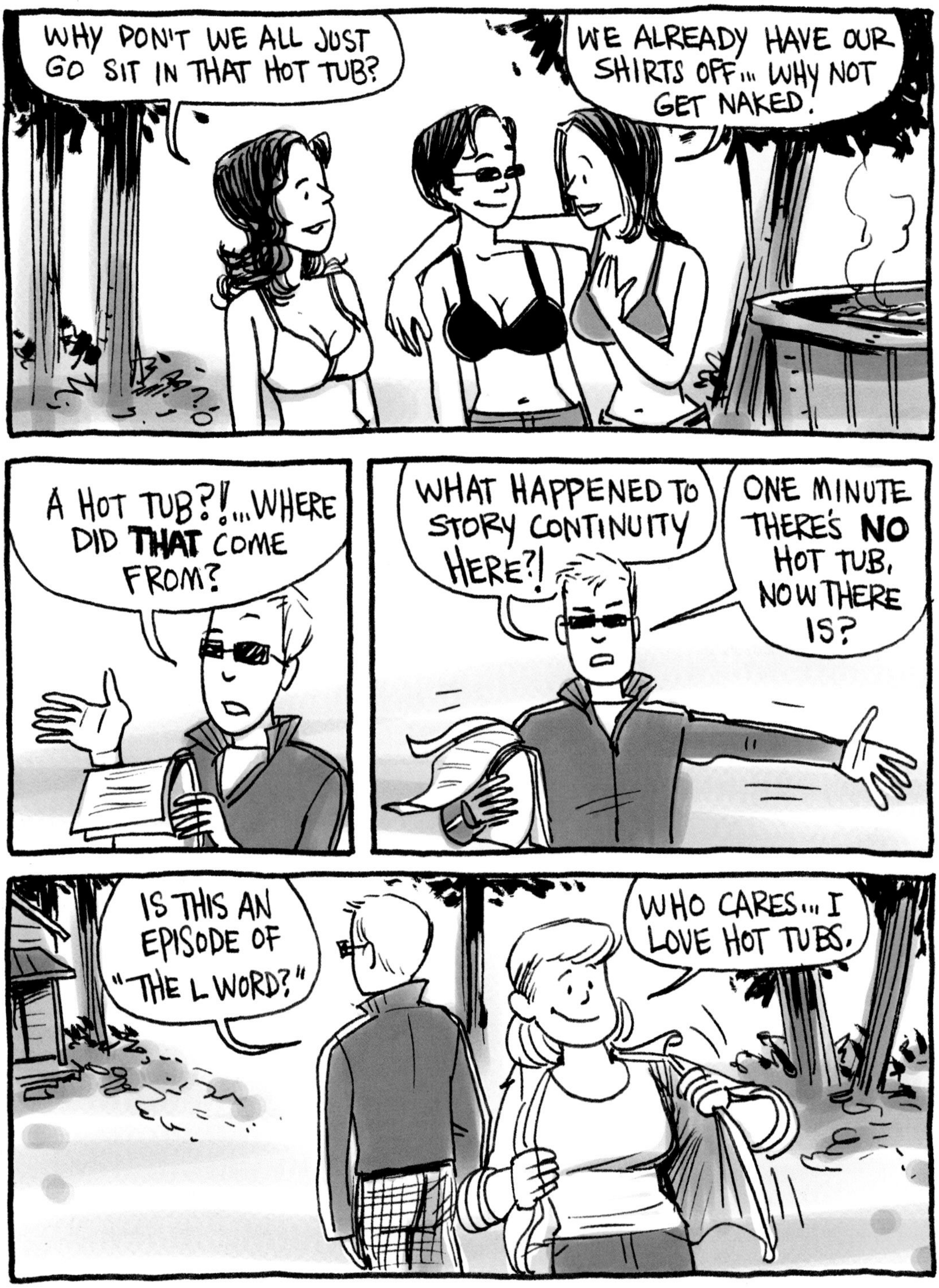
WHY DON'T WE ALL JUST GO SIT IN THAT HOT TUB?
WE ALREADY HAVE OUR SHIRTS OFF... WHY NOT GET NAKED.
A HOT TUB?!... WHERE DID **THAT** COME FROM?
WHAT HAPPENED TO STORY CONTINUITY HERE?!
ONE MINUTE THERE'S **NO** HOT TUB, NOW THERE IS?
IS THIS AN EPISODE OF "THE L WORD?"
WHO CARES... I LOVE HOT TUBS.

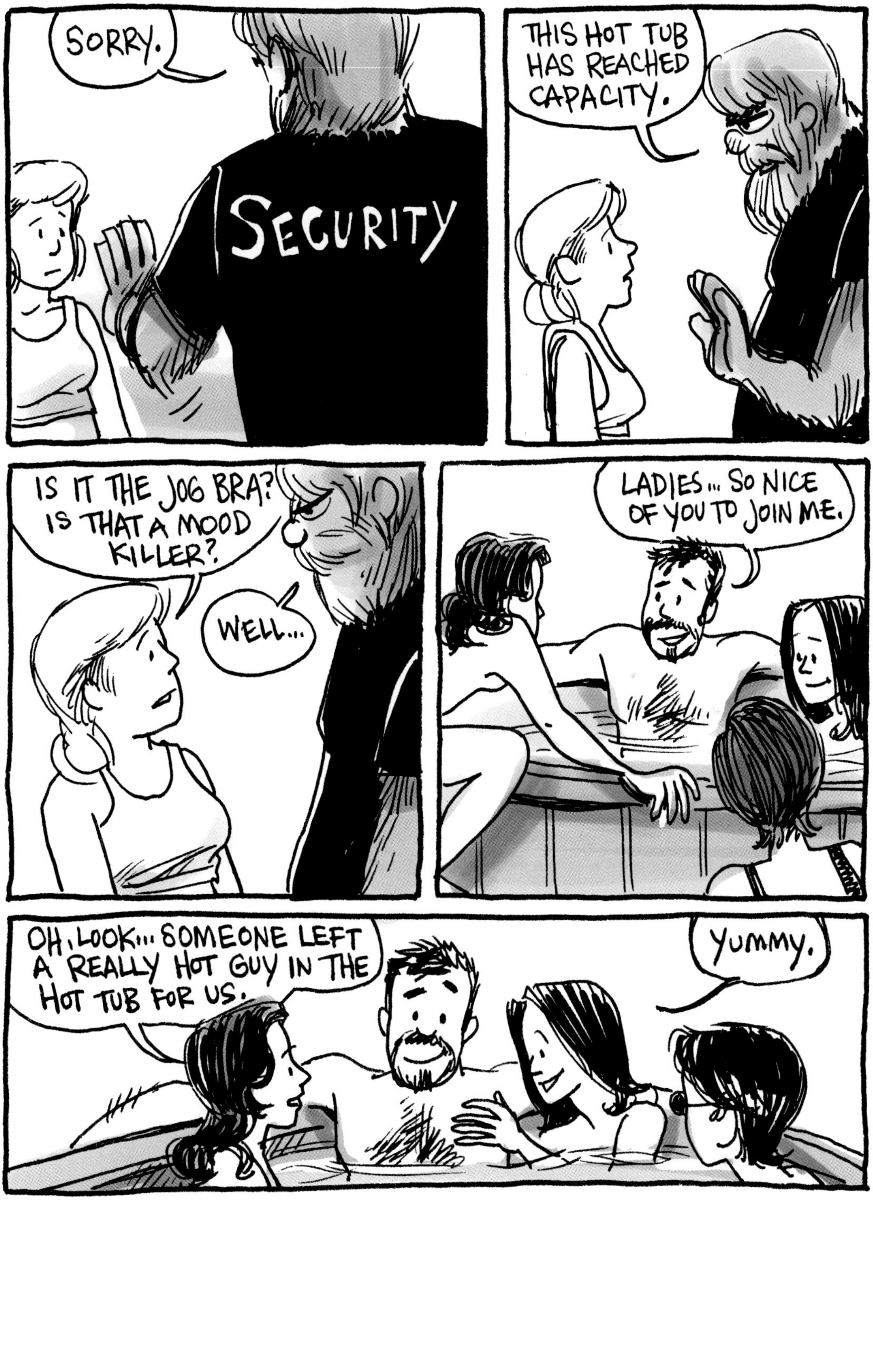
SORRY.
SECURITY
THIS HOT TUB HAS REACHED CAPACITY.
IS IT THE JOG BRA? IS THAT A MOOD KILLER?
WELL...
LADIES... SO NICE OF YOU TO JOIN ME.
OH, LOOK... SOMEONE LEFT A REALLY HOT GUY IN THE HOT TUB FOR US.
YUMMY.

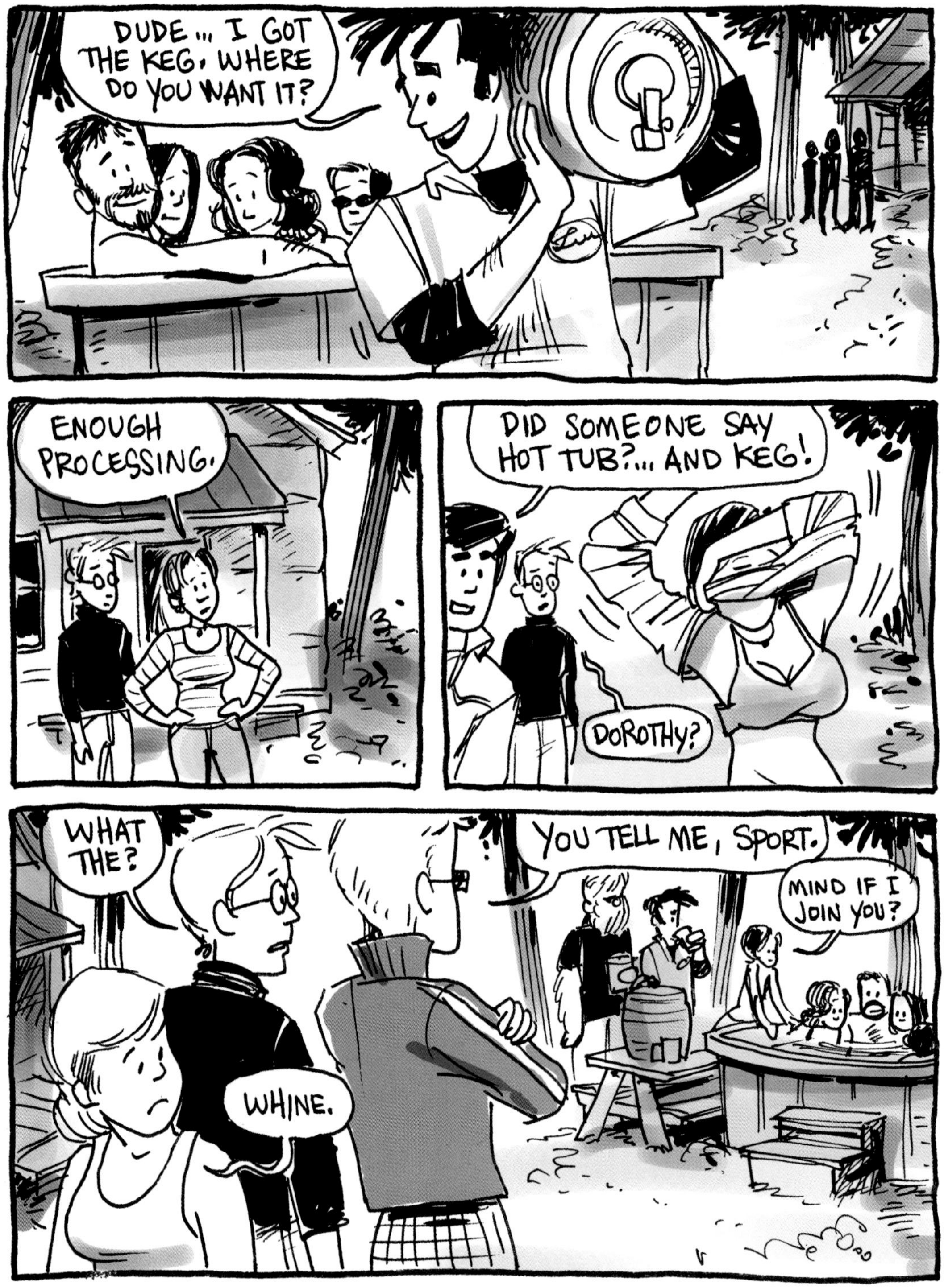
DUDE... I GOT THE KEG. WHERE DO YOU WANT IT?
ENOUGH PROCESSING.
DID SOMEONE SAY HOT TUB?... AND KEG!
DOROTHY?
WHAT THE?
YOU TELL ME, SPORT.
MIND IF I JOIN YOU?
WHINE.

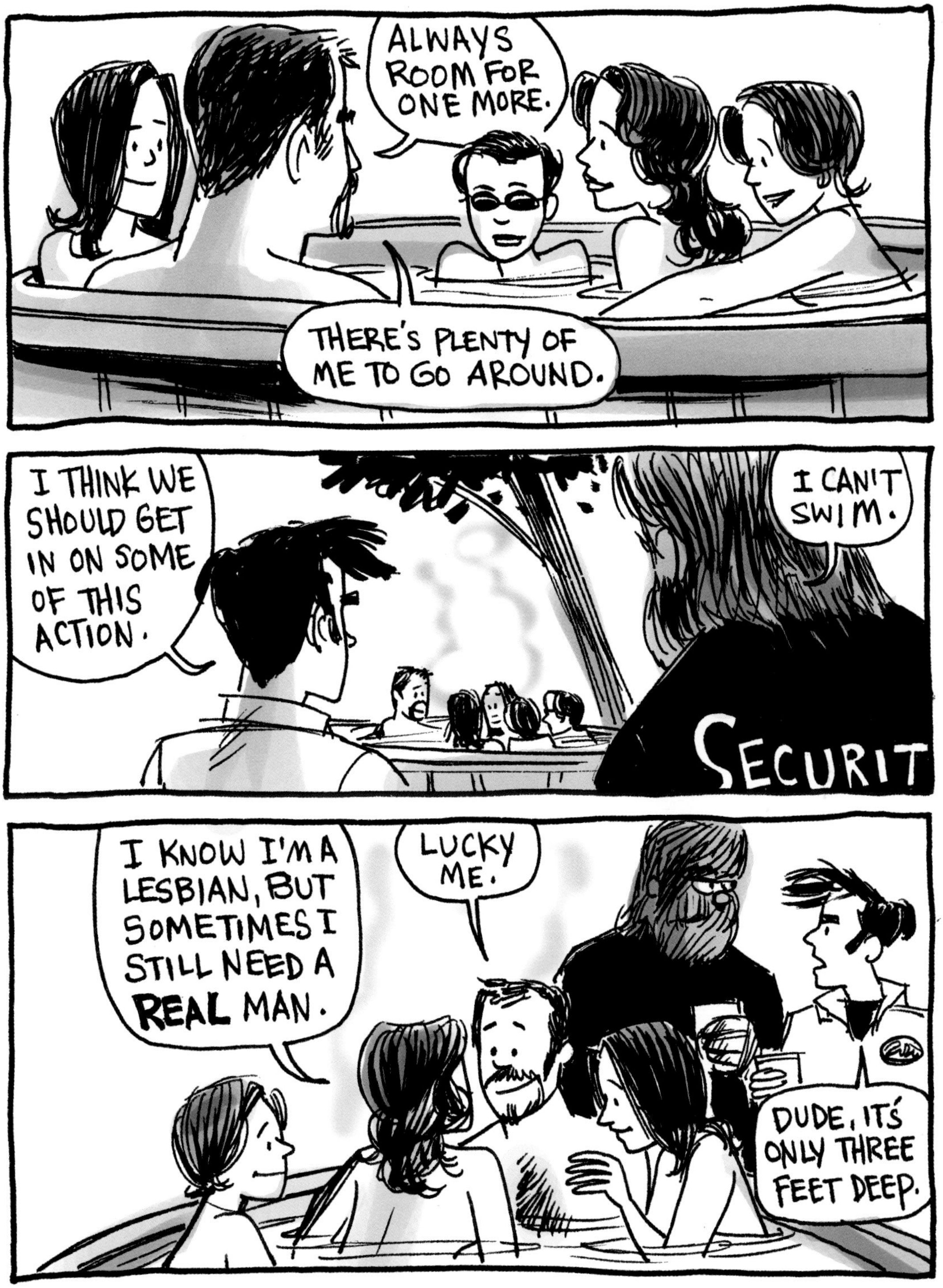
ALWAYS ROOM FOR ONE MORE.
THERE'S PLENTY OF ME TO GO AROUND.
I THINK WE SHOULD GET IN ON SOME OF THIS ACTION.
I CAN'T SWIM.
SECURIT
I KNOW I'M A LESBIAN, BUT SOMETIMES I STILL NEED A REAL MAN.
LUCKY ME.
DUDE, IT'S ONLY THREE FEET DEEP.

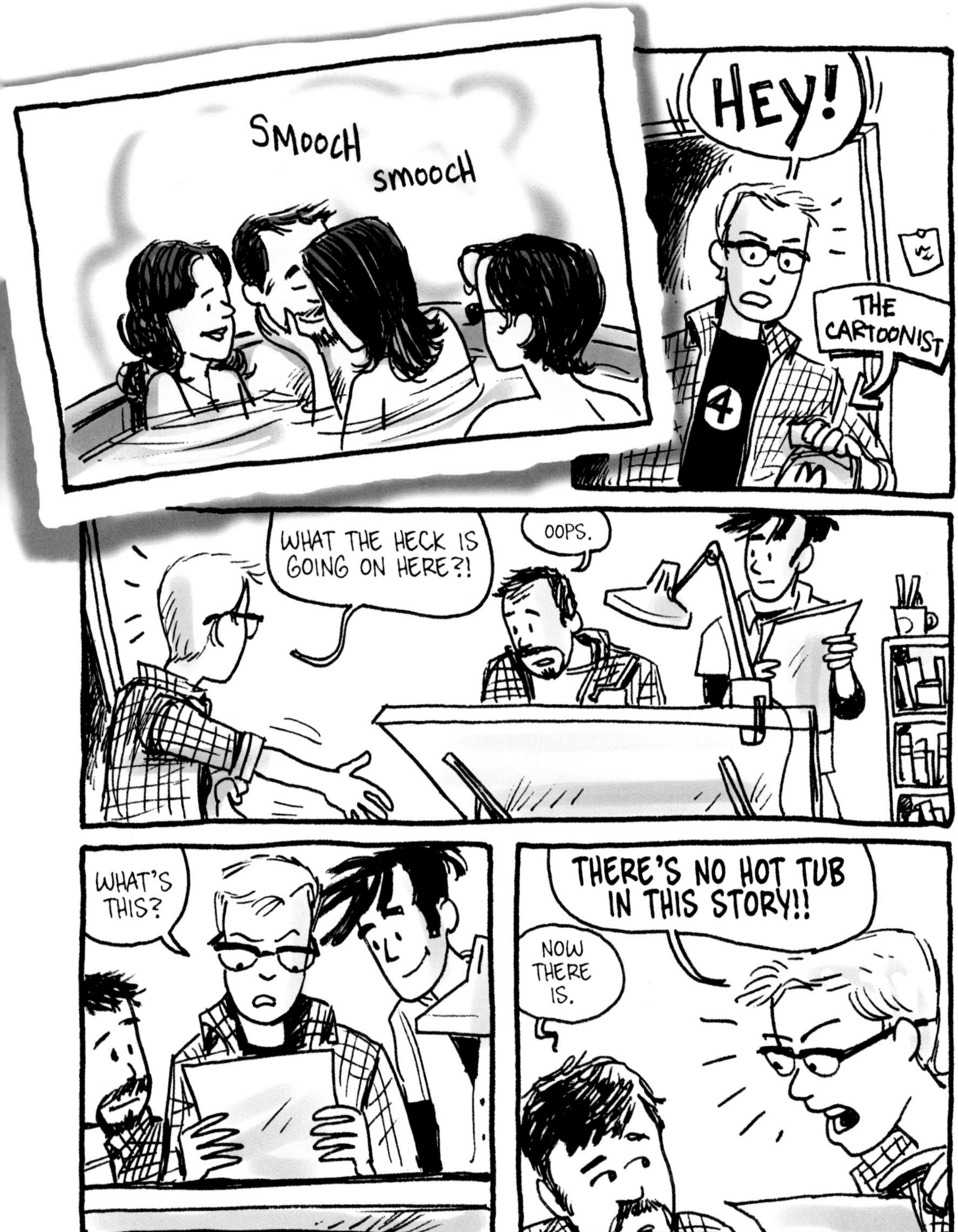
SMOOCH
SMOOCH
HEY!
THE CARTOONIST
4
WHAT THE HECK IS GOING ON HERE?!
OOPS.
WHAT'S THIS?
THERE'S NO HOT TUB IN THIS STORY!!
NOW THERE IS.

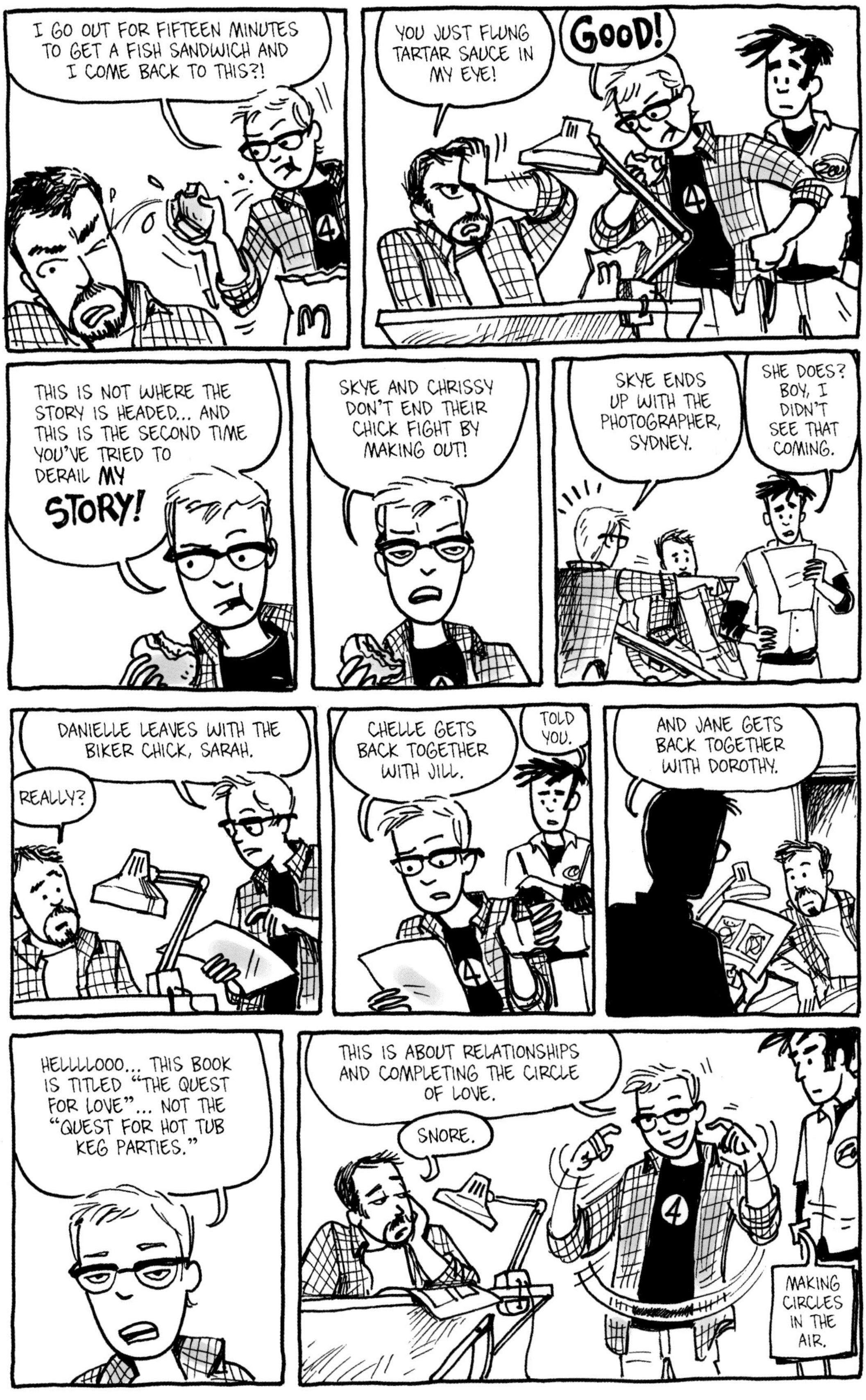

I GO OUT FOR FIFTEEN MINUTES TO GET A FISH SANDWICH AND I COME BACK TO THIS?!
YOU JUST FLUNG TARTAR SAUCE IN MY EYE!
GOOD!
THIS IS NOT WHERE THE STORY IS HEADED... AND THIS IS THE SECOND TIME YOU'VE TRIED TO DERAIL MY STORY!
SKYE AND CHRISSY DON'T END THEIR CHICK FIGHT BY MAKING OUT!
SKYE ENDS UP WITH THE PHOTOGRAPHER, SYDNEY.
SHE DOES? BOY, I DIDN'T SEE THAT COMING.
DANIELLE LEAVES WITH THE BIKER CHICK, SARAH.
REALLY?
CHELLE GETS BACK TOGETHER WITH JILL.
TOLD YOU.
AND JANE GETS BACK TOGETHER WITH DOROTHY.
HELLLLOOO... THIS BOOK IS TITLED "THE QUEST FOR LOVE"... NOT THE "QUEST FOR HOT TUB KEG PARTIES."
THIS IS ABOUT RELATIONSHIPS AND COMPLETING THE CIRCLE OF LOVE.
SNORE.
MAKING CIRCLES IN THE AIR.

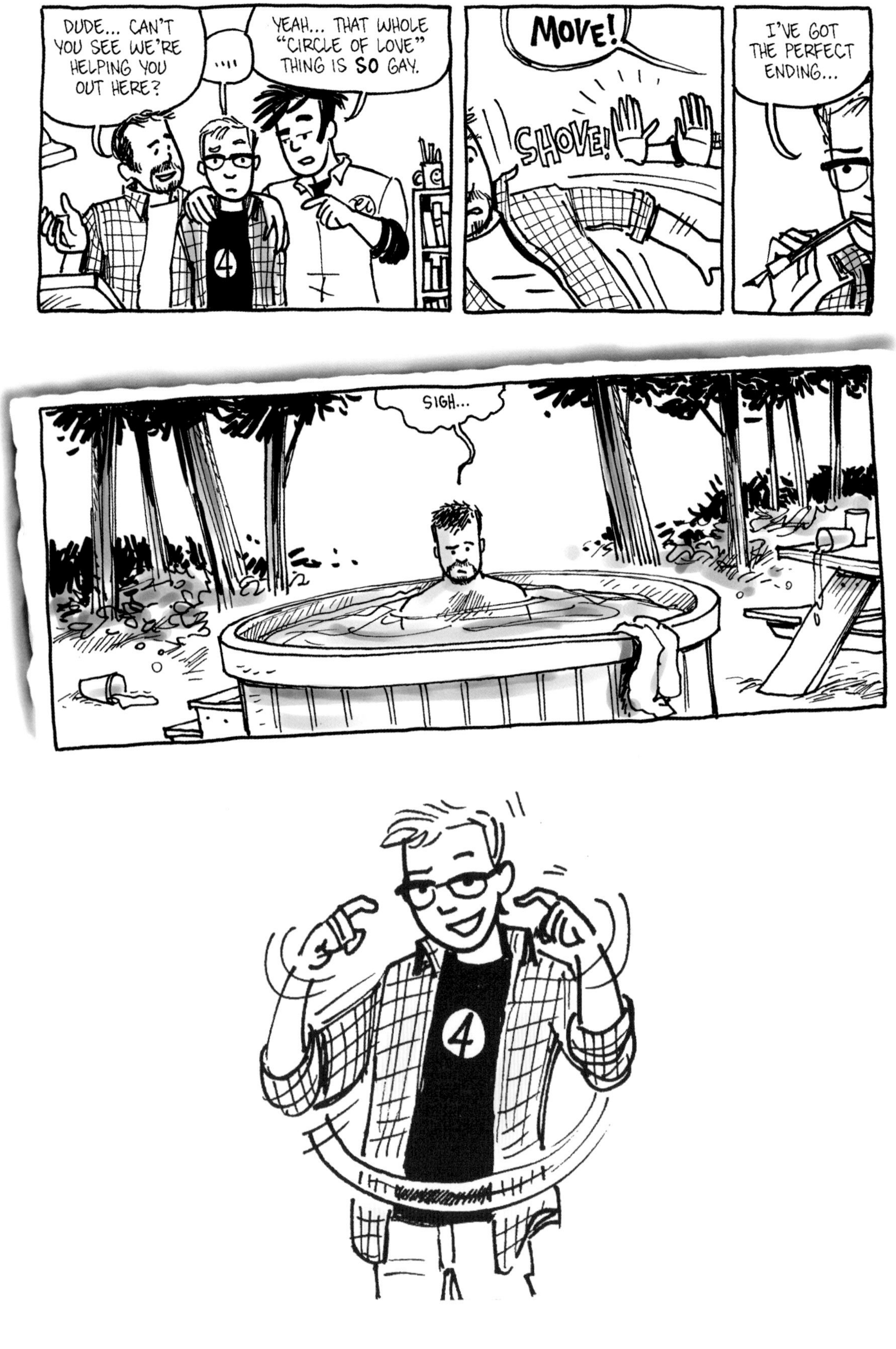
DUDE... CAN'T YOU SEE WE'RE HELPING YOU OUT HERE?
....
YEAH... THAT WHOLE "CIRCLE OF LOVE" THING IS SO GAY.
MOVE!
SHOVE!
I'VE GOT THE PERFECT ENDING...
SIGH...

EPILOGUE

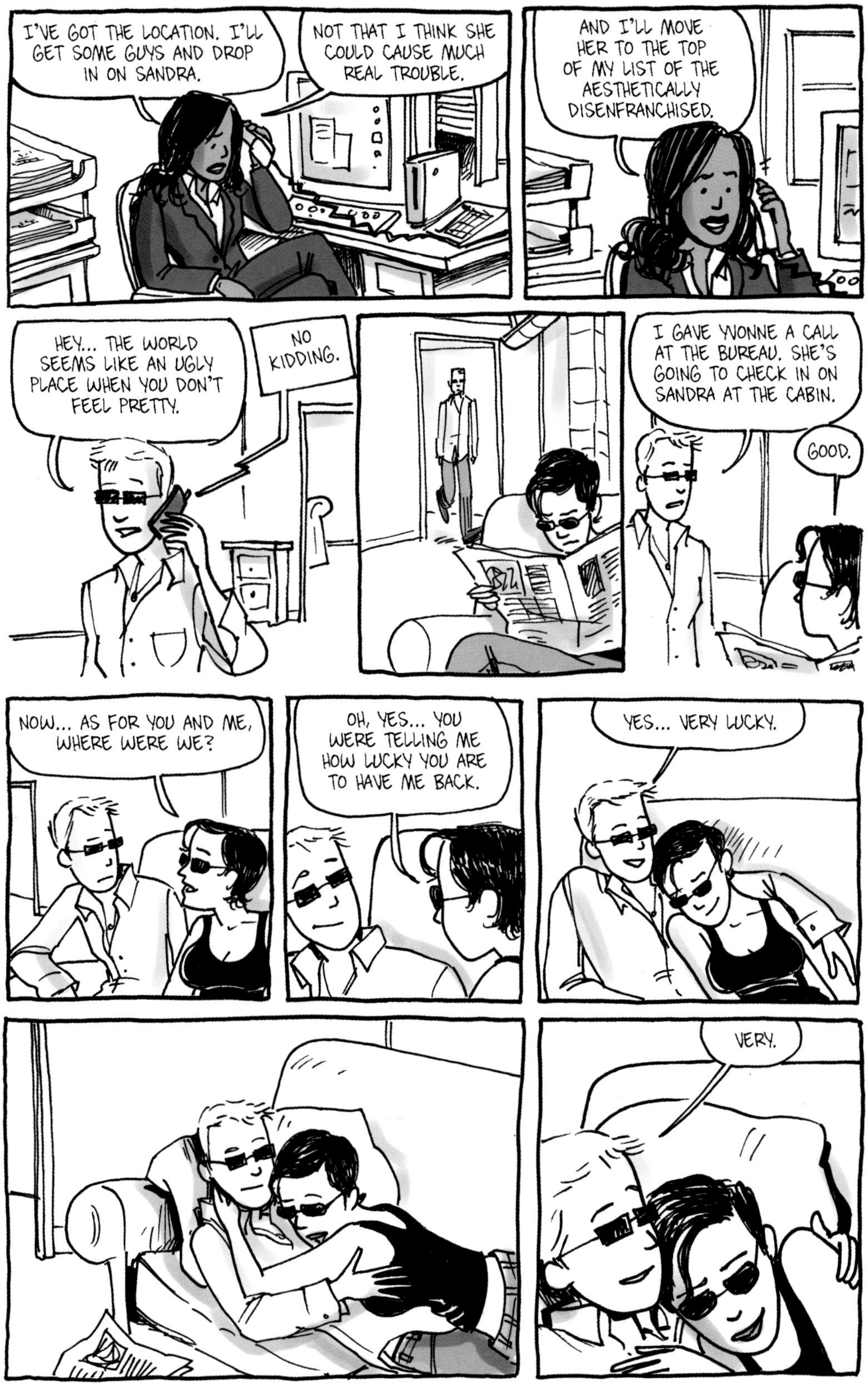
I'VE GOT THE LOCATION. I'LL GET SOME GUYS AND DROP IN ON SANDRA.
NOT THAT I THINK SHE COULD CAUSE MUCH REAL TROUBLE.
AND I'LL MOVE HER TO THE TOP OF MY LIST OF THE AESTHETICALLY DISENFRANCHISED.
HEY... THE WORLD SEEMS LIKE AN UGLY PLACE WHEN YOU DON'T FEEL PRETTY.
NO KIDDING.
I GAVE YVONNE A CALL AT THE BUREAU. SHE'S GOING TO CHECK IN ON SANDRA AT THE CABIN.
GOOD.
NOW... AS FOR YOU AND ME, WHERE WERE WE?
OH, YES... YOU WERE TELLING ME HOW LUCKY YOU ARE TO HAVE ME BACK.
YES... VERY LUCKY.
VERY.

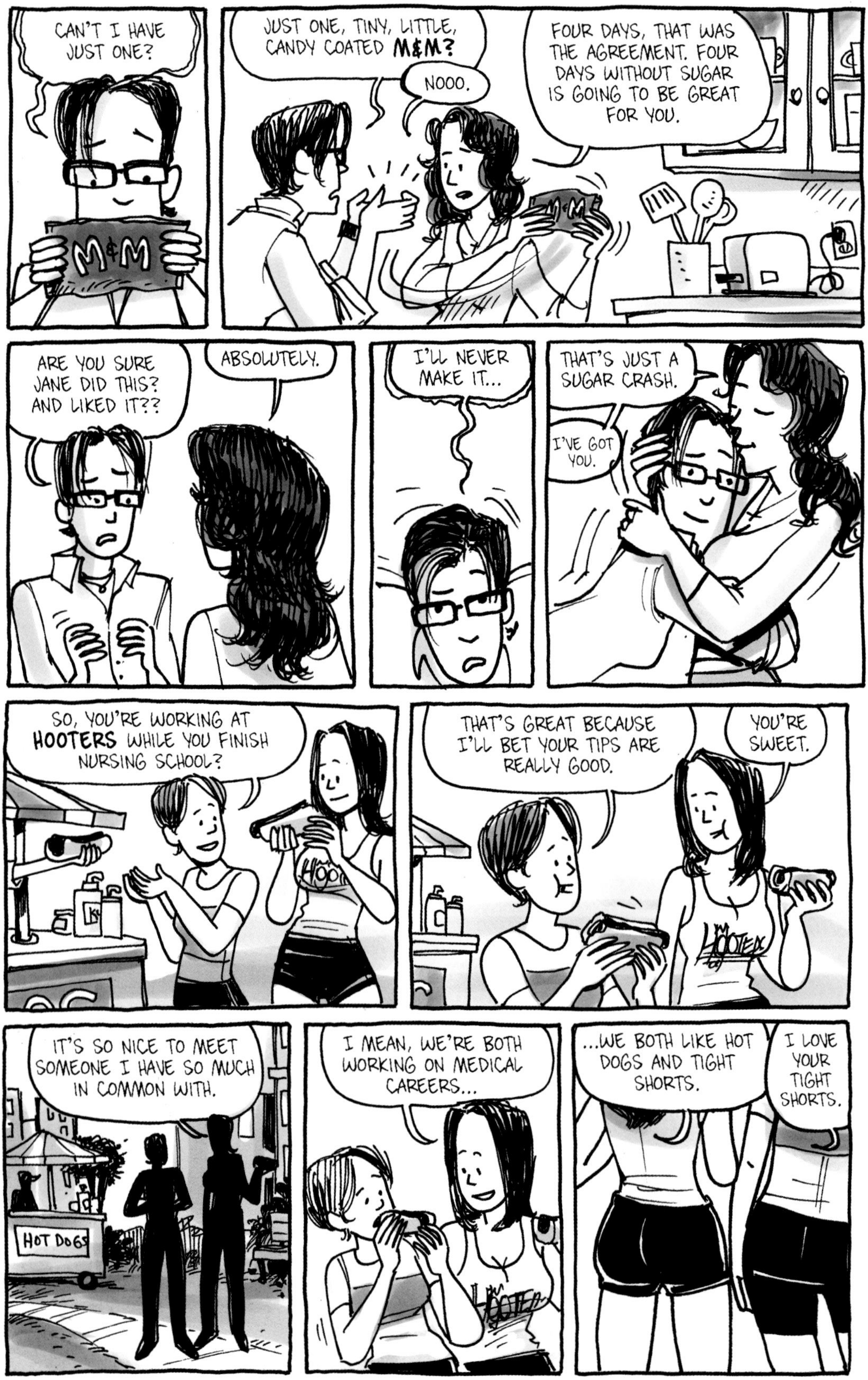
CAN'T I HAVE JUST ONE?
JUST ONE, TINY, LITTLE, CANDY COATED M&M?
NOOO.
FOUR DAYS, THAT WAS THE AGREEMENT. FOUR DAYS WITHOUT SUGAR IS GOING TO BE GREAT FOR YOU.
M&M
ARE YOU SURE JANE DID THIS? AND LIKED IT??
ABSOLUTELY.
I'LL NEVER MAKE IT...
THAT'S JUST A SUGAR CRASH.
I'VE GOT YOU.
SO, YOU'RE WORKING AT HOOTERS WHILE YOU FINISH NURSING SCHOOL?
THAT'S GREAT BECAUSE I'LL BET YOUR TIPS ARE REALLY GOOD.
YOU'RE SWEET.
IT'S SO NICE TO MEET SOMEONE I HAVE SO MUCH IN COMMON WITH.
HOT DOGS
I MEAN, WE'RE BOTH WORKING ON MEDICAL CAREERS...
...WE BOTH LIKE HOT DOGS AND TIGHT SHORTS.
I LOVE YOUR TIGHT SHORTS.

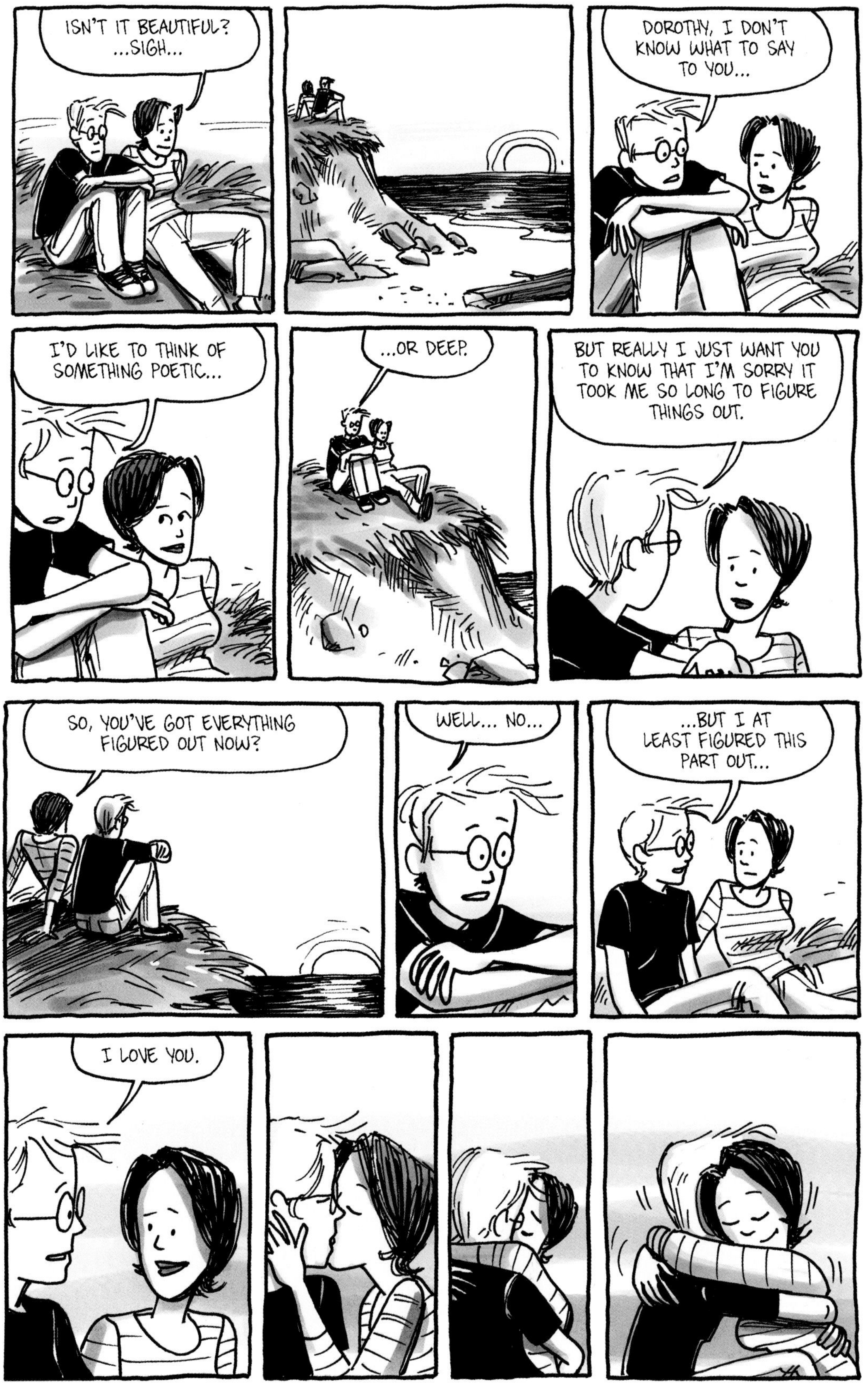
ISN'T IT BEAUTIFUL? ...SIGH...
DOROTHY, I DON'T KNOW WHAT TO SAY TO YOU...
I'D LIKE TO THINK OF SOMETHING POETIC...
...OR DEEP.
BUT REALLY I JUST WANT YOU TO KNOW THAT I'M SORRY IT TOOK ME SO LONG TO FIGURE THINGS OUT.
SO, YOU'VE GOT EVERYTHING FIGURED OUT NOW?
WELL... NO...
...BUT I AT LEAST FIGURED THIS PART OUT...
I LOVE YOU.

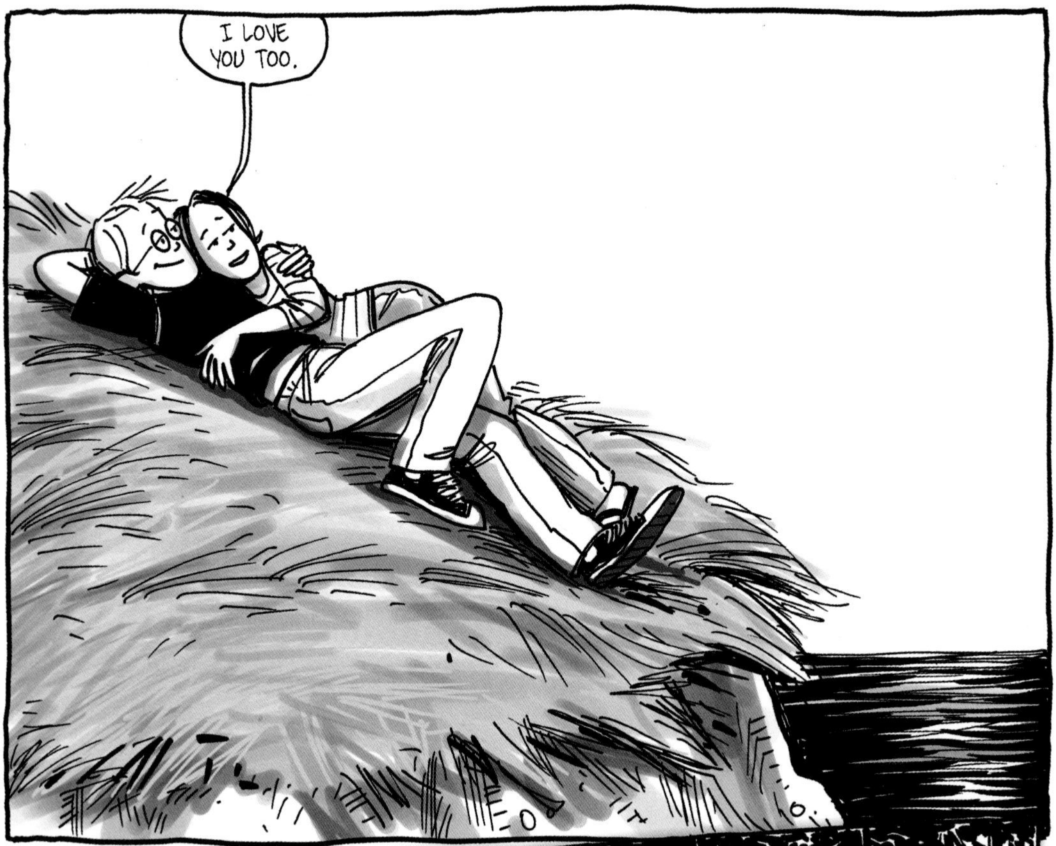
I LOVE YOU TOO.

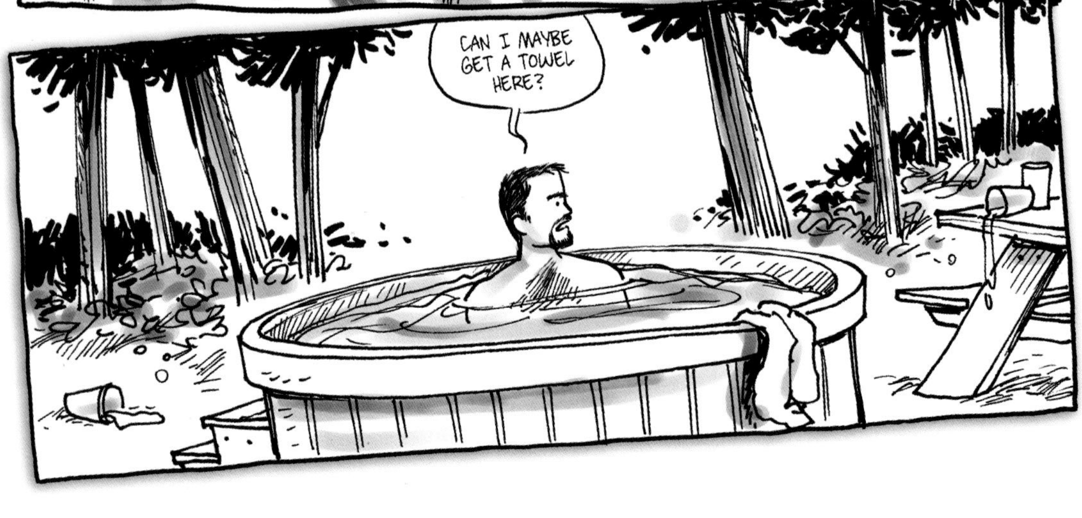
CAN I MAYBE GET A TOWEL HERE?

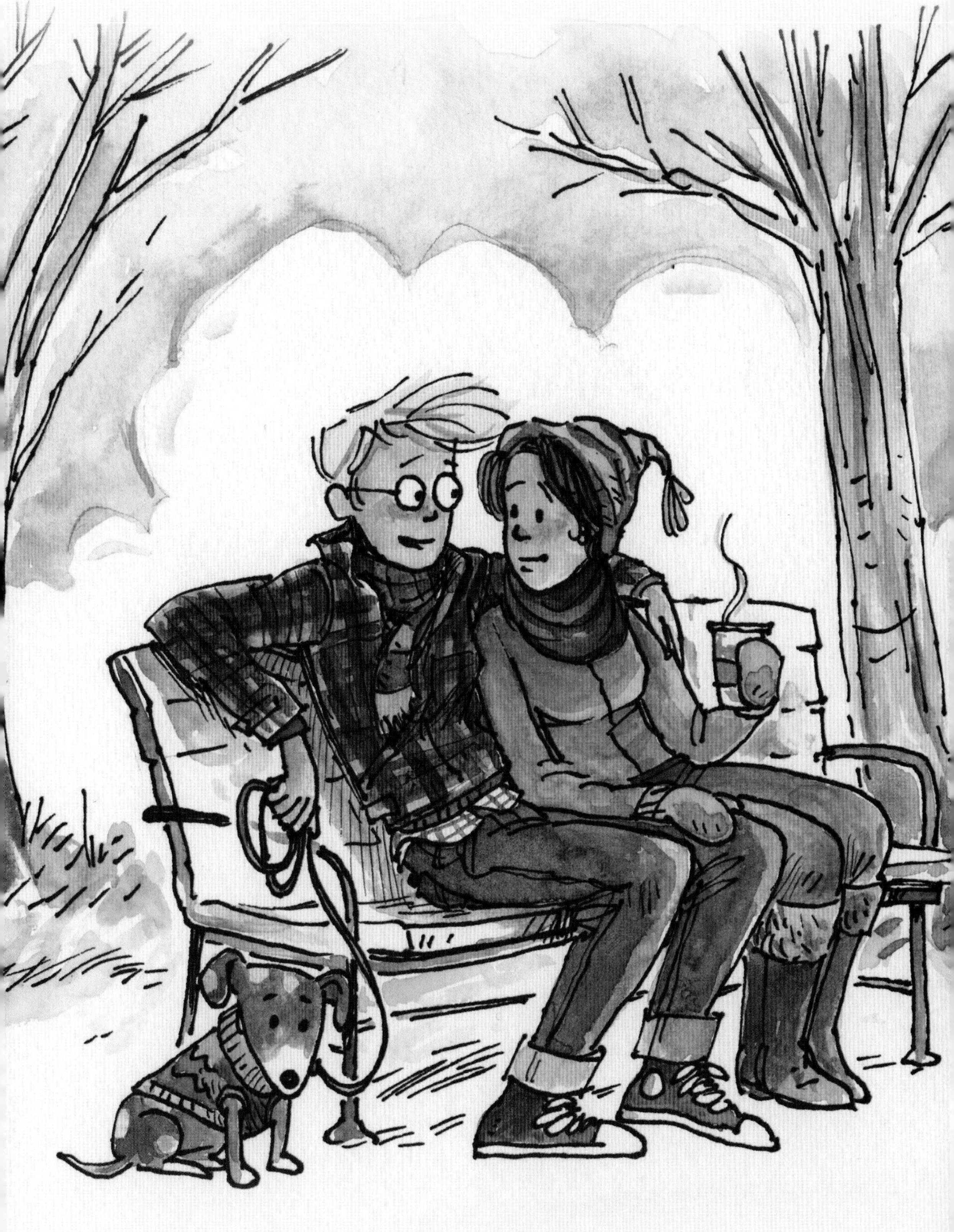

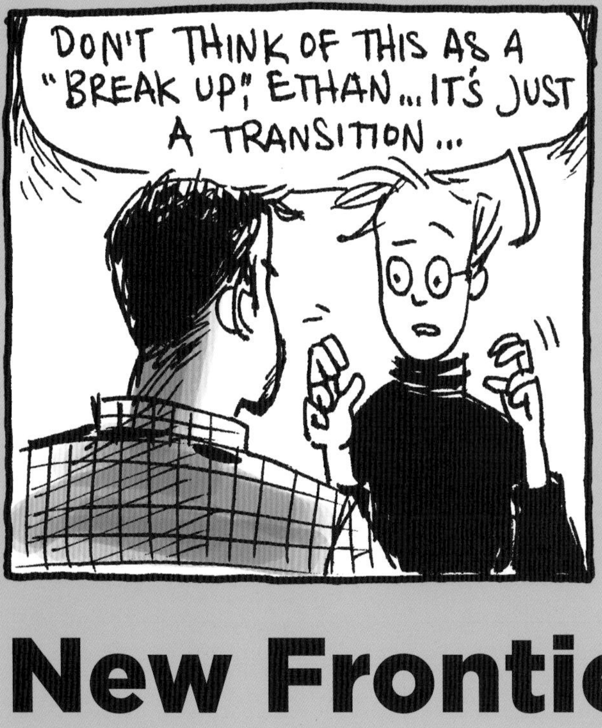
DON'T THINK OF THIS AS A "BREAK UP," ETHAN... IT'S JUST A TRANSITION...

New Frontier

Ethan and Jane aren't a couple, but even friends break up sometimes. It almost seems like Jane is growing up and becoming more mature, but...this is Jane we're talking about. Navigating a live-in girlfriend and a blended family of pets may be too much for her.

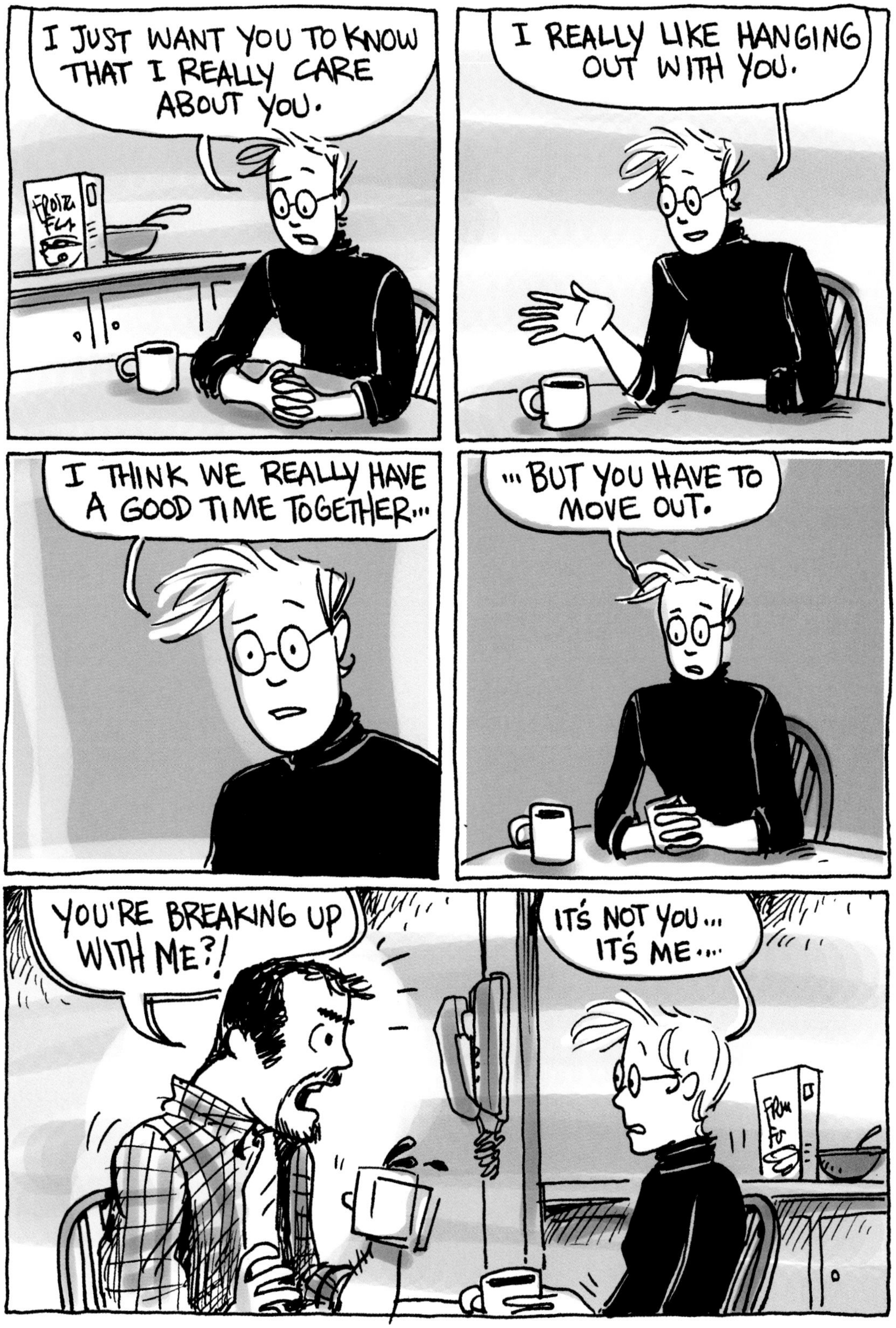
I JUST WANT YOU TO KNOW THAT I REALLY CARE ABOUT YOU.
I REALLY LIKE HANGING OUT WITH YOU.
I THINK WE REALLY HAVE A GOOD TIME TOGETHER...
...BUT YOU HAVE TO MOVE OUT.
YOU'RE BREAKING UP WITH ME?!
IT'S NOT YOU... IT'S ME....

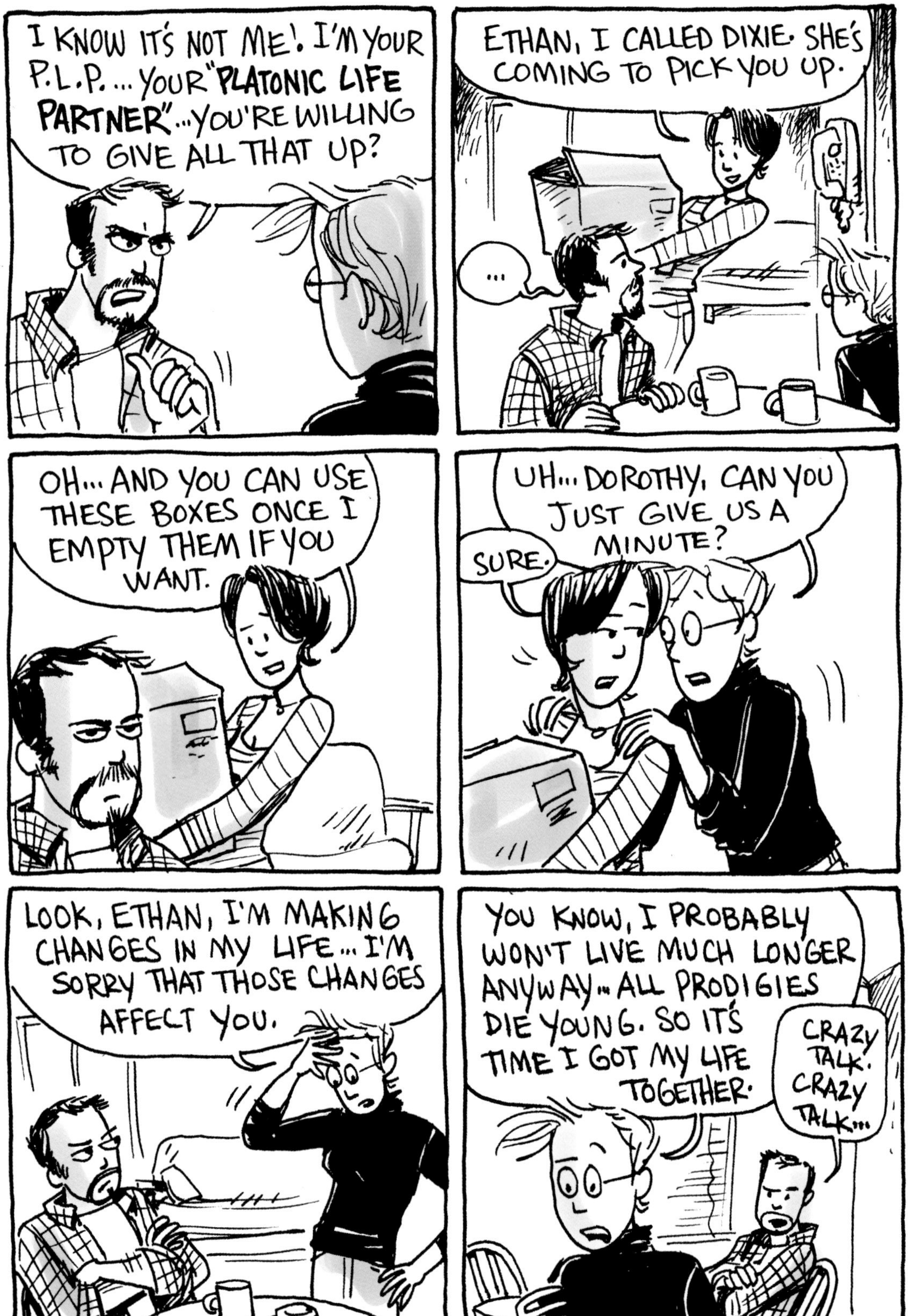
I KNOW IT'S NOT ME! I'M YOUR P.L.P. ... YOUR "PLATONIC LIFE PARTNER"... YOU'RE WILLING TO GIVE ALL THAT UP?
ETHAN, I CALLED DIXIE. SHE'S COMING TO PICK YOU UP.
...
OH... AND YOU CAN USE THESE BOXES ONCE I EMPTY THEM IF YOU WANT.
UH... DOROTHY, CAN YOU JUST GIVE US A MINUTE?
SURE.
LOOK, ETHAN, I'M MAKING CHANGES IN MY LIFE... I'M SORRY THAT THOSE CHANGES AFFECT YOU.
YOU KNOW, I PROBABLY WON'T LIVE MUCH LONGER ANYWAY... ALL PRODIGIES DIE YOUNG. SO IT'S TIME I GOT MY LIFE TOGETHER.
CRAZY TALK. CRAZY TALK...

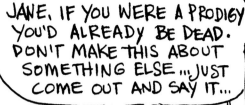

JANE, IF YOU WERE A PRODIGY YOU'D ALREADY BE DEAD. DON'T MAKE THIS ABOUT SOMETHING ELSE ... JUST COME OUT AND SAY IT...

... OUR RELATIONSHIP HAS RUN ITS COURSE. WE'VE OUTGROWN EACH OTHER.

DON'T THINK OF THIS AS A "BREAK UP", ETHAN ... IT'S JUST A TRANSITION ...

... OUR RELATIONSHIP IS EVOLVING.

GEEZ! THAT IS **SUCH** A LESBIONIC THING TO SAY!

HOW ABOUT THIS SCENARIO? YOU DIDN'T ASK ME TO LEAVE, I **CHOSE** TO LEAVE BECAUSE YOU'RE **CRAZY!**

AFTER ALL THIS TIME TOGETHER HOW COULD I NOT HAVE KNOWN YOU WERE SUCH A CHICK!

HEY!

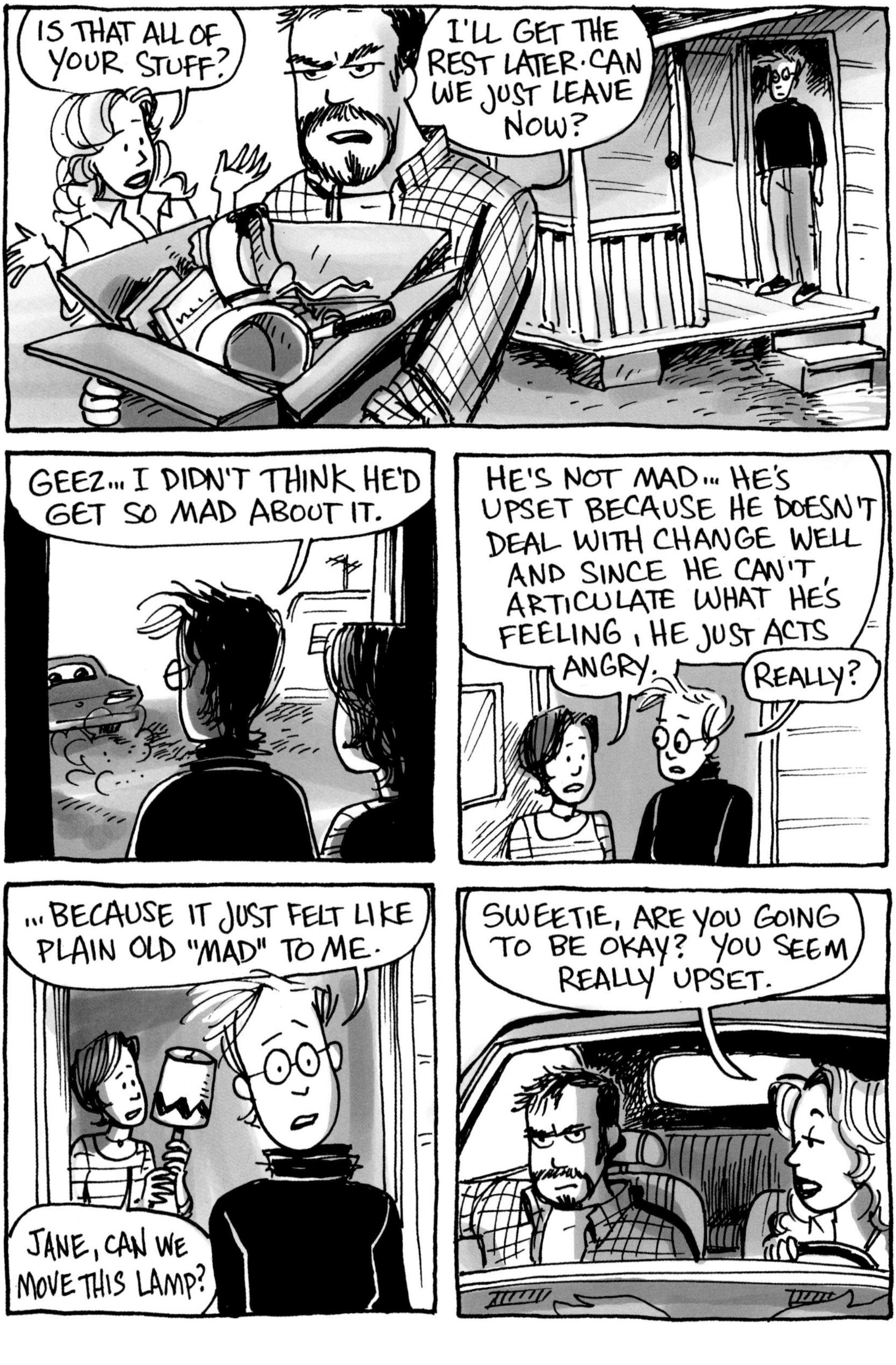
IS THAT ALL OF YOUR STUFF?
I'LL GET THE REST LATER. CAN WE JUST LEAVE NOW?
GEEZ... I DIDN'T THINK HE'D GET SO MAD ABOUT IT.
HE'S NOT MAD... HE'S UPSET BECAUSE HE DOESN'T DEAL WITH CHANGE WELL AND SINCE HE CAN'T ARTICULATE WHAT HE'S FEELING, HE JUST ACTS ANGRY.
REALLY?
...BECAUSE IT JUST FELT LIKE PLAIN OLD "MAD" TO ME.
JANE, CAN WE MOVE THIS LAMP?
SWEETIE, ARE YOU GOING TO BE OKAY? YOU SEEM REALLY UPSET.

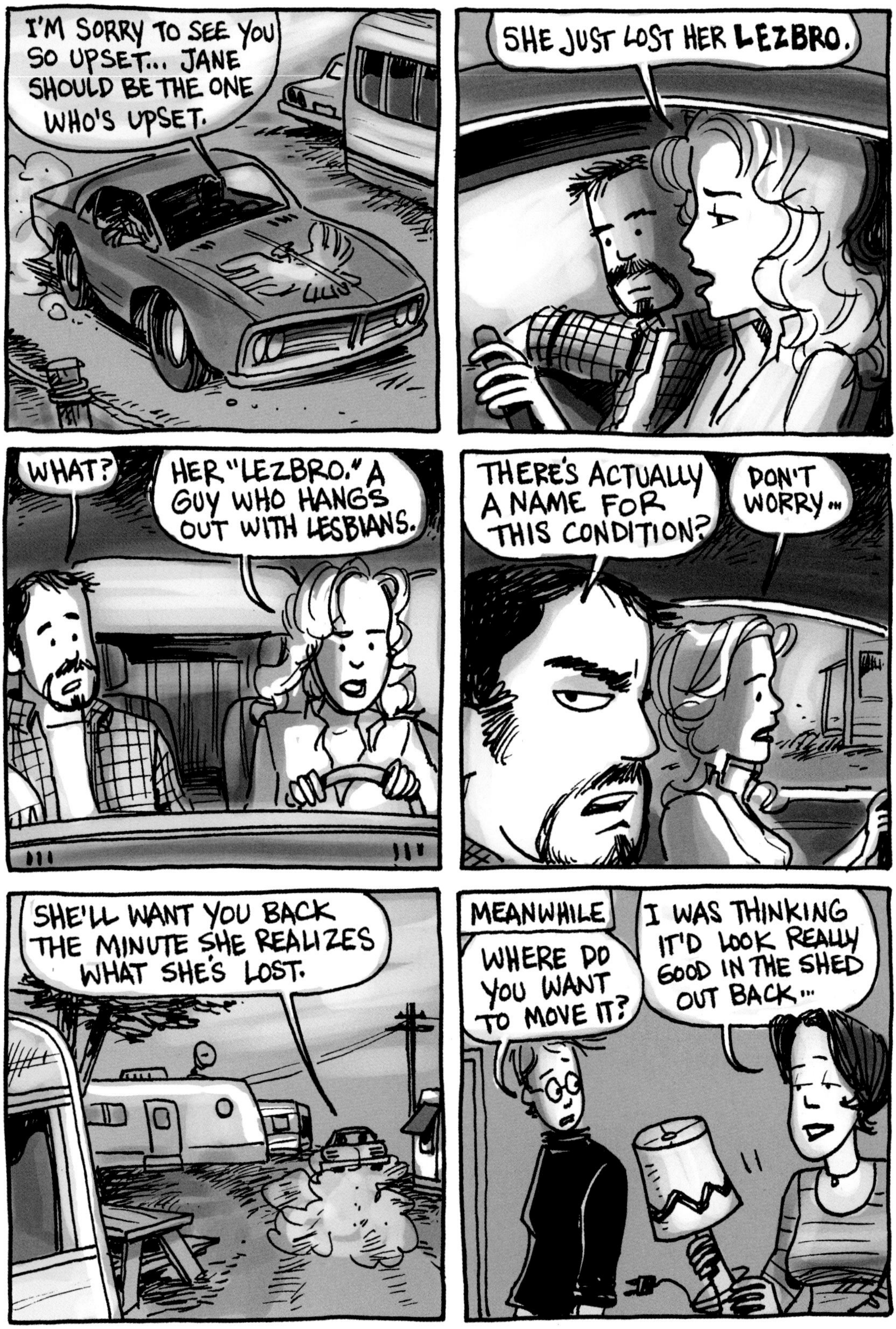
I'M SORRY TO SEE YOU SO UPSET... JANE SHOULD BE THE ONE WHO'S UPSET.
SHE JUST LOST HER **LEZBRO.**
WHAT?
HER "LEZBRO." A GUY WHO HANGS OUT WITH LESBIANS.
THERE'S ACTUALLY A NAME FOR THIS CONDITION?
DON'T WORRY...
SHE'LL WANT YOU BACK THE MINUTE SHE REALIZES WHAT SHE'S LOST.
MEANWHILE
WHERE DO YOU WANT TO MOVE IT?
I WAS THINKING IT'D LOOK REALLY GOOD IN THE SHED OUT BACK...

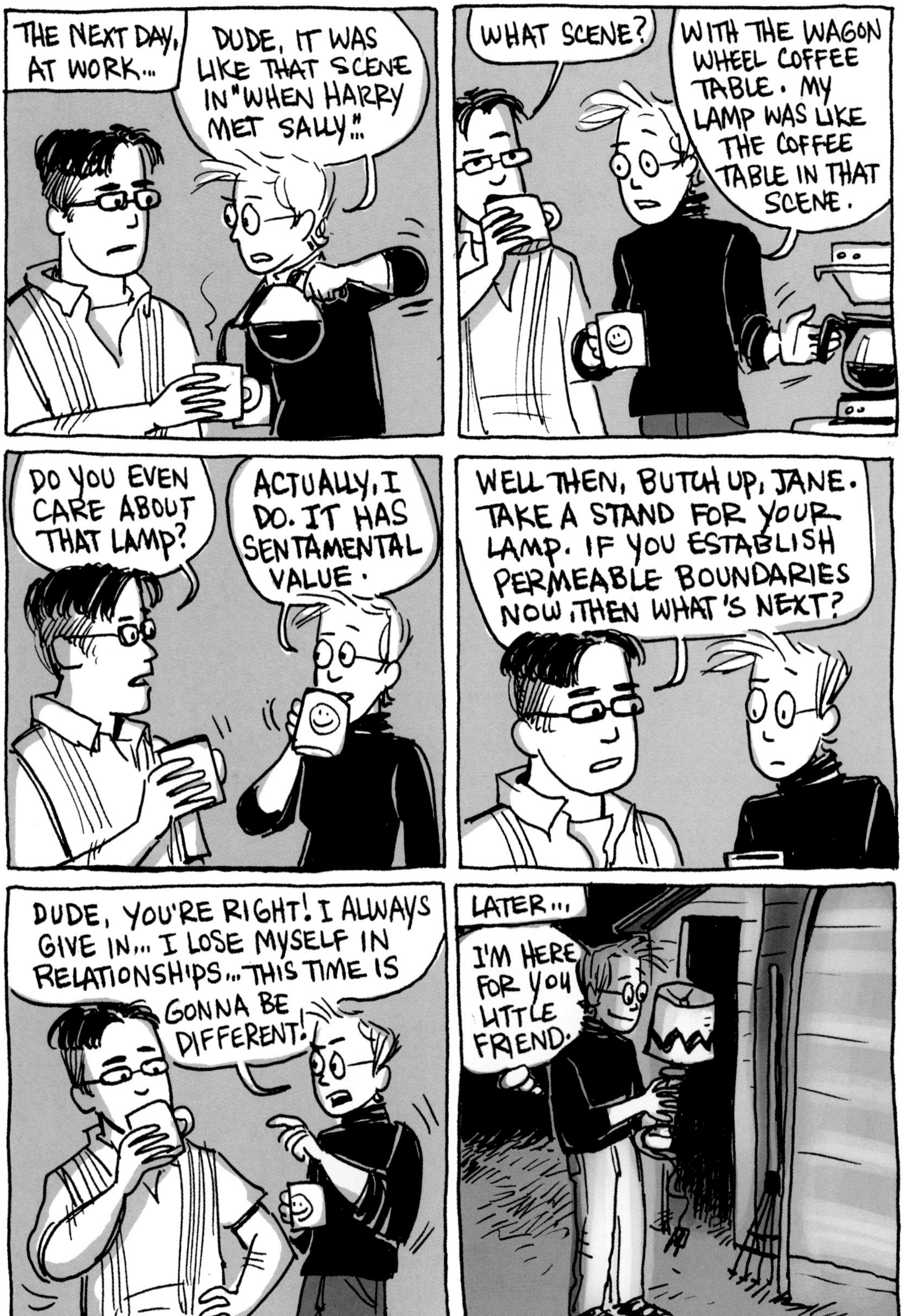
THE NEXT DAY, AT WORK...
DUDE, IT WAS LIKE THAT SCENE IN "WHEN HARRY MET SALLY."...
WHAT SCENE?
WITH THE WAGON WHEEL COFFEE TABLE. MY LAMP WAS LIKE THE COFFEE TABLE IN THAT SCENE.
DO YOU EVEN CARE ABOUT THAT LAMP?
ACTUALLY, I DO. IT HAS SENTAMENTAL VALUE.
WELL THEN, BUTCH UP, JANE. TAKE A STAND FOR YOUR LAMP. IF YOU ESTABLISH PERMEABLE BOUNDARIES NOW, THEN WHAT'S NEXT?
DUDE, YOU'RE RIGHT! I ALWAYS GIVE IN... I LOSE MYSELF IN RELATIONSHIPS... THIS TIME IS GONNA BE DIFFERENT!
LATER...
I'M HERE FOR YOU LITTLE FRIEND.

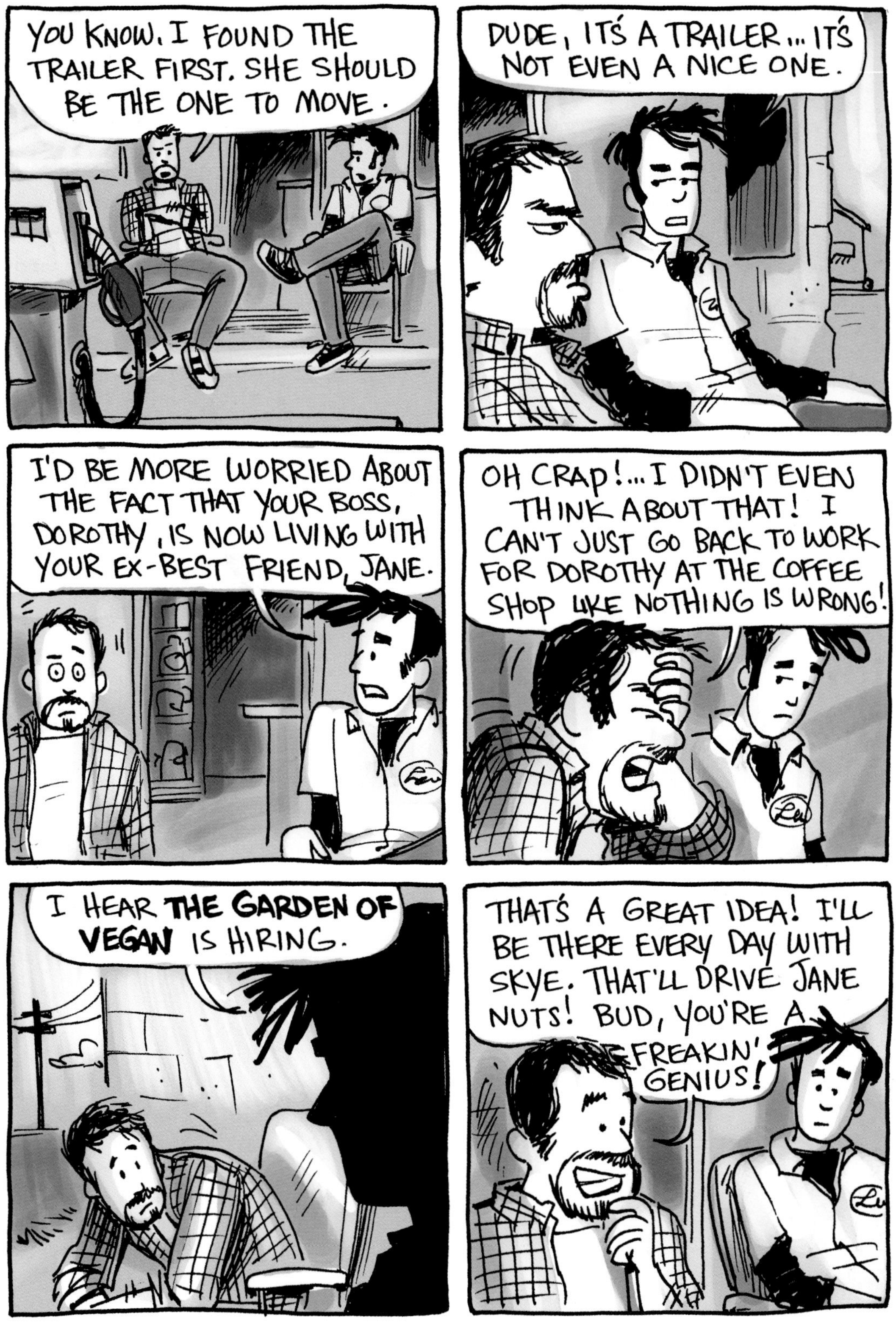
YOU KNOW. I FOUND THE TRAILER FIRST. SHE SHOULD BE THE ONE TO MOVE.
DUDE, IT'S A TRAILER... IT'S NOT EVEN A NICE ONE.
I'D BE MORE WORRIED ABOUT THE FACT THAT YOUR BOSS, DOROTHY, IS NOW LIVING WITH YOUR EX-BEST FRIEND, JANE.
OH CRAP!... I DIDN'T EVEN THINK ABOUT THAT! I CAN'T JUST GO BACK TO WORK FOR DOROTHY AT THE COFFEE SHOP LIKE NOTHING IS WRONG!
I HEAR **THE GARDEN OF VEGAN** IS HIRING.
THAT'S A GREAT IDEA! I'LL BE THERE EVERY DAY WITH SKYE. THAT'LL DRIVE JANE NUTS! BUD, YOU'RE A FREAKIN' GENIUS!

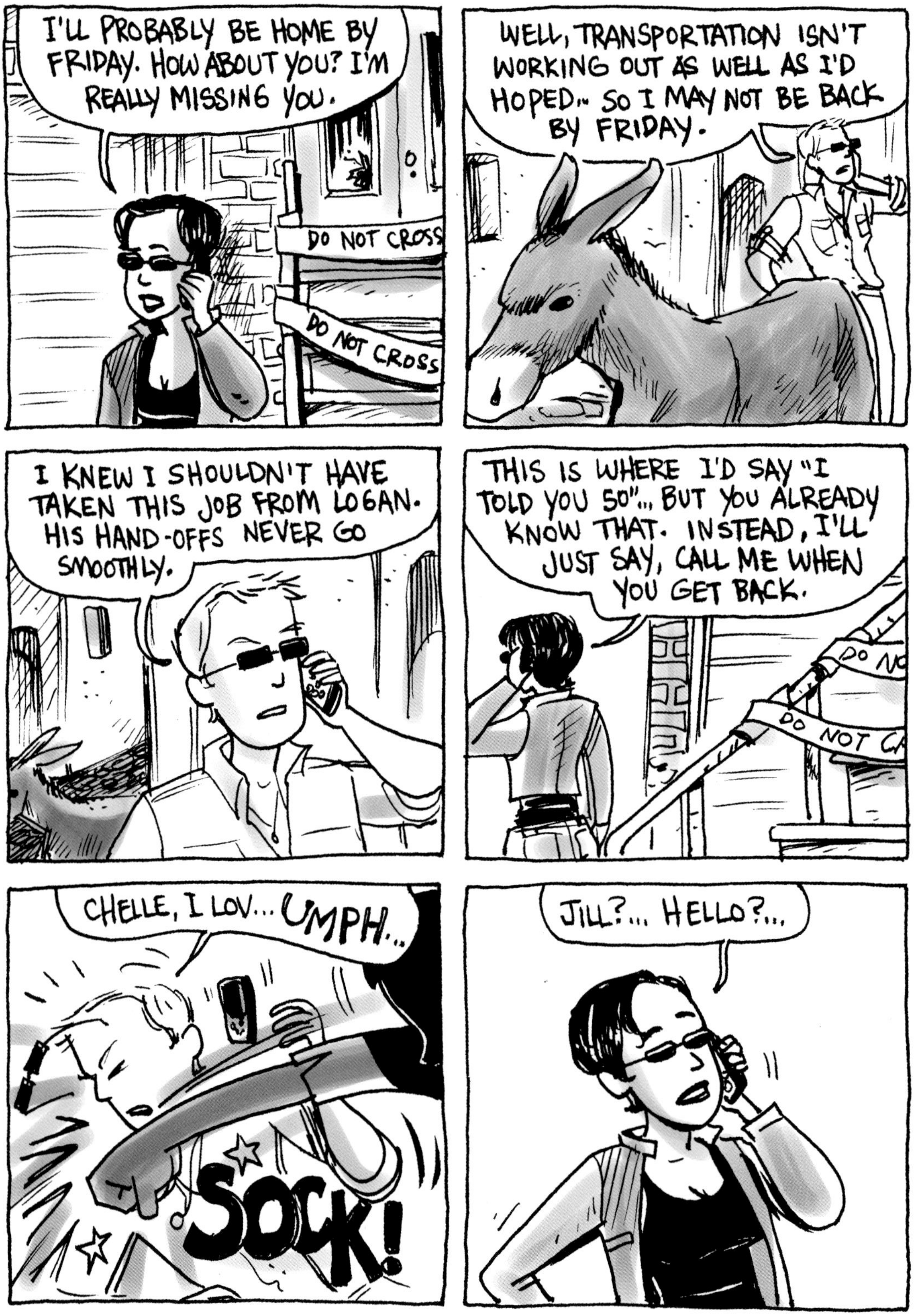

I'LL PROBABLY BE HOME BY FRIDAY. HOW ABOUT YOU? I'M REALLY MISSING YOU.
DO NOT CROSS
DO NOT CROSS
WELL, TRANSPORTATION ISN'T WORKING OUT AS WELL AS I'D HOPED... SO I MAY NOT BE BACK BY FRIDAY.
I KNEW I SHOULDN'T HAVE TAKEN THIS JOB FROM LOGAN. HIS HAND-OFFS NEVER GO SMOOTHLY.
THIS IS WHERE I'D SAY "I TOLD YOU SO"... BUT YOU ALREADY KNOW THAT. INSTEAD, I'LL JUST SAY, CALL ME WHEN YOU GET BACK.
CHELLE, I LOV... UMPH...
SOCK!
JILL?... HELLO?...

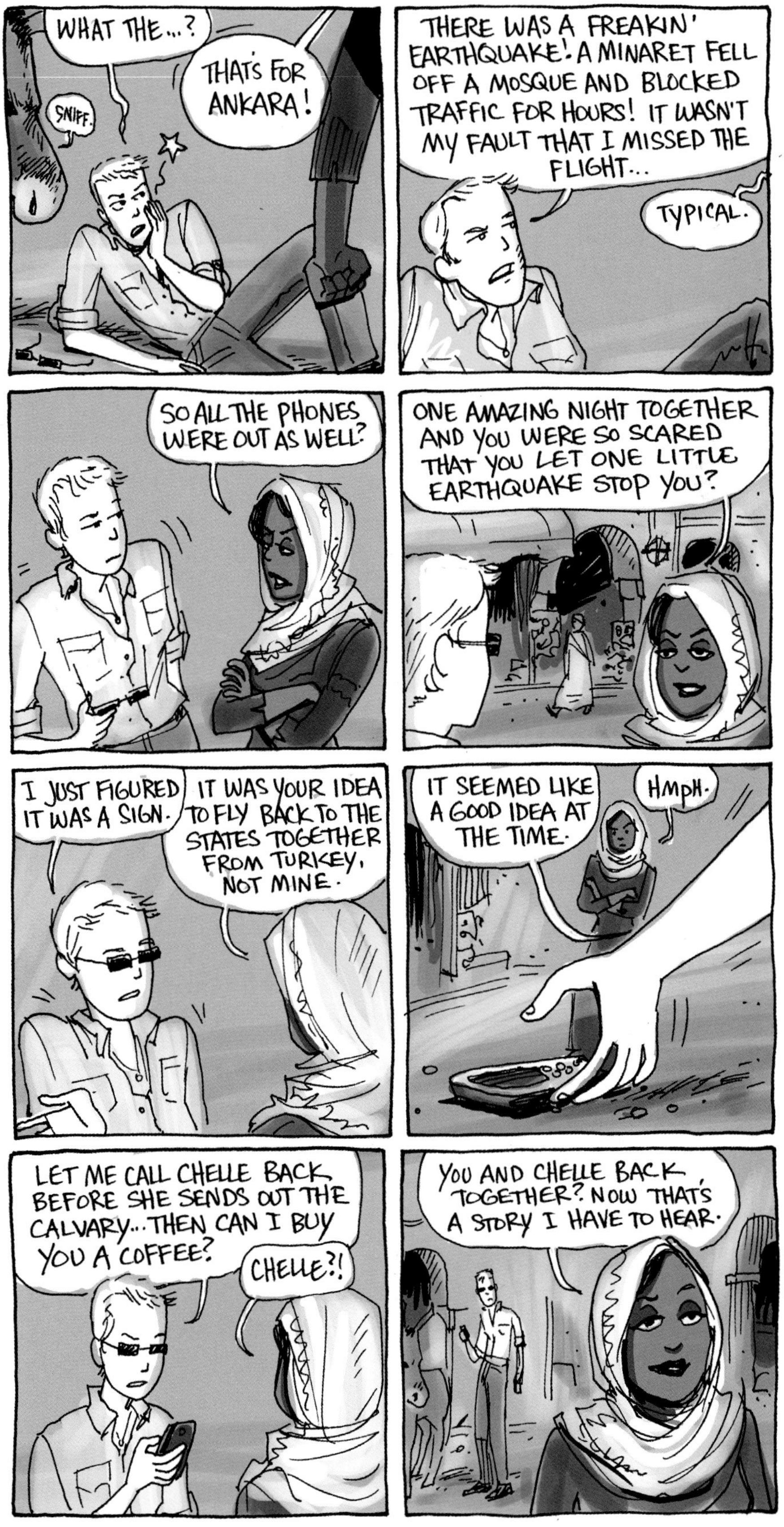
WHAT THE...?
SNIFF.
THAT'S FOR ANKARA!
THERE WAS A FREAKIN' EARTHQUAKE! A MINARET FELL OFF A MOSQUE AND BLOCKED TRAFFIC FOR HOURS! IT WASN'T MY FAULT THAT I MISSED THE FLIGHT...
TYPICAL.
SO ALL THE PHONES WERE OUT AS WELL?
ONE AMAZING NIGHT TOGETHER AND YOU WERE SO SCARED THAT YOU LET ONE LITTLE EARTHQUAKE STOP YOU?
I JUST FIGURED IT WAS A SIGN.
IT WAS YOUR IDEA TO FLY BACK TO THE STATES TOGETHER FROM TURKEY, NOT MINE.
IT SEEMED LIKE A GOOD IDEA AT THE TIME.
HMPH.
LET ME CALL CHELLE BACK BEFORE SHE SENDS OUT THE CALVARY... THEN CAN I BUY YOU A COFFEE?
CHELLE?!
YOU AND CHELLE BACK TOGETHER? NOW THAT'S A STORY I HAVE TO HEAR.

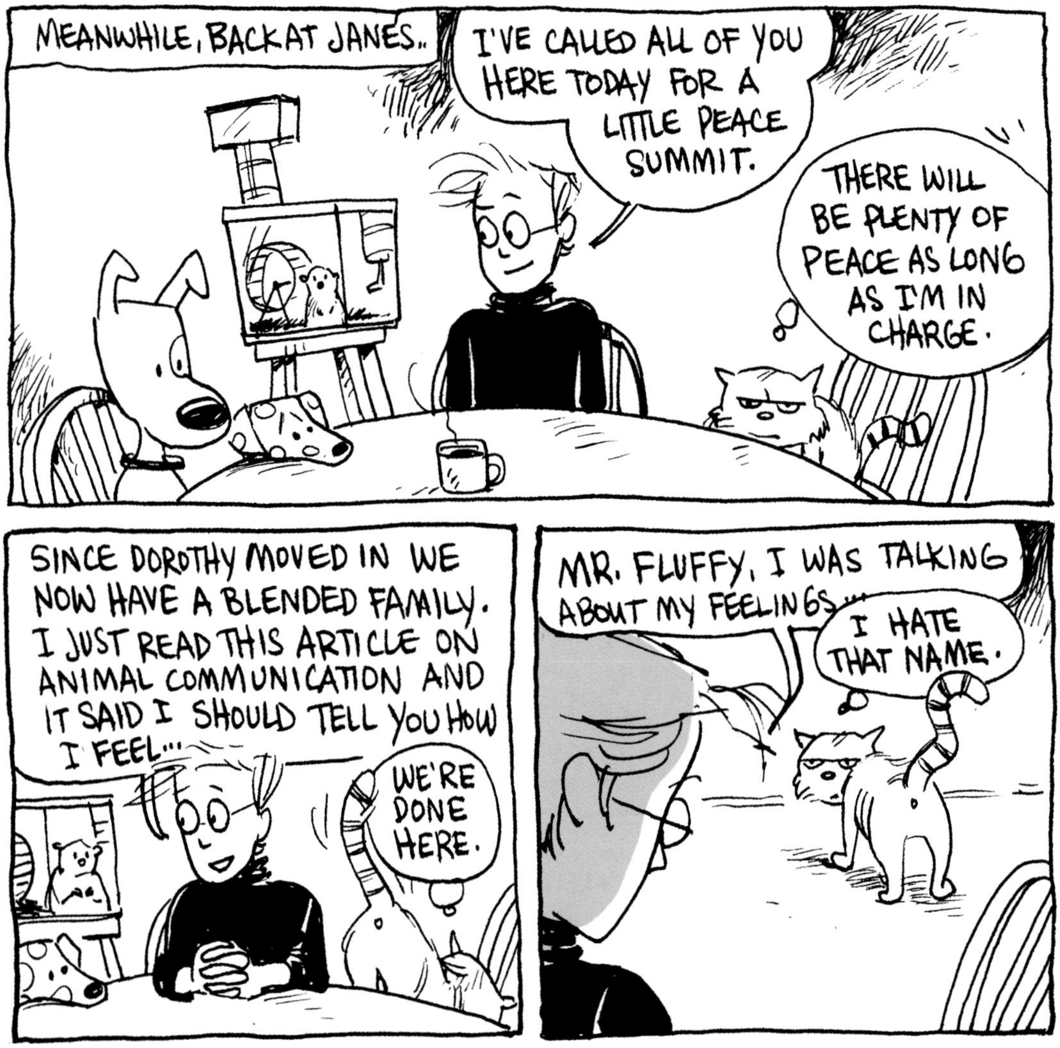
MEANWHILE, BACK AT JANES..
I'VE CALLED ALL OF YOU HERE TODAY FOR A LITTLE PEACE SUMMIT.
THERE WILL BE PLENTY OF PEACE AS LONG AS I'M IN CHARGE.
SINCE DOROTHY MOVED IN WE NOW HAVE A BLENDED FAMILY. I JUST READ THIS ARTICLE ON ANIMAL COMMUNICATION AND IT SAID I SHOULD TELL YOU HOW I FEEL...
WE'RE DONE HERE.
MR. FLUFFY, I WAS TALKING ABOUT MY FEELINGS...
I HATE THAT NAME.

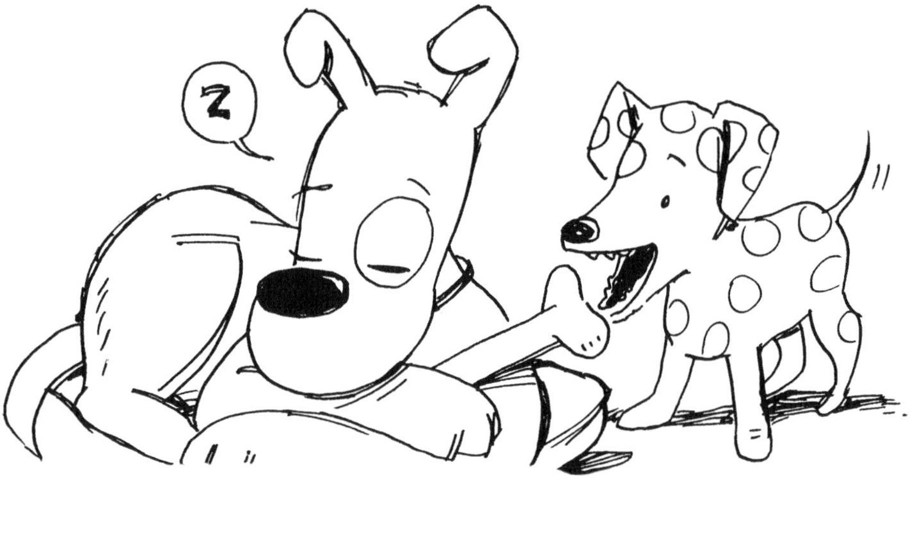
Z

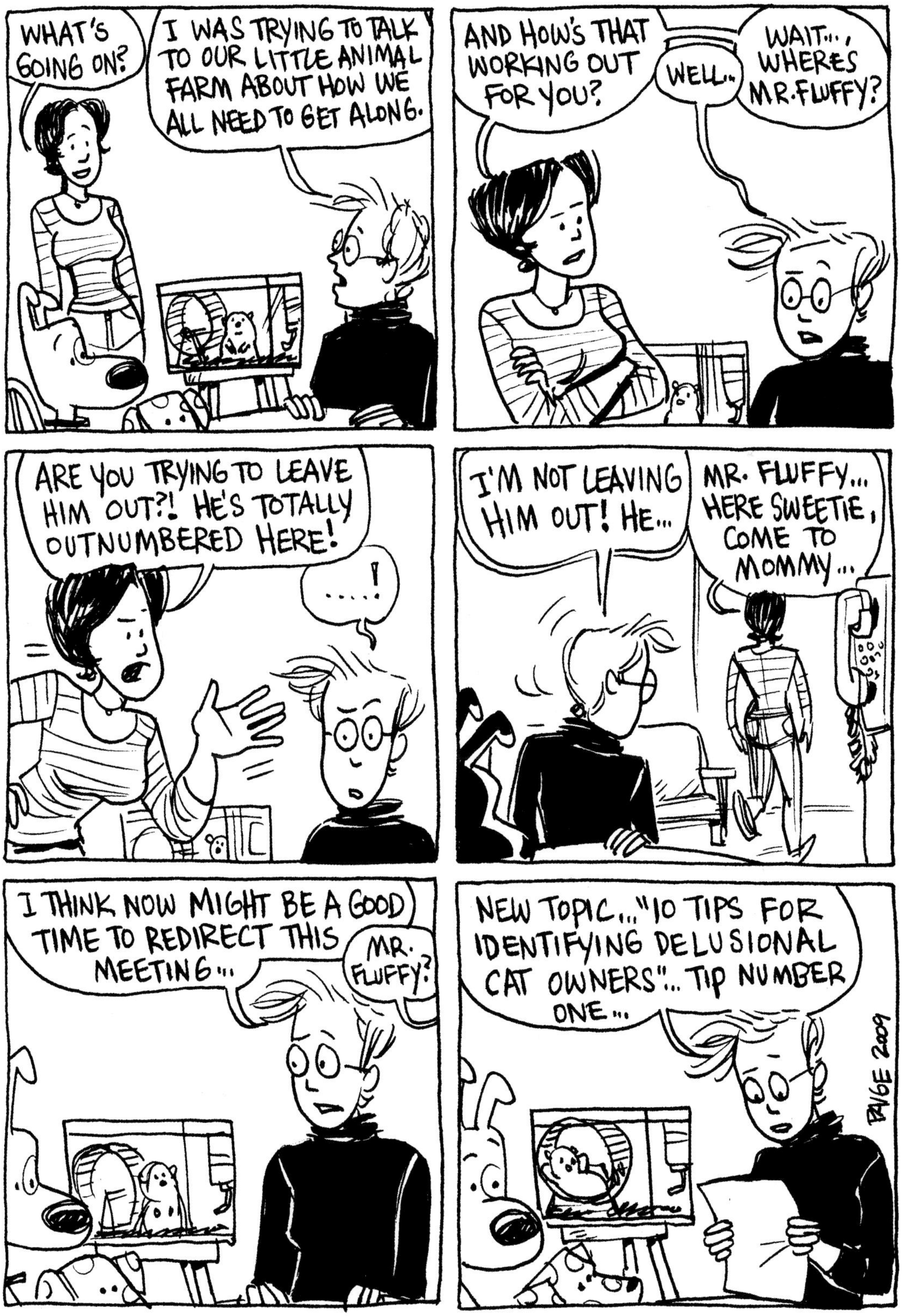
WHAT'S GOING ON?
I WAS TRYING TO TALK TO OUR LITTLE ANIMAL FARM ABOUT HOW WE ALL NEED TO GET ALONG.
AND HOW'S THAT WORKING OUT FOR YOU?
WELL..
WAIT..., WHERES MR.FLUFFY?
ARE YOU TRYING TO LEAVE HIM OUT?! HE'S TOTALLY OUTNUMBERED HERE!
.....!
I'M NOT LEAVING HIM OUT! HE...
MR. FLUFFY... HERE SWEETIE, COME TO MOMMY...
I THINK NOW MIGHT BE A GOOD TIME TO REDIRECT THIS MEETING...
MR. FLUFFY?
NEW TOPIC..."10 TIPS FOR IDENTIFYING DELUSIONAL CAT OWNERS"... TIP NUMBER ONE...
PAIGE 2009

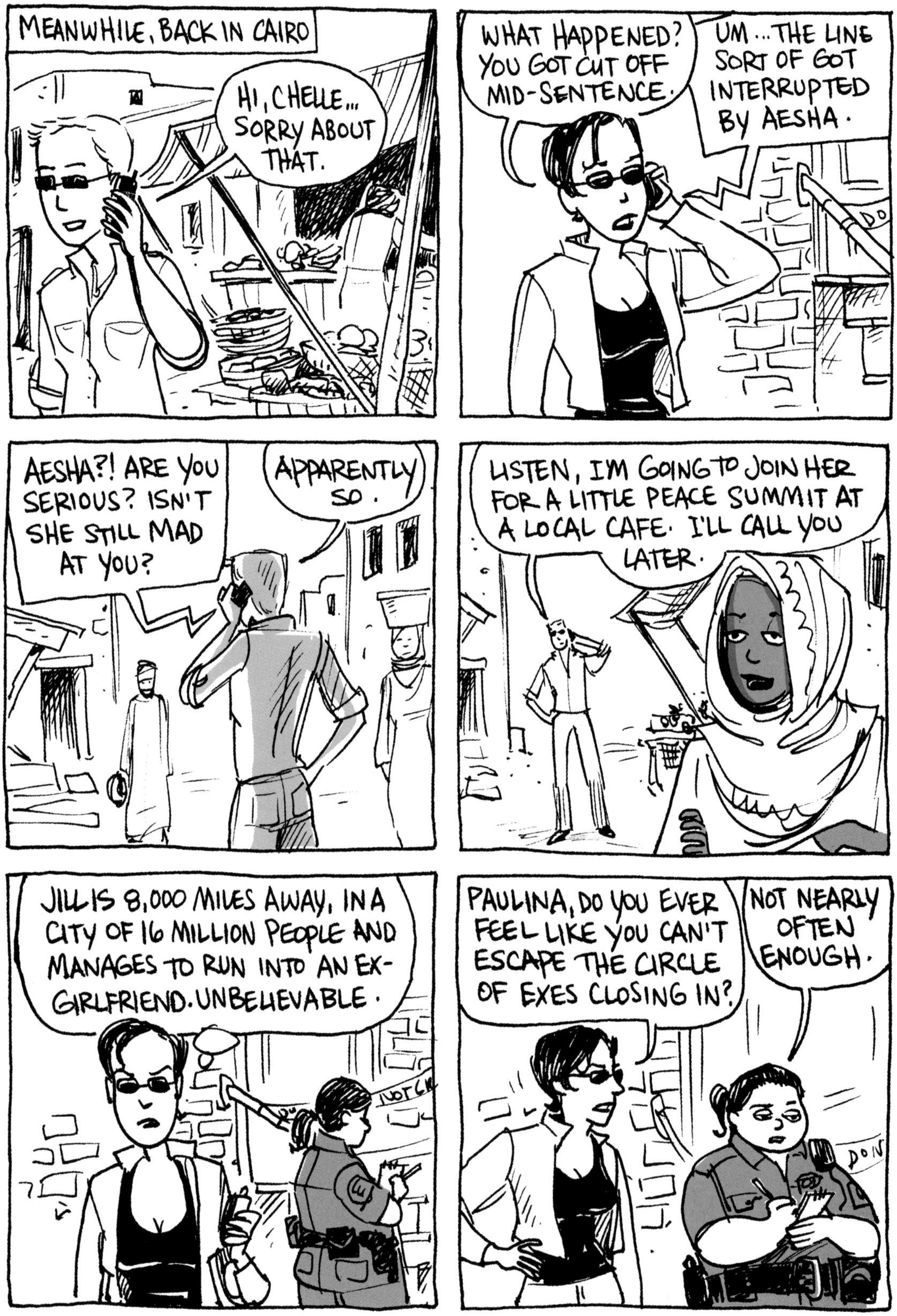
MEANWHILE, BACK IN CAIRO
HI, CHELLE... SORRY ABOUT THAT.
WHAT HAPPENED? YOU GOT CUT OFF MID-SENTENCE.
UM ... THE LINE SORT OF GOT INTERRUPTED BY AESHA.
AESHA?! ARE YOU SERIOUS? ISN'T SHE STILL MAD AT YOU?
APPARENTLY SO.
LISTEN, I'M GOING TO JOIN HER FOR A LITTLE PEACE SUMMIT AT A LOCAL CAFE. I'LL CALL YOU LATER.
JILL IS 8,000 MILES AWAY, IN A CITY OF 16 MILLION PEOPLE AND MANAGES TO RUN INTO AN EX-GIRLFRIEND. UNBELIEVABLE.
PAULINA, DO YOU EVER FEEL LIKE YOU CAN'T ESCAPE THE CIRCLE OF EXES CLOSING IN?
NOT NEARLY OFTEN ENOUGH.

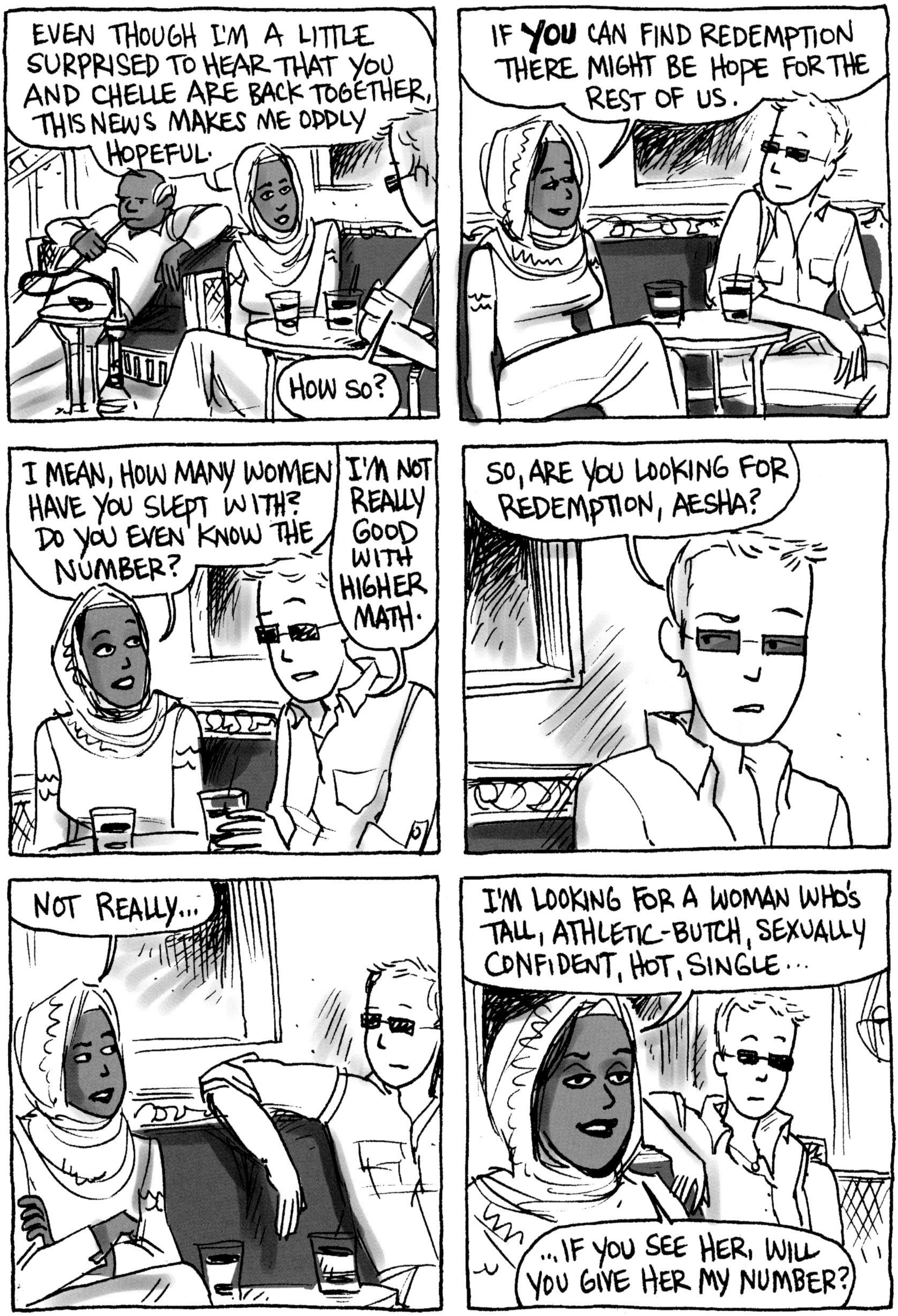
EVEN THOUGH I'M A LITTLE SURPRISED TO HEAR THAT YOU AND CHELLE ARE BACK TOGETHER, THIS NEWS MAKES ME ODDLY HOPEFUL.
HOW SO?
IF YOU CAN FIND REDEMPTION THERE MIGHT BE HOPE FOR THE REST OF US.
I MEAN, HOW MANY WOMEN HAVE YOU SLEPT WITH? DO YOU EVEN KNOW THE NUMBER?
I'M NOT REALLY GOOD WITH HIGHER MATH.
SO, ARE YOU LOOKING FOR REDEMPTION, AESHA?
NOT REALLY...
I'M LOOKING FOR A WOMAN WHO'S TALL, ATHLETIC-BUTCH, SEXUALLY CONFIDENT, HOT, SINGLE...
...IF YOU SEE HER, WILL YOU GIVE HER MY NUMBER?

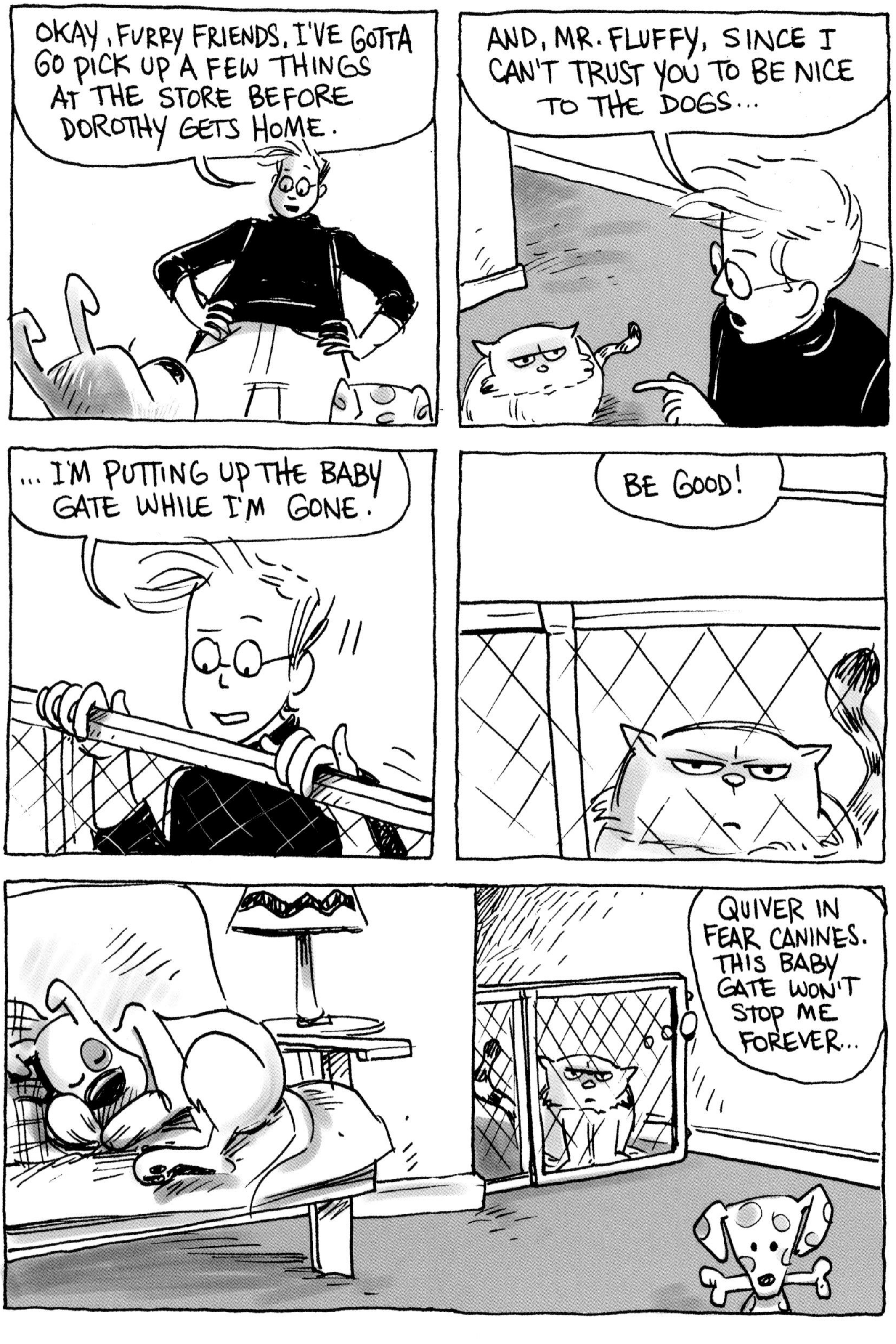
OKAY, FURRY FRIENDS. I'VE GOTTA GO PICK UP A FEW THINGS AT THE STORE BEFORE DOROTHY GETS HOME.
AND, MR. FLUFFY, SINCE I CAN'T TRUST YOU TO BE NICE TO THE DOGS...
... I'M PUTTING UP THE BABY GATE WHILE I'M GONE.
BE GOOD!
QUIVER IN FEAR CANINES. THIS BABY GATE WON'T STOP ME FOREVER...

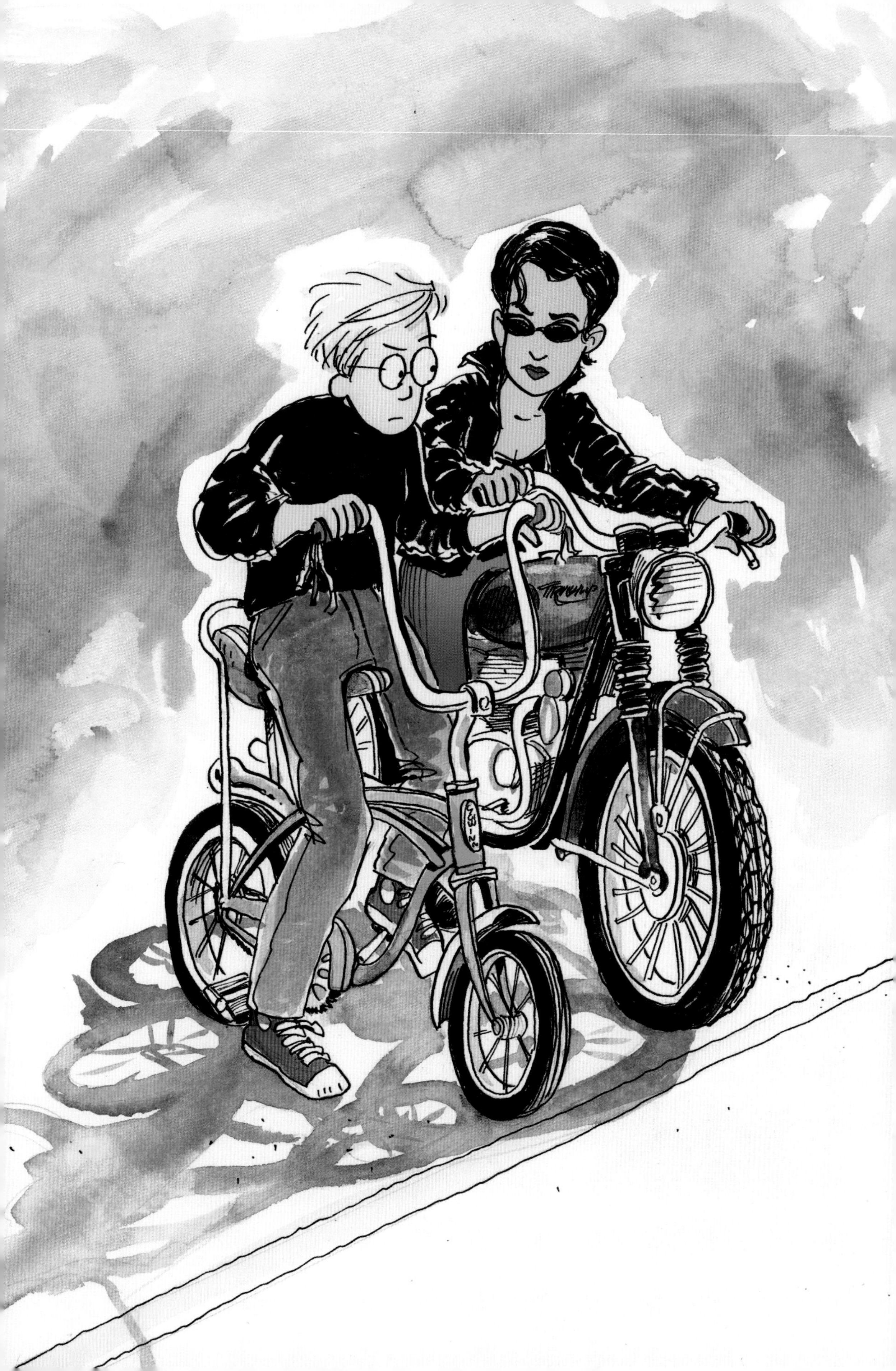

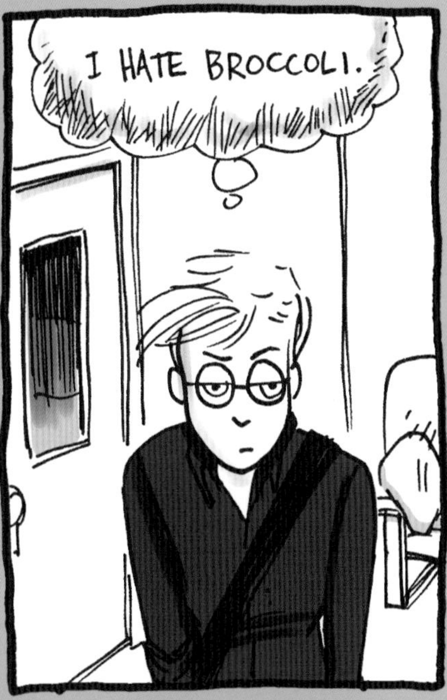
I HATE BROCCOLI.

World on Fire

Jane returns after an off-world sabbatical to find things are not quite the way she left them. Corporate managers at the newspaper have hired zombies to fill open positions. And despite her resistance to anything involving athletic exertion, Jane finds herself signed up for a lesbian soccer league.

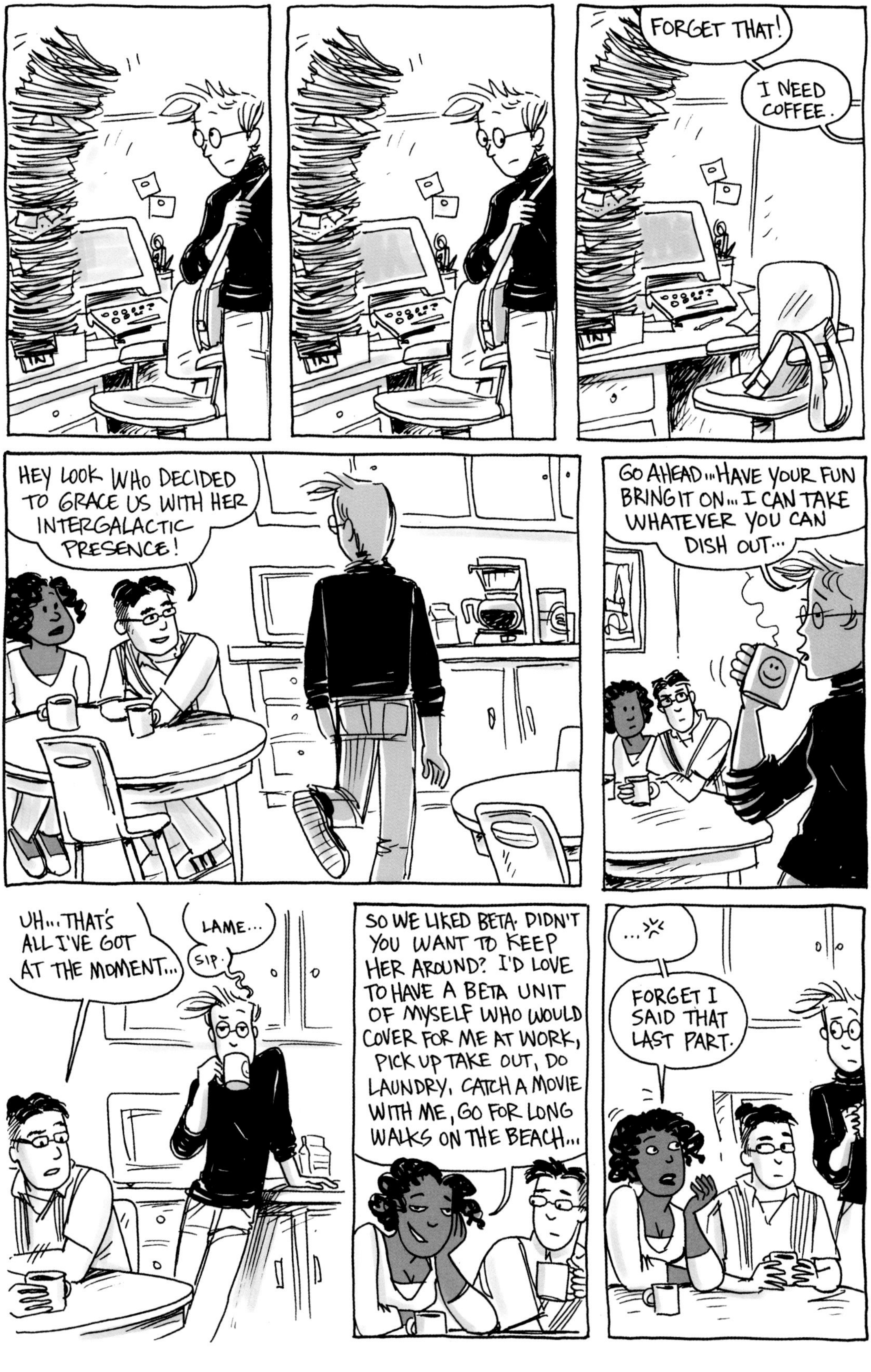
FORGET THAT!
I NEED COFFEE.
HEY LOOK WHO DECIDED TO GRACE US WITH HER INTERGALACTIC PRESENCE!
GO AHEAD... HAVE YOUR FUN BRING IT ON... I CAN TAKE WHATEVER YOU CAN DISH OUT...
UH... THAT'S ALL I'VE GOT AT THE MOMENT...
LAME...
SIP.
SO WE LIKED BETA. DIDN'T YOU WANT TO KEEP HER AROUND? I'D LOVE TO HAVE A BETA UNIT OF MYSELF WHO WOULD COVER FOR ME AT WORK, PICK UP TAKE OUT, DO LAUNDRY, CATCH A MOVIE WITH ME, GO FOR LONG WALKS ON THE BEACH...
...
FORGET I SAID THAT LAST PART.

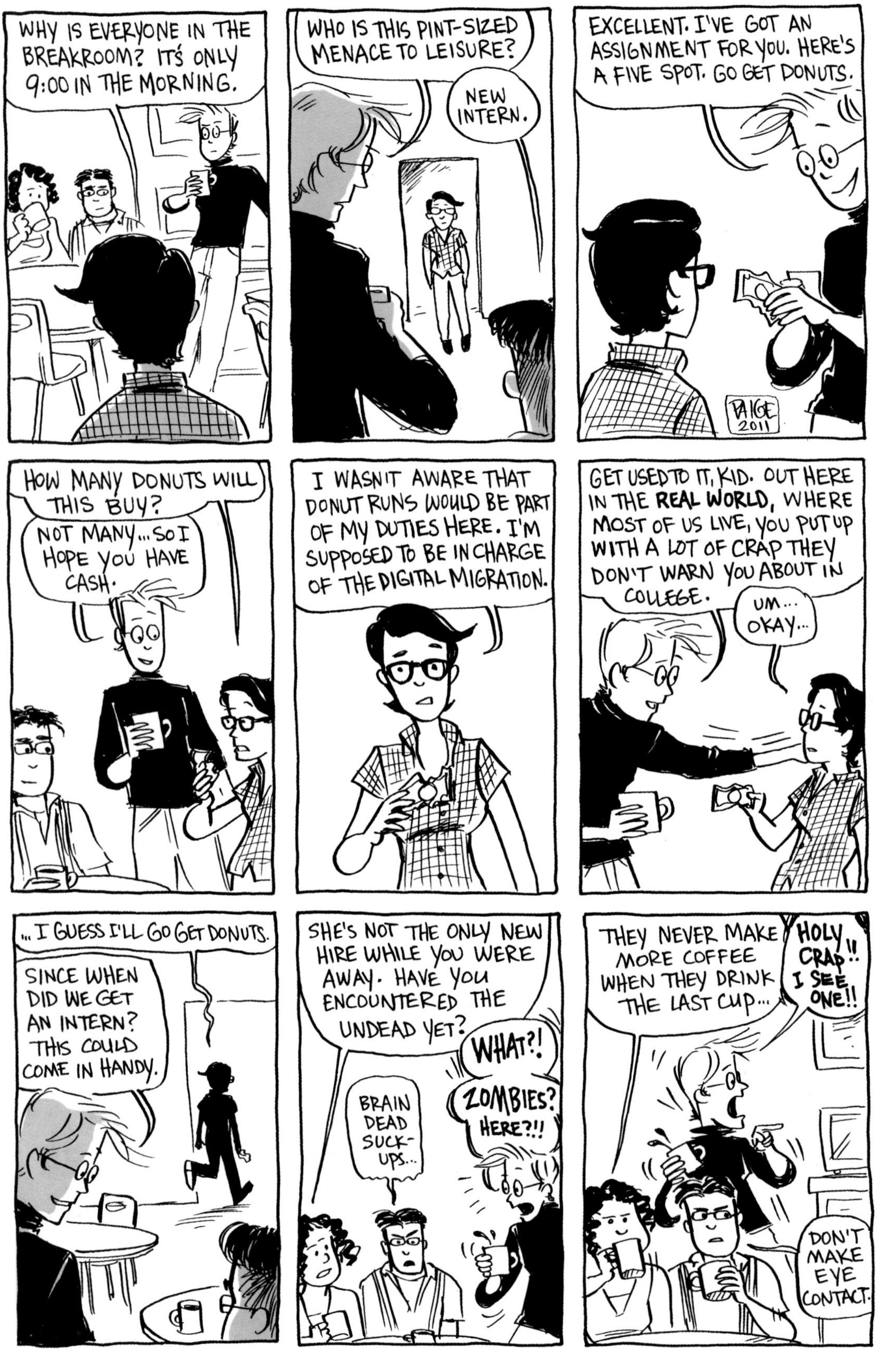
WHY IS EVERYONE IN THE BREAKROOM? IT'S ONLY 9:00 IN THE MORNING.
WHO IS THIS PINT-SIZED MENACE TO LEISURE?
NEW INTERN.
EXCELLENT. I'VE GOT AN ASSIGNMENT FOR YOU. HERE'S A FIVE SPOT. GO GET DONUTS.
PAIGE 2011
HOW MANY DONUTS WILL THIS BUY?
NOT MANY... SO I HOPE YOU HAVE CASH.
I WASN'T AWARE THAT DONUT RUNS WOULD BE PART OF MY DUTIES HERE. I'M SUPPOSED TO BE IN CHARGE OF THE DIGITAL MIGRATION.
GET USED TO IT, KID. OUT HERE IN THE REAL WORLD, WHERE MOST OF US LIVE, YOU PUT UP WITH A LOT OF CRAP THEY DON'T WARN YOU ABOUT IN COLLEGE.
UM... OKAY...
...I GUESS I'LL GO GET DONUTS.
SINCE WHEN DID WE GET AN INTERN? THIS COULD COME IN HANDY.
SHE'S NOT THE ONLY NEW HIRE WHILE YOU WERE AWAY. HAVE YOU ENCOUNTERED THE UNDEAD YET?
WHAT?!
ZOMBIES? HERE?!!
BRAIN DEAD SUCK-UPS...
THEY NEVER MAKE MORE COFFEE WHEN THEY DRINK THE LAST CUP...
HOLY CRAP!! I SEE ONE!!
DON'T MAKE EYE CONTACT.

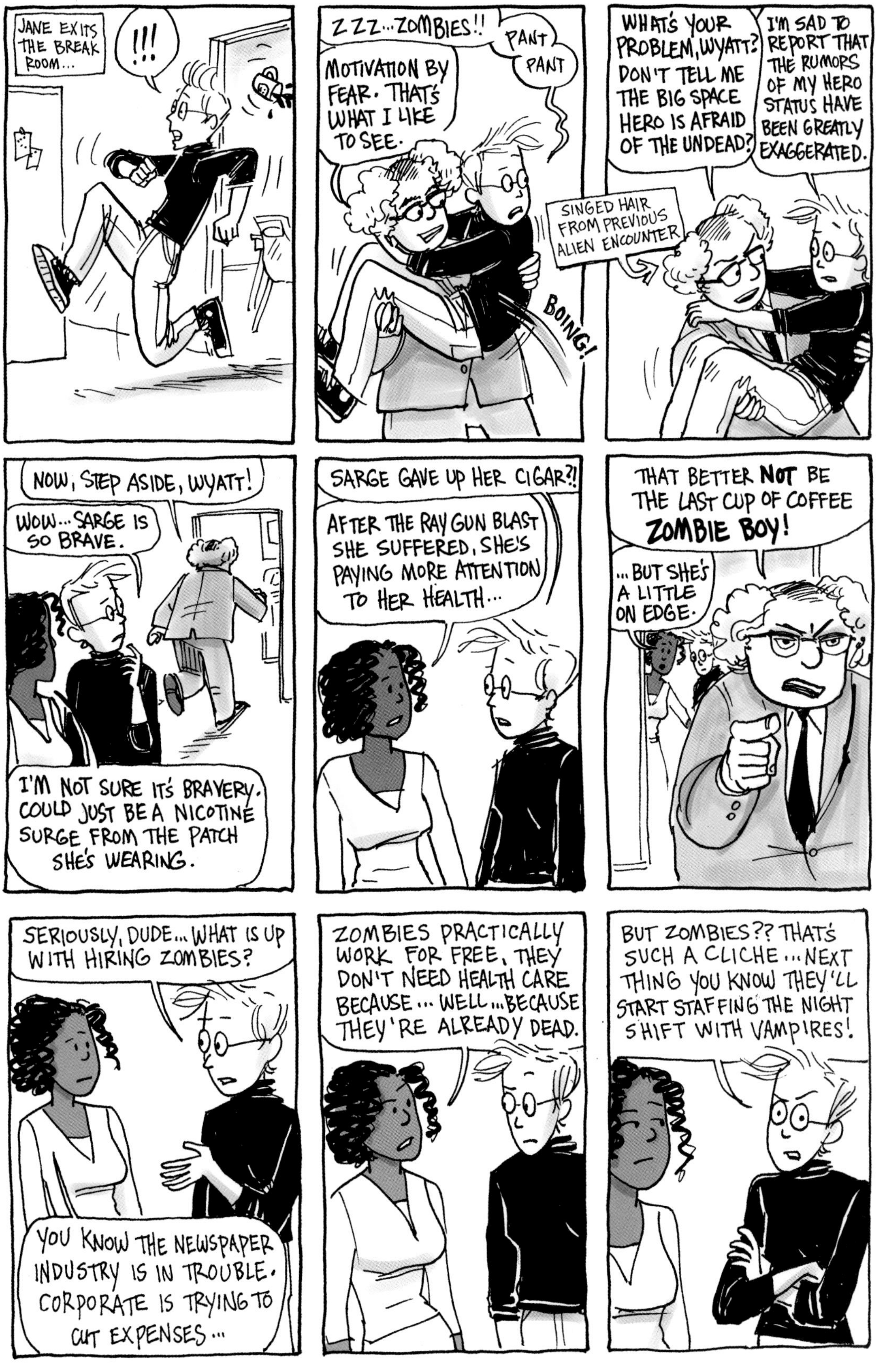
JANE EXITS THE BREAK ROOM...
!!!
ZZZ...ZOMBIES!!
PANT PANT
MOTIVATION BY FEAR. THAT'S WHAT I LIKE TO SEE.
BOING!
WHAT'S YOUR PROBLEM, WYATT? DON'T TELL ME THE BIG SPACE HERO IS AFRAID OF THE UNDEAD?
I'M SAD TO REPORT THAT THE RUMORS OF MY HERO STATUS HAVE BEEN GREATLY EXAGGERATED.
SINGED HAIR FROM PREVIOUS ALIEN ENCOUNTER
NOW, STEP ASIDE, WYATT!
WOW... SARGE IS SO BRAVE.
I'M NOT SURE IT'S BRAVERY. COULD JUST BE A NICOTINE SURGE FROM THE PATCH SHE'S WEARING.
SARGE GAVE UP HER CIGAR?!
AFTER THE RAY GUN BLAST SHE SUFFERED, SHE'S PAYING MORE ATTENTION TO HER HEALTH...
THAT BETTER **NOT** BE THE LAST CUP OF COFFEE **ZOMBIE BOY**!
...BUT SHE'S A LITTLE ON EDGE.
SERIOUSLY, DUDE... WHAT IS UP WITH HIRING ZOMBIES?
YOU KNOW THE NEWSPAPER INDUSTRY IS IN TROUBLE. CORPORATE IS TRYING TO CUT EXPENSES...
ZOMBIES PRACTICALLY WORK FOR FREE. THEY DON'T NEED HEALTH CARE BECAUSE... WELL... BECAUSE THEY'RE ALREADY DEAD.
BUT ZOMBIES?? THAT'S SUCH A CLICHE... NEXT THING YOU KNOW THEY'LL START STAFFING THE NIGHT SHIFT WITH VAMPIRES!

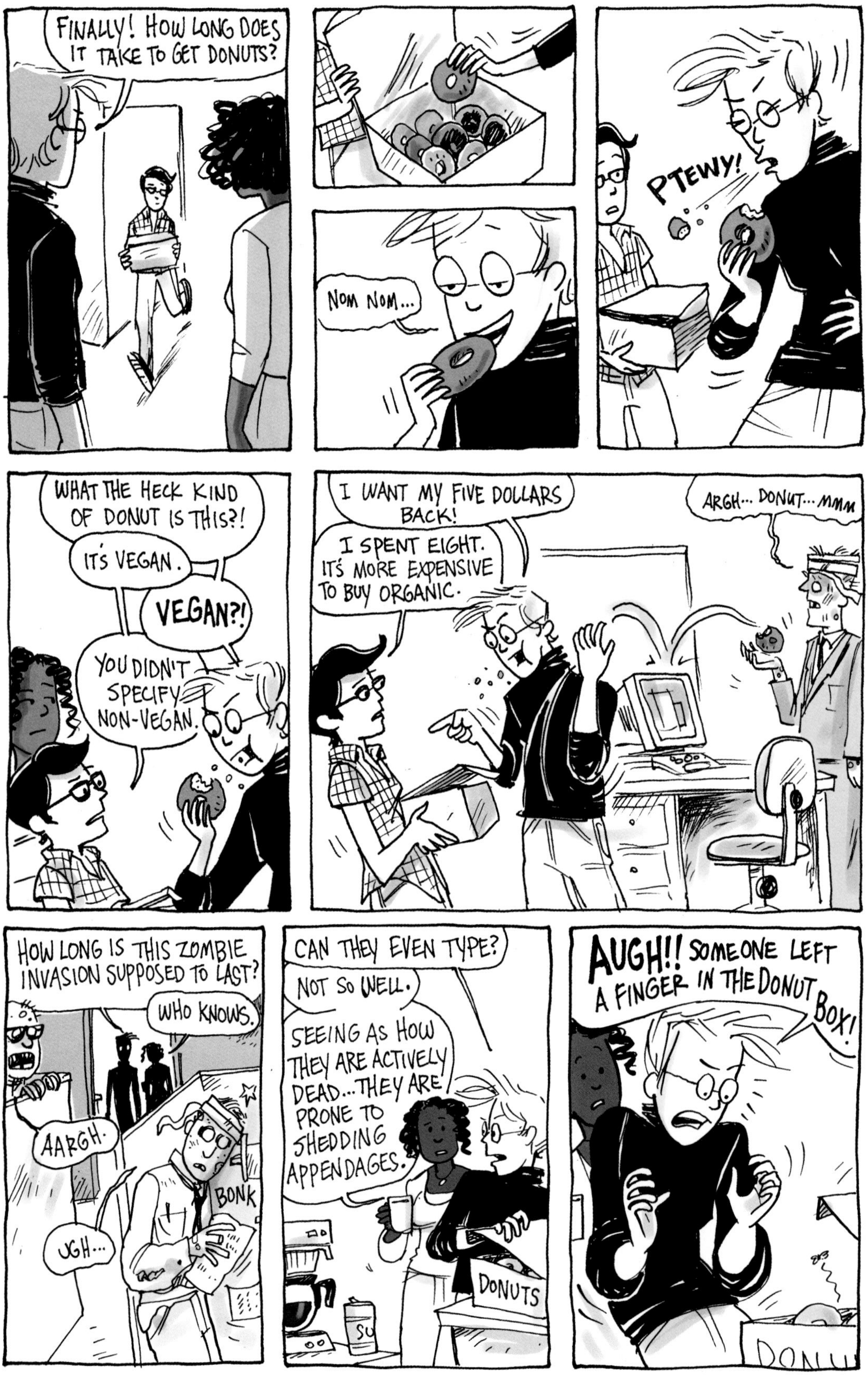
FINALLY! HOW LONG DOES IT TAKE TO GET DONUTS?
NOM NOM...
PTEWY!
WHAT THE HECK KIND OF DONUT IS THIS?!
IT'S VEGAN.
VEGAN?!
YOU DIDN'T SPECIFY NON-VEGAN.
I WANT MY FIVE DOLLARS BACK!
I SPENT EIGHT. IT'S MORE EXPENSIVE TO BUY ORGANIC.
ARGH... DONUT... MMM
HOW LONG IS THIS ZOMBIE INVASION SUPPOSED TO LAST?
WHO KNOWS.
AARGH.
UGH...
BONK
CAN THEY EVEN TYPE?
NOT SO WELL.
SEEING AS HOW THEY ARE ACTIVELY DEAD... THEY ARE PRONE TO SHEDDING APPENDAGES.
DONUTS
AUGH!! SOMEONE LEFT A FINGER IN THE DONUT BOX!

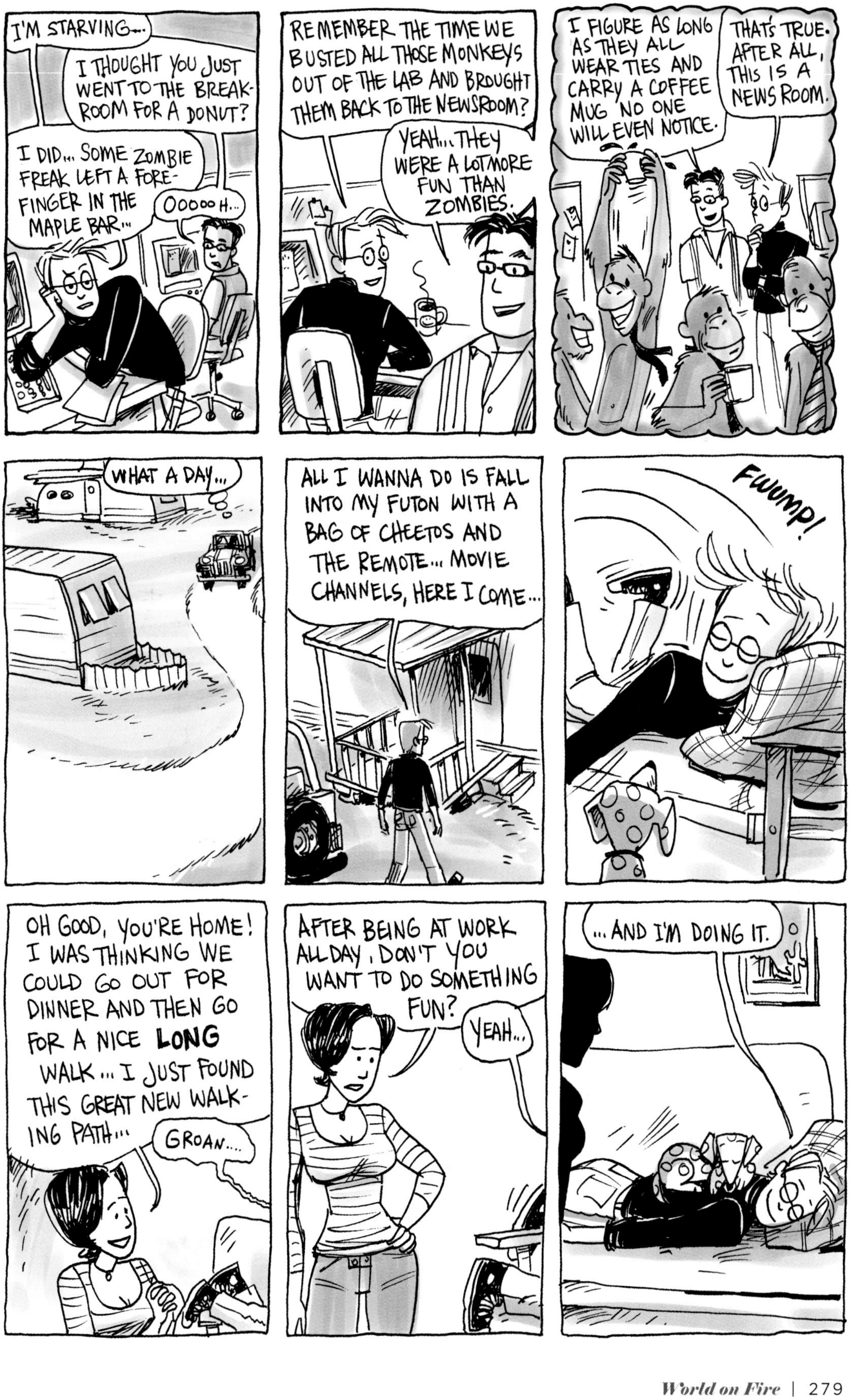
I'M STARVING...
I THOUGHT YOU JUST WENT TO THE BREAK-ROOM FOR A DONUT?
I DID... SOME ZOMBIE FREAK LEFT A FORE-FINGER IN THE MAPLE BAR...
OOOOOH...
REMEMBER THE TIME WE BUSTED ALL THOSE MONKEYS OUT OF THE LAB AND BROUGHT THEM BACK TO THE NEWSROOM?
YEAH... THEY WERE A LOT MORE FUN THAN ZOMBIES.
I FIGURE AS LONG AS THEY ALL WEAR TIES AND CARRY A COFFEE MUG NO ONE WILL EVEN NOTICE.
THAT'S TRUE. AFTER ALL, THIS IS A NEWS ROOM.
WHAT A DAY...
ALL I WANNA DO IS FALL INTO MY FUTON WITH A BAG OF CHEETOS AND THE REMOTE... MOVIE CHANNELS, HERE I COME...
FWUMP!
OH GOOD, YOU'RE HOME! I WAS THINKING WE COULD GO OUT FOR DINNER AND THEN GO FOR A NICE **LONG** WALK... I JUST FOUND THIS GREAT NEW WALK-ING PATH...
GROAN...
AFTER BEING AT WORK ALL DAY, DON'T YOU WANT TO DO SOMETHING FUN?
YEAH...
...AND I'M DOING IT.

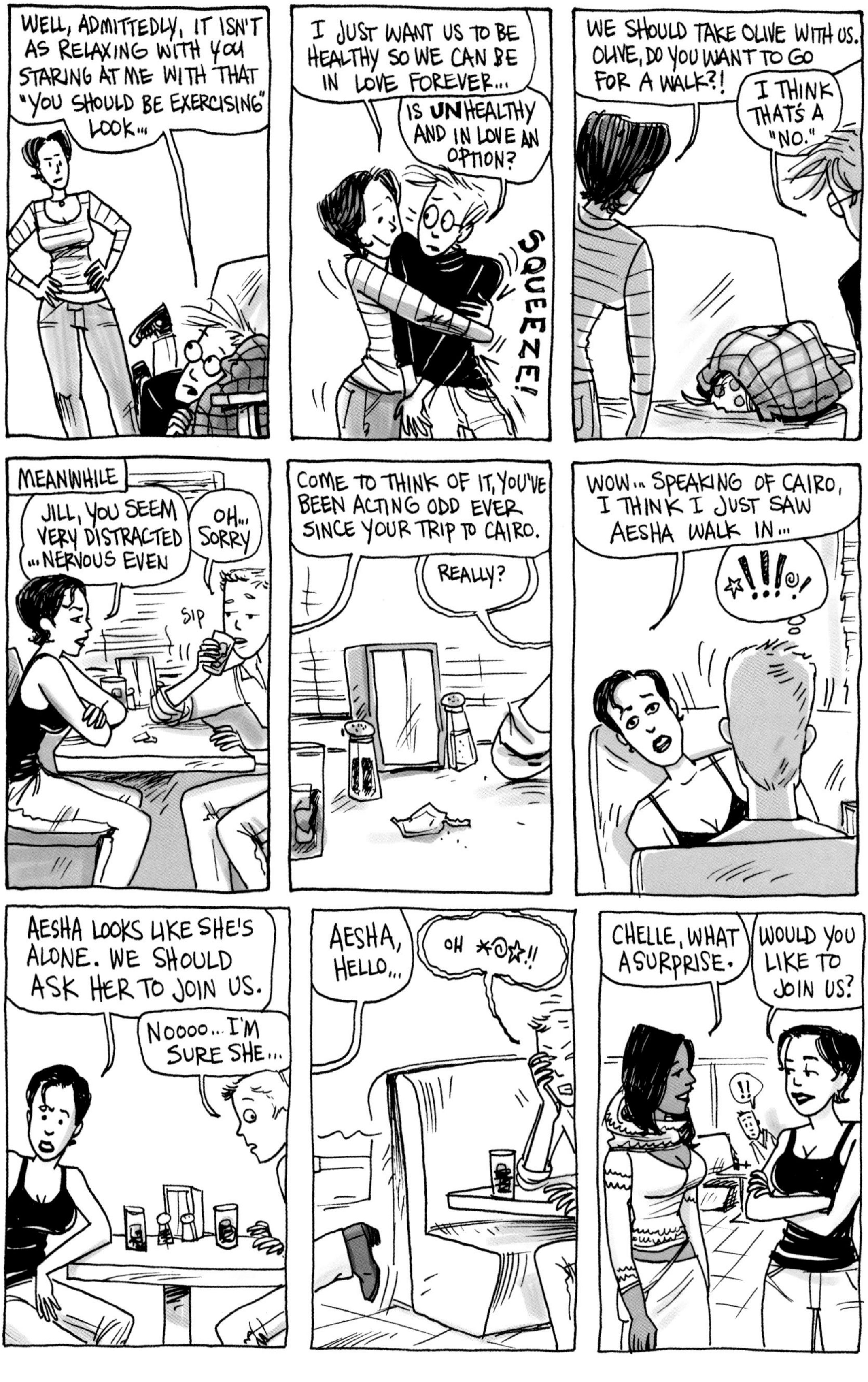
WELL, ADMITTEDLY, IT ISN'T AS RELAXING WITH YOU STARING AT ME WITH THAT "YOU SHOULD BE EXERCISING" LOOK...
I JUST WANT US TO BE HEALTHY SO WE CAN BE IN LOVE FOREVER...
IS UNHEALTHY AND IN LOVE AN OPTION?
SQUEEZE!
WE SHOULD TAKE OLIVE WITH US. OLIVE, DO YOU WANT TO GO FOR A WALK?!
I THINK THAT'S A "NO."
MEANWHILE
JILL, YOU SEEM VERY DISTRACTED ...NERVOUS EVEN
OH... SORRY
SIP
COME TO THINK OF IT, YOU'VE BEEN ACTING ODD EVER SINCE YOUR TRIP TO CAIRO.
REALLY?
WOW... SPEAKING OF CAIRO, I THINK I JUST SAW AESHA WALK IN...
AESHA LOOKS LIKE SHE'S ALONE. WE SHOULD ASK HER TO JOIN US.
NOOOO... I'M SURE SHE...
AESHA, HELLO...
OH *@☆!!
CHELLE, WHAT A SURPRISE.
WOULD YOU LIKE TO JOIN US?

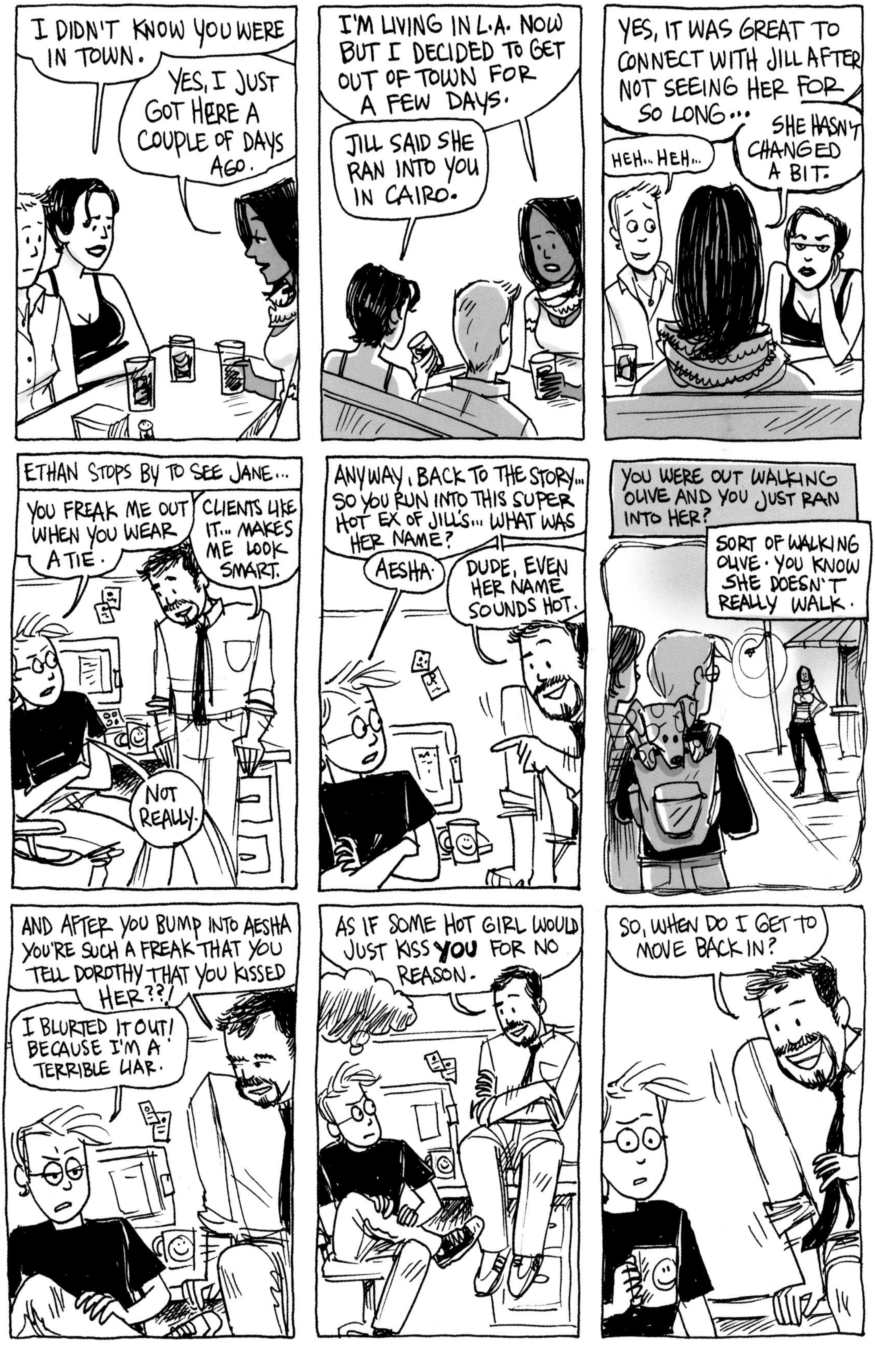
I DIDN'T KNOW YOU WERE IN TOWN.
YES, I JUST GOT HERE A COUPLE OF DAYS AGO.
I'M LIVING IN L.A. NOW BUT I DECIDED TO GET OUT OF TOWN FOR A FEW DAYS.
JILL SAID SHE RAN INTO YOU IN CAIRO.
YES, IT WAS GREAT TO CONNECT WITH JILL AFTER NOT SEEING HER FOR SO LONG...
HEH... HEH...
SHE HASN'T CHANGED A BIT.
ETHAN STOPS BY TO SEE JANE...
YOU FREAK ME OUT WHEN YOU WEAR A TIE.
CLIENTS LIKE IT... MAKES ME LOOK SMART.
NOT REALLY.
ANYWAY, BACK TO THE STORY... SO YOU RUN INTO THIS SUPER HOT EX OF JILL'S... WHAT WAS HER NAME?
AESHA.
DUDE, EVEN HER NAME SOUNDS HOT.
YOU WERE OUT WALKING OLIVE AND YOU JUST RAN INTO HER?
SORT OF WALKING OLIVE. YOU KNOW SHE DOESN'T REALLY WALK.
AND AFTER YOU BUMP INTO AESHA YOU'RE SUCH A FREAK THAT YOU TELL DOROTHY THAT YOU KISSED HER??!
I BLURTED IT OUT! BECAUSE I'M A TERRIBLE LIAR.
AS IF SOME HOT GIRL WOULD JUST KISS **YOU** FOR NO REASON.
SO, WHEN DO I GET TO MOVE BACK IN?

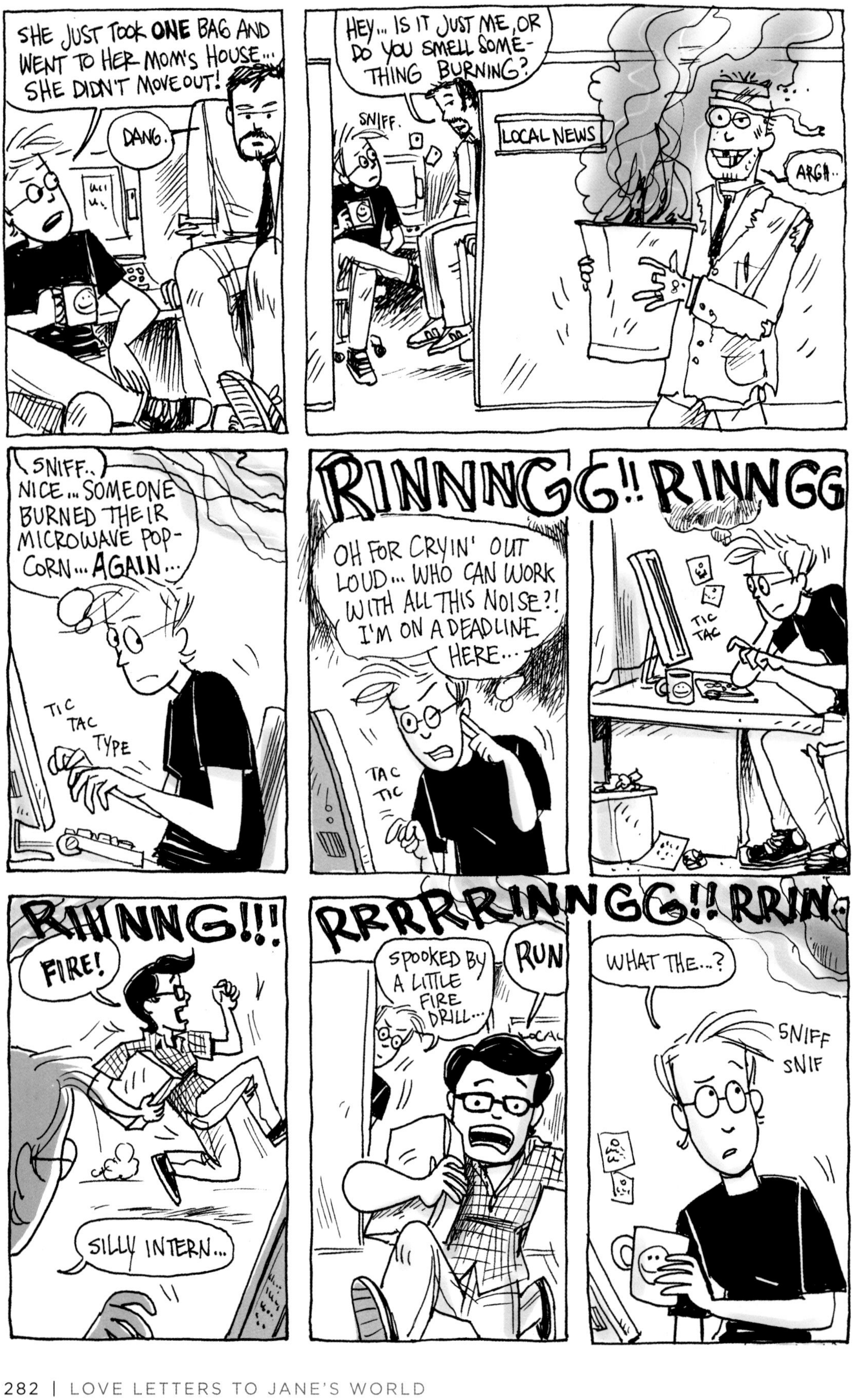
SHE JUST TOOK ONE BAG AND WENT TO HER MOM'S HOUSE... SHE DIDN'T MOVE OUT!
DANG.
HEY... IS IT JUST ME, OR DO YOU SMELL SOME-THING BURNING?
SNIFF.
LOCAL NEWS
ARGH..
SNIFF.. NICE... SOMEONE BURNED THEIR MICROWAVE POP-CORN... AGAIN...
TIC TAC TYPE
RINNNGG!! RINNGG
OH FOR CRYIN' OUT LOUD... WHO CAN WORK WITH ALL THIS NOISE?! I'M ON A DEADLINE HERE...
TAC TIC
TIC TAC
RIIINNG!!!
FIRE!
SILLY INTERN...
RRRRRINNGG!! RRIN..
SPOOKED BY A LITTLE FIRE DRILL...
RUN
WHAT THE...?
SNIFF SNIF

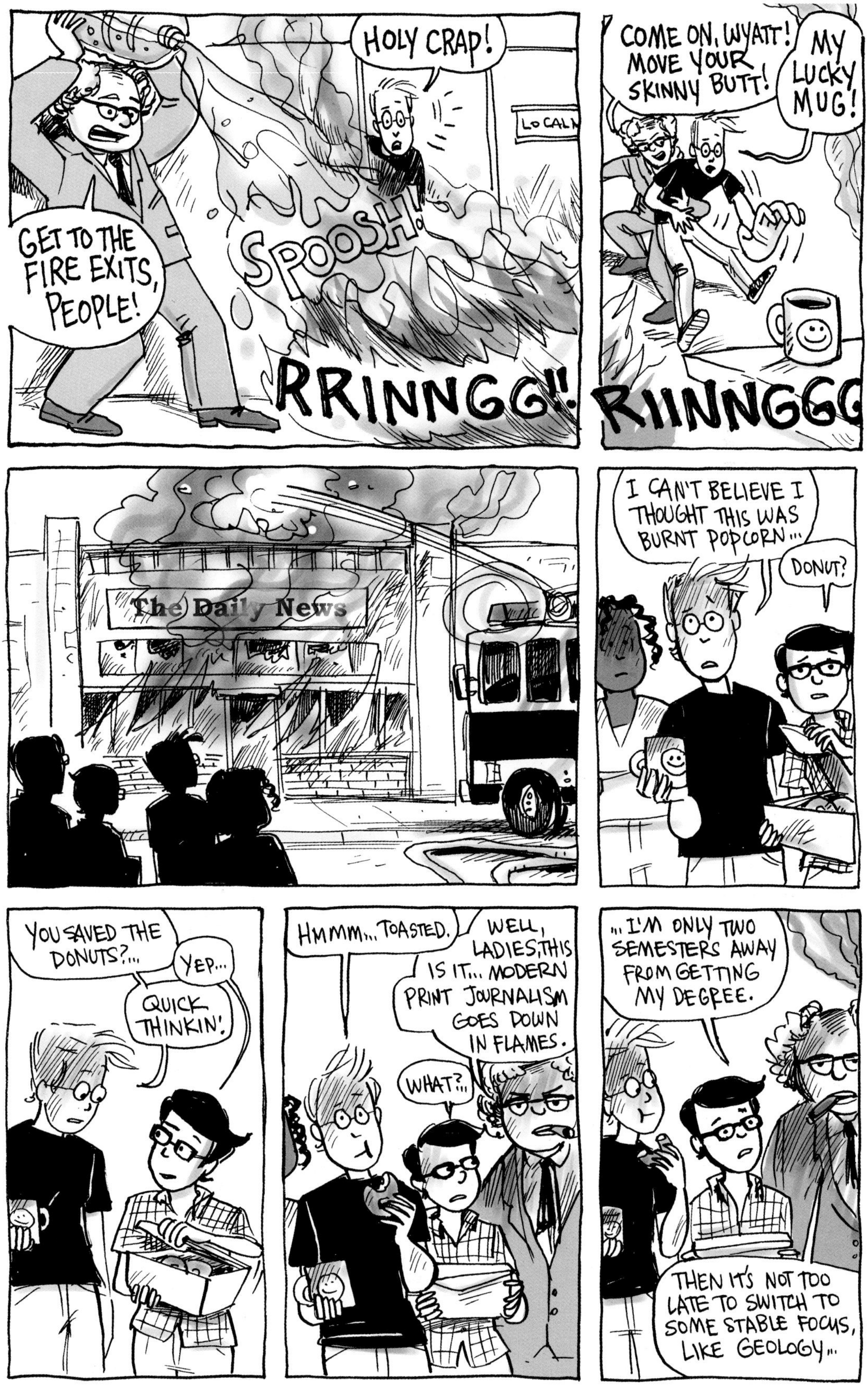
HOLY CRAP!
LOCAL
GET TO THE FIRE EXITS, PEOPLE!
SPOOSH!
RRINNGG!!
COME ON, WYATT! MOVE YOUR SKINNY BUTT!
MY LUCKY MUG!
RIINNGGG
The Daily News
I CAN'T BELIEVE I THOUGHT THIS WAS BURNT POPCORN...
DONUT?
YOU SAVED THE DONUTS?...
YEP...
QUICK THINKIN'.
HMMM... TOASTED.
WELL, LADIES, THIS IS IT... MODERN PRINT JOURNALISM GOES DOWN IN FLAMES.
WHAT?...
...I'M ONLY TWO SEMESTERS AWAY FROM GETTING MY DEGREE.
THEN IT'S NOT TOO LATE TO SWITCH TO SOME STABLE FOCUS, LIKE GEOLOGY...

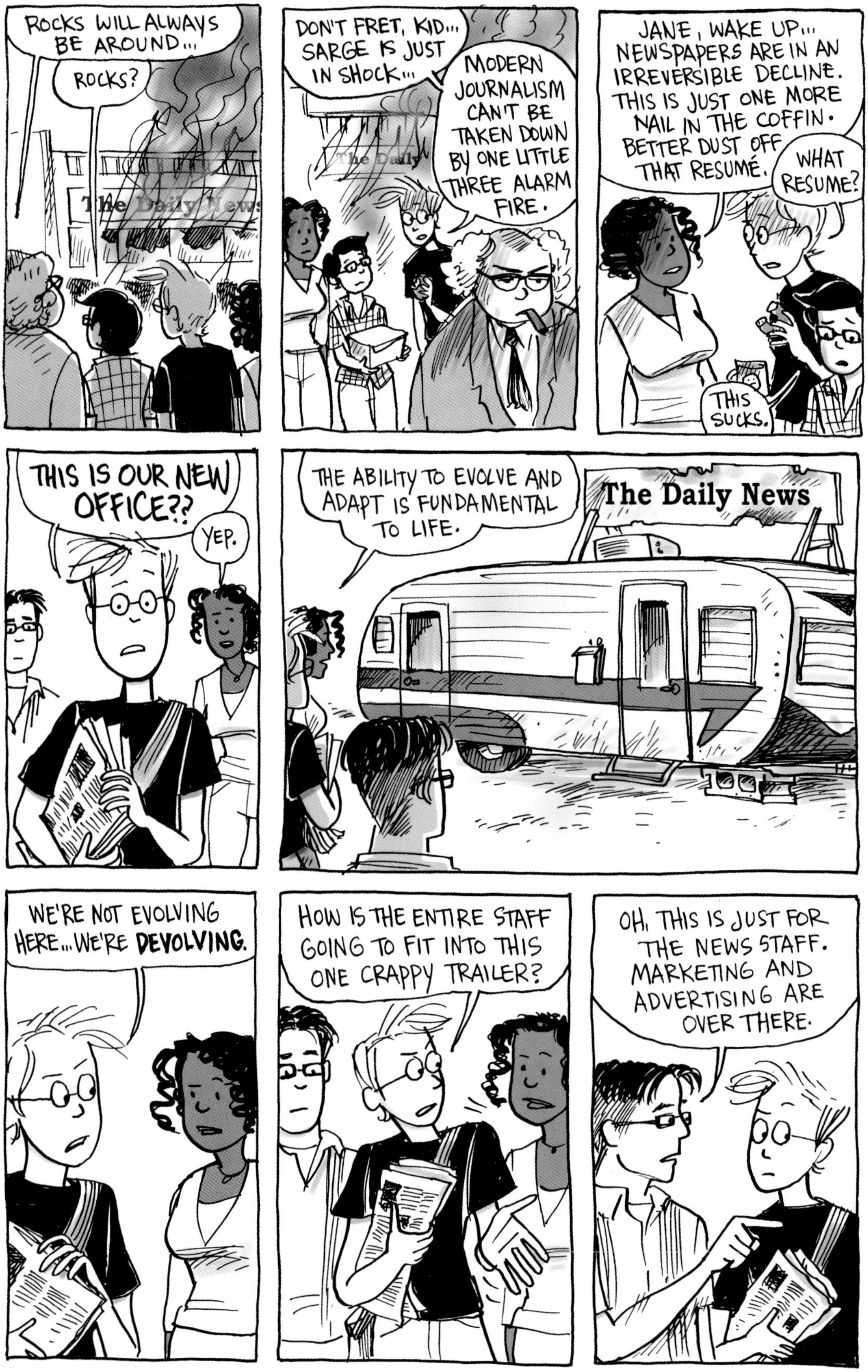
ROCKS WILL ALWAYS BE AROUND...
ROCKS?
The Daily News
DON'T FRET, KID... SARGE IS JUST IN SHOCK...
MODERN JOURNALISM CAN'T BE TAKEN DOWN BY ONE LITTLE THREE ALARM FIRE.
The Daily
JANE, WAKE UP... NEWSPAPERS ARE IN AN IRREVERSIBLE DECLINE. THIS IS JUST ONE MORE NAIL IN THE COFFIN. BETTER DUST OFF THAT RESUMÉ.
WHAT RESUME?
THIS SUCKS.
THIS IS OUR NEW OFFICE??
YEP.
THE ABILITY TO EVOLVE AND ADAPT IS FUNDAMENTAL TO LIFE.
The Daily News
WE'RE NOT EVOLVING HERE... WE'RE **DEVOLVING.**
HOW IS THE ENTIRE STAFF GOING TO FIT INTO THIS ONE CRAPPY TRAILER?
OH, THIS IS JUST FOR THE NEWS STAFF. MARKETING AND ADVERTISING ARE OVER THERE.

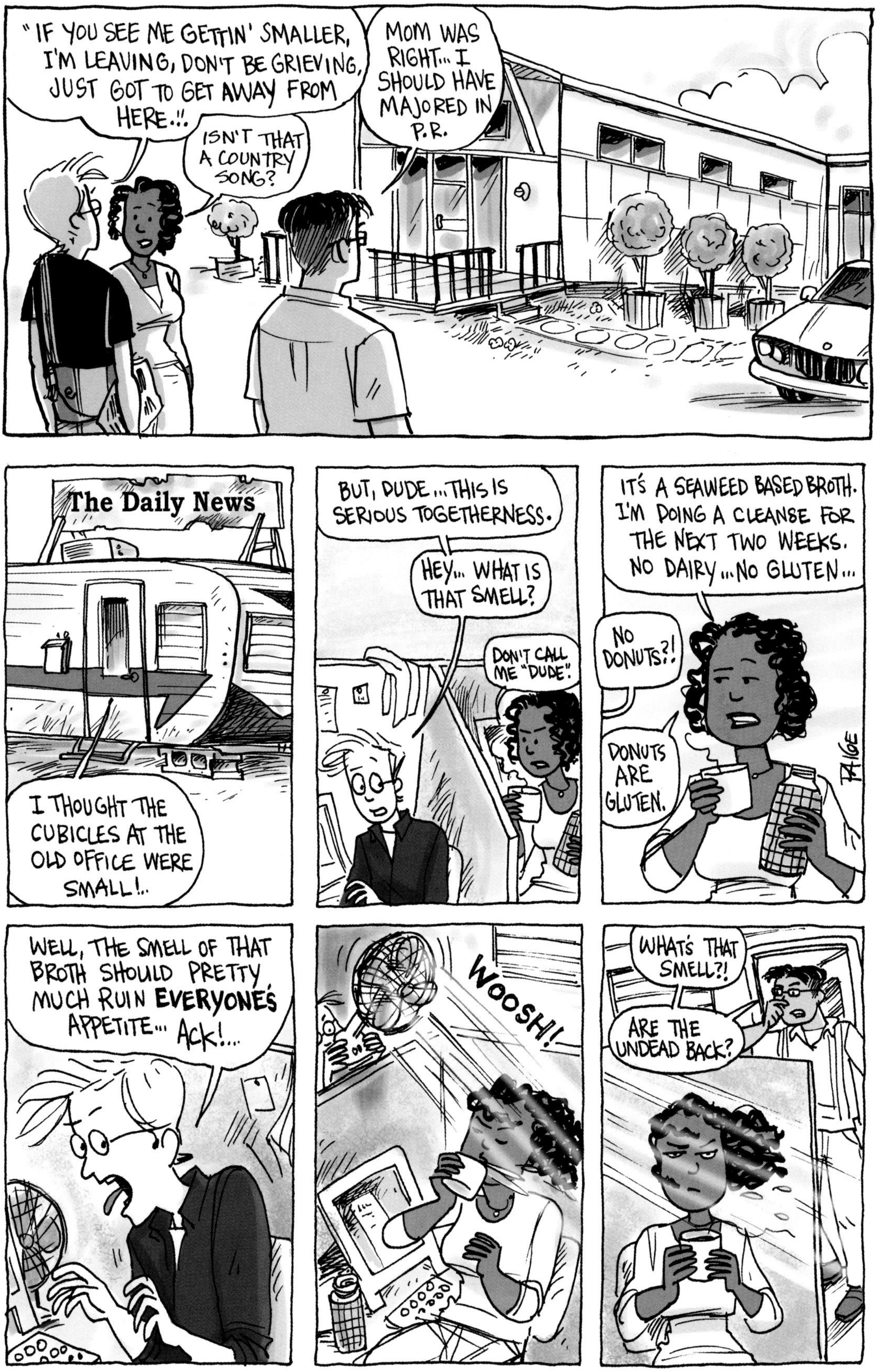
"IF YOU SEE ME GETTIN' SMALLER, I'M LEAVING, DON'T BE GRIEVING, JUST GOT TO GET AWAY FROM HERE..!"
ISN'T THAT A COUNTRY SONG?
MOM WAS RIGHT... I SHOULD HAVE MAJORED IN P.R.
The Daily News
I THOUGHT THE CUBICLES AT THE OLD OFFICE WERE SMALL!..
BUT, DUDE... THIS IS SERIOUS TOGETHERNESS.
HEY... WHAT IS THAT SMELL?
DON'T CALL ME "DUDE".
IT'S A SEAWEED BASED BROTH. I'M DOING A CLEANSE FOR THE NEXT TWO WEEKS. NO DAIRY... NO GLUTEN...
NO DONUTS?!
DONUTS ARE GLUTEN.
PAIGE
WELL, THE SMELL OF THAT BROTH SHOULD PRETTY MUCH RUIN EVERYONE'S APPETITE... Ack!...
WOOSH!
WHAT'S THAT SMELL?!
ARE THE UNDEAD BACK?

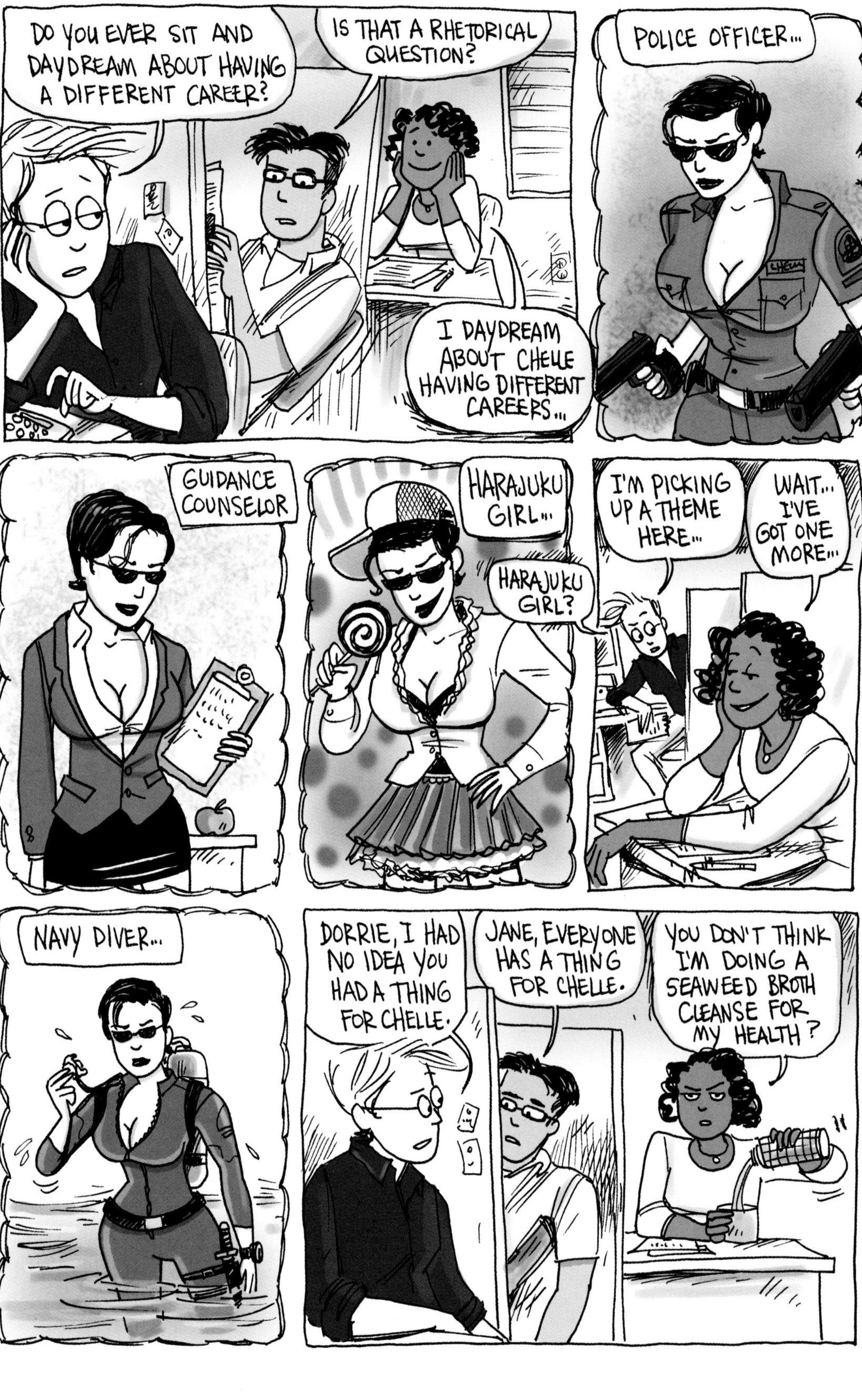
DO YOU EVER SIT AND DAYDREAM ABOUT HAVING A DIFFERENT CAREER?
IS THAT A RHETORICAL QUESTION?
I DAYDREAM ABOUT CHELLE HAVING DIFFERENT CAREERS...
POLICE OFFICER...
CHELL
GUIDANCE COUNSELOR
HARAJUKU GIRL...
HARAJUKU GIRL?
I'M PICKING UP A THEME HERE...
WAIT... I'VE GOT ONE MORE...
NAVY DIVER...
DORRIE, I HAD NO IDEA YOU HAD A THING FOR CHELLE.
JANE, EVERYONE HAS A THING FOR CHELLE.
YOU DON'T THINK I'M DOING A SEAWEED BROTH CLEANSE FOR MY HEALTH?

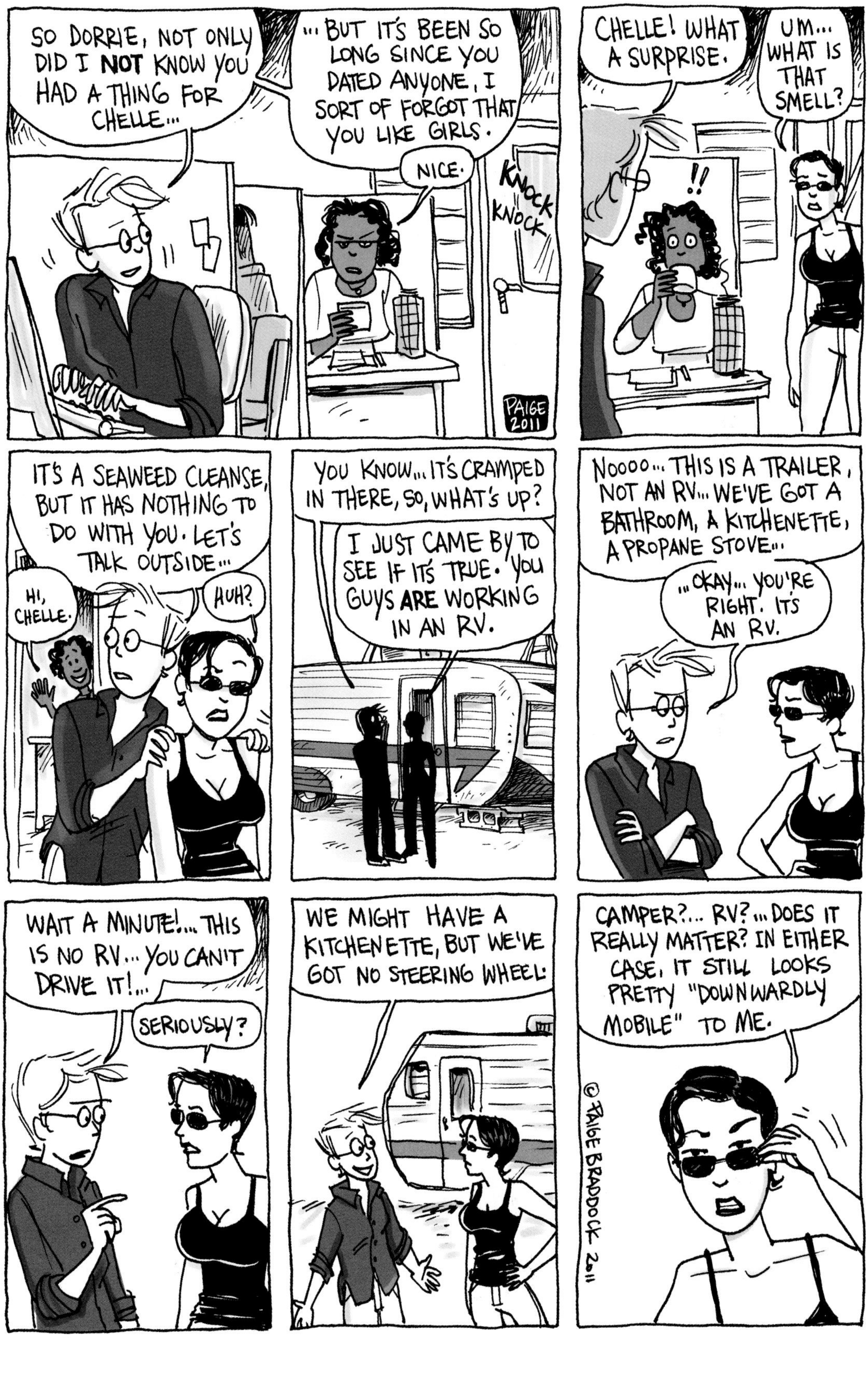

SO DORRIE, NOT ONLY DID I **NOT** KNOW YOU HAD A THING FOR CHELLE...
...BUT IT'S BEEN SO LONG SINCE YOU DATED ANYONE, I SORT OF FORGOT THAT YOU LIKE GIRLS.
NICE.
KNOCK KNOCK
PAIGE 2011
CHELLE! WHAT A SURPRISE.
!!
UM... WHAT IS THAT SMELL?
IT'S A SEAWEED CLEANSE, BUT IT HAS NOTHING TO DO WITH YOU. LET'S TALK OUTSIDE...
HI, CHELLE.
HUH?
YOU KNOW... IT'S CRAMPED IN THERE, SO, WHAT'S UP?
I JUST CAME BY TO SEE IF IT'S TRUE. YOU GUYS **ARE** WORKING IN AN RV.
NOOOO... THIS IS A TRAILER, NOT AN RV... WE'VE GOT A BATHROOM, A KITCHENETTE, A PROPANE STOVE...
...OKAY... YOU'RE RIGHT. IT'S AN RV.
WAIT A MINUTE!... THIS IS NO RV... YOU CAN'T DRIVE IT!...
SERIOUSLY?
WE MIGHT HAVE A KITCHENETTE, BUT WE'VE GOT NO STEERING WHEEL.
CAMPER?... RV?... DOES IT REALLY MATTER? IN EITHER CASE, IT STILL LOOKS PRETTY "DOWNWARDLY MOBILE" TO ME.
© PAIGE BRADDOCK 2011

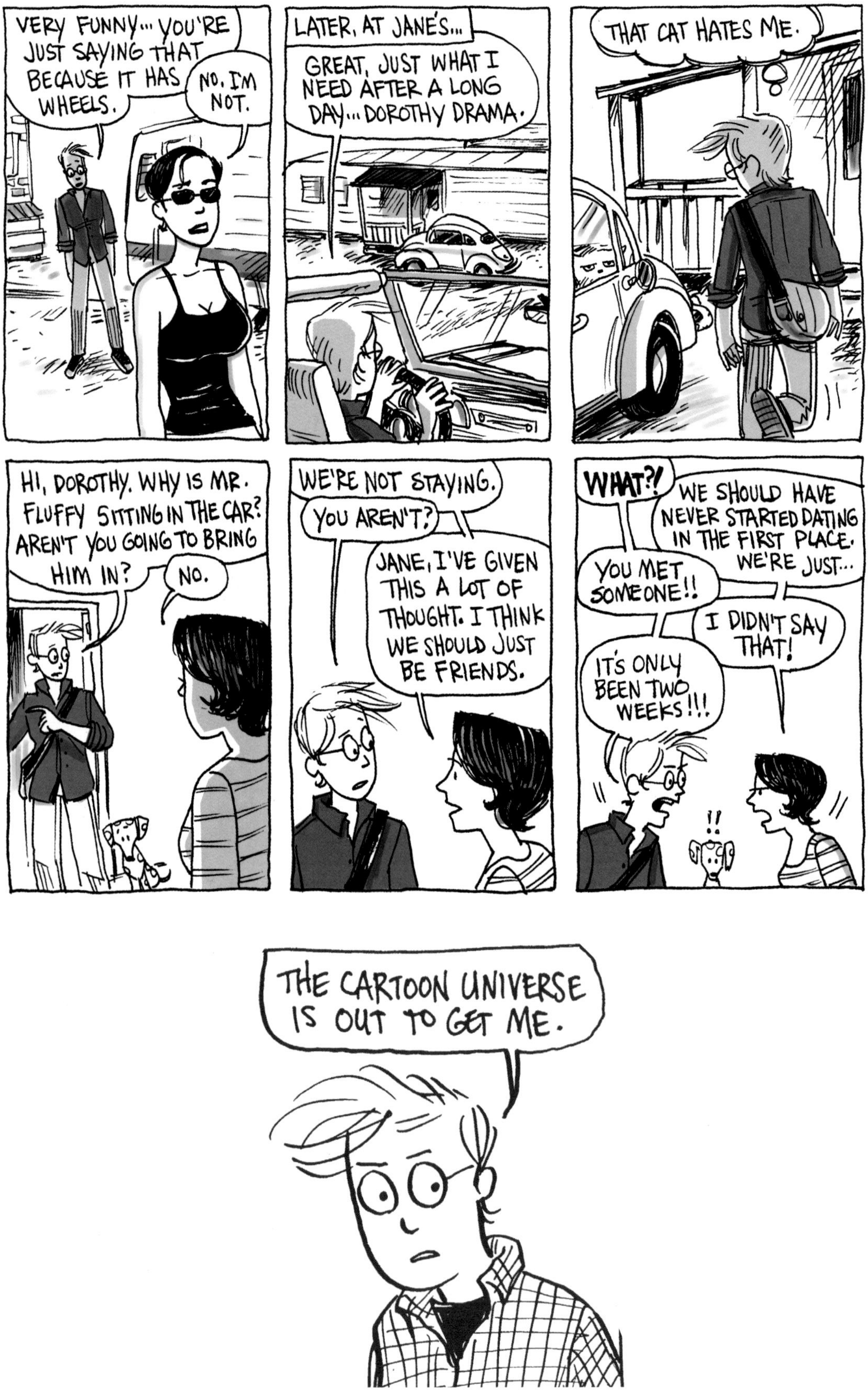
VERY FUNNY... YOU'RE JUST SAYING THAT BECAUSE IT HAS WHEELS.
NO, I'M NOT.
LATER, AT JANE'S...
GREAT, JUST WHAT I NEED AFTER A LONG DAY... DOROTHY DRAMA.
THAT CAT HATES ME.
HI, DOROTHY. WHY IS MR. FLUFFY SITTING IN THE CAR? AREN'T YOU GOING TO BRING HIM IN?
NO.
WE'RE NOT STAYING.
YOU AREN'T?
JANE, I'VE GIVEN THIS A LOT OF THOUGHT. I THINK WE SHOULD JUST BE FRIENDS.
WHAT?!
WE SHOULD HAVE NEVER STARTED DATING IN THE FIRST PLACE. WE'RE JUST...
YOU MET SOMEONE!!
I DIDN'T SAY THAT!
IT'S ONLY BEEN TWO WEEKS!!!
THE CARTOON UNIVERSE IS OUT TO GET ME.

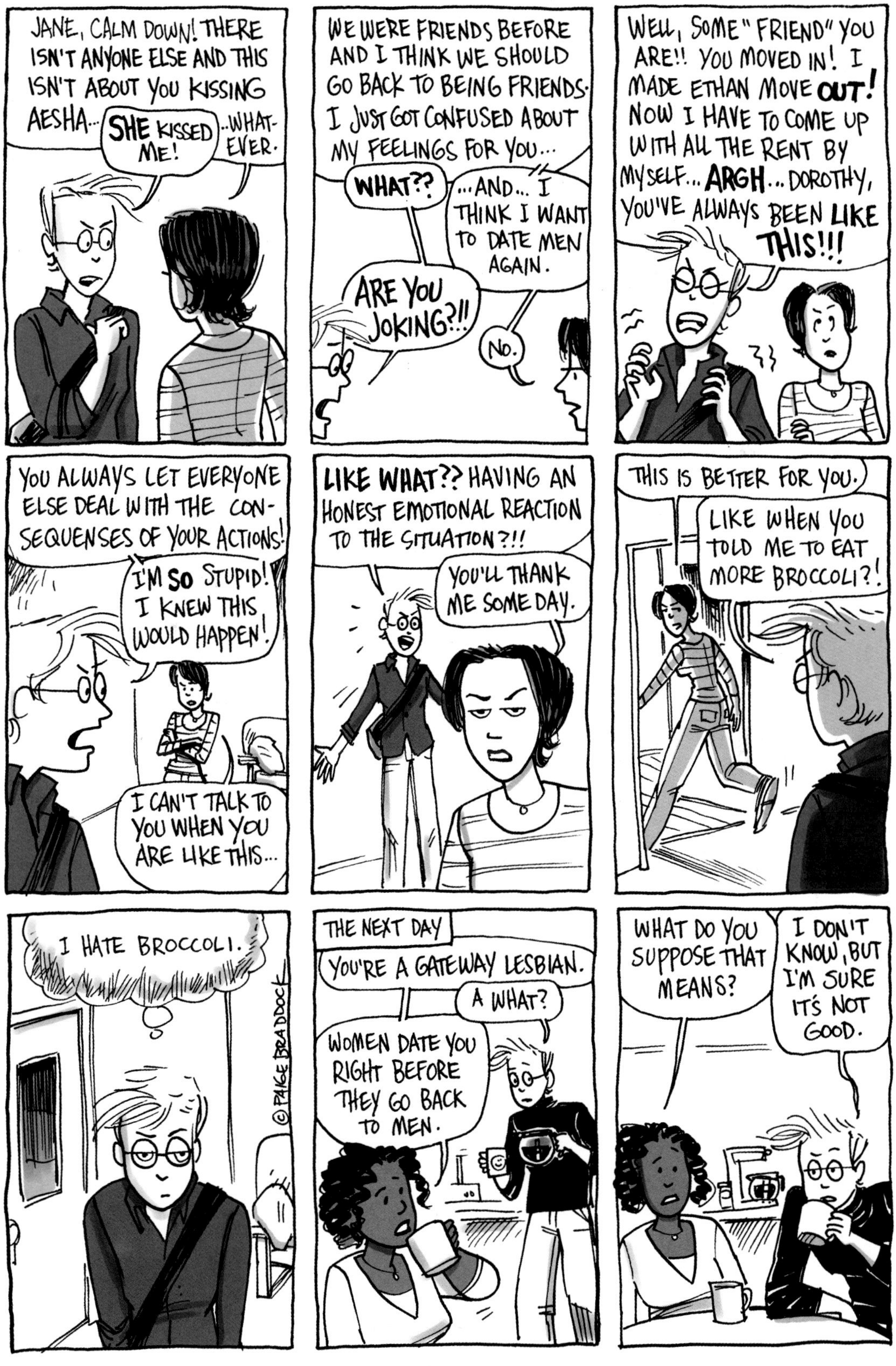
JANE, CALM DOWN! THERE ISN'T ANYONE ELSE AND THIS ISN'T ABOUT YOU KISSING AESHA...
SHE KISSED ME!
...WHAT-EVER.
WE WERE FRIENDS BEFORE AND I THINK WE SHOULD GO BACK TO BEING FRIENDS. I JUST GOT CONFUSED ABOUT MY FEELINGS FOR YOU...
WHAT??
...AND... I THINK I WANT TO DATE MEN AGAIN.
ARE YOU JOKING?!!
NO.
WELL, SOME "FRIEND" YOU ARE!! YOU MOVED IN! I MADE ETHAN MOVE OUT! NOW I HAVE TO COME UP WITH ALL THE RENT BY MYSELF... ARGH... DOROTHY, YOU'VE ALWAYS BEEN LIKE THIS!!!
YOU ALWAYS LET EVERYONE ELSE DEAL WITH THE CONSEQUENSES OF YOUR ACTIONS!
I'M SO STUPID! I KNEW THIS WOULD HAPPEN!
I CAN'T TALK TO YOU WHEN YOU ARE LIKE THIS...
LIKE WHAT?? HAVING AN HONEST EMOTIONAL REACTION TO THE SITUATION?!!
YOU'LL THANK ME SOME DAY.
THIS IS BETTER FOR YOU.
LIKE WHEN YOU TOLD ME TO EAT MORE BROCCOLI?!
I HATE BROCCOLI.
© PAIGE BRADDOCK
THE NEXT DAY
YOU'RE A GATEWAY LESBIAN.
A WHAT?
WOMEN DATE YOU RIGHT BEFORE THEY GO BACK TO MEN.
WHAT DO YOU SUPPOSE THAT MEANS?
I DON'T KNOW, BUT I'M SURE IT'S NOT GOOD.

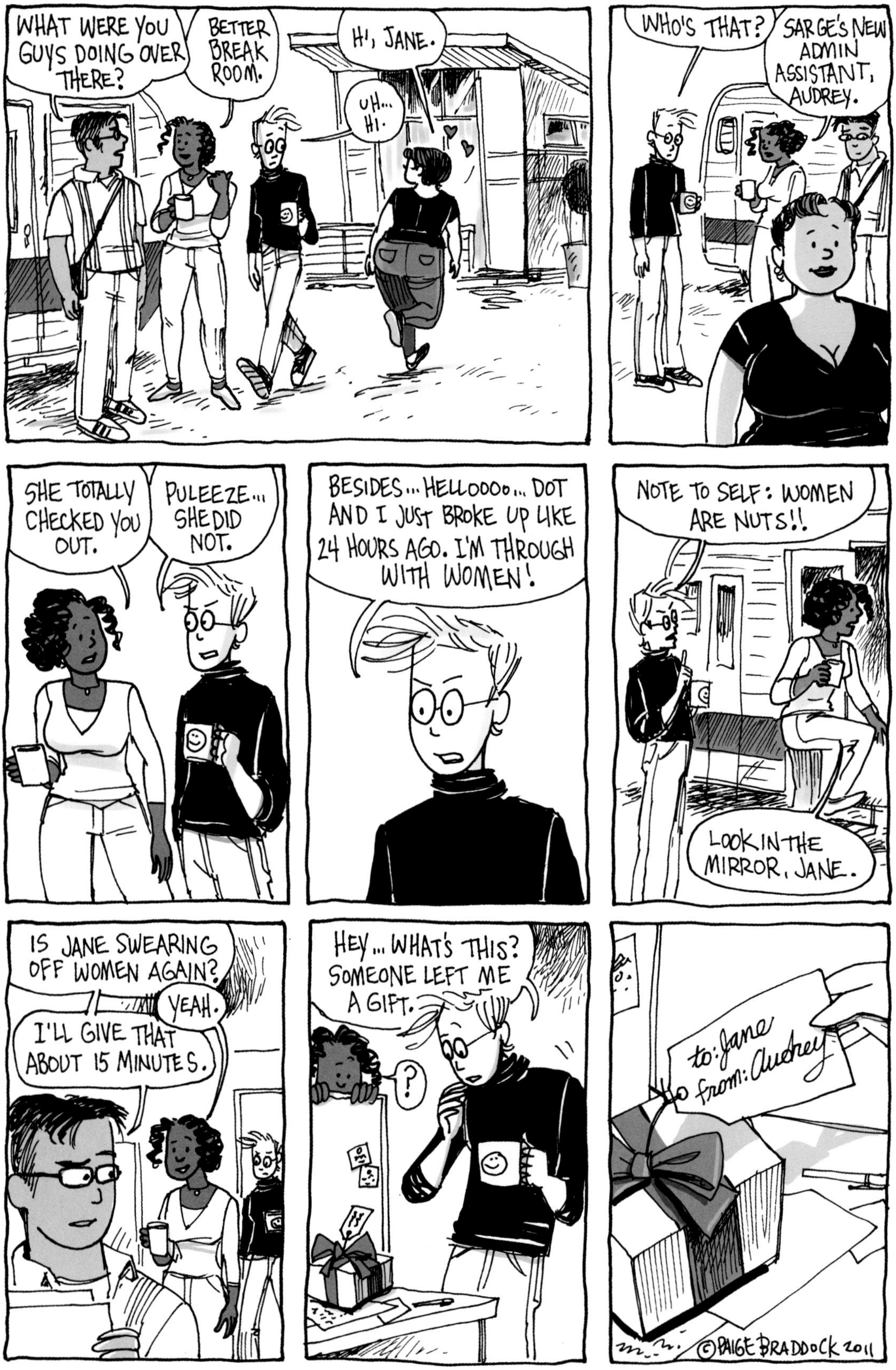
WHAT WERE YOU GUYS DOING OVER THERE?
BETTER BREAK ROOM.
H', JANE.
UH... HI.
WHO'S THAT?
SARGE'S NEW ADMIN ASSISTANT, AUDREY.
SHE TOTALLY CHECKED YOU OUT.
PULEEZE... SHE DID NOT.
BESIDES... HELLOOOO... DOT AND I JUST BROKE UP LIKE 24 HOURS AGO. I'M THROUGH WITH WOMEN!
NOTE TO SELF: WOMEN ARE NUTS!!
LOOK IN THE MIRROR, JANE.
IS JANE SWEARING OFF WOMEN AGAIN?
YEAH.
I'LL GIVE THAT ABOUT 15 MINUTES.
HEY... WHAT'S THIS? SOMEONE LEFT ME A GIFT.
?
to: Jane
from: Audrey
©PAIGE BRADDOCK 2011

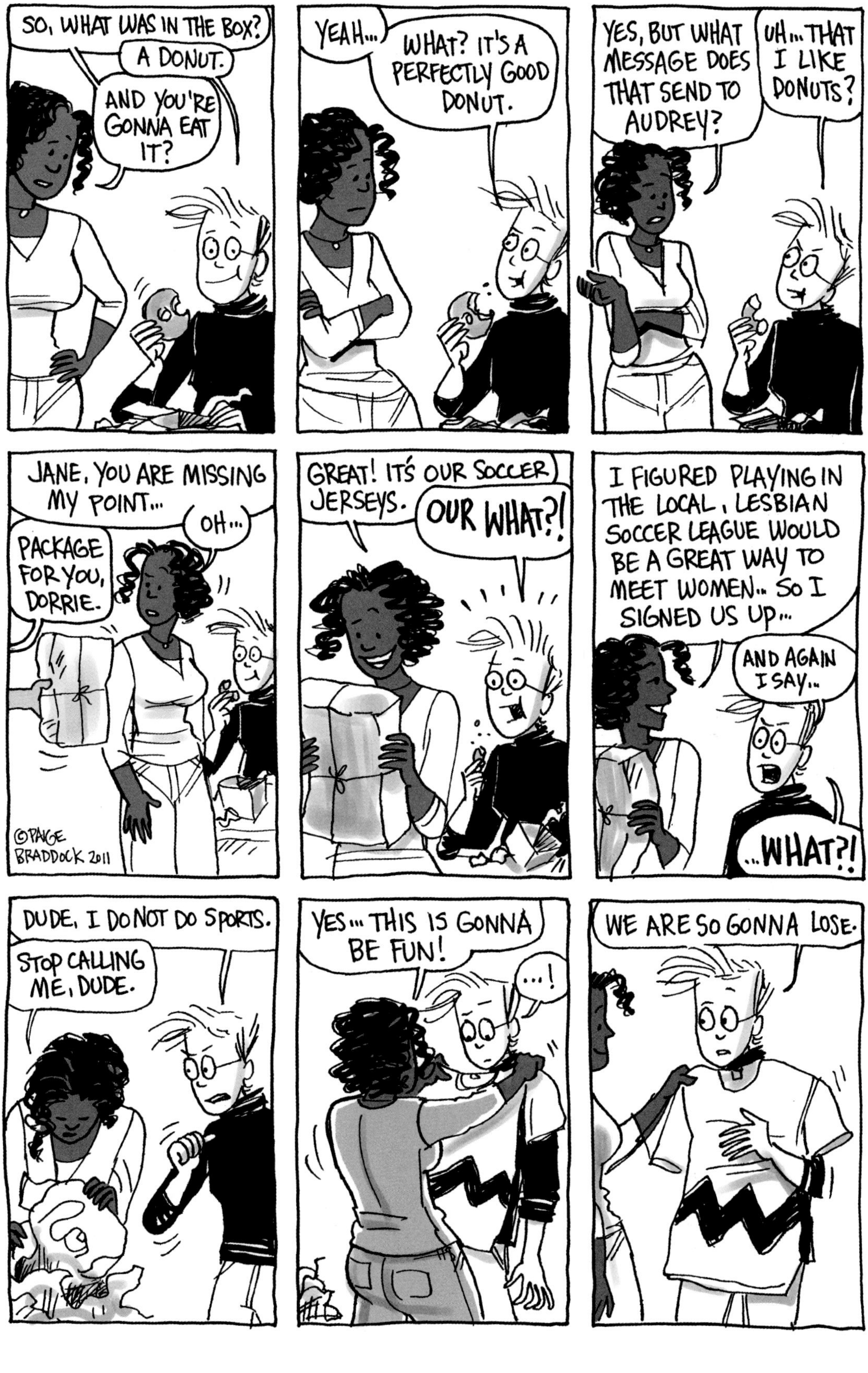
SO, WHAT WAS IN THE BOX?
A DONUT.
AND YOU'RE GONNA EAT IT?
YEAH...
WHAT? IT'S A PERFECTLY GOOD DONUT.
YES, BUT WHAT MESSAGE DOES THAT SEND TO AUDREY?
UH... THAT I LIKE DONUTS?
JANE, YOU ARE MISSING MY POINT...
OH...
PACKAGE FOR YOU, DORRIE.
©PAIGE BRADDOCK 2011
GREAT! IT'S OUR SOCCER JERSEYS.
OUR WHAT?!
I FIGURED PLAYING IN THE LOCAL, LESBIAN SOCCER LEAGUE WOULD BE A GREAT WAY TO MEET WOMEN.. SO I SIGNED US UP...
AND AGAIN I SAY..
...WHAT?!
DUDE, I DO NOT DO SPORTS.
STOP CALLING ME, DUDE.
YES... THIS IS GONNA BE FUN!
...!
WE ARE SO GONNA LOSE.

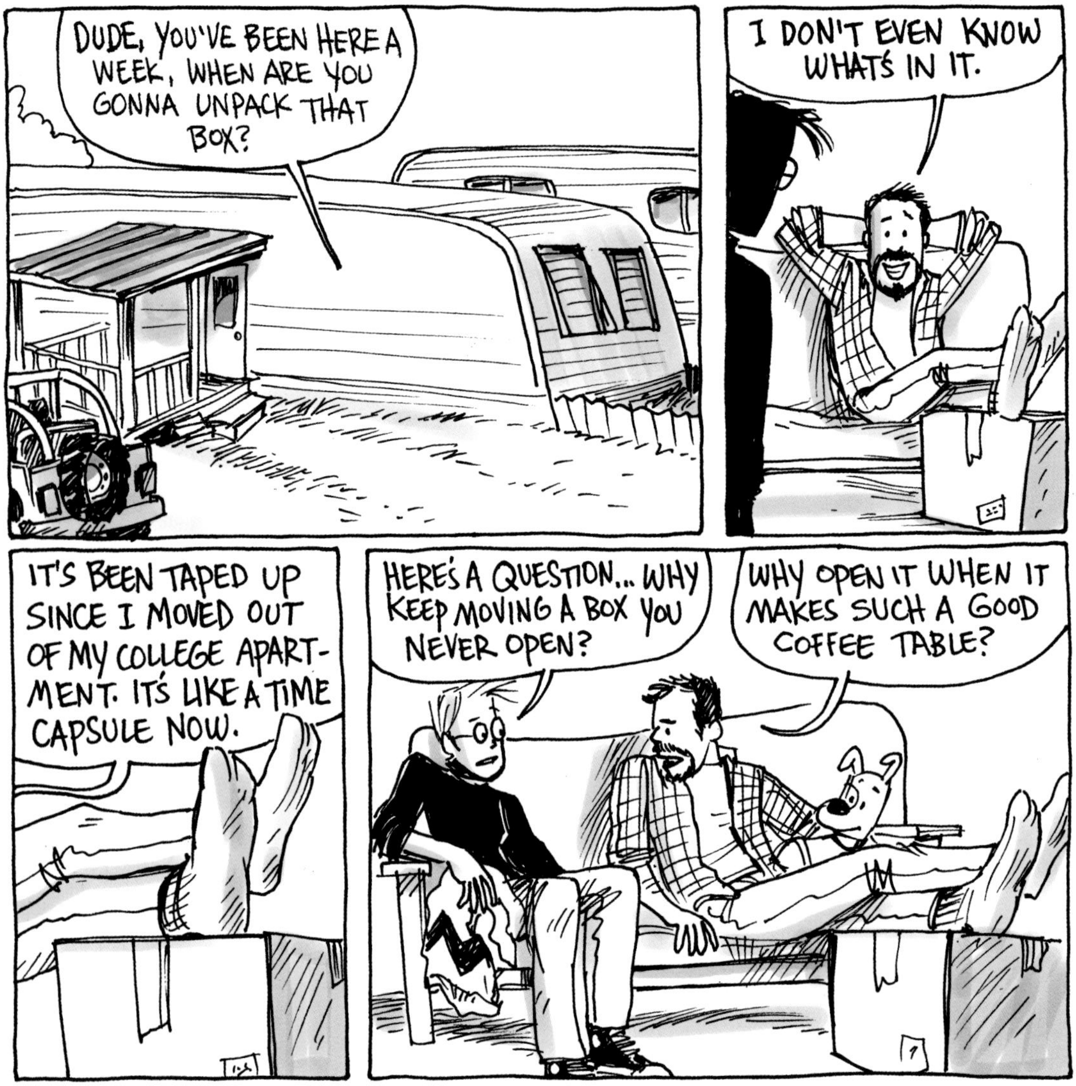
DUDE, YOU'VE BEEN HERE A WEEK, WHEN ARE YOU GONNA UNPACK THAT BOX?
I DON'T EVEN KNOW WHAT'S IN IT.
IT'S BEEN TAPED UP SINCE I MOVED OUT OF MY COLLEGE APARTMENT. IT'S LIKE A TIME CAPSULE NOW.
HERE'S A QUESTION... WHY KEEP MOVING A BOX YOU NEVER OPEN?
WHY OPEN IT WHEN IT MAKES SUCH A GOOD COFFEE TABLE?

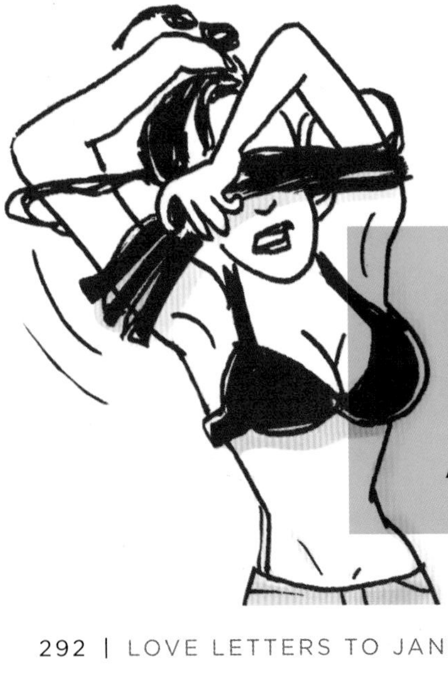

“Jane is one of the most endearing heroines in comics history. And Paige Braddock draws breasts better than anyone.”

ALISON BECHDEL

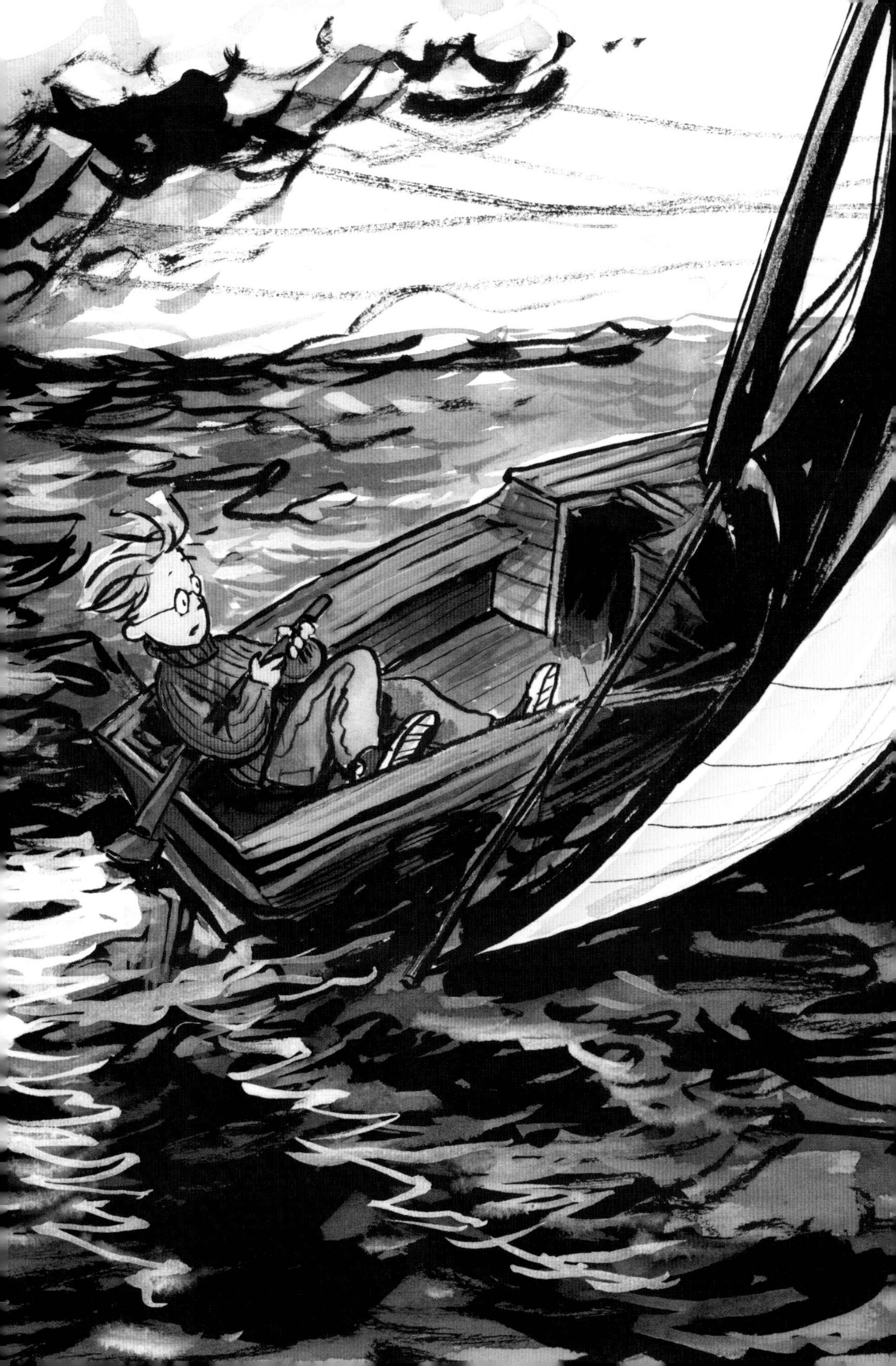

Fools Rush In

Can Jane rekindle things with her perfectly imperfect match, Dorothy? Read on, friends, and see for yourselves...

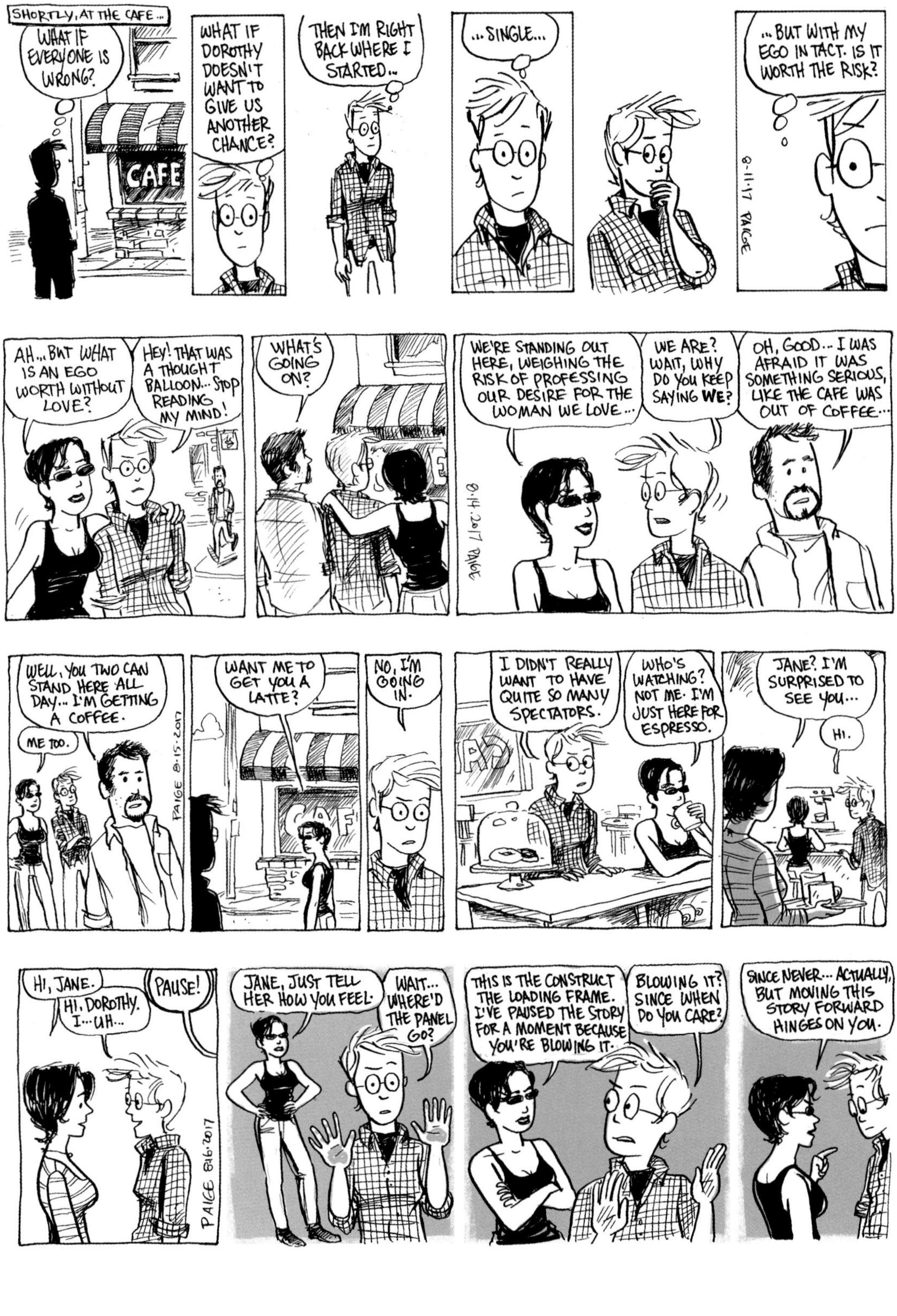
SHORTLY, AT THE CAFE...
WHAT IF EVERYONE IS WRONG?
WHAT IF DOROTHY DOESN'T WANT TO GIVE US ANOTHER CHANCE?
THEN I'M RIGHT BACK WHERE I STARTED...
...SINGLE...
...BUT WITH MY EGO IN TACT. IS IT WORTH THE RISK?
8-11-17 PAIGE
AH... BUT WHAT IS AN EGO WORTH WITHOUT LOVE?
HEY! THAT WAS A THOUGHT BALLOON... STOP READING MY MIND!
WHAT'S GOING ON?
8-14-2017 PAIGE
WE'RE STANDING OUT HERE, WEIGHING THE RISK OF PROFESSING OUR DESIRE FOR THE WOMAN WE LOVE...
WE ARE? WAIT, WHY DO YOU KEEP SAYING WE?
OH, GOOD... I WAS AFRAID IT WAS SOMETHING SERIOUS, LIKE THE CAFE WAS OUT OF COFFEE...
WELL, YOU TWO CAN STAND HERE ALL DAY... I'M GETTING A COFFEE.
ME TOO.
PAIGE 8-15-2017
WANT ME TO GET YOU A LATTE?
NO, I'M GOING IN.
I DIDN'T REALLY WANT TO HAVE QUITE SO MANY SPECTATORS.
WHO'S WATCHING? NOT ME. I'M JUST HERE FOR ESPRESSO.
JANE? I'M SURPRISED TO SEE YOU...
HI.
HI, JANE.
HI, DOROTHY. I...UH...
PAUSE!
PAIGE 8-16-2017
JANE, JUST TELL HER HOW YOU FEEL.
WAIT... WHERE'D THE PANEL GO?
THIS IS THE CONSTRUCT THE LOADING FRAME. I'VE PAUSED THE STORY FOR A MOMENT BECAUSE YOU'RE BLOWING IT.
BLOWING IT? SINCE WHEN DO YOU CARE?
SINCE NEVER... ACTUALLY, BUT MOVING THIS STORY FORWARD HINGES ON YOU.

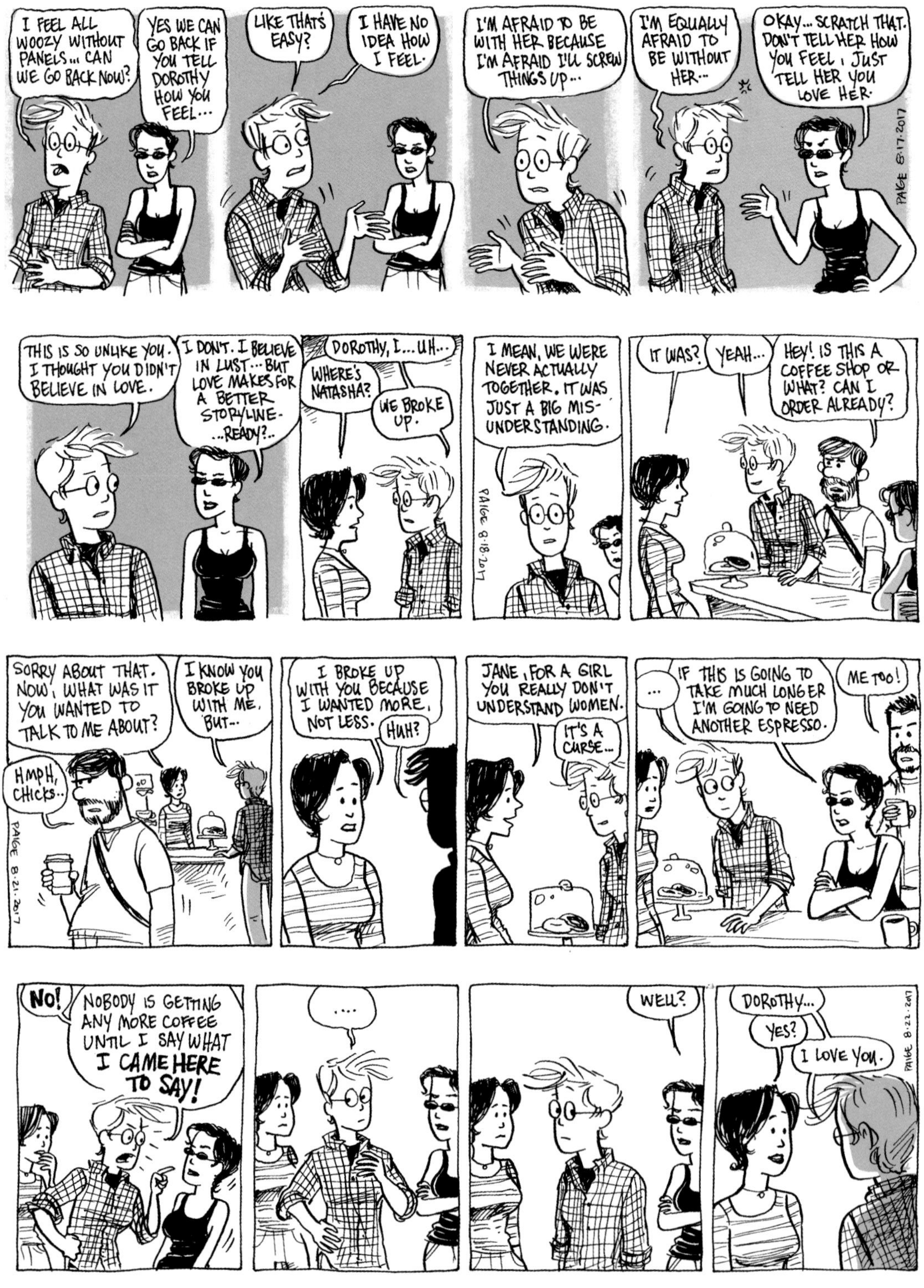

I FEEL ALL WOOZY WITHOUT PANELS... CAN WE GO BACK NOW?
YES WE CAN GO BACK IF YOU TELL DOROTHY HOW YOU FEEL...
LIKE THAT'S EASY?
I HAVE NO IDEA HOW I FEEL.
I'M AFRAID TO BE WITH HER BECAUSE I'M AFRAID I'LL SCREW THINGS UP...
I'M EQUALLY AFRAID TO BE WITHOUT HER...
OKAY... SCRATCH THAT. DON'T TELL HER HOW YOU FEEL, JUST TELL HER YOU LOVE HER.
PAIGE 8.17.2017
THIS IS SO UNLIKE YOU. I THOUGHT YOU DIDN'T BELIEVE IN LOVE.
I DON'T. I BELIEVE IN LUST... BUT LOVE MAKES FOR A BETTER STORYLINE. ...READY?..
DOROTHY, I... UH...
WHERE'S NATASHA?
WE BROKE UP.
PAIGE 8.18.2017
I MEAN, WE WERE NEVER ACTUALLY TOGETHER. IT WAS JUST A BIG MIS-UNDERSTANDING.
IT WAS?
YEAH...
HEY! IS THIS A COFFEE SHOP OR WHAT? CAN I ORDER ALREADY?
SORRY ABOUT THAT. NOW, WHAT WAS IT YOU WANTED TO TALK TO ME ABOUT?
I KNOW YOU BROKE UP WITH ME, BUT..
HMPH, CHICKS..
PAIGE 8.21.2017
I BROKE UP WITH YOU BECAUSE I WANTED MORE, NOT LESS.
HUH?
JANE, FOR A GIRL YOU REALLY DON'T UNDERSTAND WOMEN.
IT'S A CURSE...
...
IF THIS IS GOING TO TAKE MUCH LONGER I'M GOING TO NEED ANOTHER ESPRESSO.
ME TOO!
NO!
NOBODY IS GETTING ANY MORE COFFEE UNTIL I SAY WHAT I CAME HERE TO SAY!
....
WELL?
DOROTHY...
YES?
I LOVE YOU.
PAIGE 8.22.2017

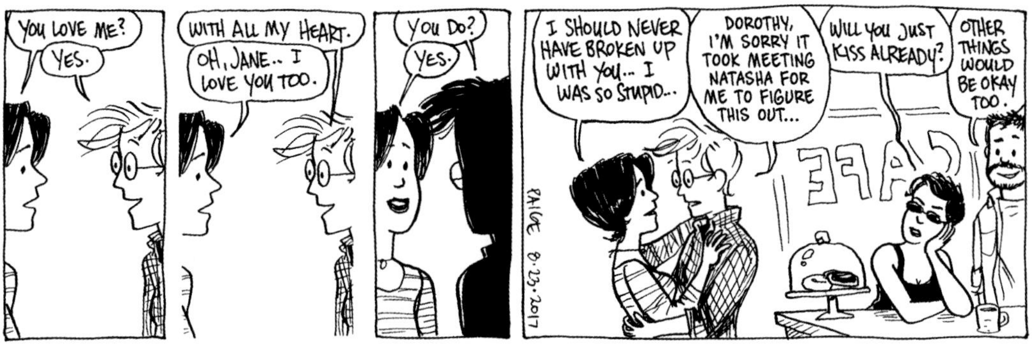
YOU LOVE ME?
YES.
WITH ALL MY HEART.
OH, JANE.. I LOVE YOU TOO.
YOU DO?
YES.
PAIGE 8·23·2017
I SHOULD NEVER HAVE BROKEN UP WITH YOU... I WAS SO STUPID...
DOROTHY, I'M SORRY IT TOOK MEETING NATASHA FOR ME TO FIGURE THIS OUT...
WILL YOU JUST KISS ALREADY?
OTHER THINGS WOULD BE OKAY TOO.
CAFE

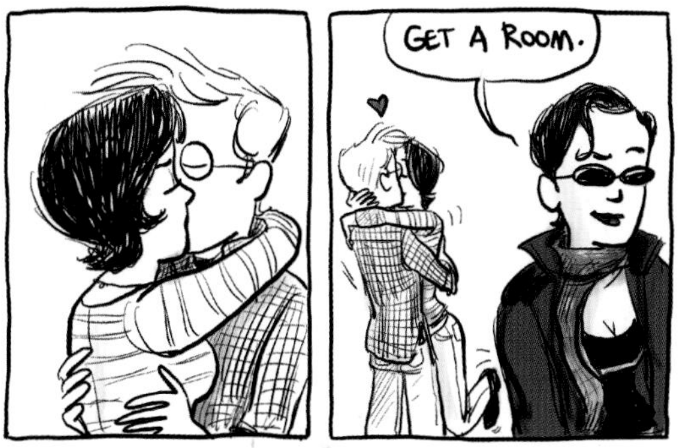
GET A ROOM.

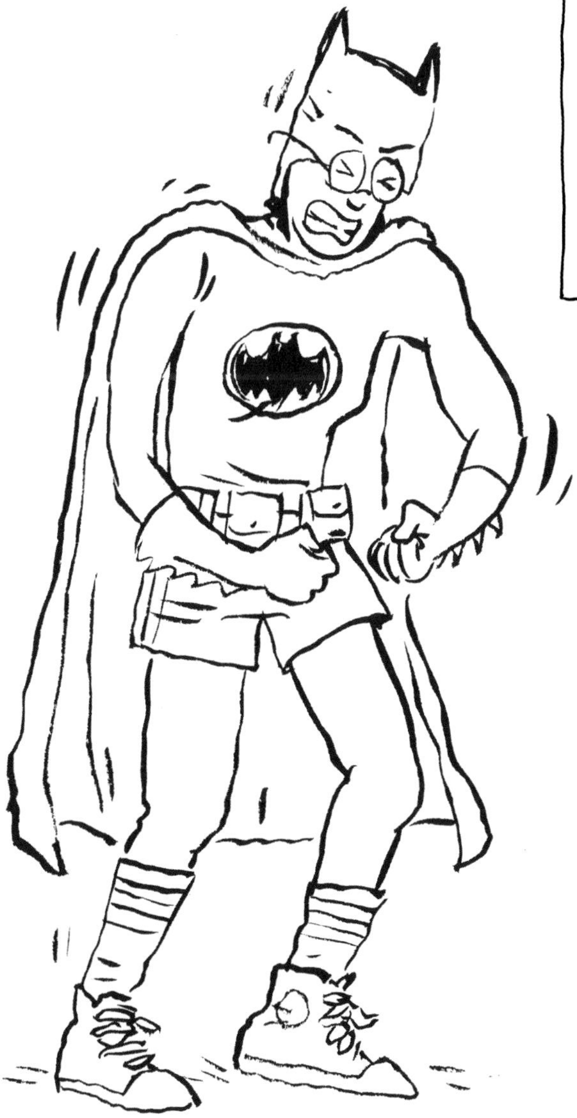

It's such a big moment the first time you walk into a comic shop and see your book along the wall with all the other monthly releases. The one thing I didn't consider was that when shelved in alphabetical order my comic book would be right next to *Justice League*: rich colors, spandex, bulging muscles, boobs...you get the idea. Needless to say, I realized immediately that I needed help making my covers pop on the shelf. Over the entire run of *Jane's World*, I've worked with an amazing colorist, Brian Miller. He really brought my inked images to life.

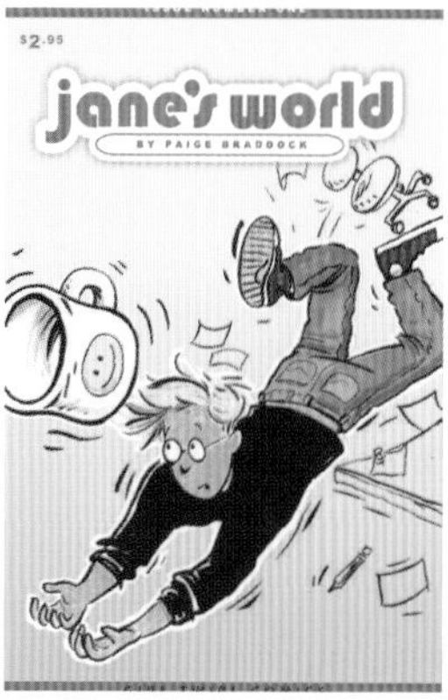
$2.95
jane's world
BY PAIGE BRADDOCK

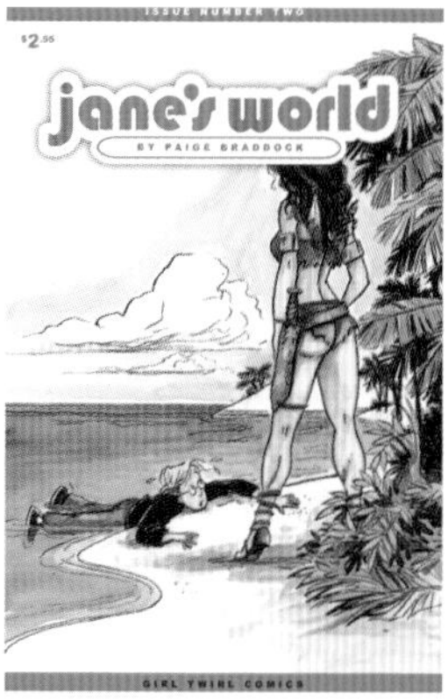
ISSUE NUMBER TWO
$2.95
jane's world
BY PAIGE BRADDOCK
GIRL TWIRL COMICS

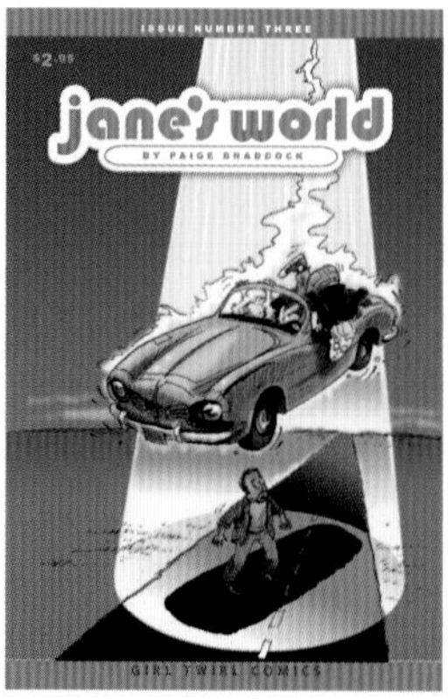
ISSUE NUMBER THREE
$2.95
jane's world
BY PAIGE BRADDOCK
GIRL TWIRL COMICS

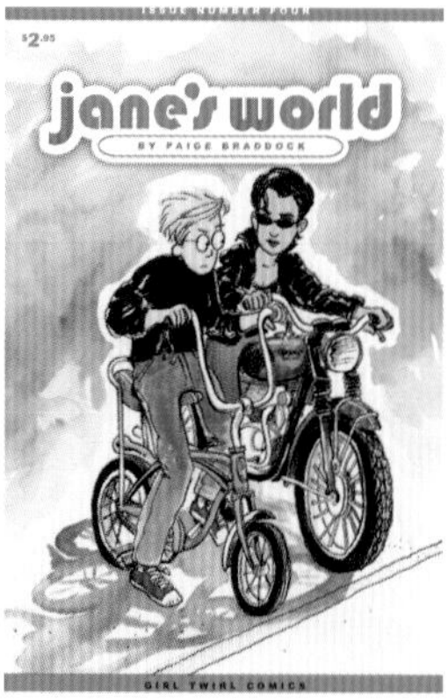
$2.95
jane's world
BY PAIGE BRADDOCK
GIRL TWIRL COMICS

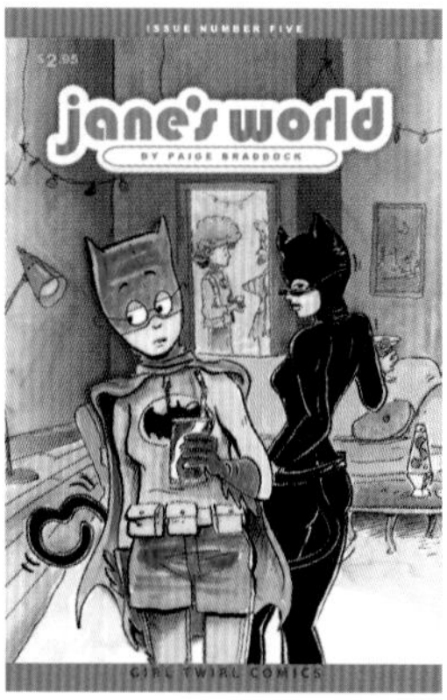
ISSUE NUMBER FIVE
$2.95
jane's world
BY PAIGE BRADDOCK
GIRL TWIRL COMICS

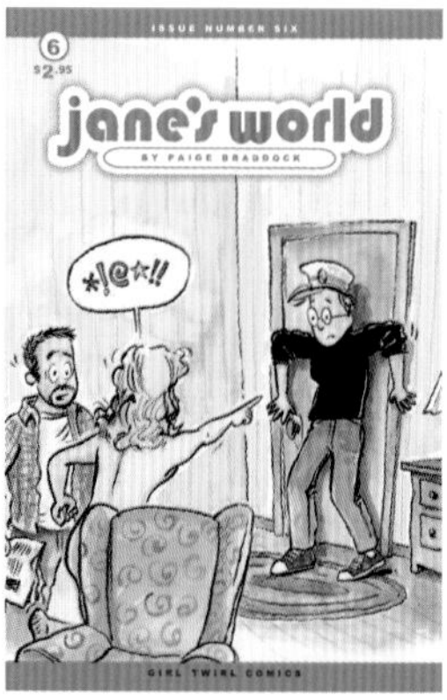
6
ISSUE NUMBER SIX
$2.95
jane's world
BY PAIGE BRADDOCK
GIRL TWIRL COMICS

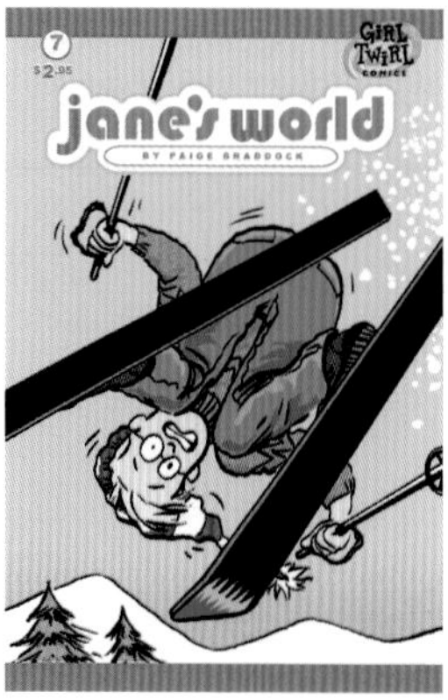
7
$2.95
GIRL TWIRL COMICS
jane's world
BY PAIGE BRADDOCK

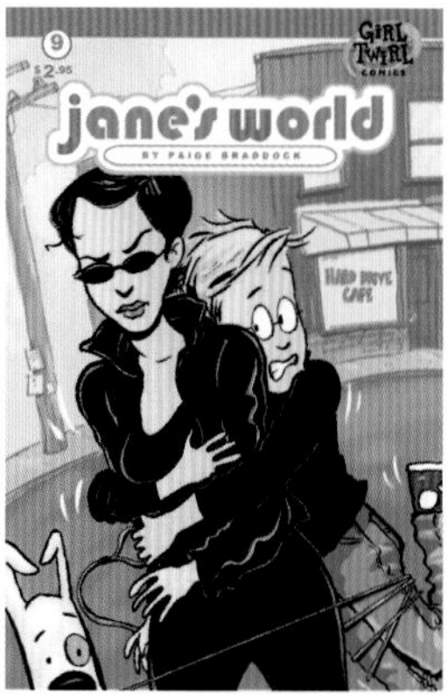
9
$2.95
GIRL TWIRL COMICS
jane's world
BY PAIGE BRADDOCK

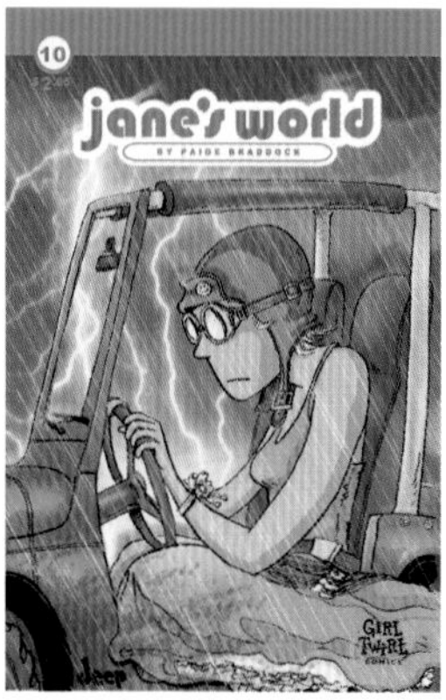
10
jane's world
BY PAIGE BRADDOCK
GIRL TWIRL COMICS

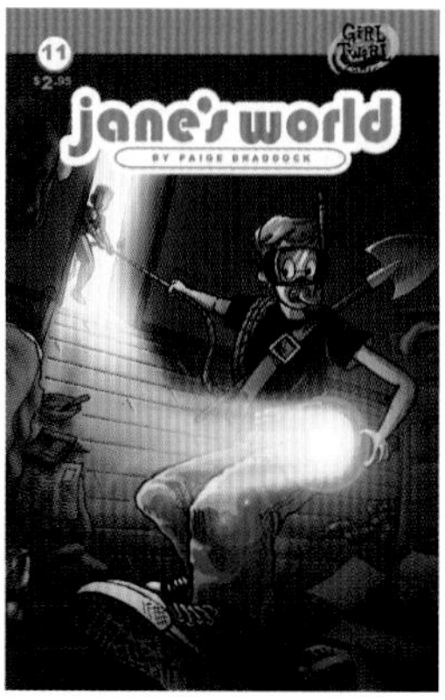
11
$2.95
jane's world
BY PAIGE BRADDOCK

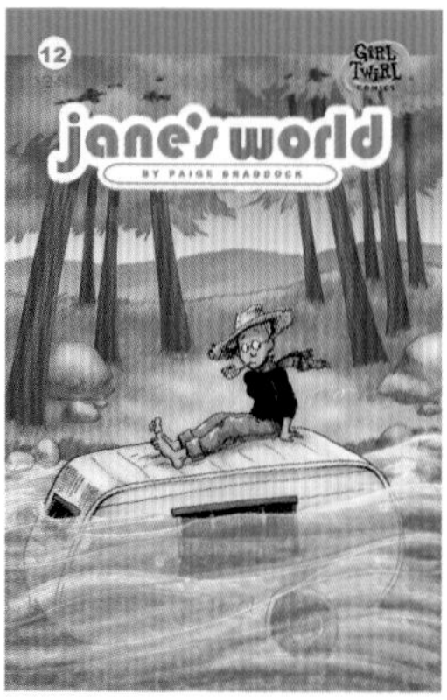
12
GIRL TWIRL COMICS
jane's world
BY PAIGE BRADDOCK

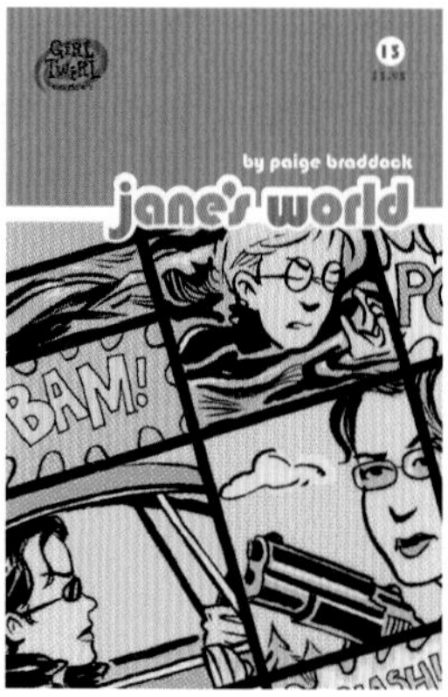
GIRL TWIRL
13
by paige braddock
jane's world
BAM!

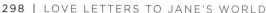

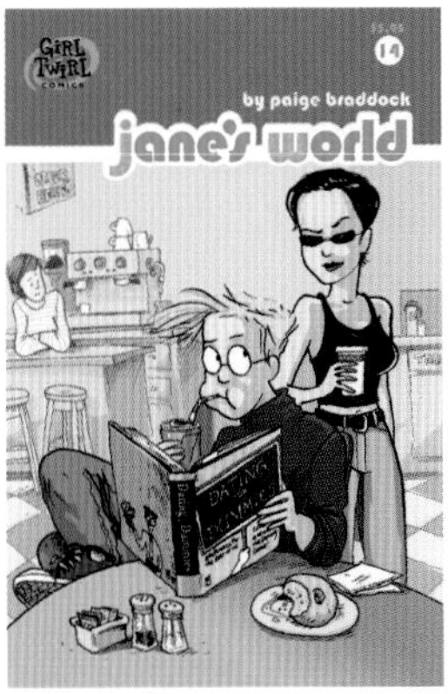
GIRL TWIRL COMICS
14
by paige braddock
jane's world

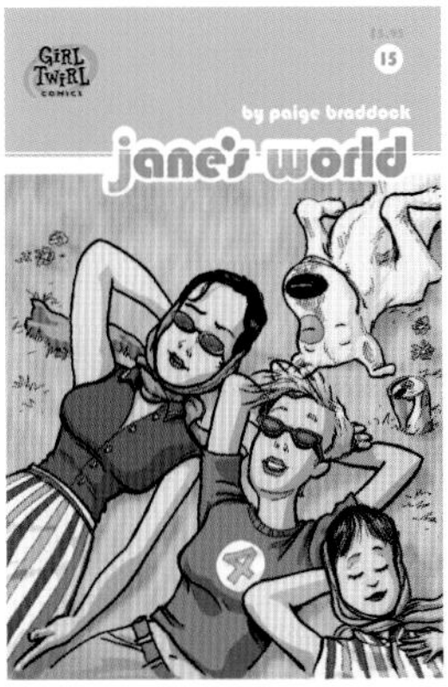
GIRL TWIRL COMICS
15
by paige braddock
jane's world

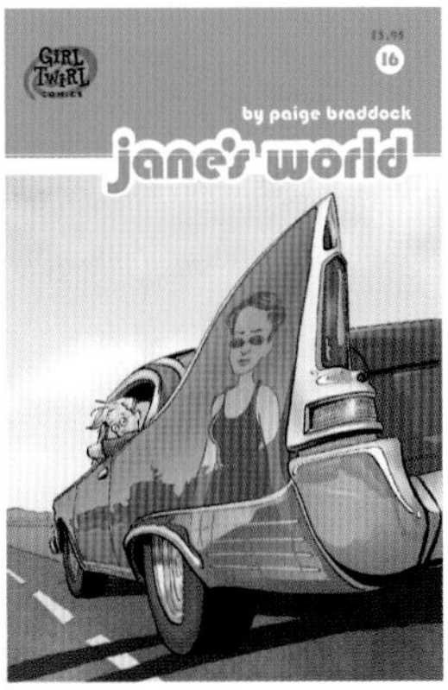
GIRL TWIRL COMICS
16
by paige braddock
jane's world

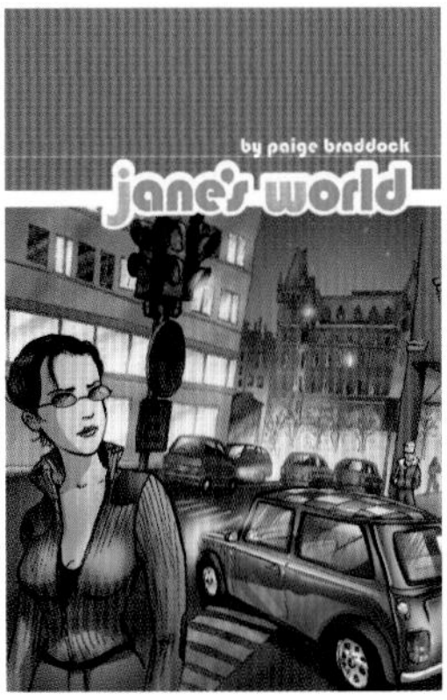
by paige braddock
jane's world

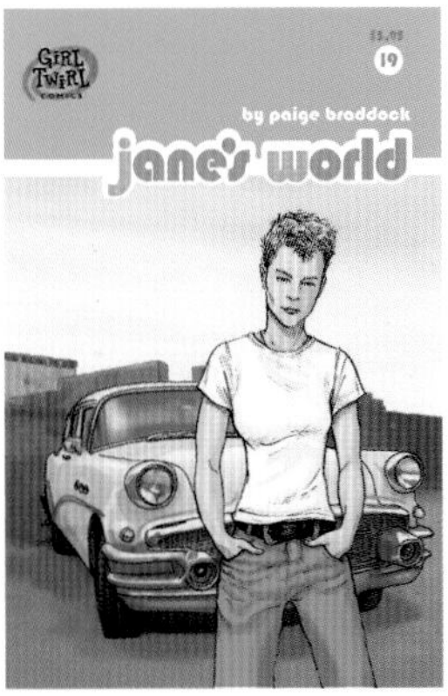
GIRL TWIRL COMICS
19
by paige braddock
jane's world

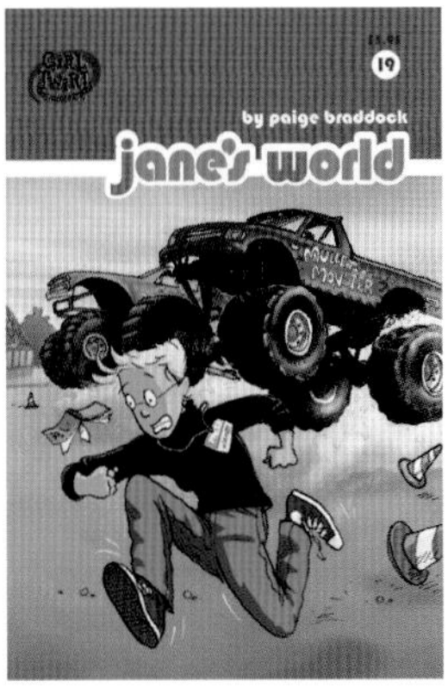
19
by paige braddock
jane's world

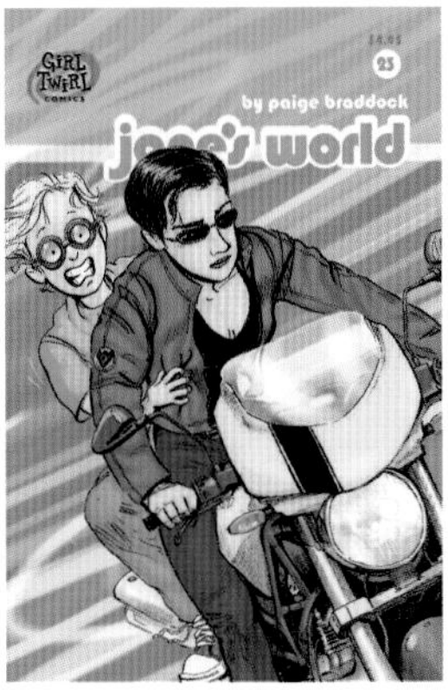
GIRL TWIRL COMICS
25
by paige braddock
jane's world

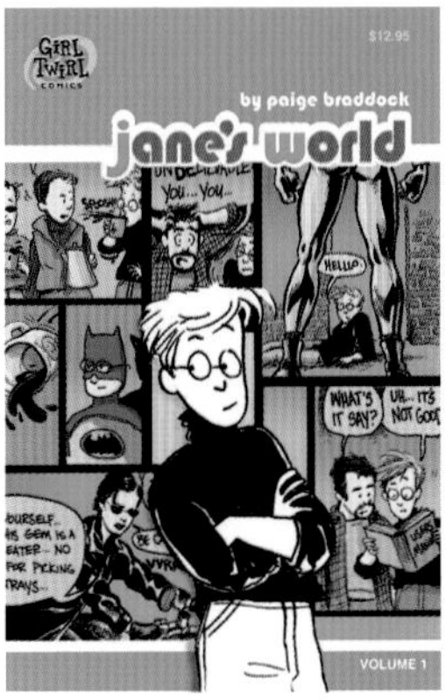
GIRL TWIRL COMICS
$12.95
by paige braddock
jane's world
VOLUME 1

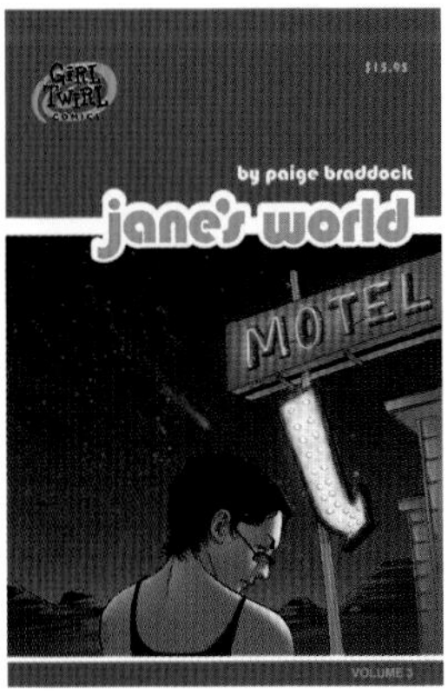
GIRL TWIRL COMICS
$15.95
by paige braddock
jane's world
MOTEL
VOLUME 3

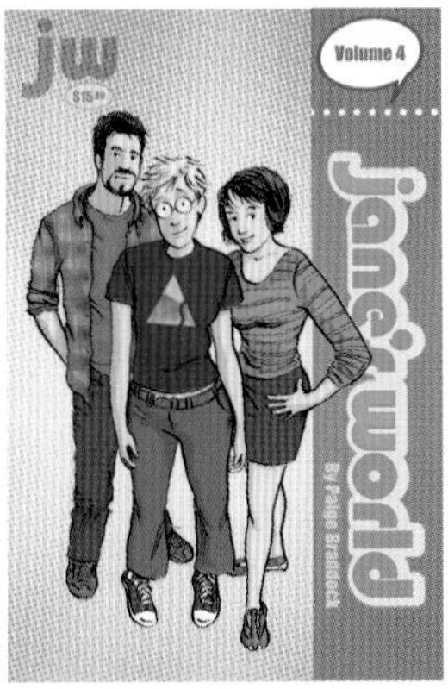
jw
Volume 4
jane's world
By Paige Braddock

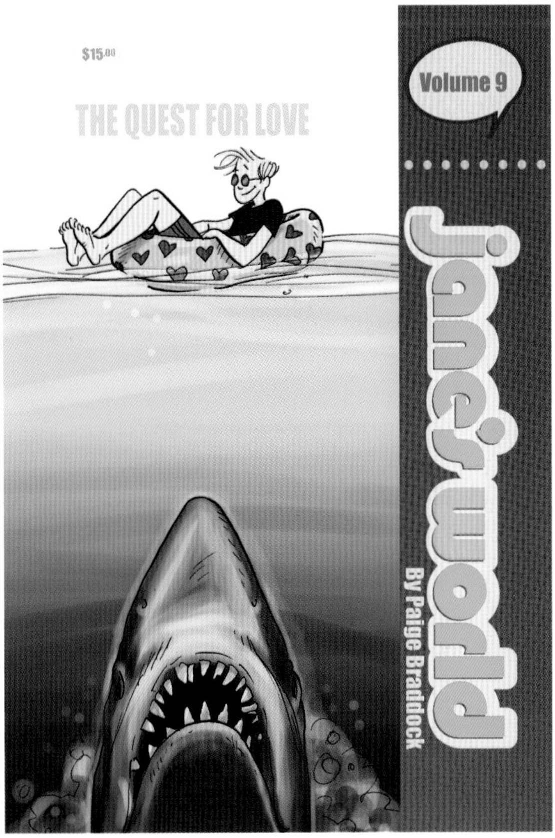
$15.00
THE QUEST FOR LOVE
Volume 9
jane's world
By Paige Braddock

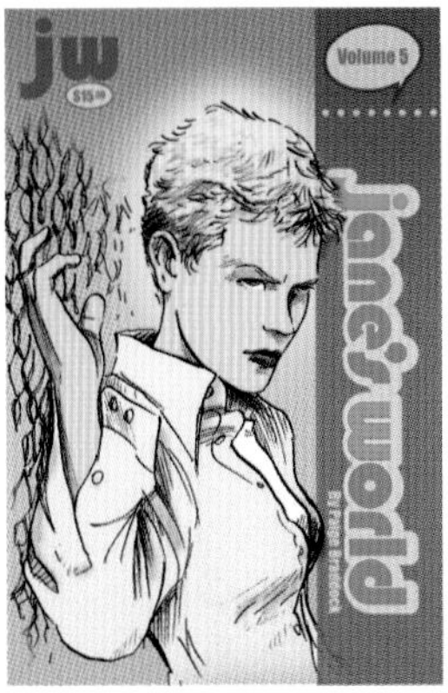
jw
Volume 5
jane's world

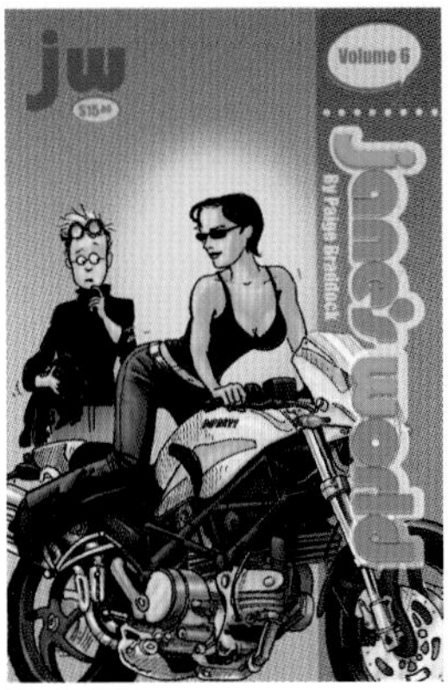
jw
Volume 6
jane's world
By Paige Braddock

CUT!
JANE'S WORLD
WE INTERRUPT OUR DAILY COMIC TO READ A BIT OF FAN MAIL...
Dear Jane, Is this really a lesbian comic if no one ever gets laid? Your friend, Steven
UH... LET'S LOOK AT ANOTHER LETTER FOLKS..
Dear Jane, When is there going to be some real action in "Jane's World?" ~Anxiously waiting, Steven
HEH, HEH..
COUGH
ONE MORE?
Dear Jane, Can someone in your comic please have sex? And when you draw the pictures can you please show some
CENSORED
!?
Voyeuristically yours, Steven
OK, FOLKS! ROLL TAPE!

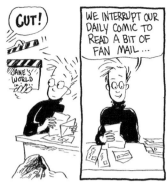

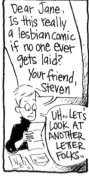

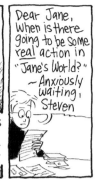

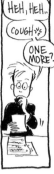

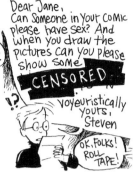

FAN MAIL

"Paige...Jane is great! Thanks for writing for the Gay/Dork faction among us. I keep recruiting all my close friends in to *Jane's World*. Any comments on SIP ending? (My comment is 'DAMN IT!')."
— HEIDY

"Hopefully God is grabbing hold of people's hearts and opening their eyes to see that what He has in mind and religion are totally different. Religion makes people act like...well, like they did on the whole Chick-fil-A thing. Ugly. Just flat ugly. I just wanted to write and say that I appreciate your comics and the talent you share with the world and your view of life and whatnot." **— JOHN**

"Hello Paige, I just wanted to write and tell you how much I hate you!!!!! I can't wait for your daily episode of *Jane*. My life is consumed with your teasingly witty episodic adventures. Please, please let the days go by faster, so that I can see what happens next...thanks for many an enjoyable morning." **— TRACY**

"I'm just an old guy, but *Jane's World* has gotten to me. It is touching and interesting." **— BOB**

"I look forward to *Jane's World* every single day. Every morning, I turn on my computer and immediately head to comics.com to check on Jane to see what is going on in her life. Thank you so much for creating *Jane's World!*"
— JEFF

"'You're a navy seal. She's just a journalist!' You really crack me up. I love *Jane's World*. Please keep up the wonderful work." **— JOE**

"You keep getting better and better. What a wonderful thrill to read your comic strip every morning. I start the day with *Jane* and *Doonesbury*...and a coffee. Life just can't get any better!"
— LOUISE

"I can relate to what Jane is going thru from my own past relationships =P it's always good to be reminded that you aren't the only one going crazy!"
— KRYSTA

"I've been enjoying the current storyline in *Jane* but I was surprised by one thing. Jane shaves under her arms?" **— MIKE**

"I am delighted every morning with your daily *Jane*; when I switch my computer on, I go to your site (and right after that, I watch for *Yu+Me* from Megan Gedris). Jane makes me laugh; I simply love her character because she is as clueless, as clumsy, as generous, as brillant, and as lovable as we all are in certain moments of the day or certain periods of our life. Voilà! Sorry if there are mistakes, English is not my mother tongue...Keep going on, and maybe see you in France for a signing!" — **ANNE-SOPHIE**

"My day has to start off with a mocha and your comic or it is just not a good start to the day." — **CHRIS**

"HELP!!!! You're killing me (I really hope you are alright)...update your *Jane* comic strip...it is still on Monday!! I live to read this every day." — **AMY**

"I just wanted to tell you how much I enjoy *Jane's World*. I love how your characters are hopelessly flawed, yet lovable—just as we all are in life—making them easily identifiable/relatable to your readers. But most of all I love your sense of humor and the way you try to have your characters play out a 'work/ life balance.' (My favorite example of this is the Jill/Skye strip when Jill is running an Op and Skye calls to ask her to bring home a bottle of wine with dinner.)" — **CHRISTINA**

"And while I'm a straight guy, I have to tell you your work is doing more for the lesbian community in terms of acceptance than somebody just getting in your face. The relationships shown in your strip are not radical in the least, just showing life from another perspective. Great stuff. If you get past the lesbian 'stigma' if you will, you have a road map for understanding your mate no matter what the gender." — **REVELL**

"My name is Jan and I've been reading *Jane's World* regularly for about a year now, but I've been reading it off and on since 2005. I love how it's more than just a comic, yet far superior than any 'soap opera comic strip' you often see in the papers. It's like a story, given to the world one tiny paragraph at a time. I adore the characters and have become very attached to them over the last year. They're so lifelike and easy to relate to that it's very easy to forget that they're not real. Thank you so much for such an amazing comic. I look forward to reading it every weekday." — **JAN**

"Loved how Jane perked up whenever anyone suggested she was butch. Loved all the bits about women being mistaken for men and how righteous some people are about the fact that they couldn't tell the difference—a life experience painfully familiar to me (well not so painful anymore!). Loved the community of exes and the sometimes painful, sometimes humorous portrayal of the complexity of these relationship webs. Loved the escape fantasies or alternate realities. Even loved the evil, two-timing, gambling butch. And I keep loving the art—it's funny, I never paid much attention to comics before, but now, maybe having met you, and seeing how prolific (and generous) you are with your artwork, I look at a picture and think about the fact that every little line, crosshatch, strand of hair, checkered pattern on clothes or other surfaces represents a mark of the pen in your hand and it is awesome." — **EVA**

"It took me a while to 'get' what *Jane* was about. When I did, it kind of blew my mind. What an incredibly novel concept! But don't you think it might be a little too daring for the 'Bible Belt'? There's people here who haven't accepted interracial marriage yet, let alone what you're talking about. Keep up the good work tho, we love you." — **CAROLE**

I wanted to be a cartoonist from the time I was seven. Looking back, I can see shades of Jane in all my previous cartoon creations. She was probably always there, waiting to be found. It wasn't until the early '90s when I was working as an illustrator for the news department of *The Chicago Tribune* that I actually gave her a name. And even then, she debuted as a single-panel comic without much of a storyline. A small cast of regular characters began to emerge, and by 1995 *Jane's World* became a comic strip that appeared fairly regularly online. This was back in the dark ages when web comics weren't really even a thing.

In 1999 I left journalism and moved to California to work with Charles Schulz in his studio. This was the first place I'd worked where comic strips were important, where comics mattered. It's hard to explain what an impact that had on me as an artist. After years of doing comics at night and on weekends while doing a "real" job during the day, finally, I was working in a studio where comics were taken seriously. *Jane's World* flourished, and so did I. The Bay Area is a great place to work in comics.

If I had to sit and explain why I do *Jane's World,* one of the main things I would say is that I do this comic because it brings me joy. *Jane's World* is a bit of an escape, where literally anything can happen: zombies, abductions by aliens from outer space, transmorphism, lethal trainees, four-alarm fires, Bigfoot, talking dogs...you name it and it has probably happened in *Jane's World*. But in addition to silly adventures, *Jane's World* is about friendship and figuring out life. The stories weave in and around one small mishap after another, but through it all runs this continuous thread of friendship and kindness. Jane, Ethan, Dorothy, and even Chelle have one thing in common: they care about each other, no matter what.

There are so many people who've populated my friend circle over the years, people who've made a difference in my life and helped *Jane's World* become what it is. I want to name of few of those folks here. Dave Graue gave me my first real cartooning lesson with a quill pen. George Breisacher talked me into joining the National Cartoonists Society. Amy Lago was the editor who picked up *Jane's World* for online syndication. Frank Camuso tabled with me at my first comic event. Terry Moore gave me tons of advice about launching *Jane's World* as a monthly comic, he even introduced me to his amazing colorist, Brian Miller. Guy Brand printed posters and gave me the first booth set up I used for Comic con. Ted, Zan, Justin, and the entire crew of Prism Comics...you're all super in my book. Tim Fish and Jason McNamara— booth mates extraordinaire. Joe and Dottie Ferrara are the two of the best pals a cartoonist can have. And that goes for Kathy Bottarini too. Jeff Smith, Chip Kidd, and Patrick McDonnell have offered friendship and support over the years, for which I'm very grateful. Special thanks to

Céline Lion, my French publisher. Jean Schulz, you support cartoonists and cartooning as an art form, along with Karen, Jessica, Tracey and the entire staff at the Charles M. Schulz Museum and Research Center. To Lex and Art and all my comics pals at Creative Associates, thanks for all the great conversations and for sharing tips for making better comics. Shena Wolf, you're a great comics editor. John Glynn, I love your goofy doodles on my royalty statements, don't ever stop being you. A big thank you to Joel Enos, Fawn Lau, Andrea Colvin, Erika Kuster, Grace Bornhoft, Tim Lynch, Annie Monette, and the team at Lion Forge for making this book a reality.

There have been so many people in my life that offered encouragement when I needed it most, including my parents, Bud and Pat, and my wife, Evelyn.

To Dean (a.k.a.: Ethan), Archie, Dorrie, and Nina (pesky, over-achieving intern), thank you for letting me name characters after you.

Special thanks to Sparky, for all the good things.

The Radio 914 nib changed my life.

Paige Braddock

Printed in China

ISBN: 978-1-5493-0275-6

Library of Congress Control Number: 2018941027

10 9 8 7 6 5 4 3 2 1

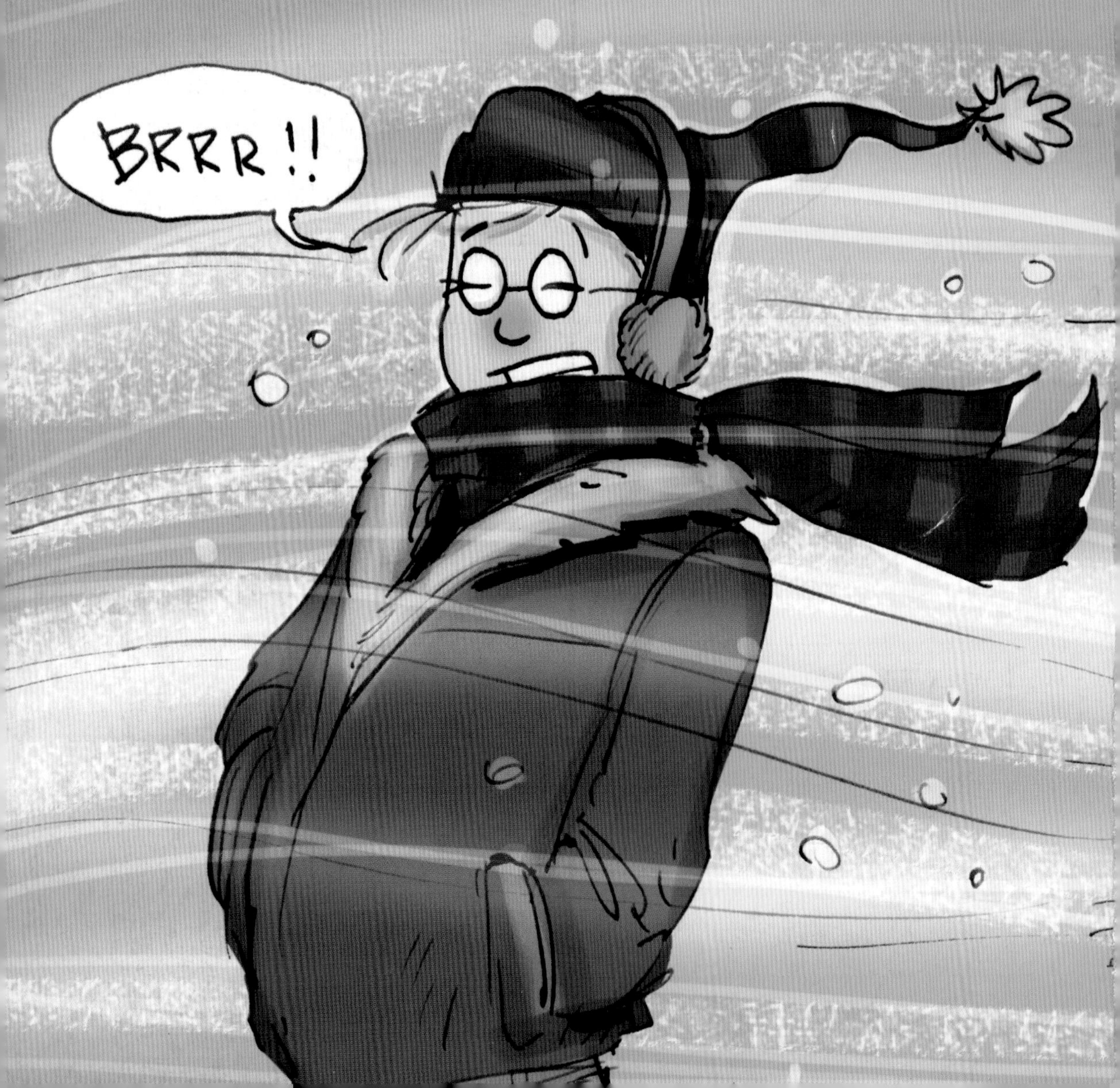
BRRR!!